second edition

Young Children with Special Needs

Richard M. Gargiulo

Jennifer L. Kilgo

THOMSON

DELMAR LEARNING

Australia Canada Mexico Singapore Spain United Kingdom United States

THOMSON

DELMAR LEARNING

Young Children with Special Needs, 2E
Richard M. Gargiulo and Jennifer L. Kilgo

Vice President, Career Education (SBU):
Dawn Gerrain

Director of Editorial:
Sherry Gomoll

Acquisitions Editor:
Erin O'Connor

Editorial Assistant:
Ivy Ip

Director of Production:
Wendy A. Troeger

Production Coordinator:
Nina Tucciarelli

Director of Marketing:
Wendy E. Mapstone

Channel Manager:
Donna Lewis

Library of Congress Cataloging-in-Publication Data

Gargiulo, Richard M.
   Young children with special needs : an introduction to early childhood special education / Richard M. Gargiulo, Jennifer L. Kilgo.—2nd ed.
      p. cm.
   Includes bibliographical references and index.
   ISBN 1-4018-6082-6
   1. Children with disabilities—Education (Early childhood) 2. Special education.
I. Kilgo, Jennifer Lynn. II. Title.

LC4019.3.G27 2004
371.9'0472—dc22

2004008080

NOTICE TO THE READER

This book is dedicated to my daughters—

Christina
Cara
Victoria
Elissa Marie

each of whom, in her own unique way, continually teaches me about what is truly important in life.

RMG

March, 2004

With much love, admiration, and appreciation, this book is dedicated to Dr. Ira B. Patton. For your sense of humor, "doctoring," wisdom, and guidance, I say thank you. No one else could have filled my dad's big shoes so well! How blessed I was to be your "adopted daughter." Your influence will be felt for the balance of my life and, in some small way, I hope I have made you proud.

Juniper

March, 2004

Contents

Preface

It is generally recognized that the early years of a child's life constitute one of its most significant developmental periods. Teachers, psychologists, and other professionals who work with young children believe that much of what happens during the earliest years of a youngster's life significantly impacts later development and learning. Unfortunately, a growing number of young children encounter less than optimal situations and circumstances. Conditions such as congenital disorders, developmental problems, and environmental factors like poverty, abuse, and even cultural and linguistic differences may place some children at-risk for future success in school. Teachers, therefore, are confronted with an increasingly diverse student population while public schools are assuming greater responsibility for the education of *all* children.

The topic of this book is children from birth through age eight; youngsters generally referred to as infants, toddlers, preschoolers, and early primary students. However, we will focus on a unique group of these individuals—some of whom have been identified as having disabilities, others who may be delayed in their development, as well as youngsters who might be at-risk for problems in learning and development due to exposure to adverse genetic, biological or environmental conditions. We wish to make one specific point about these youngsters. Throughout this text we have adopted "person first" language. This means that instead of talking about *disabled children,* we will discuss *children with disabilities.* By placing the noun before the adjective we hope to ensure that the reader realizes that the emphasis is correctly on the child, not the disability. For example, we will talk about a toddler with mental retardation instead of a mentally retarded toddler. This practice is in keeping with contemporary thinking and reflects our belief that young children with special needs are first and foremost children.

As you read this text you will encounter certain recurring themes that reflect our professional beliefs and values about programs and services for young children with special needs and their families. These themes, along with certain basic premises, provide the theoretical and philosophical foundations for this book. The following list depicts those orientations that we consider requisites for delivering high-quality services.

We value, support, and encourage:

- inclusive practices,
- family-centered services,
- transdisciplinary service delivery,
- authentic assessment,
- cultural sensitivity and competence,

- developmentally and individually appropriate practices,
- activity-based interventions,
- research-based decision making,
- coordinated and comprehensive services, and
- a holistic view of young children with special needs and their families

Features new to this edition include:

- chapter objectives that focus on key concepts;
- updated references coupled with current statistical data and research findings;
- an emphasis on instructional strategies and pedagogical recommendations necessary for creating inclusive learning environments;
- suggestions for incorporating technology in the learning environment, especially adaptive/assistive technology;
- lists of Websites providing additional sources of information appropriate to chapter content;
- a companion Website (Online Companion) offering a vast array of supporting materials for students, including:

  Web Resources—a list of helpful Websites for each chapter;

  Reflection Questions—questions to answer that will help students review and reflect on chapter content, either individually or in a group;

  Critical Reading and Analysis activities—Web activities that provide opportunities for students to research and critique articles about the most current topics in ECSE; and

  Instructor Support Slides—slides for the instructor to download, customize, and use in class.

 The Online Companion is located at http://www.earlychilded.delmar.com. Click on Online Resources, then select this book from the 2004 titles list.

- extensive use of new tables, figures, and photographs; and
- an expanded listing of resources and organizations concerned with young children with special needs and their families.

- Online Instructor's Manual with transparencies, discussion questions, and other resources for isntructors. To access, go to www.earlychilded.delmar.com. Click on Instructor Lounge and follow the steps for validation to receive a username and password.

Writing a textbook is a team effort and this one is no exception. We wish to acknowledge with deep gratitude and much appreciation the contributions of Tom Buggey (Chapter 8) and Linda L. Brady (Chapter 9). Their ideas, expertise, and professionalism greatly added to the quality of this endeavor.

We also wish to thank Juanakee McGee and Ora Owens for helping turn jumbled ideas and scribbling into flowing manuscript and expertly designed tables and figures. Their "can do" attitude and willingness to help with one more rush job made this book a reality.

Appreciation is also extended to the wonderful team at Thomson/Delmar Learning who believed in the vitality of this book and offered us the opportunity to write a second edition. We wish to thank our editor, Erin O'Connor, for her support, visionary ideas, and commitment to ensuring that *Young Children with Special Needs* is a market leader. Ivy Ip, our editorial assistant, answered countless questions, offered words of encouragement, and provided just the right amount of professional nudging. We were also blessed with a skillful copy editor whose keen eyes and command of the English language ensured the accuracy and readability of this text. Thank you to the copyeditor, Colleen Yonda, and to Nina Tucciarelli, who served as production coordinator and helped keep us attuned to various deadlines. Thank you, Ivy Ip, for your patience.

We are indebted to our reviewers. These professionals provided invaluable input and helpful suggestions. Their thoughtful commentary and insights definitely helped to shape the direction of this edition. These individuals include

Debra Ahola
Schenectady County Community College
Schenectady, NY

Alice Beyrent
Hesser College
Manchester, NH

Elaine Boski-Wilkenson
Collin County Community College
Plano, TX

Marie Brand
State University of New York, New Paltz
New Paltz, NY

Mary Cordell
Navarro College
Corsicana, TX

Paddy Favazza, Ed.D.
University of Memphis
Memphis, TN

Jeffrey Gelfer, Ph.D.
University of Nevada, Las Vegas
Las Vegas, NV

Susan Johnston, Ph.D
University of Utah
Salt Lake City, UT

Patricia Weaver
Fayetteville Technical Community College
Fayetteville, NC

Richard M. Gargiulo
Jennifer L. Kilgo

Perspectives, Policies, and Practices of Early Childhood Special Education

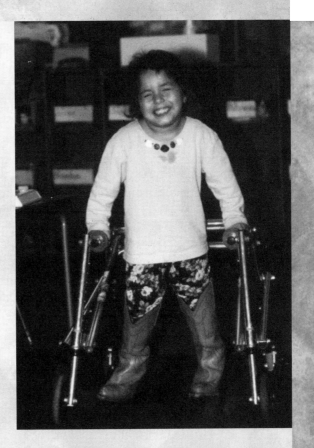

Foundations of Early Childhood Special Education

Learning Outcomes

After reading this chapter you will be able to:

- Describe the contributions of historical figures to the development of the field of early childhood education.
- Discuss the evolution of educational opportunities for children with disabilities.
- Explain the concept of compensatory education.
- Describe the purpose of Head Start and related compensatory programs.
- List four long-term benefits of preschool education.

The Origins of Early Childhood Special Education

The last thirty years have witnessed a dramatic increase in awareness, services, and opportunities for young children with special needs. Legislative initiatives, litigation, public policy, and the efforts of advocacy groups are some of the factors that have helped to focus attention on this group of children. As a distinct field, early childhood special education is relatively young but rapidly emerging. The foundation for constructing developmentally and educationally appropriate experiences for young children with special needs is built upon three related fields. The origins of early childhood special education can be traced to trends and developments in early childhood education, special education for school age pupils, and compensatory programs like Head Start (Hanson & Lynch, 1995; McCollum & Maude, 1993). In their own unique way, each movement has played a vital role in the evolution of early childhood special education. Perhaps it is best to consider the field of early childhood special education as a hybrid built upon the evolving best practices of early childhood and special education, plus the research evidence from empirical investigations documenting the effectiveness of early intervention. Figure 1–1 illustrates this three-fold foundation of the field.

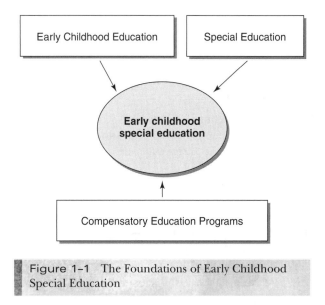

Figure 1–1 The Foundations of Early Childhood Special Education

The Development of Early Childhood Education

Early childhood education has a long history rich with tradition. The efforts of past religious leaders, reformers, educational theorists, and philosophers have helped to shape contemporary thinking about young children. The work of these individuals has also paved the way for many of the concepts and practices utilized with young children with disabilities and students who are at-risk. It is important to note, however, that the value of children and their education reflects the social, political, and economic conditions of particular time periods. Table 1–1 provides a brief summary of the early history of childhood.

Early Contributors

Although a significant historical religious leader, Martin Luther (1483–1546) is also remembered for advocating the importance of literacy and universal, compulsory education. He also was a firm believer in publicly supported schools for all children, including girls. Luther's legacy includes his visionary idea that family participation is a critical component of a child's education.

Another early religious leader and educational theorist was Jan Ámos Comenius (1592–1670). He was a strong believer in universal education, which ideally should begin in the early years due to the plasticity or malleability of the child's behavior. In *The Great Didactic* (1657), Comenius outlines his view that young children are like soft wax, capable of easily being molded and shaped. Schooling in the first six years of life should begin at home at the mother's knee ("School of the Mother's Knee") and progress throughout an individual's lifetime. Comenius also advocated that all children, including those with disabilities, should be educated (Gargiulo & Černá, 1992).

Many contemporary practices, as well as the thinking of later theorists such as Montessori and Piaget, can be found in Comenius's early ideas about children's learning and development. As an example, Comenius realized the importance of a child's readiness for an activity. He also stressed that students learn best by being actively involved in the learning process. Additionally, Comenius placed great emphasis on sensory experiences and the utilization of concrete examples.

John Locke (1632–1704) was a seventeenth-century English philosopher and physician who also influenced thinking about young children. Locke is credited with introducing the notion that children are born very much like a blank slate **(tabula rasa).**

All that children learn, therefore, is a direct result of experiences, activities, and sensations rather than innate ideas or inborn traits. Locke was a strong advocate of an environmental point of view. What a person becomes is a consequence or product of the type and quality of experiences to which they are exposed, in other words, "Children become what adults make of them" (Morrison, 2001, p. 91).

Locke's belief in the domination of the environment is reflected in the behavioral theories of B. F. Skinner and other contemporary theorists as well as today's compensatory education programs aimed at remedying the consequences of a disadvantaged environment. Early school experiences for children at-risk, such as the popular Head Start program, is a prime example. Because Locke also stressed the importance of sensory experiences, his theorizing influenced Montessori's thinking about the significance of sensory training in early education.

One social theorist and philosopher who had a significant impact on education was Jean-Jacques Rousseau (1712–1778). Through his writings, in particular, *Emile* (1762), Rousseau described his views on child rearing and education. His ideas, radical for their time, included a natural approach to the education of young children. Rousseau urged a laissez-faire approach, one void of restrictions and interference, which would thus allow the natural unfolding of a child's abilities. Childhood was viewed as a distinct and special time wherein children developed or "flowered" according to innate timetables. Rousseau emphasized the importance of early education. He also believed that schools should be based on the interests of the child (Graves, Gargiulo, & Schertz, 1996).

Educational historians typically regard Rousseau as the dividing line between the historical and modern periods of education. He significantly influenced future reformers and thinkers such as Pestalozzi, Froebel, and Montessori, all of whom have contributed to modern early childhood practices.

Pioneers in Early Childhood Education

Johann Heinrich Pestalozzi (1746–1827), a Swiss educator, is credited with establishing early childhood education as a distinct discipline. Like Rousseau,

Table 1–1	Stages in the History of Childhood				
Stage	**Time Period**	**Mode**	**Viewpoint**	**Problem**	**Solution**
1. From Bad to Worse	B.C.–300 A.D. 300–1200	Infanticide Abandonment	No apparent conception of childhood	Survival depends on pleasing the gods, controlling population, and maintaining a physically strong community	Eliminate extra mouths to feed, ensure that only the strongest are raised from childhood
2. Children Will be Children	1300–1600	Ambivalent	The emergence of the idea of childhood as a special period	Rampant disease and hardship kill many young children	Remain detached from young children, have many but don't form bonds until they survive early childhood
3. Church and State Mix	1700s	Intrusive	Parents begin to feel a responsibility for the soul of their child	Everlasting salvation of the soul is highest priority; heavenly life beyond this earthly toil is the final reward	Provide an early education so that children can learn of God's redemption
4. Parents Know Best	1800–1950	Socialization	Parents become responsible for training the child; a recognition of independence	Industrialization requires an increasing labor base; immigrant parents work long hours and neglect their children	Provide early childhood care and education to promote productive citizenship among children
5. Children Know Best	1950–Current	Helping	Children know better than the parents what they need and involve parents in fulfilling those needs	Resources are abundant enough that all people should have equal opportunity, including children	Provide early educational services to children who are poor or disabled

Note: Time periods are only approximate.

SOURCE: Adapted from V. Howard, B. Williams, P. Port, and C. Lepper, *Very Young Children with Special Needs*, 2nd ed. (Upper Saddle River, NJ: Prentice-Hall, 2001). p. 49.

Pestalozzi believed in the importance of education through nature and following the child's natural development. He also advocated developing school experiences centered around the interests of the student. Pestalozzi realized, however, that learning does not occur simply through a youngster's initiative and exploratory behavior; adult guidance is required. Teachers, therefore, need to construct "object" lessons to balance the pupil's self-guided experiences. Due to Pestalozzi's belief in the importance of sensory experiences, instructional lessons incorporated manipulative activities like counting, measuring, feeling, and touching concrete objects (Lawton, 1988).

Three additional ideas distinguish Pestalozzi's contributions to the field of early childhood education. First, Pestalozzi stressed the education of the whole child; second, he was a strong believer in involving parents in a child's early education; and, finally, he saw the merit of multiage grouping whereby older students could assist in teaching younger pupils.

Social reformer and entrepreneur Robert Owen (1771–1858) is recognized for establishing an Infant School in 1816. Influenced by the theorizing of Rousseau and Pestalozzi, Owen was concerned about the living and working conditions of the children and their parents who worked in textile mills. As the manager of a mill in New Lanark, Scotland, Owen was able to initiate his reform ideas. Very young children were prohibited from working at all and the working hours of older children were limited. Perhaps more important, however, was the establishment of a school for children between the ages of three and ten. He believed early education was critical to the development of a child's character and behavior. The early years were the best time to influence a youngster's development. By controlling and manipulating environmental conditions, Owen, like other Utopians, sought to construct a better society (Graves et al., 1996). Education was seen as a vehicle for social change.

Owen's Infant School was noted for its emphasis on the development of basic academics as well as creative experiences such as dance and music. This pioneer of early childhood education did not believe in forcing children to learn and was opposed to punishment, stressing mutual respect between teacher and learner. His ideas were immensely popular and over 50 Infant Schools were established by the late 1820s throughout Scotland, Ireland, and England. Several schools flourished in urban areas of the United States; yet, their influence diminished by the mid-1830s.

Owen's Infant Schools served as a forerunner of kindergartens. They were also seen as a way of immunizing children living in poverty from the evils of nineteenth-century urban living. This social reformer was visionary; he realized the important relationship between education and societal improvements. Owen believed, as did other reformers of that time, that poverty could be permanently eliminated by educating and socializing young children from poor families.

Graves and his colleagues (Graves et al., 1996) describe Friedrich Wilhelm Froebel[1] (1782–1852) as the one individual who perhaps had the greatest impact on the field of early childhood education. A student of Pestalozzi and a teacher in one of his schools, Froebel was a strong believer in the education of young children. He translated his beliefs into a system for teaching young children in addition to developing a curriculum, complete with methodology. His efforts have earned him the well-deserved title "Father of the Kindergarten."

Also influenced by the writings of Rousseau and Comenius, Froebel conceived an educational theory ("Law of Universal Unity") partly based on their thoughts as well as his own personal experiences and religious views. His basic idea was essentially religious in nature and emphasized a unity of all living things—a oneness of humans, nature, and God. His notion of unity led Froebel to advocate that education should be based on cooperation rather than competition. Like Comenius and Pestalozzi, he also considered development as a process of unfolding. Children's learning should, therefore, follow this nat-

---

[1]Information on Friedrich Froebel, John Dewey, Maria Montessori, and Jean Piaget is adapted from *Young Children An Introduction to Early Childhood* by S. Graves, R. Gargiulo, and L. Sluder. St. Paul, MN: West Publishing, 1996.

ural development. The role of the teacher (and parent) was to recognize this process and to provide activities to help the child learn whenever he or she was ready to learn (Graves, 1990).

Froebel used the garden to symbolize childhood education. Like a flower blooming from a bud, children would grow naturally according to their own laws of development. A kindergarten education, therefore, should follow the nature of the child. Play, a child's natural activity, was a basis for learning (Spodek, Saracho, & Davis, 1991).

Froebel established the first kindergarten (German for children's garden) in 1837 near Blankenburg, Germany. This early program enrolled youngsters between the ages of one and seven. Structured play was an important component of the curriculum. Unlike many of his contemporaries, Froebel saw educational value and benefit in play. Play is the work of the child. Because he believed that education was knowledge being transmitted by symbols, Froebel devised a set of materials and activities that would aid the children in their play activities as well as teach the concept of unity among nature, God, and humankind. Education was to begin with the concrete and move to the abstract.

Froebel presented his students with "gifts" and "occupations" rich in symbolism. In his curriculum, **gifts** were manipulative activities to assist in learning color, shape, size, counting, and other educational tasks. Wooden blocks, cylinders, and cubes; balls of colored yarn; geometric shapes; and natural objects, such as beans and pebbles, are all examples of some of the learning tools used.

Occupations were arts and craft type activities designed to develop eye-hand coordination and fine motor skills. Illustrations of these activities include bead-stringing, embroidering, paper folding, cutting with scissors, and other psychomotor skills such as weaving. Froebel's curriculum also used games, songs, dance, rhymes, and finger play. Other components of his curriculum were nature study, language, and arithmetic in addition to developing the habits of cleanliness, courtesy, and punctuality.

Teachers were to be designers of activities and experiences utilizing the child's natural curiosity. They were also responsible for directing and guiding

their students toward becoming contributing members of society (Graves, 1990). This role of the teacher as a facilitator of children's learning would later be echoed in the work of Montessori and Piaget.

Leaders of the Twentieth Century

We consider the theorizing and practices of three modern individuals—John Dewey, Maria Montessori, and Jean Piaget as having a significant influence on the field of early childhood education. We will also examine the contributions of the Russian theorist Lev Vygotsky whose work is presently attracting a great deal of attention from educators.

The influence of John Dewey (1859–1952) can be traced to the early days of the twentieth century when conflicting points of view about young children and kindergarten experiences began to emerge. Some individuals professed a strong allegiance to Froebel's principles and practices. Other professionals, known as progressives, saw little value in adhering to Froebel's symbolism. Instead, they embraced the developing child study movement with its focus on empirical study. Because of the work of G. Stanley Hall, the father of the child study movement, formal observations and a scientific basis for understanding young children replaced speculation, philosophic idealism, and religious and social values as a means for guiding the education of young children. Observations of young children led to new ideas about kindergarten practices and what should be considered of educational value for children.

Dewey, a student of Hall, was one of the first Americans to significantly impact educational theory as well as practice. He is generally regarded as the founder of a school of thought known as **Progressivism.** This approach, with its emphasis on the child and his or her interests, was counter to the then prevalent theme of teacher-directed, subject-oriented curriculum. According to Dewey, learning flowed from the interests of the child instead of from activities chosen by the instructor. Dewey, who taught at both the University of Chicago and Teachers College, Columbia University, coined the terms, "child-centered curriculum" and "child-centered schools" (Graves, 1990). Consistent with Dewey's beliefs, the purpose of schools was to prepare the student for the realities of today's world, not just to prepare for the future. In his famous work, *My Pedagogic Creed*, this philosopher emphasized that learning occurs through real-life experiences and that education is best described as a process for living. He also stressed the concept of social responsibility. Basic to his philosophy was the idea that children should be equipped to function effectively as citizens in a democratic society.

Traditionally, children learned predetermined subject matter via rote memory under the strict guidance of the teacher who was in complete control of the learning environment. In Dewey's classroom, however, children were socially active, engaged in physical activities, and discovering how objects worked. They were to be continually afforded opportunities for inquiry, discovery, and experimentation. Daily living activities such as carpentry and cooking could also be found in a Dewey-designed classroom (Graves, 1990).

Dewey (1916) advocated the child's interaction with the total environment. He believed that intellectual skills emerged from a child's own activity and play. He further rejected Froebel's approach to symbolic education.

Some have unfairly criticized Dewey as only responding to the whims of the child; this was a false accusation. Dewey did not abandon the teaching of subject matter or basic skills. He was merely opposed to imposing knowledge on children. Instead, he favored using the student's interest as the origin of subject matter instruction. Thus, curriculum cannot be fixed or established in advance. Educators are to guide learning activities, observe and monitor, and offer encouragement and assistance as needed. They are not to control their students.

Although Dewey's impact has diminished, his contributions to early childhood education in America and other countries is still evident. Many so-called traditional early childhood programs today have their philosophical roots in Dewey's progressive education movement.

As we examine the roots of modern early childhood special education, the work of Maria Montessori (1870–1952) stands out. Her contributions to the field of early childhood education are significant. A feminist, she became the first female to earn a medical degree in Italy. (Montessori also held a Ph.D. in anthropology.) She began working as a physician in a psychiatric clinic at the University of Rome. It was in this hospital setting that she came into frequent contact with "idiot children," or children with mental retardation. At the turn of the century, mental retardation was viewed as indistinguishable from mental illness. A careful observation of these youngsters led her to conclude that educational intervention rather than medical treatment would be a more effective strategy. She began to develop her theories for working with these children. In doing so, she was following an historical tradition upon which the early foundation of special education is built—the physician turned educator. Dr. Montessori was influenced by the writings of Pestalozzi, Rousseau, Froebel, and the work of Edouard Seguin, a French physician who pioneered an effective educational approach for children with mental retardation. She concluded that intelligence was not static or fixed, but could be influenced by the child's experiences. Montessori developed an innovative, activity-based sensory education model involving teaching, or **didactic materials.** She was eminently successful. Youngsters who were originally believed to be incapable of learning successfully performed on school achievement tests.

Montessori believed that children learn best by direct sensory experience. She was further convinced that children had a natural tendency to explore and

Montessori believed that children learn best by direct sensory experiences.

understand their world (Graves, 1990). Like Froebel, she envisioned child development as a process of unfolding; however, environmental influences also had a critical role. Education in the early years is crucial to the child's later development. Montessori also thought children passed through **sensitive periods,** or stages of development early in life where they are especially able, due to their curiosity, to more easily learn particular skills or behaviors. This concept is very similar to the idea of a child's readiness for an activity.

To promote the children's learning, Montessori constructed an orderly or **prepared environment** with specially designed tasks and materials. Much like Froebel's gifts, these materials included items such as wooden rods, cylinders, and cubes of varying sizes; sets of sandpaper tablets arranged according to the degree of smoothness; and musical bells of different pitches. Dr. Montessori's program also emphasized three growth periods—practical life experiences, sensory education, and academic education. Each of these components was considered to be of importance in developing the child's independence, responsibility, and productivity.

Practical life experiences focused on personal hygiene, self-care, physical education, and responsibility for the environment. Examples of this last activity include tasks such as sweeping, dusting, or raking leaves utilizing child-size equipment. Sensory education was very important in Montessori's education scheme. She designed a wide variety of teaching materials aimed at developing the student's various senses. Her didactic materials are noteworthy for two reasons. They were self-correcting, that is, there was only one correct way to use them. Thus the materials could be used independently by the children and help them become self-motivated students. The sensory training equipment was also graded in difficulty—from easiest to the most difficult and from concrete to abstract. Her sensory training materials and procedures reflected her educational belief that cognitive ability results from sensory development. The final stage, academic instruction, introduced the child to reading, writing, and arithmetic in the sensitive period, ages two to six. Various concrete and sensory teaching materials were used in the lessons of this last stage (Montessori, 1965).

Montessori's classrooms were distinguished by their attractive and child-size materials and equipment. The furniture was moveable and the beautifully crafted materials were very attractive—appealing to the child's senses. Teaching materials were displayed on low shelves in an organized manner to encourage the pupil's independent use. Children worked at their own pace selecting learning materials of their choice. They must, however, complete one assignment before starting another. Dr. Montessori fully believed in allowing children to do things for themselves. She was convinced that children are capable of teaching themselves through interaction with a carefully planned learning environment. She identified this concept as **auto-education.**

Teachers in Montessori classrooms are facilitators and observers of children's activities. By using skillfully crafted lessons, the teacher (or directress in Montessori terminology) slowly and carefully demonstrates concepts to the children. Ideas are presented to the students in small, sequential steps and build on previous experiences, which form the basis for the next level of skill development. Teachers foster the development of independence in their students. A Montessori-designed classroom is typically focused on individual student activities rather than group work.

Jean Piaget (1896–1980) is one of the major contributors to our understanding of how children think. He is considered by many to be the premiere expert on the development of knowledge in children and young adults.

Piaget is widely recognized for his ideas on the development of the intellect.

Piaget studied in Paris where he had the opportunity to work with Theodore Simon, who in conjunction with Alfred Binet, was constructing the first test for assessing children's intelligence. While standardizing the children's responses to test questions, Piaget became extremely interested in the incorrect answers given by the youngsters. His careful observations led him to notice that they gave similar wrong answers. He also discovered that the children made different types of errors at different ages. This paved the way for Piaget to investigate the thinking process that led to incorrect responses.

According to Piaget's point of view, children's mode of thinking is profoundly and fundamentally different from that of adults'. He also believed that children's thought processes are modified as they grow and mature. Because Piaget's ideas about intellectual development are complex, only his basic concepts will be presented.

First, it is important to understand Piaget's view of intelligence. He was concerned with *how* knowledge is acquired. Piaget avoids stating a precise definition of intelligence; instead, he attempts to describe it in general terms. Piaget speaks of intelligence as an instance of biological adaptation. He also looks at intelligence as a balance or equilibrium between an individual's cognitive structures and the environment. His focus is on what people *do* as they interact with their environment. Knowledge of reality must be discovered and constructed—it results from a child's actions within, and reactions to, their world. It is also important to note that Piaget is not concerned with individual differences in intelligence (Ginsburg & Opper, 1969).

Piaget's theory rests on the contributions of maturational and environmental influences. Maturation establishes a sequence of cognitive stages controlled by heredity. The environment contributes the child's experiences, which dictate how they develop. Thinking is a process of interaction between the child and the environment. Graves (1990) describes children as "active agents who interact with the social and physical world" (p. 198). Youngsters are self-motivated in the construction of their own knowledge, which occurs through activity.

One consequence of interaction with the environment is that the person soon develops organizing structures or **schema.** These schema, or mental concepts, become a basis from which later cognitive structures are established. Piaget developed three concepts that he believes individuals use to organize their personal experiences into a blueprint for thinking. He called these adaptive processes assimilation, accommodation, and equilibration. **Assimilation** occurs when the child is able to integrate new experiences and information into existing schemes, that is, what the child already knows. Children will view new situations in light of previous experiences in their world. As an illustration, when a toddler encounters a pony, she will most likely call it a dog, something the youngster is already familiar with.

Accommodation is Piaget's second process. It involves modifying existing cognitive structures so that new data can be effectively utilized. Current thought patterns and behavior are changed to fit new situations. Accommodation involves a change in understanding. For example, two-year-old Victoria visits Santa Claus at the mall. Later that day she is shopping with her mother and sees an elderly gentleman with a long white beard whom she calls Santa Claus. Victoria's mother corrects her daughter's mistake by saying that the man is old. When Victoria next meets a man with a white beard, she asks, "Are you Santa Claus or are you just old?" Victoria has demonstrated accommodation—she changed her knowledge base.

Assimilation and accommodation are involved in the final process of equilibration. Here an attempt is made to achieve a balance or equilibrium between assimilation and accommodation. Piaget believed that all activity involve both processes. The interaction between assimilation and accommodation leads to adaptation, a process of adjusting to new situations. **Equilibration** is the tendency to reach a balance, which accounts for the formation of knowledge. Intellectual growth, according to Piaget, is achieved through the interplay of these three processes.

Four stages of cognitive development were identified by Piaget. Children pass through these stages in an orderly, sequential fashion. Each stage is a prerequisite for the next one. The ages identified in Table 1–2 are

Table 1-2   Piaget's Stages of Cognitive Development

Approximate Age	Stage	Distinguishing Characteristics
Birth—1½ or 2 years	Sensorimotor	Knowledge constructed through sensory perception and motor activity. Thought limited to action schemes.
2–7 years	Preoperational	Emergence of language and symbolic thinking. Intuitive rather than logical schemes. Egocentric in thought and action.
7–11 years	Concrete operations	Beginning of logical, systematic thinking; limited, however, to concrete objects. Decreased egocentrism.
12–15 years	Formal operations	Abstract and logical thought present. Capable of solving hypothetical problems. Deductive thinking and scientific reasoning is possible.

only rough estimates of when a youngster enters each stage. Children progress at their own rate, which is influenced by their experiences and existing cognitive structures, in addition to their maturation.

Russian psychologist Lev Semenovich Vygotsky (1896–1934) was a contemporary of Piaget and another influential contributor to present understanding of how children learn and develop.

A brilliant young man (he was literate in eight languages), Vygotsky entered Moscow University in 1914 where he studied law, one of the few vocations open to a Jew in tsarist Russia. Upon graduation in 1917, he returned to the city of Gomel where he had spent most of his youth and taught in several local institutions. The massive changes brought about by the Russian Revolution provided Vygotsky with the opportunity to teach at Gomel's Teacher's College. It was here that he became attracted to the fields of psychology and education, where his lack of formal training as a psychologist proved a distinct advantage. It allowed Vygotsky to look at the field of psychology as an outsider, someone with fresh perspectives and creative ideas about child development (Berk & Winsler, 1995). A visionary thinker, Vygotsky's theories and beliefs significantly shaped contemporary thinking about children's language, play, cognition, and social development.

In his book, *Mind in Society,* Vygotsky (1978) argues that people—children in particular—are the products of their social and cultural environments. Children's development is significantly influenced by their social and cultural worlds and the individuals they come into contact with such as parents, teachers, and peers. Social experiences were very important to Vygotsky because he believed that higher order cognitive processes, such as language and cognition, necessitate social interaction. What begins in a social context is eventually internalized psychologically. In his writings Vygotsky emphasized the link between the social and psychological worlds of the youngster. Learning and development occur via social interaction and engagement.

> Learning awakens a variety of developmental processes that are able to operate only when the child is interacting with people in his environment and in collaboration with his peers. Once these processes are internalized, they become part of the child's independent developmental achievement. (Vygotsky, 1978, p. 90)

Vygotsky believed that social interaction not only fosters intellectual development, but that it is also vital to the development of social competence. Vygotsky's emphasis on the reciprocity of social relationships, however, is contrary to the theorizing of Piaget. Recall that Piaget saw children as active, yet solitary and independent discoverers of knowledge.

Perhaps the best-known Vygotskian concept is the **zone of proximal development (ZPD).** Simply described, it is a hypothetical region defined by Vygotsky (1978) as:

> the distance between the actual developmental level as determined by independent problem solving and the level of potential development as determined through problem solving under adult guidance or in collaboration with more capable peers. (p. 86)

The ZPD exists between what a youngster can presently accomplish independently and what the child is capable of doing within a supportive environment. Support is typically viewed as coming from more mature thinkers like adults and competent peers, although, according to Hills (1992), it may be derived from materials and equipment. The ZPD is actually created, Tudge (1992) writes, through social interaction. It is the arena in which learning and cognitive development takes place. Figure 1–2 portrays Vygotsky's concept of ZPD.

Scaffolding is an idea related to Vygotsky's notion of a ZPD. It refers to the assistance given a child by adults and peers that allows the individual to function independently and construct new concepts. Social interaction and collaboration with others typically provide youngsters with opportunities for scaffolding. One of the primary goals of scaffolding is to keep children working on tasks that are in their ZPD. This goal is generally obtained by providing the minimum amount of assistance necessary and then further reducing this aid as the child's own competence grows (Berk & Winsler, 1995). Within this context, "the teacher's role is one of supporting, guiding and facilitating development and learning" (Bredekamp & Rosegrant, 1992, p. 15).

As we have just seen, collaboration and social interaction are key tenets in Vygotsky's sociocultural approach to understanding children's learning and development. For Vygotsky, learning leads to development rather than following it. Learning is not itself development; rather, structured learning experiences play a major role giving impetus to developmental processes that would be difficult to separate from learning (Tudge, 1992). According to Vygotsky, devel-

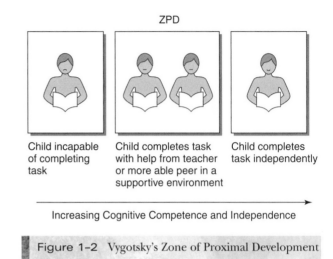

ZPD

Child incapable of completing task

Child completes task with help from teacher or more able peer in a supportive environment

Child completes task independently

Increasing Cognitive Competence and Independence

Figure 1–2   Vygotsky's Zone of Proximal Development

opment and learning are neither identical nor separate processes; instead, they are interrelated and integrative functions. This perspective sees developmental change as arising from a youngster's active engagement in a social environment with a mature partner. Growth occurs, therefore, within this zone of proximal development. His approach to education could accurately be described as one of assisted discovery, also known as guided practice or assisted performance (Berk & Winsler, 1995).

Vygotsky also spoke to the issue of children with disabilities. In fact, he enjoyed the title "Father of Soviet Defectology," which loosely translates to mean special education. Vygotsky (1993) was of the opinion that the principles that govern the learning and development of typical youngsters also apply to children with disabilities. He was firmly convinced that the optimal development of young children with special needs rested on fully integrating them into their social environment while ensuring that instruction occurs within their ZPD (Berk & Winsler, 1995). Children with learning problems should be educated, according to Vygotsky, in the same fashion as their peers without disabilities.

One of the major difficulties encountered by children with disabilities is how the impairment modifies their interaction with, and participation in, their social environment and not the disability itself. A youngster's disability results in restricted interactions with adults and peers and this contributes to the creation of a secondary—yet more debilitating—social deficit. Potentially more harmful than the primary disability, Vygotsky believed that these cultural deficits are more amenable to intervention than the original disorder is.

Several contemporary practices in early childhood special education can be traced to Vygotsky's thinking. His conceptualizations suggest that youngsters with special needs should be included as much as possible in environments designed for typically developing learners. As an early advocate of integration, Vygotsky believed that a segregated placement results in a different social climate, thus restricting students' interactions and collaborative opportunities and, thereby, limiting cognitive development. Furthermore, educators should focus on students' strengths and abilities rather than their weaknesses. What a student can do (with or without assistance) is more important than what he or she cannot do. Finally, a student's learning (social) environment should be rich with opportunities for scaffolding, which is seen as assisting in development of higher order cognitive processes.

Vygotsky's contributions to children's learning and development were not limited to children with disabilities. Many well-known instructional strategies are grounded in his theories. Teachers who engage in cooperative learning activities, peer tutoring, guided practice, reciprocal teaching, and incorporate mixed age groupings or a whole-language approach can thank Vygotsky.

A Concluding Thought Our brief examination of the historical roots of early childhood education suggest two conclusions. First, efforts on behalf of young children were, and are, frequently constrained by the political and social realities of the times. Second, much of what we often consider new or innovative has been written about and tried before. Present services for young children with disabilities have been influenced significantly by the history of education for young children. As an illustration, many contemporary programs for young children with special needs emphasize parent involvement, a child-centered curriculum, and interventions based on practical applications of child development theory. These programs also recognize that early experiences impact later social, emotional, and intellectual competency (Shonkoff & Meisels, 1990).

Table 1–3 presents a brief summary of the contributions of key individuals to the development of the field of early childhood education. We now turn our attention to the contributions emerging from our second parent field—special education.

Historical Perspectives on Children with Disabilities

The history of special education provides a second point of departure for examining the evolution of early childhood special education. Society has chosen to deal with such individuals in a variety of ways. Oftentimes, programs and practices for individuals with special needs are a reflection of the prevailing social climate, in addition to people's ideas and attitudes about exceptionality. A change in attitude is often a precursor to a change in the delivery of services. The foundation of societal attitude in the United States can be traced to the efforts and philosophies of various Europeans. We now turn our attention to the historical contributions of these individuals with vision and courage.

People and Ideas

Present educational theories, principles, and practices are the product of pioneering thinkers, advocates, and humanitarians. These dedicated reformers were catalysts for change. Historians typically trace the roots of special education to the late 1700s and early 1800s. It is here that we begin our brief examination of early leaders in the field.

One of the earliest documented attempts at providing special education were the efforts of Jean Marc Gaspard Itard (1775–1838) to educate Victor, the so-called "wild boy of Aveyron." A French physician and expert on hearing impairment, Itard endeavored in 1799 to "civilize" and teach Victor through a sensory training program and what today would be known as

Table 1–3   Key Contributors to the Development of Early Childhood Education

Sixteenth Century	
Martin Luther	Strong believer in publicly supported schools. Advocate of universal, compulsory education.
Seventeenth and Eighteenth Century	
Jan Ámos Comenius	Advanced the notion of lifelong education, beginning in the early years. Realized the importance of a child's readiness for an activity. Stressed student's active participation in the learning process.
John Locke	Believed that children are similar to a blank tablet (tabula rasa). Environmental influences strongly impact a child's development. Sensory training is a critical aspect of learning.
Jean-Jacques Rousseau	Emphasized the importance of early education, which should be natural and allow for the unfolding of a child's abilities. School should focus on the interests of children.
Johann Heinrich Pestalozzi	Advocated education through nature and following the child's natural development. Early champion of the whole child and involving parents in the education process. Promoter of sensory education.
Nineteenth Century	
Robert Owen	Theorized that the early years were important in developing a youngster's character and behavior. Linked social change and education. His Infant Schools served as a forerunner of kindergartens.
Friedrich Wilhelm Froebel	Established first kindergarten. Believed in the educational value and benefit of play. Considered development as a natural process of unfolding that provides the foundation for children's learning.
Twentieth Century	
John Dewey	Founder of the school of thought known as Progressivism. Argued that learning flows from the interests of the child rather than from activities chosen by the teacher. Coined the phrases "child-centered curriculum" and "child-centered schools." Saw education as a process for living; stressed social responsibility.
Maria Montessori	Believed that children learn best by direct sensory experience; was also convinced that there are sensitive periods for learning. Designed learning materials that were self-correcting, graded in difficulty, and allowed for independent use. Classroom experiences were individualized to meet the needs of each pupil.
Jean Piaget	Developed a stage theory of cognitive development. Cognitive growth emerges from a child's interaction with, and adaptation to, his physical environment. Youngsters are self-motivated in the construction of their own knowledge, which occurs through activity and discovery.
Lev Semenovich Vygotsky	Russian psychologist who theorized that children's development is significantly influenced by their social and cultural environments and the youngster's interactions with individuals therein. Saw learning and development as interrelated and integrative functions. Originator of the concept of a zone of proximal development (ZPD).

operant procedures. Because this adolescent failed to fully develop language after years of instruction and only mastered basic social and self-help skills, Itard considered his efforts a failure. Yet, Itard demonstrated that learning was possible even for an individual described by other professionals as a hopeless and incurable idiot. The title, Father of Special Education, is bestowed on Itard because of his groundbreaking work almost 200 years ago.

Another important pioneer was Itard's student, Edouard Seguin (1812–1880), who designed instructional programs for children his contemporaries thought to be incapable of learning. He believed in the importance of sensorimotor activities as an aid to learning. Seguin's methodology was based on a comprehensive assessment of a youngster's strengths and weaknesses coupled with an intervention plan of sensorimotor exercises prescribed to remediate specific disabilities. Seguin also emphasized the critical importance of early education. He is considered one of the first early interventionists (Shonkoff & Meisels, 1990). His theorizing also provided the foundation for Montessori's later work with the urban poor and children with mental retardation.

The work of Itard, Seguin, and other innovators of their time helped to establish a foundation for much of what we do today in special education. Table 1–4 summarizes the work of European and American pioneers whose ideas have significantly influenced special education in the United States.

The Establishment of Institutions

Taking their cues from the Europeans, other American reformers such as Boston physician and humanitarian Samuel Gridley Howe (1801–1876) spearheaded the establishment of residential programs. A successful teacher of students who were both deaf and blind, Howe was instrumental in establishing the New England Asylum for the Blind (later the Perkins School) in the early 1830s. Almost two decades later, he played a major role in founding an experimental residential school for children with mental retardation, the Massachusetts School for the Idiotic and Feebleminded Youth. The first institution for individuals with mental retardation, it is now called the Fernald State School.

Institutions at one time were very common across the United States.

SOURCE: PhotoDisc/GettyImages

Residential schools for children with disabilities received additional impetus due to the untiring and vigorous efforts of social activist Dorothea Dix (1802–1887). A retired teacher, Dix was very influential in helping to establish several state institutions for people believed to be mentally ill, a group of individuals she felt to be grossly underserved and largely mistreated.

By the conclusion of the nineteenth century, residential institutions for persons with exceptionalities were a well-established part of the American social fabric. Initially established to offer training and some form of education in a protective lifelong environment, these institutions gradually deteriorated, for a variety of reasons, in the early decades of the twentieth century. The mission of the institutions changed from training to one of custodial care and isolation. The early optimism of special education was replaced by prejudice, unproven scientific views, and fear that helped to convert institutions into gloomy warehouses for the forgotten and neglected (Shonkoff & Meisels, 1990).

Special Education in Public Schools

It was not until the latter part of the nineteenth century that special education began to appear in the public schools. In fact, in 1898 Alexander Graham Bell (1847–1922), a teacher of children who were

Table 1–4   Pioneering Contributors to the Development of Special Education

Contributors	Their Ideas
Jacob Rodrigues Pereine (1715–1780)	Introduced the idea that persons who were deaf could be taught to communicate. Developed an early form of sign language. Provided inspiration and encouragement for the work of Itard and Seguin.
Philippe Pinel (1745–1826)	A reformed-minded French physician who was concerned with the humanitarian treatment of individuals with mental illness. Strongly influenced the later work of Itard.
Jean Marc Gaspard Itard (1775–1838)	A French doctor who secured lasting fame due to his systematic efforts to educate an adolescent thought to be severely mentally retarded. Recognized the importance of sensory stimulation.
Thomas Gallaudet (1787–1851)	Taught children with hearing impairments to communicate via a system of manual signs and symbols. Established the first institution for individuals with deafness in the United States.
Samuel Gridley Howe (1801–1876)	An American physician and educator accorded international fame due to his success in teaching individuals with visual and hearing impairments. Founded the first residential facility for the blind and was instrumental in inaugurating institutional care for children with mental retardation.
Dorothea Lynde Dix (1802–1887)	A contemporary of S. G. Howe, Dix was one of the first Americans to champion better and more humane treatment of people with mental illness. Instigated the establishment of several institutions for individuals with mental disorders.
Louis Braille (1809–1852)	A French educator, who himself was blind, developed a tactile system of reading and writing for people who were blind. His system, based on a code of six embossed dots, is still used today. This standardized code is known as Standard English Braille.
Edouard Seguin (1812–1880)	A pupil of Itard, Seguin was a French physician responsible for developing teaching methods for children with mental retardation. His training program emphasized sensory motor activities. After immigrating to the United States, he helped found the organization that was a forerunner of the American Association on Mental Retardation.
Francis Gallon (1822–1911)	Scientist concerned with individual differences. As a result of studying eminent persons, he believed that genius is solely the result of heredity. Those with superior abilities are born not made.
Alfred Binet (1857–1911)	A French psychologist, Binet authored the first developmental assessment scale capable of quantifying intelligence. Also originated the concept of mental age with his colleague Theodore Simon.
Lewis Terman (1877–1956)	An American educator and psychologist who revised Binet's original assessment instrument. The result was the publication of the Stanford-Binet Intelligence Scale. Terman developed the notion of intelligence quotient (IQ). Also famous for lifelong study of gifted individuals. Credited as being the grandfather of gifted education.

deaf, advocated that public schools begin serving youngsters with disabilities. Services for pupils with exceptionalities began slowly and served only a small minority of those who needed it. The first public school class was organized in Boston in 1869 to serve children who were deaf. Children thought to be mentally retarded first attended public schools about three decades later when a class was established in Providence, Rhode Island. The Chicago public schools inaugurated a class for children with physical impairments in 1899, quickly followed by one for children who were blind in 1900 (Gargiulo, 2003). By the mid-1920s well over half of the largest cities in America provided some type of special education services. The establishment of these programs were seen as an indication of the progressive status of the school district. Still, these earliest ventures mainly served children with mild disabilities—individuals with severe or multiple impairments were kept at home or sent to institutions.

Shonkoff and Meisels (1990) assert that the economic depression of the 1930s and the ensuing world war led to the decline of further expansion of special education programs in public schools; instead, greater reliance was placed on institutionalization. The residential facilities, however, were already overcrowded and provided educationally limited experiences. The postwar years saw an increase in the recognition of the needs of Americans with disabilities. Impetus for the shift of societal attitude resulted from two related factors—the large number of men and women deemed unfit for military service and the large number of war veterans who returned home with disabilities.

With the Second World War behind the nation, the stage was set for the rapid expansion of special education. This growth has been described as a virtual explosion of services occurring at both the state and federal levels. Litigation at all levels, legislative activities, increased fiscal resources, and federal leadership, in addition to social and political activism and advocacy are some of the factors that helped fuel the movement and revitalize special education (Peterson, 1987). Significant benefits for children with exceptionalities resulted from these efforts. For example, in 1948 approximately 12% of children with disabili-

ties were receiving an education appropriate for their needs (Ballard, Ramirez, & Weintraub, 1982); yet, from 1947 to 1972 the number of pupils enrolled in special education programs increased an astonishing 716% as compared to an 82% increase in total public school enrollment (Dunn, 1973).

The last decades of the twentieth century have also witnessed a flurry of activity on behalf of students with special needs. Evidence of this trend includes the 1975 landmark legislation PL 94-142, the *Individuals with Disabilities Education Act (IDEA)* (formerly known as the *Education for All Handicapped Children Act*) and its 1986 Amendments—PL 99-457; they constitute one of the most comprehensive pieces of legislation affecting infants, toddlers, and preschoolers with special needs and their families. The growth of services for preschoolers who are at-risk or disabled, infant and toddler programs, the transition initiative, and calls for full integration of pupils with disabilities are additional indications of a changing attitude and expansion of opportunities for children and youth with exceptionalities.

Compensatory Education Programs

The **compensatory education** movement of the 1960s also played a major role in the development of early childhood special education. As the name implies, this effort was designed to compensate for or ameliorate the environmental conditions and early learning experiences of youngsters living in poverty. Such children were thought to be disadvantaged or "culturally deprived" (a popular term in the 1960s). The goal of compensatory education programs was to assist these students "by providing educational and environmental experiences that might better prepare them for the school experience" (Gearheart, Mullen, & Gearhart, 1993, p. 385). The compensatory education movement had its foundation in the idealism and heightened social consciousness that typified America over three decades ago. It was also aided by the convergence of three distinct social issues: President Kennedy's interest in the field of mental retardation, President Johnson's declaration of a War on Poverty, and the emerging civil rights movement (Shonkoff & Meisels, 1990).

In addition to sociological reasons, the compensatory education movement was aided by solid theoretical arguments. The cogent and persuasive writings of J. McVicker Hunt (1961) and fellow scholar Benjamin Bloom (1964) raised serious questions about the assumption of fixed or static intelligence. The malleability of intelligence and the importance of the early years for intellectual development was recognized by scientists and policymakers alike. Thus the powerful contribution of early and enriched experiences on later development laid the cornerstone for programs like Head Start. It also set the stage for the concept of early intervention. It was thought that the deleterious effects of poverty could be remediated by early and intensive programming. The emphasis of preschool programs shifted from custodial caregiving to programming for specific developmental gains (Thurman & Widerstrom, 1990).

Representative Compensatory Programs

Project Head Start **Project Head Start** came into existence as a result of the 1964 Economic Opportunity Act. Federally sponsored, Head Start was a critical component of a larger national agenda called the War on Poverty. As the first nationwide compensatory education program, Head Start was conceived as an early intervention effort aimed at reducing the potential for school failure in disadvantaged young children from low socioeconomic (impoverished) communities. Initiated in the summer of 1965 as an eight-week pilot program, Project Head Start served approximately 550,000 four- and five-year-old youngsters in over 2,500 communities.

According to Zigler and Valentine (1979), the first volley on the War on Poverty was constructed around three fundamental ideas:

1. compensatory experiences initiated in the preschool years would result in successful adjustment to school and enhanced academic performance;

Head Start was the first nationwide compensatory education program.

2. early intellectual growth and development is directly dependent upon the quality of care and type of experiences to which young children are exposed; and

3. socioeconomically impoverished environments include biological, environmental, and other risk factors, which can adversely affect chances of school success and impede intellectual growth.

Head Start was envisioned to be a comprehensive, multidimensional intervention effort aimed at the very roots of poverty in communities across America. It represented a coordinated federal effort at comprehensive intervention in the lives of young children (Zigler & Valentine, 1979). Head Start was unique in its emphasis on the total development of the youngster, on strengthening the family unit, and in its comprehensive nature of the services provided. The goals of the Head Start effort included increasing the child's physical, social, and emotional development; developing the youngster's intellectual skills and readiness for school; as well as improving the health of the child by providing medical, dental, social, and psychological services. Head Start was also unusual not only in its intent—to bring about a change for the child, her family, and the community, but also for its use of a multidisciplinary intervention model wherein the importance of seeing the whole child was recognized (Brain, 1979).

Parents played an unprecedented role in the Head Start program. Parent involvement and their meaningful participation was considered vitally important. They had a key voice in the local decision-making process in addition to opportunities for employment in the program or for volunteering their expertise. The inclusion of training programs for low-income adults and the establishment of a career development ladder for employees and volunteers also distinguished the Head Start program.

It is important to remember that Head Start was not specifically directed at children with special needs, although many of the youngsters served would today be identified as an at-risk population. The enactment of PL 92-424 in 1972 did require, however, that the project reserve no less than 10% of its enrollment for children with disabilities.

Fortunately, thanks to changes in federal regulations regarding Head Start, this program is now able to play a larger role in the lives of young children with special needs. In January 1993 new rules for providing services to preschoolers with disabilities enrolled in Head Start were published in the *Federal Register*. Some of the many changes guiding Head Start agencies are the following requirements:

- a model designed to locate and serve young children with disabilities and their parents;
- the development of an Individualized Education Program (IEP) for each youngster determined to be disabled;
- quicker screening of children suspected of needing special services;
- revised evaluation procedures for determining who might be eligible for a special education and related services; and
- the establishment of a disability services coordinator who would be responsible for overseeing the delivery of services to preschoolers with special needs.

These goals are to be met through a detailed and comprehensive disabilities service plan, which out-

lines the strategies for meeting the needs of children with disabilities and their families. Among the several provisions are standards that call for the assurance that youngsters with disabilities will be included in the full range of activities and services provided to other children; a component that addresses the transitioning from infant and toddler programs into Head Start as well as exiting Head Start to the next placement; and a provision stipulating that eligible children will be provided a special education with related services designed to meet their unique needs. Collectively, these changes hold the promise of significantly improving the quality of life for many young children with special needs and their families.

We consider Head Start to be a visionary program model. The framers of the project had the foresight to insist on comprehensive services, meaningful parent involvement, and a multidisciplinary approach to intervention. Many of these aspects can be found in contemporary programs and legislation. Head Start also served as a forerunner of other compensatory initiatives, which we will now briefly examine.

Project Follow-Through **Project Follow-Through** was developed in 1967 in response to controversy surrounding the effectiveness of the Head Start efforts. Some educational research data suggested that the cognitive gains of the Head Start experiment were not maintained once the children enrolled in elementary school (Cicerelli, Evans, & Schiller, 1969). Professionals quickly realized that a short-term intervention program was ineffective in inoculating young children against the deleterious effects of poverty. Follow-Through was introduced in an effort to continue the gains developed in Head Start. A new model was designed, which extended the Head Start concept to include children enrolled in kindergarten through the third grade. Like its predecessor, Project Follow-Through was comprehensive in its scope of services while maintaining the Head Start emphasis on creating change in the home and community. Unfortunately, a Congressional funding crisis precipitated a retooling of the project's original goals and objectives. According to Peterson's analysis (1987), the focus shifted from a service operation very much like Head Start to an educational experiment dedicated to assessing the effectiveness of various approaches aimed at increasing the educational attainment of young disadvantaged and at-risk students. Rather than offering a single model of early childhood education for low-income pupils, Project Follow-Through studied a variety of approaches and strategies realizing that a singular model would not meet the needs of all children. Local public schools were free to adopt the program model that they believed best met the unique needs of their communities.

Home Start In 1972 another program variation, **Home Start,** was created. Simply stated, this program took the education component typically found in Head Start centers into a child's home. The focus of Home Start was low-income parents and their preschool-aged children. Efforts were aimed at providing educational stimulation to the children in addition to developing and enhancing the parenting skills of adults. This task was accomplished through the utilization of home visitors who were skilled and trained residents of the community.

Early Head Start Early Head Start emerged from a growing recognition among service providers, researchers, policymakers, and politicians of the need to extend the Head Start model downward to the birth-to-three age group. This awareness of the need for comprehensive, intensive, and year-round services for very young children resulted in **Early Head Start** (Halpern, 2000; Meisels & Shonkoff, 2000). The 1994 reauthorization of Head Start (PL 103–252) created Early Head Start, a program focusing on low-income families with infants and toddlers as well as women who are pregnant. The mission of this program, which began in 1995, is to

- promote healthy pregnancy outcomes;
- enhance children's physical, social, emotional, and cognitive development;
- enable parents to be better caregivers and teachers to their children, and
- help parents meet their goals, including economic independence.

Early Head Start incorporates what its framers call a "four corner emphasis," which embodies child, family, community, and staff development (Halpern, 2000). Services provided through this program include high quality early education and care both in and out of the home; home visits; child care; parent education; comprehensive health services including services before, during, and after pregnancy; nutrition information; and peer support groups for parents.

Research Activities

In addition to involvement and action by the federal government, individual scientists and researchers have also been concerned about the damaging consequences of poverty on young children and their families. Two representative intervention projects include the Carolina Abecedarian Project and the Perry Preschool Project. Both of these programs focus on improving the cognitive skills of young children, thereby increasing their chances for later scholastic success.

The Carolina Abecedarian Project attempted to modify environmental forces impinging upon the intellectual development of young children living in poverty. Designed in 1972 as a longitudinal experiment, Craig Ramey and his colleagues (Ramey & Campbell, 1977, 1984; Ramey & Smith, 1977) found that youngsters enrolled in a center-based preschool intervention program who were exposed to stimulating early learning experiences achieved higher IQ scores when compared to matched age-mates who did not participate in the project. A follow-up of participants found that, at age twelve and fifteen, youngsters exposed to early intervention continued to outperform control subjects on standardized measures of intellectual development and academic achievement. Additionally, these individuals had significantly fewer grade retentions and special education placements (Campbell & Ramey, 1994, 1995). The Carolina program clearly demonstrates, as we noted earlier, the plasticity of intelligence and the positive effects of early environmental intervention.

Our second illustration is the Perry Preschool Project in Ypsilanti, Michigan. This program is one of the best examples of the long-term educational benefit of early childhood experiences. The Perry Preschool Project was designed as a longitudinal study to measure the effects of a quality preschool education on children living in poverty. Based on the work of Jean Piaget, it strongly emphasized cognitive development. More than 120 disadvantaged youngsters were followed from age three until late adolescence. The results of the investigation can be summarized as follows:

> Results to age 19 indicate long-lasting beneficial effects of preschool education in improving cognitive performance during early childhood; in improving scholastic placement and achievement during the school years; in decreasing delinquency and crime, the use of welfare assistance, and the incidence of teenage pregnancy; and in increasing high school graduation rates and the frequency of enrollment in postsecondary programs and employment. (Berrueta-Clement, Schweinhart, Barnett, Epstein, & Weikart, 1984, p. 1)

Additional follow-up (Schweinhart, Barnes, & Weikart, 1993) demonstrated that, in comparison to a control group, individuals in their mid-20s who participated in this project as preschoolers had higher incomes, were more likely to own a home, had significantly fewer arrests, and less involvement with community social service agencies.

A Concluding Thought It is safe to conclude that, generally speaking, compensatory education programs do benefit young children at-risk for success in school. The optimism exhibited by the early supporters of various intervention initiatives has been tempered, however, by a host of political, financial, and other factors. Reality has reminded educators, policymakers, and researchers that there are no quick or magical solutions to complex social problems like poverty. Yet, we must not be overly pessimistic; education does remain an important vehicle for successfully altering the lives of young children and their caregivers.

Summary

Although early childhood special education is a relatively young field, the forces that have helped to shape its identity have a rich and distinguished history. Many contemporary ideas such as individualized instruction, readiness, and parent involvement have their roots in the work of earlier philosophers, social reformers, and educational theorists. Three distinct fields—early childhood education, special education, and compensatory education—have contributed, in their own ways, to the emergence of a wide array of programs and services for young children with special needs and their families. Professionals recognize how very important the early years of a child's life are for later social, emotional, and cognitive growth and development.

Today's early childhood special education is perhaps best conceptualized as a synthesis of various theories, principles, and practices borrowed from each of its parent fields. It is a concept that continues to evolve. We are in a strong position to successfully build on the accomplishments and achievements of the past.

Check Your Understanding

1. Various religious leaders, philosophers, and educational theorists played a major role in the development of early childhood education. List five of them and their contributions found in contemporary early childhood programs.

2. Describe the "gifts" and "occupations" of Froebel's children's garden.

3. Explain Dewey's ideas about educating young children.

4. Identify the major elements of Montessori's approach to teaching young children.

5. How did Piaget believe intelligence develops?

6. Describe Vygotsky's concept of a zone of proximal development (ZPD).

7. Why would Vygotsky be considered an early advocate of integration?

8. What role did Europeans play in the development of special education in the United States?

9. Define the term *compensatory education.*

10. What is the purpose of Project Head Start?

11. List five significant events that have helped to shape the field of early childhood special education.

References

Ballard, J., Ramirez, B., & Weintraub, F. (1982). *Special education in America: Its legal and governmental foundations.* Reston, VA: Council for Exceptional Children.

Berk, L., & Winsler, A. (1995). *Scaffolding children's learning: Vygotsky and early childhood education.* Washington, DC: National Association for the Education of Young Children.

Berrueta-Clement, J., Schweinhart, L., Barnett, W., Epstein, A., & Weikart, D. (1984). Changed lives: The effects of the Perry Preschool Project on youths through age 19. *Monographs of the High/Scope Education Research Foundation, 8.*

Bloom, B. (1964). *Stability and change in human characteristics.* New York: Wiley.

Brain, G. (1979). The early planners. In E. Zigler & J. Valentine (Eds.), *Project Head Start: A legacy of the war on poverty* (pp.72–77). New York: Free Press.

Bredekamp, S., & Rosegrant, T. (Eds.). (1992). *Reaching potentials: Appropriate curriculum and assessment for young children* (Vol. 1). Washington, DC: National Association for the Education of Young Children.

Campbell, F., & Ramey, C. (1994). Effects of early intervention on intellectual and academic achievement: A follow-up study of children from low-income families. *Child Development, 65,* 684–698.

Campbell, F., & Ramey, C. (1995). Cognitive and school outcomes for high risk African-American students at middle adolescence: Positive effects of early intervention. *American Educational Research Journal, 32,* 743–772.

Cicerelli, V., Evans, J., & Schiller, J. (1969). *The impact of Head Start on children's cognitive and affective development: Preliminary report.* Washington, DC: Office of Economic Opportunity.

Dewey, J. (1916). *Democracy and education.* New York: Macmillan.

Dunn, L. (1973). *Exceptional children in the schools* (2nd ed). New York: Holt, Rinehart & Winston.

Federal Register. (1993, January 21). Head Start program final rule. *58*(12), 5492–5518.

Gargiulo, R. (2003). *Special education in contemporary society: An introduction to exceptionality.* Belmont, CA: Wadsworth.

Gargiulo, R., & Černá, M. (1992). Special education in Czechoslovakia: Characteristics and issues. *International Journal of Special Education, 7*(1), 60–70.

Gearhart, B., Mullen, R., & Gearhart, C. (1993). *Exceptional individuals.* Pacific Grove, CA: Brooks/Cole.

Ginsburg, H., & Opper, S. (1969). *Piaget's theory of intellectual development.* Englewood Cliffs, NJ: Prentice-Hall.

Graves, S. (1990). Early childhood education. In T. E. C. Smith, *Introduction to education* (2nd ed., pp. 189–219). St. Paul, MN: West.

Graves, S., Gargiulo, R., & Sluder L. (1996). *Young children: An introduction to early childhood education.* St. Paul, MN: West.

Halpern, R. (2000). Early childhood intervention for low-income children and families. In J. Shonkoff & S. Meisels (Eds.), *Handbook of early childhood intervention* (2nd ed., pp. 361–386). Cambridge, England: Cambridge University Press.

Hanson, M., & Lynch, E. (1995). *Early intervention* (2nd ed.). Austin, TX: Pro-Ed.

Hills, T. (1992). Reaching potentials through appropriate assessment. In S. Bredekamp & T. Rosegrant (Eds.), *Reaching potentials: Appropriate curriculum and assessment for young children* (Vol. 1, pp.43–63). Washington, DC: National Association for the Education of Young Children.

Hunt, J. (1961). *Intelligence and experience.* New York: Ronald Press.

Lawton, J. (1988). *Introduction to child care and early childhood education.* Glenview, IL: Scott Foresman.

McCollum, J., & Maude, S. (1993). Portrait of a changing field: Policy and practice in early childhood special education. In B. Spodek (Ed.), *Handbook of research on the education of young children* (pp. 352–371). New York: Macmillan.

Meisels, S., & Shonkoff, J. (2000). Early childhood intervention: A continuing evolution. In J. Shonkoff & S. Meisels (Eds.), *Handbook of early childhood intervention* (2nd ed., pp. 3–31). Cambridge, England: Cambridge University Press.

Montessori, M. (1965). *Dr. Montessori's own handbook.* New York: Schocken Books.

Morrison, G. (2001). *Early childhood education today* (8th ed.). Upper Saddle River, NJ: Prentice-Hall.

Peterson, N. (1987). *Early intervention for handicapped and at-risk children.* Denver: Love Publishing.

Ramey, C., & Campbell, F. (1977). Prevention of developmental retardation in high risk children. In P. Mittler (Ed.), *Research to practice in mental retardation: Care and intervention* (Vol. 1, pp. 157–164). Baltimore: University Park Press.

Ramey, C., & Campbell, F. (1984). Preventive education for high risk children: Cognitive consequences of the Carolina Abecedarian Project. *American Journal of Mental Deficiency, 88,* 515–523.

Ramey, C., & Smith, B. (1977). Assessing the intellectual consequences of early intervention with high-risk infants. *American Journal of Mental Deficiency, 81,* 318–324.

Schweinhart, L., Barnes, H., & Weikart, D. (1993). *Significant benefits: The High/Scope Perry Preschool study through age 27,* Ypsilanti, MI: High/Scope Press.

Shonkoff, J., & Meisels, S. (1990). Early childhood intervention: The evolution of a concept. In S. Meisels & J. Shonkoff (Eds.), *Handbook of early childhood intervention* (pp. 3–31). Cambridge, England: Cambridge University Press.

Spodek, B., Saracho, O., & Davis, M. (1991). *Foundations of early childhood education* (2nd ed.). Englewood Cliffs, NJ: Prentice-Hall.

Thurman, S., & Widerstrom, A. (1990). *Infants and young children with special needs* (2nd ed.). Baltimore: Paul H. Brookes.

Tudge, J. (1992). Processes and consequences of peer collaboration: A Vygotskian analysis. *Child Development, 63,* 1364–1379.

Vygotsky, L. (1978). *Mind in society: The development of higher mental processes.* Cambridge, MA: Harvard University Press.

Vygotsky, L. (1993). *The collected works of L. S. Vygotsky Vol. 2: The fundamentals of defectology.* New York: Plenum.

Zigler, E., & Valentine, J. (Eds.). (1979). *Project Head Start: A legacy of the War on Poverty.* New York: Free Press.

CHAPTER

2

The Context of Early Childhood Special Education

Learning Outcomes

After reading this chapter you will be able to:

- Define the terms *disability, handicap, developmental delay,* and *at-risk.*
- Discuss how judicial decisions and legislative enactments have benefited young children with special needs.
- Summarize the major provisions contained in the Individuals with Disabilities Education Act.
- Identify at least four benefits of early intervention for youngsters with special needs.
- Explain the concept of *ecology* and its importance to the field of early childhood special education.

Early childhood special education is a relatively young field drawing upon the long history and rich legacy of both early childhood and special education in addition to the contributions from compensatory education. Yet, early childhood special education is a distinct field having its own identity and purpose. In order to fully appreciate this discipline several topics basic to the understanding of its development need to be explored. These issues will help provide a firm foundation for the later examination of programs and services for young children with special needs and their families. Attention will be focused on key terminology, the impact of litigation and legislation on the growth of the field, the prevalence of young children with special needs, the research evidence on the efficacy of early intervention, and the validity of an ecological approach for looking at the world of young children with special needs.

Definitions and Terminology

Early childhood teachers serve a wide range of students. An increasing number of these young children exhibit disabilities, some may have developmental delays, and others might be at-risk for future school failure. What do these terms mean? Is a disability synonymous with a handicap? What is a developmental delay? What factors jeopardize a child's future academic success? Unfortunately, clear-cut answers to

these basic questions are sometimes difficult to achieve. Confusion and misinterpretation is not unusual, even among professionals. Hence, the following descriptions are an attempt to clarify key terminology and provide a common foundation for understanding infants, toddlers, and preschoolers with special needs.

Exceptional Children

Early childhood special educators will frequently identify their students as being **exceptional children.** This inclusive term generally refers to individuals

Young children with special needs are first and foremost children.

who differ from societal or community standards of normalcy. These children will, therefore, require an educational program customized to their unique needs. Some exceptionalities are obvious, while others are less obvious, such as an infant who is deaf. Furthermore, some youngsters may greatly benefit from their exceptionality in their daily lives; for example, a child who is intellectually talented, while in other situations an exceptionality may prove to be a significant problem.

Teachers must not lose sight, however, of the fact that an exceptional child is first and foremost a child—a pupil who is more like their normally developing classmates than he or she is different. The fact that a young child is recognized as exceptional should never prohibit professionals from realizing just how typical the youngster is in many other ways.

Disability and Handicap

All too often professionals, as well as the general public, use the terms *disability* and *handicap* interchangeably. These terms, however, have distinct meanings and are not synonymous. When professionals talk about a **disability,** they are referring to the inability of a preschooler to do something in a certain way. A disability may be thought of as an incapacity to perform as other children due to impairments in sensory, physical, cognitive, and other areas of functioning. A **handicap,** on the other hand, refers to the problems that a youngster with a disability encounters as she attempts to function and interact in her environment. Mandy, for example, has cerebral palsy. This is a disability. If her disability prohibits her from becoming a professional ice skater, then we would say Mandy is handicapped. Stephen, a four-year-old who is legally blind (a disability), would be handicapped if his preschool teacher inadvertently used an overhead projector while explaining a cooking activity. A disability may or may not be a handicap depending upon the specific circumstances. For instance, a four-year-old child with braces on his leg might have difficulty walking upstairs but, in the art center, his creativity and talents are easily recognized. We should only use the term *handicap* when explaining the consequences or impact imposed on a youngster by his or her disability. Gargiulo (2003) urges educators to separate the disability from the handicap.

We have chosen to use the general term *children with special needs* to describe infants, toddlers, and preschoolers with disabilities. We cannot stress enough the importance of remembering that a toddler, or any individual with a disability, is first and foremost a person. It is imperative that teachers focus on the child and not the impairment. Early childhood special educators should look for similarities between children with special needs and their typically developing classmates, not differences. Attention should also be focused on the students' strengths and abilities, not their disabilities.

Federal Definition of Disability

As we previously noted, early childhood special educators serve a variety of young children with special needs; but, who are these children? The federal government, via legislation, the *Individuals with Disabilities Education Act Amendments of 1997* (PL 105-17), defines a youngster with a disability according to thirteen distinct categories listed in the following chart. The government's interpretation of these labels is presented in Appendix A. Individual states frequently use these federal guidelines to construct their own standards and policies as to who is eligible to receive early intervention and special education services.

Federal Classification of Disabilities	
Autism	Other health impairments
Deaf-Blindness	Emotional disturbance
Hearing impairments including deafness	Specific learning disability
Mental retardation	Speech or language impairments
Multiple disabilities	Traumatic brain injury
Orthopedic impairments	Visual impairment including blindness
	Developmental delay

Developmental Delay and At-Risk

Because of the adverse effects of early labeling, young children with special needs are sometimes identified as being either developmentally delayed or at-risk for future problems in school. These labels, in fact, are incorporated in PL 99-457. This significant enactment requires that local schools provide comprehensive services to children with disabilities ages three to five. The youngsters, however, do *not* have to be identified with one of the thirteen federal disability labels. The 1991 amendments (PL 102-119) to the *Individuals with Disabilities Education Act (IDEA)* allows states to use a generic category like "children with disabilities." According to a national survey (Danaher, 2001), 17 states utilize a noncategorical description exclusively when classifying preschoolers with special needs. Examples of these generic labels include "preschool child [student] with a disability" (Colorado, Ohio, New York); "preschool special needs" (West Virginia); "individual with exceptional needs" (California); and "preprimary impaired" (Michigan). Many professionals believe that the use of a categorical disability label for most young children is of questionable value (McCollum & Maude, 1993). A noncategorical approach to serving young children with special needs is, therefore, perfectly acceptable as well as legal. Many early childhood special education programs offer services without categorizing their pupils on the basis of a disability (McCollum & Maude; Spodek & Saracho, 1994a). Thus, instead of a categorical approach, we find that programs that serve young children with special needs frequently use the broad terms *developmentally delayed* and *at-risk* when identifying their students. In fact, this is the terminology of choice when talking about children with disabilities who are younger than three years of age.

As a result of the passage of PL 105–17 it is now permissible, at the discretion of the state and local education agency, to use the label *developmentally delayed* for children ages three through nine.

Developmental Delay Congress realized that establishing a national definition of **developmental delay** would be an almost insurmountable task, and therefore, left the responsibility of developing a satisfactory definition to the individual states. One consequence of this action is the tremendous diversity of criteria found in the various meanings of this term. Many states, according to Shackelford's (2002) analysis, incorporate a quantitative approach when determining who is developmentally delayed. Typical of this strategy is a reliance on data derived from various assessment instruments. Shackelford noted three different kinds of quantitative definitions:

- a delay expressed in terms of standard deviations (SD) below the mean (Kentucky: 2 SD in one developmental area or 1.5 SD in two areas);

- a delay expressed in terms of a difference between a youngster's chronological age and their actual performance level (Iowa: 25% delay in one or more developmental areas); or

- a delay expressed in terms of performance— n number of months below child's chronological age (Texas: 2–12 months: 2-month delay; 13–24 months: 3-month delay; 25–36 months: 4-month delay).

Table 2–1 illustrates some of the various criteria used by the states when quantifying a developmental delay. Obviously, there is no one correct way to define this concept. Each approach has its advantages and disadvantages. In fact, 13 states allow for the use of a qualitative determination when considering whether or not a youngster is developmentally delayed (Danaher, 2001). Florida and Maine are but two examples of states that permit the use of professional judgment, informed team consensus, or the informed clinical opinions of members of a multidisciplinary team.

There are several advantages to using the term *developmentally delayed*. First, because it suggests a developmental status rather than a category, it is anticipated that placement of students in developmentally appropriate classrooms will be more likely. Second, it is hoped that this concept will lead to services being matched to the needs and abilities of the child rather than having services decided by a categorical label. Finally, professionals believe that the utilization of this term is likely to encourage inclusive models of service delivery instead of services being

Table 2–1   Examples of Definitions of Developmental Delay

State	Criteria
Arizona	50% delay in one or more areas
Hawaii	consensus of multidisciplinary team; no quantitative data specified
Indiana	1.5 SD in one area or 20% below chronological age: 1 SD in two areas or 15% below chronological age in two areas: informed clinical opinion
Massachusetts	age 6 months: 1.5-month delay in one or more areas; age 12 months: 3-months delay in one or more areas; age 18 months: 4-month delay in one or more areas; age 24–30 months: 6-month delay in one or more areas.
Montana	50% delay in one area or 25% delay in two areas; informed clinical opinion
Ohio	"measurable delay" or not reaching developmental milestones or informed clinical opinion
South Dakota	25% below normal age range, 6-month delay, or 1.5 SD in one or more areas
Wisconsin	25% delay or 1.3 SD in one area: atypical development; or team decision

SOURCE: Adapted from J. Shackelford. (2002). *State and Jurisdictional Eligibility Definitions for Infants and Toddlers with Disabilities Under IDEA*. NEC*TAS Notes 11. Chapel Hill, NC: National Early Childhood Technical Assistance Center.

primarily driven by a disability label (Division for Early Childhood, 1996).

At-Risk   When professionals talk about children being **at-risk,** they are speaking of youngsters "who have not been formally identified as having a disability, but who may be developing conditions that will limit their success in school or lead to disabilities. This can be the result of exposure to adverse genetic, biological, or environmental factors" (Spodek & Saracho, 1994b, p. 16). This definition parallels an earlier description of risk factors identified by Kopp (1983). She defines risk as "a wide range of biological and environmental conditions that are associated with increased probability for cognitive, social, affective, and physical problems" (p. 1081).

In both of these definitions we see that exposure to adverse circumstances *may* lead to later problems in development and learning, but it is not a guarantee that developmental problems will occur. Risk factors only set the stage or heighten the probability that differences might arise. Many youngsters are subject to a wide variety of risks, yet they never evidence developmental problems. Table 2–2 presents some of the common factors and conditions that can place a child at-risk.

Risk factors may lead to future problems in learning and development.

Our understanding of the at-risk concept has been greatly enhanced by the wide acceptance professionals have given to Tjossem's (1976) description of three at-risk categories. His tripartite classification scheme includes established, biological, and environmental risk categories. These categories are not mutually exclusive and frequently overlap. As Guralnick (1998) notes, a child identified as being biologically at-risk

Table 2-2 Representative Factors Placing Young Children At-Risk for Developmental Problems

- Maternal alcohol and drug abuse
- Children born to teenage mothers or women over age 40
- Home environment lacking adequate stimulation
- Maternal diabetes, hypertension, or toxemia
- Exposure to rubella
- Chronic poverty
- Primary caregiver is developmentally disabled
- Infections such as encephalitis and meningitis
- Oxygen deprivation
- Child abuse and neglect
- Accidents and head trauma
- Inadequate maternal and infant nutrition
- Genetic disorders such as Down syndrome, phenylketonuria, and galactosemia
- Family history of congenital abnormalities
- Exposure to radiation
- Prematurity
- RH incompatibility
- Low birth weight
- Ingestion of poisons and toxic substances by child
- Prolonged or unusual delivery

Note: Factors are not ranked in order of potential influence.

due to prematurity may also be at-risk due to environmental factors like severe poverty. As a result of this "double vulnerability," the probability for future delays and learning difficulties dramatically increases.

Established Risk. Children with a diagnosed medical disorder of known etiology and predictable prognosis or outcome are considered to manifest an established risk. Illustrations of such conditions would be a child born with cerebral palsy, Down syndrome, spina bifida, or an inborn error of metabolism such as PKU (phenylketonuria). Youngsters

identified with an established risk condition *must* be served if the state receives IDEA Part C monies.

Biological Risk. Included in this category are youngsters with a history of pre-, peri-, and postnatal conditions and developmental events that heighten the potential for later atypical or aberrant development. Examples of such conditions or complications include premature births, infants with low birth weights, maternal diabetes, rubella (German measles), anoxia, bacterial infections like meningitis, and HIV (human immunodeficiency virus) infection.

Environmental Risk. Environmentally at-risk children are biologically typical, but their life experiences and/or environmental conditions are so limiting or threatening that the likelihood of delayed development exists. Extreme poverty, child abuse, absence of adequate shelter and medical care, parental substance abuse, and limited opportunities for nurturance and social stimulation are all examples of potential environmental factors. This risk category, as well as children who are biologically at-risk, results in discretionary services. States may elect to provide early intervention if they wish to; but, they are *not* mandated to serve infants and toddlers who are biologically or environmentally at-risk. Currently, eight states have elected to serve infants and toddlers who are at-risk (Shackelford, 2002).

Given the magnitude of factors that may place a child at-risk for developing disabilities, the value of prevention and early intervention cannot be underestimated. Of course, prevention is better than remediation.

Early Intervention and Early Childhood Special Education

Finally, before leaving this section on terminology, we would like to clarify the terms early intervention and early childhood special education. Generally speaking, **early intervention** refers to the delivery of a coordinated and comprehensive set of specialized supports and services to infants and toddlers (birth through age two) with developmental delays or at-risk conditions and their families. This term can be found in federal legislation; specially, Part C of the *Individuals with Disabilities Education Act* (PL 99-457) commonly known as IDEA (to be discussed later in this chapter). Describing the nature of early intervention is not an easy task. Early intervention can be characterized according to type of service provided (physical therapy, vision services), location of service (home, special center), and even service provider (occupational therapist, nurse) to mention just some of the critical features of this concept (U. S. Department of Education, 2001).

The label **early childhood special education** is typically used when talking about the provision of customized services uniquely crafted to meet the individual needs of youngsters with disabilities between three and five years of age. It is important to note that when describing special education we are not talking about a location but rather a system of supports and services for children with disabilities (Walsh, Smith, & Taylor, 2000).

Litigation and Legislation Affecting Children with Special Needs

Key Judicial Decisions

Early childhood special education is an evolving discipline. In addition to drawing upon its three parent fields, judicial action has played a key role in the growth of the field. Litigation instigated by parents and interest groups has helped pave the way in securing numerous rights for children with disabilities and their families. Since the 1960s and early 1970s a plethora of state and federal court decisions have shaped and defined a wide range of issues that impact contemporary special education policies and procedures. Table 2–3 summarizes some of the landmark cases affecting the field of special education. Many of the judicial remedies emanating from these lawsuits form the cornerstones of both federal and state legislative enactments focusing on children with special needs. Furthermore, many accepted practices in today's special education programs, such as

nondiscriminatory assessments and due process procedures, have their roots in various court decisions.

Key Federal Legislation

Federal legislative intervention in the lives of persons with disabilities is of relatively recent origin. Prior to the late 1950s and early 1960s, little federal attention was devoted to citizens with special needs. When legislation was enacted, it primarily assisted specific groups of individuals such as those who were deaf or mentally retarded. The last 30 years, however, have witnessed a flurry of federal legislative activity, which has aided the growth of special education and provided educational benefits and other opportunities and rights to children and adults with disabilities.

Due to the multitude of the public laws (PL) affecting special education, discussion will be reserved for landmark legislation. (See the Online Companion accompanying this book for some of the early and key enactments pertaining to persons with disabilities. Go to http://www.earlychilded.delmar.com. Click on the Online Resources at the bottom of the page.) We will examine five significant pieces of legislation that have dramatically affected the educational opportunities of infants, toddlers, preschool children, and school-age children with special needs. Our initial review will focus on PL 94-142, the *Individuals with Disabilities Education Act (IDEA)*, or as it was previously called, the *Education for All Handicapped Children Act*. This change came about due to the enactment on October 30, 1990, of PL 101-476. Provisions contained in this legislation will be reviewed later.

Public Law 94-142 The *Individuals with Disabilities Education Act* is viewed as a "Bill of Rights" for children with exceptionalities and their families. It is considered by many individuals to be one of the, if not *the,* most important piece of federal legislation ever enacted on behalf of children with special needs. Some advocacy groups consider this enactment as a vital first step in securing the constitutional rights of citizens with disabilities (Allen, 1992).

Table 2–3   A Synopsis of Selected Court Cases Influencing Special Education

Case	Year	Issue	Judicial Decision
Brown v. Board of Education	1954	Educational segregation	Segregation of students by race ruled unconstitutional. Children are being deprived of equal educational opportunity. Effectively ended "separate but equal" schools for white and black pupils. Used as a precedent for arguing that children with disabilities cannot be excluded from a public education.
Hobson v. Hansen	1967	Classifying students	Grouping or "tracking" of students on the basis of standardized tests, which were found to be biased, held to be unconstitutional. Tracking systems discriminated against poor and minority children. Equal protection clause of Fourteenth Amendment violated.
Diana v. State Board of Education	1970	Class placement	Linguistically different students must be tested in their primary language as well as in English. Students cannot be placed in special education classes on the basis of tests that are culturally biased. Test items were to be revised so as to reflect students' cultures. Group administered IQ tests cannot be utilized for placement of children in programs for the mentally retarded.
Pennsylvania Association for Retarded Children v. Commonwealth of Pennsylvania	1972	Right to education	State must guarantee a free public education to all children with mental retardation, ages 6–21, regardless of degree of impairment or associated disabilities. Students were to be placed in the most integrated environment. Definition of education expanded. Case established the right of parents to participate in educational decisions affecting their children.
Mills v. Board of Education of the District of Columbia	1972	Right to education	Extended the Pennsylvania decision to include *all* children with disabilities. Specifically established the constitutional right of children with exceptionalities to a public education regardless of their functional level. Presumed absence of fiscal resources is not a valid reason for failing to provide appropriate educational services to students with disabilities. Due process procedures established to protect the rights of the child.

—continued

Table 2-3 *Continued*

Case	Year	Issue	Judicial Decision
Larry P. v. Riles	1972, 1979	Class placement	A landmark case parallel to the *Diana* suit. African American students could not be placed in classes for educable mentally retarded (EMR) children solely on the basis of intellectual assessments found to be culturally and racially biased. The court instructed school officials to develop an assessment instrument that would not discriminate against minority children. The failure to comply with this order resulted in a 1979 ruling, which completely prohibited the use of IQ tests for identifying African American students for placement in EMR classes. Ruling applies only to the state of California.
Jose P. v. Ambach	1979	Timelines and delivery of services	A far-reaching class action lawsuit that completely restructured the delivery of special education services in New York City public schools. Judgment established (1) school-based support teams to conduct evaluations and provide services; (2) stringent timelines for completing evaluations and placement; (3) due process procedures; (4) guidelines for nondiscriminatory evaluation; (5) detailed monitoring procedures; and (6) accessibility of school facilities.
Armstrong v. Klein	1980	Extended school year	States' refusal to pay for schooling in excess of 180 days for pupils with severe disabilities is a violation of their rights to an appropriate education as found in PL 94-142. The court moved that some children with disabilities will regress significantly during summer recess and have longer recoupment periods; thus, they are denied an appropriate education if not provided with a year-round education.
Tatro v. State of Texas	1980	Related services	A U.S. Supreme Court decision, which held that catheterization qualified as a related service under PL 94-142. Catheterization not considered an exempted medical procedure as it could be performed by a health care aide or school nurse. Court further stipulated that only those services that allow a student to benefit from a special education qualify as related services.

Table 2-3 *Continued*

Case	Year	Issue	Judicial Decision
Board of Education v. Rowley	1982	Appropriate education	First U.S. Supreme Court interpretation of PL 94-142. Court addresses the issue of what constitutes an "appropriate" education for a deaf student making satisfactory progress. Supreme Court ruled that an appropriate education does not necessarily mean an education that will allow for the maximum possible achievement; rather, students must be given a reasonable opportunity to learn. Parents' request for a sign language interpreter, therefore, was denied. An appropriate education is not synonymous with an optimal educational experience.
Honig v. Doe	1988	Exclusion from school	Children with special needs whose behavior is a direct result of their disability cannot be expelled from school due to misbehavior. If behavior leading to expulsion is not a consequence of the exceptionality, pupil may be expelled. Short-term suspension from school not interpreted as a change in pupil's individualized education program (IEP).
Daniel R. R. v. State Board of Education	1989	Class placement	A Fifth Circuit Court of Appeals decision that held that a segregated class was an appropriate placement for a student with Down syndrome. Preference for integrated placement viewed as secondary to the need for an appropriate education. Court established a two-prong test for determining compliance with the LRE mandate for students with severe disabilities. First, it must be determined if a pupil can make satisfactory progress and achieve educational benefit in a regular classroom through curriculum modification and the use of supplementary aids and services. Second, it must be determined whether the pupil has been integrated to the maximum extent appropriate. Successful compliance with both parts fulfills a school's obligation under federal law. Ruling affects LRE cases in Louisiana, Texas, and Mississippi, but has become a benchmark decision for other jurisdictions as well.

—continued

Table 2-3 *Continued*

Case	Year	Issue	Judicial Decision
Oberti v. Board of Education of the Borough of Clementon School District	1992	Least restrictive environment	Placement in a regular education classroom with the use of supplementary aids and services must be offered to a student with disabilities prior to considering more segregated placements. A pupil cannot be excluded from a regular classroom solely because curriculum, services, or other practices would require modification. A decision to exclude a learner from the regular education classroom necessitates justification and documentation. Clear judicial preference for educational integration established.
Agostini v. Fulton	1997	Provision of services	A U.S. Supreme Court decision that reversed a long-standing ruling banning the delivery of publicly funded educational services to students enrolled in private schools. Interpreted to mean special educators can now provide services to children in parochial schools.
Cedar Rapids Community School District v. Garret F.	1999	Related services	A U.S. Supreme Court decision which expanded and clarified the concept of related services. This case affirmed that intensive and continuous school health care services necessary for a student to attend school, and which are *not* performed by a physician, qualify as related services.

The intent of this bill was:

to ensure that all handicapped children have available to them . . . a free, appropriate public education which emphasizes special education and related services designed to meet their unique needs, to ensure that the rights of handicapped children and their parents or guardians are protected, to assist States and localities to provide for the education of all handicapped children and to assess and ensure the effectiveness of efforts to educate handicapped children. [Section 601 (c)]

In addition to these four purposes, there are six major components incorporated in this legislation:

1. *The right to a free appropriate public education (FAPE)—all* children, regardless of the severity of the disability, must be provided an education appropriate to their unique needs at no cost to the parent(s)/guardian(s). Included in this feature is the concept of related services, which requires that children receive, for example, as necessary, occupational and physical therapy, as well as speech therapy among other services.

2. *The principle of **least restrictive environment** (LRE)—* children with exceptionalities are to be educated, to the maximum extent appropriate, with typical students. Placements must be consistent with the pupil's educational needs.

3. *An **individualized education program (IEP)**—*this document, developed in conjunction with the parent(s)/guardian(s), is an individually tailored statement describing an educational plan for each exceptional learner. The IEP is required to address (a) present level of academic functioning; (b) annual goals and accompanying instructional objectives; (c) educational services to be provided; (d) the degree to which the pupil will be able to participate in regular education programs; (e) plans for initiating services and length of service delivery; and (f) an annual evaluation procedure specifying objective criteria to determine if instructional objectives are being met.

4. *Procedural due process*—the Act affords parent(s)/guardian(s) several safeguards as it pertains to their child's education. Briefly, parent(s)/guardian(s) have the right to examine all records; obtain an independent evaluation; receive written notification (in parent's native language) of proposed changes to their child's educational classification or placement; and a right to an impartial hearing whenever disagreements occur regarding educational plans for their son/daughter.

5. *Nondiscriminatory assessment*—prior to placement, a child must be evaluated in all areas of suspected disability by tests, which are neither culturally nor linguistically biased. Students are to receive several types of assessments; a single evaluation procedure is not permitted.

6. *Parental participation*—PL 94-142 mandates parental involvement. Sometimes referred to as the "Parent's Law," this legislation requires that parents participate in the decision-making process that affects their child's education. IDEA regulations currently allow assistance to parents as part of a preschooler's IEP if such assistance is necessary for the child to benefit from special education. Parental training activities are also permissible as a related service.

Congress mandated by September 1, 1980, a free appropriate public education for all eligible children age three through twenty-one. The law, however, did *not* require services to preschool children with disabilities. An exception was contained in the legislative language:

> except that, with respect to handicapped children aged three to five and eighteen to twenty-one, inclusive, the requirements . . . shall not be applied . . . if such requirements would be inconsistent with state law or practice, or the order of any court, respecting public education within such age groups within the state. [Section 612(2)(B)]

Since many states were not providing preschool services to typical children, an education for young children with special needs, in most instances, was not mandated. Although this legislation fails to require an education for our youngest students, it clearly focused attention on the preschool population and recognized the value of early education.

PL 94-142 did, however, contain benefits for children under school age. The enactment offered small financial grants (Preschool Incentive Grants) to the individual states as an incentive to serve young children with special needs. It also carried a mandate for schools to identify and evaluate children from birth through age twenty-one suspected of evidencing a disability. Finally, PL 94-142 moved from a census count to a child count, or the actual number of young children being served. The intent of this feature was to encourage the states to locate and serve children with disabilities.

Public Law 99-457   In October 1986, Congress passed one of the most comprehensive pieces of legislation affecting young children with special needs and their families—PL 99-457. This law, which was originally known as the *Education of the Handicapped Act Amendments of 1986*, changed both the scope and intent of services provided to preschoolers with special needs in addition to formulating a national policy for infants and toddlers at risk for, and with, identified disabilities.

Farran (2000) believes that one of the assumptions behind the enactment of PL 99-457 was that early intervention is cost-effective, a way of lowering

Today, education for youngsters with a disability is a right, not a privilege.

SOURCE: Photo Disc/Getty Images

future costs for special education. This rationale is vastly different from the thinking behind the passage of PL 94-142 which was rooted in the civil rights movement and saw an education for children with disabilities as a constitutional right. Thus, PL 99-457 was enacted primarily as a prevention measure.

PL 99-457 contains several parts, or in legislative terms, Titles. Our attention will primarily focus on Title II (Part B), the preschool provision as well as Title I (Part H, which is now known as Part C), a new section that allows for services to be provided to infants and toddlers with special needs.

As noted earlier, IDEA contains language that gave states the opportunity, through financial incentives, to provide an education and related services to preschool children with disabilities. This was a permissive or voluntary element of the Act, not a mandated requirement. Trohanis (1989) reported Congressional data, which revealed that less than 80% or 260,000 of the estimated 330,000 exceptional youngsters ages three to five were being served. An estimated 70,000 preschoolers were, therefore, unserved. Koppelman (1986) found that 31 states and territories did not require special education services for preschoolers with special needs. PL 99-457 was enacted to remedy this situation.

Simply stated, Title II is a downward extension of PL 94-142, including all rights and protections. It requires that as of the 1991–1992 school year, *all* preschoolers with special needs, ages three to five inclusive, are to receive a free and appropriate public education. This element of the law is a mandated requirement. States will lose significant amounts of federal preschool funding if they fail to comply. The goal of this legislation was finally accomplished in the 1992–1993 school year, when all states had mandates in place establishing a free appropriate public education for all children with disabilities ages three through five. In fact, five states (Iowa, Maryland, Michigan, Minnesota, and Nebraska) have chosen to mandate services from birth while Virginia begins a FAPE at age two. Table 2–4 shows the year that each state mandated a free and appropriate public education for children with special needs.

Other provisions of the earlier legislation remain the same, such as an education in the least restrictive environment (LRE), IEPs, due process safeguards, and confidentiality of records. Family services are also recognized as being vitally important; thus, family counseling and training are allowable as a related service. Depending on the needs of the child, service delivery models can either be home-based or center-based, full-time or part-time. As we noted earlier, states are not required to report to the U.S. Department of Education the number of children served according to a disability category. Thus, preschoolers do not have to be labeled with a specific disability, such as mental retardation.

All states were required to modify their state plans and policies to ensure compliance with the law. Funding for serving these children has also been dramatically increased.

Title I of PL 99-457 created the Handicapped Infants and Toddlers Program (Part C), a new provision aimed at children from birth through age two with developmental delays or disabilities. This component of the legislation is voluntary; states are not compelled to comply. Part C of this statute creates a discretionary program that assists states in imple-

Table 2–4   School Year in Which States Mandated a Free and Appropriate Public Education for Preschoolers with Disabilities

Year	State	Year	State
1973–1974	Illinois Michigan* Wisconsin	1991–1992	Alabama Arizona Arkansas
1974–1975	Alaska Texas		California Colorado Connecticut
1975–1976	Iowa* Virginia**		Delaware Florida
1976–1977	Massachusetts Rhode Island South Dakota		Georgia Indiana Kansas Kentucky
1977–1978	Louisiana New Hampshire		Maine Mississippi
1978–1979	Maryland*		Missouri
1979–1980	Nebraska*		New Mexico New York
1980–1981	Hawaii		North Carolina
1983–1984	District of Columbia New Jersey		Ohio Oklahoma
1985–1986	North Dakota Washington		Pennsylvania South Carolina Tennessee
1986–1987	Minnesota*		Vermont
1988–1989	Utah		West Virginia
1989–1990	Idaho	1992–1993	Oregon
1990–1991	Montana Nevada Wyoming		

*Eligible for services beginning at birth.

**Eligible for services beginning at age two.

SOURCE: Adapted from J. Danaher and R. Kraus, *Section 619 Profile* (11th ed.), 2002. Chapel Hill, NC: National Early Childhood Technical Assistance System (NEC*TAS).

menting a statewide, comprehensive, coordinated, multidisciplinary, interagency program of services for very young children with developmental difficulties and their families (Section 671). Each state that chose to participate was required to provide early intervention to children who evidence a physical or mental condition that has a high probability of resulting in a delay such as cerebral palsy or Down syndrome. At their discretion states may also offer services to youngsters who are medically or environmentally at-risk for future delays. As of September 30, 1994, all states had plans in place for the full implementation of Part C (U.S. Department of Education, 1997).

The enactment of PL 99–457 reflects a major shift in thinking regarding public policy and service provision for infants and toddlers with special needs

Table 2–5   Changes in Service Delivery for Infants and Toddlers Resulting from the Passage of IDEA (PL 99–457)

Area	Pre-IDEA Services	Post-IDEA Services
Entitlement	Served only some of the eligible children	Serve all children
Eligibility	Served only disabled children and waited until children evidenced measurable delays	Serve children with diagnosed conditions regardless of whether measurable delays are present
		May serve at-risk children in order to prevent developmental delay
Early Identification	Waited until children came to program	Find children as early as possible
Service array	Confined services to what program offered	Provide an array of services across programs
System	Provide separate, autonomous programs	Provide comprehensive, coordinated, interagency system of services
Focus	Child-centered	Family-centered
Individualization	Offered a package of services	Offer individualized services
Inclusion	Established segregated, self-contained programs	Establish inclusive programs and use of community resources
Disciplines	Disciplines worked autonomously	Disciplines working together to integrate all services (interdisciplinary, transdisciplinary)
Therapies	Provide separate and sometimes insufficient therapies	Provide sufficient integrated therapies
Procedural safeguards	Families had no recourse for complaints	Procedural safeguards in place
Transition	Unplanned traumatic transitions	Planned transition from infant and toddler program to preschool program
Funding	Single primary funding source	Coordinated and use all possible funding sources

SOURCE: Adapted with premission from G. Harbin, R. McWilliam, and J. Gallagher, Services for Young Children with Disabilities and Their Families. In J. Shonkoff and S. Meisels (Eds.), *Handbook of Early Intervention,* 2nd ed. (Cambridge, England: Cambridge University Press, 2000). p. 388.

(Harbin, McWilliam, & Gallagher, 2000). This paradigm shift is reflected in Table 2–5, which illustrates pre- and post- IDEA service delivery.

There are several features of this law that are worthy of examination. Under this Act and its accompanying amendments, infants and toddlers are eligible for services if:

- they are experiencing developmental delays in one or more of the following areas: cognitive development, physical development, communication development, social or emotional development, or adaptive development;

- they have a physical or mental condition that has a high probability of resulting in a delay (for example, cerebral palsy, Down syndrome); or

- at the state's discretion, they are medically or environmentally at-risk for substantial delay if early intervention is not provided.

Eligible children and their families must receive a multidisciplinary assessment conducted by qualified professionals and a written **individualized family service plan (IFSP).** Similar to the IEP, the IFSP is designed as a guide to the delivery of services to infants, toddlers, and their families. Developed by a multidisciplinary team, the IFSP, as promulgated in PL 99-457, must contain:

- a statement of the infant's or toddler's present levels of physical development, cognitive development, communication development, social or emotional development, and adaptive development;
- a statement of the family's resources, priorities, and concerns;
- a statement of major outcomes expected to be achieved for the infant or toddler and the family;
- a statement of specific early intervention services necessary to meet the unique needs of the infant or toddler and the family;
- the projected dates for initiation of services and the anticipated duration of such services;
- the name of the service coordinator;
- a description of the natural environments in which early intervention services will be provided; and
- the steps . . . supporting the transition of the toddler with a disability to services provided under Part B (preschool).

Unlike an IEP, the focus of the IFSP is on the family rather than the individual child, thereby resulting in a comprehensive and multidisciplinary plan. Parents are viewed as full-fledged partners with professionals. Their participation ensures that services occur within the context of the family unit and meets the unique needs of the child and his or her caregivers. This goal is clearly reflected in the IFSP statement, which addresses the issue of the "family's resources, priorities, and concerns." It is imperative for professionals to remember that while families may have a variety of needs (for example, informational, management, support), they also have strengths and resources that must not be overlooked. Best practice

dictates that services should be individualized and responsive to the goals and preferences of the parents while supporting their role as primary decision maker.

A final noteworthy aspect of Part C of IDEA is the concept of service coordination. A service coordinator originally was a professional selected from the discipline closest to the child's primary problem, for example, a speech-language pathologist for toddlers with delayed language or a physical therapist for a youngster with cerebral palsy. PL 102-119 not only changed the terminology from "case management" to service coordination and "case manager" to the less clinical term of service coordinator, but it also broadened the category of service coordinator to *any* qualified professional who is best able to assist the family. Typically, their roles are to function as an advocate for the family, to ensure the coordination of early intervention services, to monitor the implementation of the IFSP, to assist in transition planning, and to foster family empowerment among other duties. It is important to remember that the activities and responsibilities of the service coordinator are determined in conjunction with the youngster's family and are always individualized.

An IFSP must be reviewed every six months (or sooner if necessary) to assess its continual appropriateness. The infant or toddler is required by law to be reevaluated annually. Regulations further stipulate that an IFSP must be developed within forty-five days after a referral for services is made.

PL 99-457 is the culmination of many years of dedicated effort by both parents and professionals. It represents an opportunity to intervene and effect meaningful change in the lives of the nation's youngest and most vulnerable children.

Public Law 101-476 Arguably, one of the most important changes contained in this legislation was the renaming of PL 94-142 to the *Individuals with Disabilities Education Act.* The word "children" was replaced with the term "individuals" and "handicapped" became "with disabilities." This latter phrase also signifies a change in attitude to a more appropriate people-first point of view. We now realize that an individual's disability is but one aspect of her personhood.

Congress also realized the importance of preparing adolescents for a productive life after they exit from public schooling. These amendments require that each student have, no later than age sixteen, an **individual transition plan (ITP)** as part of his/her IEP. This plan calls for a coordinated set of activities and interagency linkages designed to promote the student's movement to postschool functions such as independent living, vocational training, and additional educational experiences.

PL 101-476 also expanded the scope of the related services provision by adding two services— social work and rehabilitation counseling. A final element of this legislation was the identification of autism and traumatic brain injury as distinct disability categories. Previously, these disabilities had been subsumed under other disability labels.

Public Law 102-119 In 1991, IDEA was amended again by PL 102-119, the *Individuals with Disabilities Education Act Amendment.* As we noted earlier, PL 102-119 permits states to use a noncategorical label when identifying preschoolers with special needs. Amendments to Part C require that early intervention services are to be in "natural environments" with normally developing age-mates as appropriate for each child. Transition policies and procedures are to be established so that infants and toddlers receiving early intervention services can move smoothly, if eligible, to preschool special education. States are also allowed to use an IFSP as a guide for services for children ages three through five as long as IEP requirements are met. Additionally, states were permitted to use Part C monies for preschoolers with disabilities. Likewise, these amendments allow for the use of Part B funds to serve infants and toddlers with special needs. Finally, the amount of funds allocated by Congress increased from $1,000 to $1,500 per child.

Public Law 105-17 The latest set of amendments to IDEA are incorporated in PL 105-17, the *Individuals with Disabilities Education Act Amendments of 1997.* This bill was signed into law by President Clinton on June 4, 1997. PL 105-17 restructures IDEA into four parts, revises some definitions, and revamps several key components ranging from funding to disciplining students with disabilities to how IEPs are to be developed. Highlights of this major retooling are as follows:

- Students with disabilities who bring weapons to school, possess or use illegal drugs, or pose a serious threat of injury to other pupils or themselves may be removed from their current placement and placed in an interim alternative educational setting as determined by the IEP team, but for no more than 45 days, after a due process hearing has been conducted. Students who are suspended or expelled are still entitled to receive a free and appropriate public education as addressed in their IEP.

- Pupils with disabilities who exhibit less serious infractions of school conduct may be disciplined in ways similar to children without disabilities (including a change in placement), provided that the misbehavior was not a manifestation of the student's disability. Additionally, either before taking disciplinary action, but no later than ten days after, the IEP team must conduct a functional behavioral assessment and develop (or implement) a behavior intervention plan.

- IEPs are now required to state how the student with disabilities will be involved with, and progress in, the general education curriculum. Other provisions stipulate that transition planning will begin at age 14 instead of age 16; regular educators will become part of the IEP team; short-term instructional objectives will no longer be required, rather, the emphasis will be on measurable annual goals; and lastly, the assistive technology needs of each learner must be considered by the IEP team.

- Orientation and mobility services for children with visual impairments are now included in the definition of related services.

- The present mandate of comprehensive triennial reevaluation of pupils with disabilities is lifted if school authorities and the student's parents both agree that this process is unnecessary.

- A new section on mediation requires states to offer mediation services to help resolve disputes as an alternative to using more costly and lengthy due process hearings. Parental participation is voluntary and parents still retain their right to a due process hearing.

- The category of *developmental delay* may now be used when describing children aged three through nine. The use of this term is at the discretion of the state and local education agency.

- Initial evaluations and reevaluations are not restricted to the use of formal, standardized tests. A variety of assessment tools and strategies are to be utilized in an effort to gather relevant, functional, and developmental information. Curriculum-based tests, portfolio reviews, parental input, and the observations of teachers and related service providers may be considered in determining whether or not the student has a disability and in developing the content of the IEP. A student may not be considered eligible for a special education if their educational difficulties are primarily the result of limited proficiency in English or lack of adequate instruction in math and/or reading.

- A new mechanism for distributing federal monies will occur once the appropriations reach a threshold of $4.9 billion. Upon attaining this level, states and local school systems will receive additional funding based upon 85 percent of the population of children ages three to 21 and 15 percent of the number of children ages three through 21 who are in poverty. This switch to a census-based formula instead of the current enrollment driven formula was due to a concern that some schools were overidentifying students in order to receive additional funding. No state would receive less than the amount of support it received in the year prior to the activation of this new scheme.

- The reauthorization of IDEA requires schools to establish performance goals for students with disabilities in an effort to assess their academic progress. Additionally, these youngsters are to be included in state and district-wide assessment programs or given alternative assessments that meet their unique needs.

- Early intervention services must be "family-directed" and, to the extent appropriate, these services are to be provided in noninstitutional settings such as the youngster's home.

- Child Find requirements are extended to children with disabilities who are enrolled in private schools, including students attending parochial schools. A special education and related services may be provided on the premises of a private school (including parochial) to the extent permissible by law.

- IFSP requirements are modified to include a statement justifying the extent, if any, that early intervention services are not provided in the natural environment.

Prevalence of Young Children with Special Needs

The number of young children with special needs receiving services has increased dramatically over the past several years. This growth has been spurred on due to litigation, legislative enactments (especially IDEA and its amendments), and as we will shortly see, a greater awareness of the benefits of early intervention among other factors. Figures from the U.S. Department of Education (2002) reveal that almost 600,000 preschoolers, ages three to five were served during the 2000–2001 school year under Part B of IDEA. (See Table 2–6.) This figure represents 5.0% of the population of three- through five-year-old children in the United States. Figure 2–1 portrays the ages and the percentage of youngsters receiving services through IDEA while Table 2–6 reflects the growth in the number of preschoolers receiving a special education.

Recent data provided by the U.S. Department of Education (2002) reveals that 230,853 youngsters birth through age two were receiving early intervention as of

Table 2–6	Increase in Number of Preschoolers Served under the Individuals with Disabilities Education Act (Part B)						
	Representative Years					**Change 1986–2000**	
Ages	**1986–87**	**1990–91**	**1994–95**	**1998–99**	**2000–01**	**Numbers**	**%**
3-year-olds	31,162	59,095	104,619	117,698	127,281	96,119	308.44
4-year-olds	62,327	111,787	179,825	199,924	208,677	146,350	234.80
5-year-olds	170,415	197,807	240,014	256,015	263,720	93,305	54.75
Total	265,814	368,689	524,458	573,637	599,678	333,864	125.60

Note: Data reported as of December 1 of each reporting year. Figures based upon data from the 50 contiguous states, Puerto Rico, the District of Columbia, and outlying areas.

SOURCE: U.S. Department of Education (1991–2002). *Annual Reports to Congress on the Implementation of the Individuals with Disabilities Education Act.* Washington, DC: U.S. Government Printing Office.

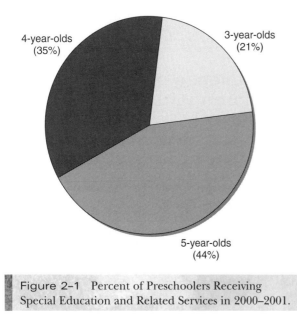

Figure 2–1   Percent of Preschoolers Receiving Special Education and Related Services in 2000–2001.

SOURCE: U.S. Department of Education. (2002). *Twenty-fourth Annual Report to Congress on the Implementation of the Individuals with Disabilities Education Act.* Washington, DC: U.S. Government Printing Office.

December 2000. This statistic represents 2.0% of the entire birth through age two population. Over the past several years, the number of infants and toddlers receiving early intervention services has steadily increased. Figure 2–2 illustrates this growth pattern. This trend reflects a 59% increase in the number of youngsters served. The U.S. Department of Education (1998) believes that this growth pattern is largely due to greater public awareness, successful Child Find efforts, and program expansion. Surprisingly, the number of youngsters served in 1998 declined. This decrease is most likely due to changes in data collection procedures, primarily in two states (U.S. Department of Education, 2002).

Slightly more than half of the children (53%) receiving early intervention in 2000 were between the ages of two and three.

The Importance of Early Intervention

Is early intervention effective? Does it really benefit young children with special needs and their families? Unfortunately, these are not simple questions and their answers are equally, if not more, complex. It is perhaps best to respond to these queries by saying, "It depends." The reason we are so vague is that our initial inquiries only give rise to additional questions. For instance, What constitutes intervention? How early is early? Are we looking for short-term or long-term

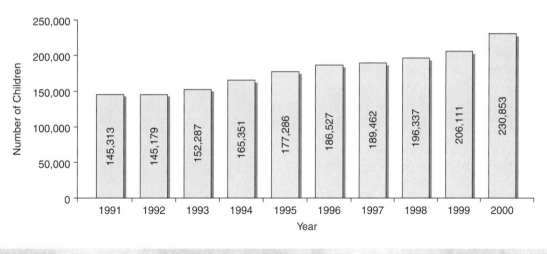

Figure 2-2   Number of Infants and Toddlers Served Under the Individuals with Disabilities Education Act

SOURCE: Adapted from U.S. Department of Education. (2002). *Twenty-fourth Annual Report to Congress on the Implementation of the Individuals with Disabilities Education Act.* Washington, DC: U.S. Government Printing Office. p. A–22.

benefits? What children are we talking about—infants and toddlers, youngsters who are environmentally at-risk, children with suspected developmental delays, or preschoolers with documented disabilities like Down syndrome or cerebral palsy? Obviously, the population we serve can affect the answer to the question.

Our initial concerns notwithstanding, we believe we can safely answer our primary questions in the affirmative. *Quality* early intervention programs *do* make a difference in the lives of young children with disabilities and their families. Guralnick (1998), in fact, considers early intervention to be "the center-piece of our nation's efforts on behalf of vulnerable children and their families" (p. 337).

We will now review the reasoning for our position that early intervention is effective. We begin by estab-lishing an understanding of what intervention is. According to Fallen and Umansky (1985), interven-tion refers to the process of intruding upon the lives of young children with disabilities and their families for the purpose of altering the direction and conse-quences of a disability or delayed development. These experts state that "the action required is indi-vidual, but it encompasses any modification or addi-tion of services, strategies, techniques, or materials required to maximize the child's potential" (p. 160).

Likewise, Peterson (1987) echoes these thoughts when she states that the purpose of intervention for young children with special needs is to:

1. minimize the effects of a handicapping [dis-abling] condition upon a child's growth and devel-opment and maximize opportunities to engage in the normal activities of early childhood;

2. prevent, if possible, at-risk conditions or early developmental irregularities from developing into more serious problems that become deviant to the extent that they are labeled as handicap-ping [disabling];

3. prevent the development of secondary handicaps [disabilities] as a result of interference from a primary disability. . . . (pp. 72–73)

More recently Bailey and Wolery (1992) sug-gested several objectives for early intervention. Their recommendations include, among other broad goals, the following:

- supporting the family in accomplishing its goals;

- facilitating the development of social compe-tency in youngsters with disabilities;

- developing the child's abilities in cognitive, motor, communication, social, and self-help skills; and

- preparing the child for the normalized experiences of early childhood.

The goals of early childhood special education are obviously diverse. McCollum and Maude (1993) describe the purpose of early intervention as one of facilitating, optimizing, minimizing, remediating, and preventing, with prevention being preferable to remediation.

Thus, we can state that, collectively, the aim of early intervention is to affect positively the overall development of the child's social, emotional, physical, and intellectual well-being. This whole child approach is important because these aspects are interrelated and dependent on each other (Zigler, 1990).

Several reviewers and investigators (Hanson & Lynch, 1995; McCollum & Maude, 1993; Peterson, 1987; Raver, 1999) have identified a variety of reasons why early intervention is important for youngsters with disabilities and children at-risk. Many of these reasons are derived from research evidence, theoretical arguments, expert opinion, and societal values. Frequently identified themes include:

- A belief that early environmental stimulation can positively facilitate subsequent development and readiness for learning.

- A critical periods hypothesis, which suggests that intervening during key periods in a child's life is vitally important if the youngster is to acquire more complex skills and competencies later on. The exclusivity of this notion, however, has been challenged by some professionals who advocate that the early years of a child's life are not the only crucial period of development; in fact, development continues across the lifespan (Clarke & Clarke, 1976). Likewise, Ramey and Ramey (1998) argue that there is no compelling evidence to support the belief of an absolute critical period of development such that interventions introduced after a certain age are ineffective. Yet, research does suggest that earlier enrollment in intervention programs produce the greatest benefit implying that it is a matter of development timing.

- An assumption that early intervention can minimize the impact of a particular disabling condi-

Early intervention can greatly benefit young children with special needs and their families.

tion like the effect of a severe hearing loss on the development of speech and language and possibly prevent or attenuate the occurrence of secondary disabilities.

- The proposition that intervention programs can ameliorate learning deficits and problems frequently attributed to certain risk factors such as environmental conditions.

- Benefits that accrue to families of youngsters with special needs and children at-risk. These children frequently present many new challenges and additional responsibilities for caregivers and can potentially impact the entire family constellation. Early childhood special education professionals can assist families by providing factual information, emotional support, and specific training as requested. A further role for professionals is to establish meaningful partnerships with parents guided by the principles of enabling and empowering parents (Dunst, Trivette, & Deal, 1988).

- Benefits that extend beyond the child and his/her family to society at large. Early intervention is cost effective. The effectiveness has been documented in terms of dollars saved and the reduced need for special education services at an older age.

In summary, early intervention for children with disabilities has definite advantages for society, the family, and, of course, the child. Early childhood special education can make a significant difference in the quality of life for young children with special needs and their families. In fact, early intervention as a strategy to prevent later problems has almost become conventional wisdom (Kamerman, 2000). Scientists have been able to consistently demonstrate that well-designed early intervention programs produce modest positive outcomes according to their intended purpose (Bailey, 2000; Ramey & Ramey, 1998; Zigler, 2000). A recent report on brain research (Shore, 1997) further substantiates the importance and efficacy of early intervention and prevention. Thus, we are in full agreement with the Ramey's persuasive argument that "early intervention can improve the course of early human development . . . ." (p. 118).

Representative Research Evidence on the Effectiveness of Intervention

During the past four decades there have been numerous investigations examining the effectiveness of early intervention with youngsters at-risk and young children with documented disabilities. Many reviews and summaries of these efforts have been published (Casto & Mastropieri, 1986; Farran, 1990; Guralnick, 1997; Shonkoff & Hauser-Cram, 1987; White, Bush, & Casto, 1986). As might be expected, the analyses revealed, for a variety of reasons, contradictory findings. As a whole, however, the reports indicate positive outcomes for early intervention, especially when a distinction is made between statistical significance and clinical significance. A group of children who learn to accomplish specific self-help skills, like feeding themselves, might not evidence statistical significance due to small sample size, but this accomplishment is important for the youngsters and their families (Bailey & Wolery, 1992). While the research evidence does provide qualified support for the effectiveness of early intervention, several reviewers comment on the difficulty of conducting methodologically sound experiments (Dunst, 1986; Dunst & Rheingrover, 1981; Farran, 1990; Guralnick, 1988, 1991). Potential problems in interpreting the research literature lie

with the appropriateness of the dependent measures; the absence of control groups; small sample sizes; improper sampling procedures; inappropriate statistical techniques; inadequate documentation of the treatment; the validity of the assessment instruments; and the variability within specific subject populations. Odom (1988) suggests that some of the research difficulties are due to the fact that early childhood special education is an applied discipline and given to answering pragmatic questions; researchers, therefore, have less control over variables in natural settings than in laboratory environments. Despite the shortcomings and the vulnerability of the research efforts, positive conclusions about the efficacy of early intervention can be drawn. Guralnick (1998), for instance, emphatically states that, "comprehensive early intervention programs for children at-risk and for those with established disabilities reveal a consistent pattern of effectiveness" (p.323). We will now review some of the research evidence.

We begin with the classic but methodologically controversial study conducted by Skeels and Dye (1939), which significantly influenced the then-current thinking about intelligence. These investigators reported an experiment where 13 children under three years of age were removed from an orphanage and placed in an institution for the mentally retarded where they received a great deal of care and attention from the female residents. A control group of 12 youngsters remained at the overcrowded orphanage and was not exposed to individual stimulation or training. Intellectual assessments were conducted at the time of transfer. When the youngsters were reevaluated 18–36 months later, significant differences were observed between the experimental and control subjects. The 13 children placed on the ward with the young women demonstrated an average gain in IQ scores of 27.5 points, while the initially higher IQ-scoring control children showed a loss of 26.2 points. Each of the children who transferred to the more enriched environment showed an increase in measured intelligence, while all except one of the controls suffered a loss; 10 children had a decrease in IQ score between 18 and 45 points.

Perhaps the most significant finding of this investigation is the long-term follow-up of the subjects into adulthood. Even as adults, the differences between the two samples are significant. Skeels (1966) reports that members of the treatment group maintained their gains and all were self-supporting. Their median grade level attainment was greater than twelfth grade, whereas the children who remained at the orphanage had a median educational attainment of less than third grade. Differences in occupational achievement were also noted with the experimental subjects enjoying greater career accomplishment while the controls remained wards of the state or largely worked as unskilled laborers.

Although the methodology of the Skeels and Dye investigation has been criticized, the study did demonstrate that environmental conditions affect development as well as pointing out that the deleterious experiences of early childhood can be reversed. The work of Skeels and Dye, as Bailey and Wolery (1992) note, "remains as one of the few truly longitudinal studies of intervention effectiveness" (p. 6).

Another pioneering study is the work of Kirk (1958), who investigated the effects of preschool experiences on the mental and social development of children with mental retardation ages three to six. Eighty-one children with IQ scores ranging from 45 to 80 were assigned to either an intervention group or served as control subjects. Two experimental groups were established containing children who lived in the community or resided in an institution. The controls also lived either at home or in a residential environment. Both intervention groups who were exposed to two years of preschool experiences demonstrated significant gains on measures of intellectual and social functioning as compared to youngsters without the benefit of intervention. The performance of the control children decreased. Follow-up indicated that the experimental subjects retained their advantage until age eight. However, some of the community-based control subjects did catch up to the experimental children after one year of school.

Kirk's research, as well as the efforts of Skeels and Dye (1939), attests to the malleability of early development in addition to providing strong evidence of the effectiveness of early intervention. As

we noted elsewhere, in the 1960s the social conscience of America was awakened. As a nation we became cognizant of the devastating effects of poverty and other social ills on the lives of young children and their families. One consequence of this heightened social awareness was the establishment of preschool intervention programs for poor children, or in contemporary terms, youngsters who are environmentally at-risk. The lasting effects of some of these projects were evaluated by the Consortium for Longitudinal Studies. Lazar and his colleagues (Lazar & Darlington, 1979; Lazar, Darlington, Murray, Royce, & Snipper, 1982) issued two major reports summarizing the results of twelve comprehensive follow-up studies of children enrolled in cognitively oriented preschools established in the 1960s. None of the projects focused specifically on children with special needs, although several selected participants on the basis of low IQ scores (range 50–85). Using original data from each program, Lazar found that environmentally at-risk enrollees had higher achievement and intelligence test scores as compared to children who did not have the benefit of preschool intervention. Their analysis also revealed that early intervention experiences significantly reduced the number of youngsters placed in special education and retained in their current grade. In comparison to control groups, preschool graduates had more positive attitudes toward school and furnished more achievement-oriented responses in follow-up interviews. Lazar and his co-workers concluded that, overall, the projects produced lasting positive outcomes and were cost effective when compared to later remediation efforts or special class placement. Table 2–7, derived from a composite of empirical investigations, summarizes some of the short- and long-term benefits that result from participating in a well-run preschool program.

The efficacy of early intervention has also been examined with children manifesting an established risk. One population that has received considerable attention is youngsters with Down syndrome. An example is the work of Guralnick and Bricker (1987). Using stringent criteria for inclusion, these investigators evaluated the outcomes of 11 projects. They con-

Table 2–7   Beneficial Outcomes of High Quality Preschool Programs

- Enhanced scholastic achievement
- Less grade retention
- Higher IQ scores
- Decreased likelihood of receiving special education services
- More positive attitudes toward school and learning
- Greater likelihood of graduating from high school
- Less likely to access public assistance
- Greater possibility of securing meaningful employment

cluded that, based on the substantial number of "first generation" studies reviewed, that the documented decline in cognitive ability with advancing chronological age typically found in children with Down syndrome can be significantly reduced, prevented, and, to some extent, reversed as a result of early intervention. This significant outcome is consistent across a wide variety of programs incorporating diverse experimental designs.

In contrast, Guralnick and Bricker report that the issue of maintenance of cognitive gains is not clear-cut, due to limited information and contradictory findings. Equally difficult to answer is the question of when is the best time to begin early intervention. The research evidence is, once again, contradictory. Both of these issues await more extensive and systematic research, which is skillfully designed to answer these questions. Despite these shortcomings, empirical investigations strongly speak to the positive benefits of early intervention with children with Down syndrome.

Another illustration of the efficacy of early intervention is the highly visible work of Casto and Mastropieri (1986). These investigators used a comprehensive statistical integration approach known as **meta-analysis.** In this method, all available research (both published and unpublished) incorporating a range of experimental designs is evaluated in an attempt to detect global statistical patterns, which yield an "effect size" reported as standard deviations (SD). Seventy-four studies of early intervention efforts of heterogeneous groups of children were analyzed. Criteria for inclusion were minimal. Overall, the meta-analysis outcomes supported the efficacy of early intervention. Modest gains were observed in children's test scores—typically standardized intelligence tests or other cognitive assessments. Cognitive measures yielded a mean effect size of .85 SD. When other dependent measures were included, such as motor and language assessments, the effect size was reduced to .68 SD. This means that the typical child with special needs in an early intervention program scored .68 of a standard deviation higher than their counterpart who was not receiving early services.

Casto and Mastropieri also reported that early intervention programs that are longer in duration and more intense usually demonstrate greater effectiveness. Two intriguing and controversial findings emerged, however, both of which were contrary to conventional wisdom and challenged two widely held beliefs of the field. First, Casto and Mastropieri found no support for the belief that the earlier the intervention commences ("earlier is better"), the greater its effectiveness. Second, their meta-analyses suggested that greater parental participation does not necessarily lead to enhanced program effectiveness.

As might be expected, professional reaction to these summary statements was swift and intense (Dunst & Snyder, 1986; Strain & Smith, 1986). Critics of the Casto and Mastropieri meta-analyses assailed the conclusions claiming that the analysis was methodologically ("apples and oranges approach") and conceptually flawed. It must be remembered, however, that this investigation was based on an enormously heterogeneous group of children incorporating different intervention methods and procedures as well as employing diverse outcome measures. It would be prudent, therefore, to draw only limited conclusions.

A subsequent and better controlled meta-analysis using a subset of the original database focusing exclusively on children younger than three years of age yielded different and more positive results (Shonkoff & Hauser-Cram, 1987). This more selective analysis revealed that youngsters with mild disabilities had better outcomes with earlier enrollment and higher levels of parent involvement were associated with greater child progress and performance.

Our final example is Guralnick's (1997) extensive examination of "second generation" research studies involving children at-risk and youngsters with a broad spectrum of established risks. This review examined the efficacy of early intervention and the variables that impede or enhance its effectiveness such as child characteristics (type and severity of disability), family characteristics, and program features (curriculum, parent-child interventions, social support). Some of the conclusions gleaned from this work support the following generalizations—the outcomes of intervention are positive, albeit modest; the sheer number of deleterious variables affecting development may be more significant than any one factor; and finally, careful consideration should be given to ecological factors affecting child-caregiver and child-family relationships.

Despite the chronic problems in conducting efficacy evaluations, it is our opinion that early intervention does make a difference in the lives of young children with special needs. It would appear that the field of early childhood special education has moved beyond the global question of whether early intervention works (we believe it does) to more precise avenues of inquiry: for whom, under what conditions, and toward what outcomes (Guralnick, 1988). Like Bailey (2000) we believe that the debate will no longer be whether to provide early intervention "but rather how much and what kind of intervention are children and families entitled to" (p. 74). A major task confronting the field will be to identify which early intervention programs work best and what elements are clearly essential to achieve maximum benefit (Zigler, 2000).

Early intervention research is not static, but rather an ongoing process. It can help guide researchers, policymakers, and educators in their quest to develop new models, programs, and services that benefit infants, toddlers, and preschoolers with special needs and their families.

An Ecological Perspective on Young Children with Special Needs and Their Families

One contemporary trend in early childhood special education is to view children as part of a larger social scheme wherein they influence, and are influenced by, various environments. This context, referred to as **ecology,** looks at the interrelationships and interactions of individuals within the environment. The primary advocate of this ecological model is Urie Bronfenbrenner (1977, 1979). From this ecological perspective, Bronfenbrenner attempts to understand the relationship between the immediate environments in which a youngster develops and the larger context of those settings. A developing child, therefore, cannot be viewed in isolation but rather as part of a larger social system. We believe it is impossible to discuss children without also describing the context in which they develop and interact—their families and communities. As an illustration, early childhood professionals must have an appreciation for the youngster's total environment—home, school, community, and the larger society, in addition to the individuals encountered therein—parents, siblings, classmates, playmates, and therapists among other people. Spodek and Saracho (1994a) support our viewpoint. They write that:

> The influence of the classroom on the young child, many educators believe, cannot be separated from the influence of the family or from the context in which both the classroom and family exist. Home, school, community, and culture are all linked to each other. (p. 80)

As we just noted, the foundation for our thinking emerges from the theorizing of Bronfenbrenner (1977), who defines the ecology of human development as:

> the scientific study of the progressive, mutual accommodation, throughout the life span, between a growing human organism and the

changing immediate environments in which it lives, as this process is affected by relations obtaining within and between these immediate settings, as well as the larger social contexts, both formal and informal, in which the settings are embedded. (p. 514)

We further accept his "unorthodox" belief (Bronfenbrenner, 1979) that development is grounded in the context in which it occurs. Basic to this notion is the idea that the contexts in which a person develops are nested, one inside the other, similar to a set of *matryoshka,* or Russian stacking dolls.

Bronfenbrenner identified four environments in which people develop:

- **microsystems** are those immediate environments in which an individual develops;

- **mesosystems** are identified as the relationships between various microsystems;

- **exosystems** are social structures that have an influence on the development of the individual, however, the person does not have a direct role in the social system; and

- **macrosystems,** which are the ideological, cultural, and institutional contexts in which the preceding systems are embedded.

These nested relationships, as they relate to young children with special needs and their families, are portrayed in Figure 2–3. This ecological context provides us with a framework for understanding the world of young children and has led to the contemporary practice of viewing families as systems embedded within other systems. The microsystem, according to Bailey, Farel, O'Donnell, Simeonsson, and Miller (1986), looks at relationships within the crucial setting of the child's family in addition to the environments typically encountered by young children—child care centers, homes of relatives or friends, and in certain circumstances, institutional settings like hospitals. The second layer, or mesosystem, relates to the relationships, at a particular point in a child's life, between caregiver and teacher or physician as well as the interaction of one professional with another. The exosystem takes into consideration the social structures that impact family functioning. Illustrations pro-

vided by Bailey et al. (1986) include neighborhood and community organizations, advocacy groups, state agencies, and school systems to name but a few. Bailey and Wolery (1992) believe that "early intervention programs probably best fit within this level of hierarchy" (p. 67). The final context is the macrosystem and includes societal values and attitudes toward individuals with disabilities, in addition to legislative enactments and judicial remedies, which in turn affect the lives of young children and their families. IDEA is a powerful example of a macrosystem in action.

Kirk, Gallagher, and Anastasiow (2000) embrace a concept very similar to Bronfenbrenner's ecological model. These writers also believe it is vital for early childhood professionals to consider the familial and social context encountered by children with disabilities. The child is seen as being at the center of successive layers of influence, with the family being the primary and frequently most influential context. Other orbits include the peer group (which may include typical and atypical youngsters), schools, and society itself (see Figure 2–3). Like Bailey et al. (1986) and Odom and Diamond (1998), Kirk and his colleagues see the child with special needs in dynamic and complex interaction with many layers of environmental forces.

Best practices in early childhood special education rely heavily on the importance of the child's family. According to Kirk et al. (2000, p. 11):

> The trend toward early intervention (before the age of 5) increases the importance of the family. Much of the intervention with young children is directed toward changing the family environment and preparing the parent or parents to care for and teach their child. At the very least, intervention tries to generate more constructive parent-child interactions.

The value of the family can be seen in the Head Start commitment to meaningful parent (caregiver) involvement and participation. It is also clearly evident in IDEA and its accompanying amendments.

Successful program planning and intervention, therefore, must take into consideration the fact that the child is part of a system that interacts reciprocally within his or her environment. Bronfenbrenner

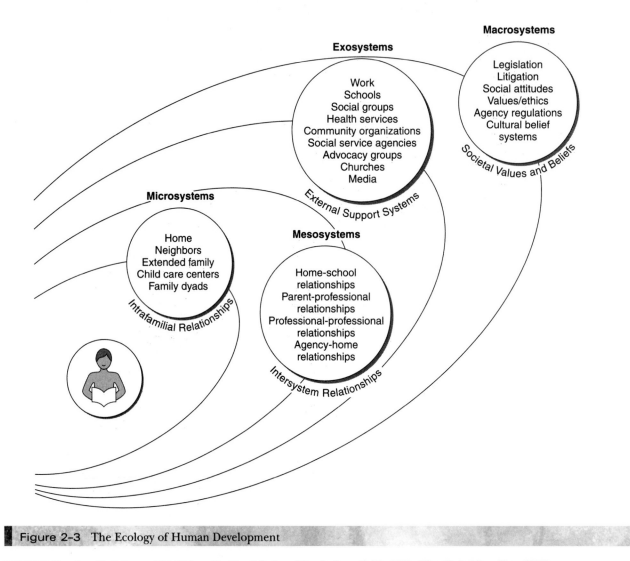

Figure 2-3   The Ecology of Human Development

SOURCE: Based on D. Bailey and M. Wolery, *Teaching Infants and Preschoolers with Disabilities* (New York: Macmillan, 1992).

(1979) observes that accomplishment of a specific task or activity "may depend no less on how he [the child] is taught than on the existence and nature of the ties between the school and home" (p. 3). Vincent, Salisbury, Strain, McCormick, and Tessier (1990) note, more recently, that "a change in the child is dependent not just on professional skills or the child's disability, but also upon complex interrela-tionships among family values, intra- and extra-family supports, and the extent to which service is offered, match what families need and want" (p. 186).

The message is clear. Quality programs for young children with special needs demand that profession-als see the child within the context of her family and, in turn, the family's interrelationships and interac-tions with other, larger social systems.

Summary

Early childhood special educators will serve a wide variety of students in a diversity of settings. Professionals will typically assign a range of labels to these youngsters such as developmentally delayed, at-risk, or even handicapped. It is imperative, therefore, that teachers have a clear understanding of the meaning of these terms. Of equal, if not greater importance, is our belief that young children with special needs are more like their typically developing peers than they are different. Teachers should focus on the child and their strengths, not their impairments. As professionals, we need to separate the youngster's abilities from their disabilities.

The growth of early childhood special education as a discipline has been aided by judicial action and federal legislation. In several instances, principles addressed in judicial remedies have found their way into both state and national legislative enactments. Many contemporary special education policies, practices, and procedures are derived from court decisions of the 1960s and 1970s. Likewise, the rights, opportunities, and benefits presently enjoyed by young children with special needs and their families are the result of federal legislative activity.

A question typically encountered by early childhood special educators is, "Is early intervention effective, does it really make a difference in the lives of young children?" Perhaps the best way to answer this difficult query is to say, "It depends." One of the reasons we are so vague is due to the documented difficulty of conducting a methodologically sound investigation. In spite of this shortcoming, there is a very strong rationale for early intervention and the efficacy of these efforts, in our opinion, has been substantially demonstrated.

The number of young children receiving special education services has grown dramatically in the past several years. This growth is partially the result of litigation, legislation, and the benefits attributed to early intervention. In the 2000–2001 school year, almost 830,500 young children were enrolled in some type of early intervention or special education program.

Contemporary thinking in early childhood special education strongly suggests the validity of viewing children as part of a larger social system, wherein they influence and are influenced by various environments. Children and their families need to be understood in the context in which they develop and interact. There is a reciprocal relationship among the various layers of environmental forces. This ecological perspective encourages early childhood professionals to be mindful of the child's total environment and the key people encountered within these several spheres of influence.

Check Your Understanding

1. What is the difference between a *disability* and a *handicap*?

2. Define and give an example of each of the four categories of eligibility for early intervention.

3. What is meant by the term *special education and related services*?

4. Identify the significance of the following court cases:
   (a) *Pennsylvania Association for Retarded Children v. Commonwealth of Pennsylvania*
   (b) *Mills v. Board of Education of the District of Columbia*
   (c) *Larry P. v. Riles*
   (d) *Board of Education v. Rowley*.

5. List the six major provisions contained in PL 94-142.

6. What is an individualized family service plan (IFSP)?

7. What is the role of a service coordinator?

8. Identify at least four benefits of early intervention for youngsters with disabilities and children at-risk.

9. What general conclusions can be drawn from the efficacy research on early intervention?

10. According to Bronfenbrenner, how should early childhood professionals relate to young children and their families?

References

Allen, K. (1992). *The exceptional child: Mainstreaming in early education* (2nd ed.). Albany, NY: Delmar.

Bailey, D. (2000). The federal role in early intervention: Prospects for the future. *Topics in Early Childhood Special Education, 20*(2), 71–78.

Bailey, D., Farel, A., O'Donnell, K., Simeonsson, R., & Miller, C. (1986). Preparing infant interventionists: Interdepartmental training in special education and maternal and child health. *Journal of the Division for Early Childhood, 11*(1), 67–77.

Bailey, D., & Wolery, M. (1992). *Teaching infants and preschoolers with disabilities* (2nd ed.). New York: Merrill.

Bronfenbrenner, U. (1977). Toward an experimental ecology of human development. *American Psychologist, 32,* 513–531.

Bronfenbrenner, U. (1979). *The ecology of human development: Experiments by nature and design.* Cambridge, MA: Harvard University Press.

Casto, G., & Mastropieri, M. (1986). The efficacy of early intervention programs: A meta-analysis. *Exceptional Children, 52*(5), 417–424.

Clarke, A., & Clarke, A. (1976). *Early experience: Myth and evidence.* New York: Free Press.

Danaher, J. (2001). Eligibility policies and practices for young children under Part B of IDEA. *NECTAC Notes, 9,* 1–18. Chapel Hill, NC: National Early Childhood Technical Assistance Center.

Division for Early Childhood. (1996). *Developmental delay as an eligibility category* (Concept paper). Reston, VA: Author.

Dunst, C. (1986). Overview of the efficacy of early intervention programs: Methodological and conceptual considerations. In L. Bickman & D. Weatherford (Eds.), *Evaluating early intervention programs for severely handicapped children and their families* (pp. 79–148). Austin, TX: Pro-Ed.

Dunst, C., & Rheingrover, R. (1981). An analysis of the efficacy of early intervention programs with organically handicapped children. *Evaluation and Program Planning, 4,* 287–323.

Dunst, C., & Snyder, S. (1986). A critique of the Utah State University early intervention meta-analysis. *Exceptional Children, 53,* 269–276.

Dunst, C., Trivette, C., & Deal, A. (1988). *Enabling and empowering families: Principles and guidelines for practice.* Cambridge, MA: Brookline Books.

Fallen, H., & Umansky, W. (1985). *Young children with special needs* (2nd ed.). Columbus, OH: Merrill.

Farran, D. (1990). Effects of intervention with disadvantaged and disabled children: A decade of review. In S. Meisels & J. Shonkoff (Eds.), *Handbook of early intervention* (pp. 501–539). Cambridge, England: Cambridge University Press.

Farran, D. (2000). Another decade of intervention for children who are low income or disabled: What do we know now? In J. Shonkoff & S. Meisels (Eds.), *Handbook of early intervention* (2nd ed., pp. 510–548). Cambridge, England: Cambridge University Press.

Gargiulo, R. (2003). *Special education in contemporary society: An introduction to exceptionality.* Belmont, CA: Wadsworth.

Guralnick, M. (1988). Efficacy research in early childhood intervention programs. In S. Odom & M. Karnes (Eds.), *Early intervention for infants and children with handicaps: An empirical base* (pp. 75–88). Baltimore: Paul H. Brookes.

Guralnick, M. (1991). The next decade of research on the effectiveness of early intervention. *Exceptional Children, 58*(1), 174–183.

Guralnick, M. (1997). *The effectiveness of early intervention.* Baltimore: Paul H. Brookes.

Guralnick, M. (1998). Effectiveness of early intervention for vulnerable children: A developmental perspective. *American Journal on Mental Retardation, 102*(4), 319–345.

Guralnick, M., & Bricker, D. (1987). The effectiveness of early intervention for children with cognitive and general developmental delay. In M. Guralnick & F. Bennett (Eds.), *The effectiveness of early intervention for at-risk and handicapped children* (pp. 115–173). New York: Academic Press.

Hanson, M., & Lynch, E. (1995). *Early intervention* (2nd ed.). Austin, TX: Pro-Ed.

Harbin, G., McWilliam, R., & Gallagher, J. (2000). Services for young children with disabilities and their families. In J. Shonkoff & S. Meisels (Eds.), *Handbook of early intervention* (2nd ed., pp. 387–415). Cambridge, England: Cambridge University Press.

Kamerman, S. (2000). Early childhood intervention policies: An international perspective. In J. Shonkoff & S. Meisels (Eds.), *Handbook of early intervention* (2nd ed., pp. 613–629). Cambridge, England: Cambridge University Press.

Kirk, S. (1958). *Early education of the mentally retarded: An experimental study.* Urbana, IL: University of Illinois Press.

Kirk, S., Gallagher, J., & Anastasiow, N. (2000). *Educating exceptional children* (9th ed.). Boston: Houghton Mifflin.

Kopp, C. (1983). Risk factors in development. In P. Mussen (Ed.), *Handbook of child psychology* (4th ed., Vol. II, pp. 1081–1188). New York: Wiley.

Koppelman, J. (1986). Reagan signs bills expanding services to handicapped preschoolers. *Report to Preschool Programs, 18,* 3–4.

Lazar, I., & Darlington, R. (1979). *Summary report: Lasting effects after preschool.* (DHEW Publication No. OHDS 80-30179). Washington, DC: U.S. Government Printing Office.

Lazar, I., Darlington, R., Murray, H., Royce, J., & Snipper, A. (1982). Lasting effects of early intervention: A report from the Consortium for Longitudinal Studies. *Monographs of the Society for Research in Child Development, 47,* (2–3, Serial No. 195).

McCollum, J., & Maude, S. (1993). Portrait of a changing field: Policy and practice in early childhood special education. In B. Spodek (Ed.), *Handbook of research in early childhood education* (pp. 352–371). New York: Macmillan.

Odom, S. (1988). Research in early childhood special education: Methodologies and paradigms. In S. Odom & M. Karnes (Eds.), *Early intervention for infants and children with handicaps* (pp. 1–21). Baltimore: Paul H. Brookes.

Odom, S., & Diamond, K. (1998). Inclusion of young children with special needs in early childhood education: The research base. *Early Childhood Research Quarterly, 13*(1), 3–25.

Peterson, N. (1987). *Early intervention for handicapped and at-risk children.* Denver: Love Publishing.

Ramey, C., & Ramey, S. (1998). Early intervention and early experience. *American Psychologist, 58*(2), 109–120.

Raver, S. (1999). *Intervention strategies for infants and toddlers with special needs* (2nd ed.). Upper Saddle River, NJ: Prentice Hall.

Shackelford, J. (2002). State/jurisdictional eligibility definitions for infants and toddlers with disabilities under IDEA. *NECTAC Notes, 11,* 1–14. Chapel Hill, NC: National Early Childhood Technical Assistance Center.

Shonkoff, J., & Hauser-Cram, P. (1987). Early intervention for disabled infants and their families: A quantitative analysis. *Pediatrics, 80,* 650–658.

Shore, R. (1997). *Rethinking the brain: New insights into early development.* New York: Families and Work Institute.

Skeels, H. (1966). Adult status of children with contrasting early life experiences. *Monographs of the Society for Research in Child Development, 31,* (3, Serial No. 105).

Skeels, H., & Dye, H. (1939). A study of the effects of differential stimulation on mentally retarded children. *Proceedings and addresses of the American Association on Mental Deficiency, 44,* 114–136.

Spodek, B., & Saracho, O. (1994a). *Right from the start.* Needham Heights, MA: Allyn and Bacon.

Spodek, B., & Saracho, O. (1994b). *Dealing with individual differences in the early childhood classroom.* White Plains, NY: Longman.

Strain, P., & Smith, B. (1986). A counter-interpretation of early intervention effects: A response to Casto and Mastropieri. *Exceptional Children, 53,* 260–265.

Tjossem, T. (1976). Early intervention: Issues and approaches. In T. Tjossem (Ed.). *Intervention strategies for high-risk and handicapped children* (pp. 3–33). Baltimore: University Park Press.

Trohanis, P. (1989). An introduction to PL 99-457 and the national policy agenda for serving young children with special needs and their families. In J. Gallagher, P. Trohanis, & R. Clifford (Eds.), *Policy implementation and PL 99-457: Planning for young children with special needs* (pp. 1–17). Baltimore: Paul H. Brookes.

U.S. Department of Education. (1997). *Nineteenth annual report to Congress on the implementation of the Individuals with Disabilities Education Act.* Washington, DC: U.S. Government Printing Office.

U.S. Department of Education. (1998). *Twentieth annual report to Congress on the implementation of the Individuals with Disabilities Education Act.* Washington, DC: U.S. Government Printing Office.

U.S. Department of Education. (2001). *Twenty-third annual report to Congress on the Implementation of the Individuals with Disabilities Education Act.* Washington, DC: U.S Government Printing Office.

U.S. Department of Education. (2002). *Twenty-fourth annual report to Congress on the implementation of the Individuals with Disabilities Education Act.* Washington, DC: U.S. Government Printing Office.

Vincent, L., Salisbury, C., Strain, P., McCormick, C., & Tessier, A. (1990). A behavioral-ecological approach to early intervention: Focus on cultural diversity. In S. Meisels & J. Shonkoff (Eds.), *Handbook of early childhood intervention* (pp. 173–195). Cambridge, England: Cambridge University Press.

Walsh, S., Smith, B., & Taylor, R. (2000). *IDEA requirements for preschoolers with disabilities.* Reston, VA: Council for Exceptional Children.

White, K., Bush, D., & Casto, G. (1986). Let the past be prologue: Learning from previous reviews of early intervention efficacy research. *Journal of Special Education, 19,* 417–428.

Zigler, E. (1990). Foreword. In S. Meisels & J. Shonkoff (Eds.), *Handbook of early childhood intervention* (pp. ix–xiv). Cambridge, England: Cambridge University Press.

Zigler, E. (2000). Foreword. In J. Shonkoff & S. Meisels (Eds.), *Handbook of early intervention* (2nd ed., pp. xi–xv). Cambridge, England: Cambridge University Press.

Introducing Two Special Children

In order to help you understand programs and services for young children with disabilities, we would like to introduce two children, Maria and T. J. We will be talking about the educational needs of Maria and T. J. over the next several chapters. It is our wish that by presenting these youngsters, you will develop a better understanding of the diversity of services required for young children with disabilities and their families.

Maria Ramirez

Bubbly, outgoing, and affectionate with a constant smile are some of the terms Maria's interventionists use when describing her. This 30-month-old with Down syndrome is the youngest child of Bruce and Catherine Ramirez. Mr. Ramirez is an executive with a local bank. Maria's mother is employed as an intensive care nurse at the regional hospital. Her two older brothers enjoy their role as protector of their little sister. The Ramirez family lives in an affluent section of a small town approximately 50 miles from a large Midwestern city.

A service coordinator comes to Maria's home one morning a week in order to provide assistance with the achievement of her IFSP outcome statements. Due to her parents' work schedule and other commitments, Maria's grandparents provide child care and are trained to work with her. Maria's entire family is committed to maximizing her potential.

Team members have recommended that Maria transition to an inclusive community-based program in order to receive Part B services. Although the family understands that with the approach of her third birthday, a change in service delivery is necessary, they are reluctant to agree to this recommendation. Maria's parents and grandparents have several concerns. Among their fears are issues of working with a new set of professionals, the length of her day, transportation, and Maria's interaction with playmates who are nondisabled.

Thomas Jefferson (T. J.) Browning

T. J. Browning is a rambunctious little boy who just celebrated his fourth birthday two months ago. He lives with his mother and a twelve-year-old stepbrother, Willy. His mom has been separated from his dad for fourteen months.

The family lives in a large apartment complex for citizens with incomes at or below the poverty level. There are few playmates his own age in the complex. T. J. does not have a close relationship with his older brother; his mom has suspicions that Willy may be involved with a neighborhood gang.

T. J. has been attending the Epps Head Start Center for the past 15 months. In the center, T. J. has few friends. The staff observe that he has a short attention span, is easily distracted, and is overly aggressive.

T. J. frequently uses his large size to get what he wants from the other children. Although well-coordinated, he has impairments with fine motor skills and his teachers suspect some cognitive deficits. T. J. receives integrated speech therapy twice a week from a speech and language pathologist. The director of the Epps Center and her staff are concerned about his readiness to attend kindergarten in the fall.

T. J.'s mother is a concerned parent who wants her son to be successful in school. Her job as a waitress limits her participation in center activities and from attending meetings and class field trips.

Family-Based Early Childhood Services

In the field of early intervention/early childhood special education, practices associated with the concept of being family-based have been increasingly advocated and used by personnel from many disciplines concerned with the well-being, education, and care of young children with known or suspected disabilities and their families. Calls have become commonplace for early childhood personnel to be family-based, to incorporate family systems theory into their professional practices, to provide support to families, and to appropriately address the needs of young children and families from diverse backgrounds. In fact, Bailey and his colleagues (1998) concluded that a family-centered perspective should permeate all aspects of early intervention/education services to include, but not be limited to, screening, assessment, team meetings, program planning, intervention activities, service coordination, and transition.

A changing view of families and their participation in their children's early intervention/education services has emerged over the last two decades. This view involves a true partnership in which families have a right to become involved in early intervention/education services, are encouraged to be involved to the degree that they choose, and to engage in shared decision-making. A variety of research studies and program models have provided evidence in support of the mutual benefits of such collaboration between families and professionals. The roles of family members and professionals have changed to a marked degree and the rationale for building effective partnerships is more compelling than in the past. Further, there has been a dramatic increase in awareness, services, and opportunities for families of young children with known or suspected disabilities. These and other factors related to family-based early childhood services will be examined in this chapter.

Historical and Legal Perspectives

It has long been recognized that the family is the fundamental social institution and the cornerstone of our society. The family is also the primary arena in which a child, with or without a disability, is socialized, educated, and exposed to the beliefs and values of his or her culture. Thus, the importance of collaboration among service providers and families in early intervention/education cannot be overstated. This collaboration often takes on even more significance when the child has a disability. It is important to note, however, that family involvement in programs for children with disabilities is not a new concept. In fact, the history of family involvement in the education of young children with disabilities has been described as an evolving process that has occurred over a number

Table 3–1	The Chronology of the Family Movement
1950s	Parents began to organize services and schools for children with disabilities in their communities. National organizations were formed and political action initiated.
1975	PL 94-142, the Education for All Handicapped Children Act (later incorporated into IDEA), established parents' roles as decision makers.
1980s	Grassroots support for parent-to-parent support groups increased.
1983	Legislation established a national program of Parent Training and Information Centers to provide assistance for families.
1986	PL 99-457 (later incorporated in IDEA) mandated that families were to be the focus of services.
1990s	Advocacy movements—early childhood, inclusion, transition, and self-advocacy—grew in numbers and influence.
1997	The 1997 IDEA Amendments placed greater emphasis on the involvement of parents in the eligibility, placement, and IEP processes.

SOURCE: Adapted from N. Flynn and C. Takemoto, The Family Perspective. 1997. In J. Wood and A. Lazzari, *Exceeding the Boundaries: Understanding Exceptional Lives.* Fort Worth, TX: Harcourt Brace College Publisher, p. 506.

of years. Table 3–1 provides a chronology of the family movement.

Among many factors contributing to the emergence of the emphasis on family involvement in the 1960s and 1970s were political, social, economic, and educational issues and events. Certain political movements, such as the civil rights and women's movements, advocacy efforts, and legislative actions have contributed to the emphasis that is now placed on the provision of quality programs for young children with special needs and their families. Influences also have come from the fields of general early childhood education, early childhood special education, and compensatory education, as well as professional organizations such as the Division for Early Childhood (DEC) of the Council for Exceptional Children (CEC).

General Early Childhood Education Influences

In the field of general early childhood education, the importance and necessity of family involvement in programs and schools for young children has been well-documented. Lasting results of the intervention programs of the 1960s and 1970s in early childhood education is a body of literature that describes the effects of various kinds of interactions and environmental influences on the development of young children (Bloom, 1964; Galinsky, 1990; Gestwicki, 1992; Gray, Ramsey, & Klaus, 1982; Lazar & Darlington, 1982; Rosenthal & Sawyers, 1996; Schweinhart & Weikart, 1980). A variety of studies suggest that the early years are of extreme importance in establishing learning patterns for young children and their families (Bloom, 1981; Dimidjian, 1989; Thompson & Hupp, 1992). It is virtually impossible to overemphasize the importance of the development that takes place in the early years and the interactions that occur among young children and their families.

Compensatory Education Influences

The Head Start program is among the longest lasting early intervention programs, having started in the mid-1960s. Studies of this program have shown that parental involvement was positively related to children's test scores, academic achievement, and self-concept, as well as parental feelings of success and involvement in community activities (Gestwicki, 1992). Another well-known intervention program was the Perry Preschool Project, which began in Ypsilanti, Michigan, in the early 1960s. The purpose of the project was to examine the immediate and long-term effects of preschool education on the lives of low-income children and their families and in the community as a whole. In this program, teachers visited parents in their homes each week. Under the auspices of this longitudinal study, preschoolers were followed through their nineteenth birthday and beyond to assess social and educational achievement. Findings included that these children received less remedial education, graduated from high school, and went on to jobs or further education at twice the rate of children who did not participate in a preschool program. In addition, they also had fewer arrests, fewer teenage pregnancies, and less welfare dependency or other problem behaviors (Berrueta-Clement, Schweinhart, Barnett, Epstein, & Weikart, 1984).

For many years in the policy and procedure guidelines of early childhood programs, parent involvement has been mandated. For example, as a community action program established by the Economic Opportunity Act of 1964, Project Head Start was required to have parent participation. In the Policy Manual, Head Start (1984) specified performance standards in four areas of parent involvement:

1. decision-making about direction and operation of the program via membership on the Policy Council;

2. participation in classrooms as volunteers, with the possibility of moving up the career ladder as paid employees;

3. parent activities planned by the parents themselves; and

4. working with their own children, along with the center staff.

According to Head Start, the rationale for parent involvement is that in order for children to reach their fullest potential, there must be an opportunity for parents to influence the character of programs that are affecting their children's development. Thus, parents have been provided with real opportunities and specific roles for active involvement in Head Start programs over the years. Through the Policy Council, parents have been involved in setting standards for hiring staff and participated in budgetary matters, as well as other administrative and program concerns.

Another example of a family-based education program is Even Start, a federal program that funds local efforts to improve the educational opportunities for the nation's children and adults. This program integrates early childhood education and adult education into a unified family program. The mandate requires program administrators to build on existing resources in the community in order to create new ranges of services. Some of these services may include: identifying and recruiting of eligible children; screening and preparing parents and children for the program; establishing instructional programs to promote adult literacy; preparing parents to support the education and growth of their children; preparing children for success in regular schools; providing special instruction for staff to develop skills to work with parents and children; and integrating instructional services through home-based programs where possible (Gestwicki, 1992).

Early Childhood Special Education Influences

As you may recall from the previous chapter, several legislative decisions have focused the country's attention on young children with disabilities and the needs and rights of their families. Parents, who have long been advocates for children with special needs, have been instrumental in the enactment of legislation. Parents have organized themselves into parent-to-parent support groups and advocacy groups. They have learned effective ways to gather information and to communicate their own needs and the needs of their children. Parent participation was mandated first in PL 94-142, the Education of All Handicapped Children's Act of 1975. This law required parent participation with professionals in planning the Individualized Education Plan (IEP). The 1986 PL 99-157, the Education of the Handicapped Act Amendments, called for a focus on the family in the delivery of early intervention services. The law specified an increased role for families in services to children ages birth to three. It also introduced the Individualized Family Service Plan (IFSP), which requires that the needs of the whole family be considered. (Extensive information about these laws is provided in Chapter 6.) In 1991, Congress reauthorized funds for special education programs as the Individuals with Disabilities Education Act (IDEA). This revision of the original law made services for 3- to 5-year-olds mandatory rather than optional.

In 1997, the 1997 Amendments to IDEA (PL 105-117) were signed into law in order to protect and enhance the fundamental rights of children with disabilities and their families. According to this legislation, children must be provided with more opportunities to be involved in the general curriculum and their parents have increased opportunities to be involved in eligibility and placement decisions. The law emphasizes the responsibility of parents and school personnel to work more closely together to ensure the effectiveness of the Individual Family Service Plan (IFSP) for infants and toddlers or the Individual Education Plan (IEP) for school age children. In all states, parents are encouraged to be active participants on the teams that are making eligibility, placement, and educational decisions about their children with disabilities (Heumann & Hehir, 1997). This legislation has substantially increased the intent and directives for parent and family involvement in the educational process for children with disabilities (Yell, 1998).

During the past few decades, a perspective that views the child within the context of the family has provided new insights into meeting the needs of young children with disabilities. In utilizing this family-based approach, close attention must be paid to the needs of the entire family and how these needs influence the desired outcomes for the child.

Influences from Professional Organizations

Recommendations from professional organizations such as the Division for Early Childhood of the Council for Exceptional Children (Sandall, McLean, & Smith, 2000), the Association of Teacher Educators (DEC, ATE, NAEYC, 1994), the National Association for the Education of Young Children (Bredekamp & Coople, 1997), and others have set standards and policies concerning parents and families. Groups like the National Association of State Boards of Education and the National Black Child Development Institute have also published documents focused on the involvement and participation of parents. These documents emphasize that the benefits of family involvement during a child's early years extend far beyond the preschool and elementary years.

The Changing American Family

As personnel attempt to provide appropriate services to families, the dramatic changes that have occurred in the composition of families over the last several decades are important to recognize. In a special issue of *Newsweek* magazine, titled "The Twenty-First Century Family," the following quote was published:

> The American family does not exist. Rather, we are creating many American families of diverse styles and shapes. In unprecedented numbers, our families are unalike; we have fathers working while mothers keep house; fathers and mothers both working away from home; single parents; second marriages bringing children together from unrelated backgrounds; childless couples; unmarried couples, with and without children; gay and lesbian parents. We are living through a period of historic change in American family life. (*Newsweek*, 1990, p. 15)

This quote emphasizes that terms such as family and parent often have different meanings to different people. The word *parent*, for example, is traditionally interpreted to mean a person's mother or father. Yet, this definition is frequently inaccurate due to a variety of reasons, such as the changing view of what constitutes a family. The term parent actually can refer to anyone who is in charge of a child's care or well-being. This responsibility can occur on a short-term or long-term basis. A child's primary caregiver might be a single parent, a parent by birth or adoption, a guardian, an aunt or uncle, a grandparent, a close friend of the mother or father, or even foster parents or surrogate parents. Thus, in this chapter, the term **parent** will be used to refer to any adult who fulfills the essential caregiving duties and responsibilities for a particular child at a particular point in the child's life.

The traditional American family was once viewed as: (a) two parents (a male and a female), who were married to each other and always had been; (b) two children (one girl and one boy) from the parents' union; (c) two sets of grandparents, living within fifty miles; (d) the mother working in the home and caring for the children; and (e) the father working outside of the home and interacting with children in the evenings and on weekends. As the *Newsweek* article points out, however, no longer is it valid to think of a family as a mom who is a full-time homemaker and a working dad along with several children who are all living together. This conventional perspective of the nuclear family has definitely changed and is continuing to change. In fact, only about 5 percent of families in the United States currently fit this description (Hodgkinson, 1992). The following statistics demonstrate some of the many ways in which the typical American family has changed:

- 58.6 percent of children under age six have a mother in the workforce,
- one out of two children live with a single parent at some point during childhood,
- over half of all marriages end in divorce,
- every 24 seconds a child is born to an unmarried mother,
- every 46 seconds a child is born into poverty, and
- families with children constitute 38% of the homeless population (Children's Defense Fund, 2003).

The preceding statistics strongly suggest that no longer is there a "typical" American family. In other words, the expression "The Cleavers don't live here anymore" is certainly accurate. It is only realistic to define families more broadly. In American families today, there may be many nuclear family configurations. The definition of **family** used in this chapter is a group of people, related by blood or circumstance, who rely upon one another for security, sustenance, support, socialization, and stimulation.

In 1990, a Task Force in New Mexico developed a poignant description of the contemporary American family that follows.

Family

We all come from families. Families are big, small, extended, nuclear, multigenerational, with one parent, two parents and grandparents. We live under one roof or many. A family can be as temporary as a few weeks, as permanent as forever. We become part of a family by birth, adoption, marriage, or from a desire for mutual support. As family members, we nurture, protect, and influence one another. Families are dynamic and are cultures unto themselves, with different values and unique ways of realizing dreams. Together, our families become the source of our rich cultural heritage and spiritual diversity. Each family has strengths and qualities that flow from individual members and from the family as a unit. Our families create neighborhoods, communities, states, and nations.

SOURCE: New Mexico's Memoria 5 Task Force on Children and Families and the Coalition for Children, 1990.

The changes that have occurred and are continuing to occur in families certainly issue a call for the utilization of an extremely individualized approach in professionals' interactions with families. Each of these family configurations adds to the complexity of interactions between families and professionals. Many factors must be taken into consideration when working with diverse family structures and the impact of these variations on family relationships with professionals. Service providers must be sensitive and

The development of relationships among families and other team members is central to early intervention/education.

aware of the unique characteristics of the families they serve. As families continue to change, personnel must carefully examine and discover the most effective methods of working with families.

Family Reactions to a Child with a Disability

When a child with a disability becomes a member of the family, whether through birth, adoption, or later onset of the disability, the ecology of the family changes and the entire family often must make adjustments. Each parent or family member responds to a child's disability in his or her own way (Winzer & Mazurek, 1998). In the same way that professionals realize that all children are individuals, they must also realize that parents are also individuals. Reactions and feelings may be dramatically different from one parent to another. Service providers, therefore, usually encounter a wide variety of behaviors and emotional responses on the part of parents and other family members.

Mistakes have been made in the past as professionals have made judgments about families based on a "stage theory" model of parental adjustment to having a child with a disability. The way in which this model evolved is surprising in that it began with a study conducted over 30 years ago, which was designed to assess parents' perceptions, feelings, and attachments to their children with disabilities (Drotar et al., 1975). Based on the results of this study, Drotar et al. (1975) developed a linear "stage theory" model of parental adjustment that followed a progression of acceptance beginning with shock and moving through denial and anger to a point of reorganization and acceptance. According to this model, parents are ready to deal with the responsibilities of their child with a disability once they have moved through the various stages of acceptance. In the 1980s, stage theories were disputed by researchers who rejected the idea of families, all of whom are unique, going through the same specific stages of acceptance. Further, they disagreed with the idea of having families' feelings being judged and categorized according

to this continuum. In fact, some researchers stated that this type of categorization was a disservice to families (Blancher, 1984).

Most professionals in the field today recognize that families respond differently to having a child with a disability based on a number of characteristics, resources, and supports that are unique to the individual family. Researchers have recognized that a variety of factors can interact to influence a family's reaction and subsequent adjustment to a child with a disability, which can include personal characteristics of family members, patterns of family interactions, health and safety factors, and others. Stress factors or needs associated with risk or disability also can effect family functioning and partnerships between professionals and families. For example, professionals who work with four-year-old T. J. must carefully consider the influences of his brother's gang-suspected activities, the neighborhood in which he lives, his parents' separation, and other family dynamics. From a more positive perspective, some family characteristics (e.g., a large family, a family with effective coping skills) may mitigate many of the stresses associated with a child with a disability (Guralnick, 1998).

The needs of the parents reflect not only their ability to cope but also their child's developmental needs. For example, the demands placed upon the professional who initially breaks the news of a child's disability to the parents may be very different from the professional who helps parents deal with the fears associated with their child's transition into a kindergarten classroom. The needs of a family of a child with a severe physical or medical disability may be different from a family of a child with delayed speech. Service providers must tailor their interactions and provide support based on the ever changing needs of families. Sometimes families of young children with disabilities, especially those of children with severe disabilities can face critical problems, some of which are listed below.

- Expensive medical treatment, surgery, or hospitalization that may occur repeatedly and for extended periods.

- Heavy expenses and financial burdens beyond medical costs, incurred by needs such as special foods and equipment.

- Frightening, energy-draining, often recurring crises, as when the child stops breathing or experiences a seizure.

- Transportation problems, especially if the child requires special equipment.

- Babysitting needs for the other children.

- Time away from jobs to get the child to consultation and treatment appointments.

- Continuous day-and-night demands on parents to provide routine but difficult caregiving tasks (for example, it may take an hour or more, five to six times during a 24-hour period, to feed a child with a severe cleft palate condition).

- Constant fatigue, lack of sleep, and little or no time to meet the needs of other family members.

- Little or no opportunity for recreational or leisure activities.

- Difficulty (and additional expense) of locating child care or babysitters qualified to care for a child with a disability.

- Lack of respite care facilities.

- Jealousy or feelings of rejection among siblings, who may feel the child with a disability gets *all* the family's attention and resources.

- Marital problems arising from finances, fatigue, differences about management of the child's disability, or feelings of rejection by husband or wife that he or she is being passed over in favor of the child. (Adapted from Allen, 2001, p. 321)[1]

It is important to remember that a team effort is required in understanding a family and its behavior. Service providers should rely on the expertise of mental health and social service professionals when working with families. It is also important to acknowledge that all families may experience a number of stresses at different points in time, and a family's behavior may seem extreme at different times in its

development. However, most families eventually achieve a healthy balance. It is important for the focus to be on the strengths and the resources of the family rather than the needs, challenges, and stresses that may be encountered by families.

Family Systems Theory

Utilization of a family systems theory model has become the recommended approach in early intervention/early childhood special education. The fundamental belief underlying **family systems theory** is that a family is an interactional system with unique characteristics and needs. The family operates as an interrelated and interdependent unit; therefore, events and experiences that have an impact on particular family members also will affect the other members of the family or the entire family unit (Minuchin, 1988, Turnbull & Turnbull 2001). Each family member may have his or her own set of needs that may or may not be congruent with the needs of other family members or with the needs of the family as a whole. Because of the relationship that exists among family members, teachers and other service providers must consider the entire family unit as the possible focus of their attention. Recommended

Children with disabilities and their families must be considered within the context of the community in which they live.

---

[1]Reproduced by permission. *The Exceptional Child: Inclusion in Early Childhood Education*, 4/e. By K. Eileen Allen and Ilene S. Schwartz. Delmar Learning, Clifton Park, New York, Copyright 2001.

practice suggests that service providers should apply family systems theory by individualizing their relationships with each family, just as they individualize their work with each child with a disability (Turnbull & Turnbull, 2001).

Family systems theory was adapted by Turnbull, Summers, and Brotherson (1984) to focus specifically on families of young children with disabilities. Their family systems conceptual framework includes the following four key elements, which are all interrelated.

1. Family characteristics are the attributes of a family, such as their cultural background, financial well-being, size, age, geographic location, abilities, and disabilities.

2. Family interactions refer to the daily relationships between and among family members.

3. Family functions are the needs and interests of family members met by the family, including social, emotional, educational, or physical needs such as health care or child care.

4. Family life cycle refers to all the changes that affect families and influence family resources, interactions, and functions.

Figure 3–1 provides a visual display of the components of the family systems theory model. What follows is a discussion of each component of the family systems theory model.

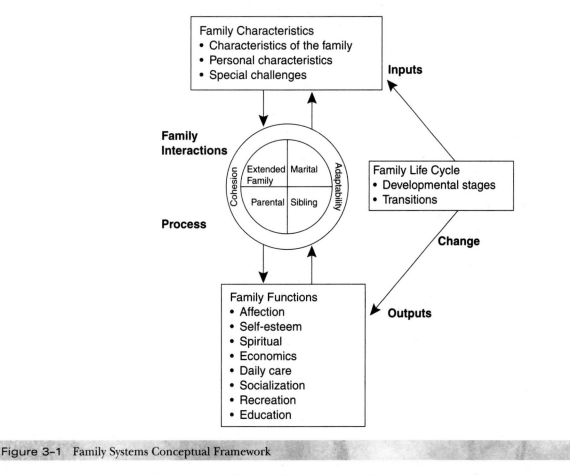

Figure 3–1   Family Systems Conceptual Framework

Adapted by permission from Turnbull, A. P., Summers, J. A., and Brotherson, M. J. (1984). *Working with families with disabled members: A family systems approach* (p. 60). Lawrence, K S: University of Kansas, Kansas Affiliated Facility.

Family Characteristics

The first element of family systems theory is **family characteristics.** As described above, family characteristics are those dimensions that make each family unique (for example, family size and form, cultural background, socioeconomic status, geographic location). Additionally, each member's health status (both physical and mental), individual coping style, and the nature and severity of the child's disability are included as personal characteristics. A final component includes special challenges that can face families, such as poverty, substance abuse, and parents who themselves have disabilities. Collectively, these variables contribute to each family's unique identity and influence interactional patterns among the members while also determining how the family responds to their child's disability. It is easy to understand how a large family living below the poverty level in a rural location might differ in their adaptation from an affluent suburban family with an only child with a disability. In both examples, the families may be successful in their adaptation; however, their responses, needs, and adaptive strategies may be very different.

Family Interactions

The second component of family systems theory is **family interactions,** which is comprised of the relationships that occur among and between the various family subsystems or subgroups. These subsystems include:

1. marital (husband-wife);
2. parental (parent-child);
3. sibling (child-child); and
4. extra-familial (family, friends, neighbors, larger community including professionals) (Turnbull & Turnbull, 2001).

How a particular family interacts depends, in part, on the degree of cohesion and adaptability in interactions. These two factors influence the quality of interactions and can only be interpreted within the context of the family's cultural background.

Cohesion that occurs in families is a type of emotional bonding that holds them together (Olsan et al., 1989). It determines the degree of freedom and independence experienced by each member of the family unit. Cohesion occurs along a continuum of behavior ranging from enmeshment to disengagement. Highly enmeshed families are overly cohesive, which can impede the development of independence in individual family members. Families who are highly enmeshed are viewed as being overly protective and having weak boundaries between the subsystems. Conversely, rigid subsystem boundaries characterize disengaged families—believed to have a low degree of cohesiveness. In this situation, families are depicted as being underinvolved and the child with a disability may experience an absence of support (Minuchin, 1988). Ideally, well-functioning families seem to achieve a balance in cohesiveness in that the "boundaries between systems are clearly defined and family members feel both a close bonding and a sense of autonomy" (Seligman & Darling, 1997, p. 9).

Adaptability has been defined as the family's ability to change its power structure, role relationships, and rules in response to crises or stressful events occurring over a lifetime (Olson, Russell, & Sprenkle, 1980). Like cohesiveness, adaptability occurs along a continuum from rigidity to chaos and is influenced by the family's cultural background and other factors. When a stressful event occurs, rigid families respond according to prescribed roles and responsibilities and are often unable to adapt to the demands of the new situation. According to Seligman and Darling (1997), this type of behavior places a family at-risk for becoming isolated and disengaged. When a child with a severe disability becomes a member of a family, some form of accommodation or adjustment is usually required. Yet, in a rigid family with a clear hierarchy of power, the child care needs will more than likely become the responsibility of the mother with little or no assistance provided by other family members. On the other hand, how a chaotic family would respond to this situation is unpredictable due to few or inconsistent rules. Turnbull and Turnbull (2001) describe chaotic families as being characterized by constant change and instability. In many situations, there is no family leader and the few existing rules are frequently altered, resulting in significant confusion particularly for young children who need parental consistency and predictability. Most well-functioning families appear to maintain a balance between the extremes of high and low adaptability.

Family Functions

The third element of the family systems theory is **family functions,** which refers to the eight interrelated activities that are necessary to fulfill the individual and collective needs of the family. These eight areas, with examples of each, are as follows.

1. *affection*—emotional commitments and display of affection.
2. *self-esteem*—personal identity and self-worth, recognition of positive contributions.
3. *spiritual*—needs related to church, religion, or God.
4. *economics*—production and utilization of family income.
5. *daily care*—day-to-day survival needs such as food, shelter, and health care.
6. *socialization*—developing social skills, establishing interpersonal relationships.
7. *recreation*—leisure time activities for both family and individuals.
8. *education*—involvement in educational activities and career choices.

Turnbull and Turnbull (2001) identify these non-prioritized functions as "outputs" and emphasize that it is impossible to discuss family functions without considering the other three main components of the family systems framework. While these tasks and activities are common to all families, they are likely to be affected by the presence of a child with a disability (Berry & Hardman, 1998). Once again, it is important to remember, however, that the effect of the presence of a child with a disability on the family unit may be positive, negative, or neutral (Turnbull & Turnbull, 2001), and can change over time.

Individual families usually have individualized priorities for each of the preceding functions. In one family, meeting the daily needs of food and shelter is of utmost importance, while for another family, the emphasis may be on education or recreation and leisure. Berry and Hardman (1998) also noted that some families may require assistance in several areas while others may need help in only a few. The amount of support families request from professionals also will vary depending upon specific family circumstances.

Family Life Cycle

Family life cycle is the fourth element in the family systems framework. This component of the theory refers to developmental changes that occur in most families over time. Most of these changes are fairly predictable; however, they can be nondevelopmental or unexpected, such as the untimely death of a family member, divorce or marriage, or the unplanned birth of a child. These changes alter the structure of the family, and in turn, impact relationships, functions, and interactions. Researchers have identified as few as six to as many as twenty-four developmental stages that occur in families (Carter & McGoldrick, 1989). Regardless of the number of stages, each stage brings with it change, additional demands, and a new set of stressors. How the family responds to these situations determines, in part, the way in which the family functions.

Without proper planning, transitions encountered by young children with disabilities and their families (e.g., graduating from preschool, beginning kindergarten) can cause increased stress.

The movement from one stage to another and the accompanying adjustment period is considered to be a transition. Transitions tend to be stressful events for families, but especially for families of young children with disabilities. For many families, it is a time of challenge and uncertainty as to what the next stage holds for the child and family as well. For instance, when a preschooler moves to kindergarten, this can cause heightened anxiety and significant stress. Not all families successfully negotiate life cycle changes.

According to family systems theory, life cycle functions are highly age related. As a family moves through the life cycle, the priorities shift when the family encounters new situations (Seligman & Darling, 1997). Turnbull and Turnbull (2001) have identified four major life cycle stages and the accompanying issues that the family of a child with disability may encounter along the family's journey. The life cycle of a family typically includes the stages of the early childhood years, the school age years, adolescence, and adulthood. Some of the developmental issues that a child with a disability presents to his or her family during the early childhood years (birth through age eight) are listed in Table 3–2. Professionals must remember, however, that the way in which a family adapts to various stages throughout the life cycle is highly individualistic.

Table 3–2   Potential Family Life Cycle Issues

Stage	Parental Issues	Sibling Issues
Early Childhood (Birth–Age 5)	• Obtaining an accurate diagnosis • Informing siblings and relatives • Locating services • Seeking to find meaning in the disability • Clarifying a personal ideology to guide decisions • Addressing issues of stigma • Identifying positive contributions of the disability • Setting great expectations	• Less parental time and energy for sibling needs • Feelings of jealousy over less attention • Fears associated with misunderstandings of the disability
School Age (Ages 5–8)	• Establishing routines to carry out family functions • Adjusting emotionally to educational implications • Clarifying issues of inclusion vs. special class placement • Participating in IEP conferences • Locating community resources • Arranging for extracurricular activities	• Division of responsibility for any physical care needs • Oldest female sibling may be at-risk • Limited family resources for recreation and leisure • Informing friends and teachers • Possible concern over surpassing younger sibling • Issues of inclusion into same school • Need for basic information on the disability

SOURCE: *Family, Professionals, and Exceptionality A Special Partnership* 2/e by Turnbull/Turnbull, © 1990. Adapted by permission of Prentice-Hall, Inc., Upper Saddle River, NJ.

Applications of Family Systems Theory

Understanding the family as a social and emotional unit embedded within other units and networks enables service providers to better grasp the complex nature of families and to work with them in more effective ways. Utilizing this view allows professionals to realize that events and changes in one unit may directly and indirectly influence the behavior of individuals in other social units. A systems perspective considers events within and between social units as supportive to the extent that they have positive influences on family functioning. Each family member is viewed as a system and as a part of many other systems such as the school, community, and society (Swick, 1993).

Internally, as described earlier, the family system has basic functions that provide a broad framework through which a variety of roles and tasks are carried out. These functions change in response to developmental shifts in the family itself, as well as individual family member shifts. The structure of the family system and any changes in the structure may have an impact on all other elements. For example, the service provider who works with 30-month-old Maria must consider that Maria's interactions with her brothers, her grandparents, people from her affluent neighborhood, the service coordinator and therapists who visit weekly, and other significant people and experiences in her life will have a profound influence on Maria. The service provider must also consider the family's fears, the parents' emotional disposition, and other family characteristics.

In this systems framework perspective, the development of individuals and families is seen as a dynamic process of person-environment relationships. Therefore, the behavior of a child, family, or a child and family is viewed as a part of a set of interrelated "systems" (that is, physical, social, economic, spiritual, psychological, and ecological) that powerfully influence one another (Swick & Graves, 1993).

Swick and Graves (1993) have added an element called **empathy** to the systems perspective, which pro-

vides the "understanding" dimension of how children and families function. It is based on the view that human behavior is purposeful and that this purpose is influenced by interactions within the family system as it relates to interactions in other social systems (Schwartzman, 1985). Utilizing this view can assist professionals in gaining an increased understanding of human behavior. By understanding (showing empathy) experiences and activities in families and assessing the influences on the family, professionals can work with families to design strategies that promote well being in the family system. For example, if Maria's teacher realizes the close relationship Maria's brothers have with their 30-month-old sister, the brothers can be encouraged to participate in some of the learning activities and strategies designed to be used at home, which will benefit Maria. Through the use of ecological-empathetic perspectives, service providers can become sensitive to observable and subtle strengths as well as needs within the family (Swick & Graves, 1993).

The phrase "understanding empathy" represents a professional's ethical and humane position that all families, regardless of their condition, have strengths, are important, and have the capacity to make decisions that yield positive results. Therefore, to understand is to engage in meaningful and supportive interactions with families. This interactive focus takes into account family needs, strengths, dynamics, and potential.

Empowerment is a concept used by many individuals in helping professions. Most professionals would agree that it is much more accurate to describe this concept as a process rather than an end state. According to Vanderslice (1984), family empowerment is a process through which individuals increase their ability to influence those people and organizations that affect their lives, as well as the lives of their children and others they care about.

Bronfenbrenner's **ecological perspective** emphasizes that power emerges from the nature and structure of human relationships (1979). For example, an infant's need to develop trust is actualized within the primary relationship system of the family. This need may also be strongly influenced by other social systems, such as the neighborhood, the child care program, and other systems. It is within the family ecology that children and parents develop their sense of power. Empowered parents and families have three enabling characteristics:

1. the ability to access and control needed resources;

2. the ability to make decisions and solve problems; and

3. the ability to interact effectively with others in the social exchange process (Dunst, Trivette, & Deal, 1988).

Since individual needs, interests, affective development, and perceptual orientation evolve within the family ecology, the underlying premises of a family systems model are highly related to the empowerment paradigm. These premises include the following (Swick & Graves, 1993):

1. behavior takes place in a systems context;

2. individual development is intimately interrelated with the family's development;

3. family development is systematic; and

4. events that influence any family member have some direct or indirect influence on the entire family system.

Within the family system, trust, attachment, self-esteem, social attitudes and behaviors, and many other processes and skills emerge in a nurturing, empowered family (Brubaker, 1993). A sense of power or a sense of powerlessness is developed in the family ecology. It is important for professionals to remember that the concept of empowerment is dynamic, interactive, and process-oriented. Professionals who believe in the empowerment paradigm share the assumption that all families have strengths. Teachers and other service providers are in a strategic position to promote positive, empowering interactions with families by providing quality programs for young children, involving parents in partnerships, and supporting families in all aspects of early intervention early childhood special education services. The following perspectives should be carefully and sensitively explored by professionals who work with

young children with disabilities (Swick & Graves, 1993, pp. 56–57).

1. Who are the families we serve? What do we know about these families that can help us to be caring professionals?

2. What do we know about ourselves as helpful early childhood professionals? How do we think about the families we serve?

3. What are the programs, services, and activities we offer families? Are they "enabling" and "empowering," in that they respond to perceived needs?

4. How do our program activities reflect family respect and family autonomy? Do we use the input provided by parents to shape program activities?

5. How is the uniqueness of each family's integrity accounted for in our programs? Do opportunities exist for service providers and families to learn about one another's needs and strengths?

6. What is the predominant view of our staff regarding families and our relationship with families? Is it one of positive-nurturing partnerships?

One of the most important functions of empowerment is to provide skills that promote self-sufficiency. Empowerment may grow through a family's changes in self-perception, increased self-confidence, ability to set goals, acquisition of skills to attain goals, and the opportunity for supported practice (Dunlap, 1997). In most cases, empowerment means promoting access to resources, competence, and self-efficacy (Heflinger & Bickman, 1997). Relationships between professionals and families can be fostered through family empowerment because professionals come to view families as part of an equal, reciprocal partnership (Swick, 1996).

A Family-Based Philosophy

Several themes have emerged for those who work with families of young children with disabilities to consider carefully. First, there is the recognition that families are all very different. They differ in concerns, resources, priorities, and other areas; therefore, an individualized approach to working with families must be used to address each family's specific needs. Secondly, families should be partners in planning, providing services, and making decisions regarding issues such as the child's placement and the family's level of involvement in early intervention/education services. This relationship must include valuing and supporting the equality within the partnership. Finally, families are viewed as the ultimate teachers and decision makers for their children. A family-based perspective should be apparent in all aspects of early childhood services. An example of a family-centered early intervention philosophy, developed at the Frank Porter Graham Child Development Center, can be seen in Table 3–3. Early childhood programs all over the country have moved towards a family-based orientation.

As described previously, this family-based philosophy in early childhood special education has evolved over time. Dunst, Johanson, Trivette, and Hamby (1991) traced the history of the role of professionals in working with families of young children with special needs in the following order: (a) professional-centered, (b) family-allied, (c) family-focused, and (d) family-centered. Most recently leaders in the field of early intervention and early childhood special education have espoused a family-based model of early intervention/education (Trivette & Dunst, 2000). The first model that they described is one of professional-centered activity, whereby the professional was the sole source and dispenser of expertise. Families were considered dysfunctional and incapable of resolving their own problems. The family-allied model came next—families served as teachers of their children, implementing family interventions prescribed by the professionals. This perspective

Table 3–3 Family-Centered Philosophy in Early Intervention

Family-centered	Professionals should recognize that the family is the constant in the child's life while the service systems and personnel within those systems may be involved only episodically.
Ecologically based	As professionals work with families, they need to consider the interrelatedness of the various contexts that surround the child and family.
Individualized	Since the needs of each child and each family may differ, services should be individualized to meet those unique needs.
Culturally sensitive	Families come from different cultures and ethnic groups. Families reflect their diversity in their views and expectations of themselves, their children, and professionals. Services should be provided in ways that are sensitive to these variations and consistent with family values and beliefs.
Enabling and empowering	Services should foster a family's independence, existing and developing skills, and sense of competence and worth.
Needs-based	Approach starts with a family's expressed interests and collaborates with families in identifying and obtaining services according to their priorities.
Coordinated service delivery	Families need access to a well-coordinated system of services.
Normalized	Programs should work to promote the integration or inclusion of the child and the family within the community.
Collaborative	Early intervention services should be based on a collaborative relationship between families and professionals.

SOURCE: Adapted from The Carolina Institute of Research on Infant Personnel Preparation, Fronk Porter Graham Child Development Center, The University of North Carolina at Chapel Hill.

gradually gave way to a family-focused emphasis. Service providers at this stage viewed families in a more positive light. Families were seen as competent and capable of collaborating with professionals; however, most professionals still believed that families needed their assistance. In early childhood special education programs today, the focus is on a family-centered model. In this model, the family is the center of the service delivery system. As such, services are planned around the family, based on its individual needs. This approach is consumer driven—professionals are working for the family. The family is the primary decision maker. Professionals provide support to families and assist them as needed in fulfilling their goals.

Using the view of the family as a system, the ecological and empathetic perspectives, and the empowerment paradigm, professional planners are acknowledging families as strong, unique, and able to identify their own concerns and resources. The concept of **family-centered practices** in this context, refers to specific techniques and methods of working with families. As described by Dunst, Johanson, Trivette, and Hamby (1991), family-centered practices stress focusing on family strengths and enhancing family skills and competencies. Families are not mere recipients of services, but are active partners in planning and implementing service delivery processes (Kilgo & Raver, 1999). The goals of each program must contain elements that assist in supporting families as they strive to meet the needs of their children with special needs.

Following an extensive literature review, researchers at the Beach Center developed the following definition of family-centered services (Allen & Petr, 1995; Beach Center on Families and Disability, 1997c, p. 2):

> Family-centered service delivery, across disciplines and settings, recognizes the centrality of the family in the lives of individuals [with disabilities]. It is guided by fully informed choices made by the family and focuses upon the strengths and capabilities of these families.

Further, researchers at the Beach Center, identified the following component of family-centered philoso-phy and practice (Beach Center on Families and Disability, 1998):

- Focus on the family, not just the child.
- Emphasize mutual respect and teamwork.
- Organize assistance according to individual family needs.
- Consider family strengths, talents, resources, attributes, and aspirations.
- Address family needs holistically (not focusing on one member).
- Give families information in a supportive manner.
- Recognize that there are typical family reactions to exceptional circumstances.
- Structure the delivery of services to make them accessible without undue disruption of the family integrity and routine.

To be successful, early childhood service providers must hold a set of values that place the family at the center of the intervention process. This marks a dramatic shift from past practices when professionals focused solely on the child and designed interventions based on what they thought was best with little or no input from the family. Professionals must exchange the role of expert for partner in a relationship where the professionals and families have equal status.

In the *DEC Recommended Practice Guidelines,* Trivette & Dunst (2000) clarify the parameters of **family-based practices,** which is the most recently used terminology to reflect recommended practice in services for families. Trivette and Dunst describe family-based practices as supplying or mediating the "resources and supports necessary for families to have the time, energy, knowledge, and skills to provide their children learning opportunities and experiences that promote child development." Thus, they emphasized that "family-based practices will have child, parent, and family strengthening and competency-enhancing consequences" (p. 39). Recommended family-based practices, which provide the foundation for high quality services for young children with disabilities and their families, are described by Trivette and Dunst (2000) in the *DEC Recommended Practice Guidelines* (see Table 3–4).

Table 3-4 DEC Recommended Practices: Family-Based Practices

Families and professionals share responsibility and work collaboratively.

F1. Family members and professionals jointly develop appropriate family-identified outcomes.

F2. Family members and professionals work together and share information routinely and collaboratively to achieve family-identified outcomes.

F3. Professionals fully and appropriately provide relevant information so parents can make informed choices and decisions.

F4. Professionals use helping styles that promote shared family/professionals responsibility in achieving family-identified outcomes.

F5. Family and professionals' relationship building is accomplished in ways that are responsive to cultural, language, and other family characteristics.

Practices strengthen family functioning.

F6. Practices, supports, and resources provide families with participatory experiences and opportunities promoting choice and decision making.

F7. Practices, supports, and resources support family participation in obtaining desired resources and supports to strengthen parenting competence and confidence.

F8. Intrafamily, informal, community, and formal supports and resources (e.g., respite care) are used to achieve desired outcomes.

F9. Supports and resources provide families with information, competency-enhancing experiences, and participatory opportunities to strengthen family functioning and promote parenting knowledge and skills.

F10. Supports and resources are mobilized in ways that are supportive and do not disrupt family and community life.

Practices are individualized and flexible.

F11. Resources and supports are provided in ways that are flexible, individualized, and tailored to the child's family's preferences and styles, and promote well-being.

F12. Resources and supports match every family member's identified priorities and preferences (e.g., mother's and father's may be different).

F13. Practices, supports, and resources are responsive to the cultural, ethnic, racial, language, and socioeconomic characteristics and preferences of families and their communities.

F14. Practices, supports, and resources incorporate family beliefs and values into decisions, intervention plans, and resources and support mobilization.

Practices are strengths- and assets-based.

F15. Family and child strengths and assets are used as a basis for engaging families in participatory experiences supporting parenting competence and confidence.

F16. Practices, supports, and resources build on existing parenting competence and confidence.

F17. Practices, supports, and resources promote the family's and professional's acquisition of new knowledge and skills to strengthen competence and confidence.

SOURCE: "Recommended Practices in Family-Based Practices," by C. M. Trivette and C. J. Dunst, in *DEC Recommended Practices in Early Intervention/Early Childhood Special Education* (pp. 45–46), by S. Sandall, M. E. McLean, and B. Smith, 2000, Longmont, CO: Sopris West.

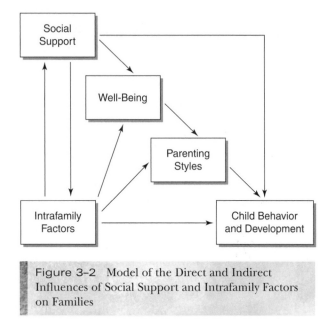

Figure 3–2 Model of the Direct and Indirect Influences of Social Support and Intrafamily Factors on Families

SOURCE: C. Trivette, & C. Dunst (2000). Recommended Practices in Family-Based Practices. In S. Sandall, M. McLean and B. Smith (Eds.) *DEC Recommended Practices in Early Intervention/ Early Childhood Special Education*. Longmont, CO: Sopris West, p. 40.

A long standing belief held by most professionals in the field is that families need both informal and formal resources and supports in order to have the knowledge and skills, as well as the physical and psychological energy and time, to engage in child rearing responsibilities and parenting activities that promote the development of their children (Bronfenbrenner, 1979). In the *DEC Recommended Practice Guidelines,* Trivette and Dunst (2000) reported evidence from research that social support has positive effects on family well-being. Figure 3–2 contains a model they used to illustrate the direct and indirect influences of social support on personal and family well-being, parent-child interactions, and child behavior and development. According to this model, "social support and resources directly influence the health and well-being of parents, both support and health/well-being influence parenting styles; and support, well-being, and parenting styles directly and indirectly influence child behavior and development" (p. 39). Through this model it is easy to recognize

the far-reaching impact of family-based practices and the importance of utilizing such an approach.

A family-based approach can result in benefits to both the child and family including, but not limited to, the following areas (Beach Center on Families and Disability, 1997):

- child functioning,
- parent skills and emotional well-being,
- parents' view of service effectiveness and sense of control over their child's care,
- problem solving ability,
- capacity of families to care for their child at home,
- service delivery,
- cost-effectiveness, and
- family empowerment.

Evidence of the effectiveness of a family-based approach, as well as direct experience, has encouraged programs throughout the country to embrace family-based practices.

Family-Professional Partnerships

One of the most important responsibilities of early childhood personnel is the development, nurturance, and maintenance of effective relationships with families. There is now a general acceptance and understanding that parents and families are the child's first and most important teachers. Recommended practice suggests that the best type of relationship that can develop between families and professionals is one in which families are viewed as full-fledged partners. This type of true collaboration requires shared trust and equality in the relationship. Like any relationship, family-professional partnerships take time and effort to sustain (Gargiulo, Schertz, & Graves, in press).

The rationale for the development of collaborative partnerships between families and professionals includes the following: (a) family members spend more time with a child who has a disability than anyone else; (b) parents have more information about their child than anyone else; (c) how a family "works"

Understanding families from a systems perspective allows professionals to approach them as partners in fostering the development and education of their children.

will determine what type(s) of intervention will "work" for the family and child; and (d) families have the ultimate control over the services provided for their children and themselves. "No matter how skilled professionals are, or how loving parents are, each cannot achieve alone what the two parties, working hand-in-hand, can accomplish together" (Peterson & Cooper, 1989, p. 208). This idea is eloquently expressed in the following poem by an unknown author.

Two Sculptors

I dreamed I stood in a studio
And watched two sculptors there.
The clay they used was a young child's mind
And they fashioned it with care.

One was a teacher; the tools she used
Were books, music and art.
One, a parent who worked with a guiding hand
And a gentle, loving heart.

Day after day the teacher toiled
With touch that was deft and sure.
While the parent labored by her side
And polished and smoothed it o'er.

And when at last their task was done.
They were proud of what they had wrought:

For the things they had molded into the child
Could neither be sold nor bought.

And each agreed he would have failed
If he worked alone:
The parents and the school,
The teacher and the home.

SOURCE: C. Salibury, 1992. Parents as team members: inclusive teams, collaborative outcomes. In B. Rainforth, J. York, and C. MacDonald Eds., *Collaborative Teams for Students with Severe Diusabilities,* Baltimore: Paul H. Brookes, p. 62.

The foundation for building positive relationships between service providers and families must include a mutual understanding of their roles in supporting children's development and learning. Table 3–5 provides examples of the contemporary roles of parents and professionals in their collaborative relationships. This process of mutual understanding can allow both parties to empathize and discover ways to support one another in their roles. Galinsky (1990) noted that the early years are not only a formative period for young children, but also a critical and challenging time for families and professionals. Parents often welcome and need support as they face the many challenges of family life during the early years of the life of a young child with disabilities.

Early childhood programs that have strong family components have proven to contribute to children's later school success. For some time, effective professionals have been participants and supporters of parent-professional partnership efforts. Initial experiences and interactions of children, parents, and professionals in early childhood programs should be positive, nurturing, and caring. Professionals should learn as much as possible about each child and family in order to maximize the possibilities of the child's success. A professional who is inviting and encouraging to parents is much more likely to build a positive relationship with the family. "It is the professional's responsibility to find ways, rather than excuses, to develop partnerships with parents and other family members. Successful relationships require that parents and professionals collaborate as equals. The ultimate beneficiaries of this partnership will be the young children with special needs" (Gargiulo & Graves, 1991, p. 178). An understanding of the family from a

Table 3–5   Changing Roles for Professionals and Families

Professionals

Traditional Role: Expert Service Provider	Contemporary Role: Partner with Families
As a professional, I am supposed to know and I must claim to know, regardless of uncertainty.	As a professional, I am presumed to know, but I recognize parents also have relevant and important knowledge. My uncertainties may be a source of learning for me and for them.
I keep distant from the parents and hold onto the expert's role. I give parents a sense of my expertise, but convey a feeling of warmth and sympathy as a "sweetener."	I seek out connections to parents' thoughts, feelings, perceptions. I allow their respect for my knowledge to emerge from their discovery of it in the situation.
I look for deference and status in the parents' response to my professional persona.	I look for the sense of freedom and of the real connection to the parents as a consequence of no longer needing to maintain a cold, distant professional role.

Families

Traditional Role: Recipient of Services	Contemporary Role: Partner with Professionals
As a parent, I put myself into the professional's hands and in doing so gain a sense of security based on faith.	As a parent, I join with the professional in making sense of my situation, and in so doing, gain a sense of increased involvement and action.
I have the comfort of being in good hands. I need only comply with the professional's advice and all will be well.	I must exercise some control over the situation. I am not wholly dependent on the professionals' information and there is action that only I can undertake.
I am pleased to be served by the best person available.	I am pleased to be able to test my judgment about the competence of the professionals. I enjoy the excitement of discovery about their knowledge, how they practice, and about myself. I feel a sense of partnership.

systems perspective will enable service providers to approach families as partners in the education and development of their young children.

Key Components of Family-Professional Collaboration

Families and professionals interact on a variety of levels in addressing the needs of young children with disabilities. Some key aspects of family-professional interactions include: (a) communication, (b) cultural responsiveness, (c) meetings and conferences, and (d) support and information exchange. What fol-

lows is a discussion of each of these dimensions with suggested strategies.

Communication

As we have come to realize, one of the most important elements in relationships between families and professionals is effective communication. Of all the skills expected of early childhood professionals, communication skills rank among the most necessary. To maximize learning and guide the child's development in positive ways, professionals and families must maintain an open, honest relationship. This type of relationship, of course, is dependent on communication.

Trust must be established between families and professionals.

The following list of suggestions for working with families is designed to facilitate effective communication, and ultimately, the development of a useful and meaningful relationship between families and professionals.

- *Listen to families!* In order for professionals to discover the family's vision for their child, communication is of the utmost importance. Professionals should probe to solicit families' perspectives. In addition, they must practice active listening and make an effort to confirm the perceptions of the family's intent and meaning. Through interactive listening and observation, attempts can be made to understand what families are saying, what they are feeling, and what they want for their child. Acknowledgement of the family's wishes and a willingness to follow the family's lead will help to establish the trust necessary for a continued working relationship.

- *Realize that the family knows their child better than anyone else.* Professionals must make every effort to learn about each child from his or her family. Families know the most about the child, his or her needs, and how those needs should be met. Therefore, professionals should show respect for the families' knowledge and understanding, and convey a feeling of acceptance of the informa-

tion they can offer. Further, opportunities should be created for parents and other family members to provide this type of meaningful information.

- *Use a two-step process when initially informing parents that their child requires early intervention/early childhood special education services.* After sharing diagnostic information, it is strongly suggested that parents be given time to comprehend and absorb the information. Parental concerns must be dealt with prior to proceeding with matters such as intervention recommendations. These issues can be addressed in follow-up meetings according to the family's readiness.

- *Explain the terminology and avoid the use of jargon.* Many families have no previous experience with individuals with disabilities. This may be their first exposure to the terminology that is used in early intervention/early childhood special education. Their conceptualization of such terms as eligibility, developmental delay, or mental retardation more than likely will be different from that of the professional; therefore, terminology used should be made clear to families. Further, everyday language should be used when possible, and jargon and acronyms (e.g., IEP, MR, PDD) should be kept to a minimum.

- *Keep families informed.* A variety of two-way communication techniques can be used when discussing a child's abilities and performance. Respect, concern, and a sincere desire to communicate and collaborate in all aspects of services must be demonstrated. Professionals should develop alliances with families based on a common goal—to help the child.

- *Be responsive to the diverse backgrounds of families.* Professionals must be sensitive to the differing levels of need for information and support desired by families from different cultural, linguistic, or ethnic backgrounds.

- *Recognize that diverse family structures and parenting styles, as well as other factors, will influence each family's interactions and level of involvement.* Open communication with families allows professionals to understand the family dynamics and individual differences that are part of each family. Professionals should respect the family's right to choose their level and style of participation in early intervention or early childhood special education services.

- *Support families in embracing realistic optimism.* In working with each family, professionals must work to achieve a balance between being optimistic and realistic about the future for each child. Children's strengths should be stressed, along with their needs. Families should be supported as they analyze, plan, and prepare for their child's future.

- *Be accountable.* If teachers and other service providers agree to assume specific responsibilities or gather information for the family, they should be certain to follow through. Accountability demonstrates to the family that they can depend on the professional. Trust, consistency, and dependability increase the chances of an effective relationship developing.

Following this list of suggestions will not necessarily ensure a successful relationship with all families, but it can assist in helping to establish a mutually respectful tone in relationships.

Effective interactions between professionals and families are vital for successful programs to be implemented for young children with special needs, which of course require communication. In its most basic form, communication is the ability of two or more people to send and receive messages. Many forms of communication are used during interactions between families and professionals, both nonverbal and verbal. Not everyone has perfected his/her communication skills; however, it is important to point out that verbal and nonverbal communication skills and strategies can be learned and improved with practice.

Nonverbal communication includes eye contact, posture, voice, physical proximity, clothing, gestures, and facial expressions. Desirable facial expressions, for example, could include eyes being at the same level as the parents', direct eye contact (except when culturally proscribed), warmth and concern reflected in facial expressions, and appropriately varied and animated facial expressions.

Verbal communication refers to both oral and written language. Well-developed listening and observation skills are necessary for effective parent-professional relationships. Table 3–6 provides tips for using active listening and observation strategies. Table 3–7 provides examples of verbal communication skills that can be used to improve the effectiveness of communication. These strategies and skills can be practiced and perfected over time.

As in any relationship, effective communication between families and professionals involves a clear understanding and knowledge of the expectations, obligations, and responsibilities of each party in the relationship. It is important for the professional to communicate clearly about the policies and practices of the program. Professionals are advised to provide parents with information at the time they enter the program and review it on an ongoing and as needed basis. Information can be provided via a program handbook, newsletter, website, etc. Parents and other family members need to know about various aspects of the program such as the assessment process, related services, health and safety requirements, daily schedules, home visits, and other program features. Having sufficient information about the program requirements helps to lay a positive foundation for an effective partnership

Effective communication must be regular and useful. Communicating information that is not useful to families or communicating too infrequently will do little to facilitate the achievement of the family's goals for their child. A number of methods of communication should be available (e.g., notes, e-mails, meetings, telephone calls, communication notebook). Regardless of the method of communication or when it occurs, professionals must be willing to listen and respect the families' points of view.

Professionals should never underestimate the importance of communication in their relationships with families and the power of their words. Table 3–8 provides a list from parents of the most helpful statements ever said to them by a professional.

Table 3–6　Tips for Active Listening and Observation

Stop talking.	Allow the person with whom you are communicating to formulate responses to your questions. You must show that you want to listen and be helpful. Be sure to pay special attention to the feelings behind the facts and avoid mentally preparing your next statement while the other person is still talking.
Put the speaker at ease.	Relax and make the appropriate amount of eye contact with the person with whom you are communicating. Remember, some cultures do not engage in direct eye contact.
Ask appropriate questions.	Be sure to ask open-ended questions, which will encourage the other person to answer with more than "yes" or "no" responses. Ask only one question at a time in a clearly phrased manner. Offer a chance for the other person to elaborate on his or her statements.
Make appropriate comments.	Be encouraging. Demonstrate attending skills, such as nodding, and making neutral vocalization, such as "yes" or "oh."
Demonstrate reflection skills.	Use reflective paraphrasing by stating what you believe the speaker has said in your own words. The speaker can then either confirm or deny your understanding and contradictions may be cleared up. Be sure to also reflect on what you perceive to be the speaker's feelings as well. For example, "You sounded distressed when. . ." or "Were you relieved when . . . ?"
Exhibit openness.	Be willing to make statements in which you reveal something that may be personal or private to you. For example, "I was sad when . . ." or "I was frightened by . . ."
Share topic selection or postponement.	Allow the person with whom you are communicating to indicate his or her preference with regard to whether or not to discuss a certain topic. The individual may wish to postpone the topic until a more favorable or comfortable time.
Remain objective.	Work to avoid jumping to conclusions in conversations. Be on the lookout for negative feelings you may already have about the other person's point of view or lifestyle. Do not allow your emotions to interfere in your conversation. Accept his or her feelings and do not take ownership of them.
Center on the other person's concerns.	Attend to the topics or issues that are important to the person with whom you are communicating. Try to listen as if you share his or her concerns.
Develop attention to detail.	Work on your skills at identifying physical characteristics of feelings. Although we generally associate certain facial expressions with certain feelings, you must really know the person with whom you are communicating. For example, they may smile most when they are the most hurt.
Focus.	Be sure to focus on the other person and focus out extraneous details. Surveying the room often gives the appearance of lack of interest and attention.

SOURCE: Information from *Families and teachers of individuals with disabilities: Collaborative orientations and responsive practices*, by D. J. O'Shea, L. J. O'Shea, R. Algozzine, D. J. Hammitte (Eds.). Boston, MA: Allyn & Bacon, pp. 260.

Table 3–7   Examples of Communication Skills

Listening Skills

Paraphrasing—Responding to basic messages.

"You are feeling positive about this approach, but you are confused as to the best way to implement it."

Clarifying—Restating a point or requesting restatement to ensure understanding.

"I'm confused about this. Let me try to state what I think you have said."

Perception checking—Determining accuracy of feeling or emotion detected.

"I was wondering if the plan you chose is really the one you want. It seems to me that you expressed some doubt. Is this correct?"

Leading Skills

Indirect leading—Getting a conversation started.

"Let's start with you describing how things are going with the first strategy."

Direct leading—Encouraging and elaborating discussion.

"What do you mean when you say there is no improvement? Give me a recent example of an incident at home."

Focusing—Controlling confusion, diffusion, and vagueness.

"You have been discussing several problems with TJ's behavior at home. Which of these is most important to you?"

Reflecting Skills

Reflecting feelings—Responding to the emotion expressed.

"It sounds as if you are feeling very frustrated with this situation."

Reflecting content—Repeating ideas in new words for emphasis.

"His behavior is making you wonder about the effectiveness of these strategies?"

Summarizing Skills

Summarizing—Pulling themes together.

"Let's take a look at what we have decided thus far. We have agreed to try a different morning schedule and to use the same strategies for one more week."

Informing Skills

Advising—Giving suggestions and opinions based on experience.

"Based on my 10 years of experience as a teacher, I can tell you that idea probably will not work!"

Informing—Giving information based on expertise, research, and training.

"I recently attended a training series on positive behavioral support techniques for group situations. Perhaps some of these strategies would help make the groups in your room work more effectively."

SOURCE: From *The Helping Relationship: Process and Skills,* 4th ed. (pp. 66–67) by L. M. Brammer, 1988, Englewood Cliffs, NJ: Prentice Hall. Adapted by permission of Prentice-Hall, Inc.

Table 3–8   What is the Most Helpful Thing a Professional Ever Said to You?

- It's not your fault. You are not capable of causing the problems your child has.
- What do you need for yourself?
- I think your son could be a success story for our agency.
- I value your input.
- Under the circumstances, you are doing the best you can do. Frankly, I don't know what I would do or how I would be able to carry on.
- If you were a perfect parent, your son would still have this condition.
- I agree with you.
- Your child has made progress and I know he can do more, so we will continue to work with him.
- Why are you taking all of the blame? It takes two to make or break a relationship.

- I don't know. I can't tell you what's wrong with your child or what caused the problem.
- Your child knows right from wrong. She knows most of society's values and that's because you taught them to her.
- There is a lot of love in your family.
- You know, it's okay to take care of yourself too.
- I don't know. I have to give that serious thought.
- I believe in your instincts. You're the expert on your child.
- You're being too hard on yourself.
- Our agency will take your case.
- Thanks so much for your participation in the group [parent support group]. Your intelligence and your calm reasonableness are important influences in the group.

SOURCE: *Family Support Bulletin* (Washington, DC: United Cerebral Palsy Association, Spring 1991), p. 20.

Cultural Responsiveness

Perhaps one of the most critical effects on the relationships that develop between families and professionals is the influence of culture. Turnbull and Turnbull (1996) defined culture in a way that is especially relevant to relationships between families and professionals:

> Culture refers to many different factors that shape one's sense of group identity, including race, ethnicity, religion, geographical location, income status, gender, sexual orientation, disability status, and occupation. It is the framework within which individuals, families, or groups interpret their experiences and develop their visions of how they want to live their lives. (p. 56)

When there are differences in the cultural beliefs and practices of professionals and families, these can serve as barriers to the development of their relationships (Harry, Kayanpur, & Day, 1999), particularly when these differences have not been identified. The importance of service providers understanding

differences between their own perspectives and those of families from other cultures and ethnic groups cannot be overstressed. In order to do this, each service provider must first carefully examine his or her own cultural background and belief system. In doing so, they will be more capable of understanding the individual perspectives that are unique to each family and how they differ from their own background and beliefs. Service providers who fail to recognize values and beliefs of families are prone to make biased and faulty judgments about parents that may weaken their relationships with them.

Early intervention and early childhood special education professionals are encouraged to use culturally responsive and respectful strategies, based on the family's unique characteristics, needs, and preferences. Specific strategies may be needed when families have linguistic differences. Examples of strategies are as follows (Parette & Petch-Hogan, 2000):

- Conduct meetings in family-friendly settings.
- Identify and defer to key decision makers in the family.

- Recognize that families from diverse cultures may view time differently from how the professionals do and schedule meetings accordingly.
- Provide transportation and childcare to make it easier for families to attend center- or school-based activities.
- Arrange for native-speaking individuals (when needed) to make initial contacts and serve as a link between family and professionals.
- Use trained interpreters (as needed) during conferences.

Collaboration between families and professional when there are cultural differences requires respect, trust, and cooperation, and it is the professional's responsibility to cope with and value differences in positive ways.

Conferences and Meetings

Most early intervention and early childhood special education programs offer a variety of meaningful activities such as home visits, group meetings, and individual conferences. In each of these activities, communication is critical. Perhaps the most utilized ways of communicating with families is through individual meetings or conferences. These meetings or conferences can take place in a variety of formats and can occur for various reasons including families' participation in the educational planning process.

Effective meetings with families require advanced planning. Families should be contacted prior to the meeting to discuss the purpose of the meeting, what is to be accomplished, and the process that will be followed during the meeting. Input should be solicited from families regarding the topics they wish to discuss. The length of the meeting should be established in advance. Families should be assured of the confidentiality of the information shared during the meeting.

At the beginning of a conference, the purpose of the meeting should be reviewed, the amount of time allotted should be restated, and again confidentiality should be emphasized. During the meeting, professionals should share any information they have about the issue(s) or topic and ask for any information or

input that the family member(s) might have. Professionals should try to keep the discussions focused on the issue(s) or topic(s) being discussed. All the information should be synthesized during the meeting. Regardless of the issue or topic, families' input should be solicited and used to establish priorities and to develop a plan to address these priorities. Families appreciate professionals who are not rushed and who discuss specific tasks, behaviors, and abilities. Any meeting should conclude with a summary and concensus regarding next steps. If possible, meetings or conversations should end on a positive and encouraging note.

One of the major ways in which families are active participants in the program planning process is through the meetings that take place in the development of the Individualized Family Service Plan (IFSP) and the Individual Education Plan (IEP). The intent of the IFSP and IEP is to provide more accountability and to increase the level of participation of families. IFSPs are written for birth to three-year-olds and IEPs for children three years and older. Detailed information about these individualized plans can be found in Chapter 6.

As mentioned previously, a specific requirement of Part C of the Individuals with Disabilities Act is to enhance the capacity of families to assist in meeting each child's special needs. Much of the literature concerning the IFSP consists of recommended practices designed to guide the development of the IFSP and the delivery of services. Dunst, Trivette, and Deal (1994) state that the IFSP is the cornerstone of the family-based model.

Several conclusions have emerged from the literature on the outcomes and implementation of IFSPs. Gallagher and Desimone (1995) reported that there are a significant number of positive outcomes that provide confidence that the IFSP procedure, when implemented correctly, can result in parents having a clearer picture of their child and the intervention program. Further, it gives the professionals a clearer view of their own goals and the strategies needed to reach them. Gallagher and Desimone (1995) offered the following suggestions for making the processes of using the IFSP more beneficial:

1. Parents and professionals should be prepared. Both parties need to be better informed about the plan, the processes, and stakeholders needed to implement the plan. An orientation meeting and a videotape of a successful session could be most helpful to families.

2. Sufficient time should be devoted to the process. The development of an effective plan, with input from all parties, requires considerable time. Just like in a relationship between professionals and parents, time is needed for the development and maintenance of the plan.

3. Reviews and updates are mandated. The document must be reviewed regularly and checked for its effectiveness. Of course, the law requires a 6-month review, but at least one person should assume the responsibility for ongoing regular review and update.

Similar to the IFSP, the IEP process provides an opportunity for families and professionals to share information and concerns about the child. Both the family and professionals can reap benefits from positive partnerships. This process can also help the family better understand the program the child is enrolled in, which in turn may boost the confidence of the parents in the way they view the program and staff. Another benefit of the IEP is that it is meeting its intended goal of providing information about the child's progress in academic and other areas of development. The literature on the use of the IEP reveals some positive outcomes including the following three advantages:

1. improved relationships between professional and family;

2. increased understanding of family about special education; and

3. provision of information about the child's academic progress, and clarification of program goals and directions (Gallagher & Desimone, 1995).

The effective use of the IFSPs and IEPs can be a tremendous help to the service providers in provid-ing appropriate services and educational programs to young children with disabilities and their families.

Regardless of the type of meeting or conference that occurs between families and professionals, strategies are needed to facilitate successful conferences and meetings. Professionals should carefully select times for conferences and strive to plan times that are mutually agreeable. Some programs provide child care and assist with transportation. Being flexible in planning to meet families' needs demonstrates to families that the professionals are committed to involving them.

Home visits are another format through which interactions occur between families and service providers. In Part C services, for birth to three-year-olds, home-based early intervention services are provided so that learning can take place in the natural environment. Through home visits, families and professionals have opportunities to develop collaborative relationships. According to Hanson and Lynch (1995), families involved in home-based services develop more positive relationships with professionals with whom they work and are more likely to follow through on recommended activities as identified in the IFSP.

As with other types of meetings between families and professionals, careful planning is required. The typical format for a home visit is as follows:

1. *Arrival and greeting.* The professional(s) usually are greeted by the family member(s), and they exchange greetings and general information.

2. *Information exchange and review.* The professional(s) and the family member(s) review and discuss the prior visit, the strategies or interventions that have been used, and the progress that has been made toward achieving the desired outcomes. The parent may explain any concerns or irregularities in the strategies being used, and any notes or information that is pertinent may be presented. Observations of the child usually take place at this time in order to review and reassess the appropriateness and success of the interventions and strategies in light of the child's progress.

3. *Development of new goals/outcomes and strategies.* Based on the review of the prior goals/outcomes and strategies, new strategies can be developed. This phase may include time for demonstration or modeling by the professional(s) and time for extensive discussions and questions by both the professional(s) and the parent or other family members. During this phase of the meeting, the home visitor should remain sensitive to the individual needs of the family and the circumstances in the home.

4. *Closure.* At the end of the home visit, the professional should summarize the discussion and allow parents or other family members to provide any additional input or pose questions. The plan for the next visit should be made at the end of the meeting if possible.

Table 3–9 provides recommendations from families describing the characteristics of a good home visit. Because home visits require professionals to enter a family's home, special consideration should be given to honor the family's privacy and preferences regarding the logistics of the meeting (e.g., time of day, location).

Support and Information

In addition to the support and information provided by early intervention/early childhood special education professionals, many families benefit from the support and guidance provided by other families who also have children with disabilities (Klemm & Schimanski, 1999). Networking with other families provides opportunities for them to problem solve regarding various issues and opportunities for enrichment often occur as well. In addition, families may want access to resources designed specifically for families or need sources for various types of information. Families who are supported and have the information that they need are more likely to respond to early intervention/education services in a meaningful way. Professionals should be familiar with the various resources that are available and be ready to share this information with families. Below are some of the most widely used sources of information and support for families of children with disabilities.

Table 3-9   A Family's Recommendations for a Good Home Visit

Be clear about agenda and roles.

Give choices in scheduling that are convenient and flexible.

Provide a record of the visit using writing, pictures, or toys.

Give ideas for activities; then help parents brainstorm.

Be flexible with the family's daily schedule: pitch in, change agenda, and reschedule.

Don't use jargon, and let the family know it's okay to ask questions.

Use modeling and reminding; don't overload with information.

Explain what you are doing and why.

Include others, e.g., siblings, grandparents, in activities and conversations.

Explain paperwork and point out progress/changes that are made.

Be sensitive to the family's need for someone to take over.

Be courteous; call if you are going to be late, absent, etc.

Respect the family's values; don't judge.

Be prepared; don't waste the family's time and energy.

Be honest with the family.

Adapted by permission from Project Dakota Outreach, Training and Consultation Services, Eagan, MN.

Summary

A specific requirement of IDEA is to enhance the capacity of families to meet the special needs of their children. This requirement explicitly acknowledges the families of young children with known or suspected disabilities as the central focus of early intervention/early childhood special education services and the primary decision makers in the service delivery process. Professionals are continuing to make changes

Beach Center on Families and Disability

311 Haworth
University of Kansas
Lawrence, KS, 66045
(913) 864-7600
Web site: http:// *www.beachcenter.org*

Funded by the National Institute on Disability and Rehabilitation Research (NIDRR) of the U.S. Department of Education, the Beach Center offers newsletters, advocacy how-to publications, opportunities for parents to make connections with other parents of children with disabilities, and information on coping strategies for a disability diagnosis, and laws that affect families.

Parent-to-Parent Programs

Beach Center
(913) 864-7600

Using mutual support, experienced parents of children with disabilities offer emotional and informational support to new parents in one-to-one matches.

Beach Center provides information about various programs. Many states have a Parent-to-Parent Network within the state. For example, below is the contact information for the Parent-to-Parent Program in New York.

Parent-to-Parent of New York State
500 Balltown Road
Schenectady, NY 12304
(518) 381-4350
Web site: *http://www.parenttoparentnys.org*

Exceptional Parent

(800) 247-8080

This is a magazine designed to be a resource for families of children with disabilities. The section titled "Parent Search and Parent Respond" is designed for parents to ask each other for assistance with finding information and meeting other needs. *Exceptional Parent* is an excellent resource that is widely recommended for families of children with disabilities of all ages.

---

in policy and practices in an attempt to move families to the center of the service delivery system.

As has been indicated throughout this chapter, a family-based philosophy is the cornerstone of recommended practice in early intervention. Rather than asking families to adjust to programs' policies and needs, recommended practice suggests that programs must adjust services according to families' concerns, priorities, and resources. Parents are seen as full partners in early intervention/early childhood special education programs.

A family-based approach is founded on a family systems model. That is, young children with special needs are viewed as part of their family system, which in turn is perceived as part of a larger network of informal and formal systems. What happens to one member of the family often affects all members, and each family member has his own needs and abilities. Thus, professionals must devise an individualized approach for each family served. To do this, profes-

sionals need a thorough understanding of how families operate and the impact that the birth of a child with a known or suspected disability, or the diagnosis of a child's disability, may have on how families function. Further, professionals must know how to engage in collaborative relationships with families and other professionals in meeting the needs of young children with disabilities.

The idea of strong relationships between families and professionals who work with young children with disabilities is proving to have many benefits. However, there have been many changes that have occurred in families, the laws, and interactions between service providers and families. These changes contribute to a complex challenge for personnel in providing appropriate learning experiences and services for young children and their families. It is very important for professionals to consider the concerns, priorities, and resources of families and to view the family as a system with many interacting forces.

Check Your Understanding

1. How has the relationship between families and professionals changed in early intervention/early childhood education over the years? What circumstances have aided this process?

2. Describe the influences of (a) general early childhood education, (b) early childhood special education, and (c) compensatory education.

3. What is the rationale behind a family systems model?

4. Identify the four key elements of a family systems model. Explain the characteristics of each of these elements.

5. How does the concept of *cohesion* differ from *adaptability* in the family systems theory model?

6. Discuss reasons why an effective family-professional relationship is a critical component of a successful program for young children with disabilities.

7. What kinds of influences have contributed to an emergence of a family-based philosophy in programs for young children with special needs?

8. Provide a rationale for the development of collaborative relationships between parents and professionals in early intervention/early childhood special education programs.

References

Allen, E., Schwartz, I. (2001). *The exceptional child: Inclusion in early childhood education* (4th ed.). Clifton Park, NY: Delmar.

Allen, R. I., & Petr, C. G. (1995). *Family-centered service delivery: A cross-disciplinary literature review and conceptualization.* Lawrence, KS: University of Kansas, Beach Center on Families and Disability, *http://www.beachcenter.org.*

Bailey, D. B., McWilliam, R. A., Dykes, L. A., Hebeler, K., Simeonsson, R., Spiker, D., & Wagner, M. (1998). Family outcomes in early intervention: A framework for program evaluation and efficacy research. *Exceptional Children, 64*(3), 313–328.

Beach Center on Families and Disabilities. (1997a). *Collaborate with the family in individualized education planning.*

Beach Center on Families and Disabilities. (1997b). Family-centered service delivery. *Families and Disability Newsletter, 8*(2), 1–3.

Beach Center on Families and Disabilities. (1997c). *Get a family-friendly IFSP.*

Beach Center on Families and Disability. (1998). *Quality indicators of exemplary family-centered programs.*

Beach Center on Families and Disability. (1999). *Quality indicators of exemplary family-centered legislation.*

Berrueta-Clement, J., Schweinhart, L., Barnett, W., Epstein A., & Weikart, D. (1984). *Changed lives: The effects of the Perry Preschool Program on youths through age 19.* Ypsilanti, MI: High/Scope Press.

Berry, J., & Hardman, M. (1998). *Lifespan perspectives on the family and disability.* Needham Heights, MA: Allyn & Bacon.

Blacher, J. (1984). Sequential stages of adjustment to the birth of a child with handicaps/Fact or Artifact? *Mental Retardation, 22,* 55–68.

Bloom, B. (1964). *Stability and change in human characteristics.* New York: Wiley.

Bloom, B. (1981). *All our children learning.* New York: McGraw-Hill.

Bredekamp, S. & Copple, C. (1997) *Developmentally appropriate practice guidelines.* Washington, DC: The National Association for the Education of Young Children (NAEYC).

Brickman, P., Kidder, L. H., Coates, D., Rabinowitz, V., Cohn, E., & Karuza, J. (1983). The dilemmas of helping: Making aid fair and effective. In J. D. Fisher, A. Nadler, & B. M. DePaulo (Eds.), *New directions in helping: Vol. 1. Recipient reactions to aid* (pp. 18–51). New York: Academic Press.

Bronfenbrenner, U. (1979). *The ecology of human development: Experiments by nature and design.* Cambridge, MA: Harvard University Press.

Brubaker, T. (Ed.) (1993). *Family relations: Challenges for the future.* Newbury Park, CA: Sage.

Carter, B., & McGoldrick, M. (1989). *The changing family life cycle* (2nd ed.). Boston: Allyn & Bacon.

Children's Defense Fund. (2003). *The state of America's children.* Washington, DC: Author.

Cochran, M., & Dean, C. (1991). Home-school relations and the empowerment process. *Elementary School Journal, 91*(3), 261–269.

DEC, the Association of Teacher Educators (ATE) and NAEYC. (1994). *Personnel standards for early education and early intervention.* Reston, VA: Author.

Dettmer, P., Dyck, N., & Thurston, L. P. (1999). *Consultation, collaboration, and teamwork.* (3rd ed.). Boston: Allyn & Bacon.

Dimidjian, V. (1989). *Early childhood at risk.* Washington, DC: National Education Association.

Dinnebeil, L. A., & Rule, S. (1994). Variables that influence collaboration between parents and service coordinators. *Journal of Early Intervention, 18,* 349–361.

Division for Early Childhood, Council for Exceptional Children. (1998). *Position statement on services for children birth to age eight with special needs.* Denver, CO: Author.

Drotar, D., Baskiewicz, A., Irvin, N., Kennell, J., & Klaus, M. (1975). The adaptation of parents to the birth of an infant with a congenital malformation: A hypothetical model. *Pediatrics, 56,* 710–716.

Dunlap, K. M. (1997). Family empowerment: One outcome of cooperative preschool education. *Child Welfare, 76*(4), 501–519.

Dunst, C. J. (1999). Placing parent education in conceptual and empirical context. *Topics in Early Childhood Special Education, 19,* 141–147.

Dunst, C. J. (2000). Revisiting "rethinking early intervention." *Topics in Early Childhood Special Education, 20,* 96–104.

Dunst, C. J., & Trivette, C. M. (1996). Empowerment, effective help giving practices, and family-centered care. *Pediatric Nursing, 22,* 334–337, 343.

Dunst, C. J., Johanson, C., Trivette, C. M., & Hamby, D. (1991). Family-oriented early intervention policies and practices: Family-centered or not? *Exceptional Children, 58*(2), 115–126.

Dunst, C., Trivette, C., & Deal, A. (1988). *Enabling and empowering families: Principles and guidelines for practice.* Cambridge, MA: Brookline Books.

Dunst, C., Trivette, C., & Deal, A. (Eds.) (1994). *Supporting and strengthening families.* Cambridge, MA: Brookline Books.

Galinsky, E. (1990). Parents and teachers/caregivers: Sources of tension, sources of support. *Young Children, 43*(3), 4–12.

Gallagher, M. J., & Desimone, L. (1995). Lessons learned from implementation of the IEP: Applications to the IFSP. *Topics in Early Childhood Special Education, 15*(3), 353–378.

Gargiulo, R. M., & Graves, S. B. (1991). Parental feelings: The forgotten component when working with parents of handicapped preschool children. *Childhood Education, 67*(3), 176–178.

Gargiulo, R., Schertz, L. & Graves, L. (in press). *Young learners: Teaching and learning in the early years.* Upper Saddle River, NJ: Prentice Hall.

Gestwicki, C. (1992). *Home, school and community relations.* Albany, NY: Delmar.

Gray, S. W., Ramsey, B. K., & Klaus, R. A. (1982). *From 3 to 20: The early training project.* Baltimore: University Park Press.

Guralnick, M. J. (1998). Effectiveness of early intervention for vulnerable children: A developmental perspective. *American Journal of Mental Retardation, 102*(4), 319–345.

Hanson, M. & Lynch, E. (1995). *Early intervention: Implementing child and family services for infants and toddlers who are at risk or disabled.* Austin, TX: Pro-Ed.

Harry, B., Kalyanpur, M., & Day, J. (1999) *Building cultural reciprocity with families. Case studies in special education.* Baltimore: Brookes.

Head Start policy manual (1984). Washington, DC: U.S. Department of Health and Human Services.

Heflinger, C. A., & Bickman, L. (1997). A theory-driven intervention and evaluation to explore family caregiver empowerment. *Journal of Emotional & Behavioral Disorders, 5*(3), 184–192.

Heumann, J. E., & Hehir, T. (1997). *Believing in children—A great IDEA for the future. Exceptional Parent,* September.

Hodgkinson, H. (1992). *A demographic look at tomorrow.* Washington, D.C: Institute for Educational Leadership.

Kilgo, J. L., & Raver, S. A. (1999). Family-Professional collaboration. In S. Raver (Ed.) *Transdisciplinary early intervention.* New York, NY: MacMillan Publishing Co.

King, G. A., Rosenbaum, P. L., & King, S. M. (1997). Evaluating family-centered service using a measure of parents' perceptions. *Child: Care, Health and Development, 23*(1), 47–62.

Klemm, D., & Schimanski, C. (1999). Parent to parent: The crucial connection. *Exceptional Parent, 29* (9), 109–112.

Lazar, I., & Darlington. R. (1982). Lasting effects of early education. *Monographs of the society for research in child development, 47,* (Serial No. 495).

Minuchin, P. (1988). Relationships within the family: A systems perspective. In R. A. Hinde & J. Stevenson-Hinde (Eds.), *Relationships within the families* (2nd ed., pp. 7–26). New York: Oxford University Press.

New Mexico's Memoria 5 Task Force on Children and Families and the Coalition for Children, 1990.

Newsweek Magazine (1990). The twenty-first century family. *Newsweek,* p. 15.

Olson, D., Russell, C., & Sprenkle, D. (1980). Circumplex model of marital and family systems II: Empirical studies and clinical intervention. In J. Vincent (Ed.), *Advances in family intervention assessment and theory* (Vol. 1) (pp. 129–179). Greenwich, CT: JAI Press.

Olson, D. H., McCubbin, H. L., Barnes, H., Larsen, A., Muxem, M., & Wilson, M. (1989). *Families: What makes them work* (2nd ed.). Los Angeles: Sage.

Parette, H. P., & Perch-Hogan, R. (2000). Approaching families: Facilitating culturally/linguistically diverse family involvement. *Teaching Exception Children, 33*(2), 4–10.

Peterson, N., & Cooper, C. (1989). Parent education and involvement in early intervention programs for handicapped children: A different perspective on parent needs and parent-professional relationships. In M. Fine (Ed.), *The second handbook on parent education* (pp. 197–234). New York: Academic Press.

Rosenthal, D. M., & Sawyers, J. Y. (1996). Building successful home/school partnerships: Strategies for parent support and involvement. *Childhood Education, 72*(4), 194–200.

Salisbury, C. (1992). Parents as team members: Inclusive teams, collaborative outcomes. From B. Rainforth, J. York, & C. MacDonald (Eds.), *Collaborative teams for students with severe disabilities*. Baltimore: Paul H. Brookes, 62.

Sandall, S., McLean, M. E., & Smith, B. J. (2000). *DEC recommended practices for early intervention/early childhood special education*. Longmont, CO: Sopris West.

Schwartzman, J. (1985). *Families and other systems*. New York: Guilford.

Schweinhart, L. J., & Weikart, D. P. (1980). *Young children grow up: The effects of the Perry preschool program on youths through age 15*. Ypsilanti, MI: High/Scope Educational Research Foundation.

Seligman, M., & Darling, R. (1997). *Ordinary families, special children* (2nd ed.). New York: Guilford Press.

Swick, K. J. (1987). *Perspectives on understanding and working with families*. Champaign, IL: Stipes.

Swick, K. J. (1996). Building healthy families: Early childhood educators can make a difference. *Journal of Instructional Psychology, 23*(1), 75–82.

Swick, K. J. (1993). *Strengthening parents and families during the early childhood years*. Champaign, IL: Stipes.

Swick, K. J., & Graves, S. B. (1993). *Empowering at-risk families during the early childhood years*. Washington, DC: National Education Association.

Thompson, T., & Hupp, C. (Eds.). (1992). *Saving children at risk: Poverty and disabilities*. Newbury Park, CA: Sage.

Thompson, L., Lobb, C., Elling, R., Herman, S., Jurkiewicz, T., & Hulleza, C. (1997). Pathways to family empowerment: Effects of family-centered delivery of early intervention services. *Exceptional Children, 64*(1), 99–113.

Trivette, C. & Dunst, C. (2000). Recommended practices in family-based practices. In S. Sandall, M. McLean & B. Smith (Eds.) *DEC recommended practices in early intervention/early childhood special education*. Longmont, CO: Sopris West, p. 40.

Trivette, C. M., Dunst, C. J., & Hamby, D. W. (1996). Social support and coping in families of children at risk for developmental disabilities. In M. Brambring, H. Raub, & A. Beelman (Eds.), *Early childhood intervention: Theory, evaluation and practice* (pp. 234–264). Berlin, Germany: de Gruyter.

Turnbull, A., Summers, J., & Brotherson, M. J. (1984). *Working with families with disabled members: A family systems approach*. Lawrence Kansas University Affiliated Facility.

Turnbull, A. P., & Turnbull, H. R. (1996). *Families, professionals, and exceptionality: A special partnership*. (3rd ed.). Columbus, OH: Merrill.

Turnbull, A. P. & Turnbull, H. R. (2001). *Families, professionals, and exceptionality: Collaborating for empowerment*. (4th ed.). Upper Saddle River, NJ: Merrill/Prentice Hall.

Vanderslice, V. (1984). Empowerment: A definition in progress. *Human Ecology Forum, 14*(1), 2–3.

Winzer, M. A., & Maszurek, K. (1998). *Special education in multicultural contexts*. Upper Saddle River, NJ: Merrill, an Imprint of Prentice-Hall.

Yell, M. L. (1998). *The law and special education*. Upper Saddle River, NJ: Prentice Hall.

Identifying and Assessing Young Children with Special Needs

Initial Assessment of Young Children with Known
or Suspected Disabilities   **Chapter 4**

Assessment for Program Planning, Progress
Monitoring, and Evaluation   **Chapter 5**

Initial Assessment of Young Children with Known or Suspected Disabilities

Key Terminology

Assessment

Screening

Diagnosis

Eligibility

Program planning

Progress monitoring and evaluation

Multidisciplinary team

Formal testing

Tests

Norm-referenced tests

Criterion-referenced tests

Curriculum-referenced tests

Reliability

Validity

Content validity

Instructional validity

Construct validity

Concurrent validity

Predictive validity

Naturalistic observation

Play-based assessment

Interviews

Authentic assessment

Portfolio assessment

Developmental domains

Cognitive skills

Gross motor skills

Fine motor skills

Communication

Language

Speech

Receptive language

Expressive language

Social and emotional skills

Self-care skills

Adaptive skills

Intelligence tests

Culturally biased assessment

Labeling

Self-fulfilling prophecy

Child Find

Referrals

Apgar Scale

PKU screening

Sensitivity

Specificity

False negative

False positive

Established risk

Diagnostic assessment

Arena assessment

Learning Outcomes

After reading this chapter, you will be able to:

- Explain the purposes of assessment in early intervention/early childhood special education.
- Describe the types of assessment procedures used in early intervention/early childhood special education.
- Discuss issues associated with traditional assessment practices used with young children.
- List recommended practices for conducting appropriate assessments of young children.
- Explain the use of the developmental delay category for children from birth to age nine.

The assessment of young children with disabilities is an integral component of early intervention/early childhood special education (EI/ECSE) services. In order to implement recommended assessment practices for young children with known or suspected disabilities, professionals must consider the major purposes of assessment, guidelines for conducting appropriate assessments, and strategies for linking initial assessment with program planning and progress monitoring. In this chapter, an overview of assessment is provided; some of the issues associated with the assessment of young children are identified; and initial assessments conducted for the purposes of screening, diagnosis, and eligibility are discussed. In the chapter that follows, the focus is on assessments conducted for the purposes of program planning and progress monitoring, as well as evaluation.

Assessment Purposes, Procedures, and Types

First, the definition of **assessment** must be considered in order to understand the comprehensiveness of the assessment process. Bailey and Wolery (1992) define assessment as "the process of gathering information for the purpose of making a decision" (p. 96). Richard and Schiefelbusch (1991) describe assessment as "a multilevel process, beginning with screening procedures and continuing through diagnosis, planning of intervention, and program monitoring and evaluation" (p. 110). These definitions suggest that assessment is a dynamic process allowing for various decisions to be made about children with known or suspected disabilities. In reality, many different types of assessment take place simultaneously and on several different levels.

Next, the origin of the word assessment should be considered. The word assessment can be traced to the Latin word *assidre,* which means to "sit beside." According to Woods and McCormick (2002), assessment in EI/ECSE should be a shared experience through which professionals and families exchange information to benefit the child. Therefore, assessment is primarily a fact-finding and problem-solving process shared by professionals and families, as will become evident as the various purposes, procedures, and types of assessment are explored in this chapter and the chapter that follows.

Assessment Purposes

Assessment information is gathered to be used in making an evaluative decision in one or more of the following areas: (a) **screening,** (b) **diagnosis,** (c) **eligibility,** (d) **program planning,** and (e) **progress monitoring** and **evaluation.** For each area of assessment, Table 4–1 provides a definition and describes the kind of information gathered, the type of decision usually made, and the time at which the information is gathered. These various assessment purposes necessitate different procedures, instruments, and skills utilized by qualified professionals.

General Assessment Considerations

The Individuals with Disabilities Education Act (IDEA) requires that a **multidisciplinary team** be involved in the assessment of young children. A multidisciplinary team refers to the involvement of two or more professionals from different disciplines (for example, physical therapy, special education, speech-language pathology) in early intervention/education activities. Thus, assessment teams are composed of family members and professionals from a variety of disciplines who address specific assessment questions. Although recommended practice and legislation call for assessments to be conducted by a team that includes the family and professionals from a variety of disciplines, professionals should be sensitive to family preferences and should realize that a large number of professionals may be confusing or overwhelming to family members. The most important aspect for professionals to remember is that the assessment process should be individualized for each family according to their wishes.

Assessment teams must consider the purpose of each assessment and gather initial information at the

Table 4-1   Types of Assessment Decisions

Type of Assessment	Type of Information Gathered	Decision(s) Usually Made	When Information Is Usually Gathered
Screening			
A procedure designed to identify children who need to be referred for more in-depth assessment.	Potential for developmental disability or delay; vision; hearing; health and physical.	Whether or not a child should be referred for more indepth assessment.	Prior to entry into a program.
Diagnosis			
The process of confirming the presence or absence of a delay or disability.	Evidence that a developmental delay or disability exists and its nature and extent.	Whether or not the child has a developmental delay or disability.	Prior to entry into a program.
Eligibility			
A comprehensive diagnostic process to determine if a child meets the criteria to be eligible for special services.	Comprehensive diagnostic information that is standardized norm-referenced, and comparative.	Whether or not a child is eligible for a program or services as specified in the state's criteria for eligibility.	Prior to entry into a program.
Program planning			
A procedure used to identify desired goals/outcomes for the IFSP/IEP and how to design instruction.	Evidences of the childs developmental skills and behaviors; family preferences and priorities; family resources and strengths; settings in which the child spends time and the demands of those settings.	What type of routines, activities, materials, and equipment to use with the individual child. What style(s) of learning to use with the child. What adult and peer interactions may work best with the child.	Intensively at the beginning of a program year, during the first several weeks of entry in a program; during and immediately after any major changes in a child's life. This is an ongoing process.
Progress monitoring and evaluation			
A process of collecting information about a child's progress, the family's satisfaction with services, and the program's effectiveness.	Evidence of the child's developmental skills and behaviors in comparison to those skills at the beginning of his/her entry into the program; family satisfaction and indication of whether or not their priorities have been met: child's ability to be successful in the setting in which he/she spends time.	To determine the effectiveness of programming for an individual child or group of children; to determine changes in a child's skill and behaviors; to determine family satisfaction; to evaluate a program's overall effectiveness.	Periodically as needed to determine whether or not intervention is effective; at the end of a program year or cycle; when dictated by administrative policy and funding sources.

SOURCE: From Davis, M. D., Kilgo, J. K., and Gamel-McCormick, M., *Young children with special needs: A developmentally appropriate approach.* Copyright © 1998 by Allyn & Bacon. Reprinted, adapted by permission.

beginning of the process. The following are some general considerations.

1. What is the purpose of this assessment or why is it being conducted (e.g., screening, diagnosis, eligibility, program planning, progress monitoring)?

2. What are the characteristics of the child or what is the child like (e.g., age, birth order, temperament, interests)?

3. What skills or behaviors are important to the child's family (e.g., walking, talking, social skills, independence)? What are the family's priorities (e.g., toilet training)?

4. What skills or behaviors are important to the child in his environment (e.g., walking, communicating, toileting, turn-taking)?

5. What adaptations are necessary for the child to display optimal skills (e.g., use of an alternative communication system, adaptive seating)?

6. Where will the assessment sessions take place (e.g., child's home, child care program, classroom, playground)?

7. How will the assessment area(s) be set up (e.g., amount of space needed)?

8. When will the assessment sessions take place (e.g., in the morning, after the child's nap)?

9. Who will be involved in the assessment (e.g., parents, early childhood special educator, related service professionals) and what roles will these individuals assume (facilitator, observer)?

10. How will the assessment be conducted (e.g., formal testing, observation, interview)?

11. What areas of development or domains will be assessed (e.g., cognitive, language, motor)?

12. What instrument(s) will be used (e.g., formal tests, checklists, play-based instruments)?

13. Who will take the lead or be in charge of coordinating the assessment (e.g., service coordinator, early childhood special educator, physical therapist)?

Based on the answers to these questions and the family's preferences, a plan can be formulated regarding how the assessment process will be implemented for each child and family.

Types of Assessment in Early Childhood

Because early childhood is a unique period of development, a number of assessment instruments have been developed specifically for young children. These tools include formal standardized measures, as well as informal measures that are usually less refined, based on observations, and specific to the situation in which they are used. According to Bagnato and Neisworth (1991), assessment for early intervention/early childhood special education:

> is not a test-based process primarily; early childhood assessment is a flexible, collaborative decision-making process in which teams of parents and professionals repeatedly revise their collective judgments and reach consensus about the changing developmental, educational, medical, and mental health service needs of young children and their families (p. xi).

In addition to direct testing, other commonly used procedures in EI/ECSE include: (a) formal testing, (b) naturalistic observations, (c) interviews, and (d) portfolios.

Formal Testing Of the different types of assessment measures used with young children, **formal testing** has been the procedure most frequently used during the initial phases of assessment. **Tests,** by definition, are a predetermined collection of questions or tasks to which predetermined types of responses are sought. Depending on the purpose of the assessment, different types of tests may be appropriate. During formal testing, standardized tests are used. Standardized tools are usually **norm-referenced tests,** which means that an individual child's performance on a test is compared to that of other children of the same age group. Thus, norm-referenced measures provide a score that is relative to other children in a particular group (that is, the source of the norms) (Cohen & Spenciner, 2003).

Criterion-referenced tests are used to determine whether a child's performance meets an established criteria or a certain level of mastery within various developmental domains (such as cognitive, motor, self-care) or set of objectives. These tools provide information about a child's attainment of specific levels of competence. **Curriculum-referenced tests** are similar to criterion-referenced measures; however, curriculum-referenced tools are used to interpret a child's performance in relation to specific curricular objectives. In most cases, curriculum-referenced tools are most relevant for program planning (Cohen & Spenciner, 2003).

Although a detailed description of the psychometric aspects of assessment instruments is beyond the scope of this chapter, it is important that these concepts be understood by those who are responsible for selection of specific assessment tools to be used during any phase of the assessment process. Reliability and validity are two of the psychometric concepts that should be considered.

Reliability refers to the consistency of the test. In other words, does the test measure what it is supposed to measure in a dependable manner? If T. J. was given the same test on different occasions, would his performance on the test be the same each time? If so, the examiner could assume with some confidence that the results were reliable. Or if several children were given the same test and received different scores on the tests, the test administrator would want to know that the variability in the scores was actually due to the differences in their abilities. The examiner needs to feel confident that the test is consistently measuring what it was designed to measure.

Another important psychometric property of an assessment instrument is validity. **Validity** may be defined as the extent to which a test measures what it was intended to measure. There are several different types of validity that should be of concern to professionals. The first is **content validity,** which refers to how well the test represents the content it purports to measure. A second type of validity is **instructional validity.** This is the extent to which the information gained from an assessment instrument would be useful in planning intervention programs for young children with disabilities. A third type of validity, **construct validity,** focuses on the degree to which a test addresses the constructs on which it was based. A fourth type of test validity is **concurrent validity.** This type of validity is concerned with how well a test correlates with other accepted measures of performance

Much information can be gathered about young children with disabilities as they interact within various settings.

administered close in time to the first. Finally, **predictive validity** focuses on the extent to which a test relates to some future measure of performance. When professionals are selecting an assessment instrument, attention should be focused on the reliability and validity information reported in the manuals.

Naturalistic Observations A **naturalistic observation** is an assessment procedure that can be defined as the systematic process of gathering information by looking at children and their environments. Most would agree that the most important influence on a young child is the nurturing quality provided by the parents or other caregivers. Assessment procedures, therefore, often include systematic observations of the interactions between children and their parents or primary caregivers and the child's behavior in familiar settings or situations.

Children cannot only be observed interacting with their parents or other caregivers, but with friends, siblings, and teachers in natural settings. Several different strategies can be used to structure the observations and organize the information that is gathered such as checklists, rating scales, and structured observations (Hanson & Lynch, 1995). Table 4–2 provides examples of the various types of information that can be gained through observations. **Play-based assessment** is one type of naturalistic observation procedure that is being used more frequently in early childhood education.

During play, children spontaneously and authentically demonstrate knowledge and skills. Play-based

---

Table 4–2   Observing an Individual Child

BODY MOVEMENTS AND USE OF BODY

Movements are usually quick or slow

Seems at ease with physical self

Small and large muscle skills and movements are about equally developed or one area is more developed than the other area

FACIAL EXPRESSIONS

Uses face to express feelings (e.g., smiles, frowns, neutral)

Reacts to experiences occurring around her/him

Shows intense feelings most of the time

Shows neutral or "deadpan" expression most of the time

SPEECH

Uses tone of voice to express feelings

Raises voice or yells when upset

Uses speech as primary communication method

Uses alternative communication (e.g., gestures, adaptive equipment)

Can imitate songs, chants, verbal expressions

Uses fluent, articulate (easy-to-understand) speech

EMOTIONAL REACTIONS

Method of exhibiting emotional reactions (e.g., smiles when happy, cries when angry)

Good balance in controlling feelings

Responds appropriately to adults/to other children

PLAY ACTIVITIES

Frequent and favorite activities

Play initiation skills and patterns of play (e.g., how play progresses and next event)

Persistence during activities or flits from one activity to another

Avoidance of certain activities (e.g., sensory materials like clay or glue)

Evidence of mastery pleasure in completing an activity

Tempo or pace of play remains even or too slow or fast. Under what circumstances?

Plays alone. Under what circumstances?

Engages in pretend play (indicate with self or partner)

Engages in dramatic play (list roles)

Tries new things

Shows curiosity about the environment, including materials, equipment, and people

Prefers to play in certain areas (list areas or indoor vs. outdoor)

Special skills in one area (e.g., music, art)

BASIC NEEDS

Typical response to food

Natural bowel and bladder control

Seems well rested most of the time

Adapted from *Seeing Young Children: A Guide to Observing and Recording Behavior,* 4e by W. Bentzen, 2001, Clifton Park, N.Y.: Delmar.

assessments provide a nonthreatening way to collect information regarding the level of development of young children (Linder, 1993). Play-based assessments support the observation of children in a play situation, which allows them to demonstrate behaviors that they typically exhibit under normal circumstances (Lifter & Bloom, 1998).

Interviews   **Interviews,** or conversations, are forms of assessment that can be used to gather information regarding the areas on which to focus during the assessment process, specific information about the child (for example, how a child responds to various situations), or other types of information that may be relevant to the assessment process. Table 4–3 provides examples of the types of assessment information that may be collected from families via an interview format. Because these interviews or conversations take place with a particular goal or goals in mind, it is important to have some structure to ensure that the

Table 4–3   Family Interview Questions

Areas of Interest	Questions
Finding out where the family wants to focus their attention.	How are things going with _____*? (Question addressed to each family member in turn, so each has a chance to respond)
Understanding the family's definition of the child's delay or disability.	What have you been told about _____ 's hearing, vision, motor skills, etc.? (Using words of family members) How does this fit with what you know and believe about _____? What else do you know about _____ difficulty? (Using words of family members) In what ways has this information been helpful or not helpful? What do you think _____ needs help with, if anything? What kinds of things have you tried that worked? What didn't work?
Understanding the family's informal and formal support system.	What kinds of advice have you been given? Whose advice has been helpful? Not helpful? What happens in a crisis? (If crisis has been described as happening in the past)
Understanding family ecology surrounding events of family members.	Is there a particular event of importance that you want to focus on (mealtime, trip to the park, etc.)? What is a typical event (mealtime, trip, etc.) like?
Focusing on solution development.	Can you think of a time that an event (mealtime, trip, etc.) went well or worked the way you wanted it to? What was happening that made it work? Who or what was helpful? Not helpful?
Understanding critical events that are not directly related to the child.	What other things are going on now that are important to you?

*Insert child's name in blanks.

SOURCE: Adapted from P. Winton and D. Bailey, *Communicating with Families: Examining Practices and Facilitating Change in Children with Special Needs* (2nd ed). Edited by J. Paul and R. Simeonsson (Ft. Worth, TX: Harcourt Brace Jovanovich. 1993). pp. 220–221.

intended goal(s) are achieved. Winton and Bailey (1988) suggest that interviews include five phases: (a) preliminary preparation (preparation for the meeting), (b) introduction (review of the purpose of the meeting), (c) inventory (discussion of the information and determination of the parents' perceptions), (d) summarizing (review of the options), and (e) closure (summary of what took place in the meeting). It is important to remember, however, that although the interviews or conversations between the professionals and family or caregivers usually need some structure, they should also be flexible enough for everyone to feel comfortable with the process.

Authentic Assessment **Authentic assessment,** by definition, is the process of observing, recording, collecting, and otherwise documenting what children do and how they do it for the purpose of making educational decisions (Pucket & Black, 1994). A type of authentic assessment that is widely used in early childhood education is the **portfolio assessment.** This is a systematic and organized collection of children's work and records of their behaviors, which can serve as evidence to be used to monitor the growth of their knowledge, skills, behaviors, and achievements over time (Artel & Spandel, 1991). Portfolio assessment is a means to provide a comprehensive overview of a child's performance on authentic, meaningful tasks in natural environments (Losardo & Notari-Syverson, 2001). Portfolios, as well as the other types of assessments, will be discussed in greater detail in subsequent chapters. Portfolios represent one way in which authentic assessment information can be collected.

Assessing Interrelated Developmental Domains

Developmental domains are the key areas typically addressed in a comprehensive assessment of young children. Most assessment instruments used with young children seek to measure development in one or more of the following domains: cognitive skills, motor skills, communication and language skills, social and emotional skills, and self-care and adaptive skills. Development during the early childhood period, however, cannot realistically be separated into isolated developmental domains. This is because the developmental domains are interdependent and interact in complex ways in young children. In fact, a direct functional relationship exists between changes in one area of development and those that occur in another area of development. When a young child learns to walk, for example, he or she is afforded new experiences that will more than likely influence skill development in other areas (such as cognitive, social, and language development). Understanding each of the developmental areas described below can be helpful in understanding the child as a whole. Typical development can be useful as a general guide for intervention and a reference point to consider when determining each child's individual strengths, needs, and progress. Appendix B contains a chart of typical developmental milestones that can be referred to in the discussions that follow. However, it is important to remember that the learning that occurs in early childhood is episodic and uneven, with great variability among children.

Cognitive Skills

Cognitive skills refer to a child's evolving mental and intellectual ability. An infant's cognitive behavior is primarily reflexive with a tremendous amount of progress being made during the first two years of life. The assessment of an infant's cognitive skills usually includes the concepts of object permanence, spatial relationships, imitation, means–end, causality, and object usage. Cognitive development occurs and is evidenced when children attend to stimuli; integrate new information with existing knowledge and skills; perform preacademic skills such as counting, sorting, and letter recognition; and perform increasingly complex problem-solving tasks. In addition, cognitive skills include the child's capacity to predict occurrences, the use of short- and long-term memory, the ability to sequence activities, the ability to detect differences among objects and events, and the ability to plan what they will do in the future. During the preschool years, the assessment of cognitive skills addresses preacademic skills, which include prereading, prewriting, and premath skills. Assessment of cognitive development during the early primary years addresses more preacademic or academic skills. At this point, children's cognitive abilities have become more sophisticated as evidenced by their knowledge of concepts, ability to tell short stories in sequence, and their quantitative abilities.

Motor Skills

The assessment of motor skills is typically divided into gross and fine motor abilities. **Gross motor skills** refer to the ability to move and get around the environment. Gross motor skills involve the movement and control of large muscle groups used for rolling, sitting, crawling, standing, walking, throwing, and jumping. **Fine motor skills** refer to the ability to use small muscle groups such as those in the hands, feet, and face. Fine motor skills are used in reaching for, grasping, and releasing a toy; building towers; tying shoes; cutting; and writing.

Infants' motor skills are solely reflexive at birth. As the brain matures and the muscles strengthen, however, the ability of children to control their movements and to move about their environment improves. Not only do most young children gain increased control of their movements, but they gain increased coordination and complexity as their motor skills develop. They improve in general strength, flexibility, endurance, and eye-hand coordination. Between the ages of two and six, children learn to perform a variety of motor tasks with more refinement such as walking and running faster, balancing, and performing many fine motor tasks with more precision (e.g., scribbling, cutting with scissors, buttoning, writing). An eight-year-old who is experiencing typical development usually has mastered gross motor skills such as the ability to perform tumbling tasks (such as cartwheels), roller skate, or ride a bicycle without training wheels, and ball handling skills (e.g., dribbling, throwing accurately). In the area of fine motor skill development, most eight-year-olds have refined their handwriting skills so that they can print most words, draw pictures with details, and can use beads, puzzle pieces, blocks, or other small objects. Motor assessments focus on development in the gross and fine motor areas with emphasis placed on the quality of the child's motor skills and how they actually use these skills.

Communication and Language Skills

In the area of communication and language skills, there are three aspects of development to consider during the assessment process. **Communication** refers to the exchange of messages between a speaker and a listener. **Language** refers to the use of symbols (that is, letter sounds that are used in various combinations to form words), or syntax (rules that guide sentence structure), or grammar when communicating with one another. **Speech** is the oral-motor action used to communicate.

The assessment of young children's communication and language skills addresses both receptive and expressive language. **Receptive language** refers to the child's ability to understand and comprehend both verbal and nonverbal information that is presented. **Expressive language** is the young child's ability to communicate his thoughts or feelings and may involve vocalizations, words, gestures, and other behaviors that are used to relay information.

The most critical period for communication and language development is before the age of five. The communication of infants is usually unintentional in the beginning; however, by the age of three, most children have acquired all of the major components of a system of communication. Language development has been conceptualized as developing through a series of stages that begin in infancy. By the time children enter school, they are usually using all of the sentence types produced by adults. When communication skills are delayed or impaired, the focus of the assessment is on communicative intent, which means that the examiner focuses on what a child is attempting to communicate in a variety of means (for example, gestures, eye gaze, vocalizations).

Social and Emotional Skills

Social and emotional skills refer to a range of behaviors associated with how children interact with others, both adults and peers, and how they react in social situations. This domain includes how children initiate interactions and respond to interactions initiated by others. When children interact with adults, they usually need skills such as how to participate in reciprocal interactions. When they interact with peers, children often need skills such as how to play cooperatively, share toys, or request a turn. Emotional skills are children's abilities to identify and communicate feelings, as well as their capacity to act on their emotions while respecting the rights of others. Skills in this area include how to control one's impulses or temper and how to resolve conflicts. During infancy, the building blocks are laid for the development of long-term social relationships with others. As children age, their personalities are defined by their early childhood experiences. The desired outcome is for children to feel good about themselves and know how to express their feelings and emotions towards others in an appropriate manner.

Self-Care and Adaptive Skills

The assessment of **self-care skills** and **adaptive skills** usually focuses on the areas of eating, personal care

The assessment of self-care skills should occur within the natural environment to determine an accurate picture of a child's level of ability and independence.

(e.g., toileting, tooth brushing, hand washing, undressing/dressing). As children mature in the other skill areas (gross and fine motor for example), the skills from these areas become integrated so that children are able to perform self-care and adaptive skills at more advanced levels of independence. In early infancy, the self-care and adaptive skill areas that predominate are sleeping and eating. However, as children mature and spend greater amounts of time interacting with their environment, they usually acquire greater independence in the areas of eating, personal care, and dressing. Eating skills progress from the suck-swallow responses of infants, to finger feeding and cup drinking in toddlers, to independent feeding with appropriate utensils in preschoolers. Toileting, handwashing, toothbrushing, and hair combing are examples of personal care skills, which also become more refined as young children practice and gain increased independence. Similarly, dressing skills progress from cooperation in undressing and dressing to independent dressing skills in most preschool age children. By the time children reach the kindergarten and the early primary grades, they can usually perform all or most of the basic self-care and adaptive skills with some assistance on some of the more difficult tasks (like buttons or snaps on blue jeans). Gradually, children increase their ability to function with greater independence across a variety of tasks (such as dressing) and in various environments (e.g., home, school, community). Assessment focuses on precision in performing self-care and adaptive skills, as well as the level of independence.

In this section, we have provided a brief overview of the interrelated areas of development that are usually the focus of assessments of young children. Young children have limited attention spans and their attention may wander or be lost if the assessment instrument has too many test items and takes too long to complete. In addition, children's current health status should also be considered. For example, young children frequently have colds leading to middle ear infections (which may result in a temporary decrease in their hearing ability). This temporary decrease in hearing could dramatically influence their test performance. Furthermore, children who are sick or not feeling well for some other reason may not demonstrate optimal performance.

Assessment procedures should be comprehensive in coverage and should focus on children's overall abilities rather than on one or two developmental areas alone. Although separate areas of development can be described or defined (e.g., motor, communication, cognition), these areas are not independent but interact in complex ways. Professionals should attempt to gain a holistic picture of children's abilities that cuts across all developmental domains.

In the section that follows, some of the problems associated with the assessment of young children will be discussed.

Issues Associated with Traditional Assessment Practices

There has been much debate in recent years regarding assessment approaches and procedures appropriate for infants and young children with known or suspected disabilities and their families (Neisworth & Bagnato, 1996; 2000). One of the biggest issues has been the use of standardized, norm-referenced tests with young children. Bronfenbrenner (1977) cautioned against the over-reliance on this type of assessment when he described the assessment of young children as, "the science of the strange behavior of children in strange situations with strange adults for the briefest possible period of time" (p. 513).

Conventional, standardized, norm-referenced assessment instruments are often inappropriate even for use with children experiencing typical development. The *inappropriateness* of such measures is even greater when used with young children with disabilities. As Bagnato, Neisworth, and Munson (1997) point out:

Assessment of infants and preschoolers remains dominated by restrictive methods and styles that place a premium on inauthentic, contrived developmental tasks, that are administered by various professionals in separate sessions using small, unmotivating toys from boxes or test kits, staged at a table or on the floor in an unnatural setting, observed passively by parents, interpreted by norms based solely on typical children, and used for narrow purposes of classification and eligibility determination. (p. 69)

Assessment measures and practices must become compatible with, rather than at odds with, the behavior and interests of young children (Neisworth & Bagnato, 2000).

Standardized, norm-referenced tests were designed to be used for screening, diagnostic, and eligibility purposes. Unfortunately, these tools too often are misused by professionals for purposes other than those for which they were intended (for example, to design intervention goals and procedures) (McLean, Bailey, & Wolery, 2003). In addition, standardized norm-referenced measures were designed to be used in conjunction with other sources of information. Too often, however, these measures are used exclusively. The real problem arises when the test results do not provide an accurate representation of a child's typical behavior or optimal performance.

As the field of early childhood has evolved, it has become increasingly apparent that traditional assessment approaches should be replaced with procedures that are more appropriate for use with young children. Table 4–4 compares the old emphasis with the new emphasis in recommended assessment practices. This shift in emphasis has occurred due to the many issues and challenges associated with the assessment of young children such as: (a) the problems associated with the use of intelligence tests with young children; (b) the nature and characteristics of young children and families; (c) the small number of appropriate instruments for use with young children, especially for those children with severe or multiple disabilities; (d) the cultural bias and lack of cultural sensitivity in traditional assessment procedures; and (e) the problem of early labeling of young children. Although there are many other issues and challenges associated with the assessment of young children, these five issues will be highlighted in the following section.

Table 4-4   Assessment Practices in Early Intervention/Early Childhood Special Education

Old Emphasis	New Emphasis
Standardized intelligence testing	Multisource information gathering
Artificial assessment environments	Assessment in natural environments
Child-Centered assessment	Family-Centered assessment
Quantitative, statistical approaches to decision making	Team decision making

Over-Reliance on Intelligence Testing

A problem that unfortunately continues to occur in early childhood is the over-reliance on **intelligence tests** to determine children's outcomes. An intelligence test is a standardized measure of intellectual functioning. The utilization of standardized assessment procedures is inappropriate and does not provide an accurate appraisal of young children's abilities (Neisworth & Bagnato, 1992, 2000; Losardo & Notari-Syverson, 2001). When a standardized assessment procedure is used, the assumption is made that children of a certain age should possess certain skills. For example, often the expectation is that a 12-month-old child should be walking, a 2-year-old child should be feeding himself, and a 4-year-old should be able to throw a ball. If children do not possess these skills within the designated age range, then they are considered to be "delayed." This approach, however, does not take into account the context in which children develop and the powerful influence that a child's environment and experiences can have on his acquisition of particular skills. For example, a child who has not been given the opportunity to use a spoon or a fork will not be likely to use these utensils proficiently. Likewise, a child who has not played with certain types of toys, such as a ball or frisbee, may not be able to throw with the same precision as other children his age. It is essential that the context in which a child lives be given appropriate consideration in the assessment process.

Although the inappropriate use of standardized tests with young children has been criticized for a number of years, the misuse and abuse has continued

(Neisworth & Bagnato, 1996; 2000). There are a number of possible explanations for the continued emphasis on intelligence testing with young children. Professionals who are responsible for assessment may be unfamiliar with more appropriate ways to determine a true estimate of the abilities of young children (McLean, Bailey, & Wolery, 2003). Another reason may be that an extensive amount of time is required to conduct a thorough assessment using multiple measures (e.g., naturalistic observations, parent interviews) across multiple settings (like home or school). Due to limited professional knowledge, time constraints, and other factors, standardized testing continues to be used in inappropriate ways with young children with known or suspected disabilities. Based on what has been learned about assessment, professionals must find ways to conduct thorough and appropriate assessments of young children.

Limited Number of Assessment Instruments Appropriate for Young Children

Another assessment problem is the relatively small number of assessment instruments available that are appropriate for young children. Most standardized tests are designed for children experiencing typical development and will not reflect the abilities and needs of children with disabilities. Thus, the presence of a disability can further complicate the task of accurately assessing the abilities of young children. When a child has a physical, communication, or sensory disability, professionals must be extremely skilled in order to obtain an accurate assessment of the child's abilities. The most effective assessment protocols rely on a sensitivity to the age of the child and the nature of the child's disability or delay. A variety of strategies may be necessary to collect accurate information such as incorporating adaptations into the assessment, using alternative sensory modalities and/or methods of communication, and gaining information from families. In addition, the developmental impact of a disability must be taken into consideration. A child with a visual impairment or physical disability, for example, may not have had some of the same experiences as nondisabled children (independent exploration of his environment, riding a tricycle or bicycle, climbing a tree and so forth). Unfortunately, given the nature of many standardized assessment instruments, families are not able to participate as equal partners in the assessment process when they are used. For example, although a parent report is included on the Bayley Scales of Infant Development (BSID II), it cannot be used for scoring purposes. Professionals must carefully select assessment measures that are appropriate for the children and families with whom they are working.

The Nature and Characteristics of Young Children and Their Families

The nature and characteristics of young children can be particularly challenging for professionals responsible for assessment. In many cases, unfortunately, professionals have continued to rely on procedures utilized with older children even though the characteristics or nature of young children make the procedures inappropriate for them. The reasons that young children are poor candidates for experiencing traditional assessment procedures include their short attention spans, their difficulty in understanding the need to follow an adult's directions, and the anxiety often produced by interactions with unfamiliar adults and/or situations. As we all know, young children are most comfortable with people with whom they are most familiar, such as their parents or primary caregivers; moreover, parents or primary caregivers are most knowledgeable about the children. Thus, assessments of young children offer a unique opportunity to involve family members in an effort to gain their input (Woods & McCormick, 2002).

Families and professionals must have ongoing opportunities to share information about the assessment process.

Families may be very anxious about the assessment process. One of their primary concerns may be whether or not something will be wrong with their child. As one parent commented following an assessment of her child, "I didn't know whether or not my daughter would pass the test." Another parent remarked that she went home from the assessment and made her child practice the skills he had missed. Professionals should make sure that parents fully understand the purpose of each assessment and why it is being conducted. Pre-assessment planning is recommended in order to provide an opportunity for professionals to share information about the assessment process and to create an opportunity for families to provide input to the professionals. Table 4–5 contains a sample format for pre-assessment planning. Another important component of any assessment procedure is a period for explaining the process and answering parents' questions, usually before and after the assessment is conducted.

Some young children may be easily distracted, which, of course, may interfere with the assessment of their typical or optimal performance. Familiar surroundings may help children feel more comfortable and yield a more accurate portrayal of their abilities. In addition, assessment results will be more accurate if professionals allow time for children to

Table 4–5 Preassessment Planning: The Setting (Project Dakota)

1. Questions or concerns others have (e.g., baby-sitter, clinic, preschool) about my child:

2. Other places you can observe my child:

   Place: _____   Place: _____

   Contact person: _____   Contact person: _____

   What to observe: _____   What to observe: _____

3. I want others to see what my child does when:

4. I prefer the assessment take place:

   _____ at home   _____ at another location   _____ at the center

5. A time when my child is alert and when working parents can be present is:

   _____ morning   _____ early afternoon   _____ afternoon

6. People whom I would like to be there other than parents and early intervention staff:

7. My child's favorite toys or activities to help him/her become focused, motivated, and comfortable:

8. During the assessment, I prefer to:

   _____ a. Sit beside my child.

   _____ b. Help with activities to explore her/his abilities.

   _____ c. Offer comfort and support to my child.

   _____ d. Exchange ideas with the facilitator.

   _____ e. Carry out activities to explore my child's abilities.

   _____ f. Permit facilitator to handle and carry out activities.

   _____ g. Other:

SOURCE: J. Kjerland and J. Kovach, Family-Staff Collaboration for Tailored Infant Assessment. In E. Gibbs & D. Teti (Eds.), *Interdisciplinary Assessment of Infants: A Guide for Early Intervention Professionals* (Baltimore, MD: Paul H. Brookes, 1990).

become familiar with them. Many children take time to "warm up" to strangers. If possible, young children should not be separated from their parents during an assessment procedure. Often young children respond to separation by becoming more anxious and do not give an optimal performance under these conditions. If children do not feel comfortable, their performance probably will not reflect their true ability.

Assessments must be designed to make young children feel comfortable and secure in order for professionals to gain an accurate appraisal of their abilities and needs. The ultimate goal of assessment should be to elicit each child's typical pattern of behavior, the skills he/she has mastered, and his optimal level of performance.

Culturally Biased Assessments

Young children who will potentially be eligible to receive early intervention or early childhood special education services are characterized by their diversity in culture, ethnicity, language, family structure, composition, values, socioeconomic status, etc. Professionals have struggled for many years with how to employ appropriate, nonbiased assessments of young children from diverse backgrounds that do not penalize them based on their background or experience. A **culturally biased assessment** is one that measures only skills and abilities valued by the dominant Western culture. Thus, those children from nondominant or non-Western cultures are placed at a unique disadvantage. Problematic situations often exist when traditional standardized assessment measures that are culturally biased are used with children from diverse backgrounds. An example of potential bias can be found in a commonly used screening tool, the *Denver Developmental Screening Test* (DDST) (Frankenburg & Dodds, 1990). The DDST contains a test item that asks 4- to 6-year-old children to indicate "what a shoe is made of" with the acceptable answer being "leather." A child whose familiarity with shoes is limited to tennis shoes or sandals would not be given credit for giving the correct answer if he or she answered "rubber," "cloth," or "plastic." This item would be missed due to the child's lack of familiarity with leather shoes. It is easy to see the many potential problems associated with cultural bias in assessment tools and processes; therefore, professionals must strive for accurate and appropriate assessments of children from diverse backgrounds, which requires attention to the uniqueness of each child's culture and experience.

Early Labeling of Young Children

An important issue associated with initial assessments of young children is the early **labeling** of children with disabilities. Although school-age children with disabilities traditionally have been assigned labels such as mentally retarded or learning disabled, most professionals in early intervention and early childhood special education believe that disability labels for young children should be avoided due to the potential detrimental effects of labeling children at a young age (DEC, 2001). This recommendation is based on a number of factors. First of all, the diagnostic results for children prior to school age are tenuous; therefore, the practice of early labeling of young children has been discouraged based on the obvious and changing individual needs of children. Second, labels are believed to bias the behavior of others towards those who are labeled. This, of course, can negatively affect the self-esteem of those who are labeled. A third reason is that labeling has not been found to facilitate program planning or intervention for young children. Diagnostic labels, which categorize the type of disability, may even accentuate the effects of a child's disability rather than assist in the search for appropriate intervention. Fourth, many pro-

fessionals feel that labels inevitably lead to a **self-fulfilling prophecy** in young children. In other words, people often expect individuals who have been labeled to achieve at a predetermined level, which may be an under- or overestimation of their true abilities or potential. Because of the many obvious problems associated with labeling, it is recommended that disability labels should *not* be assigned to young children.

Recommended Assessment Practices and Procedures for Young Children

Driven by many years of experience and research demonstrating the limitations of traditional, single-dimensional assessment procedures, a number of recommended practices have emerged. There is growing consensus that assessment should be considered a process, not a single procedure. Experts in the field of early childhood special education agree that "assessment should be an ongoing, collaborative process of systematic observation and analysis" (Greenspan & Meisels, 1994, p. 1). Table 4–6 contains a list of assessment principles and practices with examples provided of each. As can be seen in this table, assessment of young children should be multidisciplinary, multidimensional, multimethod, multisource, multicontext, multicultural, proactive, and should involve ongoing information exchange.

New Directions and Standards for Assessment in EI/ECSE

The publication of the Division for Early Childhood, *DEC Recommended Practices in Early Intervention/Early Childhood Special Education* (Sandall, McLean, & Smith, 2000), suggests new directions and professional standards for assessment in EI/ECSE. According to this document, assessment must reflect eight critical qualities. Assessment must be (1) useful, (2) acceptable, (3) authentic, (4) collaborative, (5) convergent, (6) equitable, (7) sensitive, and (8) congruent (Bagnato & Neisworth, 1999; Neisworth & Bagnato, 2000). These

Table 4–6   Assessment Principles and Practices

Principle/Practice	Example
Multidisciplinary assessment	Assessments should be conducted by a team with a equal status afforded to the family and professionals.
Multidimensional assessment	Assessment information should be collected in a number of child and family domains.
Multimethod assessment	Assessment information should be collected using a variety of techniques, such as direct testing, observation, and interviews.
Multisource assessment	Assessment information should be collected from a number of sources knowledgeable about the child, including families, caregivers, and professionals.
Multicontext assessment	Assessment should occur across a number of environmental contexts, including the home, school, child care, or other relevant environments.
Multicultural assessment	Assessment procedures should respect the uniqueness of each child and family system.
Proactive assessment	Assessment procedures should be designed to identify strengths, concerns, resources, needs, and priorities for collaborative intervention planning; emphasis should be placed on assessing resources, strengths and concerns, not deficits.
Ongoing information exchange	The collection of assessment information should be an ongoing process that facilitates collaboration.

eight qualities operationalize recommended assessment practices in EI/ECSE, each of which is described below.

The Utility of the Assessment   Above all, the assessment information that is collected must be useful. The assessment of young children requires a careful subjective and objective appraisal of a child's performance in natural learning environments. Thus, a number of individuals (e.g., educator, physical therapist, occupational therapist) from diverse backgrounds, as well as the child's family, are a part of the process. The various disciplines involved require a blending of medical and educational assessment models and an understanding of different methods and terminology used by various professionals. The assessment information must be combined to compile a useful assessment plan with information that is useful in developing meaningful goals and objectives

within the context of a child's natural environment. For example, in the case of a young child with cerebral palsy, the physical therapist may focus on the child's muscle tone and physical abilities noting spasticity, internal rotation of the hips, plantar flexion of the feet and slight hip subluxation. The occupational therapist may pay particular attention to the presence of a radial-digital grasp with limited wrist supination and the child's ability to feed himself. The early childhood special educator may collect assessment information related to the child's ability to perform skills such as walking, running, playing on playground equipment, copying, tracing, cutting, and playing with toys. Families will provide input on their priorities for their child. All of this assessment information must be combined to make important decisions about the child's need for services, his instructional objectives, and the methods to be used in providing support to the child and family.

The Acceptability of the Assessment DEC *Recommended Practice Guidelines* suggest that "the methods, styles and materials for assessment must be mutually agreed upon by families and professionals" (Neisworth & Bagnato, 2000, p. 20) in order to make the assessment process acceptable. Assessment methods may range from separate individual assessments completed by therapists and educators in a variety of settings to an arena format where all participants assess skills at the same time in the same setting. Assessment methods and styles may vary from direct testing to observations in natural contexts. The direct testing of skills can present challenges because often this requires children to have prerequisite skills such as understanding and following directions (stand on one foot) or imitation abilities (copying a model). Direct testing also presumes that children will be willing and motivated to perform skills out of context for professionals who may be unfamiliar to them. Observational information may be more acceptable and may have more social validity due to the child's comfort level in performing skills in natural environments and within the context of play. In addition, the testing materials used must be acceptable and adaptable for children with various disabilities (e.g., physical, visual, cognitive); therefore, materials within the natural environment are usually most appropriate.

The Authenticity of Assessments Establishing the authenticity of assessments may be especially important due to the number of professionals who may be involved and the diverse information that may be gathered during the assessment process. The authenticity of skills may be determined by questioning: (a) the sole use of standardized tests; (b) the use of tests that are difficult to translate into a functional assessment that guides intervention; and (c) the use of a single test, method, or source of information. By utilizing multiple sources of information collected from those most familiar with the child (e.g., family members, child care providers, teachers) and from within natural contexts will insure the authenticity of the information and result in information that is useful in determining the priorities for intervention.

Collaboration in the Assessment Process The assessment of young children requires the highest degree of collaboration due to the number of professionals who may be involved and the child's family. An initial assessment is completed by a number of professionals, along with the family, to determine if the child is eligible for services. Thereafter, the assessment team may vary in content due to the changing needs of the child. For example, a child with Down syndrome may initially need a physical therapy assessment due to the presence of abnormal muscle tone and delayed skill development. However, as the child progresses and moves from skill development (crawling, walking, etc.) to using playground equipment, the physical therapy assessment may be a lesser need, while more general assessments may be more useful. Collaboration is enhanced by the use of jargon-free language, especially when medical and educational terminology is combined. The use of the arena assessment format and the presence of a service coordinator or facilitator make the assessment process more collaborative and, therefore, more understandable and useful to all participants.

Convergence of Assessment Information Assessment requires the convergence of differing opinions that affect not only the child's progress in these skill areas, but also the areas that are greatly affected by deficits in other areas. For example, the achievement of many basic adaptive skills requires the use of many fine motor skills. Children may not be able to use utensils when eating, or zip or button clothing, without having appropriate fine motor skills (grasping objects). Therefore, many everyday routines are affected by the development of skills and should be considered when the assessment team examines results and determines objectives for children that are not only activity-based, but also routine-based.

Equity Equity in assessing young children with delays or disabilities can be a major issue when using standardized tests. For example, the materials may be difficult to manipulate if a child has muscle tone problems and/or an immature grasp or difficult to see if the child has a visual impairment. Often the demonstration of age-level skills is required to accomplish basic items on tests across all developmental areas. For example, a cognitive test item may require the child to turn pages in books or put cubes in a cup. Unfortunately, the assessment instrument may not be valid if the test materials are adapted. Recommended practices suggest the use of additional measures to accurately assess the child's skill levels. Usually a curriculum-based assessment does not have standardized materials and encourages the assessment of children in familiar environments using interesting and familiar materials. Curriculum-based measures accept responses that rely on modified responses and/or adapted materials. An additional equity issue centers around time and opportunities. Children with disabilities and/or delays often take longer to complete a task and may not do as well in a "one-shot" testing situation. Multiple observations by family members and professionals often yield more accurate results.

Sensitivity of Issues in Assessment Assessment instruments selected for children with significant delays or disabilities should reflect some type of progress over time and after repeated administrations. It would be insensitive to use inappropriate measures that repeatedly yielded no developmental gains or even showed skill regression. More appropriate observational data that indicates positive gains should be utilized. For example, some children with significant physical disabilities (e.g., quadriplegic cerebral palsy) may never "walk independently" and frequently will not progress beyond the one-to-two-year-old level in motor skills on a developmental assessment. However, this child may freely move around in all environments using a wheelchair. An appropriate assessment in this case would be an observational, functional assessment of the child's ability to move freely from one place to another.

Congruence The DEC recommended practice guidelines assert that "early childhood assessment materials and methods must be developed specifically for infants and preschool children and match the styles and interests of typical young children"

(Neisworth & Bagnato, 2000, p. 21). In assessing a young child's skills, this may be interpreted to mean that materials should be carefully selected to match the child's chronological age rather than his or her developmental level. For example, puzzles that three-year-olds use can be adapted with knobs so that children with fine motor challenges can be given the opportunity to complete the same activities as their same-age peers. Conversely, if a child is five years old and is developmentally functioning at a six-month level in terms of motor abilities, infant toys (e.g., rattles, busy box) would not be used to assess reaching and grasping skills. Instead a more age-appropriate material would be used, such as a tambourine or paint brush.

Diversity Considerations

As we have described, the appropriate assessment of young children requires careful consideration, particularly when children are from diverse backgrounds. Professionals must select the most effective strategies for gathering the needed information depending on each child's unique background. The use of standardized instruments can be particularly problematic when tools are not in the child's primary language or developmental expectations differ in the child's culture. Further, the child-rearing practices or patterns of adult-child interaction may differ in a child's culture, which may have a confounding influence in the assessment process.

Lynch and Hanson (2004) offer a number of suggestions for collecting information about children from diverse backgrounds. They suggest alternative approaches to traditional assessment, such as conducting observations and interviews. Table 4–7 provides a list of the types of questions that professionals can ask when conducting assessments in order to make them more culturally sensitive and responsive. In addition, Table 4–8 contains guidelines that professionals can use when assessing children from various cultural and linguistic backgrounds.

The remaining portion of this chapter will focus on the first three purposes of assessment. These types of assessment will be discussed in the order of screening, diagnosis, and eligibility. Two additional pur-

Table 4–7 Questions for Professionals to Ask When Conducting a Culturally Sensitive Assessment

1. With what cultural group was this assessment tool normed? Is it the same culture as that of the child I am serving?

2. Have I examined this assessment tool for cultural biases? Has it been reviewed by members of the cultural group being served?

3. If I have modified or adapted a standardized assessment tool, have I received input on the changes to be certain it is culturally appropriate? If using a standardized tool, or one to which I have made changes, have I carefully scored and interpreted the results in consideration of cultural or linguistic variation? When interpreting and reporting assessment results, have I made clear reference that the instrument was modified and how?

4. Have representatives from the cultural community met to create guidelines for culturally competent assessment for children from that group? Has information about child-rearing practices and typical child development for children from that community been gathered and recorded for use by those serving the families?

5. What do I know about the child rearing practices of this cultural group? How do these practices impact child development?

6. Am I aware of my own values and practices and the kind of information gathered in the assessment process? Can I utilize nondiscriminatory and culturally competent skills and practices in my interactions?

7. Do I utilize parents and other family members in gathering information for the assessment? Am I aware of the people with whom the child spends time, and the level of acculturation of these individuals?

8. Do I know where or how to find out about specific cultural or linguistic information that may be needed in order for me to be culturally competent in the screening and assessment process?

9. Do I have bilingual or bicultural skills, or do I have access to another person who can provide direct service or consultation? Do I know what skills are required of a quality interpreter or mediator?

10. Have I participated in training sessions on cultural competence in assessment? Am I continuing to develop my knowledge base through additional formal training and by spending time with community members to learn the cultural attributes specific to the network of peers and supervisory practitioners who are addressing these issues, and can I become a participating member?

SOURCE: Adapted from M. Anderson and P. Goldberg, (1991). *Cultural Competence in Screening and Assessment.* National Early Childhood Technical Assistance System [NEC*TAS], Chapel Hill, N.C.

poses of assessment will be discussed in the chapter that follows, program planning and progress monitoring and evaluation.

Screening Young Children

According to federal legislation, each state must establish a **Child Find** system of locating children who may have a developmental delay or disability, which makes them eligible for early intervention/early childhood special education services. Child Find requires community and interagency collaboration. Professionals from a variety of disciplines and multi-

ple agencies (e.g., Head Start, education, social services, and public health) work together to implement an effective Child Find system in each state. Usually children with known disabilities such as cerebral palsy or Down syndrome are easier to locate because of referrals from medical and other agencies. Children who are at risk or have delays or disabilities that are not as obvious during infancy and the toddler years are harder to identify. Child Find teams are set up in regions within states to find and identify those children who should undergo an indepth assessment to determine if they have a delay or disability. These teams are usually responsible for conducting public awareness campaigns to inform the community so that referrals for screening will be made. Advertisements

Table 4–8   Guidelines for Assessing Children from Diverse Backgrounds

Before the assessment

Learn about the child's and family's cultural and linguistic background, as well as the child's learning style.

   Talk directly to the family with an interpreter if necessary.

   Consult with others who are familiar with the culture.

   Read and visit local business (e.g., ethnic grocery stores).

Ask the following questions:

   What is the family's level of acculturation to the U.S. culture?

   What are the literacy practices in the home?

   Which languages can the child and family understand and speak?

During the assessment

Explain the purpose of and procedures for the assessment to the child and family members and others who will participate in the process.

Provide the child with meaningful and culturally appropriate learning experiences.

   Use culturally relevant materials and activities.

   Be aware of cultural differences in communication styles that may influence the child's responsiveness to the examiner's prompts and teaching strategies.

   Consult having a family member or an interpreter assist in the teaching if the child does not respond well to the examiners.

   Use visual nonverbal prompts and teaching strategies if the child has difficulty speaking English.

   If the child speaks more than one language or dialect, observe whether the child is aware of the differences between languages and can translate and explain words.

   Use simple words and sentences. Try to learn a few words and sentences in the child's and family's language.

After the assessment

Avoid making assumptions.

Take time to reflect on the information gathered during the assessment.

Ask caregivers for their opinions on the representativeness of the assessment results.

Solicit feedback from the family and/or the interpreter, if present, on the cultural appropriateness of communication and teaching styles.

SOURCE: Losardo, A. & Notari-Syverson, A. (2001). *Alternative approaches to assessing young children.* Baltimore, MD: Paul H. Brookes Publishing Co. p. 190.

often are done through the local media (newspapers, radio, and television) or at doctor's offices, clinics, grocery stores, shopping malls or other places frequented by families of young children. A well-informed community, which is knowledgeable of the referral process for early intervention and early childhood special education services, can result in family members themselves making the contact. Many local early intervention services have a central telephone number that accepts referrals and assigns a service provider to do an initial screening. Other sources of referral are pediatricians, child care workers, and medical professionals from hospitals (such as neonatal intensive care unit staff).

Screenings are conducted not to identify children for services but to determine whether to refer children for additional assessment. By definition, screenings are "the application of a simple, accurate means of determining which children in the population are likely to be in need of special services in order to develop optimally" (Dumars, Duran-Flores, Foster, & Stills, 1987, p. 111).

Screening Procedures and Instruments

Referrals for screenings are usually made by professionals from a variety of disciplines and services who come in contact with young children and suspect them of having delays in development. Examples of the types of professionals who frequently make referrals are physicians, nurses, or other health professionals in high-risk nurseries, health clinics, or pediatricians' offices. As a result of extensive Child Find efforts, often families and other caregivers also make referrals.

Screenings can be accomplished by using a variety of procedures including specific instruments or checklists, observations of the child, or parent interviews. A screening procedure may last anywhere from five to fifteen minutes. Screening involves a quick look to see if a child's skills are adequate or whether or not there is a discrepancy from normal expectations that warrants further assessment. The Child Find process varies from state to state. Many states offer screenings for preschoolers prior to entering kindergarten and in some states screening is mandatory before children enter kindergarten. Although the process may vary from state to state, the purpose is to identify those children with potential developmental issues, vision problems, hearing concerns, etc. Often questionnaires or interview formats are used to elicit family concerns regarding children's developmental status, health, and overall well-being (Wright & Treton, 1995). Thus, family members play an important role in the screening process because they can provide valuable information about their child's development, health, behavior, personal characteristics, etc. (Diamond & Squires, 1993). As stated earlier, the results of a screening do not satisfy the objective of determining whether or not a child has a definite problem, but only determine whether a child has the potential for developmental delay and should be referred for a comprehensive evaluation.

In reality, the screening process begins immediately following birth. Routine examinations of infants serve as a means of predicting abnormalities. One of the first screenings experienced by infants and their families is the **Apgar Scale** (Apgar & James, 1962). Infants are screened at 1-minute and 5-minute intervals following their birth in the following areas: (a) heart rate, (b) respiration, (c) reflex response, (d) muscle tone, and (e) color (see Figure 4–1). A low Apgar score may indicate that further medical assistance is needed or that a referral should be made for a more indepth assessment. The 5-minute Apgar has been found to be an accurate predictor of future developmental progress (Batshaw, 1997). In addition, blood and urine tests are routine procedures used to detect metabolic disorders such as phenylketonuria (PKU) (referred to as a **PKU screening**). Through early identification of PKU and appropriate intervention, which includes a restricted diet, many of the adverse outcomes associated with PKU, such as

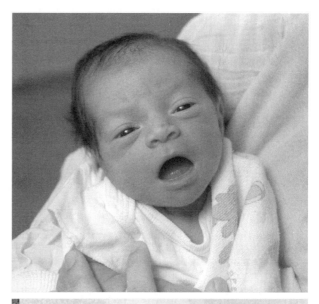

The screening process begins immediately after birth through routine examinations of newborns, using such measures as the Apgar Scale.

			1 min.	5 min.
Heart rate	Absent	0		
	Less than 100	(1)		
	100 to 140	(2)	1	2
Respiratory effort	Apneic	(0)		
	Shallow, irregular	(1)		
	Lusty cry and breathing	(2)	1	2
Reflex response	No response	(0)		
	Grimace	(1)		
	Cough or sneeze	(2)	1	2
Muscle tone	Flaccid	(0)		
	Some flexion of extremities	(1)		
	Flexion resisting extension	(2)	1	2
Color	Pale blue	(0)		
	Body pink, extremities blue	(1)		
	Pink all over	(2)	0	1
		TOTAL	4	9

Figure 4–1   The Apgar Evaluation Scale

mental retardation, can be prevented. As stated previously, the screening process may be accomplished by using a variety of specific screening instruments and procedures, by using systematic observation over time, and/or through parent report. Table 4–9 contains sample instruments that are often used for screening purposes.

When professionals select a screening tool, they should choose the instrument based on a number of specific criteria. First, a screening instrument's accuracy is important for several reasons. Some children who need services may be missed, and are, therefore, not referred if a screening tool is not accurate. Sometimes children who do not need services are referred for evaluation and, therefore, overreferral is also a problem when a tool is not accurate. A screening tool's rate of under- and overreferral is related to its sensitivity and specificity. **Sensitivity** refers to a screening instrument's ability to identify children who need additional assessment. **Specificity** refers to the capacity of a screening procedure to accurately select out children who should not be identified. In other words, a test that is specific will not refer chil-

dren who do not need further assessment. The less sensitive a screening instrument is, the greater the number of underreferrals or false negatives (See Figure 4–2). A **false negative** designates a child who needs special services but was not referred by the screening. Losses in specificity result in an increased number of overreferrals or false positives. A **false positive** designates a child who has been referred by the screening but does not need special services. In sum, the levels of sensitivity and specificity are measures of the screening tool's validity, which tells us the extent to which a test measures what it says it measures. Data on the number of false positives and false negatives should be available and at an acceptable ratio. Great care should be taken when selecting screening tools to insure that they are indeed valid and accurate.

Second, the simplicity of a screening tool is important. Instruments should be short, easy to administer, and usable by professionals from a variety of disciplines. Similarly, the scoring of the instrument should be accomplished quickly and easily. It is desirable for the screening procedures to be systematized to ensure easy implementation and repli-

Table 4-9   Selected Screening Instruments

Instrument	Publisher	Age Range	Domains
AGS Early Screening Profiles (Harrison et al., 1990).	American Guidance Service, Inc., Circle Pines, MN	2 years to 6 years, 11 months	*Profiles:* Cognitive/ Language; Motor; and Self-Help; Social *Surveys:* Articulation; Home Survey; Health History Survey; and Behavior Survey
Ages & Stages Questionnaires (ASQ) (Bricker & Squires, 1999).	Paul H. Brookes Publishing Co., Baltimore, MD	4 months through 60 months	Communication, Gross Motor, Fine Motor, Problem Solving, and Personal-Social Development
Battelle Developmental Screening Test (Newborg, 2004).	Riverside Publishing Company, Chicago, IL	Birth to 7–11 years	Personal; Social; Adaptive; Motor; Communication; Cognition
Brigance Preschool Screen (Brigance, 1998).	Curriculum Associates, North Billerica, MA	3 through 4 years	Not divided into domains; Descriptive Categories
Denver Developmental Screening (DDST) II (Frankenburg & Dodds, 1990).	Denver Developmental Materials, Denver, CO	Birth to 6 years	Personal/Social; Fine Motor/Adaptive; Language; Gross Motor
Developmental Indicator for the Assessment of Learning (DIAL-3) (Mardell-Czudnowski & Goldenberg, 1998).	American Guidance Service, Circle Pines, MN	3 through 6 years	Motor; Concepts; Language; Adaptive Social Skills; Personal and Medical Background
Early Screening Inventory—Revised (ESI) (Meisels, Marsden, Wiske, & Henderson, 1997).	Rebus Ann Arbor, MI	3 years through 4 years 6 months (ESI-P) 4 years, 6 months through 6 years (ESI-K)	Overview of Child's Development—Parent Report
First STEP (Miller, 1993).	Psychological Corporation, Hartcourt Brace, San Antonio, TX	2 years, 9 months to 6 years, 2 months	Cognition; Communication; Motor; Social/Emotional; Adaptive; Parent/Teacher Scale

cation. A third consideration is the comprehensiveness of the screening instrument. Screening tools should be multidimensional and should include screening for educational, health, behavioral, and environmental concerns. Although separate areas of development can be defined, these areas are not independent, but interact in complex ways. Ideally, screening procedures should be comprehensive in coverage and should focus on the whole child rather than one or two developmental areas alone. Another factor to consider is whether the screening instrument is cost-effective. In other words, the instrument should be inexpensive, but, at the same time, should be accurate. When an instrument is accurate, the likelihood of inappropriate referrals is minimized.

	Referred for evaluation	Not referred for evaluation
Eligible for special services	Sensitivity (Accurate referral)	False Negative (Underreferral)
Not eligible for special services	False Positive (Overreferral)	Specificity (Accurate nonreferral)

Figure 4–2   Potential Outcomes for Screening

Finally, screening tools should be sensitive to parents and provide for parent involvement or input. Because of the wide range and variations in normal development and behavior during the early years, infants and young children are often difficult to screen. Parent involvement in the screening process may alleviate some of these difficulties. Most screening tools typically involve the use of observations, parent reports, or some combination of the two. Parental report is a method most commonly used with young children. A comprehensive screening process includes the gathering of information about a wide range of children's abilities and, of course, parents have the most extensive information in such areas as motivation, interactive ability, learning style, and tolerance for learning. A technique that has been used to gather information is a parent-completed screening questionnaire. Besides the cost- and time-effective advantages that this procedure offers, parent-completed checklists can also have potential intervention effects. Although it seems that parent-completed questionnaires could provide important developmental information, not all parents are able or will choose to engage in independent questionnaire completion. This determination should be made based on each parent's abilities and desires (Henderson & Meisels, 1994).

Children who have an **established risk** generally forego the screening process. An established risk means a diagnosed medical condition that is known to have a negative impact on development (examples include Down syndrome, cerebral palsy, hearing impairment). Children who have an established risk should receive a comprehensive assessment of their abilities in multiple domains.

Diagnosis of Young Children with Disabilities

A second purpose of assessment is diagnostic in nature. **Diagnostic assessments** are designed to determine the existence of a disability in a child. If a disability is present, then questions are asked that will determine the extent of the problem and the effect the disability is having on the child's development. By clarifying the extent of the problem, a definitive diagnosis of the disability can be made. In some cases, the cause or causes of the delay or disability cannot be identified. In other cases, medical diagnoses are made by physicians or other medical professionals and they may or may not be related to the presence of a disability. In addition to the medical diagnoses, children may be involved in a number of diagnostic assessments conducted by a variety of professionals on the assessment team.

The goal of diagnosis is to identify causes and describe the nature and severity of a child's disability. Diagnostic information may come from input provided by families, reports of professionals from a variety of disciplines, and direct observations of the child. Following the collection of information about the child's abilities, a diagnosis can be made that describes the nature of the problem, severity of the problem, possible causes, and maintaining factors. This step in the assessment process should provide a foundation for the more indepth and finely tuned assessment procedures that follow (McLean & McCormick, 1993).

Determining Eligibility for Services

After a young child is found to be in need of further assessment, a complete eligibility assessment should be conducted to determine whether a child is, in fact, eligible for early intervention or early childhood special education services. In other words, does the child meet the eligibility requirements to receive the services? This phase of the process is most often conducted by a team of qualified individuals from several disciplines (such as special education, speech-language pathology, physical therapy and others). These professionals collaborate to determine a child's eligibility for services by (a) reviewing the child's health records and medical history, (b) determining the child's current level of functioning in major development areas, and (c) assessing the child's individual strengths and needs.

Eligibility Criteria

Over the past several years, there has been much discussion regarding eligibility criteria and categories for young children with known or suspected disabilities. Recall from Chapter 2 that through the 1991 Amendments to IDEA, PL 102-119, states were given the option to use an additional developmental delay eligibility category for preschoolers. Table 4–10 pro-

vides eligibility guidelines for infants, toddlers, and preschoolers as specified in the IDEA Amendments of 1991. This means that in the absence of an identified disability, children can be determined eligible for receiving services based on the particular eligibility criteria established within his or her state (for example, 25% delay in one or more developmental domains). Of course, this decision will depend on federal, state, and local eligibility criteria that specify precisely how eligibility is determined in a particular area.

The 1997 Reauthorization of IDEA, PL 105-117, allowed for the developmental delay eligibility category to be extended through age nine if states desire. Table 4–11 provides the eligibility guidelines established by the 1997 Reauthorization of IDEA that pertains to three- through nine-year-olds. States and localities are still required by IDEA and its amendments, however, to develop definitions of developmental delay thoughtfully so that the outcome will be eligibility procedures that are based on knowledge of young children and will ensure appropriate services for young children with disabilities and their families.

Eligibility Procedures and Instruments

Procedures must be used to determine if a child's skills are significantly different from a large group of children whose development falls within the normal

---

Table 4–10   PL 102-119 IDEA Amendments of 1991

Infant and Toddler Eligibility

Each infant or toddler with a disability and the infant's or toddler's family shall receive—

(1) a multidisciplinary assessment of the unique strengths and needs of the infant or toddlers and the identification of services appropriate to meet such needs.

(2) a family-directed assessment of the resources, priorities, and concerns of the family and the identification of the supports and services necessary to enhance the family's capacity to meet the developmental needs of their infant or toddler with a disability.

Preschool Eligibility

Allows states to service children aged 3 to 5 to be found eligible for Part B services if they are—

(1) experiencing developmental delays as defined by the State and as measured by appropriate diagnostic instruments and procedures, in one or more of the following areas: physical development, cognitive development, communication development, social or emotional development, or adaptive development; and

(2) who, by reason thereof, need special education and related services.

Table 4–11   PL 105-476 IDEA Amendments of 1997

Eligibility for Ages 3 through 9

The term "child with a disability" for a child aged 3 through 9 may be, at the discretion of the State and the LEA, a child who is experiencing developmental delays (as defined by the State and as measured by appropriate diagnostic instruments and procedures, in one or more of the following areas: physical development, cognitive development, communication development, social or emotional development, or adaptive development), and who, by reason thereof, needs special education and related services.

range. This determination is made by comparing a child's performance to the expected performance of children of the same age. Thus, the assessment procedures that follow involve administering instruments in a controlled manner. For example, the same materials, directions, and scoring procedures are used each time a tool is administered. The types of instruments that are used for eligibility determination include the *Bayley Scales of Infant Development-II (BSID-II)* (Bayley, 1993), the *Battelle Developmental Inventory (BDI)* (Newborg, Stock, Wnek, Guidubaldi, & Svinicki, 1988), the *Developmental Assessment of Young Children* (DAYC) (Voress & Maddox, 1998) or one of many other instruments. What these instruments have in common is that they all measure a child's skills and development as compared to a norm group of children who have previously completed the test. When a child's test scores fall significantly below the scores of the children in the norm group, this serves as a signal that the child may have a developmental delay and may be eligible for early intervention or early childhood special education services.

It is important to note that recommended practice suggests that no major decision about a child's eligibility should be made based *solely* on the results of a single test. Decisions regarding eligibility should be based on observations and other multiple-assessment measures. Another important recommendation is that professionals should be allowed the flexibility to make appropriate decisions guided by informed clinical opinion. Observations and other assessment procedures should be used to support the findings of an assessment instrument. Standardized, norm-referenced assessment instruments do not guarantee that the examiner will be able to determine if the child has a delay or is at-risk for developing a delay or disability. By collecting additional information from the child's family and other caregivers and by observing the child's behavior in natural settings, examiners can make an informed decision about the presence of a developmental delay or whether or not the child is developing at a significantly different rate from his or her same age peers. Parents and other family members can add valuable information to the eligibility decision by participating in the assessment

process in a variety of ways. Parents can provide information informally through discussions with team members; they can complete questionnaires, checklists, or parent reports; and/or they can be present in the room with their child during the assessment. Often they can provide feedback regarding the skills or behaviors the child is demonstrating (e.g., whether this is typical behavior, other skills or abilities the child has demonstrated, or supplemental information).

Professionals are encouraged to be sensitive to families when discussing eligibility assessment information. Following is a list of tips developed by Cohen and Spenciner (2003) for sharing eligibility information with families:

- Provide family members with an opportunity to receive the assessment report in a one-to-one setting rather than during a large IFSP of IEP team meeting. This meeting allows the family time to ask questions with an empathetic professional and to reflect on the information prior to the larger, full-staff meeting.
- Share information with both parents (or major caregivers) at the same time.
- Be honest and straightforward regarding the disability.
- Be willing to say when you don't know.
- Allow time for families to express their feelings.
- Be sensitive to families if they are not ready to hear details.
- Offer to provide additional information.
- Suggest additional resources.
- Be available to the family for further discussions.
- Arrange to have a native-language interpreter available if families need assistance (p. 328).

Recent recommendations regarding eligibility assessment indicate a need to focus more on the *process* of assessment rather than just the *product* of assessment (McLean, Bailey, & Wolery, 2003; Neisworth & Bagnato, 2000). One recommended informal method through which this can be accomplished is an **arena assessment** process. Arena assessments are conducted by a group of professionals from various disciplines and the child's family. This group of professionals and family members is referred to as a transdisciplinary team. As you may recall from the previous chapters, transdisciplinary teams plan and provide services within and across discipline boundaries to deliver integrated services. This team jointly collects information about specific developmental areas as well as the interrelatedness of these areas within the child. One or more of the team members usually conduct the assessment while other team members, including the parents, observe the assessment process. An integrated assessment report is then completed by the participating professionals, including input from the family. Figure 4–3 provides a visual example of the participants in an arena assessment.

Summary

Recommended practice suggests that assessment is a process rather than a single procedure. Assessments of young children are conducted to help professionals and families to make informed, evaluative decisions at several levels. The type of decision to be made will determine the purpose of the assessment (that is, whether the objective is screening, diagnosis, eligibility, program planning, or progress monitoring and evaluation), as well as the assessment tools to be used or the processes that will be followed. Depending on the purpose of the assessment, the assessment process can be formal and/or informal and can include direct testing, observations, interviews, portfolios, and/or other procedures.

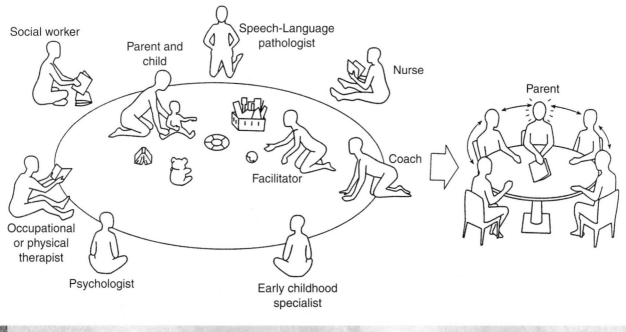

Figure 4–3   Example of Arena Assessment

SOURCE: M. J. McGonigel, G. Woodruff, & M. Roszmann-Millican, The transdisciplinary team: A model for family-centered early intervention. In L. J. Johnson, R. J. Gallagher, M. J. LaMontagne, J. B. Jordan, J. J. Gallagher, P. L. Hutinger, & M. B. Karnes (Eds.) *Meeting early intervention challenges, issues from birth to three* (2nd ed.), 1994. Paul H. Brookes, Baltimore.

Conducting appropriate assessments of young children has been the topic of discussion and debate for several years. Some of the issues have included: (a) the over-reliance on intelligence testing, (b) the limited number of tools appropriate for young children, (c) the nature and characteristics of young children, (d) culturally biased assessments, and (e) early labeling of young children. In this chapter, a number of issues have been discussed and strategies have been suggested for conducting appropriate assessments of young children.

Recommended assessment practices have changed dramatically over the last several years. Because of the limitations of standardized and formal assessment tools, informal procedures are more widely used with young children. It is important to remember that the key component of an appropriate assessment is for the assessment team members to gain an accurate representation of the child's current abilities and behaviors in the context of his natural environment as he interacts with key adults and peers. Thus, recommended practice suggests that assessment should include multiple observations of the child over a period of time in a variety of environments or contexts. This process will enable team members to have a better understanding of a child's true abilities. Assessment must be useful, acceptable, authentic, collaborative, convergent, equitable, sensitive, and congruent (Bagnato & Neisworth, 1999; Neisworth & Bagnato, 2000). These eight qualities operationalize the concept of recommended assessment practice for early intervention/early childhood special education.

As has been illustrated in this chapter, assessment is an ongoing process that begins with screening and continues with diagnosis, eligibility, and program planning, as well as progress monitoring and evaluation. Assessments conducted for three different purposes have been described in this chapter—screening, diagnosis, and eligibility. First, screenings are conducted to identify children who may have a delay or disability. Through screenings, the determination is made if children should undergo more indepth assessment procedures. Second, diagnostic assessments are conducted to determine if a delay or disability exists, the nature of the problem, and the possible cause or causes of the delay or disability. Third, eligibility assessments determine if children meet the requirements of a given program or service. In other words, based on children's abilities, do they qualify for special services according to a program's established criterion? In the next chapter, two additional purposes of assessment will be discussed: program planning and progress monitoring and evaluation.

Check Your Understanding

1. Provide a definition of assessment as it applies to early intervention/early childhood special education (EI/ECSE).

2. Identify and describe the five purposes of assessment in EI/ECSE.

3. Briefly describe legislative requirements from the IDEA regarding the assessment of young children.

4. Describe four different types of assessment procedures commonly used in EI/ECSE.

5. Briefly define each of the developmental domains: (a) cognitive, (b) communication and language, (c) social and emotional, (d) motor, and (e) self-care and adaptive skills.

6. Discuss how the interrelatedness of the developmental domains contribute to the development of the whole child.

7. Discuss some of the problems or issues associated with the assessment of young children and provide suggestions for addressing them.

8. List at least five recommended guidelines for conducting appropriate assessments of young children.

9. Describe procedural assessment considerations as reflected in *DEC Recommended Practice Guidelines*.

10. Describe how professionals can ensure that assessments are culturally appropriate.

11. Describe recommended screening practices and provide two examples of screening instruments.

12. Differentiate between assessment conducted for diagnostic purposes and assessment designed to determine eligibility.

13. Explain why the category of "developmental delay" is used for children under age nine rather than categorical labels, such as learning disability or mental retardation.

References

Anderson, M., & Goldberg, P. (1991). *Cultural competence in screening and assessment*. National Early Childhood Technical Assistance System (NEC*TAS) topical paper. Chapel Hill, NC.

Apgar, V., & James, L. (1962). Further observation on the Newborn Scoring System. *American Journal of Diseases of Children, 104*, 419–428.

Arter, J. A., & Spandel, V. (1991). *Using portfolios of student work in instruction and assessment*. Portland, OR: Northwest Regional Education Laboratory.

Bailey, D., & Wolery, M. (1992). *Teaching infants and preschoolers with disabilities* (2nd ed.). New York: Merrill.

Bagnato, S. J., & Neisworth, J. T. (1991). *Assessment for early intervention: Best practices for professionals*. New York: Guilford.

Bagnato, S. J., & Neisworth, J. T., & Munson, S. M. (1997). *LINKing: Assessment and early intervention*. Baltimore: Brookes.

Bagnato, S. J., & Neisworth, J. T. (1999). Collaboration and teamwork in assessment for early intervention. *Child and Adolescent Psychiatric Clinics of North America, 8*(2), 347–363.

Bagnato, S. J., & Neisworth, J. T. (2000, Spring). Assessment is adjusted to each child's developmental needs. *Birth through 5 Newsletter, 1*(2), 1.

Batshaw, M. J. (1997). *Children with disabilities* (4th ed.). Baltimore: Brookes.

Bayley, N. (1993). *Bayley scales of infant development-II (BSID-II)*. New York: Psychological Corporation.

Bondurant-Utz, J. (2002). *Practical guide to assessing infants and preschoolers with special needs*. Upper Saddle River, NJ: Merrill/Prentice Hall.

Brazelton, T. B., & Nugent, J. K. (1995). *Neonatal behavioral assessment scale* (3rd. ed.). London: MacKelth Press.

Bredekamp, S., & Copple (1997). *Developmentally appropriate practice in early childhood programs serving children from birth through age 8*. Washington, DC: National Association for the Education of Young Children.

Bricker, D., (2002). *Assessment, evaluation, and programming system for children*. Baltimore: Brookes.

Bricker, D., & Squires, J. (1999). *Ages and stages questionnaires: A parent-completed child monitoring system*. (2nd ed.). Baltimore, MD: Brookes.

Brigance, A. H. (1991). *BRIGANCE inventory of early development-revised*. No. Billerica, MA: Curriculum Associates.

Brigance, A. H. (1998). *BRIGANCE preschool screen for three- and four-year-old children*. North Billerica, MA: Curriculum Associates.

Bronfenbrenner, U. (1977). Toward an experimental ecology of human development. *American Psychologist, 32*(7), 513–531.

Cohen, L. G., & Spenciner, L. J. (2003). *Assessment of children and youth with special needs*. Boston, MA: Allyn & Bacon.

Davis, M., Kilgo, J., & Gamel-McCormick, M. (1998). *Young children with special needs: A developmentally appropriate approach*. Boston, MA: Allyn & Bacon.

Diamond, K. E., & Squires, J. (1993). The role of parental report in the screening and assessment of young children. *Journal of Early Intervention, 17*, 107–115.

Division for Early Childhood (DEC) (2001). *Concept paper on Developmental Delay as an Eligibility Category*. Missoula, Montana: DEC Executive Office.

Dumars, D., Duran-Flores, D., & Foster, C., & Stills, S. (1987). Screening for developmental disabilities. In H. M. Wallace, R. F. Biehl, L. Taft, & A. C. Oglesby (Eds.). *Handicapped children and youth* (pp. 111–125). New York: Human Science Press.

Foley, G. (1990). Portrait of the arena evaluation: Assessment in the transdisciplinary approach. In E. Gibbs & D. Teti (Eds.), *Interdisciplinary assessment of infants: A guide for early intervention*. Baltimore, MD: Brookes.

Frankenburg, W. K., & Dodds, J. B. (1990). *Denver II screening manual*. Denver, CO: Denver Developmental Materials.

Greenspan, S., & Meisels, S. (1994). Toward a new vision for the developmental assessment of infants and young children. *Zero to Three, 14*(6), 1–8.

Greenspan, S., & Meisels, S. (1996). Toward a new vision for the developmental assessment of infants and young children. In S. Meisels & E. Fenichel (Eds.), *New visions for the developmental assessment of infants and young children.* (pp. 27–52). Washington, DC: National Center for Infants, Toddlers, and Families.

Hanson, M., & Lynch, E. (1995). *Early intervention: Implementing child and family services for infants and toddlers who are at risk* (2nd ed.). Austin, TX: PRO-ED.

Harrison, P. L., Kaufman, A. S., Kaufman, N. L., Bruininks, R. H., Rynders, J., Ilmer, S., Sparrow, W. W. & Cicchetti, D. V. (1990). *AGS early screening profiles.* Circle Pines, MN: American Guidance Service.

Henderson, L., & Meisels, S. (1994). Parental involvement in the developmental screening of their young children: A multiple-source perspective. *Journal of Early Intervention, 18*(2), 141–154.

Kilgo, J., & Raver, S. (1999). Family-professional collaboration. In S. Raver (Ed.) *Transdisciplinary early intervention.* New York, NY: McMillan.

Kjerland, L., & Kovach, J. (1990). Family-staff collaboration for tailored infant assessment. In E. Gibbs & D. Teti (Eds.), *Interdisciplinary assessment of infants: A guide for early intervention professionals.* Baltimore, MD: Brookes.

Lifter, K., & Bloom, L. (1998). Internationality and the role of play in the transition to language. In S. F. Warren & J. Reichle (Series Eds.) & A. M. Weatheby, S. F. Warren, & J. Reichle (Vol. Eds.). *Communication and language intervention series: Vol. 6. Transiting in prelinguistic communication* (pp. 161–195). Baltimore: Brookes.

Linder, T. W. (1993). *Transdisciplinary play-based assessment: A functional approach to working with young children* (rev. ed.). Baltimore, MD: Brookes.

Losardo, A., & Notari-Syverson, A. (2001). *Alternative approaches to assessing young children.* Baltimore, MD: Brookes.

Lynch, E., & Hanson, M. (2004). *Developing cross-cultural competence: A guide for working with children and their families.* Baltimore: Brookes Publishing Company.

Mardell-Czudnowski, C., & Goldenberg, D. (1998). *Developmental indicators for the assessment of learning-revised (DIAL-3).* Circle Pines, MN: American Guidance Service.

McCormick, K., McLean, M., Danaher, J., Kilgo, J., & Schakel, J. (2000). *Developmental delay as an eligibility category.* Concept Paper of the Division for Early Childhood (DEC) of the Council for Exceptional Children (CEC).

McGonigel, M., Woodruff, G., & Roszmann-Millican, M. (1994). The transdisciplinary team: A model for family-centered early intervention. In L. J. Johnson, R. J. Gallagher, M. J. LaMontagne, J. B. Jordan, J. J. Gallagher, P. L. Hutinger, & M. B. Karnes (Eds.). *Meeting early intervention challenges, issues, from birth to three.* (2nd Ed.), Baltimore, MD: Brookes.

McLean, M., Bailey, D., & Wolery, M. (2003). *Assessing infants and preschoolers with special needs.* Columbus, OH: Merrill.

McLean, M., & McCormick, K. (1993). Assessment and evaluation in early intervention. In W. Brown, S. K. Thurman, & L. F. Pearl (Eds.), *Family-centered early intervention with infants and toddlers: Innovative cross-disciplinary approaches* (pp. 43–79). Baltimore: Brookes.

McLean, M., & Odom, S. (1993). Practices for young children with and without disabilities: A comparison of DEC and NAEYC identified practices. *Topics in Early Childhood Special Education, 13*(3), 274–292.

Meisels, S. (1985). A functional analysis of the evolution of public policy for handicapped young children. *Educational Evaluation and Policy Analysis, 7,* 115–126.

Meisels, S. (1996). Charting the continuum of assessment and intervention: Toward a new vision for the developmental assessment of infants and young children. In S. Meisels & E. Fenichel (Eds.), *New visions for the developmental assessment of infants and young children* (pp. 11–26). Washington, DC: National Center for Infants, Toddlers, and Families.

Meisels, S., & Provence, S. (1989). *Screening and assessment: Guidelines for identifying young disabled and developmentally vulnerable children and their families.* Washington, DC: National Center for Clinical Infant Programs.

Meisels, S. J., Marsden, D. B., Wiske, M. S., & Henderson, L. W. (1997). *Early screening inventory-revised (ESI-R).* Ann Arbor, MI: Rebus.

Miller, L. J. (1993). First STEP. *Screening test for evaluating preschoolers.* San Antonio, TX: The Psychological Corporation, Harcourt Brace.

Neisworth, J., & Bagnato, S. (1992). The case against intelligence testing in early intervention. *Topics in Early Childhood Special Education, 12*(1), 1–20.

Neisworth, J., & Bagnato, S. (1996). Assessment for early intervention: Emerging themes and practices. In S. Odom & M. McLean (Eds.). *Early intervention/early childhood special education: Recommended practices.* (pp. 23–58). Austin, TX: PRO-ED.

Neisworth, J., & Bagnato, S. (2000). Recommended practices in assessment. In S. Sandall, M. McLean, & B. Smith (2000). *DEC Recommended practices for early intervention/early childhood special education.* p. 17–27. Longmont, CO: Sopris West.

Newborg, J., Stock, J., Wnek, L., Guidubaldi, J., & Svinicki, J. (1988). *Battelle developmental inventory.* Allen, TX: Developmental Learning Materials.

Puckett, M., & Black, J. (1994). *Authentic assessment of the young child: Celebrating development and learning.* New York: Merrill.

Richard, N., & Schiefelbusch, R. (1991). Assessment. In L. McCormick & R. Schiefelbusch (Eds.), *Early language intervention.* Columbus, OH: Merrill.

Sandall, S., McLean, M. E., & Smith, B. J. (2000). *DEC Recommended practices for early intervention/early childhood special education.* Longmont, CO: Sopris West.

Voress, J. K., & Maddox, T. (1998). *Developmental assessment of young children* (DAYC). Austin, TX: PRO-ED.

Winton, P., & Bailey, D. (1988). The family-focused interview: A mechanism for collaborative goal-setting with families. *Journal of the Division for Early Childhood, 12,* 195–207.

Winton, P., & Bailey, D. (1993). Communicating with families: Examining practices and facilitating change. In J. Paul & R. Simeonsson (Eds.), *Understanding and working with parents of children with special needs* (2nd ed.) New York: Holt, Rinehart, & Winston.

Woods, J., & McCormick, K. (2002). Toward an integration of child and family centered practices in the assessment of preschool children: Welcoming the family. *Young Exceptional Children, 5*(3), pp. 2–11.

Wright, A., & Treton, H. (1995). Child-development days: A new approach to screening for early intervention. *Journal of Early Intervention, 19,* 253–263.

CHAPTER 5

Assessment for Program Planning, Progress Monitoring, and Evaluation

Learning Outcomes

After reading this chapter, you will be able to:

- Differentiate between assessment for determining eligibility and assessment for program planning in early intervention/early childhood special education (EI/ECSE).
- Explain the importance of family preferences being emphasized in the EI/ECSE program planning process.
- Describe four methods that can be used to collect assessment information.
- Identify the steps in an ecological assessment process.
- Explain the levels of an overall evaluation plan for EI/ECSE programs.
- Differentiate between the purposes of formative and summative evaluation.

Assessment in early intervention/early childhood special education (EI/ECSE) is an ongoing process. McCormick (1997) noted "assessment, planning, intervention, and evaluation are overlapping activities" (p. 223). According to Bricker (1993):

> Assessment refers to the process of establishing a baseline or entry-level measurement of the child's skills and desired family outcomes. The assessment process should produce the necessary information to select appropriate and relevant intervention goals and objectives. Intervention refers to the process of arranging the physical and social environment to produce the desired growth and development specified in the formulated intervention plan for the child and family. Evaluation refers to the process of comparing the child's performance on selected intervention goals and objectives before and after intervention, and comparing the family's progress toward established family outcomes (p. 12).

In the previous chapter, initial assessments that are conducted for the purposes of screening, diagnosis, and eligibility were described. Two additional reasons to conduct assessments include (a) program planning and (b) progress monitoring and evaluation. These two components of assessment are the focus of this chapter.

Assessment for Program Planning

In order to plan efficient, effective programs and interventions for young children with delays or disabilities, appropriate **program planning assessment** must occur. Assessment conducted for the purpose of program planning must be a continuous process that focuses on each child's skill level, needs, background, experiences, and interests, as well as the family's preferences and priorities. Ongoing assessment provides the basis for constructing and maintaining individualized programs for young children with disabilities.

As discussed in the preceding chapter, the initial assessment procedures used to determine eligibility are distinctly different from the assessment procedures necessary for program planning. Table 5–1 illustrates the major ways in which these two types of assessments differ.

Recommended practice in EI/ECSE recognizes the importance of the link between assessment and curriculum in order to insure that program content is meeting the needs of the child and the concerns of the family (Bagnato et al., 1997; Neisworth & Bagnato, 2000). In recent years, formal assessments have been found to be inappropriate for program planning, resulting in a shift away from the use of formal assessment measures toward the use of informal means of assessment, such as curriculum- or criterion-based instruments, observations, family

Table 5–1   Comparison of Assessment for Eligibility and Programming Decisions

Assessment for Eligibility	Assessment for Program Planning
Compares a single child to a large group of children.	Identifies the child's current levels of developmental skills behaviors, and knowledge.
Uses instruments, observations, and checklists with predetermined items or skills.	Determines the skills and behaviors necessary for a child to function in the settings where he or she spends time.
Determines if a child's skills or behaviors fall below a specified cut-off level.	Determines those skills, behaviors, and knowledge that the child's family and primary caregivers have set as priorities for the child to learn.
Designed to differentiate children from one another.	Designed to determine the individual child's strengths and learning style.
Assessment instrument items do not necessarily have significance in the everyday lives of young children.	Assessment instrument items are usually criterion based or focus on functional skills that may have importance in the everyday lives of young children.

SOURCE: From Davis, M. D., Kilgo, J. K., and Gamel-McCormick, M., *Young children with special needs: A developmentally appropriate approach.* Copyright © 1998 by Allyn & Bacon. Reprinted/adapted by permission.

reports, and play-based measures. Each of these methods will be discussed later in this chapter. Assessment procedures that are appropriate for determining a child's eligibility for services (standardized, norm-referenced instruments) should not be used in isolation and should not be used to plan instructional programs or interventions for young children with disabilities (Neisworth & Bagnato, 1996, 2000).

Assessment for program planning purposes must focus on the whole child within the context of his or her natural environment(s) (such as home, school, child care setting, community in which he or she lives, etc.) in order to make an accurate appraisal of the child's strengths and needs. Collecting information of this nature is critical to designing individualized programs and planning appropriate interventions and supports for young children and their families.

Purpose of Assessment for Program Planning

The purpose of program planning assessment is to answer a number of questions related to the child's abilities, the desired child and family outcomes, the

Assessment is a process requiring a collaborative effort between families and professionals that occurs on an ongoing basis.

types of services to be provided, and the intervention strategies to be used. Table 5–2 describes the potential questions, purposes, and procedures associated with program planning assessment. Figure 5–1 provides a schematic of a linked assessment, goal/outcome development, intervention, and evaluation approach to early intervention/ early childhood spe-

Table 5-2   Program Planning: Assessment Questions, Purposes, and Procedures

Assessment Questions	Purposes	Possible Procedures
What type of EI/ECSE and/or related services should be provided?	To plan the child's program	Family-directed assessment
At what location(s) should the child and family receive services?	To determine family concerns, priorities, and resources	Norm-referenced instruments
What environmental modifications and adaptations should be made?	To determine the locations and type of service(s) to be received	Curriculum-based assessments
What factors impede learning; what strategies, interventions, and supports should be included?	To assess the physical, learning, and social environments	Criterion-referenced assessments
		Observations
	To understand the child's knowledge or skill level	Probes
What is the child's knowledge or skill level?	To determine where intervention or instruction should begin	Interviews
What are the family's concerns, priorities, and resources?		Checklists
		Parent-professional (team) meetings or conferences
Where should intervention or instruction begin?		Parent report
		Review of developmental history

Adapted from: Cohen, Libby G., & L. J. Spenciner (2003), *Assessment of young children*, White Plains, NY: Longman.

cial education with collaborative professional and family participation in the process.

Assessment information collected for program planning purposes is used to develop an Individualized Family Service Plan (IFSP) or Individualized Education Program (IEP) for each child and family. Recall from Chapter 1 that the IFSP and IEP are intended to be planning documents used to shape and guide the day-to-day provision of services to young children with developmental delays or disabilities. The IFSP is required for the provision of early intervention services for eligible infants and toddlers, ages birth to three, and their families. The IEP is used for special education services delivered to eligible children ages three and older. IFSPs and IEPs contain individualized outcomes and goals that can be determined by conducting an inventory of the skills needed by the child to participate in a variety of natural environments as just described. This process, an ecological inventory, allows information to be gathered that has relevance to each child and family. When this method is used, the IFSP or IEP should be developed according to the family's routines (at home and other environments) and priorities. Thus, goals and objectives contained in the IEP or IFSP should be developed to reflect the necessary skills the child will need to participate in natural environments and routines within those environments (Noonan & McCormick, 1993).

When conducting assessments for the purpose of program or intervention planning for young children with disabilities, Bailey and Wolery (1992) suggest that the following goals be accomplished:

1. the identification of developmentally appropriate and functional goals;

2. the identification of the unique styles, strengths, and coping strategies of each child;

3. the identification of parents' goals or outcomes for their children and their needs or priorities for themselves;

4. the formation and reinforcement of families' sense of competence and worth;

5. the development of a shared and integrated perspective across professionals and among

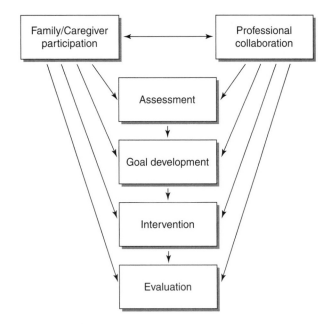

Figure 5-1 A Linked Assessment, Goal Development, Intervention, and Evaluation Approach to Early Intervention/Education with Collaborative Professional and Family Participation

SOURCE: Bricker, D. (2002). *Assessment, evaluation, and programming system for children* (Volume 1). Baltimore: Paul H. Brookes, p. 19.

professionals and family members regarding the child's and family's needs and resources; and

6. the creation of a shared commitment to the collaboratively established intervention goals. (pp. 97–99)

Through the accomplishment of these goals, the team members (family, teachers, therapists and other professionals) should be provided with the information necessary to make program planning decisions regarding the activities and strategies to meet the unique goals or outcomes of individual children and families.

Family Involvement in the Assessment Process

It has long been recognized that parents and other family members can provide a wealth of information about the child, as well as information about the family as a whole. Although addressing family concerns, priorities, and resources is not a new concept in EI/ECSE, it has received increased attention in recent years due to the emphasis on IFSPs for families with children under age three and an increased emphasis on family-based practices in all aspects of services for young children with special needs ages three through eight. Thus, it is most important that family members be encouraged to become active members of the assessment team. If family members are willing and able to play an active role in the assessment process, their involvement will ensure the validity of the established goals and outcomes. An approach that has been used to help make certain that the family has input into the assessment process is referred to as "top-down" or "outcome-driven" assessment (Campbell, 1991). This model suggests using family-identified outcomes for the child as the starting point of the assessment. In other words, in this model, the family's vision for their child becomes the central focus of the assessment process. At what level would the family like to see their child functioning in terms of skills and abilities (in the next six months, year, three years)? What are their priorities? For example, one family's top priority might be for their child to be able to communicate and feed herself, while another family might want their child to be toilet trained and develop friendships with peers. In what environments would they like their child to be able to participate? For example, would they like their child to be in an inclusive preschool or kindergarten program?

Gathering assessment information from families must occur on an ongoing basis, must be an integral part of the planning process, and should be a collaborative effort. Before family information is gathered, however, it is essential that families be assured that the assessment process will maintain their privacy and integrity. Families deserve respect, confidentiality, the recognition that they have unique needs, interests, and beliefs, and that they are integral members of the team. An effective early childhood professional recognizes the uniqueness of each family and realizes the importance of families having opportunities to provide input into the assessment process.

A family-based approach suggests that families participate in the assessment process according to what they feel is appropriate for them. Regardless of the degree to which a family chooses to participate in the assessment process, the manner in which they participate, or the format for providing information, the families' participation and the information they can provide serve an invaluable purpose in program planning. According to Turnbull and Turnbull (1997), families should be offered options for participating in the assessment process. Some of the areas in which families can provide input include the following:

- Collaborate with professionals in planning the assessment process (where, when, and how it will take place, who will be involved).
- Determine to what extent they want to be a part of the assessment process.
- Determine on which domains and skills to focus during the assessment,
- Provide information about their child's developmental history, play and interaction preferences, and daily routines and schedule.
- Provide information about the settings where their child spends time and the demands placed upon their child in those settings.
- Report on their child's current skills, where and how those skills are used by the child, and under what circumstances the skills are exhibited.
- Report on their child's strengths, abilities, and needs.
- Emphasize their child's skills in multiple settings.
- Provide a perspective as to the importance of a child's performance results on an assessment instrument in comparison to their everyday skills.
- Share information about their child that would not be gained through traditional measures.
- Share their vision for their child's future.
- Collaborate with professionals in constructing authentic assessments.
- Share their priorities, resources, and concerns, particularly during infant and toddler assessments.

Some potential areas in which information can be gathered from families include their need for support, information, education, services, etc. Information can be collected from families in a variety of ways—through parent interviews, observational methods, parent reports, instruments, checklists, etc. Each family's preferences must be considered before information is gathered. Summers et al. (1990) suggest using an ongoing conversational approach with families in lieu of formal family interviewing. A "Conversation Guide," developed by Turnbull and Turnbull (2001), can be used to promote relaxed and natural conversation with families. Some families may prefer providing information through a written format, such as a family needs questionnaire or checklist. Informal tools (as opposed to norm-referenced, standardized tools) are preferred in most instances. Examples of such measures are recommended in the *Guidelines and Recommended Practices for the Individualized Family Service Plan* (NECTAS & the Association for the Care of Children's Health, 1991) and *Practical Strategies for Family-Centered Early Intervention* (McWilliam, Winton, & Crais, 1996). In addition, the CLAS Early Childhood Research Institute Website *(http://clas.uiuc.edu)* offers some guidelines to consider when selecting family information gathering tools or methods (Banks, Santos, & Roof, 2003).

Along with the different instruments available to identify family concerns, priorities, and resources, some EI/ECSE programs have developed their own measures. Regardless of the measures used, families should be encouraged to identify their own concerns and resources and determine their own priorities for their child and the family as a whole. Professionals should realize that the range of concerns families may have is considerable. Families of young children with known or suspected disabilities often feel overwhelmed and unsure of where to begin. Professionals can provide information to help them sort out their concerns and make decisions about their priorities. It is likely, however, that their concerns and priorities will change over time. Examples of possible family concerns include how their child's medical needs can be met or how their child will be treated when he or she begins preschool. Examples of family priorities could be how to learn more about their child's disability or how to communicate with their child. Family resources might include reliable transportation, relatives who live nearby, and community support. The belief behind family information gathering is that with the right kind of resources matched to each family's concerns and priorities, families can support the development of children with special needs (Kilgo & Raver, 1999).

Ecological Assessment

As we have emphasized in the preceeding chapters, assessment information is not very useful when little or no emphasis is placed on the context in which children develop and the influence the environment has on skill acquisition. In order to assess a child's skills for the purpose of program planning, it is essential that the environment(s) in which a child functions and the skills needed to be successful in those environments are considered during the assessment process. Thus, **ecological assessments** are increasingly being used to replace traditional assessment practices when planning interventions for young children with disabilities. An ecological assessment provides for functional goals and objectives to be generated within the natural environment. McCormick (1997) emphasizes the twofold purpose of an ecological assessment:

1. To generate information about the social, educational, and functional activities and routines in natural environments where the child wants and needs to be an active and successful participant; and

2. to determine what resources and supports the child will need to participate in and receive maximum benefits from activities and routines in the classroom and other environments. (p. 237)

Bronfenbrenner's (1979) theory of human ecology stresses that the interconnections between environments (e.g. the connection between home and school) influence what actually takes place within an environment (e.g. a child's learning in school). Figure 5–2 shows that the focus of assessment should

be on a child's skills and abilities within the context of his environments.

As discussed in the previous chapter, children's skills do not develop and are not displayed in isolation. Instead, each child's development is strongly influenced by the demands or expectations that are placed on him or her within their environment. Some environments require advanced gross motor skills, while others call for strong social or communication skills. There are some very important aspects of a child's environment that must be considered in program planning: (a) the expectations of the family or primary caregivers, (b) the cultural parameters, and (c) the expected level of participation due to the child's age and disability. The demands placed upon children by these contextual aspects of the environment can have a tremendous influence on their development and the skills or behaviors they display. For example, if T. J. lives in a neighborhood in which all of the children learn to ride bicycles at an early age, then he might be motivated to learn to ride his bike at a young age. Or if a family lives in a warm climate and goes to the beach or pool on a frequent basis as a family activity, then the children may be likely to learn to swim or participate in water sports at an early age.

An ecological assessment considers the skills needed by an individual child in order to participate in his or her environment throughout the day. The specific environments, expectations, and levels of participation are defined by the child, his or her family and other primary caregivers, the community, and the family's culture. This type of assessment is distinctly different from the type of traditional child assessment in which the child's skills are observed and recorded based on his or her skill level. The product of an ecological assessment is not the skill level at which a child is functioning. Instead, the end result of an ecological assessment is a greater understanding of the context and expectations that are important for the child. For example, when conducting an ecological assessment of T. J. at a Head Start center, the observer notices that there are several times in which the children are required to make transitions from one activity to another during the morning routine. The teacher expects the children

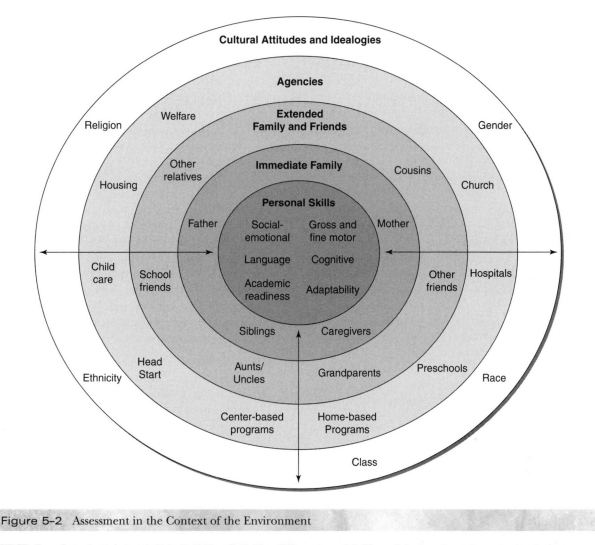

Cultural Attitudes and Idealogies

Agencies

**Extended
Family and Friends**

Immediate Family

Personal Skills

Religion

Welfare

Gender

Other
relatives

Cousins

Housing

Church

Father

Social-
emotional

Gross and
fine motor

Mother

Child
care

School
friends

Language

Cognitive

Other
friends

Hospitals

Academic
readiness

Adaptability

Siblings

Caregivers

Head
Start

Aunts/
Uncles

Grandparents

Preschools

Ethnicity

Race

Center-based
programs

Home-based
Programs

Class

Figure 5-2   Assessment in the Context of the Environment

SOURCE: From Introduction (pp. 1–8) by E. V. Nuttall, K. Nuttall-Vazquoz, and A. Hempel, in *Assessing and screening preschoolers: Psychological and educational dimensions.* E. Vazquoz Nuttall, I. Romero, and J. Kalesnik (Eds.). 1999. Needham Heights, MA: Allyn & Bacon.

to be able to make the transition (or move) from one activity to another when prompted. These transitions are an important part of this particular environment. The purpose of this observation is not to determine whether or not T. J. has the ability to make these transitions, but the fact that the transitions take place within the environment in which he will be participating. With this information, the team conducting

the assessment will know to focus on T. J.'s ability to make transitions like the ones that occur in his early childhood program.

The contexts, conditions, and expectations identified through an ecological assessment assist the team members in identifying those skills that should be examined during the assessment process. Furthermore, the ecological assessment allows the assessment team to determine the skills necessary for the child to be successful in his current settings. In other words, the result of the ecological assessment is a **protocol,** or assessment format, that can be followed to decide the skill areas on which to focus and the specific skills to be observed during the assessment.

An ecological assessment regards the family members and other primary caregivers as being critical to the assessment process. Family members and caregivers may include parents, siblings, grandparents, other relatives, child care providers, babysitters, or other significant people in a child's life, such as neighbors. These individuals, in addition to professionals such as teachers, occupational therapists, physical therapists, speech-language pathologists, and others, will determine which of the individual child's skills are important to focus on during the assessment. Conducting ecological assessments of children within their natural environments requires a step-by-step approach. By assessing the environments in which children live and the expectations associated with those environments, the skills to be targeted can be better determined. Program planning can logically grow from the assessment information that is collected. What follows is a step-by-step process for conducting an ecological assessment.

Step 1. *The ecological process begins by determining the child's important environment(s).* For most children, there will be at least two important settings: the child's home and a child care or school setting. For many children, there may be one or more additional environments that are important to them (for example, a child care facility, a classroom setting, a neighborhood play group, a grandparent's or other relative's house, or a babysitter's house). Any place that the child spends significant amounts of time are important environments. These important environments can be determined by asking the child's parents and/or care providers to identify the child's daily and weekly experiences.

Step 2. *The child's routine within each of the important environments is then determined.* The primary caregiver(s) (either parent, teacher,

babysitter or others) in each environment can be asked to identify the child's routine within that environment. For example, at home Maria's mother, father, or grandparents can be asked to describe her morning routine, which might include awakening, eating breakfast, bathing, getting dressed, and playing with toys or reading books. Sometimes another primary caregiver, such as a teacher or babysitter, will describe the routines that take place in different environments. In most cases, it is usually best to talk with the person(s) directly responsible for the child's activities in that environment. A parent may know the general schedule or routine at the child care center, but the teacher or child care provider will probably have more specific information about the child's routine. When possible, it is best to gather information directly from the person(s) most responsible for the child in the particular environment.

Step 3. *The skills that are important for the child to possess in each environment should be determined by the family.* As we have emphasized throughout this text, the family has the greatest influence on a young child's development. The family often will have specific preferences and beliefs about what skills are most important in various environments. For example, a family with an active social life may feel that the ability to greet and interact with other children is more important than preacademic skills because of its value regarding social interaction. Or a family that is involved in athletics may place more importance on gross motor skill development than social skill development.

It is important to remember that in some cases, parents, care providers, and professionals may identify different skills as being most important for a child to develop in specific environments. For example, the parents may identify the need for their child to learn to feed himself, dress himself, and be toilet trained as soon as possible. A teacher may identify important skills needed in the classroom environment, such as the child being able to independently choose an activity or to put away his or her belongings. A child care provider may identify the ability to share with other children or to wait for his or her turn as important skills for a child to possess in a child care situation.

Step 4. *All identified skills can be prioritized in terms of the importance of the skills.* After a complete list is compiled of the skills identified as being important to the child in all environments, the family can be asked to prioritize the importance of each of the skills with input from other team members when appropriate. The skills that are important across all or many environments often become the top priorities.

Step 5. *The list of identified skills can then be given to the assessment team members.* The list of skills generated should be communicated to all team members, including the family, who will be participating in the assessment process. This information will allow the assessment team members to know what the most important skills are for this child within his natural environment(s) and will help the team to focus on the child's ability to perform these skills.

Assessment information must be collected within the child's natural environment in order to determine the necessary skills.

The list of skills generated by this process will be those skills that are important for the child to have in all of the settings in which he currently participates. This list can serve as a map that can guide the child's individual assessment. Depending upon which skills are identified, decisions can be made regarding (a) where the child's assessment should take place; (b) over what period of time the assessment should take place; (c) what assessment instruments should be used; (d) what materials should be included; and (e) which disciplines should be involved in the assessment. Each of these questions will be discussed in the section that follows.

Where should the child's assessment take place? The best place to determine if a child has a **functional skill** is in the environment(s) where he or she uses that skill. A functional skill is a basic skill that is required on a frequent basis (such as eating, toileting, requesting assistance, turn taking, etc.) in the natural environment. Conducting an ecological assessment will help members of the assessment team in determining the location of the assessment. For example, if eating independently during meal time is an important skill for a particular child, the assessment team will know to conduct some portion of the assessment during a meal, either at home, school or another setting.

When should the assessment take place? Certain skills need to be assessed over time and/or in a number of different settings. If it has been determined that a child's ability to initiate interactions is important, the team may want to conduct some portion of the assessment at the beginning of the school day to see how the child greets other children and adults. The ecological assessment process should provide the team members with the information they need to determine the time of day or the portion(s) of a child's routine in which they need to assess the skills that are important to functioning well in specific environments.

What assessment instrument(s) should be used? Depending on which skills are identified as important to the family and service providers, some assessment instruments will be more useful than others. As a general rule, criterion-based or curriculum-based assessment instruments will provide clear, specific criteria by which the evaluators can determine whether

Conducting observations of children's skills and behavior can provide useful information for program planning.

or not the child possesses a skill. In addition, teacher-made tests or checklists and play-based assessment instruments are often used.

What assessment materials or activities should be used? Children will have clear preferences for certain materials and activities based on their experiences. The ecological assessment will help the assessment team members to determine which materials and activities may be best to use during the assessment process.

Which discipline representatives should be included on the assessment team? The list of skills generated through the ecological assessment process will assist in determining which professionals from specific disciplines should be involved. If the list of skills includes initiating conversations and communicating wants and needs, a speech/language pathologist would be a crucial team member. If pulling to a stand and walking are identified as important skills, a physical therapist would be important to include. At all times, on all teams, family members should be included to the greatest extent possible. Because family members will have extensive information about their child across many of the environments, their input will be very important.

An ecological assessment approach usually will result in a more precise child assessment. The assessment team will know what skills on which to focus, what materials or activities the child prefers, and which setting(s) in which to conduct the assessment. The end result of a thorough, ecological assessment is a road map for the program planning phase of the assessment process. The outcome of an ecological assessment can be seen in Table 5–3.

Methods and Procedures for Collecting Information

As described previously, the *DEC Recommended Practice Guidelines* (Sandall, McLean, & Smith, 2000) suggest standards to address when gathering useful information for planning intervention. As emphasized throughout this document, the whole child should be considered when planning programs for young children with disabilities rather than segmenting their abilities in the various of developmental areas.

Table 5–3   Ecological Assessment of Walking from the Bus to the Classroom

Name: Jimmy **Environment: School, home, community**
Activity: Walking **Subenvironment: From bus to classroom**

Tests Required	Jimmy	Steps Can Acquire	Steps May Not Acquire	Compensatory Strategies	Objectives for Intervention
1. Walk down bus steps	Can bear weight as he is lifted down each step, cannot go down steps independently.	Go down steps independently	Going down steps reciprocally	None	Yes—going down bus steps
2. Walk from bottom of bus steps to the two steps of the school entrance	Can grasp walker and walk to steps.	Walk faster and without falling	Walking without walker	Will use a walker, which the bus driver will put at the bottom of the bus steps, evaluate whether or not another type of walker would be more helpful	Yes—walking faster and without falling
3. Walk up the two steps	Steps are wide and deep enough for the walker, he can put walker up on the first step, but cannot stand up.	Walk up steps with a walker	Walk up without walker	No change	Yes—walk up steps with walker
4. Walk from the top of the steps to the door	Can do this, but loses balance occasionally and is slow.	Walk faster and without falling	Walk without walker	No change	Yes—see 2 above
5. Open the door of the school and go in	Cannot open or hold door to go through if it is opened for him, lacks needed strength, coordination, and balance.	May be able to learn to open the door and walk through	Walk without walker	Team may need to request installation of automatic door	Yes—opening door and walking through
6. Walk from inside the door to the classroom (50 feet)	Can only walk about 15 feet before tiring and losing balance. With assistance can walk about 25 feet.	Walk faster and walk without falling from the door to the classroom		No change	Yes—see 2 above

In Maria's case, for example, she has a diagnosis of Down Syndrome with delays in several developmental domains (communication, self-care, and cognitive skills). In order to meet her multiple needs, program planning assessment should address all areas of development, which must function together to perform most tasks. As we all know, most activities or tasks require the combined use of several different skill areas. Thus, in order for program planning assessments to focus on the whole child, a variety of measures (such as criterion- and curriculum-referenced tools, observations, interviews) should be used in a variety of settings (home, child care, school, playground, etc.). Using arena assessment format (as described in the previous chapter) provides optimal opportunities for families and professionals to cooperatively plan intervention goals from the same perspective using an appropriate assessment instrument whose purpose is to link assessment with intervention. The types of measures that are most often used are criterion- or curriculum-referenced assessments.

Criterion-referenced instruments and **curriculum-referenced instruments** provide the team with useful information that can assist in program planning (Bagnato, Neisworth, & Munson, 1997; Neisworth & Bagnato, 2000). Children are assessed on various objectives and then evaluated on the achievement of the targeted objectives. On criterion-referenced measures, each individual child's performance is then compared to a predetermined standard or criteria, rather than to a norm group. The criteria used to determine if a child has acquired a skill is often a flexible criteria that can have different interpretations for different settings. On curriculum-referenced measures, each assessment item relates directly to a specific educational objective in the program's curriculum. Curriculum- and criterion-referenced measures provide a level of flexibility that is not available with standardized, norm-referenced instruments. Because the skills being assessed with these types of instruments are in-context, represent specific skills that have been determined by the child's family and other team members to be valuable to his or her development, and are generally listed in a developmental sequence, they often can be very useful in

program planning. On a cautionary note, however, it is important to remember that many criterion- and curriculum-referenced instruments are often drawn from items on standardized tests, thus decreasing their relevance to the child's unique needs and to the necessary program planning to meet those needs. Curriculum-referenced measures do allow team members to determine how important skills are within the context (environment) of their use.

One of the DEC recommended practices for assessment noted by Neisworth and Bagnato (2000) is that the EI/ECSE team use only those measures that have high treatment validity (i.e., that link assessment, individual program planning, and progress evaluation). In order to insure that the entire process is linked, the selection of appropriate instruments and measure are of critical importance. Criterion- or curriculum-based instruments are recommended for program planning and establishing a link between assessment and intervention. Bagnato and colleagues developed an excellent assessment resource describing this link for young children with disabilities (see Bagnato et al., 1997).

Table 5–4 contains a list of some curriculum- and criterion-referenced assessment instruments that are frequently used in early childhood special education. For each instrument included in the table, the following information is provided: (a) domains addressed, (b) age range covered, (c) theoretical base, (d) specific features, and (e) the publisher. As described previously, these tools can be useful in providing a strong, direct linkage between assessment and intervention in programs serving young children with disabilities.

An example of a widely-used curriculum-referenced instrument that provides a strong linkage to intervention planning and implementation is the *Assessment, Evaluation, and Programming System (AEPS)* (Bricker, 2002). This comprehensive instrument is designed to use observational techniques to obtain assessment information within the context of the natural environment. The *AEPS* and other curriculum-based measures usually are multi-domain instruments that subdivide major developmental milestones into smaller increments. For example, the *AEPS* (Bricker, 2002) subdivides fine motor skills into three strands: reach, grasp-and-release, and functional use of fine

Table 5-4 Early Childhood Assessment Instruments that Assist with Instructional Programming for Young Children with Disabilities

Instrument	Domains	Age Range	Theoretical Base	Important Features	Publisher
Assessment, Evaluation, and Programming System (AEPS) for Infants and Children (Bricker, 2003)	Cognitive, fine motor, gross motor, adaptive, social-communication, social	Birth to 36 months; 3 to 6 years	Developmental; functional	Criterion-referenced; easy transition to curriculum goals and objectives from assessment items; has periodic assessments of child's progress, sensitive tracking; activity-based, developmentally appropriate instruction; strong family involvement	Paul H. Brookes, Baltimore, MD
Battelle Developmental Inventory (BDI-2) (Newborg, 2004)	Personal-social adaptive, motor, communication, cognitive	Birth to 95 months	Developmental	Curriculum-referenced; merges norm-based and curriculum-based assessment; has adaptive features; requires family input	Riverside Publishing Co., Itasca, IL

Table 5–4 Early Childhood Assessment Instruments that Assist with Instructional Programming for Young Children with Disabilities *(continued)*

Instrument	Domains	Age Range	Theoretical Base	Important Features	Publisher
BRIGANCE Diagnostic Inventory of Early Development (Revised Ed.) (BDIED-R) (Brigance, 1991)	Preambulatory motor, gross motor, fine motor, self-help, speech and language, general knowledge and comprehension, social-emotional development, readiness, basic reading skills, manuscript writing, basic math	Birth to 7 years	Development	Criterion-referenced; is frequently used owing to ease of use; blends assessment with selection of objectives and evaluation of progress; appropriate only for children who are at-risk or have mild disabilities; lacks field validation with children with disabilities	Curriculum Associates, North Billerica, MA
Carolina Curriculum for Infants and Toddlers with Special Needs (2nd Edition) (Johnson-Martin, Jens, Altermeier, & Hacker, 1991)	Cognitive; fine motor; gross motor; social adaptation; communication; all domains have extensive subdomains	Birth to 2 years	Piagetian	Criterion-referenced; has an accompanying curriculum; ordinal in nature; very detailed cognitive development domain; family involvement; good data collection system; functional activities	Paul H. Brookes, Baltimore, MD

Table 5–4   Early Childhood Assessment Instruments that Assist with Instructional Programming for Young Children with Disabilities *(continued)*

Instrument	Domains	Age Range	Theoretical Base	Important Features	Publisher
Carolina Curriculum for Preschoolers with Special Needs (Johnson-Martin, Altermeier, & Hacker, 1990)	Cognitive; fine motor; gross motor; social adaptation; communication; all domains have extensive subdomains	2 to 5 years	Piagetian	Criterion-referenced; has an accompanying curriculum; detailed subdomain in the cognitive section; good data collection system; specifics on the impact of various disabilities, task analyses & alternative activities	Paul H. Brookes, Baltimore, MD
Developmental Programming for Infants and Young Children (Revised DPIYC) (Rogers & D'Eugenio, 1981)	Cognition; language; adapt; gross motor; fine-motor/perceptual; social/emotional	Birth to 36 months	Developmental	Criterion-referenced; has accompanying curriculum; parent activity suggestions also included	University of Michigan, Ann Arbor, MI
Developmental Programming for Infants and Young Children (Brown et al., 1981)	Perceptual/fine motor, cognition, language, social-emotional, adaptive, gross motor	3 to 6 years	Developmental	Criterion-referenced; focuses on parents for intervention program; provides short-term goals and suggested activities; designed especially for interdisciplinary teams; adaptations for various disabilities	University of Michigan, Ann Arbor, MI

Table 5–4   Early Childhood Assessment Instruments that Assist with Instructional Programming for Young Children with Disabilities (continued)

Instrument	Domains	Age Range	Theoretical Base	Important Features	Publisher
Hawaii Early Learning Profile (HELP) (Parks et al., 1994)	Cognitive; expressive language; gross motor; fine motor; social-motional and adaptive	Birth to 3 years	Developmental	Criterion-referenced; accompanying manual provides intervention suggestions	VORT Corporation, Palo Alto, CA
Hawaii Early Learning Profile (HELP) for Preschoolers (VORT, 1995)	Adaptive; motor; communication; social; and learning/cognitive; extensive subdomains	3 to 6 years	Developmental	Curriculum-based; accompanying manual provides activities for intervention	VORT Corporation, Palo Alto, CA
Infant-Preschool Play Assessment Scale (Flagler, 1996)	Cognitive, communication, sensorimotor, fine motor, gross motor, and social-emotional skills	Birth through 5 years	Developmental	Criterion-referenced	Chapel Hill Training-Outreach Project, Chapel Hill, NC
Infant-Toddler Developmental Assessment (IDA) (Provence, Erikson, Vater, & Palmeri, 1995)	Motor, language, cognitive adaptive, feelings, social adaptation personality	Birth to 42 months	Developmental	Facilitates integrated approach to assessment and decision making; provides link between assessment and intervention; ensures parent participation	Riverside Publishing Co., Itasca, IL

Table 5–4   Early Childhood Assessment Instruments that Assist with Instructional Programming for Young Children with Disabilities (continued)

Instrument	Domains	Age Range	Theoretical Base	Important Features	Publisher
Early Learning Accomplishment Profile (E-LAP) (Glover, Preminger & Sanford, 1995)	Fine motor, gross motor, language, self-help, social-emotional, cognition	Birth to 3 years	Developmental	Easy to use but some domains have fewer number of items; some items lack teachability; does not provide adaptations for special needs; encourages multidisciplinary use; includes supplemental materials and audiovisual aids	Chapel Hill Training-Outreach Project, Chapel Hill, NC
Learning Accomplishment Profile-Revised (LAP-R) (Glover, Preminger, Sanford, & Zelman, 1995)	Fine motor, gross motor, language, prewriting, self-help, personal-social, cognition	30 to 72 months	Developmental	(same as above)	Chapel Hill Training-Outreach Project, Chapel Hill, NC
Transdisciplinary Play-Based Assessment (Revised edition) (Linder, 1993)	Cognitive; sensorimotor; social-emotional; communication and language	Infancy to 6 years	Developmental	Framework for determining skills within the context of play; assists in interpreting the information observed during play sessions; very individualized; natural and functional	Paul H. Brookes, Baltimore, MD

motor skills. Each of the strands is further divided into goals and objectives that link the assessment process to the preparation of an educational plan that guides intervention.

The items on the *AEPS,* as is usually true with curriculum-based measures, follow a typical developmental progression. The curriculum activities that correspond to test items are designed to teach skills related to the identified needs of the individual child. For example, the *Carolina Curriculum* (Johnson-Martin, Lens, Attemeier, & Hacker, 1991) provides developmental markers for assessing young children across developmental domains. The *Carolina Curriculum* also provides suggestions for modifying test items for children with motor or sensory impairments. Another instrument, the *Hawaii Early Learning Profile (HELP),* provides developmental assessment and the *HELP at Home* provides curriculum activities and activity sheets for parents across the developmental domains (Parks et al., 1992).

Criterion- or curriculum-referenced tools represent one method of collecting information that can be used for program and intervention planning. Other methods include: informal, teacher-made checklists or tests; play-based measures; observations in the natural environment (home, classroom, playground, etc.); and interviews with the family or other primary care providers. Table 5–5 provides a description of the characteristics of program planning assessment and examples of the various types of information that can be gathered to plan programs for young children with disabilities.

In program planning for T. J., the team could use a criterion-referenced instrument to measure his abilities in cognitive, communication, and motor development. In addition, they could devise some situations in which the team determines how T. J. performs particular skills in the context of the natural environment(s), such as riding a tricycle or eating a meal. More than likely the team would also observe social interactions during a play situation with his peers.

Progress Monitoring and Program Evaluation

The final purpose of assessment to be discussed involves **progress monitoring** and **program evaluation.** As previously described, the efficacy of EI/ECSE has received much attention during recent years with the result being an increased awareness of the importance of ongoing progress monitoring and evaluation as it relates to the improvement and expansion of EI/ECSE programs.

A necessary component of any EI/ECSE program is a set of procedures for collecting and using data to monitor the effectiveness of program efforts (Sandall & Schwartz, 2002). A comprehensive evaluation plan in EI/ECSE programs should represent the scope of the most important features of intervention: the child, the family, and the program. Without this critical feedback regarding all of these interlocking components, EI/ECSE can never fully meet the individual needs of young children with disabilities and their families. Table 5–6 shows the questions, purposes, and procedures that are the focus of assessment conducted for program monitoring and evaluation.

In order to improve and expand EI/ECSE services, it has been suggested that evaluation in early childhood programs be multidimensional (Johnson & LaMontagne, 1994). For children enrolled in EI/ECSE programs, the measurement and outcome procedures should match the specific goals of the interventions for which they are designed. This usually includes information that reflects the children's attainment of goals stated on their IEPs or IFSPs. In addition, programs should measure the outcomes of various family variables such as family satisfaction, independent resource management, or the utilization of support networks. Last, the program should measure specific aspects of the overall program, such as whether the program meets recommended practice standards such as those

Table 5–5 Characteristics of Program Planning Assessment and Examples for T. J.

Characteristic	Description	Example
Assessment should include a variety of measures in a variety of settings.	The assessment procedures include the use of curriculum-referenced tests, teacher-devised and informal tests, direct observation in natural settings (e.g., home, classroom), and interviews with people who know the child best.	The teacher uses developmental scales to assess T. J.'s communication, motor, and cognitive development. She devises some testing situations to determine how he performs particular skills. She observes him during play sessions with other children to note his social interaction, play, and language skills. She observes him at lunch and in the bathroom to identify his self-care skills. She interviews his parents, former teachers, and therapists to secure additional information.
Assessment results should provide a detailed description of the child's functioning.	The results include a description of (a) the child's developmental skills across all relevant areas. (b) what the child can and cannot do, and (c) what factors influence the child's skills/abilities.	The teacher analyzes the results of her assessment activities, summarizes what T. J. can and cannot do in each area, and describes what factors appear to influence his performance (e.g., what toys he appears to like, which children he interacts with, what help he needs on different tasks, and what appears to motivate his behavior).
Assessment activities should involve the child's family.	The family should fulfill the following roles: receive information from professionals, observe the assessment activities, provide information about the child's development and needs, gather new information, and validate the assessment results.	The teacher plans the assessment with the family. She asks them about how T. J. performs different skills, how he spends his time, and what concerns and goals they have for him. She allows them to observe the testing. She asks them to gather information on some skills at home. She reviews the results with them and asks them to confirm, modify, and qualify, and—if necessary—refute the findings.
Assessment activities should be conducted by professionals from different disciplines.	Frequently, assessment from the following disciplines is needed; speech/language therapy, physical therapy, audiology, social work, health (e.g., nurses, physicians), psychology, nutrition, special education, and possibly others.	The teacher coordinates the assessment activities of the team. Because of T. J.'s communication delays, a speech/language pathologist assesses him. An audiologist assesses his hearing, a physical therapist and an occupational therapist assess his motor skills, and the special education teacher assists the kindergarten teacher in assessing his social and cognitives skills.
Assessment activities should result in a list of high-priority objectives.	Assessment activities will identify more skills than are possible to teach; therefore, those of most value are identified. All team members, including the family, are involved in this decision. Skills are selected to be focused on if they are useful to the child, have long-term benefits, and/or are important to the family.	After the results have been analyzed, the team (including the parents) meets to review the findings. They discuss which skills T. J. needs to learn, which ones will be most useful, which will result in long-term benefits and which are most important to his family. The most important skills are listed as goals on his individualized Educational Program (IEP).

SOURCE: Adapted from M. Wolery, P. Strain, and D. Bailey, Jr., Reaching Potentials of Children with Special Needs, in *Reaching Potentials: Appropriate Curriculum Assessment for Young Children* (Vol. 1). Edited by S. Bredekamp and T. Rosegrant, (Washington, DC: The National Association for the Education of Young Children, 1990), p. 100.

Table 5–6   Program Monitoring and Program Evaluation: Assessment Questions, Purposes, and Procedures

Assessment Questions	Purposes	Procedures
Once intervention or instruction begins, is the child making progress? Should the intervention or instruction be modified?	To monitor the child's program To understand the appropriate pace of intervention To understand what the child is capable of doing prior to and following intervention or instruction	Curriculum-based assessments Criterion-referenced assessments Observations Probes Interviews Checklists Parent-professional conferences Portfolios Journals
Has the child met the goals of the IFSP or IEP? Has the child made progress? Has the program been successful for the child and family? Does the child continue to need services? Has the program achieved its goals?	To determine whether the program was successful in meeting the child and family goals (IFSP) To determine if the program was successful in meeting the child's IFSP/IEP goals To determine if the child continues to need services To evaluate program effectiveness	Curriculum-based assessments Criterion-referenced assessments Observations Probes Interviews Checklists Questionnaires Parent-professional conferences Portfolios Journals Surveys

Adapted from: Cohen, Libby G., & L. J. Spenciner (2003). *Assessment of young children*, White Plains, NY: Longman.

jointly promulgated by the Division for Early Childhood (DEC) of the Council for Exceptional Children and the National Association for the Education of Young Children (NAEYC).

Bricker and Littman (1982) recommended an ongoing evaluation plan that encompasses an ongoing schedule of data collection. This schedule includes initial program planning assessments, daily and weekly monitoring of child acquisition of IFSP or IEP outcomes, family outcomes, quarterly evaluations of program effectiveness, and annual evaluation across all program participants. Ongoing examination of child outcomes provides the team with realistic feedback about child progress. In addition, systematic data-based evaluations hold professionals accountable not only to themselves but to the children and families they serve. All measures should be conducted on both a **formative evaluation** (during program operation) and a **summative evaluation** (at the completion of services) schedule.

Monitoring Child Progress and Outcomes

Collecting individual child-focused information can serve as a valuable monitoring tool to be used in updating the child's program and to provide input about program effectiveness. Data should be collected regularly and systematically and used in making educational decisions. Such data may be collected through direct observation of specific child behaviors; the use of developmental checklists; permanent product samples, such as videotapes or audiotapes; ongoing performance data collection; and family reporting.

Regardless of the methods used, it is critical for data to be linked to a child's goals and be used to adjust the intervention and program activities in accordance with changes in a child's development and progress made towards achieving the goals. According to Bricker and Littman (1982), child eval-

Assessment information is needed about how a child performs meaningful tasks, such as eating a meal and cleaning up afterwards.

portfolio assessment process. A portfolio is a type of authentic assessment that is a means to provide a comprehensive view of the child's performance across a variety of situations and environments. It recognizes that a person's behavior is influenced by a broad variety of contextual factors and that the assessment process must use several methods to obtain information from diverse sources on the child's behaviors across multiple environments. Although it may also include information on a child's performance in contrived situations (e.g., standardized tests), it is primarily an assessment that documents a child's functioning in authentic, meaningful tasks that are part of his/her daily routine.

No specific rules dictate a portfolio's appearance. A portfolio can be described simply as a container for carrying documents (LaBoskey, 2000). Examples of the types of containers that can be used are ring notebooks, file boxes, expandable file holders, pizza boxes (covered in contact paper), laser disks, or computer files. A portfolio should be well organized, however, so that relevant materials can be located with minimal effort. These collections are used as evidence to monitor the growth of the child's skills, behavior, knowledge, and even their interests,

uation serves the following distinct, yet complementary, functions:

1. It guides the development of individual programming.
2. It provides feedback about the success of individual programming.
3. It provides a system for determining the value of an intervention system designed to benefit groups of children.

There are many ways to collect data and record children's progress. Table 5–7 provides a description of some of the different methods or monitoring devices that can be used. Figures 5–3, 5–4, 5–5, and 5–6 show several different examples of the various processes that can be used to collect observational data regarding a child's progress including anecdotal recording, interval recording, and time sampling.

As discussed in Chapter 4, one way to keep a record of children's progress is through the use of a

Children's artwork can be collected systematically and used to document progress over time.

Table 5–7   Methods of Data Collection for Monitoring Child Progress and Outcomes

Monitoring Device or Method	Description of Data Collection Procedure
Developmental Checklists	Teacher uses a formal or informal developmental checklist to record child's continuous progress in mastering developmental milestones or skills and to track a child's progress in comparison with the age level at which most normally developing children acquire each skill. Some teacher-made checklists allow for recording the date on which the child attains each new skill, as well as some measure of the level of proficiency (or independence) with which the skill is performed (e.g., brushes teeth independently, with physical prompts, verbal prompts).
Behavior Rating Scales	Teacher rates child's behavior at regular intervals by means of a checklist or rating scale on which presence or absence of certain behaviors or skills is noted (either appropriate or inappropriate behaviors). A child's behavior may be rated on a dichotomous measure (yes-no), a continuum (always-frequently-sometimes-never), or a qualitative judgment (poor-acceptable-excellent). Rating scales help a teacher identify problematic behaviors, behavioral deficits where more experience should be given to improve skills, or good behaviors that should be given more attention and praise.
Permanent Product Samples	Teacher obtains samples of a child's work at regular intervals for qualitative comparisons with later products and to provide concrete examples of the child's progress over time (e.g., drawings of a person, writing of name or numbers, art work, sample worksheets on preacademic work). Audiotapes of a child's speech or videotapes of a child's skills. This method of data collection is especially useful in showing parents what the child can do and concrete evidence of progress.
Anecdotal Recording	Teacher makes notes on significant events concerning a child's behavior and activities or records observations of the child's physical or emotional state on a given day—which may be factual or an interpretive form of data. If information recorded is a teacher's subjective interpretation, this could be made clear in the written narrative. Anecdotal records may entail written notes on specific behaviors, including events that preceded and followed each behavior observed (e.g., what words a child uses during certain activities and in what situations a child engages in spontaneous verbalizations). Or anecdotal records may involve more lengthy written narratives describing the sequence of events when a child exhibits a certain behavior (e.g., temper tantrum, seizure, accident involving the child). Anecdotal records usually focus on the content or style of behavior or situations in which behavior occurs rather than its frequency or duration.
Collection of Ongoing Performance Data:	
• Frequency Data	Behavior is monitored in regard to the number of occurrences. Teacher takes a simple count of the number of discrete events of a particular behavior as it occurs during a given observation period (e.g., how many tantrums a child has in a day; how many times a child asks a question).
• Percentage Data	Behavior or skill learning is monitored in terms of the proportion of correct to incorrect responses. Teacher takes a count of the number of discrete events of a specific behavior against the number of opportunities the child has to perform the behavior (e.g., a child labels 12 objects correctly out of a total of 20 objects: $12/20 \times 100 = 60\%$).
• Rate Data	Behavior is monitored in regard to how fast a child performs a given skill. Teacher takes a count of the number of responses given in a specified, timed observation period (e.g., a child discriminates 3 red objects from other colored objects in 1 minute).

Table 5-7   Methods of Data Collection for Monitoring Child Progress and Outcomes *(continued)*

Monitoring Device or Method	Description of Data Collection Procedure
Collection of Ongoing Performance Data *(continued):*	
• Duration Data	Behavior is monitored in regard to how long it lasts. Teacher uses a stopwatch to measure the total amount of time a child engages in a specific appropriate or inappropriate behavior (e.g., how many minutes a child spends having a temper tantrum).
• Latency Data	Behavior is monitored in regard to the time that elapses before a child gives response. Teacher uses a stopwatch to measure how long it takes the child to begin a task after instructions are given (e.g., how many seconds the child takes to begin putting away toys after being told to do so).
• Interval Recording	Behavior is monitored in terms of whether defined behaviors occur or do not occur within specified time intervals. Teacher establishes a specific observation period and divides the session into a number of predetermined time intervals (e.g., 30-second intervals or 15-second intervals). Using a stopwatch, the teacher or a staff person observes the child and records the presence or absence of the behavior during each interval. At the end of the observation period, the number of intervals in which the behavior occurred is counted and divided by the total number of intervals observed to obtain a ratio of total intervals in which the child exhibited the specific behavior. Example: A child is observed to be engaged in cooperative play in 5 of 15 intervals observed when the child had the opportunity of exhibiting social behavior, 5 divided by 15 shows a rate of 33% of cooperative play.)
• Time Sampling	Behavior is monitored by observing a child at designated time intervals to note presence or absence of specified behaviors. Teacher predetermines the length of time between conservations (e.g., 5 minutes, 30 minutes, 1 hr.) And observations are taken exactly at the defined time intervals. At the end of the observation session, teacher counts the number of observations during which the child exhibited the behavior, dividing this court by the total number of observations to obtain a percentage measure.

From Peterson, N. (1987). *Early intervention for handicapped and at risk children.* Denver: Love Publishing Co. pp. 311–12.

attitudes, or personal reflections. The official definition of portfolios tend to vary; however, portfolios seem to share four essential characteristics. Portfolios are collections of children's work that are:

1. longitudinal in nature;
2. diverse in content;
3. collaborative in their selection and evaluation; and
4. place emphasis on strengths, development of skills, improvement, and personal reflections and expectations.

In addition, portfolios can serve as a record of teachers' and other team members' observations and comments about children's activities and behaviors; video or audiotapes of significant activities; checklists of skills (for example, vocabulary words used spontaneously); photographs of children's work or activities in which they have engaged; a wide selection of the child's work (such as art work, writing samples); summaries of teacher observations; anecdotal records of specific events; information shared by parents or family members; and any other evidence of children's skills and progress. The information and materials that are included in a portfolio can be selected by any member of the team (the teacher, therapists, paraprofessionals, family members, or even the child) (Grace & Shores, 1990). Depending

Child's name: *T.J.*   Date: *1/22*   Time: *9:20 a.m.*

Observer's Name: *J.K.*   Location: *Preschool Classroom*

Anecdote: **Comment:**

T.J. was playing with the small blocks. He was putting one block on top of another. He was having difficulty balancing the blocks on top of each other. He attempted to build a tower of 3 blocks. His teacher approached him and he turned away. Just then A.K., another child in the room, walked over to where T.J. was playing. T.J. picked up the blocks and started to take A.K.'s blocks. A.K. began to retrieve the blocks. Teacher noticed this incident and encouraged A.K. to move to another part of the room.

Need to find out why he was having difficulty balancing the blocks.

Why did T.J. turn away from his teacher?

Need to observe T.J. in other settings.

Figure 5-3 Example of Anecdotal Recording

Behavior	Child	Total	Percentage	Interval									
				1	2	3	4	5	6	7	8	9	10
Requests help	Maria	9	90%	X	X	X	X	X	X	X	X	X	0

Figure 5-4 An Interval Record Using One-Minute Intervals

Child's name: *T.J.*   Date: *3/19*   Time: *11:10*

Observer's Name: *J.K.*   Location: *Preschool Classroom*

Time	Observation	Comment:
11:10	Watching block building	
11:12	Watching A.K. color	Switches hands
11:14	Writing name	
11:16	Moves to block area	
11:18	Playing with blocks	
11:20	Playing with blocks	Switches from right hand to left, right again
11:22	Playing with blocks	

Figure 5-5 Time Sampling

Name: _Maria_____   Date:_2-17-04_____

Objective: _Maria will urinate when placed on potty_____

Key: D = dry   W = wet   V = vocalized
        P = placed on potty
        + = urinated in potty   -- = did not urinate in potty

Time	Monday	Tuesday	Wednesday	Thursday	Friday
8:00	D	D	D	D	D
8:30	W	W	P--	VP+	P+
9:00	D	D	W	D	D
9:30	D	D	D	D	D
10:00	D	VP--	D	D	D
10:30	VP--	D	D	VW	VP+
11:00	W	W	VP+	D	D
11:30	D	W	D	D	D

Figure 5–6   Time Sampling

on the specific purpose, the portfolio can be divided into different sections according to IFSP or IEP goals, types of documents (e.g., photographs, drawings, anecdotal notes, test results), developmental or curriculum areas, sources of information (e.g., teachers, specialists, family), or context (e.g., classroom, home, community). Table 5–8 provides guidelines for implementing a portfolio assessment process.

The information that is collected via the portfolio assessment process meets many of the criteria required in program planning and progress monitoring. That is, it is collected over time; it relies on multiple sources of information; it collects information from many different individuals about children's skills; and most importantly, it collects skill information in the setting where the child has demonstrated the skill. The information collected is used to document progress that is being made toward the accomplishment of each child's individual goals and objectives contained in the IEP or outcome statements on the IFSP.

Family Input

If collected properly, family input is invaluable in monitoring child and family status within the larger context of determining program effectiveness. As IFSPs and IEPs are implemented, information should be collected from families regarding the appropriateness of the goals and outcomes, the success of the plan in meeting the child's needs, and the family's concerns and priorities. The IFSP or IEP should be modified based on the feedback provided by the family or upon the family's request. In addition to families having opportunities to evaluate the effectiveness of the IFSP or IEP, they also should have multiple opportunities to provide input into the overall effectiveness of the early intervention program and the services they are receiving. Information can be collected regarding their perceptions of the program staff, the policies and procedures, the team process, etc. Table 5–9 is an example of a family scale that can be used to determine a family's satisfaction with the services and supports they have received.

Table 5–8   Guidelines for Implementing Portfolio Assessment

Start portfolios at the beginning of the year.
Caregivers and other team members should identify in advance the purpose for the portfolio, as well as expectations for children's work.
Children should be told the purpose of their portfolios.

Establish types of documentation for each goal and criteria for evaluating work.
Develop plan for when and how data will be collected and by whom.
Date all work promptly.
Determine who will evaluate the portfolio.
Identify ways to involve the child and the family in work selection and evaluation. If necessary, teach children the skills needed to participate in this process.

Portfolio contents should be representative of children's work, growth, and accomplishments.
Explain to caregivers and children the reasons for selecting samples.

Decide how to organize the portfolio.
Content areas
IEP goals
Themes
Chronological order of work

Decide who owns the portfolio and where it will be stored.
Establish clear, agreed-on guidelines to manage access to the portfolio and ensure confidentiality.

Determine criteria for monitoring children's progress.
Practitioners can schedule quarterly conferences with children, family, teachers, and other team members to review the portfolio.
At these meetings, discuss team member observations and documentation to check for subjectivity and bias.
Daily debriefings with other team members can help track the various types of documentation being gathered.
Criteria for evaluating the portfolio may include:
    Quantity, quality, and diversity of items,
    Organization of the portfolio,
    Level of student involvement,
    Meaningfulness of caption statement,
    Quality of summary statements about growth and change.

Adapted from: Losardo, A. & Notari-Syverson, A. (2001). *Alternative approaches to assessing young children.* Baltimore, MD: Paul H. Brookes Publishing.

Overall Program Effectiveness

Program evaluation has been defined as an objective, systematic process for gathering information about a program, or set of activities, which can be utilized for the following purposes: (a) to ascertain a program's ability to achieve the originally conceived and implemented goals; (b) to suggest modifications that might lead to improvement in quality and effectiveness; and (c) to allow well-informed decisions about the worth, merit, and level of support a program warrants. In order for evaluation to be effective, it must be designed with a specific purpose in mind. Few early childhood programs have well-developed purposes and evaluation plans prior to the beginning of services, thus compromising their program's ability to document outcomes.

Early childhood programs that serve infants and young children with disabilities and their families must consider a number of issues when designing evaluation plans. Bailey and Wolery (1989) recommended several questions to provide insight into the overall quality of a program. These questions are as follows:

Table 5-9   Sample Family Evaluation Scale

Early intervention Control Scale
by Kimberly Boyd and Carl J. Dunst

This scale includes a series of statements that describe different ways people sometimes feel about supports and services they receive from the early intervention or preschool program serving their child and family. Please read each statement and circle the response that best describes whether the statement is true for you and your family. Please answer all of the questions; and remember, your opinions and feelings are most important in answering the questions.

Please indicate to what extent each of the following statement is true for you:	Rarely True	A Little True	Sometimes True	Generally True	Almost Always
1. I can get the type of support and services I want most for my family from this early intervention or preschool program.	1	2	3	4	5
2. My previous experiences at getting support and services from this early intervention or preschool program have been successful.	1	2	3	4	5
3. I am able to get services from this early intervention or preschool program during times of the day that are convenient to my family's schedule.	1	2	3	4	5
4. I have "good feelings" about myself whenever I successfully arrange for supports and services from this early intervention or preschool program.	1	2	3	4	5
5. I am satisfied with the supports and services I am able to get for my family from this early intervention or preschool program.	1	2	3	4	5

From: Boyd, K. & Dunst, C. (1997). *Early intervention control scale.* (Unpublished scale). Orelena Hawks Puckett Institute, Asheville, NC.

1. Can the program demonstrate that their methods, materials, and overall service delivery represent the best educational practice?

2. Can the program demonstrate that the methods espoused in the overall philosophy are implemented accurately and consistently?

3. Can the program demonstrate that it attempts to verify empirically the effectiveness of interventions or other individual program components for which the best educational practice has yet to be verified?

4. Can the program demonstrate that a system is in place for determining the relative adequacy of client progress and service delivery?

5. Can the program demonstrate that it is moving toward the accomplishment of program goals/objectives?

6. Can the program demonstrate that the goals, methods, materials, and overall service delivery system are in accordance with the needs and values of the community and clients it serves?

These answers can provide a clear and realistic framework for understanding and monitoring program operations and effectiveness.

Summary

Assessments conducted for program planning, intervention, progress monitoring, and overall program effectiveness are overlapping activities in programs serving young children with disabilities and their families. In this chapter, we have addressed assessments conducted for the purposes of (a) program planning and (b) progress monitoring and program evaluation.

In order to design and provide the most effective services for young children with disabilities, appropriate program planning assessment must take place. These assessment procedures are distinctly different from the assessment procedures necessary to determine eligibility for services. Program planning assessment is designed to collect information about the child's intervention needs. This means that program planning assessment must focus on what skills and behaviors the child needs to function in his natural environment rather than only pinpointing what skills are missing from his repertoire, based on traditional assessment measures. Thus, program planning requires that ongoing assessment take place within the context of the child's natural environment, which can then be directly linked to intervention. There must be a strong linkage between assessment and intervention activities in order for young children with disabilities to receive the maximum intended benefits. Recommended practice suggests that an ecological assessment approach, such as the one presented in this chapter, is a model to be used in order to provide a strong, direct linkage between assessment and intervention.

In order to determine the effectiveness of intervention, children's progress towards the attainment of their individual goals and outcomes must be monitored, as well as family outcomes. Progress monitoring should be conducted regularly and frequently and should take place in authentic, naturalistic settings. This will provide a record of children's progress and indicate whether any interventions should be changed. Furthermore, information should be collected regarding family satisfaction and overall program effectiveness.

Check Your Understanding

1. Describe the difference between assessment to determine eligibility and assessment for program planning purposes.

2. Describe the characteristics of assessment procedures that represent recommended practice for young children with disabilities.

3. Describe the importance of considering family preferences in the program planning process.

4. Describe four different methods that can be used to collect assessment information.

5. Define what is meant by an ecological assessment and identify the steps in an ecological assessment.

6. Provide a rationale for considering (as part of the assessment process) the environments or settings in which children spend time and the demands that are placed on them in those environments.

7. Explain how each of the following levels of evaluation should be addressed in the overall evaluation plan of an early childhood program in which children with disabilities are served: (a) child level, (b) family level, and (c) program level.

8. Explain the importance of monitoring the progress of young children with disabilities.

9. Differentiate between formative and summative evaluation.

References

Bagnato, S. J. & Neisworth, J. T. (1990). *System to plan early childhood services (SPECS)*. Circle Pines, MN. American Guidance Service.

Bagnato, S. J., Neisworth, J. T. & Munson, S. M. (1997). *LINKing assessment and early intervention: An authentic curriculum-based approach*. Baltimore MD: Brookes.

Bailey, D., & Simeonsson, R. (1988). *Family assessment in early intervention*. Englewood Cliffs, NJ: Merrill/Prentice Hall.

Bailey, D., & Wolery, M. (1992). *Teaching infants and preschoolers with disabilities.* (2nd ed.). New York: Merrill.

Banks, R. A., Santos, R. M. & Roof. (2003). Discovering family concerns, priorities, and resources: Sensitive family information gathering. *Young Exceptional Children. 6*(2), pp. 1–7.

Boyd, K., & Dunst, C. (1997). *Early intervention control scale.* Genesis Press.

Bricker, D., & Cripe, J. (1992). *An activity-based approach to early intervention.* Baltimore, MD: Paul H. Brookes.

Bricker, D. (2003). *Assessment, evaluation, and programming system for children.* Baltimore, MD: Paul H. Brookes.

Bricker, D., & Cripe, J. (1993). *Assessment, evaluation, and programming system for children: AEPS measurement from birth to three years* (Vol. 1). Baltimore, MD: Paul H. Brookes.

Bricker, D., & Littman, D. (1982). Intervention and education: The inseparable mix. *Topics in Early Childhood Special Education, 1,* 23–33.

Bricker, D. & Squires, J. (1999). *Ages and stages questionnaires: A parent-completed child monitoring system* (2nd edition). Baltimore, MD: Paul H. Brookes.

Brigance. A. H. (1991). *BRIGANCE inventory of early development-revised.* No. Billerica, MA: Curriculum Associates.

Bronfenbrenner, U. (1979). *The ecology of human development: Experiments by nature and design.* Cambridge, MA: Harvard University Press.

Brown, S. L., D'Eugenio, D. B., Drews, J. E., Haskin, B. S., Lynch, E. W., Moersch, M. S., & Rogers, S. J. (1981). *Preschool developmental profile.* Ann Arbor: University of Michigan Press.

Bruder, M. (1997). Early childhood intervention. In J. Wood & A. Lazzari. *Exceeding the boundaries: Understanding exceptional lives* (pp. 539–569). Fort Worth, TX: Harcourt Brace College Publishers.

Campbell, P. (1991). Evaluation and assessment in early intervention for infants and toddlers. *Journal of Early Intervention, 15*(1), 36–45.

CLAS Institute (2001). *Family information gathering review guidelines.* Retrieved April 7, 2003, from the CLAS Early Childhood Research Institute Website: *http://clas.uiinc.edu*

Cohen, Libby G., & Spenciner, L. J. (2003) *Assessment of young children.* White Plains, NY: Longman.

Cooney, M. H. & Barbanan, M. (2001). Documentation: Making assessment visible. *Young Exceptional Children 4*(3). 10–16.

Flager, S. (1996). *Infant-preschool play assessment scale.* Lewisville, NC: Kaplan.

Furunno, S., O'Reilly, K., Hosaka, C. M., Inatsuka, T. T., Zeisloft-Falbey, B., & Allman, T. (1994). *Revised HELP checklist: Birth to three years.* Palo Alto, CA: Vort.

Glover, E., Preminger, J., & Sanford, A. (1995). *Early learning accomplishment profile (E-LAP).* Chapel Hill, NC: Chapel Hill Training-Outreach Project.

Glover, E., Preminger, J., Sanford, A., & Zelman, (1995). *Learning accomplishment profile (LAP-R).* Chapel Hill, NC: Chapel Hill Training-Outreach Project.

Grace, C., & Shores, E. (1990). *The portfolio and its use: Developmentally appropriate assessment of young children.* Little Rock, AR: Southern Association on Children Under Six.

Johnson, L., & LaMontagne, M. (1994). Program evaluation: The key to quality programming. In L. Johnson, R. Gallagher, M. LaMontagne, J. Jordon, J. Gallagher, P. Hutinger, & M. Karnes (Eds.), *Meeting early intervention challenges: Issues from birth to three* (pp. 185–216). Baltimore, MD: Paul H. Brookes.

Johnson-Martin, N., Attermeier, S., & Hacker, B. (1990). *The Carolina curriculum for preschoolers with special needs* (2nd. ed.). Baltimore, MD: Paul H. Brookes.

Johnson-Martin, N., Jens, K., Attermeier, S., & Hacker, B. (1991). *The Carolina curriculum for infants and toddlers with special needs* (2nd. ed.). Baltimore, MD: Paul H. Brookes.

Johnson-Martin, N., Jens, K., Attermeier, S., & Hacker, B. (1991). *The Carolina curriculum for infants and toddlers with special needs* (2nd ed.) Baltimore, MD: Paul H. Brookes.

Kilgo, J. & Raver, S. (1999). Family-professional collaboration. In S. Raver (Ed.). *Transdisciplinary early intervention.* New York, NY: McMillan.

Kramer, S., McGonigel, M., & Kauffman, R. (1991). Developing the IFSP: Outcomes, strategies, activities, and services. In M. McGonigel, R. Kaufmann, & B. Johnson (Eds.), *Guidelines and recommended practices for the individualized family service plan* (pp. 57–66). Bethesda, MD: Association for the Care of Children's Health.

LaBoskey, V. K. (2000). Portfolios here, portfolios there . . . Searching for the essence of 'educational portfolios.' *Phi Delta Kappan, 81*(8), 590–595.

Lifter, K., & Bloom, L. (1998). Internationality and the role of play in the transition to language. In S. F. Warren & J. Reichle (Series Eds.) & A. M. Weatheby, S. F. Warren, & J. Reichle (Vol. Eds.). *Communication and language intervention series: Vol. 6. Transiting in prelinguistic communication.* (pp. 161–195). Baltimore, MD: Paul H. Brookes.

Linder, T. W. (1993). *Transdisciplinary play-based assessment: A functional approach to working with young children* (Rev. ed.). Baltimore, MD: Paul H. Brookes.

McCormick, L. (1997). Ecological assessment and planning. In L. McCormick, D. Loeb, & R. Schiefelbusch (Eds.), *Supporting children with communication difficulties in inclusive settings: School-based language intervention* (pp. 223–256). Boston: Allyn & Bacon.

McWilliam, P. J., Winton, P., & Crais, E. R. (1996). *Practical strategies for family-centered early intervention.* San Diego, CA: Singlular.

NECTAS & the Association for the Care of Children's Health. (1991). Guidelines and recommended practices for the individualized family service plan (2nd ed.) Chapel Hill, NC: National Early Childhood Technical Assistance Systems (NECTAS).

Nehring, A. D., Nehring, E. F., Bruni, J. R., & Randolph, P. L. (1992). *Learning accomplishment profile.* Lewisville, NC: Kaplan Early Learning Company.

Neisworth, J., & Bagnato, S. (1996). Assessment for early intervention: Emerging themes and practices. In S. Odom & M. McLean (Eds.), *Early intervention/early childhood special education: Recommended practices* (pp. 23–58). Austin, TX: PRO-ED.

Neisworth, J. & Bagnato, S. (2000). Recommended practices in assessment. In S. Sandall, M. McLean, & B. Smith (2000). *DEC Recommended practices for early intervention/early childhood special education.* p. 17–27. Longmont, CO: Sopris West.

Newborg, J., Stock, J. R., & Wnek, L. (1988). *Battelle developmental inventory.* Itasca, IL: Riverside.

Newborg, J. (2004). *Battelle Developmental Inventory (BDI)* (2nd ed.). Scarborough, ON, Canada: Nelson Thomson Learning.

Noonan, M. J., & McCormick, L. (1993). *Early intervention in natural environments: Methods and procedures.* Pacific Grove, CA: Brooks/Cole.

Parks, S., Furuno, S., O'Reilly, K., Inatsuka, T., Hosaka, C., Zeisloft-Falbey, B. (1994). *Hawaii Early Learning Profile.* Palo Alto, CA: Vort Corporation.

Parks, S. et al. (1992). *Help at home: Activity sheets for parents.* Palo Alto, CA: Vort Corporation.

Provence, S., Erickson, J., Vater, S. & Palmeri, S. (1995). *Infant-toddler developmental assessment (IDA).* Chicago, IL: Riverside.

Rogers, S. J. & D'Eugenio, D. B. (1981). *Preschool developmental profile.* Ann Arbor MI: University of Michigan Press.

Sandall, S., McLean, M. E., & Smith, B. J. (2000). *DEC Recommended practices for early intervention/early childhood special education.* Longmont, CO: Sopris West.

Sandall, S., & Schwartz, L. (2002). *Building blocks for teaching preschoolers with special needs.* Baltimore, MD: Paul H. Brookes.

Summers J. A., Dell'Oliver, C., Turnbull, A. P., Benson, H. A., Santelli, E., Campbell, M. & Siegel-Causey, E. (1990). Examining the IFSP process; What are family and practitioner preferences? *Topics in Early Childhood Special Education, 10,* 78–99.

Turnbull, A. P., & Turnbull, H. R. (1997). *Families, professionals, and exceptionality* (3rd ed.). Upper Saddle River, NJ: Merrill/Prentice Hall.

Turnbull, A. P., & Turnbull, H. R. (2001). *Families, professionals, and exceptionality: Collaborating for empowerment.* (4th ed.). Upper Saddle River, NJ: Merrill/Prentice Hall.

Voress. J. K., & Maddox, T. (1998). *Developmental assessment of young children.* Austin, TX: PRO-ED.

VORT Corporation (1995). *Hawaii early learning profile (HELP) for preschoolers.* Palo Alto, CA: Vort Corporation.

Wolery, M., Strain, P., & Bailey, D. (1992). Reaching the potential of children with special needs. In S. Bredekamp & T. Rosegrant (Eds.) *Reaching potentials: Appropriate curriculum and assessment for young children* (Vol. 1) (pp. 92–111). Washington, DC: National Association for the Education of Young Children (NAEYC).

Zirpoli, S. (1997). Issues in early childhood behavior. In T. J. Zirpoli & K. J. Melloy (Eds.), *Behavior management: Applications for teachers and parents* (2nd ed., pp. 383–417). Upper Saddle River, N.J.: Merrill.

Planning and Organizing Educational Programs

CHAPTER

6

Delivering Services to Young Children with Special Needs

Learning Outcomes

After reading this chapter you will be able to:

- Identify the advantages and disadvantages of center-based and home-based service delivery models.
- List five benefits of providing services in inclusive settings.
- Define the concept of least restrictive environment.
- Outline the steps needed to ensure effective transitions.
- Explain the differences between multi-, inter-, and transdisciplinary team models.
- List the required components of an individualized family service plan (IFSP) and an individualized education program (IEP).

A goal of early intervention efforts and early childhood special education is to provide at-risk and young children with special needs with the best possible beginning. As a field, early childhood special education has been driven by the recognition of the importance of providing services and interventions to youngsters with disabilities "as early and comprehensively as possible in the least restrictive setting" (Carta, Schwartz, Atwater, & McConnell, 1991, p. 4). One of the questions this chapter will attempt to answer is whether the need for specialized services necessitates restricted environments. The literature strongly suggests that segregated settings are not called for (Sandall, McLean, & Smith, 2000; Sandall & Ostrosky, 2000). The challenge to early childhood professionals, as Carta and colleagues (1991) note, is to develop delivery systems that provide services in integrated environments. This leads us to our second question, which also provides a framework for this chapter—how to best design services for young children with disabilities and those at-risk in a manner that is responsive to the needs of the child and the family's goals and priorities.

The primary objective of this chapter is to examine the variety of placement options or models available for providing interventions. The importance of carefully planned transitions will also be considered. We will also look at the vehicles for delivering services, that is, individualized education programs (IEPs) and individualized family service plans (IFSPs). Finally, our attention will focus on professional collaboration and cooperation. This teamwork is so necessary if programs are to effectively function and meet the needs of young children with special needs and their families.

Service Delivery Models

There are a variety of administrative options for providing services to young children with special needs and their families. These arrangements are usually referred to as service delivery approaches—where intervention or education is provided. The location of service delivery, according to Graves, Gargiulo, and Sluder (1996), is frequently dependent on the age of the child (infant vs. preschooler), geographical considerations (rural vs. urban), child characteristics (severity and type of disability), and community resources as well as child/family goals and objectives. Additionally, the philosophy and beliefs of the agency, program, or school regarding the integration of pupils with special needs with their typical peers may also influence where intervention/education is rendered.

Yet, as we will see shortly, contemporary thinking strongly supports the notion that intervention and other services for young children with disabilities should occur in **natural environments;** that is, those locations viewed as normal or typical for individuals of similar chronological age without disabilities. These locations might include child care settings, the youngster's home, or a neighborhood play group.

Places viewed as "not natural" include, for example, hospitals, rehabilitation centers, clinics, therapists' offices, or segregated group settings. This preference for offering services in the natural environment parallels the concept of least restrictive environment (LRE) or inclusive settings for preschoolers with disabilities—to the extent appropriate, children with disabilities must be educated along side their typically developing peers (Walsh, Rous, & Lutzer, 2000).

Traditionally, programs for young children with special needs are identified as center-based, home-based, or combination models. Like many other professionals we agree with this conventional classification scheme. Yet, it should be remembered that there is no single, accepted standard regarding where youngsters with special needs should be served (Peterson, 1987). Furthermore, we believe that a decision as to where services are provided primarily resides with the child's parents. They should be the primary decision makers in this regard and in all other aspects of programming affecting their son or daughter.

Even though there is no one best model, best practice guidelines for the delivery of early intervention and special education services have been formulated. Regardless of where services are provided, McDonnell and Hardman (1988) suggest that programs include the following dimensions:

- Integrated placements: systematic contact with nondisabled peers.
- Comprehensive: full range of services available.
- Normalized: age-appropriate skills and intervention strategies; instruction across a variety of settings.
- Adaptable: flexible procedures meeting individual needs of the child.
- Peer and family referenced: parents perceived as full partners; curriculum geared toward child, family, peers, and community (that is, an ecological approach).
- Outcome-based: developing skills with present and future usefulness; preparation for integrated settings.

Several years ago, the Division for Early Childhood (DEC) of the Council for Exceptional Children convened a task force, which developed a set of indicators of quality and recommended practices for early childhood special education programs. The DEC Task Force on Recommended Practices (1993) incorporated five general principles that guided the selection of best practice indicators. These principles include (1) placement in the least restrictive environment or most natural setting; (2) family-focused services; (3) the use of a transdisciplinary service delivery approach; (4) the inclusion of both developmentally and individually appropriate practices; and (5) the inclusion of empirically sound as well as value-driven practices. The task force developed standards for home-based, center-based, clinic-based, and hospital-based delivery models. Table 6–1 presents ten indicators, which the task force believes traverse each of the delivery options.

We need to keep in mind that the practices identified by McDonnell and Hardman (1988) and DEC are simply recommended indicators of quality. As such, they should be used as guidelines for early childhood special education programs. The needs of individual children with disabilities and their families dictate where, how, and what services are provided. Furthermore, as the DEC task force astutely notes, any recommended or best practice suggestions are inherently time-bound. What is considered best or recommended at one point in time might be obsolete in a few years. We now turn our attention to examining three traditional service delivery models.

Home-Based Programs

For some young children, especially infants and toddlers, the most appropriate location for providing services is in their home. Here interventions can individually be provided by the primary caregiver in the youngster's most natural environment—their home (Graves et al., 1996). The caregiver, typically a parent, works cooperatively with various professionals on implementing specific intervention strategies developed by an interdisciplinary team with the parent's input. Service providers make regular and frequent visits to the home to work directly with the child, to assist and support the parent, and to monitor the youngster's progress. Forming meaningful partner-

Table 6-1   DEC Recommended Practices for Service Delivery Models

Indicators Across All Models of Service Delivery

- Program staff coordinate early intervention services with all other modes of service delivery available to, and needed by, the child and family.
- Services include a measure of effectiveness and results should be communicated in a timely fashion to the family.
- The nature of services provided are based upon families informed selection from an array to viable options.
- The early intervention program frequently monitors delivery of services to ensure that agreed upon procedures and outcomes are achieved in a timely fashion.
- Programs are staffed by personnel who have received competency-based training with children of the age being served.

- Someone in the program or immediately available to the program speaks the family's preferred language.
- Program staff individualize services in response to children's characteristics, preferences, interests, abilities, and health status.
- Staff monitor interventions frequently, and make changes in programming as needed.
- Staff employ a variety of strategies and interventions to address individual child and family needs.
- Staff design services to allay children's fears and anxieties regarding separation, medical interventions, and other intervention-related issues.

SOURCE: DEC Task Force on Recommended Practices, *DEC Recommended Practices: Indicators of Quality in Programs for Infants and Young Children with Special Needs and Their Families* (Reston, VA: Division for Early Childhood, Council for Exceptional Children, 1993), p. 47.

ships with parents is crucial to the success of home-based programs. Although service providers are primarily concerned with advancing the developmental status of the youngster, they are also concerned with enhancing the well-being and competency of the family (Raver, 1999).

Delivering services in the child's home has multiple advantages. The primary advantage is that services are provided in a setting that is familiar to the child and by the youngster's first teacher—the parent. Parents also have the opportunity to intervene on an ongoing basis as behaviors naturally occur. Furthermore, skills learned in a child's natural environment are easier to maintain. Finally, disruption to the child's and family's routines are frequently minimized. With **home-based programs,** costs may be less, transportation is not a concern, and services are responsive to family needs. The potential for family involvement with the interventions is also greater. This model is especially appropriate for children living in rural or sparsely populated communities and,

as we noted earlier, infants and toddlers. Sixty-eight percent of infants and toddlers receiving early intervention get these services in their home (U.S. Department of Education, 2002).

There are certain disadvantages to home-based models. A commonly noted drawback is the commitment required by, and the responsibilities placed upon, the caregiver. Not all parents are capable of providing effective intervention nor is it a role they wish to assume. Providing intervention in a child's home also dictates that professionals demonstrate cultural sensitivity with families having different values, beliefs, and customs (Wayman, Lynch, & Hanson, 1991). Furthermore, in some situations the effectiveness of this model may be diminished due to family circumstances such as a single parent household, conditions of poverty, and other risk factors. Opportunities for social interaction with other children are sometimes also absent in home-based models. Finally, a considerable amount of the professional's time is usually spent traveling from one home to another.

Center-Based Programs

As the name implies, **center-based programs** are located away from the child's home. Settings may be in churches, child care centers, preschools, public schools, or other accessible locations. Center-based models are very common settings for three- and four-year-old children with special needs (Bailey & Wolery, 1992). Youngsters are transported to the site, where they receive intervention from professionals representing a variety of disciplines such as physical and occupational therapists or speech-language pathologists. This strategy is in concert with the interdisciplinary approach of working with at-risk and children with special needs. In this model, professionals from a variety of disciplines share their information and expertise while working cooperatively as a team in delivering an individualized education program. The primary direct service provider for preschoolers with disabilities is typically the child's teacher. Center-based programs typically stress the acquisition of developmental, social, cognitive, and self-help skills necessary for success in elementary school (Umansky & Hooper, 1998).

Many center-based programs like to involve parents as part of the team. Professionals consider the parents' participation to be both necessary and beneficial. Parental involvement increases the effectiveness of the interventions (Bailey, 1994). Children usually attend a program for several hours each day. Some youngsters participate in daily programs while others attend only two or three times a week. (See Feature 6–1 for a mother's experience with a center-based program serving infants and toddlers.)

Experts (Bailey & Wolery, 1992; Peterson, 1987; Raver, 1999) consider center-based models to have several advantages. Frequently identified aspects include:

1. the development of social skills plus opportunities for social interaction between typical and atypical age-mates;

2. access to comprehensive services from specialists representing many different disciplines;

3. availability of specialized equipment and materials;

4. enhanced efficiency of staff time;

5. parental involvement and the chance to develop social networks with parents; and

6. exposure to experiences and the development of skills which will aid in the transition to kindergarten programs.

Center-based programs are not without limitations and drawbacks. Disadvantages include:

1. The cost of transportation to and from the center (considered a related service according to IDEA).

2. Extended periods of travel time to and from the center.

3. The expense of maintaining the center and its equipment.

4. In comparison to a home-based delivery system, the possibility of limited opportunity for establishing meaningful working partnerships with parents.

Feature 6–1   A Mother's Story

Our son Ryan was diagnosed with multiple handicaps at the age of five months and I was thrown into a world I would never have chosen. Not for him and not for us.

Ryan was seven months old when we enrolled him in the Center's Infant Intervention Program. For an hour a week a therapist from the Center would work with Ryan, using toys and rattles, mirrors and music in an attempt to elicit a response.

The Center revolves around the philosophy that early intervention can substantially boost a child's development, especially a child whose handicaps may prevent him from interacting with his world the way other children can. Patiently, the therapist showed me how to position Ryan to encourage the strengthening of certain muscles, how to recognize his responses which signaled his interest in a toy and how to interpret other subtle signals from him.

I remember one of these days very vividly. Ryan was lying on the mat and the therapist was shaking and rattling toys in an attempt to get him to hold his head up and look at the object. While she tried toy after toy, he just lay there motionless. There were two graduate students observing and two therapists evaluating. The quiet in that room was deafening. In my head I kept saying over and over: *Please look at the rattle . . . please look at the rattle.* Silently I tried to will him to move—to do something astounding.

One of the therapists reached over and turned on a musical windmill and suddenly that little head popped up off the mat and looked all around trying to locate the sound. The therapist sitting closest to me laughed and said under her breath, "Why, you little stinker!" They had found a motivator—music is what they would use to urge Ryan to do the things that were so difficult for him.

When he turned a year old he entered the Infant/Toddler classroom attending school twice a week for three-hour sessions. During those sessions he would receive motor and speech therapy.

Ryan's motor ability was, and still is, severely limited. To even bring a toy to his mouth was a monumental achievement, often requiring repeated attempts. So he was put on a motor program to help him improve in this area. As a first step, he was given a battery-operated toy, which was operated by a switch. Ryan's training would involve repeated attempts (under the direction of his therapist) to hit the switch and activate the toy. Soon, they were substituting tape recorded songs for the toy. In addition to developing a certain, consistent reach in Ryan which might be useful in operating a wheelchair, the activity allowed him to finally control something himself.

One day while I sat and cheered him on, a therapist came in to watch. I had never met her but obviously she knew Ryan. She stood quietly watching as his arm swung out into wide arc, attempting over and over to hit the switch. When at last he made contact she bent over and kissed the top of his head. "Good job, Ryan," I heard her say softly to him. I sat in the corner and cried over the very special encouragement my child had received. I knew that in this school he would learn many things, perhaps the most important being that he was lovable and worthy of our best efforts.

It hurts to watch your child struggle so hard to do the things that come naturally to other children. By Spring, in Ryan's Infant/Toddler classroom the others were all walking, or learning. Ryan was unable to even sit alone by himself, and sometimes activities that were perfect for the rest of the class seemed inappropriate for Ryan. One day I came in and found his teachers had placed him on the floor on his back and formed a circle around him with all the children. They sang "Ring-a-Round-the-Rosie" as they skipped around him. Ryan loved it, watching each face as it passed and squealing happily to the music.

As I watched him I realized that while Ryan's handicap was severe, it didn't need to limit him. He was as much a part of the class that day as any other child in the room. I will always be grateful to his teachers, Margo and Dawn, for finding ingenious ways to involve Ryan and for helping me to see that Ryan didn't have to sit back and watch life go by—he could be a part of it.

Source: M. Hunt. A mother's story. *Children's Progress,* *16*(2), 1988, pp. 4–6. Used by permission of Children's Hospital Medical Center of Akron.

DEC Recommended Practices for Center-Based Programs

- Environments are safe and clean, barrier free, and physically accessible to families. Toys and materials are appropriate to the age and needs of the youngsters.

- Service providers employ pull-out services only when activity-based services fail to meet identified needs.

- Services for children with disabilities are non-categorical.

- Environments stimulate children's interactions and choices while promoting high levels of engagement.

- Service providers communicate on a regular basis with family members and professional colleagues.

- The ratio of adult staff to children maximizes safety, health, and promotion of specific goals.

Source: Adapted from DEC Task Force on Recommended Practices, *DEC Recommended Practices: Indicators of Quality in Programs for Infants and Young Children with Special Needs and Their Families* (Reston, VA: Division for Early Childhood, Council for Exceptional Children, 1993), p. 48.

In some situations, administrators of center-based programs are also confronted with the difficult task of providing services within a normalizing environment as mandated by IDEA. Unfortunately, too few public schools provide preschool programs for typical pupils; therefore, creative and alternative ways for serving youngsters with disabilities are being developed. A growing number of early childhood programs are including youngsters with disabilities and are meeting their special needs by utilizing consultants or itinerant professionals for the delivery of specialized services. (Sadler, 2003). Recent data provided by the U.S. Department of Education (2002) reveals that 36 percent of preschoolers with disabilities are being served in an early childhood setting. We suspect that this will become an increasingly prominent model for providing needed services while addressing the issue of a normalizing environment.

In other instances, dual enrollments are being utilized. A youngster with multiple impairments, for example, might attend a program specifically for young children with disabilities in the morning while in the afternoon care is provided in a proprietary setting like La Petite Academy or Kinder Care. Thanks in part to the expanding influence of the Americans with Disabilities Act, children with disabilities are enjoying greater access to programs designed for typical youngsters.

Combination Programs

Services to young children with disabilities and those who are at-risk may require that program philosophies be merged in order to best serve and meet the unique needs of the child and his or her family. **Combination programs** provide this flexibility and reflect the advantages of both settings. According to Karnes and Stayton (1988), a growing number of intervention programs include aspects of both models. For example, in some instances a toddler with cerebral palsy may attend an integrated child care center two mornings a week where she is the recipient of physical therapy while also receiving weekly home visits from a speech-language pathologist and an occupational therapist. Parent involvement and participation, however, remain a key component of this approach. In fact, because parent involvement is so crucial, many programs are now adopting a family-focused approach to providing services rather than the traditional child-focused approach. These models aim to provide support and assistance to the entire family while building upon their strengths and resources.

No service delivery model is superior to another. *Where* services are delivered does not define the quality nor the effectiveness of an intervention program. A best practice approach suggests that a range of options be available so that parents may choose the

Feature 6–2

It is difficult to imagine how it feels to call an early childhood program and rather than inquiring about what kind of curriculum they have or types of activities, you first have to ask them if they accept children with disabilities. Because of inclusion, the dream of my child having the opportunity to go to the same early childhood program and to develop friendships with her normally developing peers has finally been realized.

Source: M. Davis, J. Kilgo, and M. Gamel-McCormick, *Young Children with Special Needs* (Needham Heights, MA: Allyn & Bacon, 1998), p. 52.

service delivery option that best fits their needs and those of their son or daughter. Many special education professionals believe that what is most important is matching the services to the needs of the child while reflecting the priorities, needs, and values of the family. What is an appropriate program for one family may be inappropriate for another. Meyen (1996) believes that "the optimal model for service delivery depends on family and child characteristics and needs, intensity of services, and geographic characteristics of the service area" (p. 171). Cook and her colleagues (Cook, Tessier, & Klein, 2000) are in agreement with this argument. They too believe that no one location is best for all children and their families. They also remind us that any setting for delivering services must be culturally compatible with the values and child-rearing practices of the family.

Inclusive Settings

As noted in the preceding section, home-based and center-based models are, in many instances, viable options for delivering services to infants, toddlers, and preschoolers with special needs. Yet, with the advent of IDEA (PL 99-457, PL 102-119, PL 105-17) and support from the Americans with Disabilities Act (ADA), the service delivery landscape has dramatically changed. Services for infants and toddlers are required to be provided in normalized, natural environments. This provision is generally interpreted to mean those settings that are typical or natural for the youngster's peers who are not disabled, and includes

a variety of community placements (see Feature 6–2). Services for preschoolers with special needs are now under the jurisdiction of local public schools who are mandated to serve these children according to the provisions of IDEA—including providing services in the least restrictive environment (LRE). While there is growing support for providing services in a normalized context, we must remember that where early intervention and education are provided, they must be appropriate to the needs of the child and in concert with the goals and values of the youngster's family.

The idea of providing services to young children with special needs in normalized settings is not new.

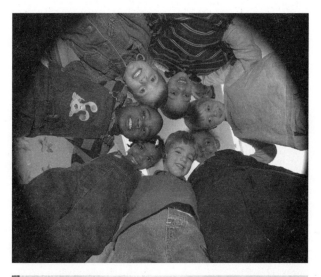

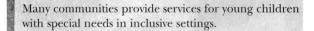

Many communities provide services for young children with special needs in inclusive settings.

Early childhood special educators have been challenged by this issue for many years. Many professionals and parents have long advocated for the provision of services in natural environments that include both typically and atypically developing youngsters (Harbin, Mc William, & Gallagher, 2000). One of the problems, however, with the implementation of this principle is the absence, in many communities, of appropriate placements or settings for infants, toddlers, and preschoolers with disabilities. To fully appreciate this contemporary practice we need to review its conceptual evolution and understand key terminology.

The 1970s saw the establishment of a strong foundation for merging early childhood programs that integrated youngsters with and without disabilities (Guralnick, 1994). The decade of the 1980s, according to Guralnick (1990), witnessed the repeated demonstration that early childhood mainstreaming programs could effectively be implemented. The challenge facing professionals in the 1990s was to construct program models that would allow for services to be delivered in nonspecialized or natural settings (Carta et al., 1991). We predict that in the coming years the most common setting for serving infants, toddlers, and preschoolers with special needs will be in programs designed primarily for typical youngsters. Across the United States, this idea is gaining momentum, driven in part by a growing recognition that it is essential to provide intervention for children with special needs as early as possible in the most normalized setting (Carta et al., 1991). As McLean and Hanline (1990) contend, the need is *not* for special placements or environments but rather for specialized teaching that meets the individual needs of the child.

Over twenty-five years ago, Bricker (1978) and more recently, Bailey, McWilliam, Buysse, and Wesley (1998), identified social-ethical, legal-legislative, and psychological-educational arguments supporting the educational integration of young children with disabilities. In recent years Bricker's arguments have been reinforced by an expanding research knowledge base, judicial decisions, and legislative enactments. Today, many professionals and parents alike appreciate the benefits and opportunities that have accrued to young children with and without special needs and their families (see Table 6–2). They are the result of many years of arduous effort. Still, in spite of these gains, there are some professionals (and parents too), who believe that we have not done enough in advocating for the full inclusion of all children with disabilities into all aspects of society—but especially into educational programs. We see this call for full inclusion as having a potentially significant impact on the field of early childhood special education.

The debate surrounding the full inclusion movement is an emotionally and value-laden one with the potential for polarizing the field of special education. Across the country, advocates of this movement view it as the next great revolution in special education while opponents see it as the start of the return of the "dark ages" of special education; namely, the pre-PL 94-142 era. We suspect that the truth lies somewhere between these two extremes. The intensity of this debate is fueled by several factors, one of which is the inconsistent use of key terminology. As frequently happens in arguments, people are often saying the same thing only they are using different words. Therefore, we offer the following interpretations, which are frequently encountered in describing this movement.

Mainstreaming

The first potentially confusing term is **mainstreaming,** or in contemporary language, inclusion. We define this term as the social and instructional integration of children with disabilities into educational programs whose primary purpose is to serve typically developing individuals. The term *mainstreaming* represents the popularized version of the principle of educating children with disabilities, including preschoolers, in the least restrictive environment (LRE). Bricker (1995), however, questions the applicability of this term when talking about programming for infants with disabilities. Interestingly, the word itself does not appear in any piece of federal legislation.

The idea of mainstreaming has been woven into the fabric of American education for approximately

Table 6-2 Benefits of Preschool Integration

Beneficiary	Benefit
Children with disabilities	• They are spared the effects of separate, segregated education—including the negative effects of labeling and negative attitudes fostered by lack of contact with them. • They are provided with competent models that allow them to learn new adaptive skills and/or learn when and how to use their existing skills through imitation. • They are provided with competent peers with whom to interact, and thereby learn new social and/or communicative skills. • They are provided with realistic life experiences that prepare them to live in the community. • They are provided with opportunities to develop friendships with typically developing peers.
Children without disabilities	• They are provided with opportunities to learn more realistic and accurate views about individuals with disabilities. • They are provided with opportunities to develop positive attitudes toward others who are different from themselves. • They are provided with opportunities to learn altruistic behaviors and when and how to use such behaviors. • They are provided with models of individuals who successfully achieve despite challenges.
Communities	• They can conserve their early childhood resources by limiting the need for segregated specialized programs. • They can conserve educational resources if children with disabilities, who are mainstreamed at the preschool level, continue in regular as compared to special education placements during the elementary school years.
Families of children with disabilities	• They are able to learn about typical development. • They may feel less isolated from the remainder of their communities. • They may develop relationships with families of typically developing children who can provide them with meaningful support.
Families of children without disabilities	• They may develop relationships with families who have children with disabilities and thereby make a contribution to them and their communities. • They will have opportunities to teach their children about individual differences and about accepting individuals who are different.

SOURCE: M. Wolery and J. Wilbers, Introduction to the Inclusion of Young Children with Special Needs in Early Childhood Programs, in *Including Children with Special Needs in Early Childhood Programs,* M. Wolery and J. Wilbers (Eds.), (Washington, DC: National Association for the Education of Young Children, 1994), p. 11.

thirty years. Despite significant barriers and obstacles to implementing mainstream programs at the preschool level (Odom & McEvoy, 1990), many successful programs have been established across the United States. Demchak and Drinkwater (1992) argue that preschoolers with disabilities should use the same facilities, equipment, and materials as their typical peers and participate fully with their classmates in a wide variety of activities, such as center activities, free play, and field trips.

The judicial system also supports the concept of mainstreaming. An analysis of IDEA's LRE mandate by Osborne and DiMattia (1994) reveals that the courts interpret "that the right to associate with peers without disabilities was [is] a fundamental value of the right to a public education . . ." (p. 11). Yet, an integrated program must provide an appropriate education to the student. Mainstreaming is judicially viewed as secondary to the provision of an appropriate education. It is recognized as one of the many components of an appropriate education (Osborne & DiMattia, 1994; Yell, 1995). Judicial decisions, however, seem to be wavering somewhat from this earlier posture, and currently, the LRE provision is on equal footing with the mandate for an appropriate education. This "judicial activism" has resulted in the courts "telling us that the time to fully implement the LRE has arrived" (Osborne & DiMattia, 1995, p. 583). Parents no longer have to prove that their son or daughter should be included; rather, schools must justify their position to exclude and prove that they have made a good faith effort at integration or present strong evidence that an inclusionary setting is unsatisfactory (Osborne & DiMattia, 1995; Yell, 1995). PL 105–17 currently supports this thinking.

The key to understanding mainstreaming is that it must provide the student with an appropriate education based on the unique needs of the child. According to Rose and Smith (1993), "mainstreaming is meant to enhance the child's education through provision of a normalized social context for learning" (p. 62). The framers of IDEA never envisioned that mainstreaming would be interpreted to mean that *all* young children with special needs must be placed in integrated placements; to do so would mean abandoning the idea of determining what is the most appropriate placement for a particular child. IDEA clearly stipulates that, to the maximum extent appropriate, children with disabilities are to be educated with their typical peers. We interpret this provision to mean that, for some youngsters, an integrated or mainstream setting, even with supplementary aids and services, might be an inappropriate placement due to the child's unique characteristics. A least restrictive environment does not automatically mean placement with typical learners. Special educators need to make the distinction between the concepts of appropriateness and restrictiveness (Gargiulo, 2003).

The notion of mainstreaming flows from the principle of **normalization,** which advocates providing services in as culturally normative a fashion as possible (Wolfensberger, 1972). Accordingly, individuals with disabilities should be integrated, to the maximum extent possible, into all aspects of everyday living. Bailey and McWilliam (1990) believe that early childhood special education programs should adopt the concept of normalization.

Mainstreaming is but one dimension of the normalization principle. According to the DEC Task Force on Recommended Practices (1993), regardless of the type of setting selected for delivering intervention, the normalization principle still applies to the manner in which services are provided. The primary concern is the needs of the child. One must carefully assess the setting into which the youngster is placed. Merely placing a child with disabilities into a typical early childhood facility does not guarantee that the normalization principle has been upheld.

Least Restrictive Environment

The terms *mainstreaming* and **least restrictive environment (LRE),** while closely linked, should not be used interchangeably. Their meanings are educationally distinct. As we have just seen, mainstreaming refers to the integration of pupils with disabilities into general education programs. LRE, on the other hand, is a legal term interpreted to mean that young children with special needs are to be educated in settings as close as possible to a regular education environment. "Mainstreaming is one means of meeting the LRE requirement; but IDEA does not require mainstreaming in all cases" (Osborne & DiMattia, 1994, p. 7). The goal of the LRE principle is to prevent the unwarranted segregation of students with disabilities from their typical classmates. An LRE is not a place but a concept.

The determination of the LRE is individually defined for each child. It is based on the student's educational needs—not his or her disability. The LRE mandate applies equally to preschoolers and the school age population. The provision for educating preschoolers with disabilities as much as possible with typical youngsters also requires that service delivery options be available. A continuum of educational placements has been devised to meet the LRE requirements. Figure 6–1 portrays one possible option.

As we mentioned earlier, professionals who work with preschoolers encounter special problems in their attempts to implement the LRE mandate due to the absence of appropriate sites for delivering services. One of the primary difficulties is that most public school systems do not routinely provide preschool experiences for typical three- and four-year-olds (McCollum & Maude 1993; U.S. Department of Education, 1994).

Fortunately, a solution for resolving this dilemma exists. Guidance has been provided by the federal government in the rules and regulations accompanying IDEA. Schools may utilize a variety of alternative community-based placements or "options" for achieving the LRE requirements when serving three- to five-year-old children with disabilities (Federal Register, 1989). Variations in service delivery might include, among other possibilities, community preschool programs, child care settings, university child development centers, Head Start programs, and private agencies—all of which are normalized preschool settings. Many opportunities are thereby created for integration across a variety of community programs. Fifteen states have recently formulated inclusion guidelines/statements specifically for preschoolers with disabilities (Danaher & Kraus, 2002). As a result of the Americans with Disabilities Act (PL 101-336) integrated placement options for infants and toddlers with disabilities will also likely emerge.

The continuum illustrated in Figure 6–1 reflects varying degrees of restrictiveness, which refers to the

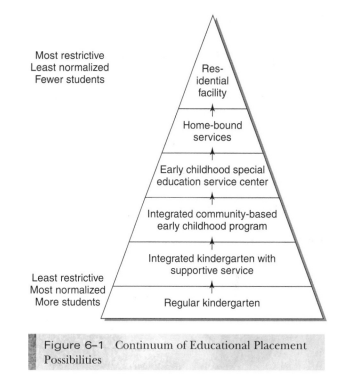

Figure 6–1   Continuum of Educational Placement Possibilities

amount of available contact with typical learners. Being only with children with special needs is considered restrictive, while placement with nondisabled youngsters is viewed as least restrictive. As we ascend the continuum, the environments provide fewer and fewer opportunities for interaction with typically developing age-mates, hence greater restrictiveness. While contact with typical students is highly desirable, it must be balanced by the requirement of providing an education appropriate to the unique needs of the youngster. Consequently, an integrated environment may not always be the most appropriate placement option. Each situation must be individually assessed and decided on a case-by-case basis. The idea of a continuum of service delivery options allow for, in limited situations, the removal of a child from integrated environments if it is in the best educational interest of the student. Segregation, while not desirable, might be necessary in some situations in order to provide an appropriate education as outlined in the pupil's IEP or IFSP (Yell, 1995). As an

The least restrictive environment is individually determined for each child.

example, Bricker (1995) contends that placement in a nonintegrated setting may be the placement of choice especially if it increases the youngster's chances for future placement in a general education program. Judicially speaking, the courts have allowed, under certain circumstances, segregated placements for students with disabilities (Osborne & DiMattia, 1994). Yet we recognize, as do many other special educators, that maximum integration with typically developing children is highly desirable and should be one of our major goals. The question then, as posed by Gargiulo (2003), is when, where, with whom, and to what extent are young children with special needs to be integrated.

Regular Education Initiative

The third concept that requires attention is the **regular education initiative (REI).** While not directly aimed at young children with special needs, REI is an important link in the evolution of the full inclusion movement and is conceptually relevant. The term was introduced in 1986 by former Assistant Secretary of Education (Office of Special Education and Rehabilitative Services) Madeline Will, who questioned the legitimacy of special education as a separate system of education and called for a restructuring of the rela-

tionship between general and special education. She endorsed the idea of shared responsibility or a partnership between regular (general) and special education resulting in a coordinated delivery system (Will, 1986a). It is interesting to note, that despite its name, this idea was initiated by a special education professional. Her comments have been interpreted in many ways, which have contributed to the current debate about the roles of special and general educators in delivering services to children with disabilities as well as youngsters enrolled in remedial and compensatory programs. At one end of the spectrum are those who consider regular and special education as unnecessary dual systems (Wang & Reynolds, 1985) and thus advocate the elimination of special education as a distinct delivery system (Gartner & Lipsky, 1987; Stainback & Stainback, 1987). Some professionals believe that *all* children, including those with severe impairments, should be educated in regular classrooms (Stainback & Stainback, 1989). This proposal, of course, would radically reform special education as we presently know it and is genuinely counter to the basic tenets of special education.

Part of the difficulty in understanding the complexities of REI is that it has been misrepresented and, therefore, misunderstood. Some of the problem arises from the fact that Will (1986a) fails to clearly define what she means by a partnership between general and special educators, thereby providing the impetus for diverse interpretations of her call. A careful reading of her position finds that Will (1986b) does not suggest that special education be consolidated into general education. A question also arises as to which population REI is aiming. Will (1986a) talks about students with learning difficulties, the educationally disadvantaged, and those who learn slowly—she does not describe a particular disability group for whom REI would be appropriate. Some interpret her remarks to mean that *all* children, regardless of the severity of their disability, should be educated in one consolidated delivery system (Gartner & Lipsky, 1989; Stainback & Stainback, 1984). Lieberman (1990) observes that the goal of these educators is to fully integrate "any and all children into regular classrooms regardless of condition, disability, fragility, vulnerability, or need" (p. 561). Professionally speaking, we

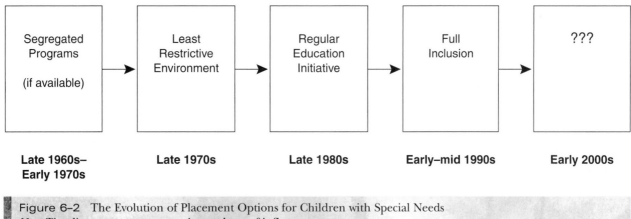

Figure 6-2   The Evolution of Placement Options for Children with Special Needs
Note. Timeline represents approximate dates of influences.

question the wisdom of such a plan and wonder, as does Kauffman (1989), if a child's right to an appropriate education in the LRE would be abused by such an explanation. What Will does advocate is bringing services for children with special needs into inclusive environments. She writes, "The basic issue is providing an educational program that will allow them [children with learning problems] to learn better" (Will, 1986a, p. 21). Will (1986a) believes that educators must also "visualize a system that will bring the program to the child rather than one that brings the child to the program" (p. 21). As early childhood special educators, most of us can embrace this idea. Furthermore, few would argue that special education services would be enhanced if there was greater coordination and cooperation between general and special educators. The true test of the efficacy of REI, however, according to Jenkins, Pious, and Jewell (1990), is whether or not it matches or improves educational outcomes for pupils with disabilities as well as students in general education programs.

Full Inclusion

We see the movement toward **full inclusion** as an extension of REI and earlier thinking about where children with disabilities should be educated. Figure 6–2 illustrates the evolution of this thought process.

As we noted in the introduction to this section, the issue of full inclusion is a potentially explosive concept

with vocal supporters as well as detractors. It has emerged as one of the most controversial and complex practices in the field of early childhood education (Peck, Odom, & Bricker, 1993). As with other controversial topics, an agreed-upon definition is difficult to develop. We offer the following succinct interpretation: full inclusion is a belief that *all* children with disabilities should be taught exclusively (with appropriate supports) in general education classrooms located in their neighborhood schools, that is, the same school and classrooms they would otherwise attend if they were not disabled. This will most likely require extensive curricular modifications along with professional collaboration and teaming between general and special educators (Stainback & Stainback, 1992). Recall that Will (1986a) originally proposed this call for partnership in her regular education initiative. While the trend in judicial interpretations is toward inclusionary placement (Osborne & DiMattia, 1995), the LRE mandate of IDEA does *not* require all pupils to be educated in regular classrooms nor does the legislation require that students be educated in their neighborhood schools (Osborne & DiMattia, 1994).

Advocates of full inclusion believe, according to Gargiulo (2003), that the present pull-out system of serving students with special needs is ineffective. Children are labeled and stigmatized, their programming fragmented, and regular educators assume little or no ownership for special education students. Placement in a regular classroom, with a true

Table 6–3   Key Elements of Full-Inclusion Models

- **"Home School" Attendance.** Defined as the local school the child would attend if nondisabled.

- **Natural Proportion at the School Site.** The percentage of special needs children enrolled in a particular school is in proportion to the percentage of exceptional pupils in the entire school district; in regular education classes this would mean approximately two to three students with disabilities.

- **Zero Rejection.** All students are accepted at the local school, including those with severe impairments; pupils are not screened out or grouped separately because of their disability.

- **Age/Grade Appropriate Placement.** A full-inclusion model calls for serving children with special needs in regular classrooms according to their chronological age rather than basing services according to the child's academic ability or mental age.

- **Site-Based Management Coordination.** Recent trends in school organizational reform suggests a movement away from central office administration for special education programs to one where the building principal (or other administrator) plays a large role in planning and administering programs for all children in the school.

- **Use of Cooperative Learning and Peer Instructional Models.** Instructional practices that involve children learning in a cooperative manner rather than in a competitive fashion and using students to assist in the instruction of classmates with disabilities can be effective strategies for integrating exceptional learners in the regular classroom.

SOURCE: Sailor, Gerry, & Wilson, 1991; Stainback & Stainback, 1992.

partnership between special education teachers and general education teachers, would result in a better education for students with special needs and it would occur within the least restrictive environment. See Table 6–3 for a summary of the key components of most full-inclusion models.

When correctly instituted, full inclusion is characterized by its virtual invisibility. Students with disabilities are not segregated but dispersed into classrooms they would normally attend if they were not disabled. "They are seen," Gargiulo (2003) writes, "as full-fledged members of, not merely visitors to, the general education classroom" (p. 70). Special educators provide services in the regular classroom alongside their general education colleagues.

Full inclusionists advocate the elimination of a continuum of service delivery options such as those illustrated in Figure 6–1. The concept of LRE, however, is not an all or nothing proposition. Only if a full continuum of settings is available can one reasonably ensure that an appropriate placement will be made (Yell, 1995). The true litmus test for advocates of full

inclusion is whether or not this model is more effective than the programming options presently available. The answer awaits the research evidence.

Full inclusion has met with considerable resistance in some professional circles. Critics of this movement (Fuchs & Fuchs, 1991; Kauffman, 1991; Lieberman, 1992; Vergason & Anderegg, 1992) argue that general educators are ill prepared to teach students with special needs, regular classrooms are already overcrowded, and funding as well as support services are inadequate to meet present needs. Special educators, on the other hand, are specially trained to work with children with special needs and an individually determined special education placement is a more appropriate setting for delivering interventions and specialized instruction. Hallahan and Kauffman (2003) remind us that IDEA, as presently interpreted, gives parents the right to choose which environment they, not the full inclusionists, believe is most appropriate and least restrictive for delivering services to their son or daughter. The notion of making decisions based on the indi-

Feature 6–3   The Division for Early Childhood (DEC) Position on Inclusion

Adopted: April 1993
Revised: December 1993
Reaffirmed: December 1996
Revised: June 2000

Inclusion, as a value, supports the right of all children, regardless of abilities, to participate actively in natural settings within their communities. Natural settings are those in which the child would spend time had he or she not had a disability. These settings include, but are not limited to home, preschool, nursery schools, Head Start programs, kindergartens, neighborhood school classrooms, child care, places of worship, recreational (such as community playgrounds and community events) and other settings that all children and families enjoy.

DEC supports and advocates that young children and their families have full and successful access to health, social, educational, and other support services that promote full participation in family and community life. DEC values the cultural, economic, and educational diversity of families and supports a family-guided process for identifying a program of service.

As young children participate in group settings (such as preschool, play groups, child care, kinder-

garten) their active participation should be guided by developmentally and individually appropriate curriculum. Access to and participation in the age appropriate general curriculum becomes central to the identification and provision of specialized support services.

To implement inclusive practices DEC supports: (a) the continued development, implementation, evaluation, and dissemination of full inclusion supports, services, and systems that are of high quality for all children; (b) the development of preservice and inservice training programs that prepare families, service providers, and administrators to develop and work within inclusive settings; (c) collaboration among key stakeholders to implement flexible fiscal and administrative procedures in support of inclusion; (d) research that contributes to our knowledge of recommended practice; and (e) the restructuring and unification of social, educational, health, and intervention supports and services to make them more responsive to the needs of all children and families. Ultimately, the implementation of inclusive practice must lead to optimal developmental benefit for each individual child and family.

Endorsed by the National Association for the Education of Young Children: April 1994, April 1998

---

vidual needs of the child is fundamental to the foundation of special education. Yet, advocates of full inclusion summarily dismiss the idea of individualized decision making by the very nature of their advocacy for full integration (Lieberman, 1990). To assert "that *all* [italics added] students must be educated in integrated settings," Yell (1995) writes, "is as discriminatory as educating all students with disabilities in segregated settings" (p. 400).

As we understand it, full inclusion has come to mean the education of *all* students with exceptionalities in the general education classroom, especially during the preschool and elementary school years (Sailor, Gerry, & Wilson, 1991). Of particular importance to early childhood special education is one proposal where full inclusion is advocated for day care, preschool age youngsters, and kindergartners regard-

less of the type or severity of the child's disability (Sailor, Anderson, Halvorsen, Doering, Filler, & Goetz, 1989). The Association for Childhood Education International (ACEI) supports this viewpoint. In an association position paper crafted by Sexton, Snyder, Sharpton, and Stricklin (1993), ACEI affirms their support for full inclusion for the very youngest of children with disabilities. ACEI believes that young children with special needs should be served in settings designed for their age peers without disabilities. A single inclusive system of care, intervention, and education is considered best for all children and their families. The Division for Early Childhood of the Council for Exceptional Children (CEC) also advocates inclusion, although their position statement (see Feature 6–3) reflects an interpretation broader than just education.

Yet, there is one perplexing issue that must be resolved. If we have accurately interpreted full inclusion, then it represents a radical departure from the concept of a cascade of services (see Figure 6–1) and may well be a violation of current federal law (Gargiulo, 2003). We suspect that the resolution of this debate may well reside in courtrooms across America.

As professionals in the field of early childhood special education, each individual will need to develop his or her own position on the issue of full inclusion for young children with special needs. The topic is certainly controversial; yet, as Rogers (1993) astutely notes, the debate has produced much heat but little light. We fully support the principle of integrating young children with special needs to the maximum extent appropriate. We believe, however, that professionals should formulate their decisions on the basis of skillfully conducted research while considering what is best for the child (and their family) rather than aligning themselves with whomever is banging the drum the loudest.

Transition

Change is inevitable in the lives of young children with special needs. When it occurs, it generally affects the children, their caregivers, and service providers. Change also brings with it the potential of stress due to the disruption of patterns of behavior and fearfulness of new situations and environments. Yet, a typical dimension in the lives of toddlers and preschoolers with disabilities and their families is change, or transition, to new service programs. We succinctly define **transition** as the process of moving from one type of placement to another. A transition can also occur within a particular program and is exemplified when a youngster begins working with a new teacher or is placed in a different classroom. Key elements of the transition process include planning, coordination, cooperation, and follow-up.

One of the main goals of early childhood special education programs is successful transition (Conn-Powers, Ross-Allen, & Holburn, 1990). If accomplished, it presents to children and their families

opportunities for growth and development. It can be an enabling experience. Poorly orchestrated transitions, however, lead to anxiety, uncertainty, and feelings of vulnerability (DEC Task Force on Recommended Practices, 1993).

Program transitions can occur at any time during the early childhood years. For toddlers with disabilities, it may occur upon leaving an early intervention program and entering one devoted to serving preschoolers. For preschoolers with disabilities, it occurs upon entering a preschool special education program and exiting from it. Youngsters may enter from day care, early intervention programs, or from being at home and they leave to be placed in kindergartens, resource rooms, and other appropriate placement options. Inherent in the concept of transition is allegiance to the philosophy of normalization. An attempt is usually made to place a child in a program less restrictive or more normalized than the preceding one (Noonan & Kilgo, 1987). Our goal should always be to serve the youngster in the most natural and normalized setting.

The goal of the transition process is to accomplish the following objectives as identified by the DEC Task Force on Recommended Practices (1993).

1. Ensure continuity of service.
2. Minimize disruption of the family system.
3. Promote child functioning in the natural environment or the least restrictive environment (e.g., home, mainstream preschool program, Head Start, day care, etc.).
4. Involve planning, preparation, implementation, and evaluation within and between programs and with the family. (p. 105)

Conn-Powers and colleagues (1990) developed seven goals for transition through their demonstration project funded by the Handicapped Children's Early Education Program. They believe that the desired outcomes of transition and the planning process itself should focus on:

1. [Promoting] the speedy adjustment of the child and the family to the new educational setting.
2. [Enhancing] the child's independent and successful participation in the new educational setting.

3. [Ensuring] the uninterrupted provision of appropriate services in the least restrictive school setting.

4. [Supporting and empowering] the family as an equal partner in the transition process.

5. [Promoting] collaboration among all constituents in the transition process.

6. [Increasing] the satisfaction of all constituents with
   a. the outcomes of the transition process, and
   b. the transition process itself, including their participation.

7. [Increasing] the likelihood that the child is placed and maintained in the regular kindergarten setting and elementary school mainstream. (p. 94)

The need for effective transitioning is clearly articulated in IDEA and its accompanying rules and regulations. The legislation is very specific about this issue. Part C, which focuses on infants and toddlers, specifies that the individualized family service plan (IFSP) must include a transition plan that outlines the procedures to be undertaken as infants and toddlers move from early intervention to preschool special education programs. Language in Part B, the preschool grant program, also emphasizes the importance of carefully planned transitions. The intent is undeniable—there must be a continuity of services. Almost all states have developed, or are in the process of constructing, policies and agreements that will guide and provide for a seamless system of services for youngsters birth through age five (Danaher & Kraus, 2002). This effort is in concert with legislative intent (PL 105-17) and calls for continuity of services (Sainato & Morrison, 2001).

When a transition occurs it impacts more than the toddler or preschooler. Recall that we assert that change also effects families and professionals as well. It is a crucial time for all involved. Bronfenbrenner (1977) supports this idea and contends that transitions produce "ripple effects" within systems. Like a pebble being dropped in a pond, when a youngster moves from an infant program to a preschool program or from a preschool special education program to a kindergarten, this change in ecology disturbs the existing ecological structure. Obviously, the young-

Planning is crucial for successful transitions.

ster's microsystem is changed. Parents will establish new parent-professional relationships, thus the mesosystem is also modified. Furthermore, involvement with a variety of new and different agencies (ecosystems) is possible and encounters with different regulations, rulings, and even values (macrosystem) is very likely. Professionals must be sensitive to how families react to these changes. The more that existing behavior patterns and routines are disrupted, the greater the likelihood that stress and anxiety will develop. One remedy for this problem is careful and skillful preparation for transitioning. A smooth transition relies on proactive and comprehensive planning. Preparation, by necessity, involves the child, family, and service providers. We now turn our attention to strategies for meaningfully involving key team members.

Child Involvement

A critical component of successful transition is the preparation of the child. A smooth transition depends, in a large part, on the child demonstrating the skills and behaviors required in the new environment. This information is usually gathered by future environment surveys, which describe behaviors needed in the receiving program. There must be a match between the skills in the child's repertoire and the requirements and expectations of the new placement (DEC Task Force on Recommended Practices, 1993). This will require, according to Fowler, Schwartz, and Atwater (1991), an assessment of the youngster's strengths and needs and subsequent instruction in the essential social, behavioral, and academic requirements of the new setting. Identifying and teaching critical skills and routines will enable the student to participate with greater independence and success in the new setting (Conn-Powers et al., 1990).

Key transitional skills have been identified by the DEC Task Force on Recommended Practices (1993, p. 101). This noninclusive list includes the following:

- Social behaviors and self-help skills.
- Motivation and problem-solving skills.
- Preacademic or academic support skills.
- Task-related behaviors.
- Conduct behaviors.
- Communication skills.

Likewise, Noonan and her colleagues (Noonan, Ratokalau, Lauth-Torres, McCormick, Esaki, & Claybaugh, 1992) developed a preschool "survival skills" checklist as part of a demonstration project called Preschool Preparation and Transition. Three clusters of skills were identified: self-help, classroom routines, and communication/socialization skills. Interestingly, eleven skills identified as preschool skills also appear on several kindergarten checklists; the difference being the competency level exhibited by the child. Thus, the following skills are useful for gauging both entering and exiting behavior (Noonan & McCormick, 1993, p. 361) :

- Follows general rules and routines.
- Expresses wants and needs.
- Cooperates with/helps others.
- Complies with directions given by adult.
- Shares materials/toys with peers.

- Socializes with peers.
- Takes turns.
- Interacts verbally with adults.
- Interacts verbally with peers.
- Focuses attention on speaker.
- Makes own decisions.

Any discussion of survival or critical skills needed in a future environment must keep in mind an important caveat: identified survival skills are optimal goals and *not* behavioral prerequisites for placement in a new setting (Salisbury & Vincent, 1990). A youngster's failure to demonstrate specific skills on a checklist should not prohibit the child's movement to the new placement (Noonan & McCormick, 1993).

A list of survival behaviors that facilitate a smooth transition is a necessary, but not sufficient, condition. As Fowler et al. (1991) note, a successful transition requires that the student not only possesses the necessary classroom survival skills, but also uses these skills in the appropriate context. We fully agree with Fowler and her colleagues that, as early childhood special educators, our aim should be to develop strategies for identifying, teaching, and promoting the generalization and maintenance of essential classroom skills rather than attempting to create comprehensive checklists of key behaviors.

Family Involvement

The family of a young child with special needs plays a vital role in the transition process. Recall that in Chapter 2, we argue for professionals to see the child within the context of their family and their family in interaction with larger social systems. A transition from a preschool special education program to a public school kindergarten provides us with a good example. An effective transition requires that professionals not only prepare the child but also fully involve and prepare the parents for movement (see Feature 6–4). A change in programs can be especially stressful for families—routines and schedules are altered, new relationships are established, and old

Feature 6–4   Family Participation in Transition Planning

With the approach of Maria Ramirez's third birthday, her early intervention team members have recommended to Mr. and Mrs. Ramirez that Maria transition from her home-based program to an inclusive, community-based program in order to begin receiving Part B services. Her parents, and grandparents too, are very reluctant to agree to this recommendation. They have expressed their concerns to their service coordinator. Among their worries are working with a whole new staff, the length of Maria's school day, her involvement with typical playmates, her social readiness, transportation difficulties, and other potential problems.

We offer the following suggestions illustrating specific activities that may assist Mr. and Mrs. Ramirez in understanding the transition process, in addition to diminishing their anxieties about their daughter's success in a new setting. Remember, successful transitions depend, in part, on being sensitive to the needs and concerns of the parents.

- Service coordinator schedules meeting with parents (and grandparents if desired) to discuss their preferences, explain transition process and rationale, review legal rights, and ascertain parents' need for support.

- Arrange for Maria and Mr. and Mrs. Ramirez (and grandparents) to visit the facility. Opportunity for parents to meet staff, teachers, and related service providers. Maria visits her classroom and meets other children and staff.

- As desired by Maria's parents, service coordinator arranges meeting with parents of other children enrolled in the class and/or provides Mr. and Mrs. Ramirez with appropriate written materials.

- At least 90 days prior to Maria's third birthday, her service coordinator, in cooperation with Maria's parents, other early intervention team members, and professionals from the program jointly develop a transition plan.

- With parents' permission, service coordinator arranges for program staff to observe Maria's therapy sessions to ensure continuity of service and to answer parents' questions.

- Service coordinator arranges for Maria to visit her classroom on several different occasions. Parents (and grandparents) are provided an opportunity to qualitatively assess impact of attendance on their daughter.

ones relinquished. Attendance at meetings is necessary as well as helpful in establishing new objectives and expectations for their son or daughter (Fowler et al., 1991). An active role in the decision-making process and meaningful involvement can minimize the adverse effects of change. Families must be integrally involved in the transition planning. Professionals must view the child's family as an equal member of the transition team (DEC Task Force on Recommended Practices, 1993).

While parents have much to offer professionals, as well as much to gain by their involvement in the transition process, professionals must be sensitive to the needs and priorities of the individual family. Each family has its own preferred level of involvement. Professionals need to ascertain what the optimal level of involvement is for each family (Fowler et al., 1991).

Teachers and other service providers should not assume that all parents want to be involved in the transition process nor are all parents prepared for the responsibility. Shea and Bauer (1991) point out that many parents will require support, information, and training in order to actively participate in the transition process. Conn-Powers and his colleagues (1990) agree with this viewpoint. They write that "establishing a transition process that enables families to participate as equal partners requires professionals to provide information, support, and opportunity that addresses family-identified needs and goals" (p. 96).

Successful transitions can be accomplished. They require, however, adherence to what we identify as the three Cs: **C**ollaboration, **C**ommunication, and **C**omprehensive planning with families.

Professional Involvement

The third component of our tripartite strategy (see Figure 6–3) for ensuring smooth transitions requires the involvement of a variety of service providers. Professionals from the program the child is exiting (sending program), as well as providers from the program the child is entering (receiving program) must be involved. Team members will most likely include general and special educators, administrators, physical and occupational therapists, speech-language pathologists, service coordinators, and a host of other professionals involved in providing services to the child with disabilities and their family. It is very important that professionals from both the sending and receiving programs work together and understand one another's goals and procedures (Noonan & McCormick, 1993). Cooperative and collaborative planning between both groups will help to facilitate a smooth transition. Formal program/agency policies and procedures will also aid in the transition process. Joint involvement is important due to the number of logistical and programmatic issues that need to be addressed. Examples of these concerns include the identification of program exit criteria, coordination responsibilities, transfer of records, and the selection of placement options (Fowler et al., 1991).

Parents should perceive the transition process as routine and predictable. Services should be minimally interrupted, if at all. Unfortunately, this often is not the case. In some instances programs have not established formal procedures for facilitating the movement of youngsters from one program to another (U.S. Department of Education, 2001). Although effective transition policies are seen as crucial to the development of a coordinated system of transitioning children from one service delivery system to another, parents frequently perceive the process as frustrating and traumatic (Harbin et al., 2000).

Noonan and McCormick (1993) recommend that service providers attempt to minimize the differences between sending and receiving environments. If at all possible, the transition should be gradual, rather than abrupt, and should commence anywhere from six to twelve months before the tod-

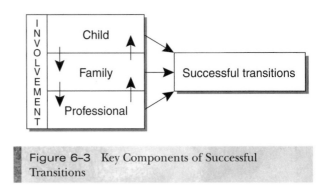

Figure 6–3 Key Components of Successful Transitions

dler or preschooler exits his or her current program. Children in transition need time to adjust to the demands and expectations of the new setting. These experts offer the following five steps that teachers from the sending program can undertake to facilitate movement to the new program—in this example a kindergarten.

1. *Field trips to the "new" school.* Ideally such tours would include lunch in the cafeteria, some time for play on the playground, and participation in a few kindergarten activities.

2. *Reading stories about the fun of new adventures and new friends.* Read (or make up) stories about new experiences.

3. *Helping the children create a scrapbook about kindergarten.* Each child's scrapbook could include photos taken during the field trip, as well as pictures of kindergarten activities created by the child.

4. *Role playing "going to the new school."* In the course of role-play sessions, encourage the children to express their feelings about the new experiences.

5. *Invite kindergarten teachers to visit the class.* Try to arrange for each receiving kindergarten teacher to visit the preschool class. The goal is for the kindergarten teachers to get to know the children in familiar setting. (p. 370)

These steps provide an excellent illustration of the type of activities T. J. Browning's teachers could use to facilitate his movement from the Epps Head Start Center to kindergarten.

Table 6–4   Steps in Planning Transitions

1. Form a transition team—including parents, current program staff, and staff of the most likely receiving programs.

2. Schedule meetings—the first meeting will be to develop an initial written plan; the later meetings will consider specific transition tasks.

3. Identify possible receiving settings.

4. Identify basic transition tasks—what will be necessary to implement the transition?

5. Agree on assignments—specifically, who will perform each of the different transition tasks.

6. Establish timelines—including the referral date and dates for pre-placement activities.

7. Decide communication procedures—including transfer or records and other information.

8. Agree on pre-placement activities—such as

   a. Parent visits to potential receiving environments.

   b. Information sharing between teaching staff in sending and receiving agencies.

   c. Observations in the receiving setting to determine needed adaptations.

   d. Arrangements for whatever family support will be provided.

   e. Therapy and other special services.

   f. Future consultative interactions.

9. Plan for follow-up activities—should be planned and carried out between the family and the agencies involved.

10. Place the child—after needed environmental adaptations have been completed.

11. Provide consultation and therapy services.

12. Follow up and evaluate.

SOURCE: M. Noonan and L McCormick, *Early Intervention in Natural Environments.* Copyright © 1993 Wadsworth Inc. Reprinted by permission.

Steps for Planning Effective Transitions

Smooth transitions don't just happen; they demand extensive preparation on the part of everyone involved. Effective transitions require adherence to a series of well planned out steps. Utilizing the following strategies and recommendations can help to minimize the disruption of services; reduce stress for the child, parents, and service providers; and ensure that movement from one program to another progresses as smoothly as possible. The intent of transition planning is to maximize the students' chances for success in their future environment.

Lazzari and Kilgo (1989) believe that transitions involve three distinct phases: preparation, implementation, and follow-up. Each of these elements are evident in the following transition planning activities. The steps outlined in Table 6–4 serve a dual purpose—they function as an outline for movement from an early intervention program to a preschool program in addition to offering suggestions on transitioning from a preschool special education placement to a kindergarten. We recommend that these responsibilities and procedure be incorporated when planning transitions.

Likewise, the twelve activities generated by Fowler and her colleagues (Fowler et al., 1991) also give us guidance on conducting smooth transitions. Although originally produced to aid in the movement of a student from an early childhood special education program to a kindergarten, we believe that these suggestions are equally valid for the transitioning of toddlers. Their recommendations, illustrated in Table 6–5, represent a synthesis of the thinking of various experts on transitioning.

Collectively, the preceding procedures and strategies provide professionals with a blueprint for constructing a successful transition plan. Effective transition planning, however, also requires attention

Table 6–5   Recommended Transition Planning Activities

1. Agreement on exit criteria from [early intervention or] preschool.

2. Discussion with families regarding the exit criteria, timeline for child's transition from the program, consent for release of information, and the parents' role in planning the transition.

3. Notification of the receiving agency or agencies that [the] child will be entering their service system.

4. Evaluation of [the] child to determine current level of development.

5. Staffing of the child with representatives from the sending and receiving program and family members to determine eligibility for continued special services.

6. Development of the IEP [IFSP] if the child is eligible for continued special education services.

7. Identification of placement options based on principle of least restrictive environment, but only after the child's needs are determined to ensure that placement is appropriate and not based simply on what classrooms are available.

8. A visit to each placement option by parents and by sending program staff; a visit to the sending program by staff from the receiving school.

9. Decision regarding placement by family and staffs.

10. A review of procedural safeguards and transfer of appropriate records.

11. A visit by child and parent to the new classroom and discussion of home-school communication strategies.

12. Follow up by sending and receiving programs to determine if the transition has produced a good fit between child and family and the new program.

SOURCE: S. Fowler, I. Schwartz, and J. Atwater, 1991. Perspectives on the Transition from Preschool to Kindergarten for Children with Disabilities and Their Families, *Exceptional Children, 58*(2), p. 142.

to the barriers which may work against the implementation of the process. Frequently identified barriers include the absence of administrative support, lack of planning time, financial barriers, and the need for inservice training and staff development activities (Conn-Powers et al., 1990; Fowler et al., 1991).

Finally, we believe it is important to point out that the transition planning process does not terminate upon a youngster's entry into the receiving program; rather, it is an ongoing process. Transition team members should continue to serve as resources for the parents and each other even after the child transitions. This provides an avenue for quickly and positively resolving any problems that may develop (Conn-Powers et al., 1990).

Professional Teaming and Collaboration

The idea of professionals working together in a cooperative manner has been part of the fabric of special education almost 30 years. Since the implementation of PL 94-142, attention has been focused on how

professionals from a variety of disciplines can work collaboratively in the planning and delivering of services to young children with special needs and their families. In fact, the concept of collaboration is an integral part of the philosophical foundation of PL 99-457. It should be apparent that no one discipline, agency, or professional possesses all of the resources or clinical skills needed to devise appropriate interventions or construct appropriate educational plans for youngsters with disabilities, many of whom have complex needs. Furthermore, collaboration can be the vehicle by which services are provided in an integrated rather than fragmented fashion (McCollum & Maude, 1993). Some of the benchmarks of successful inclusive programs for young children with special needs are collaborative relationships among early childhood teachers and the service providers needed to provide an appropriate education (Odom & Diamond, 1998). Bailey and Wolery (1989) identified several other reasons why collaboration is beneficial: (1) erroneous placement recommendations are reduced; (2) assessments are more likely to be nondiscriminatory; and (3) more appropriate service plans and intervention goals are

Table 6-6   Professions Typically Serving Young Children with Special Needs

Audiology

To provide and coordinate services to children with auditory difficulties, including detecting the problem and managing any existing communication disabilities.

Early Childhood Special Education

To ensure that environments for infants and preschoolers with disabilities facilitate the development of social, motor, communication, self-help, cognitive, and behavioral skills that enhance children's self concept, sense of competence and control, and independence.

Medicine

To assist families in promoting optimal health, growth, and development for their infants and young children by providing health services.

Nursing

To diagnose and treat actual and potential human responses to illness; for infants and preschoolers with disabilities, this means (1) promoting the highest health and development status possible and (2) helping families cope with changes in their lives resulting form the child's disability.

Nutrition

To maximize the health and nutritional status of infants and preschoolers through developmentally appropriate nutrition services within family and community environments.

Occupational Therapy

To promote children's independence, mastery, and sense of self-worth in their physical, emotional, and psychosocial development; purposeful activity is used to expand the child's functional abilities, such as self-help skills, adaptive behavior play skills, sensory, motor, and postural development; these services are designed to help families and other caregivers improve children's functioning in their environment.

Physical Therapy

To enhance the sensory motor development, neurobehavioral organizations, and cardiopulmonary status of at-risk infant's or those with disabilities and preschool children within a family and community context.

Psychology

To derive a comprehensive picture of child and family functioning and to identify, implement, or evaluate psychological interventions.

Social Work

To improve the quality of life for infants and toddlers and their families who are served by IDEA through the provision of social work services.

Speech/Language Pathology

To promote children's communication skills in the context of social interactions with peers and family members, in school, and in the community.

SOURCE: Adapted from L. Rossetti, *Infant-Toddler Assessment*, (Austin, TX: Pro-Ed, 1990). p. 215. Original source adaptation: Carolina Institute for Research on Infant Personnel Preparation (1998). *Proceedings of a Working Conference*. Unpublished manuscript.

generated as a result of professional teaming. Additionally, a team approach, according to Sexton, Snyder, Lobman, Kimbrough, and Matthews (1997), improves the efficiency of professionals delivering early intervention. Yet, effective collaboration requires a high degree of cooperation and mutual respect among the various service providers.

A variety of disciplines are involved in delivering services to children at-risk and youngsters with specific learning or development problems. Teams differ according to their membership. Some of the professionals typically involved in the assessment and delivery of services to young children with special needs are identified in Table 6–6.

Teams also differ according to their structure and function. Three types of team organizations are utilized in delivering services. The three most common approaches identified in the professional literature (McGonigel, Woodruff, & Roszmann-Millican, 1994; Noonan & McCormick, 1993) include

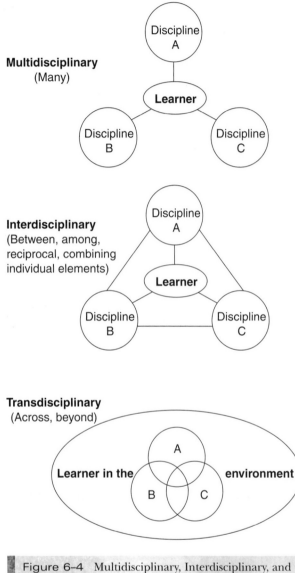

Multidisciplinary
(Many)

Interdisciplinary
(Between, among,
reciprocal, combining
individual elements)

Transdisciplinary
(Across, beyond)

Figure 6–4   Multidisciplinary, Interdisciplinary, and Transdisciplinary Team Models

SOURCE: M. Giangreco, J. York, & B. Rainforth, 1989. Providing Related Services to Learners with Severe Handicaps in Educational Settings: Pursuing the Least Restrictive Option, *Pediatric Physical Therapy, 1*(2), p. 57.

multidisciplinary, interdisciplinary, and transdisciplinary teams. Each of these approaches are interrelated; and, according to Roberts-DeGennaro (1996), represents a historical evolution of teamwork. This

evolutionary process can be portrayed as concentric circles with each model retaining some of the attributes of its predecessor. Figure 6–4 illustrates these various configurations.

Multidisciplinary

The idea of a **multidisciplinary** team can be found in PL 94-142. This approach, whose origins are grounded on a medical model, utilizes the expertise of professionals from several disciplines, each of whom usually perform assessments and other tasks (e.g., report writing, goal setting) independent of one another. Each individual contributes according to his or her own specialty area with little regard for the actions of other professionals. There is a high degree of professional autonomy and minimal integration. It is viewed as a team only in the sense that each person shares a common goal. There is very little coordination or collaboration across discipline areas.

Families often meet with each team member individually. They are generally passive recipients of information about their son or daughter. Because information to the parents flows from several sources, some parents may encounter difficulty synthesizing all of the data and recommendations from the various experts. We do not consider the multidisciplinary model to be especially "family-friendly." It is also contrary to contemporary thinking regarding family involvement and empowering parents (Dunst, Trivette, & Deal, 1988). Effective team models provide opportunities for parental input; they are part of the decision-making process.

Interdisciplinary

PL 99-457 stresses the concept of **interdisciplinary** collaboration. With an interdisciplinary team, members perform their evaluations independently; however, program development and recommendations are the result of sharing information, joint planning, and mutual decision-making. Significant cooperation exists among the team members, leading to an integrated plan of services. Coordination and collaboration are the hallmark of this model. Direct services, however, such as physical therapy, are usually provided in isolation from one another. Families typically meet with the team or its representative; for the infant or toddler with special needs this role is fulfilled by the service coordinator.

In addition to the potential for "professional turf" protection among team members, Noonan and McCormick (1993) call attention to another possible flaw with this model. They observe that information generally flows in one direction—from the various professionals involved in the assessment to the service provider. There is no mechanism in this model for the provider to give feedback as to the appropriateness of the intervention recommendations; for example, are they practical, functional, and meeting the needs of the youngster and their family?

Transdisciplinary

The **transdisciplinary** approach to providing services builds upon the strengths of the interdisciplinary model. It is distinguished, however, by two additional and related features: role sharing and a primary therapist. Professionals in the various disciplines conduct their initial evaluations; yet, they relinquish their role (role release) as service providers by teaching their skills to other team members, one of whom will serve as the primary interventionist. For preschoolers with special needs, this role is usually filled by the early childhood special educator. This individual relies heavily on the support and consultation provided by his or her professional peers. Team members trust in each other's competencies and rely on each other's expertise (Roberts-DeGennaro, 1996). Discipline-specific interventions are still available, although they occur less frequently.

"The primary purpose of this approach," according to Bruder (1994), "is to pool and integrate the expertise of team members so that more efficient and comprehensive assessment and intervention services may be provided" (p. 61). The aim of the transdisciplinary model is to avoid compartmentalization and fragmentation of services. It attempts to provide a more coordinated and unified or holistic approach to assessment and service delivery; team members func-

tion as a unit. Professionals from various backgrounds teach, learn, and work together in order to accomplish a common set of goals (Bruder, 2001). A transdisciplinary service delivery model also encourages a whole-child and whole-family approach (Raver, 1999). Families are full members of the team and share in the decision-making process. This model is currently the recommended model in early intervention and early childhood special education (Bruder, 2001; Davis, Kilgo, & Gamel-McCormick, 1998; Sandall et al., 2000).

"A transdisciplinary model," according to Davis and his colleagues (Davis et al., 1998), "lends itself to integrated therapeutic services in the natural environment" (p. 57). This approach, which is growing in popularity (Guralnick, 2001), is recommended over a "pull-out" model whereby children are removed from a normalized setting in order to receive various services. Young children learn best "through ongoing interactions with their natural environment rather than in isolated lessons or sessions (Sandall et al., 2000, p. 49). Integrated therapies that incorporate the youngster's typical routines and natural activities result in increased skill acquisition (Bruder, 1994).

Professionals generally agree that an interdisciplinary team model is superior to a multidisciplinary approach. Considerable debate exists, however, as to the advantages and disadvantages of a transdisciplinary model (Bailey & Wolery, 1989). Despite the fact that a transdisciplinary approach is sometimes difficult to implement because of the required degree of collaboration, it is slowly evolving as the optimal model for the design and delivery of services for young children with special needs who are enrolled in early childhood programs (Bruder, 1994). The transdisciplinary model is equally appropriate for infants and toddlers with special needs, due to its emphasis on family involvement and cross-disciplinary collaboration. It is also recommended as the vehicle for ensuring mutual decision making and effective inclusionary practices in early intervention (Bruder, 2001). Individuals who embrace this approach, however, need to be cautious that they do not overstep the boundaries of their professional competency and expertise.

Transdisciplinary teams

Most Collaborative
Most Cooperative
Most Coordinated
Most Integrative
High Family
   Involvement

Interdisciplinary teams

Multidisciplinary teams

Least Collaborative
Least Cooperative
Least Coordinated
Least Integrative
Low Family
   Involvement

Figure 6–5   Characteristics of Team Models

In conclusion, we predict that, for a variety of reasons (economic, personnel shortages, complexity of child/family needs), there will be a growing recognition of the importance of integrating interventions across developmental domains (DEC Task Force on Recommended Practices, 1993) in spite of the difficulty inherent with interprofessional collaboration. Professional teaming will become the key to delivering services in a judicious fashion. Parents and professionals will increasingly find themselves linked together as program partners. Figure 6–5 highlights, in hierarchical fashion, some of the characteristics of each team model we discussed.

Delivering Individualized Services

Effective programs for infants, toddlers, and preschoolers with special needs require that professionals and parents work together as a team. Perhaps nowhere else is this linkage more crucial than in the development of an **individualized family service plan (IFSP)** and an **individualized education program (IEP).** By mandate of federal law (IDEA), each youngster identified as disabled and in need of special education is required to have an individualized program plan of specially designed instruction that addresses the unique needs of the child and his or her family. The design and delivery of customized services and instruction is guided by one of these documents.

Individualized Family Service Plan

Recall from Chapter 2 that the IFSP is the blueprint behind the delivery of early intervention services to infants and toddlers who are at-risk or disabled. While primarily focusing on children younger than age three, changes in thinking now allow the document to be used with preschoolers who require a special education. In an effort to minimize the differences between early intervention and preschool special education services, the government has encouraged states to establish "seamless systems" designed to serve youngsters birth through age five (Stowe & Turnbull, 2001). As a result of this policy decision, states now have the authority to use IFSPs for preschoolers with special needs until the child's sixth birthday. States are reminded that when a free and appropriate public education is provided by an IFSP that the Part B rights and protections still apply (U.S. Department of Education, 1994). As of May 2002, one state is studying the feasibility of using IFSPs for its preschool population; Oregon and Maine use IFSPs as statewide policy; while 17 additional states allow local discretion in using the IFSP for delivering preschool services (Danaher & Kraus, 2002).

The shift in policy is partly derived from a belief that similarities in service delivery for youngsters birth through age five are greater than the differences. Additionally, the needs of children are generally best met with a single system of service (U.S. Department of Education, 1993). While there are several exchangeable features of IEPs (which we will discuss shortly) and IFSPs, a few distinguishable components stand out; for example, the IEP is silent regarding the issue of service coordination and transition planning for young children. Another difference is the IFSP acknowledgment of the family as the focal point of services in contrast to the emphasis in the IEP on the individual child and their educational needs. Our final illustration relates to the role of the parents and their interaction with professionals. Strickland (1993) succinctly captures the difference between both systems.

> Whether by design or as a result of implementation, parents, upon entering the public school system, primarily participate in procedural and decision-making capacities. There is little, if any, provision for assessment of, or services to, the parents or family of school-aged children with disabilities. (p. 233)

The IFSP is developed by a team consisting of professionals and the child's parents who are the key members of the team. Additionally, parents may invite other family members to participate as well as an advocate. Typically, the service coordinator who has been working with this family, those professionals involved in the assessment of the youngster, and the service providers constitute the remainder of the group charged with the responsibility of writing the IFSP. Figure 6–6 portrays recommended practices and guiding principles needed for crafting effective IFSPs.

An IFSP, which is to be developed within 45 days of referral, must include the following components. These requirements are the result of the enactment of PL 105-17 and were effective July 1, 1998:

- A statement of the infant's or toddler's present levels of physical development, cognitive development, communication development, social or emotional development, and adaptive development.

- A statement of the family's resources, priorities, and concerns.

- A statement of major outcomes expected to be achieved for the infant or toddler and the family including criteria, procedures, and timelines used to assess progress toward outcomes.

- A statement of early intervention services necessary to meet the unique needs of the infant or toddler and the family. (See Table 6–7 for a list of representative early intervention services.)

- The projected dates for initiation of services and the anticipated duration of such services.

- The name of the service coordinator.

- A statement of the natural environments in which early intervention services shall be provided . . . or justification if services are not provided in said environment.

- The steps . . . supporting the transition of the toddler with a disability to services provided under Part B (preschool).

Obviously, the preceding features are important to the development of an effective plan for delivering services to infants and toddlers with special needs. Yet, according to De Gangi, Royeen, and Wietlisbach (1992), the truly important element is the creation of a plan based on mutual respect and trust among all of the participants. In fact, these authorities believe that it is fair to say that the *process* itself is more important than the plan *per se*. We are in agreement with their analysis. As we noted in Chapter 3, professionals need to form partnerships with families, while realizing that different goals and priorities for the child may legitimately exist.

The IFSP was intentionally designed to preserve the family's role of primary caregiver. Well-constructed IFSPs fully support the family and encourage their active and meaningful involvement. (See page 182 for an IFSP completed for Maria Ramirez and her family.) This thinking is in keeping with an empowerment model, which views families as capable (with occasional assistance) of helping themselves (Turbiville, Turnbull, Garland, & Lee, 1996). This point of view allows

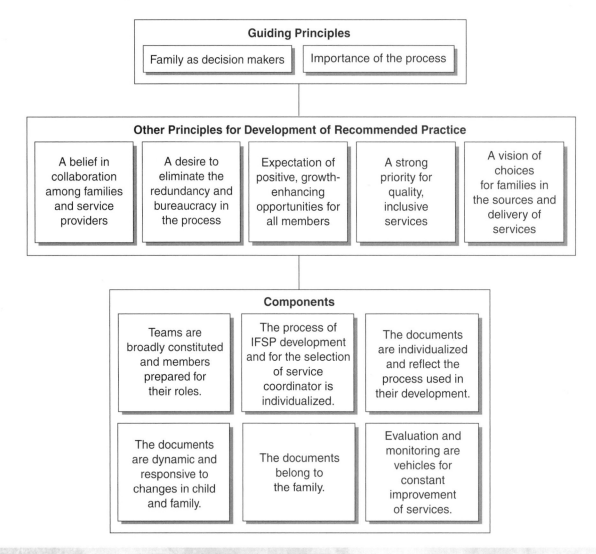

SOURCE: Adapted from DEC Task Force on Recommended Practices, *DEC Recommended Practices: Indicators of Quality in Programs for Infants and Young Children with Special Needs and Their Families* (Reston, VA: Division for Early Childhood, Council for Exceptional Children, 1993), p. 31.

parents to retain their decision-making role, establish goals, and assess their needs among other functions. It is also in keeping with our support of an ecological perspective (Bronfenbrenner, 1979), which argues that one cannot look at a child without considering the various systems and spheres of influence that provide support; in this instance, the infant's or toddler's family and community.

Various features of the IFSP reflect a family focus. One feature in particular, however, stands out—the assessment of the family's resources, priorities, and concerns. Although IDEA encourages early intervention programs to gather this information, family assessment is to be a voluntary activity on the part of the families. While a personal interview with key family members is to be conducted by trained personnel,

Table 6-7 Representative Early Intervention Services Available to Infants/Toddlers and Their Families	
Assistive technology devices and services	Physical therapy
Audiology	Psychological services
Family training, counseling, and home visits	Service coordination
Health services	Social work services
Medical services (only for diagnosis and evaluation)	Special education
Nursing services	Speech-language pathology
Nutrition services	Transportation (direct and related costs)
Occupational therapy	Vision services

considerable debate exists among professionals as to the best and most appropriate strategies for obtaining information about the family (McLean, Bailey, & Wolery, 1996). Furthermore, any information obtained must be gathered in a culturally sensitive fashion and reflect the family's perception of their resources, priorities, and concerns.

This concept of family assessment has been an evolving one. PL 99-457 originally referred to a statement of family needs and strengths. PL 102-119 modified this language because many families objected to the idea of being "needy" and requiring help from professionals. Contemporary thinking emphasizes that while families may have concerns about their young child, they also possess certain resources and strengths. It is the task of professionals to build on these attributes and to instill in families a sense of confidence and competence (Turnbull, & Turnbull, 2001).

"The primary role of professionals," Bailey (1994) writes, "is to seek to understand how families view their child and what kinds of services they would like from early childhood programs" (p. 34). Bruder (2001) more recently urges professionals to carefully listen to what families have to say so that they may better understand what is important for the family. We fully agree with this thinking and encourage service providers to appreciate the concerns and understand the priorities of the family from the family's perspective. We would like to reiterate our earlier point—families need to be the primary decision makers

about what is best for them and their son or daughter. Our job is to help them in this effort.

Information obtained from the family and data about the infant's developmental status are used to generate outcome statements or goals for the child and his or her family. Practitioners are increasingly emphasizing real-life or authentic goals for infants and toddlers (as well as preschoolers) with special needs (Notari-Syverson & Shuster, 1995). These goals are reflected in the ISFP's required outcome statements. Best practice suggests that these statements focus on the priorities and concerns of the family.

Interventionists no longer teach skills in isolation; rather, goals are developed that are relevant to the daily activities of the youngster and their families. These statements need to be practical and functional, reflecting authentic situations that occur in the natural environment. Contemporary thinking encourages practitioners to structure learning opportunities that emphasize the acquisition of competence in natural settings. According to Notari-Syverson and her colleague (1995), five components are necessary for meaningful objectives:

- *Functionality*—skills necessary for independently interacting within the daily environment.
- *Generality*—general vs. specific skills which are adaptable to meet the individual needs of the child.
- *Ease of integration*—skills that can be used in a variety of natural environments such as the home, classroom, or playground.

INDIVIDUALIZED FAMILY SERVICE PLAN

I. Child and Family Information

Child's Name _Maria Ramirez_

Date of Birth _12–14–01_   Age in Months _30_   Gender _F_

Parents(s)/Guardian(s) _Bruce & Catherine Ramirez_

Address _2120 Valley Park Place_   _Middletown, IN_   _46810_

        Street   City   Zip Code

Home Telephone No. _(513) 555–0330_

Work Telephone No. _(513) 555–1819_

Preferred Language _English_

Translator Appropriate _____ Yes _X_ No

II. Service Coordination

Coordinator's Name _Susan Green_

Agency _Indiana Early Intervention Program_

Address _105 Data Drive_   _Burlington, IN_   _46980_

        Street   City   Zip Code

Telephone No. _(513) 555–0214_

Appointment Date _6–10–04_

III. IFSP Team Members

Name	Agency	Telephone No.	Title/Function
Susan Green	Indiana Early Intervention (EI) Program	513–555–0214	Service Coordinator
Mr. & Mrs. B. Ramirez	N/A	513–555–0330	Parents
Barbara Smith	Indiana EI Program	513–555–0215	Speech/Language Pathologist
Martha King	Indiana EI Program	513–555–0213	Occupational Therapist
Libby Young	Middletown Preschool Program	513–555–3533	Preschool Teacher

IV. Review Dates

Date of IFSP _6–10–04_   Six Month Review _12–10–04_   Annual Evaluation _6–10–05_

V. Statements of Family Strengths and Resources

Maria's parents are well-educated professional individuals with realistic goals for her educational development. The entire family unit, including her grandparents, are committed and motivated to assist her in any way. Because of the family's geographical location, limited resources are available for service delivery at this time.

IX. Transition Plans

If eligible, the following steps will be followed to transition **_Maria Ramirez_** to Part B services on or about **_12–14–04_**

Child's Name   Projected Transition Date

1. The service coordinator will schedule meeting with parents to explain the transition process and rationale, review their legal rights, and ascertain their preferences and need for support.

2. The service coordinator will arrange for Maria and her parents (and grandparents) to visit the center and meet teachers, staff, and children.

3. The service coordinator will arrange for Maria to visit her classroom on at least three occasions in the month prior to her transition date.

4. At least 90 days prior to Maria's third birthday, the service coordinator will convene a meeting to further develop Maria's transition plan.

X. Identification of Natural Environments

The home environment is considered to be Maria's natural environment at this time.

Justification for not providing services in natural environment: not applicable.

XI. FAMILY AUTHORIZATION

We (I) the parent(s)/guardian(s) of _Maria Ramirez_ hereby certify that we (I) have had the opportunity to participate in the development of our (my) son's/daughter's IFSP. This document accurately reflects our (my) concerns and priorities for our (my) child and family.

We (I) therefore give our (my) permission for this plan to be implemented.

     X
   ──────   ──────
   Yes   No

Catherine Ramirez	_6–10–04_	_Bruce Ramirez_	_6–10–04_
Signature of Parent/Guardian	Date	Signature of Parent/Guardian	Date

I agree to facilitate this plan and provide appropriate assistance and guidance to the family.

Susan Green	_6–10–04_	_Barbara Smith_	_6–10–04_
Signature	Date	Signature	Date

Martha King	_6–10–04_	_Libby Young_	_6–10–04_
Signature	Date	Signature	Date

- *Measurability*—skills must be capable of being measured such as their frequency or duration.
- *Hierarchical relationship*—complex skills need to be logically sequenced building upon earlier behaviors.

Table 6–8 provides a checklist constructed by Notari-Syverson and Shuster for determining whether or not the IFSP statements fulfill the preceding criteria.

Individualized Education Program

The IEP is part of an overall strategy designed to deliver needed services appropriate to the individual preschooler (and older students). By the time we reach the IEP stage, the appropriate permissions have been gathered, assessments conducted, and a disability determination has been made. We are now at the point where the IEP is developed, followed by

Table 6–8   Checklist for Writing IFSP (and IEP) Goals and Objectives for Infants and Young Children

Functionality

1. Will the skill increase the child's ability to interact with people and objects within the daily environment?
   The child needs to perform the skill in all or most of environments in which he or she interacts.

Skill:	Places object into container.
Opportunities:	Home—Places sweater in drawer, cookie in paper bag.
	School—Places lunch box in cubbyhole, trash in trash bin.
	Community—Places milk carton in grocery cart, rocks and soil in flower pot.

2. Will the skill have to be performed by someone else if the child cannot do it?
   The skill is a behavior or event that is critical for completion of daily routines.

Skill:	Looks for objects in usual location.
Opportunities:	Finds coat on coat rack, gets food from cupboard.

Generality

3. Does the skill represent a general concept or class of responses?
   The skill emphasizes a generic process, rather than a particular instance.

Skill:	Fits objects into defined spaces.
Opportunities:	Puts mail in mailbox, places crayons in box, puts cutlery into sorter.

4. Can the skill be adapted or modified for a variety of disabling conditions?
   The child's sensory impairment should interfere as little as possible with the performance.

Skill:	Correctly activates simple toy.
Opportunities:	Motor impairments—Activates light, easy-to-move toys (e.g., balls, rocking horse, toys on wheels, roly-poly toys).
	Visual impairments—Activates large, bright, noise-making toys (e.g., bells, drums, large rattles).

5. Can the skill be generalized across a variety of settings, materials, and/or people?
   The child can perform the skill with interesting materials and in meaningful situations.

Skill:	Manipulates two small objects simultaneously.
Opportunities:	Home—Builds with small interlocking blocks, threads lace on shoes.
	School—Sharpens pencil with pencil sharpener.
	Community—Takes coins out of small wallet.

Table 6–8   Checklist for Writing IFSP (and IEP) Goals and Objectives for Infants and Young Children *(continued)*

Instructional Context

6. Can the skill be taught in a way that reflects the manner in which the skill will be used in the daily environments?
   The skill can occur in a naturalistic manner.

Skill:	Uses object to obtain another object.
Opportunities:	Use fork to obtain food, broom to rake toy; steps on stool to reach toy on shelf.

7. Can the skill be elicited easily by the teacher/parent within the classroom/home activities?
   The skill can be initiated easily by the child as a part of daily routines.

Skill:	Stacks objects.
Opportunities:	Stacks books, cups/plates, wooden logs.

Measurability

8. Can the skill be seen and/or heard?
   Different observers must be able to identify the same behavior.

Measurable skill:	Gains attention and refers to object, person, and/or event.
Nonmeasurable skill:	Experiences a sense of self-importance.

9. Can the skill be directly counted (e.g., by frequency, duration, distant measures)?
   The skill represents a well-defined behavior or activity.

Measurable skill:	Grasps pea-sized object.
Nonmeasurable skill:	Has mobility in all fingers.

10. Does the skill contain or lend itself to determination of performance criteria?
    The extent and/or degree of accuracy of the skill can be evaluated.

Measurable skill:	Follows one-step directions with contextual cues.
Nonmeasurable skill:	Will increase receptive language skills.

Hierarchical Relation Between Long-Range Goal and Short-Term Objective

Is the short-term objective a developmental subskill or step thought to be critical to the achievement of the long-range goal?

Appropriate: Short-Term Objective—Releases object with each hand.
Long-Range Goal—Places and releases object balanced on top of another object.

Inappropriate: 1. The Short-Term Objective is a restatement of the same skill as the Long-Range Goal with the addition of an instructional prompt. (e.g., Short-Term Objective—Activates mechanical toy with physical prompt. Long-Range Goal—Independently activates mechanical toy) or a quantitative limitation to the extent of the skill (e.g., Short-Term Objective—Stacks five 1-inch blocks; Long-Range Goal—Stacks ten 1-inch blocks).
2. The Short-Term Objective is not conceptually or functionally related to the Long-Range Goal (e.g., Short-Term Objective—Releases objects voluntarily; Long-Range Goal—Pokes with index finger).

SOURCE: A. Notari-Syverson and S. Shuster, 1995. Putting Real-Life Skills into IEP/IFSP's for Infants and Young Children, *Teaching Exceptional Children, 27* (2), p. 29.

placement in the most appropriate and least restrictive setting with reviews occurring at least annually. (Parents may request a review prior to the annual review.) A complete reevaluation of the pupil's eligibility for special education must occur every three years. PL 105–17 waives this stipulation, however, if both parents and school officials agree that such a review is unnecessary.

Bateman and Linden (1998) make a very important point about *when* the IEP is developed. They feel that IEPs are often written at the wrong time. Legally, the IEP is to be developed within thirty days following the evaluation and determination of the child's disability but *before* a placement recommendation is formulated. Placement in the LRE is based on a completed IEP, not the other way around. (See Fig. 6–7.) A commonly noted abuse is developing the IEP on the basis of available placements or simple administrative convenience. Although professionals frequently follow this procedure, it is illegal. What often happens is that we wind up fitting children into programs rather than planning programs to meet the needs of the students. The IEP is not to be limited by placement options or the availability of services. The IEP, once developed, serves according to Strickland (1993), "as the basis for determining how and in what setting special education and related services will be provided" (p. 243).

The benchmark of early childhood special education is individualization. Instead of fitting the child into the program (curriculum), a curriculum is tailored that meets the individual needs of the student. One of the cornerstones of constructing appropriate curricula for young children with special needs is their IEP. Based upon a multidisciplinary educational evaluation of the pupil's strengths and needs, an individualized plan of learning activities and objectives is prescribed. It is perhaps best to envision the IEP as a management tool or planning vehicle, which ensures that children with disabilities receive an individualized education appropriate to their unique needs. This focus is in concert with both the intent and spirit of IDEA.

The purpose of the IEP is interpreted differently by various authorities in special education. Polloway, Patton, Payne, and Payne (1989) identify what they believe to be the most prominent purposes of an IEP. First, IEPs furnish instructional direction acting as a blueprint to providing integrated instruction. Next, an IEP can serve as a basis for evaluation. Goals can function as a measure of instructional effectiveness and student progress. Finally, well-written IEPs have the potential to improve communication among team members—educators, parents, and other professional staff. Likewise, Strickland (1993) believes that the single most important purpose of an IEP meeting is one of establishing positive and trusting relationships among all parties. In turn, this provides a strong foundation for mutual planning and joint decision making on behalf of the child. Our view of the purpose of an IEP is most clearly reflected in the thinking of Goodman and Bond (1993). Like these

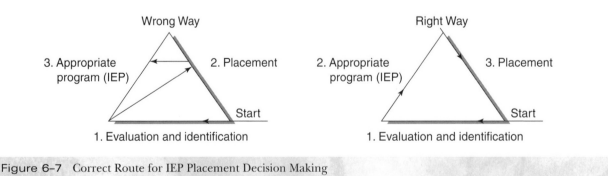

Figure 6-7   Correct Route for IEP Placement Decision Making

SOURCE: B. Bateman and M. Linden, *Better IEPs: How to Develop Legally Correct and Educationally Useful Programs,* 3rd ed., (Longmont, CO: Sopris West, 1998). p. 66.

IEPs and IFSPs are written by a team.

two experts, we see the original purpose of the IEP as an instrument of professional accountability, which has slowly evolved into an instructional and evaluative mechanism. We do not necessarily view this shift as totally inappropriate or unreasonable. It is important to remember, however, that some contemporary interpretations of the IEP have drifted from its original intent—to "ensure adequate service by insisting on individualized program planning and professional accountability" (Goodman & Bond, 1993, p. 409).

Like the IFSP, IEPs are written by a team. At a minimum, participation must include one or both parents/guardians; the child's teachers (including a special educator and at least one general education teacher); an individual capable of interpreting evaluation results; and a representative from the school district. When appropriate, the student and other professionals whose expertise is desired may participate at the discretion of the parent or school. Parents have a legal right to meaningfully participate in this planning and decision-making process; they serve as the child's advocate. While IDEA mandates a collaborative role for parents, it does not stipulate the degree or extent of their participation. As Strickland (1993) notes, the legislation is "not a mandate to measure up to an established standard of participation" (p. 236). The parents choose the extent to which they wish to be involved. They alone define

their role on the team. Professionals must respect the parents' right to choose their level of involvement and participation. Table 6–9 contains a list of strategies professionals can use to enhance parental involvement in the IEP conference.

The role of the regular and special education teacher is crucial in the IEP development process; these professionals are usually ultimately responsible for implementing the team's decisions. Pavia (1992) believes that both the special educator and early childhood teacher should jointly be viewed as the child's teacher. Their role in developing the IEP is complementary and mutually supporting. Unfortunately, general educators sometimes express dissatisfaction with the IEP process. Among their concerns is a lack of meaningful involvement and believing that they are not a valued member of the team (Menlove, Hudson, & Suter, 2001). The failure of these professionals to meaningfully collaborate will often limit the effectiveness of the IEP.

The required components of an IEP that must be in effect at the beginning of each school year include:

- A statement of the child's present levels of educational performance, including a statement of how the pupil's disability affects the child's involvement in general curriculum; or for preschoolers, a statement of how the disability affects participation in appropriate activities.

- A statement of measurable annual goals and accompanying short-term instructional objectives or benchmarks, which address the student's involvement and progress in the general education curriculum and objectives related to meeting the child's other educational needs.

- A statement of special education, related services, and supplementary aids and services to be provided . . . including a statement of program modifications or supports necessary to advance toward attainment of annual goals; to be involved and progress in the general education curriculum, extracurricular, and nonacademic activities; and to be educated and participate in activities with other children with disabilities and nondisabled children.

Table 6-9 Strategies for Facilitating Parent Participation in IEP Planning

1. Provide appropriate written notices to parents regarding their involvement in IEP committees, including the requirements of stating the purpose of the IEP, arranging a mutually convenient time and location, and informing parents of the persons who will be attending the meeting.

2. Demonstrate skills in informing parents of evaluation results and IEP involvement using, in addition to the written notice, the strategies of parent-teacher conferences, phone calls, and home visits.

3. Prepare parents for meaningful IEP involvement prior to their attendance at the conference by training them in their specific roles and responsibilities.

4. Create an atmosphere in the initial portion of IEP committees that will contribute to effective parental involvement such as greeting parents, making introductions, and ensuring that parents understand their particular role and responsibilities as committee members.

5. Communicate with parents by displaying respect for the child, sensitivity to the parents' feelings, recognition of the parents' right to the confidentiality of their private life, and the willingness to listen to and respect the parents' viewpoints.

6. Initiate strategies for involving parents in active decision making, if they do not automatically assume this role, by modeling the role of asking questions and stating diverse viewpoints, reinforcing parental responses, and directing questions to parents.

7. Inform parents of their legal rights in understandable and jargon-free terminology.

8. Review evaluation results with parents in terms of specific strengths and weaknesses of their child and relating this information to the child's performance at school and home.

9. Discuss and negotiate the following aspects of IEP development with parents: (a) levels of performance; (b) annual goals; (c) short-term objectives; (d) evaluation procedures; (e) special education placement and related services; (f) extent of time in the regular class; and (g) method of reviewing the IEP on at least an annual basis.

10. Elicit special concerns from parents related to their child and ensure that these concerns are carefully considered by the IEP committee.

11. Clarify with parents the particular follow-up responsibilities of IEP committee members and negotiate preferred strategies for parent-teacher communication throughout the school year.

12. Devise strategies for appointing, training, and involving parent surrogates for the IEP conference when the child's parent (biological, guardian, foster, or adoptive) cannot be located.

SOURCE: B. Strickland, Parents and the Educational System. In J. Paul and R. Simeonsson (Eds.), *Children with Special Needs*, (Fort Worth, TX: Harcourt Brace Jovanovich, 1993) p. 238.

- An explanation of the extent, if any, to which the student will *not* participate in the general education classroom.
- A statement of any individual modifications needed for child to participate in state- or district-wide assessments; if student will not participate, a statement why the assessment is inappropriate and how the pupil will be assessed is required.

- Projected date for initiation of services; expected location, duration, and frequency of such services.
- Beginning at age 14, a statement of transition service needs to focus on student's course of study; beginning at age 16 (or earlier if determined by IEP team), a statement of needed transition services, including a statement of inter-agency responsibilities; and at least one year prior to reaching age of majority,

information must be provided regarding trans-feral of rights to student upon reaching age of majority.

- A statement of how progress toward annual goals will be measured and a statement of how student's parents (guardians) will be regularly informed of such progress.

In addition to the preceding components, federal regulations require that the IEP team consider the following factors when developing a youngster's IEP (or IFSP).

- For a child with limited English proficiency, consider the language needs of the child as those needs relate to the child's IEP or IFSP;

- For a child who is blind or visually impaired, provide for instruction in Braille and the use of Braille unless the IEP teams determines, after an evaluation of the child's reading and writing skills, needs, and appropriate reading and writing media (including an evaluation of the child's future needs for instruction in Braille or the use of Braille), that instruction in Braille or the use of Braille is not appropriate for the child;

- For a child who is deaf or hard of hearing, consider the child's language or communication needs, opportunities for direct communication with peers and professional personnel in the child's language and communication mode, academic level, and full range of needs, including opportunities for direct instruction and the child's language and communication mode; and

- Consider whether the child requires assistive technology devices and services. (Walsh, Smith, & Taylor, 2000, p. 30)

Unfortunately, these elements, which were effective July 1, 1998, do not contain any provision for family goals and services as found in PL 99-457 (see Table 6–10). Yet, there is no empirical or theoretical reason, Bailey and Wolery (1992) believe, for excluding this component. We agree with this point of view. In fact, it could reasonably be argued that this element is equally important for preschool children with disabilities and their families as it is for infants and

toddlers. The DEC Task Force on Recommended Practices (1993) also believes that IEPs should be more family-centered, reflecting family priorities rather than only school or child priorities. A possible remedy for this dilemma would be to use an IFSP instead of an IEP as permitted by state law.

Regrettably, some teachers frequently see the IEP only as a burdensome paperwork requirement instead of a vehicle for providing a customized instructional program. It is viewed as developed primarily for compliance rather than for guiding instruction (Smith & Simpson, 1989). Effective teachers realize, however, that an IEP serves as the basis for constructing a tailor-made plan of instruction for each preschooler with disabilities who needs a special education. These educators appreciate the underlying relationship between assessment data, the formulation of instructional objectives, and the delivery of the instruction itself. In essence, according to Gargiulo (2003), an IEP serves as "a management tool that stipulates *who* will be involved in providing a special education, *what* services will be offered, *where* they will be delivered, and for *how long*. In addition, an IEP gauges *how successfully* goals have been met" (pp. 60–61).

IEPs are not designed to be so detailed or complete that they serve as the entire instructional agenda (Gargiulo, 2003) nor are they intended to prescribe curriculum (Goodman & Bond, 1993). IEP goals and objectives are designed, according to Cook et al. (2000), "to target remediation of particular developmental lags or to accelerate learning" (pp. 156–157). These goals and objectives, listed by priority, form the foundation from which daily lesson plans are developed within the developmental domains, which are the framework of curricular content in early childhood special education (Peterson, 1987). Typical areas might include speech and language, motor skills, social development, cognitive activities, or self-help skills.

Among the several components of an IEP, two are especially noteworthy: annual goals and the accompanying short-term or instructional objectives (benchmarks). Writing meaningful goals and objectives can be an especially challenging and difficult task for the IEP team (Gargiulo, 2003). The primary purpose of this team, Bateman and Linden (1998)

Table 6–10 Comparable Components of an IEP and IFSP

Individualized Education Program	Individualized Family Service Plan
• A statement of child's present levels of educational performance . . . including involvement and progress in general education curriculum . . .	• A statement of the infant's or toddler's present levels of physical, cognitive, communication, social/emotional, and adaptive development
• No comparable feature	• A statement of the family's resources, priorities, and concerns . . .
• A statement of annual goals including benchmarks or short-term instructional objectives . . .	• A statement of major outcomes expected to be achieved for the infant or toddler and the family . . .
• A statement indicating progress toward annual goals and a mechanism for regularly informing parents/guardians of such progress . . .	• . . . criteria, procedures, and timelines used to determine the degree to which progress toward achieving the outcomes is being made . . .
• A statement of specific special education and related services and supplementary aids and services to be provided and any program modifications . . .	• A statement of specific early intervention services necessary to meet the unique needs of the infant or toddler and the family
• An explanation of the extent to which the child will not participate in general education programs	• A statement of the natural environments in which early intervention services shall appropriately be provided or justification if not provided . . .
• Modifications needed to participate in state- or district-wide assessments . . .	• No comparable feature
• The projected date for initiation of services and the anticipated duration, frequency, and location of services	• The projected dates for initiation of services and the anticipated duration of services
• No comparable feature	• The name of the service coordinator . . .
• At age 14, a statement of transition service needs that focuses on student's course of study; at age 16, a statement of needed transition services, including interagency responsibilities . . .	• The steps to be taken to support the transition of the child to other services at age 3

SOURCE: Adapted from Individuals with Disabilities Education Act Amendments of 1997, Title 20 U.S. Code (U.S.C.) 1400 *et seq* Part B Section 614 (d)(1)(A) and Part C Section 636 (d).

believe, is to plan a program of instruction that is "reasonably calculated to enable the child to receive educational benefit" (p. 32). It is this portion of the youngster's IEP that addresses the issue of what specially designed instruction will be provided to the child.

Based on the pupil's present level of performance, goals are drafted that represent reasonable estimates of the child's progress. Goal-setting is a complex process. It is exceedingly difficult to project accomplishments for preschool children who exhibit cognitive, social, and emotional disabilities (Good-

man & Bond, 1993). Priorities for annual goals are formulated on the basis of critical needs—what the child needs in order to meaningfully participate in present and future environments (Noonan & McCormick, 1993). As noted earlier, Notari-Syverson and Shuster (1995), drawing upon the work of Bronfenbrenner (1979), advocate that educational goals should reflect skills that are relevant to everyday functioning and focus on real-life situations.

Goals statements are purposely broad. Their intent is to provide long-range direction to a child's educational program and not to define exact instructional tasks (Spodek & Saracho, 1994). The business of guiding instruction is the role filled by short-term objectives, typically one to three months in duration. These statements, written after goals have been crafted, describe the sequential steps the pupil will take to meet the intent of the goals statement(s). Instructional objectives are usually written by the teacher.

Criteria for effective short-term objectives or benchmarks include three components: a description of the behavior using observable and measurable terminology; a statement of conditions under which the behavior will be exhibited; and finally, a standard or performance criterion for assessing the adequacy of the student's accomplishment (Lignugaris/Kraft, Marchand-Martella, & Martella, 2001). Writing meaningful instructional objectives is not an easy task. Regular and special educators are sometimes confused about what constitutes a useful objective. Recall that Notari-Syverson and Shuster (1995) believe that high-quality objectives should be functional, measurable, generalizable, and easily integrated into daily routines, as well as being conceptually related to the goal statements. These indicators of quality are appropriate for developing IEPs and IFSPs.

In conclusion, the quality of an IEP largely depends on having well-written and appropriate goals and objectives that address the unique needs of the child. The IEP should be viewed as a "living" or dynamic document, guiding the delivery of special education services to young children with special needs. It is not something to be filed away and forgotten until the end of the academic year approaches. IEPs are the vehicle for ensuring that a specially designed educational program is provided. (See p. 194 for a typical IEP developed for four-year-old T. J. Browning.)

Summary

Young children with special needs receive services in a variety of locations. Traditionally, these settings have been identified as center-based, home-based, or combination programs; yet, no one service delivery approach is necessarily superior to another. The delivery of services must be tailored to the individual needs of the infant, toddler or preschooler, and his or her family. The field is presently experiencing a thrust toward more integrated and normalized environments for young children with disabilities. Our challenge, as we begin the twenty-first century, is to develop models that allow for the delivery of comprehensive services in the most integrated setting.

One subject that has sparked considerable debate among professionals is the movement toward full inclusion of preschoolers with special needs into early childhood programs designed for typical youngsters. Portrayed as an evolving concept, this issue has its vocal advocates as well as opponents. Calls for full inclusion represent a radical departure from present day service delivery models. While we fully endorse the principle of maximum integration, we believe that any placement decision should be formulated based on the child's best interest, while also respecting the wishes of the parent(s). There is no one ideal placement capable of meeting the needs of *all* learners.

Movement or transitioning from one type of placement to another is an important element of early intervention and early childhood special education programs. Successful transitions are enabling experiences for both the child and family. The intent is to provide for continuity of services. Smooth transitions dictate comprehensive planning and collaboration in addition to ongoing communication among all parties involved. The preparation for transitioning must involve the child and the parent(s), as well as both current and new service providers.

Young children with special needs typically receive services from a multitude of professionals. The idea of professionals from various disciplines working together is a well-established aspect of early childhood special education. No one discipline, agency, or professional possesses all of the skills or resources needed to develop appropriate educational experiences for infants, toddlers, and preschoolers with disabilities. Professionals need to work together, usually forming teams. Three common team structures typically encountered by young children with special needs and their families are multidisciplinary,

INDIVIDUALIZED EDUCATION PROGRAM

I. STUDENT INFORMATION AND INSTRUCTIONAL PROFILE

Student _Thomas Jefferson (T.J.) Browning_   Date of Birth _8-3-98_   Student Number _000-60-0361_

Parent's/Guardian's Name _Angela Browning_   Address _141 Boulder Ave. Apt. 16-A_   _Franklin, SC_   _42698_
                                                        Street   City   Zip Code

Parent's/Guardian's Phone No. _803-555-1920_   Student's Present School _Epps Head Start_   Grade _Pre-K_

Date of IEP Meeting _May 6, 2003_   Date of Eligibility _April 14, 2002_   IEP Review Date _May 6, 2004_

Child's Primary Language _English_   Limited English Proficiency _No_   Braille Instruction _No_
                                                    Yes/No   Yes/No

Assistive Technology Needs _No_   Language/Communication Needs _Yes_   Behavior Needs _Yes_
                  Yes/No   Yes/No   Yes/No

II. STUDENT PERFORMANCE PROFILE

T.J. is an energetic, creative four-year-old. He loves outdoor play and has age-appropriate gross motor skills. He demonstrates age-appropriate skills in self-care. Like many of his peers, he still has some difficulty with tying his shoes and buttoning smaller-sized buttons.

T.J. is able to communicate his wants and needs. Generally in conveying his message, T.J. uses a lot of gestures to support his verbal language. A language sample conducted on May 1, 2003, indicated that, on average, T.J. was using two–three word sentences. Within the classroom T.J. often will not respond to questions asked of him or directives given to him. Classroom observations conducted throughout the school year show that T.J. has the greatest difficulty in answering questions beginning with "Why," "What," and "When." Standardized tests administered on May 1, 2003 place T.J. in the age range of a child 3 years, 4 months and 3 years, 8 months for auditory comprehension and verbal abilities, respectively. Specific areas of difficulty include: vocabulary, recalling details in sequence, language usage, and classification of objects.

T.J. loves to please adults. He is very responsive to praise. T.J. prefers solitary play. He will typically choose activities in which he demonstrates competence. In 4 out of 5 opportunities, these activities involve object assembly such as Legos or blocks. T.J. has difficulty playing cooperatively and sharing. Due to his language delays he tends to rely on aggressive behavior, rather than on verbal interaction, when trying to resolve conflict with his peers. Although T.J. does know the classroom rules, he requires frequent redirection to task. He has a short attention span, usually staying no more than five minutes with any given activity.

Visual-motor integration seems to be difficult for T.J. within fine motor activities. He has difficulty copying shapes and designs using pencil or crayon. T.J. is able to cut on a 1/4" straight line, but needs continued practice with cutting other shapes.

Mrs. Browning, T.J.'s mother, states that she is concerned about his ability to communicate and play (interact) with children of his own age at school and at home. She worries about his aggressive behaviors toward his peers at school and church. At home she has noticed that T.J. has difficulty following directions.

The members of the IEP team have identified T.J.'s delayed communication skills, short attention span, poor social interaction, and the fine motor skills as areas of concern that impact his achievement in the general education classroom.

III. PROGRAM ELIGIBILITY

Eligible _X_   Not Eligible _____   Area(s) of Disability _Language Impairment_   _Not applicable_

                                                              Primary   Secondary

Rationale for Eligibility _Delayed receptive and expressive language is significantly below language of same age peers._

Student T.J. Browning   Date of Birth 8-3-98   Student Number 000-60-0361

INDIVIDUALIZED EDUCATION PROGRAM

IV. Annual Goals and Benchmarks

Area: Communication/Language

Annual Goal: To improve T.J.'s overall performance in receptive and expressive communication.

Benchmark	Provider	Evaluation Method	Initiation Date	Check Date	Mastery Date
Speaks in expanded sentences of 4–5 words	General educator Speech/language pathologist	(a.) Data collection b. Teacher/Text test c. Work samples (d.) Classroom observation e. Grades (f.) Other: language sample	9/5/03	1/5/04 5/5/04	
Correctly answer "wh" questions	General educator Speech/language pathologist	a. Data collection b. Teacher/Text test c. Work samples (d.) Classroom observation e. Grades f. Other:	9/5/03	1/5/04 5/5/04	
		a. Data collection b. Teacher/Text test c. Work samples d. Classroom observation e. Grades f. Other:			

Student *T.J. Browning*   Date of Birth *8-3-98*   Student Number *000-60-0361*

INDIVIDUALIZED EDUCATION PROGRAM

Area: *Cognitive/Language*

Annual Goal: *To increase language concepts associated with literacy/writing.*

Benchmark	Provider	Evaluation Method	Initiation Date	Check Date	Mastery Date
Verbally retells simple stories stating at least 3 events in sequence	*General educator* _____ *Special educator* _____ _____	ⓐ Data collection b. Teacher/Text test c. Work samples ⓓ Classroom observation e. Grades ⓕ Other: *tape recorded retellings*	*9/5/03*	*1/5/04* *5/5/04*	_____
Appropriately uses vocabulary associated with kindergarten classroom and curriculum	*General educator* _____ *Special educator* _____ _____	ⓐ Data collection b. Teacher/Text test c. Work samples ⓓ Classroom observation e. Grades f. Other	*9/5/03*	*1/5/04* *5/5/04*	_____
Verbally names/describes objects found within picture book illustrations	*General educator* _____ *Special educator* _____ _____	a. Data collection b. Teacher/Text test c. Work samples ⓓ Classroom observation e. Grades f. Other: _____	*9/5/03*	*1/5/04* *5/5/04*	_____

Student _T.J. Browning_   Date of Birth _8-3-98_   Student Number _000-60-0361_

INDIVIDUALIZED EDUCATION PROGRAM

Area: _Social/Behavioral_

Annual Goal: _To demonstrate age-appropriate behavior in social interactions._

Benchmark

	Provider	Evaluation Method	Initiation Date	Check Date	Mastery Date
Responds to conflict with peers without aggression	General educator Special educator	a. Data collection b. Teacher/Text test c. Work samples ⓓ Classroom observation e. Grades ⓕ Other: _behavior contract_	9/5/03	1/5/04 5/5/04	

Benchmark

	Provider	Evaluation Method	Initiation Date	Check Date	Mastery Date
Follows adult instructions and directions with less than two reminders	General educator Special educator	a. Data collection b. Teacher/Text test c. Work samples ⓓ Classroom observation e. Grades ⓕ Other: _behavior contract_	9/5/03	1/5/04 5/5/04	

Benchmark

	Provider	Evaluation Method	Initiation Date	Check Date	Mastery Date
Participates in an activity for 10 minutes	General educator Special educator	ⓐ Data collection b. Teacher/Text test ⓒ Work samples ⓓ Classroom observation e. Grades f. Other:	9/5/03	1/5/04 5/5/04	

Student _T.J. Browning_   Date of Birth _8-3-98_   Student Number _000-60-0361_

INDIVIDUALIZED EDUCATION PROGRAM

Area: _Fine Motor_

Annual Goal: _To function independently with fine motor activities in the kindergarten curriculum._

	Provider	Evaluation Method	Initiation Date	Check Date	Mastery Date
Benchmark					
Recognizably prints his first	_General educator_	a. Data collection	_9/5/03_	_1/5/04_	
and last name		b. Teacher/Text test		_5/5/04_	
		ⓒ Work samples			
		d. Classroom observation			
		e. Grades			
		f. Other:			
Benchmark					
Copies, cuts, glues, and	_General educator_	a. Data collection	_9/5/03_	_1/5/04_	
assembles classroom		b. Teacher/Text Test		_5/5/04_	
art projects		ⓒ Work samples			
		d. Classroom observation			
		e. Grades			
		f. Other:			
Benchmark					
		a. Data collection			
		b. Teacher/Text test			
		c. Work samples			
		d. Classroom observation			
		e. Grades			
		f. Other:			

Student _T.J. Browning_   Date of Birth _8-3-98_   Student Number _000-60-0361_

INDIVIDUALIZED EDUCATION PROGRAM

V. Supplementary Aids and Related Services

Services/Related Services	Provider	Hours per week	Location
Instructional support	Special educator	2	General education environment
Speech/language therapy	Speech/language pathologist	2	General education environment

Aids/equipment/program modifications needed to attain annual goals and progress in general education curriculum: _Not applicable at this time_

Frequency of use: _Not applicable_

VI. Special Education Placement

Student to be placed in the following least restrictive environment (LRE):

Location of Services	Duration (No. of hours in location/total no. of school hours)	Extent of Participation
General education classroom	35 hours per week / 35 hours per week	100%
Special education environments:		
Special day school		
Residential school		
Hospital school		
Homebound services		
Other (e.g. Head Start, preschool program)		
Rationale for placement in setting other than general education class	Not Applicable	

Page 6 of 8

Student _T.J. Browning_   Date of Birth _8-3-98_   Student Number _000-60-0361_

INDIVIDUALIZED EDUCATION PROGRAM

VII. Special Services

Physical Education: Regular _X_   Adaptive _____

Transportation: Regular _X_   Special _____   Not Applicable _____

Is student provided an opportunity to participate in extracurricular and nonacademic activities with nondisabled peers? _Yes_
                                                                                                                              Yes/No

Are supports necessary? _No_   Describe: _____
                          Yes/No

Rationale for nonparticipation: _Not applicable_ _____

VIII. Transition   (no later than age 14, earlier if appropriate)

Transition Service Needs   _Not applicable at this time_
Focusing on Course of Study

Employment Outcome   _Not applicable at this time_

Community Living Outcome   _Not applicable at this time_

Identify Needed Transition Services   _Not applicable at this time_

Identify Interagency   _Not applicable at this time_
Responsibilities and
Community Linkages

IX. Assessment Modifications

Is student able to participate in state- or district-wide assessments? _Yes_
                                                                         Yes/No

Are modifications required? _No_
                             Yes/No

Identify type of modifications: _Not Applicable_ _____

Rationale for nonparticipation and alternate assessment plan: _Not Applicable_ _____

Student _T.J. Browning_ Date of Birth _8-3-98_ Student Number _000-60-0361_

INDIVIDUALIZED EDUCATION PROGRAM

X. Progress Report

Parents will be informed of child's progress toward annual goals using same reporting methods used for children without disabilities.

Method Frequency

- Written Progress Report _Yes_ Every _9_ weeks
  Yes/No

- Parent Conference _Yes_ _As needed_
  Yes/No

- Other _behavior contact_ _Weekly_
  Identify

- Other _____
  Identify

XI. Transferal of Rights

I understand that the rights under the Individuals with Disabilities Education Act will transfer to me upon reaching my eighteenth birthday.

_____ _____
Student's Signature Date

XII. Recommended Instructional and/or Behavioral Interventions

Behavior contract designed to reduce frequency of aggressive interactions with peers.

_____

_____

XIII. IEP Development Team

Name	Team Member's Signature	Position/Title
Angela Browning	_Angela Browning_	Parent/Guardian
		Parent/Guardian
Patricia Gwin	_Patricia Gwin_	LEA Representative
Ann Martin	_Ann Martin_	Special Education Teacher
Cecelia Watkins	_Cecelia Watkins_	General Education Teacher
		Student
Melanie Spangler	_Melanie Spangler_	Other Speech/language pathologist

interdisciplinary, and transdisciplinary models. Each model has its own unique features and serves a specific function. We see value in the importance of teaming and professional collaboration. It serves as the foundation for delivering services in a judicious fashion.

States have recently been encouraged to develop seamless systems for providing services to youngsters with special needs birth through age five. One consequence of this shift in government policy is that individualized family service plans (IFSP) can be used to guide the delivery of services to preschoolers with disabilities as well as infants and toddlers. We see this as a commendable effort at providing for continuity and minimizing the disruption of services to young children with special needs and their families.

The IFSP is the driving force behind the delivery of services to infants and toddlers who are disabled or at-risk. The IFSP acknowledges the youngster's family as the focal point of services. This focus is clearly evident in the required statement of the family's resources, priorities, and concerns. A well-developed IFSP encourages the parents' full and meaningful involvement while supporting their role as primary decision maker for their son or daughter.

An individualized education program, more commonly referred to as an IEP, is the vehicle that ensures that preschoolers with disabilities receive an individualized education appropriate to their unique needs. Written by a team, it is the basis for constructing a customized plan of instruction. At the heart of an IEP are well-written goals and objectives. An IEP is not developed solely for compliance purposes; rather, it is a dynamic document and the primary tool for providing a specially designed educational program.

Check Your Understanding

1. Identify some of the advantages and disadvantages of center-based and home-based service delivery models.

2. What are normalized environments for young children with disabilities?

3. Describe the evolution of the movement toward full inclusion.

4. Take a position either for or against full inclusion. Support your viewpoint.

5. List five outcomes or goals of the transition process.

6. What roles do the child, their parents, and service providers play in the transition process?

7. Identify the differences between multidisciplinary, interdisciplinary, and transdisciplinary team models.

8. Why is a transdisciplinary approach to providing services currently viewed as best practice?

9. What is the rationale for using IFSPs for preschool children with special needs?

10. List the required components of an IFSP.

11. Identify at least five types of early intervention services available to infants/toddlers and their families.

12. What are the reasons for including families in the development of an IFSP?

13. What is the purpose of an IEP?

14. How does an IEP differ from an IFSP?

References

Bailey, D. (1994). Working with families of children with special needs. In M. Wolery & J. Wilbers (Eds.), *Including children with special needs in early childhood programs* (pp. 23–44). Washington, DC: National Association for the Education of Young Children.

Bailey, D., & McWilliam, R. (1990). Normalizing early intervention. *Topics in Early Childhood Special Education, 10* (2), 33–47.

Bailey, D., McWilliam, R., Buysse, V., & Wesley, P. (1998). Inclusion in the context of competing values in early childhood education. *Early Childhood Research Quarterly, 13*(1), 27–47.

Bailey, D., & Wolery, M. (1989). *Assessing infants and preschoolers with handicaps.* Columbus, OH: Merrill.

Bailey, D., & Wolery, M. (1992). *Teaching infants and preschoolers with disabilities* (2nd ed.). New York: Macmillan.

Bateman, B., & Linden, M. (1998). *Better IEPs: How to develop legally correct and educationally useful programs* (3rd ed.). Longmont, CO: Sopris West.

Bricker, D. (1978). A rationale for the integration of handicapped and nonhandicapped preschool children. In M. Guralnick (Ed.), *Early intervention and the integration of handicapped and nonhandicapped children* (pp. 3–26). Baltimore: University Park Press.

Bricker, D. (1995). The challenge of inclusion. *Journal of Early Intervention, 19*(3), 179–194.

Bronfenbrenner, U. (1977). Toward an experimental ecology of human development. *American Psychologist, 32,* 513–531.

Bronfenbrenner, U. (1979). *The ecology of human development: Experiments by nature and design.* Cambridge, MA: Harvard University Press.

Bruder, M. (1994). Working with members of other disciplines: Collaboration for success. In M. Wolery & J. Wilbers (Eds.), *Including children with special needs in early childhood programs* (pp. 45–70). Washington, DC: National Association for the Education of Young Children.

Bruder, M. (2001). Inclusion of infants and toddlers. In M. Guralnick (Ed.), *Early childhood inclusion: Focus on change* (pp. 203–228). Baltimore: Paul H. Brookes.

Carta, J., Schwartz, I., Atwater, J., & McConnell, S. (1991). Developmentally appropriate practice: Appraising its usefulness for young child with disabilities. *Topics in Early Childhood Special Education, 11*(1), 1–20.

Conn-Powers, M., Ross-Allen, J., & Holburn, S. (1990). Transition of young children into the elementary education mainstream. *Topics in Early Childhood Special Education, 9*(4), 91–105.

Cook, R., Tessier, A., & Klein, M. (2000). *Adapting early childhood curricula for children in inclusive settings* (4th ed.). Upper Saddle River, NJ: Prentice-Hall.

Danaher, J., & Kraus, R. (Eds.). (2002). *Section 619 profile* (11th ed.). Chapel Hill, NC: National Early Childhood Technical Assistance Center.

Davis, M., Kilgo, J., & Gamel-McCormick, M. (1998). *Young children with special needs: A developmentally appropriate approach.* Needham Heights, MA: Allyn & Bacon.

DEC Task Force on Recommended Practices. (1993). *DEC recommended practices: Indicators of quality in programs for infants and young children with special needs and their families.* Reston, VA: Council for Exceptional Children.

DeGangi, C., Royeen, C., & Wietlisbach, S. (1992). How to examine the individualized family service planning process: Preliminary findings and a procedural guide. *Infants and Young Children, 5*(2), 42–56.

Demchak, M., & Drinkwater, S. (1992). Preschoolers with severe disabilities. The case against segregation. *Topics in Early Childhood Special Education, 11*(4), 70–83.

Dunst, C., Trivette, C., & Deal, A. (1988). *Enabling and empowering families: Principles and guidelines for practice.* Cambridge, MA: Brookline Books.

Federal Register. (1989, April 27). Assistance to states for education of handicapped children. *54*(80), 18253–18256. Washington, DC: U.S. Government Printing Office.

Fowler, S., Schwartz, I., & Atwater, J. (1991). Perspectives on transition from preschool to kindergarten for children with disabilities and their families. *Exceptional Children, 58,* 136–145.

Fuchs, D., & Fuchs, L. (1991). Framing the REI debate: Abolitionists versus conservationists. In J. Lloyd, N. Singh, & A. Repp (Eds.), *Regular education initiative: Alternative perspectives on concepts, issues and models* (pp. 241–255). Sycamore, IL: Sycamore.

Gargiulo, R. (2003). *Special education in contemporary society.* Belmont, CA: Wadsworth.

Gartner, A., & Lipsky, D. (1987). Beyond special education: Toward a quality system for all students. *Harvard Educational Review, 57,* 367–395.

Gartner, A., & Lipsky, D. (1989). New conceptualizations for special education. *European Journal of Special Needs Education, 4*(1), 16–21.

Goodman, J., & Bond, L. (1993). The individualized education program: A retrospective critique. *Journal of Special Education, 26*(4), 408–422.

Graves, S., Gargiulo, R., & Sluder, L. (1996). *Young children: An introduction to early childhood education.* St. Paul: West.

Guralnick, M. (1990). Major accomplishments and future directions in early childhood mainstreaming. *Topics in Early Childhood Special Education, 10*(2), 1–17.

Guralnick, M. (1994). Mothers' perceptions of the benefits and drawbacks of early childhood mainstreaming. *Journal of Early Intervention, 18*(2), 163–168.

Guralnick, M. (2001). A framework for change in early childhood inclusion. In M. Guralnick (Ed.), *Early childhood inclusion: Focus on change* (pp. 3–35). Baltimore: Paul H. Brookes.

Hallahan, D., & Kauffman, J. (2003). *Exceptional learners* (9th ed.). Needham Heights, MA: Allyn & Bacon.

Harbin, G., McWilliam, R., & Gallagher, J. (2000). Services for young children with disabilities and their families. In J. Shonkoff & S. Meisels (Eds.), *Handbook of early childhood intervention* (2nd ed., pp. 387–415). Cambridge, England: Cambridge University Press.

Jenkins, J., Pious, C., & Jewell, M. (1990). Special education and the regular education initiative: Basic assumptions. *Exceptional Children, 56*(6), 479–491.

Karnes, M., & Stayton, V. (1988). Model programs for infants and toddlers with handicaps. In J. Jordan, J. Gallagher, P. Hutinger, & M. Karnes (Eds.), *Early childhood special education: Birth to three* (pp. 67–108). Reston, VA: Council for Exceptional Children.

Kauffman, J. (1989). The regular education initiative as Reagan-Bush education policy: A trickle-down theory of education of the hard-to-teach. *Journal of Special Education, 23*(3), 256–278.

Kauffman, J. (1991). Restructuring in sociopolitical context: Reservations about the effects of current reform proposals on students with disabilities. In J. Lloyd, N. Singh, & A. Repp (Eds.), *The regular education initiative: Alternative perspectives on concepts, issues, and models* (pp. 57–66). Sycamore, IL: Sycamore.

Lazzari, A., & Kilgo, J. (1989). Practical methods for supporting parents in early transition. *Teaching Exceptional Children, 22*, 116–125.

Lieberman, L. (1990). REI: Revisited . . . again. *Exceptional Children, 56*(6), 561–562.

Lieberman, L. (1992). Preserving special education . . . for those who need it. In W. Stainback & S. Stainback (Eds.), *Controversial issues confronting special education: Divergent perspectives* (pp. 13–25). Boston: Allyn & Bacon.

Lignugaris/Kraft, B., Marchand-Martella, N., & Martella, R. (2001). Writing better goals and short-term objectives or benchmarks. *Teaching Exceptional Children, 34*(1), 52–58.

McCollum, J., & Maude, S. (1993). Portrait of a changing field: Policy and practice in early childhood special education. In B. Spodek (Ed.), *Handbook of research in early childhood education* (pp. 352–371). New York: Macmillan.

McDonnell, A., & Hardman, M. (1988). A synthesis of "best practices" guidelines for early childhood services. *Journal of the Division for Early Childhood, 12*, 328–341.

McGoningel, M., Woodruff, C., & Roszmann-Millican, M. (1994). The transdisciplinary team: A model for family-centered early intervention. In L. Johnson, R. Gallagher, M. LaMontagne, J. Jordan, J. Gallagher, P. Hutinger, & M. Karnes (Eds.), *Meeting early intervention challenges* (pp. 95–131). Baltimore: Paul H. Brookes.

McLean, M., Bailey, D., & Wolery, M. (1996). *Assessing infants and preschoolers with special needs* (2nd ed.). Englewood Cliffs, NJ: Prentice-Hall.

McLean, M., & Hanline, M. (1990). Providing early intervention services in integrated environments: Challenges and opportunities for the future. *Topics in Early Childhood Special Education, 10*(2), 62–77.

Menlove, R., Hudson, P., & Suter, D. (2001). A field of IEP dreams. *Teaching Exceptional Children, 33*(5), 28–33.

Meyen, E. (1996). *Exceptional children* (3rd ed.). Denver: Love.

Noonan, M., & Kilgo, J. (1987). Transition services for early age individuals with severe mental retardation. In R. Ianacone & R. Stodden (Eds.), *Transition issues and directions* (pp. 25–37). Reston, VA: Council for Exceptional Children.

Noonan, M., & McCormick, L. (1993). *Early intervention in natural environments.* Pacific Grove, CA: Brooks/Cole.

Noonan, M., Ratokalau, N., Lauth-Torres, L., McCormick, L., Esaki, C., & Claybaugh, K. (1992). Validating critical skills for preschool success. *Infant-Toddler Intervention, 2*(3), 187–202.

Notari-Syverson, A., & Shuster, S. (1995). Putting real-life skills into IEP/IFSPs for infants and young children. *Teaching Exceptional Children, 27*(2), 29–32.

Odom, S., & Diamond, K. (1998). Inclusion of young children with special needs in early childhood education: The research base. *Early Childhood Research Quarterly, 13*(1), 3–25.

Odom, S., & McEvoy, M. (1990). Mainstreaming at the preschool level: Potential barriers and tasks for the field. *Topics in Early Childhood Special Education, 10*(2), 48–61.

Osborne, A., & DiMattia, P. (1994). The IDEA's least restrictive mandate: Legal implications. *Exceptional Children, 61*(1), 6–14.

Osborne, A., & DiMattia, P. (1995) Counterpoint: IDEA's LRE mandate: Another look. *Exceptional Children, 61*(6), 582–584.

Pavia, L. (1992). Introducing the early childhood teacher to IEPs. *Day Care and Early Education, 19*, 38–40.

Peck, C., Odom, S., & Bricker, D. (1993). *Integrating young children with disabilities into community programs.* Baltimore: Paul H. Brookes.

Peterson, N. (1987). *Early intervention for handicapped and at-risk children.* Denver: Love.

Polloway, E., Patton, J., Payne, J., & Payne, R. (1989). *Strategies for teaching learners with special needs* (4th ed.). Columbus, OH: Merrill.

Raver, S. (1999). *Intervention strategies for infants and toddlers with special needs* (2nd ed.). Upper Saddle River, NJ: Prentice Hall.

Roberts-DeGennaro, M. (1996). An interdisciplinary model in the field of early intervention. *Social Work in Education, 18*(1), 20–30.

Rogers, J. (1993, May). The inclusion revolution. *Phi Delta Kappan Research Bulletin,* No. II, 1–6.

Rose, D., & Smith, B. (1993). Preschool mainstreaming: Attitude barriers and strategies for addressing them. *Young Children, 48*(4), 59–62.

Sadler, F. (2003). The itinerant special education teacher in the early childhood classroom. *Teaching Exceptional Children, 35*(3), 8–15.

Sailor, W., Anderson, J., Havorsen, A., Doering, K., Filler, J., & Goetz, L. (1989). *The comprehensive local school: Regular education for all students with disabilities.* Baltimore: Paul H. Brookes.

Sailor, W., Gerry, M., & Wilson, W. (1991). Policy implications of emergent full inclusion models for the education of students with disabilities. In M. Wang, H. Walberg, & M. Reynolds (Eds.), *Handbook of special education* (Vol. 4, pp. 175–193). New York: Pergamon Press.

Sainato, D., & Morrison, R. (2001). Transition to inclusive environments for young children with disabilities: Toward a seamless system of service delivery. In M. Guralinick (Ed.), *Early childhood inclusion: Focus on change* (pp. 293–306). Baltimore: Paul H. Brookes.

Salisbury, C., & Vincent, L. (1990). Criterion of the next environment and best practices: Mainstreaming and integration 10 years later. *Topics in Early Childhood Special Education, 10*(2), 78–89.

Sandall, S., McLean, M., & Smith, B. (2000). *DEC recommended practices in early intervention/early childhood special education.* Longmont, CO: Sopris West.

Sandall, S., & Ostrosky, M. (2000). *Natural environments and inclusion.* Longmont, CO: Sopris West.

Sexton, D., Snyder, P., Lobman, M., Kimbrough, P., & Matthews, K. (1997). A team-based model to improve early intervention programs: Linking preservice and inservice. In P. Winston, J. McCollum, & C. Catlett (Eds.), *Reforming personnel preparation in early intervention* (pp. 495–526). Baltimore: Paul H. Brookes.

Sexton, D., Snyder, P., Sharpton, W., & Stricklin, S. (1993). Infants and toddlers with special needs and their families. *Childhood Education, 69*(5), 276–286.

Shea, T., & Bauer, A. (1991). *Parents and teachers of children with exceptionalities* (2nd ed.). Needham Heights, MA: Allyn & Bacon.

Smith, S., & Simpson, R. (1989). An analysis of individualized education programs (IEPs) for students with behavior disorders. *Behavioral Disorders, 14,* 107–116.

Spodek, B., & Saracho, O. (1994). *Dealing with individual differences in the early childhood classroom.* White Plains, NY: Longman.

Stainback, S., & Stainback, W. (1987). Integration versus cooperation: A commentary on "Educating children with learning problems: A shared responsibility." *Exceptional Children, 54*(1), 517–521.

Stainback, S., & Stainback, W. (1989). No more teachers of students with severe handicaps. *TASH Newsletter, 15*(2), 9.

Stainback, S., & Stainback, W. (1992). Schools as inclusive communities. In W. Stainback & S. Stainback (Eds.), *Controversial issues confronting special education: Divergent perspectives* (pp. 29–43). Boston: Allyn & Bacon.

Stainback, W., & Stainback, S. (1984). A rationale for the merger of special and regular education. *Exceptional Children, 51*(2), 102–111.

Strickland, B. (1993). Parents and the educational system. In J. Paul & R. Simeonsson (Eds.), *Children with special needs* (2nd ed., pp. 231–255). Fort Worth, TX: Harcourt Brace Jovanovich.

Stowe, M., & Turnbull, H. (2001). Legal considerations of inclusion for infants 'and toddlers and preschool-age children. In M. Guralnick (Ed.), *Early childhood inclusion: Focus on change* (pp. 69–100). Baltimore: Paul H. Brookes.

Turbiville, V., Turnbull, A., Garland, C., & Lee, I. (1996). Development and implementation of IFSPs and IEPs: Opportunities for empowerment. In S. Odom & M. McLean (Eds.), *Early intervention/early childhood special education recommended practices* (pp. 77–100). Austin, TX: Pro-Ed.

Turnbull, A., & Turnbull, H. (2001). *Families, professionals and exceptionality: A special partnership* (4th ed.). Upper Saddle River, NJ: Prentice Hall.

Umansky, W., & Hooper, S. (1998). *Young children with special need* (3rd ed.). Upper Saddle River, NJ: Prentice Hall.

U.S. Department of Education. (1993). *Fifteenth annual report to Congress on the implementation of the Individuals with Disabilities Education Act.* Washington, DC: U.S. Government Printing Office.

U.S. Department of Education. (1994). *Sixteenth annual report to Congress on the implementation of the Individuals with Disabilities Education Act.* Washington, DC: U.S. Government Printing Office.

U.S. Department of Education. (2001). *Twenty-third annual report to Congress on the implementation of the Individuals with Disabilities Education Act.* Washington, DC: U.S. Government Printing Office.

U.S. Department of Education. (2002). *Twenty-fourth annual report to Congress on the implementation of the Individuals with Disabilities Education Act*. Washington, DC: U.S. Government Printing Office.

Vergason, G., & Anderegg, M. (1992). Preserving the least restrictive environment. In W. Stainback & S. Stainback (Eds.), *Controversial issues confronting special education* (pp. 45–54). Needham Heights, MA: Allyn & Bacon.

Walsh, S., Rous, B., & Lutzer, C. (2000). The federal IDEA natural environments provision. In S. Sandall & M. Ostrosky (Eds.), *Natural environments and inclusion* (pp. 3–15). Longmont, CO: Sopris West.

Walsh, S., Smith, B., & Taylor, R. (2000). *IDEA requirements for preschoolers with disabilities*. Reston, VA: Council for Exceptional Children.

Wang, M., & Reynolds, M. (1985). Avoiding the "catch-22" in special education reform. *Exceptional Children, 51*(6), 497–502.

Wayman, K., Lynch, E., & Hanson, M. (1991). Home-based early childhood services: Cultural sensitivity in a family systems approach. *Topics in Early Childhood Special Education, 10,* 56–75.

Will, M. (1986a). *Educating students with learning problems: A shared responsibility*. Washington, DC: U.S. Department of Education, Office of Special Education and Rehabilitative Services.

Will, M. (1986b). Educating children with learning problems: A shared responsibility. *Exceptional Children, 52*(5), 411–415.

Wolfensberger, W. (1972). *Normalization: The principle of normalization in human services*. Toronto: National Institute on Mental Retardation.

Yell, M. (1995). Least restrictive environment, inclusion, and students with disabilities: A legal analysis. *Journal of Special Education, 28*(4), 389–404.

Curriculum for Young Children with Special Needs

Learning Outcomes

After reading this chapter, you will be able to:

- Explain the influence of various curriculum models on curriculum development for young children with disabilities.
- Describe factors to be considered in developing curricula for young children with disabilities.
- Describe the three components of developmentally appropriate practice (DAP).
- Discuss the similarities and differences between DAP from general early childhood education (ECE) and practices from early childhood special education (ECSE).
- Explain a model for blending recommended practices from ECE and ECSE.

This chapter provides an overview of curriculum content and examines current practices in curriculum development and implementation for young children with disabilities. After curriculum is defined, a brief overview follows of the major theoretical perspectives that have influenced curriculum development in early intervention/early childhood special education (EI/ECSE). A description is then provided of the curriculum development process in programs serving young children with disabilities. The chapter concludes with a discussion of recommended practices from the fields of EI/ECSE and general early childhood education (ECE). Emphasis is placed on the similarities and differences in EI/ECSE and ECE practices and how these perspectives can be blended to best meet the needs of young children with disabilities and their families.

Definition of Curriculum

The curriculum is one of a number of program features that contribute to the effectiveness of early intervention/education for children with disabilities (Bruder, 1997). Many definitions of **curriculum** can be found in the early childhood literature. In the past, the term *curriculum* represented, at least to some, a purchased package of materials, objectives, and activities designed to guide instruction. This, of course, is an extremely narrow and limited view of curriculum because the content is predetermined without gaining input from the child, his or her family, and other care providers. In this chapter, we move beyond this narrow view of curriculum and recognize the importance of the child's environment, each child's unique needs and interests, and each family's priorities.

Most professionals today define curriculum in terms of a theoretical model reflecting beliefs about what should be taught and in what sequence. Dunst (1981) defined a curriculum for infants and young children with disabilities as consisting of:

> a series of carefully planned and designed activities, events, and experiences intentionally organized and implemented to reach specified objectives and goals, and which adhere and ascribe to a particular philosophical and theoretical position, and whose methods and modes of instruction and curriculum content are logically consistent with the psychological perspective from which it has been derived. (p. 9)

Others define curriculum to include planned, as well as unplanned, experiences. In other words, curriculum is viewed as everything that happens throughout the day in an early childhood program. This perspective of curriculum includes the theoretical and philosophical foundation on which programming is based. For young children with disabilities, this perspective should be coupled with the individual needs of children and the environmental demands that are placed on them.

McCormick (1997) suggests that it is easier to define curriculum in terms of what it is not rather than what it is. She states that "curriculum is *not* teaching methods and procedures and it is *not* a set of activities: It is *what* is to be learned" (p. 268). We agree with the premise that curriculum supplies a basis for early childhood programs and the intervention provided to young children and their families. In this chapter, the focus is on *what* is to be learned by young children with known or suspected disabilities. The chapter that follows addresses instructional methods and procedures.

Historical and Legislative Influences on Curriculum

To best understand curriculum in EI/ECSE, it is helpful to consider the historical roots of the field. As described previously, EI/ECSE and the various curriculum models for young children with disabilities have been developed from three different fields of education: general early childhood education, special education (e.g., for older children), and compensatory education (e.g., Head Start). Each of these areas represents a different point of view about young children and their development and learning. The field of general early childhood education, for example, underscores the young child's need to construct his or her own knowledge through active engagement with and exploration of the environment (Bredekamp & Copple, 1997). On the other hand, special education emphasizes the use of remedial instruction and the provision of related services to facilitate skill acquisition. Compensatory education is founded on the perspective that early intervention/education can help to minimize or alleviate the effects of environmental influences such as poverty and other risk factors.

In addition to these influences, research in the field of child development has provided an opportunity to broaden the focus of intervention for young children to include children's caregiving environments. The transactional view of child development (Sameroff & Chandler, 1975), for example, proposes that a child's developmental status varies as a function of the transactions occurring between the child's biological characteristics and the environmental or contextual conditions in which he or she lives. The emphasis placed on a child's relationship with his or her family and other primary caregivers has greatly influenced early childhood curricula.

Another strong influence on curricula in EI/ECSE has been federal legislation, in particular the Individuals with Disabilities Education Act (IDEA). In fact, the explicit requirements of the IFSP and IEP have altered the nature of curricula. In most instances, a broad-based application of curricula is used in EI/ECSE with the IEP and IFSP used to individualize the experiences of children with disabilities (Noonan & McCormick, 1993).

Theoretical Influences on Curriculum Development

As described previously, most professionals in early childhood agree that an integral component of any curriculum is the theoretical perspective on which it is based (Mallory, 1992). A number of such theoretical perspectives have been identified in EI/ECSE (Bailey & Wolery, 1992; Hanson & Lynch, 1995; Noonan & McCormick, 1993), which have influenced the development of curricula. These curriculum perspectives have included (a) developmental, (b) developmental-cognitive, (c) academic (or preacademic) skills, (d) behavioral, and (e) functional. Each of these perspectives is discussed in this section; however, it is important to note that, in practice, most early childhood programs rely on a combination of theoretical approaches. That is, different components of any one or more of the various theoretical perspectives are combined to match the needs of a given group of children, which is often referred to as an eclectic approach to curriculum development in early childhood. Hanson and Lynch (1995) emphasize that it is not surprising that most curricula for young children with disabilities are eclectic. They attributed this to the fact that the field of EI/ECSE has such a diverse background of historical, theoretical, and legislative influences.

Developmental Perspective

The most traditional early childhood curriculum models seem to primarily reflect a developmental focus. The developmental perspective is based on theories of typical child development. The sequences of skills in this model include physical development (that is, gross motor and fine motor), adaptive development (such as self-care and daily living skills), social development, and communication and language development (receptive and expressive language for example) based on child growth and maturation studies (Gesell & Amatruda, 1947). According to the developmental model, children's development is genetically predetermined, suggesting that children who are experiencing typical development usually acquire skills in a fairly predictable sequence (for instance, in the gross motor area, children usually learn to roll over, sit, crawl and stand before they learn to walk). By using a developmental model, it was originally assumed that teaching the same sequences of skills to young children with disabilities would help them to overcome many of their developmental delays or disabilities.

Curricula based on a developmental model contain a list of developmental milestones in the sequence in which they are expected to develop and accompanying activities to facilitate the development of these skills. The skills are determined that each child has or has not acquired as compared to the age-related norms of children who are experiencing typical development. Children's active interaction with the physical and social aspects of the environment is thought to be critical to the acquisition of more advanced developmental skills. Thus, children are supported as active participants in the learning process. Instructional strategies are designed to simulate activities engaged in by nondisabled children.

The developmental focus in early childhood curricula may be partly due to the eligibility criteria for

Curriculum development requires extensive planning to address children's individual differences and family preferences.

EI/ECSE services that emphasize a discrepancy between a child's chronological age and his or her developmental abilities. Although a development focus is prevalent, it is important to realize that a developmental approach has a number of limitations when designing curricula for young children with disabilities. Rainforth, York, and Macdonald (1992) noted that a curriculum based on a linear model of development tends to focus on the skills that children need to develop next when compared to age-related norms of children who are experiencing typical development. A developmental curriculum does not reference the natural environments and expectations of those environments for children with disabilities. For example, the skills required to be successful during group time at T. J.'s child care program (such as raising his hand to have a turn) would not be addressed in a developmental curriculum. Further, it is likely that individual differences and family preferences would not be given appropriate consideration.

Developmental-Cognitive Perspective

Another major influence on curriculum development for young children is the developmental-cognitive perspective. The developmental-cognitive model has been described as a theory-driven model that is based on the work of Piaget (Noonan & McCormick, 1993). As discussed in the first chapter, Piaget theorized that cognitive development occurs as a result of physiological growth and the child's interaction with the environment.

The developmental-cognitive model is defined by the content that is covered and the instructional methods that are used. The content of the developmental-cognitive-model is very similar to the developmental model; however, the cognitive skill domain is emphasized. The cognitive domain consists of skill sequences derived from Piaget's description of the various periods of intellectual development (for example, the sensorimotor period) (Piaget, 1952). The instructional approach utilized in a developmental-cognitive model, like the one used in a developmental model, focuses on children's interaction with a stimulating, well-planned environment (Hanson & Lynch, 1995).

The criticisms of a developmental-cognitive model are similar to those of the developmental model. The major drawback is that children's functional skills are not addressed in this model. Functional skills are those skills that will be useful to the child and will be used often by the child in his natural environment (examples include greeting others, eating independently). It is easy to understand why functional skills are important to children with disabilities. Because the developmental-cognitive model does not address functional skills, it has limited utility in designing curricula for children with disabilities.

Academic (or Preacademic) Perspective

Closely related to the developmental and developmental-cognitive curriculum models is the basic academic (or preacademic) skills perspective. This approach makes the assumption that the development of nondisabled children is based on a group of core skills that are typically taught to children during the preschool years (usually referred to as preacademics) and the early primary years (academics). Skills such as counting, using money, telling time, reading, and writing a story are analyzed into their component preacademic or academic skills. These skills are then taught to young children.

There are a number of disadvantages in applying this preacademic or academic approach to curriculum development for young children with disabilities. First, a preacademic or academic curriculum primarily focuses on the traditional subject areas of reading, writing, and arithmetic. Nonacademic skills that children with disabilities need to acquire, such as appropriate social skills (greeting others, turn-taking behaviors, etc.) and adaptive or self-care skills (that is, dressing, toileting, etc.), may not be addressed. Second, preacademic or academic skills are often taught in isolation during separate time periods of the day with separate materials and tasks. Yet, participation in most activities within the natural environment requires that young children are able to perform several different skills within the same activity (for example, playing a board game usually requires fine motor, cognitive, communication, and social skills, as well as some basic academic skills such as reading or counting). Another concern is that children with disabilities will be unable to generalize skills learned in isolation to the functional context in which they are actually performed in daily life. As one mother commented, "My son learned to count to 20 and to recognize coins, but he never learned to pay for his own hamburger at McDonald's." Third, the basic preacademic or academic skills that are taught may be different from those needed by children with disabilities to perform functional tasks in natural contexts (rather than just counting money out of context, they need to learn all the skills necessary to use money to buy things within their natural environment).

Behavioral Perspective

The behavioral perspective is based on the learning principles of behavioral psychology. Behaviorists (such as Skinner, Bijou, and Baer) believe that children are extrinsically motivated and describe child development and learning as resulting from environmental factors. From a behavioral point of view, emphasis should be placed on the activities in which a child engages within his environment and the skills that are necessary to participate in those activities in an age-appropriate manner. According to a behavioral approach, skills are important only to the extent to which they are adaptive and related to increasing children's independence. Curricula based on a behavioral model emphasize direct instruction through a prescribed sequence of instructional activities (Hanson & Lynch, 1995). According to this approach, antecedent events and consequences related to behavior are examined and then direct instruction and reinforcement are applied to change the behavior. Instructional procedures such as prompting, shaping, or reinforcing are used to facilitate children's acquisition of skills. Skill acquisition is then monitored through frequent data collection. Based on the amount of progress that the children make, modifications are made in instructional activities.

Instead of following a developmental sequence for curricular content, behavioral interventionists apply remedial logic to the selection of skills. The focus is on the identification of targeted behaviors with the application of direct instructional techniques designed to increase or decrease certain behaviors. The major problem with a behavioral curriculum approach is the degree of structure and precision required in the implementation. Furthermore, this approach is more difficult to blend with the theoretical perspectives espoused in most general early childhood programs.

Functional Perspective

Somewhat related to a behavioral model is a functional curriculum model (Strain, McConnell, Carta, Fowler, Neisworth, & Wolery, 1992). In recent years, many early childhood special educators have adopted a functional skills approach to developing curricula for young children with disabilities, especially for children with severe disabilities. Within this perspective, functional skills or behaviors that are useful for the child to adapt to current or future anticipated environmental demands are identified and facilitated (Bailey, Jens, & Johnson, 1983). Thus, skills having immediate relevance to a child are emphasized, such as interacting in a typical manner based on the demands of the environment and performing skills

required for daily tasks such as dressing, eating, and many other functional skills performed at home, at child care, at school, and all other community settings. Developmental age is of less importance than is the child's proficiency in acquiring important age-appropriate skills. Functional skills geared toward daily living activities are the focus rather than preacademic, academic, or developmental sequences. In some cases, relevant skills are task-analyzed into a sequence of observable and measurable subskills. For example, a skill such as eating with a fork would be broken down into steps, beginning with picking up the fork, stabbing the food with the fork, and, finally, returning the fork to the plate.

According to Rainforth et al. (1992) and others, the functional approach has several advantages over developmental and other theoretical approaches for children with disabilities. First, the curriculum is based on functional and chronologically age-appropriate skills needed by children in a number of natural settings within the community. Learning to perform these skills usually enables children to function more independently in a variety of settings. When children with disabilities perform in a competent manner, those observing often raise their expectations of them. A second advantage of the functional curriculum approach is that many of the skills taught are performed by nondisabled children. Learning many of the same day-to-day tasks performed by nondisabled children increases opportunities for children with disabilities to be successfully included within the natural environment. Third, the use of task analysis as a strategy to identify specific responses to be taught facilitates individualization. A particular task may be analyzed into any number of discreet steps, based on the unique strengths and needs of the child. For example, different steps and strategies will be involved in teaching dressing skills to a child with cerebral palsy than when teaching dressing skills to a child who is blind.

There appears to be only one major disadvantage of the functional skills approach in that it lacks a clear organizational framework. Because there are no universal or generally accepted criteria for determining what skills are functional and relevant for children, the potential exists for idiosyncratic curricular content that is specific to each child. Difficulty can arise when teachers attempt to address the unique skills that each and every child needs (Rainforth et al., 1992).

This description of the various approaches to curriculum development is an extreme oversimplification. Furthermore, there is rarely a strict adherence to any one curriculum model in early childhood programs, and, in fact, a combination of approaches is typically used in program planning for young children with known or suspected disabilities. Hanson and Lynch (1995) stress that curriculum content is most often based on developmental, cognitive, and/or functional theoretical approaches. Instructional strategies, on the other hand, are often derived from a behavioral theoretical approach.

Most curriculum developers and service providers recognize that the perspectives described above are not necessarily mutually exclusive approaches. In fact, many would agree that a combination of approaches may be most effective.

A number of factors differentiate the various approaches to curriculum. Bailey (1997) points out that one of the primary features to distinguish curriculum approaches is the role of the teacher (or sometimes the parent) in relation to the child. Approaches that are directive or adult-centered emphasize teacher planning of curriculum activities, setting objectives for children, and engaging in planned instructional activities. On the other hand, approaches considered to be responsive or child-centered emphasize the child as the initiator of interactions with the adult responding to children's interests in a facilitative manner. The perspectives described above and the dichotomies that exist as defining characteristics of curriculum approaches (developmental versus functional approaches to curriculum content; directive versus responsive approaches to teaching) serve as the focus of much discussion in the professional literature.

Each teacher must use a tentative approach to curriculum development with which he or she feels comfortable, which usually evolves over time, and seems to be appropriate for the children being served. There are a number of other factors to consider in curriculum development for young children with disabilities, which are discussed in the section that follows.

Curriculum Development

As described previously, curricula in EI/ECSE are influenced by a number of complex factors. In addition to subscribing to a particular theoretical perspective, curricula can vary along a variety of dimensions. Curricula can focus on one or more developmental domains (e.g., motor, cognitive, social) or the focus can be on more broad-based, integrated constructs such as play (Linder, 1993b). The target of curricula can vary as well, with the target being the child only, the family only, or both. This dimension also varies according to the focus of the intervention (e.g., direct intervention vs. relationship-oriented) depending on the age of the child, etc. Curricula also can vary according to the contexts in which they are implemented, such as when directed toward the home or community environment. Finally, the implementation of the curriculum can range from highly structured, teacher-directed learning episodes to more naturalistic activities (Wolery & Sainato, 1996). Further, it must be emphasized that these dimensions are neither mutually exclusive nor exhaustive (Bruder, 1997).

Curriculum in early childhood is essentially all of the specific components of the intervention plan that the teacher, families, and other team members have selected for a group of young children. In this section, the focus is on the content of curricula. Although the theoretical basis and content of the curriculum usually vary from program to program, the salient feature is that the skills, behaviors, abilities, and patterns of interaction that are important for children to acquire are reflected in the curriculum.

Curriculum Content

Identifying the content of the curriculum that will be the target of intervention for each child with a disability is an ongoing process. The curriculum should have a mechanism for assisting the teacher, family, and other team members in identifying the skills that are most important for an individual child. Ongoing assessment can be used to determine the targets of intervention by examining the characteristics of the child, the demands of the environment, and the necessary skills to be successful. This process can help the team understand the ecological demands of children's environments.

The content of the curriculum for young children with disabilities usually includes a broad range of skills that would be appropriate for most young children who are nondisabled (Wolery & Sainato, 1996). Curriculum content encompasses all potential skills that are relevant to a child with a disability. Children's skills in the various developmental domains and the relationships among these domains can serve as a guide in determining curriculum content. In addition, the idiosyncratic skills that children need to function in their unique ecologies should be considered. The ordering or sequencing of skills also plays a role in determining curriculum content. Goals for children are derived by considering all of the aforementioned factors. Table 7–1 indicates the phases involved in curriculum development in early childhood programs where children with disabilities are served.

Team members can work together to adapt the curriculum as needed to address children's goals or outcomes stated on their IFSPs or IEPs. These goals or outcomes are broken down into benchmarks/objectives. Basically, objectives represent learning expectations and are based on a child's strengths, needs, and the family's preferences. Objectives differ from goals or outcomes in that they separate the goal into smaller components. The team must decide what objectives to teach, the routines in which to teach them, the appropriate teaching strategies to use, and ways to record progress. In order for curricula to have optimal utility, it must be flexible, functional, and adaptable.

The scope of early intervention/education services often includes information and support for the family in addition to services for the child. Services for the child, of course, specifically address the child's identified disability or delay. In Maria's case, services are provided to address the outcomes stated

Table 7–1   **Phases of Curriculum Development**
Phase 1
Determine what goals or outcomes are desired for each child.
Phase 2
Determine what skills each child must learn in order to achieve these goals or outcomes.
Phase 3
Determine the expectations of the environment(s) and the functional skill requirements.
Phase 4
Determine how the skills will be taught based on each child's learning style, activity preferences, and experiences.
Phase 5
Determine how the goals or outcomes will be evaluated.
Result
Information that can be used to make decisions about the curriculum.

on her IFSP in the areas of gross and fine motor skills, communication, and cognition. The type of services that would provide information and support to her family might include assisting her parents and grandparents so that they will be able to interact with her in ways that will facilitate communication and cognitive skill development. Another example of a service that would provide information and support to Maria's family would be the provision of assistance with transition planning to the preschool program that they feel is appropriate for Maria.

Commercial Curriculum Guides

In addition to collecting information specific to each child and family in designing the curriculum, there are a number of commercial curriculum guides organized in a sequenced format that are used in early childhood programs serving young children with disabilities. Many of these commercial curriculum guides promote functional and individually appropriate activities for young children. Often these guides are referred to as curriculum-based assessment systems because they usually contain an assessment scale and an accompanying curriculum guide (Neisworth & Bagnato, 1996). Examples of widely used curriculum-based measures are included in Table 7–2.

The *AEPS Curriculum for Birth to Three Years* and *AEPS Curriculum for Three to Six Years* is a frequently used system, which is divided into two volumes. The AEPS allows professionals to match the child's established IFSP/IEP goals and objectives with age-appropriate, activity-based interventions that correspond to the six areas scored on the *AEPS Test*. Because the test and curricula use the same numbering system, users can easily locate activities in the curricula that correspond to specific goals and objectives identified with the test—a feature that also helps with ongoing evaluation. In both volumes, professionals are provided with sample teaching tactics, instructional sequences, recommendations for environmental arrangements, and strategies for incorporating the activities into the child's daily routine. To reflect the individual learning styles many children acquire by ages three to six, the *Curriculum for Three to Six Years* is more flexible in that it provides general intervention considerations and suggested activities rather than specific instructional sequences.

Most teachers find curriculum guides to be helpful in planning activities in early childhood programs. The following questions have been adapted from Hanson and Lynch (1995) for teachers and other team members to consider when evaluating the quality and appropriateness of curriculum guides:

1. Is the curriculum organized around a theoretical rationale? Is this philosophical approach clearly stated?

2. Is the philosophical approach consistent with or appropriate to the EI/ECSE program's approach and the population to be served?

3. Does the curriculum include a wide range of items/activities (scope), such that the needs of the full range of children in the program will be met? Are items appropriate for use with children with different disabilities (if so, which ones) and of different ages? If so, what are the age ranges?

4. Are the directions for curriculum use clearly and specifically stated?

5. Are the curricular items sequenced in a developmentally appropriate order?

6. Can items be further "branched" or broken down to accommodate children for whom items may be too difficult? Are instructions for this branching provided?

7. Do items meet the test of being both developmentally and functionally appropriate for young children?

8. Is family involvement encouraged and is it a central focus? If so, how? Can the curriculum be implemented by parents or other caregivers?

9. Is the selection of curricular items integrally linked with assessments and observations of child behavior? Are the goals and objectives clearly stated so that the child's progress can be assessed?

10. Are the goals and activities written in a jargon-free manner so that they can be easily and consistently used?

11. Is the amount of time needed to implement the curriculum appropriate to the needs of the program?

12. Can the curriculum be used with various group sizes and, if so, is it appropriate for the group size(s) of the program?

13. Are the target environments or settings in which the curriculum is to be implemented appropriate to the goals and needs of the program?

14. Are the teaching techniques and areas of expertise required to implement the curriculum consistent with those of the staff members?

15. Are special materials or equipment needed? If so, are these readily available to early childhood program staff members and/or family members?

Table 7-2   Commercial Curriculum Guides

Title	Author	Date	Publisher	Ages	Domains	Assess Log
The Assessment, Evaluation, Programming System (AEPS) Curriculum for Infants and Children	Bricker	2002	Paul H. Brookes	Birth–6 years	All domains	Yes; separate book; also progress log
Active Learning for Infants, Ones, Twos, and Threes	Cryer, Harms, & Bourland	1987	Addison Wesley Longman	Birth–3 years	Communication, physical/creative	No
Active Learning for Children with Disabilities	Biley, Cryer, Harms, Osborne, & Kniest	1996	Dale Seymour Publications	Birth–5 years	All domains	No
Carolina Curriculum for Preschoolers with Special Needs	Johnson-Martin, Jens, Attermier, & Hacker	1991	Paul H. Brookes	3–5 years	All domains	Yes; separate protocol; also progress charts
Help at Home	Parks	1998	VORT	Birth–3 years	All domains	Yes
Instructional Activities for Children at Risk	Dolimar, Boser, & Holm	1994	DLM	2–6 years	All domains	No
Teaching Young Children Using Themes	Kostelnik & Howe	1991	Goodyear Books	2–6 years	Themes: social science, numbers, language	No
Transdisciplinary Play-Based Intervention	Linder	1993	Paul H. Brookes	Birth–5 years	All domains, including mastery motivation	Yes; separate assessment book

16. Is the cost of the curricular package reasonable and economically feasible for the program?

17. Are the curricular items nonracist, nonsexist, and culturally nonbiased?

18. Does the curriculum include strategies to foster the generalization of skills to other people, places, or materials?

19. Has the curriculum been tested on the populations for which it was designed? Are these validation data present?

20. Were professionals from different disciplines involved with and reflected in the curricular content?

21. Can the curriculum be used in formative and summative evaluations of child progress? Can the effectiveness of the curricular approach be evaluated as part of program evaluation? (p. 199)

Curriculum Planning and Activities

There is an increasing recognition that the concept of curriculum is much broader than the traditional view of a packaged set of goals and activities. Most would agree that the curriculum is, or at least is highly influenced by, the entire set of experiences provided in an early intervention/education program, including teacher-child ratios and group size, the degree of structure, teaching activities, therapeutic services, the physical environment, and peers (Graham & Bryant, 1993). The remainder of this chapter is based on a broad-based view of curriculum, to include curriculum planning and the full range of activities provided by the EI/ECSE program and experienced by the children participating in that program.

Curriculum planning in early childhood education programs often involves the development of integrated thematic units. They are usually developed around topical areas of interest to young children (e.g., animals, holidays, special events such as the circus). Davis et al. (1998) recommend at least five factors to be considered when integrated thematic units are selected for classrooms in which young children with disabilities are served. They recommend that the theme topic should be:

- broad enough to address the wide range of abilities of the children,

- one in which the children's IEP or IFSP objectives can be addressed,

- generated based on the interests and experiences of the children,

- selected based on the availability of resources and materials necessary, and

- designed based on the interests of the teacher and other team members.

Depending on the thematic units selected, curriculum activities can be planned that address multiple areas of development. This approach provides a flexible method for addressing children's IEP or IFSP goals/outcomes.

In implementing the curriculum, multiple child-directed, play-based activities, such as center activities that are part of the early childhood classroom routine, are utilized (Fox, Hanline, Vail, & Galant, 1994), as well as teacher-directed activities such as circle time. Activities are selected that naturally require children to perform targeted skills and ensure that by performing the skills, children will become more independent within their routines. By considering children's individual characteristics and unique needs, the team plans ways to make adaptations or modifications to activities and determines how various levels of support will be provided to ensure that all children are able to participate.

A curriculum approach that is widely used with young children with disabilities has been termed **activity-based instruction** (Bricker & Cripe, 1992). Bricker and Cripe (1992) developed an "activity-based" curriculum model of instruction that integrates the theories of Vygotsky, Piaget, and Dewey while using behavioral learning principles. This model is based on the assumption that the fundamental goal of EI/ECSE is "to improve children's acquisition and use of important motor, social, affective, communicative and intellectual (e.g., problem solving) behaviors that, in turn, are integrated into response repertoires that are generative, functional, and adaptable" (Bricker, 2002, p. 11). Thus, an activity-based curriculum model uses a transactional approach that (a) is child-directed;

(b) embeds predetermined objectives into a range of routines, adult-planned activities, and child-initiated activities; (c) uses contexts and consequences that are logical and natural in the child's life; and (d) promotes the development of skills that are useful. This approach has been described as "a child-directed, transactional approach, that embeds training on a child's individual IFSP or IEP goals and objectives into routine or planned activities and uses logically occurring antecedents and consequences to develop functional and generalizable skills" (Bricker & Cripe, 1989, p. 253). As such, this type of approach utilizes the many naturally occurring events and opportunities that exist in a young child's life as "intervention opportunities." By capitalizing on the child's interests, preferences, and actions, emphasis is placed on the child's initiations rather than on the teachers' choices. In addition, the interventions encourage the acquisition of functional skills that can be generalized to other settings, people, or materials. Skills are acquired by crossing developmental domains in the same activity, using naturalistic instructional strategies, and promoting creativity and independence. For example, during snack time, objectives from several developmental domains may be targeted such as self-care, communication, and fine motor skills. In using this approach, professionals must be keen observers of child behavior, be aware of ways to arrange the environment to facilitate child initiations, and maximize adult responsiveness to child-initiated interactions within social and nonsocial environments. An activity-based instructional approach will be discussed in greater detail in the chapter that follows.

Curriculum Evaluation

Ongoing with curriculum implementation is documentation regarding the children's progress in relation to the broader curriculum goals, as well as each child's individual goals/outcomes and benchmarks/objectives/activities. Record keeping and reevaluation are important for meeting the changing needs of children as well as families. To ensure that an objective has been met on a child's IFSP or IEP, early childhood professionals must demonstrate that a child has attained mastery of his/her objectives.

The portfolio process, described in Chapter 5, is one approach that embraces family-based practices and merges general early childhood and early childhood special education practices. Progress can be documented on children's individual objectives by observing a child's performance and by collecting permanent products. Observational recording techniques include the use of anecdotal notes, running records, teacher reflections, checklists or inventories, responses to questions or requests, rating scales, family input, and other child progress monitoring procedures. Observations can focus on spontaneous performance or may involve asking the child to engage in a specific activity. Examples of products could include writing samples, drawings, and other art samples; audiotapes of children retelling or dictating stories; videotapes of story reenactments or play activities; photographs of large projects or completed projects; and logs of books that were read to or by children (Southern Association for Children Under Six, 1991). Records can be collected in chronological order and filed by area of development in each child's portfolio.

Families can be better informed about their children's progress when portfolios are used to organize

Activity-based instruction promotes skills from several domains within a routine or planned activity.

collected data. Recent observational records and products are compared to previous records and products to determine whether progress has been made on each child's individual objectives. In order to determine if the IFSP or IEP objectives have been achieved, mastery at criteria levels specified on the IFSPs or IEPs must also be documented. Modifications can be made in the curriculum based on the data that is collected to document each child's progress.

Regular communication about children's progress should be maintained with families using methods that they have selected. When children with disabilities are included in the same environments as their nondisabled peers, the family, along with the general early childhood, early childhood special education, and related service professionals can discuss ways to coordinate their communication about children's progress. For example, early childhood special education and related service professionals might schedule joint parent conferences with the general early childhood teacher during the same times that conferences are offered for all families or they might use a system where professionals can exchange information with the family by writing in a notebook that the child brings to and from school.

As discussed in this chapter thus far, curriculum development in an early childhood program is an ongoing process that involves determining: (a) the theoretical or philosophical approach on which the curriculum is based, (b) the curriculum content to be addressed, (c) the curriculum implementation process to be followed, and (d) the curriculum evaluation procedures to be used. Any evaluation of a particular curriculum guide or approach should take into consideration additional curriculum components when making judgments about its effectiveness. A number of other current influences on curriculum in EI/ECSE are the focus of the remainder of this chapter.

Current Influences on Curriculum

The designation of recommended practice in curriculum development for infants and young children with disabilities has been evolving for a period of years. Perhaps the most dramatic influence has been the input coming from the fields of both general early childhood education (ECE) and early childhood special education (ECSE) that has occurred as the inclusion movement has grown. Within the two disciplines of ECE and ECSE, professionals who represent the major professional bodies have constructed documents that represent contemporary thought regarding practices that should be used in the education of young children.

The question that arises is how do we reconcile the apparent pedagogical and philosophical differences between these two approaches. We believe that common ground must be established with the increased legal, legislative, and educational emphasis on including children with disabilities in programs alongside their nondisabled peers. We begin this task by briefly exploring recommended practices from ECE and ECSE, followed by analysis of the applicability of DAP to young children with special needs, and conclude with support for a blended approach to curriculum development and implementation in programs serving children with disabilities.

Recommended Practices in General Early Childhood Education (ECE)

One of the most widely used descriptors of recommended practice in early childhood curriculum is **developmentally appropriate practice (DAP)** (Bredekamp, 1987; Bredekamp & Copple, 1997). DAP, which is the term more commonly used to refer to developmentally appropriate practice, is a set of guidelines established by the National Association for the Education of Young Children (NAEYC) to articulate appropriate practices for the early education of young children. The idea of constructing a statement of DAP was inaugurated in 1987 as a vehicle for providing information to early childhood programs seeking accreditation through NAEYC (National Association for the Education of Young Children, 1991). The document also served as a reactionary statement to the growing fears of the increasingly academic demands and expectations encountered by young children in preschool and early primary programs (Carta et al., 1991; Udell, Peters, & Templeman, 1998).

Many in the early childhood community were concerned that too many programs were focusing on academic preparedness and not providing young children with enough opportunities to engage in play and other less structured activities that typify early childhood. As one mother explained, "although I'm not an educator, I know from experience that four-year-olds should not be expected to sit at a table and complete work sheets for an hour at a time! No one should be expected to do the same task for that long without getting bored and misbehaving!"

The DAP guidelines were developed to emphasize the unique learning needs of young children, to offer guidance to early childhood educators in providing learning opportunities for young children through a play-oriented approach, and to point out the inappropriateness of rigid academic instruction for this age group. In addition, the guidelines were developed to provide guidance to those early childhood programs that were expanding their services to infants and toddlers. A fundamental premise of DAP is the belief that "early childhood programs should be tailored to meet the needs of children, rather than expecting children to adjust to the demands of a specific program" (Bredekamp, 1987, p. 1).

After a decade of extensive dissemination, the 1987 position statement became the most widely recognized guideline for recommended practice in the field of early childhood education. In 1997, NAEYC published revised guidelines titled *Developmentally Appropriate Practice in Early Childhood Programs* (Bredekamp & Copple, 1997). The revised guidelines were developed in response to the overwhelming amount of discussion that occurred in response to the 1987 DAP guidelines and to clarify the misunderstandings and misinterpretations related to the original position statement.

Before highlighting some of the provisions of DAP, we need to point out that the guidelines themselves are purposefully general and allow professionals to interpret what is appropriate for young children. The DAP guidelines were conceived as a living document and not as educational dogma. They were also conceptualized as a dynamic and evolving statement of recommended practices (Wolery & Bredekamp, 1994). As a working hypothesis, the guidelines are subject to change and amenable to revisions as thinking and recommended practices (which are necessarily time-bound) change. This position represents an attempt by NAEYC to define developmental appropriateness as a major, rather than the sole or exclusive, indicator of quality programs for young children.

According to NAEYC, DAP has three important dimensions: (a) age appropriateness, (b) individual appropriateness, and (c) cultural appropriateness (Bredekamp & Copple, 1997). These components are central to the concept of DAP, as well as the role of the child and teacher in the learning environment. In addition, another key aspect of developmentally appropriate practice is that teaching must take place in the child's natural context rather than in any artificial environment.

The first dimension, **age appropriateness,** refers to the universal nature of the course of human development during the early childhood years. According to research in child development, there are universal, predictable sequences of growth and change that occur in young children during the first nine years of life across various development domains (physical, emotional, social, and cognitive, etc.) Based on their knowledge of typical development in children, teachers are able to prepare the learning environment and plan appropriate experiences.

Individual appropriateness, the second dimension, refers to the uniqueness of children. Children have individual patterns and timing of growth, as well as individual personalities, strengths, interests, backgrounds, and experiences. According to the DAP guidelines, for the learning environment and curriculum to be responsive to the individual differences teachers must design to meet the needs of each child.

The third dimension of the DAP guidelines, **cultural appropriateness,** refers to the teacher's ability to understand each child and his or her unique social and cultural contexts. The curriculum and meaningful learning experiences, which are relevant to individual children, can be planned when the teacher has firsthand knowledge of each child's social and cultural background.

When applying these concepts to curriculum development, the goals underlying curriculum con-

A developmentally appropriate curriculum is tailored to meet the needs of young children and provides opportunities for them to engage in play and other less-structured activities.

tent and activities should reflect what professionals know about the typical sequence of child development and, at the same time, should be responsive to the individual variances in development, personality, ability, interest, learning style, and culture. Curriculum is age appropriate when knowledge of typical child development is used to plan experiences that are based on the ages of the children in the program. Curriculum is individually appropriate when it is responsive to unique differences in children (Bredekamp, 1987; Bredekamp & Copple, 1997). Curriculum is culturally appropriate when learning experiences are designed based on the social and cultural contexts in which children live (Bredekamp & Copple, 1997). In addition, curriculum is flexible, allowing for content that meets a wide range of abilities, interests, and backgrounds of the children (Bredekamp & Rosegrant, 1992). Teachers and other professionals should be aware of cultural differences of the children and families they serve and adapt curricula accordingly. Cultural diversity is addressed in many curriculum resources available in early childhood education.

What follows is a discussion of some of the widely accepted beliefs or premises of developmentally appropriate curriculum in general early childhood education.

1. *The process of learning is just as important, if not more important, as the end product.* Children's active engagement within their environment with peers, materials, and adults is valuable and necessary in order for them to be active participants in the learning process. Experiences occur on a continuum from child-initiated to teacher-guided, depending on the needs of each child and the context of the activity.

2. *Children learn through play and through concrete "hands-on" activities that are relevant to their lives.* Opportunities for children to interact with others and to play with real objects provide the context for learning. In T. J.'s Head Start classroom, a cooking activity, such as making cinnamon toast, could be used to explore measurement (of the sugar, cinnamon, etc.) and numbers (how many pieces of bread, how many napkins), as well as to develop fine motor skills (pouring, stirring, eye-hand coordination).

3. *Heterogeneous grouping is embraced with the belief that appropriate educational experiences meet the needs of young children with a wide range of abilities, cultural backgrounds, and interests.* It is believed that educational experiences should be flexible as children are allowed to work on different levels and at their own pace. The curriculum should not only celebrate diversity, but should challenge prejudice, stereotyping, and bias (related to gender, ability, race, etc.).

According to Bredekamp and Rosegrant (1992), when planning appropriate curriculum content and activities for young children, the following characteristics should be evident:

- the children's interests are acknowledged;
- the activities are meaningful and relevant to the children's everyday experiences;
- social interaction is encouraged;
- activities draw on children's previous knowledge; and
- many forms of participation for active engagement are provided for while promoting the acquisition of skills and knowledge.

Table 7–3   Constructing Appropriate Curriculum

1. Developmentally appropriate curriculum provides for all areas of a child's development: physical, emotional, social, linguistic, aesthetic, and cognitive.

2. Curriculum includes a broad range of content across disciplines that is socially relevant, intellectually engaging, and personally meaningful to children.

3. Curriculum builds upon what children already know and are able to do (activating prior knowledge) to consolidate their learning and to foster their acquisition of new concepts and skills.

4. Effective curriculum plans frequently integrate across traditional subject matter divisions to help children make meaningful connections and provide opportunities for rich conceptual development; focusing on one subject is a valid strategy at times.

5. Curriculum promotes the development of knowledge and understanding, processes and skills, as well as the dispositions to use and apply skills, and to continue learning.

6. Curriculum content has intellectual integrity, reflecting the key concepts and tools of inquiry of recognized disciplines in ways that are accessible and achievable for young children, ages 3 through 8.

7. Curriculum provides opportunities to support children's home culture and language while also developing all children's abilities to participate in the shared culture of the program and the community.

8. Curriculum goals are realistic and attainable for most children in the designated age range for which they are designed.

9. When used, technology is physically and philosophically integrated in the classroom curriculum and teaching.

SOURCE: Adapted from S. Bredekamp, and C. Copple, *Developmentally appropriate practice in early childhood programs* (Revised Edition). (Washington, DC: National Association for the Education of Young Children, 1997), p. 20.

By responding to children's interests, teachers and others can provide learning activities that are stimulating and increase the probability that children will have sustained involvement with high interest materials, behaviors, and people. By creating educational experiences that are similar and meaningful to children's real-life experiences, teachers address their current needs and provide learning activities that are directly applicable to their reality.

A variety of procedures may be used by early childhood professionals to identify suitable and meaningful curriculum. For example, regular observations of individual children can be useful in determining their unique strengths, needs, and interests. Table 7–3 provides suggestions from NAEYC for constructing appropriate curriculum for young children (Bredekamp & Copple, 1997). A variety of intervention strategies can be used to teach these curricular goals based on children's individual needs (Bredekamp & Rosegrant, 1992; Richarz, 1993). (These strategies will be discussed in detail in subsequent chapters.)

Recommended Practices in Early Childhood Special Education (ECSE)

The field of ECSE did not have a set of guidelines comparable to the DAP guidelines until 1993, when the Division for Early Childhood (DEC) of the Council for Exceptional Children (CEC) published the first document to provide recommendations for programs serving young children with special needs and their families and indicators of quality in these programs (DEC Task Force on Recommended Practices, 1993). As described earlier, DEC published a set of guidelines titled *DEC Recommended Practices in Early Intervention/Early Childhood Special Education* (Sandall, McLean, & Smith, 2000) that synthesizes the knowledge found in the scientific/professional literature and the knowledge from experience of parents, practitioners, and administrators about those practices that produce the best outcomes for children. Further, and perhaps most important to this discussion, the guidelines contain many recommendations that have relevance to curriculum development and implementation. In designing early childhood curriculum for young children with disabilities and their families, it is important to consider the principles underlying the DEC recommended practices and quality indicators that support the goals of early childhood special education.

Principles Underlying DEC Recommended Practices   The DEC guidelines delineate the underlying six principles of curriculum content and experiences for young children with disabilities. These principles are discussed in the following section.

- *Educational experiences should be family-based.* This means that the curriculum should be responsive to families' goals and priorities for their children. As described in Chapter 3, a dramatic shift in advocated practices has occurred in early childhood special education over the years, from a solely child-oriented approach to a family-based approach. Although federal legislation is largely credited with providing the rationale for basing services on the family, the law put into policy what had been an already burgeoning movement. Family participation is now guided by the goal of a partnership of equals being built between the family and the EI/ECSE service system (such as family-based service delivery model). The spirit of this family movement is based on the belief that the vision families have for their children should provide the foundation for program planning. Family preferences play a vital role in planning the curriculum content and strategies. Thus, family input is encouraged and supported, and families' rights to make decisions about their children's EI/ECSE experiences are respected.

- *Educational experiences should be research-based or value-based.* That is, specific strategies that early childhood special education professionals use should have some empirical support or be value-driven (supported by current values held by professionals in the field and the family). This implies that professionals must continually examine their current practices and procedures to ensure their effectiveness and social validity.

DEC's *Recommended Practices* provide suggestions that have relevance to curriculum development and implementation for young children with disabilities.

- *Educational experiences should be consistent with a multicultural perspective.* Appropriate educational experiences should reflect the diverse values, backgrounds, and experiences of children and families served within a program, acknowledging the individuality of children and families. The cultural backgrounds of the children and families should help to guide curriculum development.

- *Educational experiences should provide for multidisciplinary input.* Because children with disabilities often have a need for services such as physical therapy, speech-language therapy, occupational therapy, and/or other related services, there are often many different professionals who work with the child and family. Practices should reflect a team approach, whereby all team members share information and expertise, communicate frequently, and participate in joint decision making. Input from the various disciplines should be integrated into the design of the curriculum.

- *Educational experiences should be developmentally and chronologically appropriate.* Wolery et al. (1992) stress that the DAP guidelines may not be sufficient when addressing the needs of children with disabilities. The key to developing appropriate educational experiences (for any child) is to create a match between the unique, individual needs of the child and the curriculum. Making this match for children with disabilities may require paying attention to the physical and social environment, adapting or using specialized equipment and materials, and/or utilizing specialized instructional strategies and techniques to support each child's development and learning.

- *Educational experiences should be normalized.* Nirje (1976) defined normalization as making available to all persons with disabilities ". . . the patterns of life and conditions of everyday living which are as close as possible to the regular circumstances and ways of life of society" (p. 231). Normalization is often narrowly interpreted to mean that children with disabilities should be placed in inclusive settings. While that is one application of normalization, placement within inclusive settings does not ensure that the normalization principle is being addressed. When applied to young children with disabilities, it includes examining a number of different aspects of each child's educational placement to include educational programming, teaching strategies, the physical and social environment, and family-based practices.

Along with these general principles, the DEC Task Force on Recommended Practices (1993) provides more specific guidelines related to skill development across the developmental domains and many other areas including, but not limited to, assessment, family participation, and transition planning.

Potential Benefits or Outcomes of ECSE

The underlying premises of DEC recommended practices described above support the general goals of early educational experiences for young children with disabilities (Bailey & Wolery, 1992; Bricker et al., 1998; Sandall, McLean & Smith, 2000). The potential benefits or outcomes of ECSE are described as follows.

- *Families are supported in achieving their goals.* Children with disabilities may have complex needs that are better understood when professionals interact with families and learn about the priorities that parents have for their children. As the mother of a 3-year-old with cerebral palsy told her child's teacher, "All I want is for my child to learn to walk." Thus, this mother's priority became the focus of intervention. Although the child never actually learned to walk, he did learn to use an electronic wheelchair to get from place to place independently. If professionals do not have knowledge of the families' priorities, the likelihood of success will be diminished. It is critical for professionals to understand that families function as a system. Thus, they must develop rapport with families, have ongoing interactions with them, and support them in achieving the goals they have for their children (Turnbull & Turnbull, 2001).

- *Child engagement, independence, and mastery are supported.* Through the ECSE curriculum, each child's engagement with the people, materials, and activities in his or her natural environment (home, school, etc.) is supported, which enables him or her to master the demands associated with each of these environments. A mother of a 4-year-old child with Turner's Syndrome encouraged professionals to examine the routines and demands of the general early childhood program where her daughter was enrolled in order to determine the focus of intervention. In order for Kathryn to become more independent and to be successful in this setting, the focus of her program needed to be on what was expected of her within this setting. Efforts should be made to "promote active engagement (participation), initiative (choice making, self-directed behavior), autonomy (individuality and self-sufficiency) and age-appropriate abilities in many normalized contexts and situations" (Wolery & Sainato, 1996, p. 53).

- *Development is promoted in all areas.* Experiences for young children with disabilities should be designed to promote progress in each of the key areas of development already described (e.g., cognitive, motor, communication, social). Many activities in which young children participate require the integrated use of skills from various domains. For example, when Maria is participating in a snack time activity, she is using skills from several areas including fine motor, language, social, and self-care skills. Often young children with disabilities are behind their typically developing age-mates and, therefore, individual goals are targeted for each child and instructional strategies are used that lead to rapid learning in order to help the child with disabilities move closer to normal developmental levels (Wolery & Sainato, 1993, 1996).

- *The development of social competence is supported.* Most would agree that social skills (e.g., developing friendships, getting along with peers, playing cooperatively) are among the most important skills for young children to learn. Young children with special needs reportedly engage in less sophisticated and less frequent social interactions than their nondisabled peers (Guralnick, 1990). Therefore, many children with disabilities have difficulty developing these skills and must be taught to interact effectively and properly (Goldstein, Kaczmarek, & English, 2001). As a result, one of the primary benefits of ECSE is that the social competence of young children with disabilities is often further developed. As one mother noted, "My son needed to learn the social expectations of the general education classroom. His kindergarten teacher didn't seem to mind that he couldn't write his name, but she did expect him to walk in a line with his classmates to the lunchroom and to stay in his seat during group time."

- *The generalized use of skills is emphasized.* Skill generalization is especially important when teaching young children with disabilities who have extreme difficulty with generalizing or applying what they learn to different situations, people, and materials (Drew, Logan, & Hardman, 1992). Bethany is a 4-year-old with Down syndrome who learned to communicate at preschool by using sign language along with a few words. After her initial success with communicating at preschool, the emphasis of her program expanded to using her communication skills at home, the babysitter's house, and other environments. As Wolery and Sainato (1993) point out, "Early interventionists should not be satisfied if children learn new skills; they should only be satisfied if children use those skills when and wherever they are appropriate" (p. 54).

- *Children are provided with, and prepared for, "normalized" life experiences.* Because IDEA and its amendments reflect the normalization principle (previously discussed), services for young children with disabilities should be provided to the extent possible in settings that are as much like the typical settings in which young children without disabilities play and learn (Cook, Tessier, & Klein, 2000). Therefore, a primary purpose and potential benefit of early education for young children with disabilities is to provide a "normalized" curriculum, which should prepare them for "normalized life experiences." Some of the normalized learning environments for a 2-year-old child might be a play group with other children in the neighborhood, a child care program, or a babysitter's house. Some normalized life experiences for T. J. might be going to church, attending birthday parties, or eating at McDonald's. The literature describes the benefits of placements in inclusive settings and suggests strategies for effective inclusive early childhood programs (Guralnick, 2001; Sainato & Strain, 1993; Sandall, McLean, & Smith, 2000; Sandall & Schwartz, 2002; Wolery & Wilbers, 1994).

- *The emergence of future problems or disabilities is prevented.* A final benefit of the EI/ECSE curriculum is to prevent the development of additional problems in young children with disabilities. For example, Audrey is a 4-year-old with cerebral palsy who spends most of her day in a wheelchair or other adaptive seating devices that provide trunk support. Without the trunk support and continued physical therapy, she probably will develop scoliosis, or a curvature of the spine. Jimmy is a 3-year-old who is blind. As a result of his visual impairment, he does not receive the same visual stimulation as other children his age, does not move around to explore his environment, and exhibits few social initiations. Without encouragement and support to explore his surroundings and initiate interactions with others, Jimmy may develop delays in related areas such as cognitive, social, and/or motor development. In each of these examples, the child has a primary disability that will lead to secondary problems unless he/she is provided with a curriculum that meets his/her individual needs (including attention to the environment, materials, equipment, and instruction).

These principles and potential benefits or outcomes undergird curriculum content and experiences for young children with disabilities. Based on the DEC guidelines, a number of strategies can be used by professionals who develop and implement appropriate curricula for young children with disabilities. The questions that emerge include: (a) are the DAP guidelines appropriate for use with young children with disabilities, and (b) how can recommended practices from both NAEYC (general early childhood education) and DEC (early childhood special education) be combined to meet the needs of children with differing abilities?

The Utility of the DAP Guidelines for Children with Disabilities

Bredekamp and Rosegrant (1992) emphasized that the principles of developmentally appropriate practice, as specified by the NAEYC, are appropriate for all children. However, over the years there has been much debate in the literature over the applicability of developmentally appropriate practice for children with disabilities (Atwater, Carta, Schwartz, & McConnell, 1994; Carta et al., 1991; Bredekamp, 1993a;

NAEYC's *Developmentally Appropriate Practice (DAP) Guidelines* have utility for young children with disabilities; however, adaptations and instructional techniques must be tailored to each child's individual needs.

Carta, Atwater, Schwartz, & McConnell, 1993; Fox et al., 1994; Johnson & Johnson, 1992; Mallory, 1992; Mallory & New, 1994; Safford, Sargent, & Cook, 1994; Wolery, Strain, & Bailey, 1992). Within the field of ECSE, most professionals agree that curriculum models emphasizing DAP are desirable, but are usually insufficient without adaptations and instructional techniques individually tailored to meet the needs of children with disabilities (Carta, 1994; Carta et al., 1991; Johnson, 1993; Wolery & Bredekamp, 1994). As Wolery et al. (1992) pointed out, "a program based on the guidelines alone is not likely to be sufficient for many children with special needs" (p. 106). Carta and her colleagues also share this viewpoint. Their analysis of the 1986 DAP guidelines revealed the following inadequacies as it pertained to young children with special needs:

- Programs serving young children with special needs must offer a range of services that vary in intensity based on the needs of the children they serve.

- Programs serving young children with special needs must develop individualized teaching plans consisting of goals and objectives that are based on a careful analysis of the child's strengths and weaknesses and on skills required for future school and nonschool environments.

- Assessment must be derived from many sources, be carried out across settings, and be frequent enough to monitor children's progress toward their individual goals and objectives.

- Instructional methodologies/procedures for teaching young children with special needs should be effective, efficient, functional, and normalized.

- Whatever types of instructional procedures are employed by the teacher, they should result in high levels of active involvement and participation in activities.

- Programs serving young children with special needs should focus on strengthening the abilities of families to nurture their children's development and to promote normalized community adaptation.

- Programs serving young children with special needs must be outcome-based, with specific criteria, procedures, and timelines used to determine if individual children progress toward stated outcomes. (pp. 3–7)

Carta et al. (1991) stated that the preceding seven statements represent basic premises of early childhood special education; they also serve as indicators of deficiency in the DAP guidelines. Carta and colleagues clearly acknowledge that the DAP guidelines have much in common with the underlying principles of the field of ECSE; yet, they provide several illustrations for each of their points where the DAP guidelines are considered insufficient for meeting the needs of young children with special needs and their families. Our interpretation of the Carta et al. position is that DAP is not necessarily *wrong;* it just doesn't go far enough as a vehicle for guiding the development of curriculum and the delivery of instruction to young children with disabilities.

But perhaps the biggest challenge to the utilization of DAP for young children with disabilities is a difference in the purpose or focus of instruction. Carta et al. (1991) explain that essentially, typically developing young children require a "safe, carefully planned environment that encourages . . . cognitive and social interaction" (p. 8). DAP is also an opponent of unwarranted acceleration of academic progress in nondisabled children. Early childhood special education, on the other hand, is driven by an environmentalist, rather than a constructivist position, which attempts to accelerate developmental progress and the acquisition of skills that typically would not occur without the benefit of direct intervention or instruction. This, in fact, is the explicit mission of early childhood special education. We, therefore, seem to be confronted with somewhat of a dichotomy. On one side, we have a present-oriented, teacher-facilitated, and child-initiated philosophy. The other side contains a structured, teacher-led, skill-focused, future-oriented philosophy (Safford et al., 1994). Are these positions that far apart? Is it at all reasonable to expect a blending of viewpoints? Do we have a true dichotomy or is it a continuum of approaches? We believe that the apparent difference between these two positions is due, in a large part, to the fact that DAP has been misinterpreted and misunderstood. Myths and misconceptions abound.

Bredekamp (1993a) examined the status of the relationship between what she believes to be the two complementary fields of ECE and ECSE. Her analysis revealed that while diversity exists in both fields, there is a growing movement toward resolving pedagogical and philosophical differences. Artificial barriers sometimes diminish opportunities for collaboration among professionals from both ECE and ECSE. As an illustration, commonly accepted misconceptions about DAP exacerbate differences between early childhood special educators and professionals in general early childhood education. Bredekamp identifies three misconceptions that have a direct bearing on serving young children with disabilities.

Her first example focuses on the NAEYC position regarding direct instruction of children. The DAP guidelines identify the following practice as inappropriate for nondisabled children: "using highly structured, teacher-directed lessons almost exclusively" and using "large group, teacher-directed instruction most of the time" (Bredekamp, 1987, p. 54). Unfortunately, this has been interpreted as suggesting that teachers should never use direct instruction with individual learners or in small groups. This representation is simplistic and unproductive (Burton, Hains, Hanline, McLean, & McCormick, 1992) while contributing to the disbelief that teachers in a DAP classroom do not teach and their students control the room (Bredekamp, 1993b). NAEYC advocates that the *exclusive* use of teacher-directed instruction is inappropriate for any child—partly because it denies opportunities for social interaction with classmates that research has validated to be vitally important for young children with special needs (Bredekamp, 1993a).

Curriculum in a classroom utilizing developmentally appropriate practices is construed as solely emerging from children's interest. This is an inaccurate portrayal, which has contributed to confusion about the role of goals (outcomes) in DAP. Goals are emphasized in DAP programs but not to the same degree as found in early childhood special education classrooms. Because DAP is—by definition—age, individually, and culturally appropriate, a teacher could not possibly affect individual appropriateness without careful planning and assessment of a student's individual interests and needs (Bredekamp & Copple, 1997). Bredekamp believes that some of the confusion surrounding this issue is due to a difference in interpretation of individualization. Early childhood educators look at individualization as responding to the interests of their children while their colleagues in ECSE interpret the term in relationship to IEP goals and objectives or IFSP outcome statements. This difference is one of language rather than substance as both ECE and ECSE address the individual needs and interests of their students.

DAP is built around the belief that it is applicable to *all* children. Yet, it has falsely been interpreted as applying to only *some* children—generally assumed to be middle-class and Caucasian. This is not a valid assumption. It is correct, however, that the NAEYC position fails to directly address the issue of young children with special needs; however, the 1986 document was not written for this population. The guidelines do require that teachers cater to the individual differences found among their students.

Johnson and Johnson (1992) also identified typical misrepresentations of DAP. For instance, they noted that Carta et al. (1991) stated that "the philosophy of early education . . . proposed that preschool programs should be child-centered" (p. 2). This statement is an invalid interpretation of DAP. Johnson and Johnson believe that DAP is neither child-centered nor age-based; rather, it is more appropriately considered child-sensitive, experience-based, and interaction-centered. DAP correctly recognizes the interactional process of instruction and learning and seeks to balance them.

Johnson and Johnson provide another illustration of a common misinterpretation. Looking at the Carta et al. article (1991), again they observe that DAP is accused of being overly restrictive and advocating a "single approach for teaching" (Carta et al., 1991, p. 6). This simply is not true. DAP guidelines, as we noted earlier, are flexible and allow for various instructional approaches to be utilized in the classroom.

Finally, Kostelnik (1992), in an attempt to clear up the confusion about what DAP actually entails, generated a list of nine myths frequently identified with developmentally appropriate programs. "These myths represent collected opinions that are based on false assumptions or are the product of fallacious reasoning" (p. 17). These common misinterpretations are exhibited in Table 7–4.

Hopefully, we have been able to address some of the confusion that surrounds the issue of developmentally appropriate practices and the applicability to children with disabilities. Discussion predicated on false information and misinterpretation serves no real purpose. As service providers, if we are to effectively serve all children and their families, we must consider what is in their best interest rather than entrapping ourselves with professional bickering. Remember, the DAP guidelines are a thinking person's document to be used wisely by professionals.

Blending ECE and ECSE Recommended Practices

As we have described, there has been much discussion across and within general ECE and ECSE fields about the similarities and differences in the guide-

Table 7-4   Myths Associated with Developmentally Appropriated Programs (DAP)

- There is one right way to implement a developmentally appropriate program.
- Developmentally appropriate practice requires teachers to abandon all their prior knowledge and experience. Nothing they have learned or done in the past is acceptable in the new philosophy.
- Developmentally appropriate classrooms are unstructured classrooms.
- In developmentally appropriate classrooms, teachers don't teach.
- To be developmentally appropriate elementary teachers and administrators have to "water down" the traditional curriculum. Children will learn less than they have in the past.
- Developmentally appropriate programs can be defined according to dichotomous positions. One position is always right; the other position is always wrong.

SOURCE: *Developmentally appropriate programs in early childhood education* by Kostelnik, © 1993. Adapted by permission of Prentice-Hall, Inc., Upper Saddle River, NJ.

lines of NAEYC and DEC related to philosophical origins, language, and emphases within practices used with young children. Nonetheless, both the fields of ECE and ECSE have provided excellent guidelines that should be utilized when creating educational experiences for young children with disabilities (Bredekamp & Copple, 1997; Bredekamp & Rosegrant, 1992; Sandell, McLean, & Smith, 2000). An effort has been underway for some time now to determine how ECE and ECSE practices can be blended or used in combination, while remaining true to what is recommended in their respective fields.

As stated previously, the growing interest in blending ECE and ECSE recommended practices that has emerged in recent years can be attributed primarily to the inclusion movement. This movement has been spurred by public laws (for example, the IDEA Amendments, and the Americans with Disabilities Education Act) and the belief that services for young children with disabilities should be provided in settings they would attend if they did not have a disability. As we saw in Chapter 6, young children with disabilities increasingly are being included in general early childhood settings throughout the country (Fox et al., 1994). Obviously the inclusion movement has had, and will continue to have, a tremendous impact on curriculum development for young children with disabilities.

We support the notion that greater collaboration is needed between general early childhood education and early childhood special education professionals. Most of the philosophical and pedagogical differences have been resolved (Bredekamp, 1993a). As Burton and her colleagues (1992) emphasized, working partnerships must be established as the demand for services outstrip available resources in both fields. Goodman (1994) also notes that as greater numbers of young children with special needs are being served in inclusive settings, "the theoretical divide between special education and regular education becomes increasingly problematic" (p. 113).

According to this authority, a merging of practices is necessary, which does justice to the diversity of children, instructional objectives, and instructional methods. We are inclined to agree with the analysis of Burton et al. (1992) that differences between ECE and ECSE are merely reflections of different developmental pathways and not an expression of deep philosophical differences.

As described earlier, DAP has been championed as an approach for working with *all* young children, including those with disabilities (Bredekamp, 1993a; Bredekamp & Rosegrant, 1992). We also find that strategies valued by professionals in early childhood special education are compatible with what is viewed as important for teaching typically developing children (Fox et al., 1994).

Current consensus is that the DAP guidelines do not conflict with practices recommended for children with disabilities by the Division for Early Childhood (DEC) of the Council for Exceptional Children (McLean & Odom, 1993; Sandall,

McLean, & Smith, 2000). Similarities have been documented across both DAP and the DEC guidelines in a number of areas (Fox et al., 1994) including:

- the importance placed on individualization,
- the de-emphasis of standardized assessment,
- the integration of curriculum and assessment,
- the importance of child-initiated activities,
- the importance of a child's active engagement with the environment,
- the emphasis on social interaction, and
- the importance of cultural diversity.

In fact, there appear to be no areas of major disagreement in practices advocated by either general early childhood educators or early childhood special educators (McLean & Odom, 1993). The two fields share much common ground. When differences do emerge, it is typically one of intensity or emphasis and not an indication of conflict. Differences are

found in the application and emphasis of certain guidelines within each field (Carta et al., 1993). In particular, these differences include:

- the role of the family, and
- service delivery models.

As emphasized earlier, current consensus is that DAP is a necessary condition for programs serving all young children, including those with disabilities (Fox & Hanline, 1993; Garalnick, 1993); however, DAP may be insufficient for children with disabilities (Carta, 1994; Carta et al., 1993; Fox et al., 1994; Wolery, 1991).

A conceptual model has been developed at the Teaching Research Early Childhood Program at Western Oregon University that views DAP as the foundation on which individualized programs are built. Early childhood special education practices are added as needed for individual children (Udell, Peters, & Templeman, 1998). According to Udell

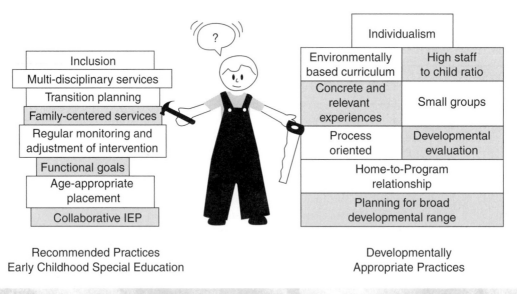

Combining ECSE and DAP

Recommended Practices
Early Childhood Special Education

Developmentally
Appropriate Practices

Figure 7–1   Builder with Two Sets of Materials: ECSE and DAP

SOURCE: T Udell, J. Peters, & T. P. Templeman, 1998. From philosophy to practice in inclusive early childhood programs. *Teaching Exceptional Children, 30*(3), p. 48.

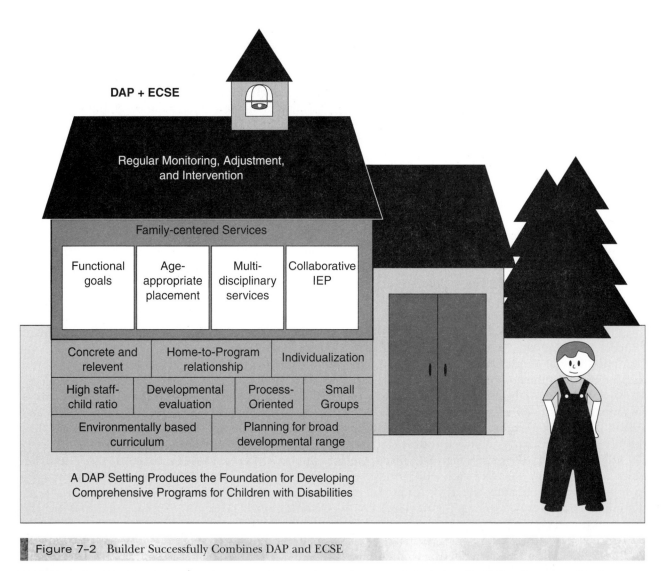

Figure 7-2   Builder Successfully Combines DAP and ECSE

SOURCE: T. Udell, J. Peters, & T. P. Templeman, 1998. From philosophy to practice in inclusive early childhood programs. *Teaching Exceptional Children, 30*(3), p. 49.

et al. (1998), both developmentally appropriate practices and early childhood special education practices can exist within the same setting. They have illustrated the conceptual base for dealing with the issue of combining recommended practice from ECSE and DAP. Figure 7–1 shows a builder who is trying to combine ECSE and DAP practices in constructing a program. Figure 7–2 shows how this issue is reconciled by

using the DAP guidelines as the foundation and ECSE practices as the material to complete the structure. Udell and his colleagues encourage professionals to recognize that the ECE and ECSE practices serve as very different types of resources to be used appropriately with individual children.

In order for DAP to serve as the foundation for programs serving young children with disabilities, a number of steps must be taken. First and foremost, ECE and ECSE professionals must have a clear understanding of what constitutes recommended practice in their respective fields. Furthermore, they must understand the congruencies and differences between ECE and ECSE philosophies and practices. This will allow them to reconcile these differences and move towards a model in which DAP is the framework upon which appropriate programming for any child can be built. Finally, early childhood programs across the country must learn to incorporate ECSE requirements and techniques into developmentally appropriate programs. The end result should be stimulating programs that meet the needs of *all* young children and their families.

In conclusion, we believe that the DAP guidelines are indeed appropriate for young children with disabilities. Yet, we must remember to gauge the appropriateness of suggested practices by how well they meet the needs of the *individual* child (Carta, 1994). Effective practices associated with the field of early childhood special education within the DAP framework neither prohibit nor inhibit their use (Fox et al., 1994). Early childhood special education programs, however, that are *exclusively* constructed around DAP guidelines, are likely to be insufficient for meeting the needs of many young children with disabilities (Wolery et al., 1992). Programming that reflects the best thinking in the fields of early childhood and early childhood special education is likely to result in the improved delivery of services for all young children and their families. Our task as early childhood professionals is "to identify the practices that are relevant for all children and to understand when and under what conditions differences and adaptations of practices are required" (Wolery & Bredekamp, 1994, p. 335).

Summary

In this chapter, we have provided an overview of curriculum in early childhood with an emphasis on determining curricula content to be addressed in programs serving young children with disabilities.

Several theoretical perspectives of curriculum for young children were reviewed, which included the developmental, developmental-cognitive, academic or preacademic, behavioral, and functional curriculum models. There are a number of problems when traditional models such as the developmental model are applied to curriculum development for young children with disabilities. In this chapter, an approach to curriculum development for young children with disabilities was described that recognizes the importance of the child's environment and his or her unique interests (that is, the functional curriculum model).

In this chapter, we have also focused on various aspects of curricula for young children with special needs, including curriculum content, commercially available curriculum packages, curriculum implementation, and curriculum evaluation. Professionals must make decisions regarding curriculum based on the unique abilities, needs, backgrounds, and interests of the children and families they serve.

Curriculum development for young children with disabilities has had various influences—including recommended practices from the fields of both general early childhood education (ECE) and early childhood special education (ECSE). Organizations that support the education of young children offer guidelines on curricula. There has been much discussion of the developmentally appropriate practice (DAP) guidelines (Bredekamp, 1987; Bredekamp & Copple, 1997) published by the National Association for the Education of Young Children (NAEYC) regarding their application to curriculum development for young children with disabilities. The Division for Early Childhood (DEC) published a similar set of guidelines (McLean & Odom, 1993) with recommended practices for young children with disabilities. The similarities and differences in these two approaches were discussed in this chapter, as well as how these approaches can be merged to develop appropriate curriculum for young children with disabilities.

Over the last several years, the dialogue that has emerged between ECE and ECSE has served a number of important functions in that many misconceptions have been clarified and an increased understanding of the unique perspectives of both fields has been the result. For programs serving young children with disabilities, many professionals suggest a curriculum approach that merges practices from ECE and ECSE. The DAP guidelines have laid the groundwork for a widely accepted definition of what represents quality early childhood programs for young children. Many professionals suggest that the DAP guidelines should provide the foundation for all early childhood programs and that strategies and adaptations from ECSE should be applied as needed for young children with disabilities.

Professionals need to be aware of recommended practices and stay current with changing curricula trends. As pointed out by Cook, Tessier, and Klein (2000), early intervention and early childhood special education are evolving fields. Each decade brings new challenges and new ideas for curriculum development. Much research is needed in order to determine the appropriateness and effectiveness of various curricula models and practices in an ever-changing field.

Check Your Understanding

1. Define "curriculum" as it applies to programs serving young children with disabilities.

2. (a) Name the curriculum models that have influenced early childhood special education curricula.
   (b) Discuss the advantages and disadvantages of each perspective when applied to curriculum development for young children with disabilities.

3. Describe important features of commercially available curriculum guides.

4. Describe the factors that must be considered in developing curricula for young children with disabilities.

5. Explain the importance of curriculum evaluation.

6. (a) Describe what is meant by *developmentally appropriate practice.*

   (b) Explain how the components of age appropriateness, individual appropriateness, and cultural appropriateness influence curriculum in early childhood.

7. Describe the conclusions that have been drawn in the fields of general ECE and ECSE regarding the applicability of the DAP guidelines to young children with disabilities.

8. Summarize the goals of ECSE.

9. Discuss the similarities and differences between recommended practices from ECE and ECSE.

10. Describe a model for blending recommended practices from ECSE and ECE.

References

Atwater, J., Carta, J., Schwartz, I., & McConnell, S. (1994). Blending developmentally appropriate practices and early childhood special education: Redefining best practices to meet the needs of all young children. In B. Malloy & S. New (Eds.), *Diversity and developmentally appropriate practice challenges for early childhood education* (pp. 185–201). New York: Teachers College Press.

Bailey, D. B. (1997). Curriculum alternatives for infants and preschoolers. In M. J. Guralnick (Ed.), *The effectiveness of early intervention* (pp. 227–247). Baltimore: Brookes.

Bailey, D. B., Jens, K. G., & Johnson, N. (1983). Curricula for handicapped infants. In S. G. Garwood & R. R. Fewell (Eds.), *Educating handicapped infants* (pp. 387–415). Rockville, MD: Aspen Publishers.

Bailey, D., & Wolery, M. (1992). *Teaching infants and preschoolers with disabilities* (2nd ed.). Columbus, OH: Merrill.

Barnett, D. W., Bell, S. H., & Carey, K. T. (1999). *Designing preschool interventions: A practitioner's guide.* New York: Guilford.

Bredekamp, S. (Ed.). (1987). *Developmentally appropriate practice in early childhood programs serving children from birth to age 8* (Exp. ed.). Washington, DC: National Association for the Education of Young Children.

Bredekamp, S. (1993a). The relationship between early childhood education and early childhood special education: Healthy marriage or family feud? *Topics in Early Childhood Special Education, 13,* 258–273.

Bredekamp, S. (1993b). Myths about developmentally appropriate practice: A response to Fowell and Lawton. *Early Childhood Research Quarterly, 8*(1), 177–120.

Bredekamp, S., & Copple, C. (1997). *Developmentally appropriate practice in early childhood programs* (Rev. ed.). Washington, DC: National Association for the Education of Young Children.

Bredekamp, S., & Rosegrant, T. (1992). *Reaching potentials: Appropriate curriculum and assessment for young children*. Washington, DC: National Association for the Education of Young Children.

Bricker, D. (2002). *Assessment, evaluation, and programming system for children:* Baltimore, MD: Paul H. Brookes.

Bricker, D., & Cripe, J. (1989). Activity-based intervention. In D. Bricker (Ed.), *Early education of at risk and handicapped infants, toddlers and preschoolers* (pp. 251–274). Palo Alto, CA: VORT.

Bricker, D., & Cripe, J. (1992). *An activity-based approach to early intervention.* Baltimore, MD: Paul H. Brookes.

Bricker, D., & Cripe, J. (2003). *An activity-based approach to early intervention* (2nd ed.). Baltimore, MD: Paul H. Brookes.

Bricker, D., Preto-Fromtezsk, K., & McComas, N. (1998). *An activity-based approach to early intervention* (2nd ed.). Baltimore: Paul H. Brookes

Brigance, A. H. (1999). *Brigance Diagnostic Comprehensive Inventory of Basic Skills—Revised.* N. Billerica, MA: Curriculum Associates.

Brophy, J., & Alleman, J. (1991). Activities as instructional tools: A framework for analysis and evaluation, *Educational Researcher, 20*(4), 9–23.

Bruder, M. B. (1997). Curriculum for children with disabilities. In M. Guralnick (Ed.). *The effectiveness of early intervention* (pp. 523–548). Baltimore: Paul H. Brookes.

Burton, C., Higgins-Hains, A., Hanline, M., McLean, M., & McCormick, K. (1992). Early childhood intervention and education: The urgency of professional unification. *Topics in Early Childhood Education, 11*(4), 53–69.

Carta, J. (1994). Developmentally appropriate practices: Shifting the emphasis to individual appropriateness. *Journal of Early Intervention, 18*(4), 342–343.

Carta, J., Schwartz, I., Atwater, J., & McConnell, S. (1991). Developmentally appropriate practice: Appraising its usefulness for young children with disabilities. *Topics in Early Childhood Special Education, 11* (11–20).

Carta, J. J., Atwater, J. B., Schwartz, L. S., & McConnell, S. R. (1993). Developmentally appropriate practices and early childhood special education: A reaction to Johnson and McChesnery Johnson. *Topics in Early Childhood Special Education, 13,* 243–254.

Cook, R. E., Tessier, A., & Klein, M. D. (2000). *Adapting early childhood curricula for children in inclusive settings* (5th ed). Englewood Cliffs, NJ: Merrill.

DEC Task Force on Recommended Practices. (1993). *DEC recommended practices: Indicators of quality in programs for infants and young children with special needs and their families.* Reston, VA: Council for Exceptional Children.

Davis, M., Kilgo, J., & Gamel-McCormick, M. (1998). *Young children with special needs: A developmentally appropriate approach.* Boston, MA: Allyn & Bacon.

Drew, C., Logan, D., & Hardman, M. (1992). *Mental retardation* (5th ed.). New York: Merrill/Macmillan.

Dunst, C. J. (1981). *Infant learning: A cognitive-linguistic intervention strategy.* Hingham, MA: Teaching Resources Corp.

Fowler, S. A., Donegan, M., Lueke, B., Hadden, D. S., & Phillips, B. (2000). Evaluating community collaboration in writing interagency agreements on the age . . . . *Exceptional Children, 67,* 35–50.

Fox, L., & Hanline, M. F. (1993). A preliminary evaluation of learning within developmentally appropriate early childhood settings. *Topics in Early Childhood Special Education, 13*(3), 308–327.

Fox, L., Hanline, M. F., Vail, C., & Galant, K. (1994). Developmentally appropriate practices: Applications for young children with disabilities. *Journal of Early Intervention, 18*(3), 243–257.

Gesell, A., & Amatruda, C. (1947), *Developmental diagnosis* (2nd ed.) New York: Harper & Row.

Goldstein, H., Kaczmarck, L. A., & English, K. M. (2001). *Promoting social communication: Children with developmental disabilities from birth to adolescence.* Baltimore: Paul H. Brookes.

Goodman, J. (1994). "Empowerment" versus "best interests": Client-professional relationships. *Infants and Young Children, 6*(4), vi–x.

Graham, M. A., & Bryant, D. M. (1993). Characteristics of quality, effective service delivery systems for children with special needs. In D. M. Bryant & M. A. Graham (Eds.), *Implementing early intervention: From research to effective practice* (pp. 233–252). New York: Guilford.

Guralnick, M. (2001). *Early childhood inclusion: Focus on change.* Baltimore, MD: Paul H. Brookes.

Guralnick, M. (1990). Major accomplishments and future directions in early childhood mainstreaming. *Topics in Early Childhood Special Education, 10*(2), 1–17.

Guralnick, M. J. (1997). *The effectiveness of early intervention.* Baltimore: Paul H. Brookes.

Guralnick, M. J. (1993). Developmentally appropriate practice in the assessment and intervention of children's peer relations. *Topics in Early Childhood Special Education, 13*(3), 344–371.

Hanson, J., & Lynch, E. (1995). *Early intervention: Implementing child and family services for infants and toddlers who are at-risk or disabled.* (2nd ed.). Austin, TX: Pro-Ed.

Johnson, C. (1993). Developmental issues: Children infected with human immunodeficiency virus. *Infants and Young Children, 6*(1), 1–10.

Johnson, J., & Johnson, K. (1992). Clarifying the developmental perspective in response to Carta, Schwartz, Atwater, and McConnell. *Topics in Early Childhood Special Education, 12*(4), 439–457.

Johnson, K. M., & Johnson, J. E. (1993). Rejoinder to Carta, Atwater, Schwartz, and McConnell. *Topics in Early Childhood Special Education, 13*, 255–257.

Johnson-Martin, N., Attermeier, S., & Hacker, B. (1990). *The Carolina curriculum for preschoolers with special needs* (2nd ed.). Baltimore, MD: Paul H. Brookes.

Johnson-Martin, N., Jens, K., Attermeier, S., & Hacker, B. (1991). *The Carolina curriculum for infants and toddlers with special needs* (2nd ed.). Baltimore, MD: Paul H. Brookes.

Kostelnik, M. J. (1992). Myths associated with developmentally appropriate programs. *Young Children, 47* (4), 17–23.

La Paro, K. M., Pianta, R. C., & Cox, J. J. (2000). Teachers' reported transition practices for children transitioning into kindergarten and first grade. *Exceptional Children, 67,* 7–20.

Linder, T. W. (1993a). *Transdisciplinary play-based assessment: A functional approach to working with young children* (Rev. ed.). Baltimore: Paul H. Brookes.

Linder, T. W. (1993b). *Transdisciplinary play-based intervention: Guidelines for developing a meaningful curriculum for young children.* Baltimore: Paul H. Brookes.

Mallory, B. (1992). Is it always appropriate to be developmental? Convergent models for early intervention practice. *Topics in Early Childhood Special Education, 11*(4), 1–12.

Mallory, B. J., & New, R. S. (1994). *Diversity and developmentally appropriate practices: Challenges for early childhood education.* New York: Teachers College Press.

McCormick, L. (1997). Ecological assessment and planning. In L. McCormick, D. Loeb, & R. Schiefelbusch (Eds.), *Supporting children with communication difficulties* (pp. 223–256). Boston, MA: Allyn & Bacon.

McLean, M., & Odom, S. (1993). Practices of young children with and without disabilities: A comparison of DEC and NAEYC identified practices. *Topics in Early Childhood Special Education, 13*(3), 274–292.

McWilliam, R. A., Wolery, M., & Odom, S. L. (2001). Instructional perspectives in inclusive preschool classrooms. In M. J. Guralnick (Ed.), *Early childhood inclusion: Focus on change.* Baltimore: Brookes.

National Association for the Education of Young Children (NAEYC) & National Association of Early Childhood Specialists in State Departments of Education (NAECS/SDE) (1991). Guidelines for appropriate curriculum content and assessment in programs serving children ages 3 through 8. *Young Children, 46*(3), 21–38.

Neisworth, J., & Bagnato, S. (1996). Assessment for early intervention: Emerging themes and practices. In S. Odom & M. McLean (Eds), *Early intervention/early childhood special education: Recommended practices* (pp. 23–58). Austin, TX: Pro-Ed.

Neisworth, J. & Bagnato, S. (2000). Recommended practices in assessment. In S. Sandall, M. McLean, & B. Smith (Eds.), *DEC Recommended practices for early intervention/early childhood special education,* (pp. 17–27). Longmont, CO: Sopris West.

Nirje, B. (1976). The normalization principle. In R. Kugel & A. Shearer (Eds.), *Changing patterns in residential services for the mentally retarded.* Washington, DC: President's Committee on Mental Retardation.

Noonan, M., & McCormick, L. (1993). *Early intervention in natural environments: Methods and procedures.* Belmont, CA: Wadsworth, Inc.

Notari, J., Cripe, J., Slentz, K., & Ryan-Seth, B. (1992). Cognitive domain. In J. Cripe, K. Slentz, & D. Bricker (Eds.), *Assessment, evaluation, and programming system (AEPS) for infants and children,* Vol. 2., Baltimore, MD: Paul H. Brookes.

Parks, S., Furuno, S., O'Reilly, K., Hosaka, C., Inatsuka, T., & Zeisloft-Talby, B. (1998). *Hawaii early learning profile at home.* Palo Alto, CA. Vort.

Piaget, J. (1952). *The origins of intelligence in children.* New York: Norton.

Rainforth, B., York, J., & McDonald, C. (1992). *Collaborative teams for students with severe disabilities.* Baltimore: Paul H. Brookes.

Richarz, S. (1993). Innovations in early childhood education: Models that support the integration of children of varied developmental levels. In C. Peck, S. Odom, & D. Bricker (Eds.), *Integrating young children with disabilities into community programs: Ecological perspectives on research and implementation* (pp. 83–108). Baltimore: Paul H. Brookes.

Safford, P., Sargent, M., & Cook, C. (Eds.). (1994). Instructional models in early childhood special education: Origins, issues, & trends. In P. Safford (Ed.), *Early childhood special education* (pp. 96–117). New York: Teachers College Press.

Sainato, D. M., & Strain, P. S. (1993). Increasing integration success for preschoolers with disabilities. *Teaching Exceptional Children, 25*(2), 36.

Sameroff, A. J. & Chandler, M. J. (1975). Reproductive risk and the continuum of care-taking casualty. In F. D. Horowitz, M. Hetherington, S. Scarr-Salapatek, & G. Siegel (Eds.). *Review of child development research* (Vol. 4) (pp. 187–244). Chicago: University of Chicago Press.

Sandall, S., & Ostrosky, M. (2000). *Natural environments and inclusion: Young exceptional children.* Monograph series No. 2. Reston, VA: Council for Exceptional Children. Division for Early Childhood.

Sandall, S., & Schwartz, L. (2002). *Building blocks for teaching preschoolers with special needs.* Baltimore: Paul H. Brookes.

Sandall, S., Joseph, G., Chou, H. Y., Schwartz, J. S., Horn, E., Limber, J., Odom, S. L., & Wolery, R. (2000). *Talking to practitioners: Focus group report on curriculum modifications in inclusive preschool classrooms.* Unpublished manuscript.

Sandall, S., McLean, M. E., & Smith, B. J. (Eds.) (2000). *DEC recommended practices in early intervention/early childhood special education.* Reston, VA: Council for Exceptional Children. Division for Early Childhood.

Sandall, S., Schwartz, L., & Joseph, C. (2000). A building blocks model for effective instruction in inclusive early childhood settings. *Young Exceptional Children, 4*(3). 3–9.

Shonkoff, J. P., & Meisels, S. J. (2000). *Handbook of early childhood intervention* (2nd ed.). Cambridge, UK: Cambridge University Press.

Southern Association on Children Under Six (1990). *Developmentally appropriate assessment: A position paper.* Little Rock, AR: Author.

Spodek, B., & Brown, P. C. (1993). Curriculum alternatives in early childhood education: A historical perspective. In B. Spodek (Ed.), *Curriculum alternatives in early childhood education: A historical perspective* (pp. 91–104). New York: Macmillan.

Strain, P., McConnell, S., Carta, J., Fowler, S., Neisworth, J., & Wolery, M. (1992), Behaviorism in early intervention. *Topics in Early Childhood Special Education, 12*(1):121–41.

Turnbull, A. P., & Turnbull, H. R. (2001). *Families, professionals, and exceptionality: Collaborating for empowerment* (4th ed.). Upper Saddle River, NJ: Merrill/Prentice Hall.

Udell, T., Peters, J., & Templeman, T. (1998). From philosophy to practice in inclusive early childhood programs. *Teaching Exceptional Children,* Jan./Feb., 44–49.

Widerstrom, A. H., Mowder, B. A., & Sandall, S. A. (1997). *Infant development and risk* (2nd ed.). Baltimore: Brookes.

Wolery, M. (1991). "Instruction in early childhood special education: Seeing through a glass darkly . . . knowing in part." *Exceptional Children, 58*(2), 127–135.

Wolery, M., & Bredekamp, S. (1994). Developmentally appropriate practices and young children with disabilities: Contextual issues in the discussion. *Journal of Early Intervention, 18*(4), 331–341.

Wolery, M., & Sainato, D. (1996). General curriculum and intervention strategies. In S. Odom & M. McLean (Eds.), *Early intervention/early childhood special education: Recommended practices* (pp. 125–158). Austin, TX: PRO-ED.

Wolery, M., & Wilbers, J. S. (1994). *Including young children with special needs in early childhood programs.* Washington, DC: National Association for the Education of Young Children.

Wolery, M., Anthony, L, & Heckathorn, J. (1998). Transition-based teaching: Effects on transitions, teachers' behavior and children's learning. *Journal of Early Transition, 21* 117–131.

Wolery, M., Ault, M. J., & Doyle, P. M. (1992). *Teaching students with moderate to severe disabilities.* New York: Longman.

Wolery, M., Strain, P., & Bailey, D. (1992). Reaching potential of children with special needs. In S. Bredekamp & T. Rosegrant (Eds.), *Reaching potentials: Appropriate curriculum and assessment for young children* (Vol. 1) (pp. 92–111). Washington, DC: National Association for the Education of Young Children.

Zirpoli, T. J. & Melly, K. J. (2001). *Behavior management: Applications for teachers* (3rd ed,). Upper Saddle River, NJ: Merrill.

Designing Learning Environments for Young Children with Special Needs

CHAPTER

8

Contributed by Tom Buggey, Ph.D. University of Memphis

Learning Outcomes

After reading this chapter you will be able to:

- Describe the key characteristics of a well-designed indoor learning environment.
- Outline the types of learning centers typically found in preschool classrooms.
- List the requirements of an accessible learning environment.
- Describe a safe and healthy learning environment.

One of the most important responsibilities of an early childhood special educator is to construct an environment that facilitates the delivery of an effective instructional program. This role of classroom designer and architect has been referred to as "environmental engineering" (Neisworth & Buggey, 2000). It is important for teachers to be aware of the impact that the environment has on influencing the behavior of children. Educators must also be cognizant of how to manipulate the learning environment to enhance learning. Over the past twenty-five years, proponents of diverse theoretical models of learning such as behaviorism, constructivism, and social learning have increasingly stressed the importance of environmental elements in their learning and instructional paradigms. Maria Montessori, for example, through her concepts of auto-education and the "prepared classroom," emphasized environmental considerations in the educational process. The focus of her work was based on the premise that, during early development, an enriched learning environment could offset the effects of impoverished living conditions. The schools of Reggio Emilia in Italy, which are gaining in popularity across the world, have the "beautiful environment" as one of the three major components of their program. In these programs, the environment is seen as the "third teacher" (Gandini, 1993).

In this chapter our focus will be on environmental arrangements for school and center-based programs primarily designed for preschoolers. Yet, many of the same principles and practices that are applied in these settings can be adapted to fit programs for toddlers and for home-based programs. The key is to provide environments that promote both nurturance and learning. We will investigate how to effectively arrange space, consider environmental factors that maximize learning, and discuss how to provide safe and accessible learning environments.

Considerations in Designing the Learning Environment

Human learning is primarily based on experiences gained in interacting with the environment. The environment is constantly providing messages to the learner. If one finds an experience pleasant, he or she will seek to return to the conditions that provided that sensation. If persons experience pain, discomfort, or failure they tend to avoid all the environmental stimuli associated with the experience. In a sense, we become what we experience. If we can construct a classroom environment that communicates the messages "This is a safe place," "This is a fun, happy place," and most importantly, "You can learn here and have a good time," then we will have set the stage for maximizing instructional efficiency.

The positive effects of a secure, pleasant working/learning environment are many. Researchers (Carta, Sainato, & Greenwood, 1988; Odom & Bailey, 2001; Warren & Kaiser, 1988) have found that manipulation of environmental conditions can promote learning in young children, facilitate instruction and planning, improve working conditions as well as self-esteem, and help minimize undesirable behaviors. Knowledge of how the environment impacts learners can be used to create learning environments that can maximize, and even magnify, a teacher's instructional effectiveness.

The design of a preschool classroom should be based on a fundamental knowledge of learning theory, advice from expert practitioners, best practice guidelines from professional associations, and research evidence. Effective environmental arrangements are also related to issues of:

- Available space
- Age of the students
- Population density
- Responsiveness
- Visual appeal
- Accessibility
- Safety and health
- Organization/scheduling
- Budget
- Student-teacher ratios

Knowledge of these factors leading to informed application will help determine the look and feel of the learning environment.

Classroom Dimensions

The ratio of classroom size (area) and the child population is an important factor in the preschool design. Early research findings suggest that within some classrooms, aggressive behaviors among children increase as the classroom population increases (Hutt & Viazey, 1966). Conversely, Brown, Fox, and Brady (1987) along with Trawick-Smith (1992) found that positive social interactions are more likely to occur when learning areas are small and proximity is maximized. On the surface, the findings of these investigations may seem contradictory. However, there are other variables that effect quality of socialization other than square footage per child. For example, it has been shown that the amount of play materials available influences children's interactions. Researchers note that fewer toys often leads to heightened disruption and conflict among children (Odom & Bailey, 2001) while a sufficient quantity of

play items can reduce conflict between youngsters (McWilliam, Wolery, & Odom, 2001). It is possible that there is an optimal space/population/material ratio for specific classrooms that is dependent on the interactions of many variables, including the quality of environmental arrangement, type of activity, and student characteristics. It is important that the early childhood special educator understand the group dynamics involved in environmental interactions (both social and physical) in various forms of activities and in the different areas of the classroom.

The National Association for the Education of Young Children (NAEYC) (1991) recommends that preschools should maintain 35 square feet of space per child for indoor settings and 75 square feet for outdoor spaces. Many states have adopted these figures for inclusion in their licensing regulations and specifications for early childhood programs. Dimension requirements for infant and toddler programs tend to be slightly smaller due to the more limited mobility of the children. As stated above, the square footage provided per child may not be as significant a factor as the way in which the available space is arranged.

Providing Spaces

Many teachers divide their classroom space into activity or interest areas. There can be a permanent site in the classroom for such centers as reading (literacy), arts and crafts, gross motor, and fine motor, while centers can also be temporary or rotating such as in a "discovery" or science area. Centers or areas tend to give a sense of order to the room and can serve as the focal points of daily scheduling and programming. Center content also may vary depending on the age and abilities of the children.

Areas for Infants and Toddlers   Developmentally appropriate practice tends to support the trend to have infant centers focused on sensory and motor stimulation. Cataldo (1983) suggests the following centers for infants: a rattle area, a reaching and manipulation center, a sensory stimulation area, a water table, an exercise mat, an interaction-game area, and a puppet theater and dollhouse structure. Areas should also be provided for changing, sleeping, feeding, and quiet and active play. Infants with developmental delays may have much of their program prescribed by specialists in physical and occupational therapy. Inclusive infant/toddler care environments, however, will often structure their programs around activities of daily living such as dressing, eating, or going to the bathroom. These tasks are just as important for youngsters with delays and disabilities as they are for typically developing children (O'Brien, 2001).

Due to the increased mobility and developing cognitive skills of toddlers, centers can become increasingly complex and varied. Cataldo (1983) recommends that toddler centers be built around the themes of music, creative play, construction and blocks, personal identity, problem solving, sand/water play, and fine and gross motor activities. Spaces for role-playing, outdoor play, and privacy should also be provided. Figure 8–1 provides one example of an infant/toddler classroom arrangement.

Preschool Areas A question that often arises when planning the space for preschoolers is whether to construct open- or closed-plan facilities. Open-plans tend to have undivided internal spaces within a large room while closed-plan facilities usually entail several self-contained rooms connected by corridors or hallways. Moore (1987) investigated the effects these types of environments have on children and found possible flaws with both designs. Moore found that open-plans contributed to random behaviors resulting in less time on task and that the closed-plans tended to promote withdrawal behaviors and more time spent in transitioning between activities. As with many opposing views in education, a compromise between the two extremes may best serve children's needs. Moore suggested a modified open-plan as the best solution. This type of environment would make use of both large and small activity sites that provided youngsters with some protection from distraction, while allowing them to be able to view other areas in the room and the activities available to them.

Olds (1987) suggests the use of "fluid boundaries" for separating areas of the preschool. Fluid boundaries consist of environmental clues that a change of area has occurred while placing no physi-

cal barriers to impair mobility. For example, an activity site may be differentiated from other areas by lowering the ceiling with a parachute canopy rather than surrounding the area with bookcases or storage units. Painted lines on the floor (or colored tape if the floor is carpeted) can form effective boundaries as can differentiating carpet colors. The use of stimulus-control to arrange areas is closely related to this concept and will be discussed later.

It is safe to say that at least several activity centers should be present in all preschool classrooms. The terms "learning center/area" and "activity center/area" are sometimes used interchangeably. It is often necessary for the reader to use the context in which the terms are used to discriminate whether one is referring to a section of a classroom set aside for a general use (e.g., block area, gross-motor center, language area) or an arrangement within the room for a specific activity ("cut and paste a valentine" area, "life cycle of a frog" center, or "letter match" area). Suffice it to say that there may be specific activities within areas (or centers within areas). Bailey and Wolery (1992) define **activity areas** as "space within the room designed to accommodate different types of activities for children and adults" (p. 212.). Typically these areas are designed to accommodate small groups and an adult supervisor, although some areas such as a circle area for introductory or circle-time/sharing activities may be designed to accommodate the entire class. The preschool should include centers that are age-, ability-, and interest-appropriate, while linked to individual outcomes and goals as outlined on the youngster's individualized family service plan (IFSP) or individualized education program (IEP).

The classroom environment exerts a powerful influence on children. Room arrangement and materials play a vital role in a youngster's educational experience (Gordon & Browne, 2004). Learning activities must be organized so as to encourage the meaningful participation of pupils who exhibit a wide range of skills and abilities. Selection of materials and the arrangement of learning centers should reflect age-appropriateness and individual-appropriateness (Bredekemp & Copple, 1997). Table 8–1 offers a list of representative classroom materials and equipment

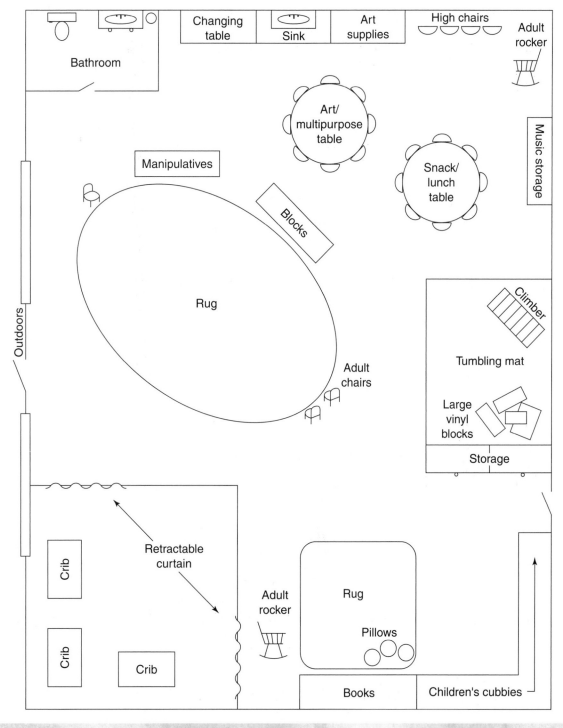

Figure 8-1   Infant/Toddler Classroom Design

SOURCE: M. Henniger, *Teaching Young Children.* (Upper Saddle River, NJ: Prentice Hall, 1999), p. 228.

Preschool classrooms typically have areas devoted to specific activities.

that can be used to furnish developmentally appropriate centers for children of different ages.

Olds (1979) also recommends that preschools contain at least the following six general types of activity areas. These suggested activity areas can be found in many of today's classrooms.

1. Gross-motor area
2. Quiet, calm area
3. Discovery area
4. Dramatic play area
5. Therapeutic area
6. Arts and crafts area

The National Association for the Education of Young Children (1991) recommends that space be divided to facilitate a range of small group and individual activities including block building, sociodramatic play, art, music, science, math, manipulative, and quiet reading. Feeney and her colleagues

(Feeney, Christensen, & Moravcik, 2001) recommend the addition of computer, writing, and sensory training areas. Within these general areas, an almost endless number of specific centers can be arranged. The quiet, calm area may include the literacy (reading) language center, a private space, a listening center, and a nap area. During the day, an area's use may change, taking on dual or triple roles. For example, the quiet, calm area may first be used for language activities, then as a listening center with a tape recorder with multiple headphones, and then as the nap area. The discovery area could have rotating centers based on the theme of the week or special projects. This is a good site for hands-on science activities and as a home for classroom pets.

The dramatic play area should have activities that promote creative expression and real-life simulations. Materials should be provided to stimulate role playing such as dress-up clothes, mirrors, play kitchen, and store. Also, human figures or dolls representing

Table 8-1   Guide to Equipping Developmentally Appropriate Centers

	Infants 6 weeks to 1 year	Toddler 1 year to 2½ years	Preschool 2½ years to 5 years	School Age 5 years to 9 years

Classroom Furnishings	Couch/futon
	Changing counter
	Adult rocker
	Cribs/cradles
	Infant bounce chair
	Cubbies/bins
	High chair/chair with
	  tray
	Child access shelves
	Nest/wading pool
		In addition:
		Book display
		Chairs/seating
		  cubes
		Lunch tables
		Child rockers
		Block cart
		Small water table
		Cots/mats
		Pillows
			In addition:
			Activity counters
			Small play tables
			Work bench
			Room dividers
			Small rugs
			Sand/water table
				In addition:
				Easy chairs
				Bunk beds
				Tents
				Hammock

Large Motor	Mats/pillows Beach balls Push/pull toys Small wagon Foam rolls Tunnel 4–6 Passenger carts Strollers Sling/backpack	*In addition:* Stairs/slide Rocking boat Barrel Wheelbarrows No-pedal trikes Variety of balls Simple climber	*In addition:* Balance beam Pedal wheel toys Large wagons Shovels/rakes Hula hoops Planks/triangles	*In addition:* Sports balls Roller/ice skates Basketball hoop Jump ropes Skateboards Scooters
Dramatic Play	Baby dolls Stuffed animals Rubber animals Rubber people Puppets Hats Plexiglass mirrors	*In addition:* Large doll furniture Dress-up clothes and hats Child-size furniture Plastic cooking sets Blankets Tents Boxes Cars/trucks Pots/pans	*In addition:* Doll houses Plastic food Clothespins Play money Cash register Kitchen utensils Prop boxes Purses/luggage Play telephone	*In addition:* Small dolls Castle sets Mobile Balance scale Microphone Stage Fabric Planks/boxes

Blocks/ Construction	Fiberboard blocks
	Foam blocks
	Bucket and blocks
		In addition:
		More blocks
		Large trucks
		Large train
		Snap blocks
		Waffle blocks
			In addition:
			Unit blocks
			Hollow/perma
			  blocks
			Planks
			Derrick/pulleys
			Wheelbarrow
			Wood working
			  tools/hat/belts
			Dominoes/lots of
			  blocks
				In addition:
				More hollow blocks
				More planks
				Plastic crates
				More tools
				Tri-wall cardboard
				Traffic signs/train set
				Plastic/wood wheels,
				  nuts, bolts

(continued)

Table 8–1   Guide to Equipping Developmentally Appropriate Centers *(continued)*

	Infants *6 weeks to 1 year*	Toddler *1 year to 2½ years*	Preschool *2½ years to 5 years*	School Age *5 years to 9 years*
Creative/ Art	Finger paint Simple prints Wall hangings Sculpture Mobiles Messy mats	*In addition:* Block crayons Large brushes Chalk/markers Chalkboard Playdough Ink stamps Paste	*In addition:* Easel Small brushes Water colors Modeling clay and wax Collage material Glue Scissors	*In addition* Tri-wall cardboard Styrofoam pieces Clay Sewing machine Badge maker Camera Camcorder

**Sensory/Sand/
Water/Science**
	Dish/garden tubs
	Tub toys
	Sponges
	Plants
	Aquariums/
	  birdfeeders
	Animals
	Windchimes
		In addition:
		Buckets/jars
		Funnels/sifters
		Measuring
		  cups/pitchers
		Magnifiers
		Large magnets
		Flashlights
			In addition:
			Electric frying pan
			Incubator
			Ant farm
			Balance scales
			Thermometer
			Magnets/prisms
				In addition:
				Microscopes
				Rock tumblers
				Tape measures
				Oven
				Motors

**Books/
Language/
Music**
	Cloth books
	Hard board books
	Posters
	Photos
	Records/tapes
	Music boxes
	Musical mobiles
		In addition:
		Picture books
		Read-to books
		Play telephones
		Simple instruments
		Listening center
			In addition:
			More books
			Magnetic
			  letters/lotto
			Typewriter
			Telephones
			Thick pencils
			Musical keyboard
			Instrument set
			Scarves/ribbons
				In addition:
				Computer and
				  software
				Easy-read books
				Chapter books
				Time/Life-type books
				Maps
				Dictionary/encyclopedias
				Historical books
				Notebooks

**Perceptual
Motor/Games/
Manipulatives/
Math**
	Mobiles
	Cradle gyms
	Busy boxes
	Rattles
	Prisms
		In addition:
		Pop beads
		Stack/nesting toys
		Large pegboards
		Lock boards
		Pounding bench
		Poker chips
		Sorting boxes
			In addition:
			Small pegboards
			Puzzles
			Thread boards
			Table blocks/parquet
			  blocks
			Tyco/Lego/Lazy
			  blocks
			Abacus
			Lacing boards
			Nuts and bolts
				In addition:
				Board games
				Skill games
				Cards/checkers
				Dominoes
				Looms
				Cuisenaire rods
				Calculators
				Models

SOURCE: J. Greenman, 1990, Guide to Equipping the Developmentally Appropriate Center, *Child Care Information Exchange,* 76, p. 33.

various ages, ethnic backgrounds, and occupations should be provided. Although this may be considered an area devoted to creative play, there is much a teacher can do in this area to promote learning of new language behaviors and social behaviors such as tolerance for differences, sharing, and working through disputes.

The range of activities provided in the arts and crafts area should be limited only by the media available through the school's budget; and then, the creative teacher can often work around this limitation. If possible, this area should be located in proximity to the bathroom or a sink to ease cleanup and the flooring should be slip-proof tile or linoleum. Child-size easels are recommended and space should be provided for the display of the children's work. Besides traditional coloring and painting, other activities might include woodworking projects, clay or play-dough pottery, collage making, basketry, sewing (for example, class patchwork quilts), and printmaking. In classes with students with motor and physical disabilities, it is particularly important to have a variety of media available so that all children can be working at a project appropriate for their skills and specific abilities.

Recent research has upheld Olds' (1979) earlier contention that therapeutic space be provided within the classroom setting. However, the idea of having a separate area within the classroom for therapies may not be as progressive as embedding therapies throughout the environment. There is a rapidly increasing body of empirical evidence that suggests that for therapies (interventions) to be effective they should be delivered during naturally occurring, ongoing, routine events (Harbin, McWilliam, & Gallagher, 2000; McWilliam et al., 2001; Rule, Losardo, Dinnebeil, Kaiser, & Rowland, 1998). This thinking is also in keeping with the contemporary preference for service delivery in inclusive settings. The inclusion of speech-language therapy, for example, in the natural environment can usually be accomplished with minimal adaptations. Although environmental arrangements are important for certain language interventions, major adaptations to the environment are rarely needed. The introduction of physical and occupational therapies within a class-

room setting, on the other hand, may require the addition of adaptive equipment that necessitates additional space for use and storage. Teachers and related service providers using naturalistic approaches generally want to limit the amount of adaptations necessary to accommodate the needs of the children. There are two reasons for this. One is a social consideration of limiting the amount of undue attention given to the youngster with a disability. The second reason is functional—children with disabilities must learn to navigate and communicate as much as possible within the constraints of a normalized environment (Noonan & McCormick, 1993).

Another area that should be included in all preschools is a greeting area. A bright and cheerful welcome arrangement will be the first area experienced by children and parents as they enter the classroom. Along with the pleasing aesthetics, this area should be quite functional. This is a good site to display children's work and to post information and announcements for parents. Rubber mats and indoor/outdoor carpet can prevent the spread of mud and water to other areas. This would also be an appropriate site for color coded and name-personalized cubbies or lockers provided for coats, boots, and personal belongings.

A popular site in many preschools is the sand and water area. This is an area that can be used to meet many social and learning objectives. It is a sensory stimulation area and can be used to help children learn about shapes, textures, weight, quantity, and other basic physical science concepts. As in the other areas that involve role-playing activities, sand and water play can promote cooperative play and problem solving while facilitating language development.

Floor surfaces in this area should be noncarpeted or contain indoor/outdoor carpeting. Nonslip linoleum may be the best choice. A location close to the bathroom will aid in cleanup. Raised tables with lockable wheels, central drains, and removable lids are preferable features. These items make the tables mobile and ease cleanup. Basins, wash tubs, and plastic wading pools are appropriate substitutes.

Materials used in the tables need not be limited to sand and water. Rice, beans, sawdust, pasta of various shapes, and even Jell-O can serve to add textural experiences to the center. The use of any material should be based on individual safety factors and the area should be closely supervised to limit mouthing of materials and to prevent accidents.

Early childhood educators often suggest that time and space be provided for individual private areas (Bailey & Wolery, 1992; Brewer, 2001) both in terms of social time (or lack thereof) and privacy for storage and care of belongings. Children's sense of independence and need for privacy can be managed by providing them with individual "cubbies" for storage of personal items and attractive and comfortable areas designed specifically for individuals to have private time as an option. It is important that these areas be viewed by the children as positive or neutral areas.

Some preschools may have a "time-out" area where a disruptive youngster is placed for brief periods of social isolation (generally one minute for each year of chronological age—thus, two minutes of time out for a two year old). The sites for time out and personal quiet areas should be clearly delineated so that no negative connotations are associated with the privacy areas. Picture books, listening material, and items of personal value should be available in the privacy areas. The arrangement of the time out area should not present the child with overly distracting stimuli; but, could benefit from decorations illustrating children exhibiting appropriate behaviors and receiving positive feedback for their actions.

When designing classroom space, it is important to consider factors related to the needs of the adults. As children should be provided space for private time, so should adults. An adult area can be used for parent meetings and for storage of child files and records. Amenities such as a refrigerator, microwave, and sofa will make the environment more teacher-friendly and serve to enhance the total teaching experience. Figure 8–2 is a representative floor plan for a preschool consistent with NAEYC's space guidelines. Over time, teachers change the environment based on their own experiences and the needs of the children presently in the class. Once again, the teacher acting as an "environmental engineer" must weigh the benefits of providing a consistent environment against the need for new opportunities for exploration.

Outdoor Spaces   Every preschool should have some form of outdoor play space. Outdoor play is an integral part of any child's natural environment and provides children the opportunity to receive the health benefits associated with sunshine and fresh air as well as providing breaks for both children and adults from the indoor routines. Properly designed outdoor settings not only benefit the youngster's physical development but support the child's cognitive and social-emotional development as well. Outdoor play is also an essential component of developmentally appropriate practices for young children (Bredekamp & Copple, 1997). A large, accessible, grassy area with interactive and exploratory equipment, plus traditional swings and slides is generally recommended. For toddlers and other youngsters who are developmentally unable to safely participate, adaptive equipment appropriate to the abilities of the child should be available. Playhouses can provide space for socialization and role-playing activities. Space for outdoor eating should also be available and the entire area should be fenced in for safety purposes. Paved surfaces connecting equipment and play areas will allow for wheelchair accessibility. Areas under the play equipment should be lined with bark, pea gravel, sawdust, or sand to cushion any falls. The material should be deep enough to prevent serious injury. For example, it is recommended that pea gravel be at least eight inches deep to be effective (Morris, 1990). The safety issue should be the number one factor when considering outdoor play design. The U.S. Consumer Product Safety Commission (1997) offers a useful handbook on playground safety.

The number of accidents requiring medical attention that occur on playgrounds is alarming. Emergency rooms report between 100,000 and 150,000 cases of children who are hurt on playgrounds each year (Taylor & Morris, 1996). The majority of the these accidents occur with swings, slides, and climbing equipment. A contributing factor to these numbers may be that children are involved with activities or equipment that are beyond their developmental levels. If the outdoor space involves a mix of toddlers and preschoolers or preschoolers and elementary age students, then the

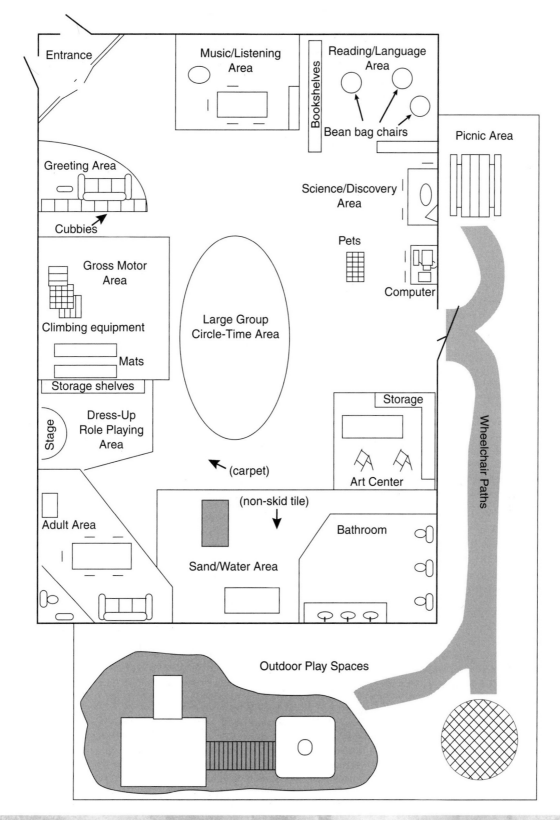

Figure 8-2 Sample Preschool Design

Outdoor play is an important component of developmentally appropriate practices.

design should incorporate activities and equipment developmentally appropriate for each group. In situations with varying levels of students, scheduling of separate outdoor play time for each group based on developmental level is advised. We tend to equate playgrounds with "equipment;" however, we should not undervalue the use of open, natural outdoor spaces. A natural space with several height levels and simple material to develop balance and other gross motor skills might be just as effective as more complex designs especially in terms of safety and cost. According to White and Coleman (2000), developmentally appropriate outdoor environments provide children with a variety of natural and commercially produced landscape elements.

All children, including those with delays and disabilities, profit from playing outdoors. Play, which is the work of the child, can be the vehicle through which children, regardless of individual differences, grow, develop, and learn; it provides a natural opportunity for integrative experiences (Jambor & Gargiulo, 1987). In some circumstances, the outdoor environment needs to be modified to accommodate the child with special needs with accessibility and safety—two of the primary concerns. Pathways, for example, need to be wider for use by children in wheelchairs, handrails may need to be installed, wider gates might be necessary, and playground surfaces designed so as to be accessible by children with motor impairments. (See Figure 8–3 for an example of an inclusive outdoor playground.)

Promoting Engagement

The efficacy of every lesson introduced by the teacher and the degree of learning demonstrated by the child is dependent upon the engagement of the child in the environmental interaction. The motivation needed by a child to engage in a task or activity can be facilitated by providing enticing, attractive environmental arrangements.

Bailey and Wolery (1992) offer five suggestions for improving the initial attractiveness of activities and materials to facilitate engagement.

- *Provide appealing materials.* Colorful materials are better than drab. Three-dimensional objects are more appealing than two-dimensional. Toys that provide immediate feedback (sounds, visual displays, movement) are also motivating.

- *Make participation a privilege rather than a duty.* Have some high-interest activities be a reward for helping or exhibiting appropriate behaviors.

- *Give children immediate roles in activities.* Children could use puppets, stuffed animals, or their imaginations to take on roles of characters during story time. Clearly define student's roles—each child, for example, should have a specific responsibility matched to their ability level when involved in a group art activity.

- *Use instructions to initiate or prompt interactions.* Children who sit idly in an activity may need a model or prompt to begin.

- *Identify children's preference for materials.* The most motivating materials are those the child plays with most, and these materials vary among children.

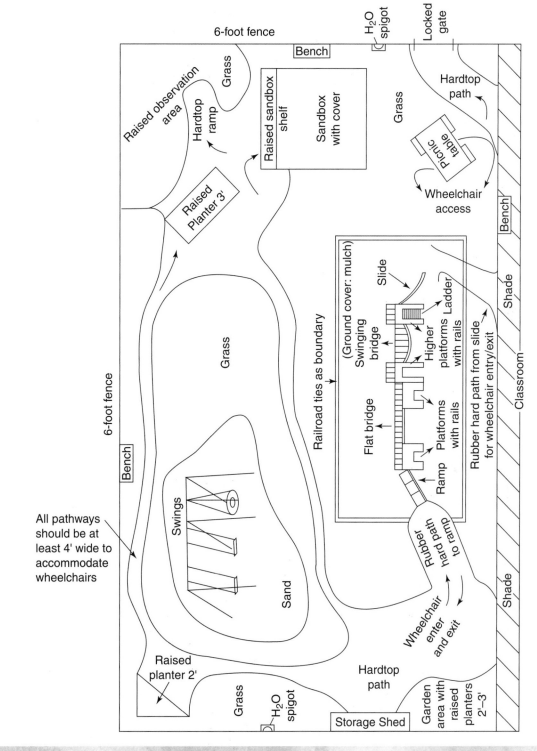

Figure 8–3 Example of an Inclusive Outdoor Playground

SOURCE: M. Henniger, *Teaching Young Children* (Upper Saddle River, NJ: Prentice Hall, 1999). p. 319

The Learning Environment and Stimulus-Control

It is important that skills and behaviors being taught to a child generalize to other situations beyond the environment in which they were learned. Careful manipulation of environmental settings can be a powerful tool in ensuring that generalization occurs and can cue desired behaviors within areas of the classroom. An important behavioral principle related to environmental arrangement is stimulus-control. **Stimulus-control** refers to the fact that behaviors are more apt to occur in the presence of stimuli present while the behavior is being reinforced. Thus, physical prompts in the learning environment can be used to cue desired behaviors. For example, many homes are designed so that rooms fill a specific purpose. The den or study is decorated and furnished to promote quiet, studious pursuits. A fireplace, bookshelves, and comfortable seating all serve to stimulate behaviors related to quiet study. If one places other stimuli in the room such as a TV or pool table, the mood is changed and other types of behaviors are promoted. Each room can exert power over the observer based on the experiences that person associates with this particular environmental arrangement. Why do we alter our voices to whispers when entering a church or library? The contingencies of those environments obviously shape our speaking behavior.

In a similar manner, teachers often manipulate stimulus-control in designing learning areas (Bailey & Wolery, 1992; McEvoy, Fox, & Rosenberg, 1991; Wolery, 2000). The reading area, for example, might be decorated with letters, posters of children reading, and attractive book covers, which serve as prompts for looking at picture books and other reading materials. In this manner, stimulus-control also can be used to promote and hold engagement. Classroom management can be facilitated by color coding the areas. Brightly colored free play and gross-motor areas can cue the children that louder noise levels are permissible. Softer, pastel hues in the reading and math areas can serve to prompt quiet behavior. In order to limit distractions and interference, quiet areas should not be in proximity to noisier areas. Movement within the classroom can be cued by using functional objects. A simulated stop sign or red light can cue children that an area is off-limits for the time being. A green light can signal areas children may visit. By allowing the environment to provide cues about classroom routine and rules, the teacher can save him- or herself time and energy. Children will tend to monitor peer behavior and there will be less temptation for students to test limits when a visual prompt is present.

Stimulus control is also relevant to generalization or transfer of learned behaviors across settings and individuals. Behaviors taught in isolation (or in settings not reflecting the milieu one would expect for the behavior) do not automatically transfer to new situations. For example, language skills taught in traditional "pull out" language therapy sessions have been found to be mastered within the clinic, but the same behaviors may not occur outside of the therapy setting. Research in language intervention (Kaiser, Yoder, & Keetz, 1992; Warren & Bambara, 1989; Warren & Gazdag, 1990; Wolery, Ault, & Doyle, 1992) suggests that the transfer of verbal skills is facilitated when the behavior is taught in the milieu where you expect the skills to naturally occur, such as at home, during snack time, or at free-play. Vocational schools also provide a good example. They often make use of stimulus-control to prepare their students for the world of work. As an illustration, food preparation courses are taught in situations resembling those expected in the work environment (a kitchen) and auto body repair courses are taught in garage-type settings. It is extremely doubtful whether a traditional lecture approach could produce graduates who could easily transition to a restaurant or automotive repair shop.

In the preschool, kitchen areas provide an excellent opportunity for applying stimulus-control techniques. Generalization of learned skills in etiquette, nutrition, and cooking will more likely occur when taught in an environment that includes or resembles the circumstances present in the other environments in which the behaviors will be used. A general practice that can be applied across the curriculum for young children with disabilities is to analyze objectives in terms of where, when, and with whom the desired skills could or should occur. If instruction cannot take place in the exact site in which you wish the behaviors to occur, instruction should then take place in simulated environments that closely approximate these outcome settings.

Similarly, stimulus-control can be used in preparing children for transition from a preschool setting to a kindergarten (Buggey, DeHaas-Warner, & Bagnato, 1991; McEvoy et al., 1991). The preschool setting can be altered to approximate the kindergarten environment as transition time draws near. Social and academic skills acquired in this transition area tend to more easily generalize to the kindergarten setting.

Reinforcement and Responsivity

Elements of the preschool environment can also serve as a reinforcer for children's behavior. Learning areas can be manipulated so that children receive immediate feedback and reinforcement. For example, a child working in the math learning center who successfully completes a task may be rewarded with time to work on the class computer or another reinforcer that has high value to the child. Learning centers can easily be designed so that they permit flexible sequencing of child activities. The Premack principle (Premack, 1962) is a method that can be used for scheduling activities so that children move from less- to more-desirable activities. **Premacking** involves sequencing activities so that less-probable or low-probability activities are followed by high-probability (motivating) activities. College students often apply this principle when they interrupt periods of tedious studying by inserting an activity that allows them to relax or unwind. If a child is uninterested in the reading area and highly motivated by the gross-motor area, time in the gross-motor area can serve as a reinforcer following participation in the reading area. Likewise, if a child enjoys the dress-up center, they can attend this area contingent on completion of prescribed activities in a less desirable setting such as the listening center.

Related to the idea of reinforcement is the concept of **responsivity.** Researchers have identified responsivity as an environmental factor closely linked to academic gain (Bailey & Wolery, 1992; Wolery, 2000). A responsive environment is one that provides the learner with predictable and immediate outcomes from any environmental interaction. Toy manufacturers make great use of responsivity in the production of material for infants. Crib-hanging learning centers and mobiles provide the infant with a visual or auditory response for any action done to it. For instance, push a rubber bulb and you get a ding, run a hand across a cylinder and you get a spinning, jingling response. The infant's verbal and facial reactions to these types of immediate feedback indicate the strength of responsivity to promote engagement. The child will return again and again to these stimuli because she understands that her actions can influence the environment.

A setting that provides immediate and consistent reinforcement of behaviors will permit children to acquire a sense of power and security in controlling their environment. This sense of empowerment can be an important motivator for young children with disabilities and serves to encourage them to explore the next nook or cranny. The antithesis to the concept of empowerment is **learned helplessness** and is typical of many students with special needs. Children develop this sense of helplessness when their interactions with the environment prove futile or produce inconsistent results. Children may shy away from risk and new experiences because they are unsure of the results their actions will bring.

A responsive environment offers immediate and predictable consequences.

Self-correcting materials are a good example of instructional technologies that can provide immediate feedback. Because self-correcting materials can be completed by the child or a small group of students with or without the teacher being present, children will also develop independence. Montessori preschools have long used self-correcting material in their preschool designs. Many computer software programs developed for preschool-aged children use a self-correcting format. An animated creature will appear on the screen and say "good work" or will provide a soft form of correction and urge the child to try again.

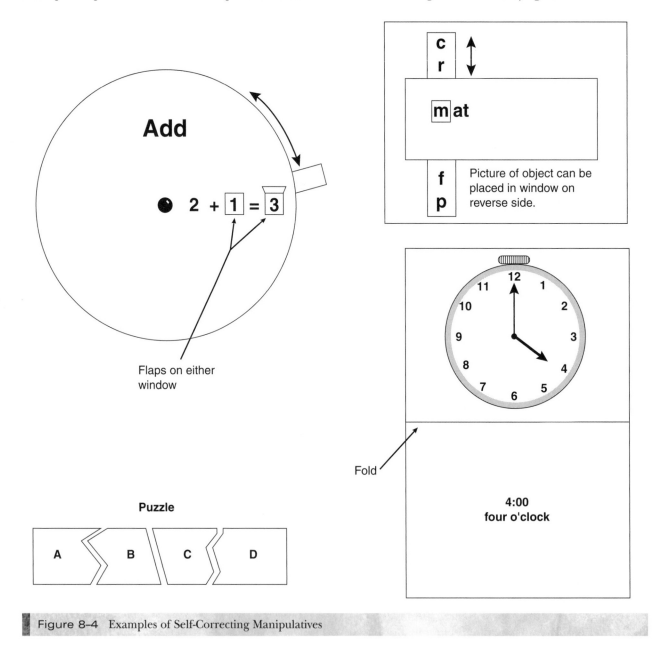

Figure 8–4   Examples of Self-Correcting Manipulatives

Teachers can make use of the same procedures when making their own self-correcting material. Windows and flaps that conceal the correct response or a picture of the correct response can be easily incorporated into either two-dimensional or three-dimensional manipulative materials constructed from cardboard or posterboard. Some examples of these materials are presented in Figure 8–4.

Responsivity can be greatly facilitated when working with children with physical or multiple disabilities through the use of switches and adapted materials. Any battery-operated toy can be easily adapted to operate when pressure is applied to a connected switch. Switches come in a variety of shapes and sizes to fit the specific mobility abilities of the user. They can be placed on a lap board on a child's wheelchair for hand use, on the top side of the wheelchair for response to head movement, and can even be connected to sip-and-puff devices that respond to air pressure.

For the nonverbal child, auditory output devices can be provided that allow a child to use a switch to scan possible responses to center activities. For example, in storytime, the teacher may be reading a Beatrix Potter story. Beforehand an assistant records the terms "Peter," "Flopsy," and "Mopsy" into the device and places corresponding pictures in spaces provided. When the teacher asks comprehension questions, the child can scan the device by pressing the switch and, by pressing again, can stop the scan on the answer she wishes to give. The answer will then be stated verbally. With the emergence of adaptive equipment and advancing technology it is now possible for just about all children with disabilities to meaningfully participate and interact with their learning environment and their peers.

Methods Based Primarily on Environmental Arrangement

It is possible for the environment to actually control the increase and maintenance of acquired behaviors. Baer and Wolf (1970) introduced this concept through their technique of **behavior trapping.** The key to behavior trapping is to provide an environment that is powerfully motivational to the child and yet requires only a basic response in order to participate. Once engaged, the natural reinforcers of the arrangements will serve to increase the rate and maintain the behavior. Behavior trapping is often used to promote social behaviors. A child with a disability may be introduced to a peer group once he or she has acquired some basic social interaction skills and the peer group has received some coaching by the teacher. Once accepted by the peer group, the child's use of the social skills will be maintained and developed by the contingencies and stimuli present in the peer interactions. This concept is related to the principle of stimulus-control discussed earlier.

Social interactions can easily be manipulated through environmental arrangements. Some materials and equipment naturally lend themselves to promoting cooperative interaction. A classic example of this is the playground teeter-totter where its enjoyment necessitates cooperation. Other gross-motor equipment can be adapted to encourage cooperation such as two-seater swings, slides wide enough for pairs, and water and sand play areas. Materials that promote sharing and cooperation include blocks, musical instruments, role-playing figures, and vehicles. Activity centers that facilitate role-playing, such as housekeeping and dress-up, can also promote interaction and thus increase desired behaviors such as sharing, assisting, and communicating.

Special adaptations will most likely be necessary so that children with physical disabilities have access to most social activities. This is especially true for outdoor activities. Paved walkways can provide access to outdoor equipment and peer teaming can facilitate social interactions. A wheelchair, for example, can be a focus of social activities. Children can take turns riding and pushing the wheelchair under the teacher's supervision. There is also an element of empathy training involved in this activity as children develop an appreciation for the skills necessary to manipulate the wheelchair.

The physical contexts of activity arrangements can also be manipulated to promote sharing, social interactions, and communication. Noonan and

McCormick (1993) suggest that there are three basic dimensions to consider in arranging activities: (1) structure built into the activity itself, as found in collaborative games; (2) structure imposed by the material and toys, as in dress-up centers; and (3) structure resulting from the teacher's role, as he or she determines the extent of involvement and direction needed in a given activity. In order to get the desired effect, it is important to know how these various dimensions interact to affect child behaviors. Some early childhood professionals believe that children interact best when left to their own creativity to structure play activities, but there is evidence to suggest that when teachers arrange the structure by setting rules, assigning roles, and establishing themes, social interactions increase compared to when the teacher takes a passive role (Odom, McConnell, & McEvoy, 1992).

An innovation in the instruction of language behaviors first described by Hart and Risely (1978) has been to administer language interventions in natural environments (or milieus) and to manipulate these environments to promote the desired language behaviors. Warren and Bambara (1989) describe **milieu teaching** as having three components: dispersed training trials, using the child's attentional lead as a basis for instruction, and teaching the form and content of language in the context of normal use. Because of the child's selection of stimuli, this approach has also been referred to as "incidental teaching" (Fey, 1986). One example of manipulating the environment to promote language development is to place desired objects just out of reach of the student in order to stimulate requesting verbalizations. Getting access to the material is then contingent on the child verbalizing a request.

Although incidental teaching strategies have been used primarily in teaching language skills, the methods have also been used to successfully teach other skills. Dunst and McWilliam (1988) describe a five-step plan for applying incidental teaching techniques to the teaching of cognitive skills.

- *Arrange the environment to maximize child interest and enjoyment.* Know which stimuli attract and hold a student's attention.

- *Arrange to have reinforcers in the environment that are actually reinforcing.* Do not take for granted that frequently used rewards will be reinforcing for all students. Know each child's interests and preferences and apply reinforcers for appropriate behavior.

- *Promote interaction with persons and objects in the environment.* The more interactions with the environment, the more opportunities for learning. Be prepared to apply natural reinforcers contingent on performance of desired behaviors.

- *Use prompting, modeling, or environmental arrangements to elicit progressively more complex behaviors.* Encourage successive approximations toward the desired behavior. Promote variations or novel demonstrations of the behavior and shape newly acquired behaviors toward fluency and proficiency.

- *Focus on functional skills.* Skills that can be used in the child's daily routines to achieve desired goals will tend to be practiced more and will receive natural reinforcements.

Results from milieu intervention research (McWilliam et al., 2001) have indicated very positive results, especially in regard to promoting generalization of learned skills to other settings. There may be a broader lesson here for educators—the closer we can arrange the learning environment to resemble the environment in which the behavior naturally occurs, the easier it will be for the child to generalize and apply the new skill.

Selecting Materials

Teachers must think from the child's point of view as to what will be most appealing. A consistent source of dismay among parents at gift-giving times, such as Christmas or birthdays, is when their toddler spends hours playing with the cardboard box and wrapping paper and ignores the bright, expensive toy contained within. Early childhood professionals must be good consumers and consumer advocates, not always

Table 8-2   Considerations for Purchasing Instructional Materials

I. General Considerations
1. Cost and durability
2. Target population
3. Research and field-test data
II. Instructional Considerations
1. Sequencing of skills
2. Organization of materials:
   • Teacher-friendly?
   • Individualized?
   • Chapters?
   • Units?
   • Evaluation?
3. Stimulus-response modality combinations, sensory modalities used
4. Effective teaching practices:
   • Activities for maintenance and generalization
   • Progress assessment
   • Corrective feedback procedures
   • Practice to mastery activities
   • Advance organizers/models
III. Classroom Management Considerations
1. Space/time requirements
2. Evaluation and data recording
3. Extent of teacher involvement
4. Interest levels
5. Reinforcement needed

deciding on purchasing that which is widely advertised and neatly packaged. The money that is spent on resources for our programs must be spent wisely as the amount of money typically available seems to decrease every year. An outline of considerations for purchasing materials is presented in Table 8–2.

General Considerations

A key consideration when purchasing or creating material is to ensure its durability. Almost all two-dimensional materials can and should be laminated or covered with clear plastic to facilitate cleaning and promote longevity. The preschool environment can be rough on materials, especially material used frequently. Even material designed specifically for teacher use such as curricula, kits, teacher idea books, or thematic units can receive a lot of wear in a short time.

Because most commercially made material can be costly, it is highly recommended that teachers accumulate their own teacher-made materials. Not only will this save on expense, but it is much easier for teachers to create materials geared to specific student needs. Many teachers find the making of materials worthwhile for intrinsic reasons. Having one's own material in the classroom provides a sense of investment and self-fulfillment. The concept of personal pride and investment can also be applied to the activities of children and their parents. An investment in the physical design of the classroom may promote parent involvement and child interest. In addition to being an environmental engineer, the teacher often must take on the role of architect and interior design expert.

Before the purchase of any material such as prepackaged kits or curricula, the early childhood special educator should examine any available information on its development and field-testing. Information obtained can be helpful in determining whether this material is suitable for a specific group and the specific purposes behind its development. The appropriateness of material both in terms of age and ability becomes especially relevant when dealing with children with developmental delays. Material field-tested with populations that did not include children with disabilities may turn out to be inappropriate for similar aged populations with disabilities and delays.

Instructional Considerations

Some materials are designed more than others to be teacher- and curriculum-friendly. When purchasing or constructing materials, the teacher must consider how the material will be used in relation to time, the curriculum, the specific needs of the youngsters, and how well a particular material lends itself to multiple uses. Some materials will come "as is" with little in the way of teacher support, while some will come with more detailed suggestions for class use. Look for ideas concerning incorporating the material into a program, descriptions of skills the material was designed to enhance, developmental sequences of skills to be taught, adaptations for those with physical or sensory impairments, suggestions or guides for evaluation, and tips for presentation or actual lesson plans. How the materials are organized will go a long way in determining their ease of use and eventual effectiveness with children.

A final major consideration is how the material will fit into the physical environment and schedule of the preschool. Many early childhood special education classrooms follow a daily schedule of activities while typically being short of storage space. Any new material entering the classroom will need to be evaluated as to how it will impact on space and time requirements.

The Nurturing Preschool

The Accessible Environment

The Americans with Disabilities Act (PL 101-336) requires that reasonable accommodations be made to ensure that public facilities, including child care centers and preschool programs, are accessible to individuals with disabilities. Accessibility of the preschool environment is crucial if inclusion of youngsters with disabilities is to be successful (Odom & Bailey, 2001). White and Coleman (2000) observe that "developmentally appropriate classrooms allow for the inclusion of all children" (p. 288).

While the term **accessibility** often is used in the context of providing equal opportunity to enter into an environment, this term is more encompassing in education circles. Accessibility in educational contexts includes adaptations necessary to ensure successful goal attainment by children with disabilities.

This may require changes in the communication methods as well as the physical arrangements. Programs that cater to individual needs will be relatively easy to adapt for children with sensory or physical disabilities. In these programs, modifications to meet the needs of students are part of the presentation of daily activities. Programs that are more free-form, relying on child-directed activities will need more adaptation to accommodate children with special needs. We recommend that early childhood programs conduct accessibility assessments.

As a rule, adaptations to an environment to accommodate a child should be kept to a minimum. In other words, adaptations should be as unobtrusive as possible to minimize pointing out the differences in the child with the disability. The adaptations needed will depend on the type and severity of the disability. Preschoolers with severe physical disabilities will need additional space for maneuvering and therapy and may require a range of adaptive equipment to facilitate therapy and to aid in accessing aspects of the preschool program. (See Feature 8–1 for a list of modifications appropriate for a child in a wheelchair.) Equipment often used in this context includes wedges, wheelchairs, prone standers, sidelyers, posture chairs, and support bars. Examples of adaptive equipment used to assist students with physical disabilities to access their environment are presented in Figure 8–5. Teachers must work closely with physical and occupational therapists and parents to ensure that individual needs for successful participation are met. For example, the purpose of a wedge is to give the lower trunk and torso support so that head, arms, and hands are free to manipulate objects. A child using a wedge may freely participate in activities such as block play, art, and role-playing with human figures and dolls. Sidelyers and prone standers serve the same purpose for youngsters with a variety of physical disabilities.

Adaptations to the communication environment may require the adoption of augmentative or alternative communication material. This may include a range of materials and methods such as signing, communication boards, flip-picture cards, as well as high-tech devices such as scanning computer keyboards that can be operated with switches adapted for a par-

Feature 8-1   Is Your Classroom Wheelchair-Accessible?

Check for the following modifications to be certain that your classroom is accessible for a child in a wheelchair. What other modification might be necessary?

_____ Adjustable table legs to raise table height

_____ Table size and shape modified for easier wheelchair access

_____ Wide paths created to accommodate wheelchair movement

_____ Adjustable storage shelves for easier wheelchair access

_____ Rearrangement of toilets for easier wheelchair access

_____ Handrails added to facilitate child's transfer from wheelchair to the toilet

_____ Toilets raised to facilitate child's transfer from wheelchair to the toilet

_____ Wheelchair-accessible sinks

Source: Adapted from C. White and M. Coleman, *Early Childhood Education: Building a Philosophy for Teaching* (Upper Saddle River, NJ: Prentice Hall, 2000). p. 209.

Feature 8-2   Thinking about Environmental Accommodations

Maria Ramirez will soon transition to an inclusive community-based preschool program. Because of her cerebral palsy and complicated by the typical motor delays associated with Down syndrome, Maria will require some environmental adaptations in order to maximize her educational program. Maria's recent evaluation revealed that accommodations for her physical and communicative abilities will most likely be necessary. What types of modifications might be required in order for Maria to fully participate and successfully interact with her classmates and the learning environment? How would you plan on meeting her unique needs? One way of thinking and planning for Maria's needs would be through simulation. Although it would be impossible to accurately reproduce what Maria feels and senses, empathy and understanding of her situation can be gained through simulation activities. Maria's fine motor ability might be reproduced, to a degree, by wearing mittens. What play objects and instructional material would be difficult or impossible to manipulate? How could these material be made accessible? Books, for example, have historically been inaccessible to persons with cerebral palsy without someone's assistance. The inability to turn a page has prevented many from accessing literacy. For Maria there may be two options. One would be through a computer with a switch interface and the appropriate literacy software. The second option is simpler: a small rubber ball attached to a pencil. Maria has the gross motor skills necessary to grasp the pencil and drag the ball across the page causing it to turn. One could also try navigating the preschool in a wheelchair. This would let a person evaluate firsthand the accessibility to areas and materials. Maria will need access to the sand and water table. Can you think of creative ways to accomplish this? What types of adaptive equipment would give Maria access to classroom centers?

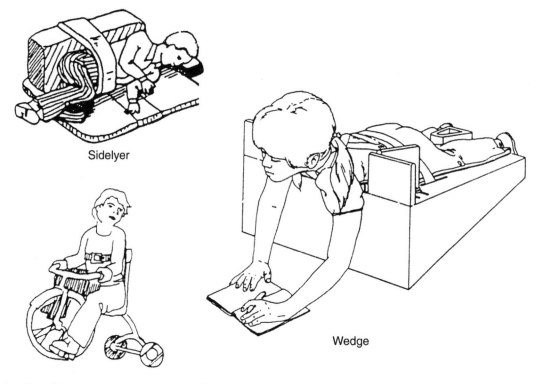

Sidelyer

Wedge

Tricycle with built-up back and pedals. Adult three-wheeled bikes are available for larger children and adolescents.

Figure 8-5   Examples of Adaptive Equipment

SOURCE: J. Bigge, S. Best, and K. Heller, *Teaching Individuals with Physical, Health, and Multiple Disabilities* (4th ed.), (Upper Saddle River, NJ: Merrill, 2001). p. 99.

ticular disability. It may be necessary to modify bulletin boards and other classroom materials to accommodate these alternative forms of communication. The use of signs or symbols with the printed word on materials may facilitate learning of these techniques by all class members, thus improving accessibility of children who are nonverbal by providing a universal method of classroom communication.

When thinking about adapting your classroom to include children with special needs it would be helpful to remember the following three key concepts: accessibility, usability, and developmental appropriateness (Winter, Bell, & Dempsey, 1994). Youcha and Wood (1997) suggest that teachers ask themselves the following questions:

1. Can the child get where she needs to be in the classroom to learn something?

2. Once the child is in that location, can she use the materials and equipment and participate in the activity as independently as possible to learn something?

3. Are the learning activities arranged and scheduled to meet the individual learning needs of all the children, including the child with disabilities? (p. 46)

Remember, it is not always necessary for children with delays and disabilities to participate in an activity to the same degree as their typical classmates for the activity to be enjoyed. The concept of "partial participation states that, regardless of severity of disability, individuals can be taught to participate in [a] variety of activities to some degree, or activities can be adapted to allow participation" (Sheldon, 1996, p. 116). Adaptations to activities can increase opportunities for interaction and enhance the quality of participation so that the environment is exciting and interesting for all youngsters. Table 8–3 offers a checklist of environmental adaptations needed to accommodate children with diverse abilities.

The Safe Environment

Keeping children safe and healthy is job number one. Regulations governing these two critical areas are found in all licensing and accreditation standards. It is imperative that teachers are committed to the safety and well-being of their pupils. While keeping youngsters safe is a matter of common sense, the responsibility for a safe environment resides with the teacher (Feeney et al., 2001).

The teacher's task of providing a safe environment for young children with special needs has been made easier due to the development of safer toys and equipment, and by the production of safer building material. Many early childhood programs are now equipped with slip-proof linoleum with a rubber underlining to help prevent breakage. This product can be essential in making bathrooms, wet areas, and art areas safer for children.

As matters of safety and efficiency, learning areas can be partitioned by using shelving or dividers that are approximately three feet high (two feet for toddlers). This allows the teacher to have a clear field of vision across the classroom, provides a sense of privacy to the areas, and places storage of materials adjacent to the site where they will most likely be used.

Consumer protection groups have worked diligently to ensure that toys and material are nontoxic and fire retardant. Most children's toys now carry labels and warnings concerning age appropriateness and possible safety problems experienced by infants and toddlers. Although these improvements have decreased potential dangers, teachers must be ever-vigilant to identify environmental conditions that may put children at risk of injury. For example, a throw rug used in a high traffic area of the room will invariably lead to an unplanned tumble. This arrangement will also tend to limit accessibility for a child with a visual or motor impairment.

A particularly frightening source of accidents in the preschool is electrical shock and resulting burns. The effects of burns are always painful and often irreparable. The effect of electrical shock is often heart failure. It is much easier to work on preventative measures than to initiate treatment after the accident. Wall sockets are very attractive to young children wishing to explore a newfound cranny. In new construction, wall outlets should be teacher-height, approximately five to six feet off the floor. Extension cords should be used with extreme care or be completely excluded from preschool settings (National Resource Center for Health and Safety in Child Care, 1996). Young children can easily separate an extension cord and place the exposed end in their mouth. This can cause severe burns to the tongue, lips, and other soft parts of the oral cavity and, in some instances, can be fatal. Although we believe that all preschool teachers should be trained in first-aid and CPR, an ounce of prevention will better serve the children.

A final topic related to safety is classroom orderliness and organization. A cluttered room is not safe; thus, a clean-up time between activities is important. Not only is cleanup desirable for safety factors, but also to promote good work habits and responsibility among the students.

We recommend that early childhood teachers consult the following two resources for guidance on establishing a safe and secure learning environment.

- *Stepping Stones to Caring for Our Children* (National Resource Center for Health and Safety in Child Care, 1997)
- The ABCs of Safe and Healthy Child Care (Centers for Disease Control and Prevention, 1997)

Table 8–4 offers specific suggestions for maintaining a safe classroom.

Table 8–3   Checklist for an Accessible Environment

Physical Environment

Questions to think about:

- How do different children use their bodies or the space around them for learning?
- How can we enhance or adapt the physical environment for children who have difficulty moving (or who move too much)?
- How can we capitalize on the physical environment for children who learn by moving?

Accessing the environment safely:

❑ Are doorway widths in compliance with local building codes?

❑ Ramps in addition to or instead of stairs?

❑ Low, wide stairs where possible (including playground equipment)?

❑ Hand rails on *both* sides of stairs?

❑ Easy handles on doors, drawers, etc.

❑ At least some kids' chairs with armrests?

- "Cube" chairs are great!
- Often a footrest and/or seat strap will provide enough stability for a child to do fine motor activities.

❑ When adapting seating, mobility, and/or gross motor activities for a specific child with physical disabilities, consult a physical therapist.

Learning through the environment:

❑ Does the environment and equipment reflect variety?

- Surface, heights (textured, smooth, low, high, etc.).
- Space for gross motor activity (open spaces, climbing structures, floor mats).
- Quiet/comfort spaces (small spaces, carpet, pillows).
- Social spaces (dramatic play area, groups of chairs or pillows, etc.).

❑ Are toys and equipment physically accessible?

- Glue magnets to backs of puzzle pieces and attribute blocks and use on a steel cookie tray.
- Attach large knobs or levers to toys with lids, movable parts.
- Attach tabs to book pages for easier turning.

❑ An occupational therapist can provide specific suggestions for adapting materials and activities so a child with physical disabilities can participate.

Visual Environment

Questions to think about:

- How do different children use their vision for learning?
- How can we enhance the visual environment for a child with low or no vision?
- How can we capitalize on the visual environment for children who learn by seeing?

Table 8-3   Checklist for an Accessible Environment *(continued)*

Accessing the environment safely:

❑ Are contrasting colors used on edges and when surfaces change (e.g., tile to carpet, beginning of stairs)?

❑ Can windows be shaded to avoid high glare?

  • Also consider darker non-glossy floors and table tops.

  • Some children's behavior and learning may improve dramatically once a strong glare is eliminated.

❑ Is visual clutter avoided on walls, shelves, etc.?

  • Visual clutter can interfere with learning, predictability, and safety.

❑ Is "spot lighting" (e.g., swing arm lamp) in a dimmer room available?

  • Spot lamps help some children pay attention and work better on table tasks.

❑ Orientation and mobility specialists help children with visual impairments learn to navigate the environment.

Learning through the environment:

❑ Are objects and places in the environment labeled ("door," "chair," etc.)?

❑ Are the size and contrast of pictures and letters adequate for the children with visual impairments in your program?

❑ Are visual displays at the children's eye level?

❑ Are large-print materials, textured materials, and auditory materials available (e.g, big books, sandpaper letters, books on tape)?

❑ Is the daily schedule represented in words and pictures?

  • A velcro schedule that allows children to post the schedule and then remove items as activities are completed can help children to stay focused and transition more easily from one activity to the next.

❑ Are children with low vision seated close to the center of activity and away from high glare?

❑ Teachers for the visually impaired assist in selecting and adapting materials for children with low vision.

❑ Children who are blind may need a "running commentary" of events, places, etc. Pictures in books and food on plates, for example, should be described.

Auditory Environment

Questions to think about:

  • How do different children use their hearing for learning?

  • How can we enhance the auditory environment for a child who is deaf, hearing impaired, or has poor auditory discrimination skills?

  • How can we capitalize on the auditory environment for auditory learners?

Accessing the environment safely:

❑ Does background noise (from indoor or outdoor sources) filter into the area?

❑ Is there a way to eliminate or dampen background noise (using carpeting, closing windows and doors)?

  • Some kids are unable to do the automatic filtering out of background noises that we do so unconsciously.

(continued)

Table 8–3   Checklist for an Accessible Environment *(continued)*

❏ Is "auditory competition" avoided?

- Raising one's voice to compete with a roomful of noisy children is rarely as effective as "silent signals," such as holding up a peace sign or encouraging children who notice to do the same until the room is full of quiet children holding up peace signs.

❏ Are non-auditory signals needed to alert a child with a hearing impairment?

- Turning the lights on and off is a common strategy.
- Ask the child's parents what strategies are used at home.

Learning through the environment:

❏ Are auditory messages paired with visual ones (e.g., simple sign language, flannel boards, picture schedules)?

❏ Are children with hearing impairment seated so they can see others' faces and actions?

❏ Teachers for the hearing impaired can provide strategies for modifying activities for children with hearing impairments.

❏ A child who is deaf will need a teacher or aide who uses sign language.

Social Environment

Questions to think about:

- How do different children use social cues for learning?
- How can we adapt the social environment for children with impulsive behavior, attention deficits, or behavior problems?
- How can we capitalize on the social environments for children who learn by relating to others?

Accessing the environment safely:

❏ Is the schedule predictable? Are children informed of schedule changes?

❏ Does the schedule provide a range of activity level (e.g., adequate opportunities for physical activity)?

❏ School psychologists and behavior specialists can help analyze misbehavior and modify the environments or schedule to minimize problems for children with attention deficits or behavior problems.

Learning through the environment

❏ Does the environment have a positive impact on self-esteem?

- Allows all children to feel safe?
- Invites all children to participate?
- Maximizes all children's opportunities for independence?

❏ Do learning materials and toys include representations of all kinds of people, including children and adults with disabilities?

- People with disabilities should be represented in active and leadership roles, not just as passive observers.

Table 8-3   Checklist for an Accessible Environment *(continued)*

❑ Does the schedule include opportunities for a variety of groups (pairs, small groups, whole class) as well as quiet time or time alone?

- Pairing or grouping children with complementary abilities eases the demands on the teacher and enables children to help one another.
- When given a chance, peers often come up with the most creative ways for children with disabilities to participate.
- Creative use of staffing may be needed to provide additional support for some children during some activities.

❑ Does the schedule provide both structured and open activity times?

- Children who have difficulty with a particular type of activity may need extra support at those times.

Additional Strategies When Adapting the Environment for Individual Children

❑ Make use of the diverse strengths of the various people on the child's team.

- Early childhood educators are among the most sensitive and creative when it comes to developing multisensory, inclusive activities that take individual children's skills and needs into account!
- Be on the lookout for how kids modify environments and activities for themselves and their peers. They often come up with the most creative solutions!
- Include parents when making accommodations for children with special needs. Parents know their own children better than anyone else.
- Some children qualify for special education services through state-wide infant or preschool intervention services. The specialists in these programs can assist in assessing a child's needs and providing suggestions and/or parameters for modifying the environment (and instructional strategies).

❑ Respect for each child's strengths and needs is the most important ingredient in creating appropriate environments for all children.

SOURCE: Adapted from K. Haugen, 1997. Using Your Senses to Adapt Environments: Checklist for an Accessible Environment, *Child Care Information Exchange, 114*, pp. 50, 55–56.

A Healthy Environment

Another key responsibility in providing a safe environment for children is to protect them from the spread of communicable diseases. Teaching good hygiene habits is a central element of many preschool programs and is often an integral component of a functional curriculum. Some children with disabilities are particularly at-risk for certain infections due to related problems with immune systems, heart conditions, or chronic illnesses. Infectious diseases that tend to be of particular concern with infants and young children include hepatitis A and B, cytomegalovirus (CMV), herpes simplex Type 1, and AIDS (Noonan & McCormick, 1993). CMV will produce only flulike symptoms in children, but can be devastating if transmitted to a teacher or parent who is pregnant. Both hepatitis B (the more virulent form of hepatitis) and herpes simplex are incurable and can be spread through bodily fluids. Herpes simplex Type 1 and CMV are probably the most infectious of these diseases because they can be spread through airborne effects of coughing and sneezing. AIDS has the least transmission likelihood in child care centers and preschools because of the need for there to be semen or blood transference. (The issue of children with AIDS is discussed in Chapter 10.)

The spread of these and other communicable diseases can be controlled by applying good health practices such as hand washing which is considered

Table 8–4 Classroom Environment Safety Checklist

1. Check the environment, both inside and outside, for any hazards. Check electrical outlets and cords; make sure children cannot pull over any equipment (television sets, VCRs); remove dangerous plants; cover sharp edges; make sure fences are sturdy and exit gates are childproof; and eliminate any other hazards to children's safety.

2. Practice emergency procedures on a regular basis. Children's and teachers' responses to fire drills (and in some areas, tornado and earthquake procedures) must become automatic.

3. Make sure that the classroom contains a fire extinguisher and that all staff know how to use it.

4. All teachers and staff members should be trained in first aid and cardio-pulmonary resuscitation (CPR). At minimum, one person with such training should be present at all times. Staff should be required to have special training in CPR for infants, if the program accepts children that young.

5. Post a list of the names of all children and a map of fire exit routes near each exit.

6. Each classroom should be equipped with a well-stocked first aid kit. Keep it in a specific location so staff members can quickly find it. A second kit should be available for use on field trips and outdoor outings.

7. Keep cleaning agents, insecticides, and other such items (including medications) out of the reach of children— preferably in a locked cabinet.

8. Maintain an up-to-date list of emergency phone numbers (parents, relatives, doctors, and hospitals) for each child. Take a copy of this information with you when going on field trips or other excursions.

9. Keep the number for the poison control center posted near the telephone.

10. Post a list of children's allergies (including reactions to ant, wasp, bee stings, or certain foods) and check it before planning any food experiences or outdoor activities.

11. Keep a list by the door of the adults authorized to pick up each child. Do not release a child to any unauthorized person.

12. Make all posted information readily available to substitute teachers.

SOURCE: Adapted from J. Brewer, *Introduction to Early Childhood Education* (4th ed.). (Needham Heights, MA: Allyn & Bacon, 2001). p. 107.

by many health care professionals to be the most effective way of controlling the spread of disease and illness. This hygiene practice, commonly referred to as "universal precautions," also requires that the cleansing of materials and surfaces with disinfectant become a regular part of an adult's duties in the classroom. Surfaces such as toilet seats, positioning boards, wheelchair trays, and eating areas should receive special attention. Toys and materials should be washed after use and adults should pay special attention to material handled by children with runny noses and toys placed in or near the mouth. A rule in the classroom could be that anything touching the mouth is immediately taken and placed in a tub to be cleaned. Adults should always wash their hands following any contact involving bathroom assistance, positioning, feeding, or diaper changing. A good practice is to wear disposable latex gloves during these duties. Any open cuts or sores noticed on adults or children should be covered with bandages. Adapting these hygiene procedures into the daily routine not only helps to prevent the spread of disease, but serves as a model of safety behavior for children.

A topic of environmental safety that has only recently begun to be addressed is that of indoor pollutants. Childhood illnesses and developmental disorders have been linked to ingestion of noxious substances (Lin-Fu, 1985; Noyes, 1987). Children can be exposed by inhaling gases and particulates, by food intake, or by touch. The effects of lead and asbestos on human health have been well-documented, but other substances commonly found in preschool environments are also becoming suspect

Universal precautions are necessary for maintaining a healthy environment.

(Weiser, 1991). Formaldehyde, a material commonly used in bookbinding, particle board, and plywood, has been found to be particularly noxious. Children with asthmatic conditions or allergies may be especially sensitive to particulate matter from tempera paints, chalk dust, or dry clay, and from irritants emanating from gas stoves or teachers' perfume or cologne. While it is impossible to shield children from all noxious environmental substances, one can work to minimize the potential hazards and be sensitive to individuals who exhibit symptoms that may be environmentally related.

Evaluating Learning Environments

In order to provide and maintain an environment that facilitates maximum learning for each child, a method of evaluation must be developed to measure environmental impact. Bailey and Wolery (1992) suggest five steps in the evaluation process.

- Identify outcomes associated with each activity or area.
- Periodically review each child's performance at centers. Performance factors include time in engagement, specific skills learned at the site, and the amount of inappropriate behaviors.
- Attempt to understand the reasons for problems student may have at the centers (for example, low interest for a child, too cluttered and distracting, problems with peers).
- Attempt to make corrections based on these reasons.
- Reevaluate once modifications to the area are made.

This method of evaluation is similar to that which could be applied to any instructional method and underscores the fact that environmental arrangements may be considered an instructional technique.

One method for evaluating the total preschool environment based on the concepts and techniques presented in this chapter is the *Preschool Environmental Rating Scale (PERS)* located in Appendix B. The PERS is a judgment-based measure based on criteria of suggested best practices in six basic areas:

- Physical design
- Materials
- Basic care needs
- Curriculum
- Adult/Interpersonal needs
- Activities

Because of the judgment-based nature of the scale, it is important that the PERS be administered by several individuals. Judgment-based evaluations are prone to evaluator bias. Thus ratings by multiple raters should be averaged to determine a mean score in each area. Due to the fact that the PERS has not been field-tested, it should not be used to compare different preschool sites. It is meant to serve only as a starting point for self-evaluation of a preschool setting.

Other commercially available environmental rating scales with established validity and reliability are available. One of the most frequently used assessments is the recently revised *Early Childhood Environment Rating Scale (ECERS-R)* (Harms, Clifford, & Cryer, 1998). This scale provides an overall indicator of environmental quality in addition to evaluating seven specific features of the classroom. Using a Likert-type scale (1 = inadequate, 7 = excellent) evaluators can assess the following environmental features:

- Personal care routines
- Furnishings and displays
- Language-reasoning experience
- Fine and gross motor activities
- Creative activities
- Social development
- Adult needs

Mean ratings of 5 or higher are judged "good," scores of 3–4 are viewed as "mediocre," and a rating below 3 is considered "poor." Administration of the ECERS-R usually requires a half day of observation as well as staff interviews. This scale provides an effective way of gauging the strengths and limitations of the learning environment.

A similar scale, the *Infant/Toddler Environmental Rating Scale (ITERS)* (Harms, Cryers, & Clifford, 1990) is available for assessing center-based programs for children under 30 months of age. A seven category or subscale format is also used with this assessment instrument. The seven subscales include:

- Personal care routines
- Furnishings and displays
- Listening and talking
- Learning activities
- Interaction
- Program structure
- Adult needs

Administration requirements are similar to the ECERS.

Another measure, the *Early Childhood Physical Environment Scales (ECPES)* (Moore, 1982) is composed of two subscales and primarily focuses on use of space. One subscale rates the overall organization and space of the center, the other is used to evaluate specific rooms or centers. Both subscales measure several different dimensions. The overall center subscale assesses visual connection between spaces, closure of spaces, spatial separation, mixture of large and small spaces, separation of staff and children's areas, separation of age groups, circulation, visibility, and connection between indoor and outdoor spaces. The subscale evaluating individual areas measures spatial definition of activity areas, visual connections among centers, size, storage and work space, concentration of same-use resources, softness, flexibility, variety of seating and working positions, amount of resources, and proximity of activity centers from circulation paths. The primary outcome of the ECPES evaluation is to provide a representation of the atmosphere and arrangements of the preschool. Moore recommends combining this assessment with other measures to build a more complete picture of the preschool environment. All three of the preceding measures have been shown to have good reliability and validity and provide practical feedback for evaluating the learning environment.

Summary

Environmental arrangements are critically important in the education of young children with special needs. Teachers must become environmental engineers in their own classroom to maximize the impact of their instruction. Development of this ability is dependent on a basic understanding of how children learn and how the environment effects the learning process.

Early childhood special educators must constantly monitor the effect the environment is having on individuals and modify the arrangements to best meet the needs of the children. Maintaining an interesting, stimulating environment will require creativity and energy on the part of the teacher, but can be a source of much intrinsic reward and fun. As the youngsters are creating imaginary scenarios in their role playing activities, the teacher actually participates in a similar activity by creating a real-life scenario for his or her own teaching.

Two overriding considerations for any learning environment must be to provide a setting which is both safe and accessible to all students. Providing a safe environment not only serves to reduce accidents and injuries, but also facilitates child independence. Children feel freer to explore their world when they know they can depend on the adults and their environment to provide safety and security. It should be noted that while providing a safe and secure environment, we should not eliminate all risk from the child's experiences. An environment free of risk would mean an environment free of novel experiences and one in which children could not benefit from learning from their mistakes. Risk-taking is an important component of learning new skills, and teachers and parents must be able to make informed decisions about what constitutes constructive risk versus what arrangements present undue danger.

Safety is a critical element of accessibility; however, accessibility also implies equal opportunity of participation for all children. For example, a raised stage area of the preschool should be wheelchair accessible. Yet, beyond providing access, the ramp leading to the stage should provide as much safety for the child in the wheelchair as other children have in scaling one or two steps. This would require a ramp wide enough for the child to easily negotiate and curb features (raised edges of the ramp or a side wall) to deter tipping accidents. For a child with a sensory or physical impairment, the message that must be transmitted by the environment is, "Your disability will not handicap your ability to interact here." Accessibility is a primary element of environmental design. For if children are denied participation due to inaccessibility, the teacher has set the stage for frustration and resistance to learning.

Getting Connected

Visit the following Websites for useful information about chapter content.

❑ Centers for Disease Control and Prevention, http://www.cdc/gov/

❑ Gigglepotz—ideas for creating learning centers, http://www.gigglepotz.com/pres_centers.htm

❑ Head Start Center Design Guide, http://www.headstartinfor.org/publications/designguide/index.cfm

❑ National Clearinghouse on Educational Resources, offers extensive list of resources, for example—classroom design, healthy school environments, early childhood centers, http://www.edfacilites.org

Check Your Understanding

1. Discuss how interactions with the environment can help shape a child's learning and development.

2. How can the dimensions of the classroom affect children's behavior and performance?

3. Identify the various types of learning centers typically found in most preschool classrooms and describe the components of each.

4. How can stimulus control enhance learning?

5. Describe the concept of Premacking.

6. Why is responsivity important for learning in young children with disabilities?

7. What factors should a teacher consider when selecting instructional materials?

8. List the steps you would take to ensure a safe and healthy learning environment for young children with special needs.

References

Baer, D., & Wolf, M. (1970). The entry into natural communities of reinforcement. In R. Ulrich, T. Stachnik, & M. Mabry (Eds.), *Control of human behavior* (Vol. 2, pp. 319–324). Glenview, IL: Scott Foresman.

Bailey, D., & Wolery, M. (1992). *Teaching infants and preschoolers with disabilities* (2nd ed.). Columbus, OH: Merrill.

Bredekamp, S., & Copple, C. (Eds.). (1997). *Developmentally appropriate practice in early childhood programs* (rev. ed.). Washington, DC: National Association for the Education of Young Children.

Brewer, J. (2001). *Introduction to early childhood education* (4th ed.) Needham Heights, MA: Allyn & Bacon.

Brown, W., Fox, J., & Brady, M. (1987). The effects of spatial density on the socially directed behavior of three and four year old children during freeplay: An investigation of a setting factor. *Education and Treatment of Children, 10,* 247–258.

Buggey, T., DeHaas-Warner, S., & Bagnato, S. (1991). Can professionals forecast and plan for kindergarten success? In S. Bagnato & J. Neisworth (Eds.), *Assessment for early intervention: Best practices for professionals* (pp. 142–163). New York: Guilford Press.

Carta, J., Sainato, D., & Greenwood, C. (1988). Advances in ecological assessment of classroom instruction for young children with handicaps. In S. Odom & M. Karnes (Eds.), *Early intervention for infants and children with handicaps: An empirical base* (pp. 217–239). Baltimore: Paul H. Brookes.

Cataldo, C. (1983). *Infant and toddler programs: A guide to very early childhood education.* Reading, MA: Addison-Wesley.

Centers for Disease Control and Prevention. (1987). *The ABCs of safe and healthy child care.* Atlanta, GA: Author.

Dunst, C., & McWilliam, R. (1988). Cognitive assessment of multihandicapped young children. In T. Wachs & R. Sheehan (Eds.), *Assessment of developmentally disabled children* (pp. 213–438). New York: Plenum.

Feeney, S., Christensen, D., & Moravcik, E. (2001). *Who am I in the lives of children* (6th ed.). Upper Saddle River, NJ: Prentice Hall.

Fey, M. (1986). *Language interventions with young children.* Boston: College Hill Press.

Gandini, L. (1993). Fundamentals of the Reggio Emilia approach to early childhood education. *Young Children, 49*(1), 4–8.

Gordon, A., & Browne, K. (2004). *Beginnings and beyond* (6th ed.). Clifton Park, NY: Delmar.

Harbin, G., McWilliam, R., & Gallagher, J. (2000). Services for young children with disabilities and their families. In J. Shonkoff & S. Meisels (Eds.), *Handbook of early intervention* (2nd ed., pp. 387–415). Cambridge, England: Cambridge University Press.

Harms, T., Clifford, R., & Cryer, D. (1998). *Early Childhood Environment Rating Scale* (rev. ed.). New York: Teachers College Press.

Harms, T., Cryers, D., & Clifford, R. (1990). *Infant/Toddler Environmental Rating Scale.* New York: Teachers College Press.

Hart, B., & Risely, T. (1978). Promoting productive language through incidental teaching. *Education and Urban Society, 10,* 407–429.

Henniger, M. (1999). *Teaching young children.* Upper Saddle River, NJ: Prentice Hall.

Hutt, C., & Viazey, M. (1966). Differential effects of group density on social behavior. *Nature, 209,* 1371–1372.

Jambor, T., & Gargiulo, R. (1987). The playground: A social entity for mainstreaming. *Journal of Physical Education, Recreation, & Dance, 58*(1), 18–24.

Kaiser, A., Yoder, P., & Keetz, A. (1992). Evaluating milieu teaching. In S. Warren & J. Reichle (Eds.), *Causes and effects in communication and language intervention* (pp. 9–47). Baltimore: Paul H. Brookes.

Lin-Fu, J. (1985). Forward. In D. Kane, *Environmental hazards to young children.* Phoenix: Oryx.

McEvoy, M., Fox, J., & Rosenberg, M. (1991). Organizing preschool environments: Suggestions for enhancing the development/learning of preschool children with handicaps. *Topics in Early Childhood Special Education, 11,* 18–28.

McWilliam, R., Wolery, M., & Odom, S. (2001). Instructional perspectives in inclusive preschool classrooms. In M. Guralnick (Ed.), *Early childhood inclusion: Focus on change* (pp. 503–527). Baltimore: Paul H. Brookes.

Moore, G. (1982). *Early Childhood Physical Environment Scales.* Milwaukee, WI: Center for Architecture and Urban Planning Research.

Moore, G. (1987). Effects of the spatial definition of behavior settings on children's behavior: A quasi-experimental field study. *Journal of Environmental Psychology, 6,* 205–231.

Morris, S. (1990, June). Safe play surface buying guide. *Child Care Information Exchange, 73,* 48–54.

National Association for the Education of Young Children. (1991). *Accreditation criteria and procedures of the National*

Academy of Early Childhood Programs (rev. ed.). Washington, DC: Author.

National Resource Center for Health and Safety in Child Care. (1996). *National health and safety performance standards: Guidelines for out-of-home child care programs.* Denver: Author.

National Resource Center for Health and Safety in Child Care. (1997). *Stepping stones to caring for our children.* Washington, DC: U.S. Department of Health and Human Services.

Neisworth, J., & Buggey, T. (2000). Behavior analysis and principles in early childhood education. In J. Roopnarine & J. Johnson (Eds.), *Approaches to early childhood education* (3rd ed., pp. 123–148). Upper Saddle River, NJ: Prentice Hall.

Noonan, M., & McCormick, L. (1993). *Early intervention in natural environments: Methods and procedures.* Pacific Grove, CA: Brooks/Cole.

Noyes, D. (1987). Indoor pollutants: Environmental hazards to young children. *Young Children, 42,* 57–65.

O'Brien, M. (2001). Inclusive child care for infants and toddlers. In M. Guralnick (Ed.), *Early childhood inclusion: Focus on change* (pp. 229–251). Baltimore: Paul H. Brookes.

Odom, S., & Bailey, D. (2001). Inclusive preschool programs. In M. Guralnick (Ed.), *Early childhood inclusion: Focus on change* (pp. 253–276). Baltimore: Paul H. Brookes.

Odom, S., McConnell, S., & McEvoy, M. (Eds.). (1992). *Social competence of young children with disabilities: Issues and strategies for intervention.* Baltimore: Paul H. Brookes.

Olds, A. (1979). Designing environmentally optimal classrooms for children with special needs. In S. Meisels (Ed.), *Special education and development: Perspectives on young children with special needs* (pp. 91–138). Baltimore: University Park Press.

Olds, A. (1987). Designing settings for infants and toddlers. In C. Weinstein & T. Edward (Eds.), *Spaces for children: The built environment and child development* (pp. 117–138). New York: Plenum Press.

Premack, D. (1962). Reversibility of the reinforcement relation. *Science, 136,* 255–267.

Rule, S., Losardo, A., Dinnebeil, L., Kaiser, A., & Rowland, C. (1998). Translating research on naturalistic instruction into practice. *Journal of Early Intervention, 21*(4), 283–293.

Sheldon, K. (1996). "Can I play too?" Adapting common classroom activities for young children with limited motor abilities. *Early Childhood Education Journal, 24*(2), 115–120.

Sorohan, E. (1995). Playgrounds are us. *The Executive Educator, 17*(8), 28–32.

Taylor, S., & Morris, V. (1996). Outdoor play in early childhood settings: Is it safe and healthy for children? *Early Childhood Education Journal, 23,* 153–158.

Trawik-Smith, J. (1992). How the classroom environment affects play and development: Review of research. *Dimensions, 20*(2), 27–30.

U.S. Consumer Product Safety Commission. (1997). *Handbook for public playground safety.* Washington, DC: U.S. Government Printing Office.

Wachs, T. (1979). Proximal experience and early cognitive-intellectual development: The physical environment. *Merrill-Palmer Quarterly, 25,* 3–41.

Warren, S., & Bambara, L. (1989). An experimental analysis of milieu language intervention: Teaching the action-object form. *Journal of Speech and Hearing Disorders, 54,* 448–461.

Warren, S., & Gazdag, G. (1990). Facilitating early language development with milieu intervention procedures. *Journal of Early Intervention, 14,* 62–86.

Warren, S., & Kaiser, A. (1988). Research in early language intervention. In S. Odom & M. Karnes (Eds.), *Early intervention for infants and children with handicaps: An empirical base* (pp. 89–108). Baltimore: Paul H. Brookes.

Weiser, M. (1991). *Infant/toddler care and education.* New York: Macmillan.

White, C., & Coleman, M. (2000). *Early childhood education.* Upper Saddle River, NJ: Prentice Hall.

Winter, S., Bell, M., & Dempsey, J. (1994). Creating play environments for children with special needs. *Childhood Education, 71*(1), 28–32.

Wolery, M. (2000). Behavioral and educational approaches to early intervention. In J. Shonkoff & S. Meisel (Eds.), *Handbook of early childhood intervention* (2nd ed., pp. 179–202). Cambridge, England: Cambridge University Press.

Wolery, M., Ault, M., & Doyle, P. (1992). *Teaching students with moderate and severe disabilities.* White Plains, NY: Longman.

Youcha, V., & Wood, K. (1997). Enhancing the environment for ALL Children. *Child Care Information Exchange, 114,* 45–49.

Strategies for Teaching Young Children with Special Needs

Contributed by Linda L. Brady, University of Alabama at Birmingham

Learning Outcomes

After reading this chapter you will be able to:

- Describe teaching strategies that facilitate inclusion of young children with special needs in home and school settings.
- Identify adaptations for children with sensory delays, motor delays, cognitive delays, social and emotional delays, and communication and language delays.
- list materials and assistive technologies for children with special needs.
- summarize instructional strategies for children with special needs in each specific delay area.

Children with disabilities are first and foremost children. They can and do learn. They may learn at a different rate, use different strategies, or learn through another modality, but they do learn. They may learn through exploration and child-initiated activities or with the additional support of peers and direction from a teacher. The key in creating appropriate educational experiences for any child is to *create a match* between the individual needs of the child and the environment, materials, and instruction. This may result in teachers and parents using a variety or combination of strategies to facilitate development and learning.

IDEA and its amendments stress that children be educated "to the maximum extent individually appropriate in the least restrictive environment (LRE)." These laws provide support for educational services for children with disabilities between the ages of three and five with the placement of choice being with typically developing children (Odom, 2000). This concept has been written about since the early 1970s and has emerged as the service delivery model of choice for children and families in recent years. The most common interpretation of this aspect of the law is that children be placed in educational settings alongside typically developing peers. One current application of the least restrictive environment clause is referred to as inclusion. Within inclusive settings, children can be functionally included, achieve social integration (full participation), and engage in the typical classroom setting without support (Haring, 1991). This level of participation requires that teachers examine the child

in each setting to determine if he/she is actively engaged in all aspects of the environment.

This chapter provides suggestions for including young children with special needs in normalized settings. A wide range of strategies proven to be effective in promoting child engagement is presented (see Wolery, 1994a; 1994b; 1994c for an extensive review). The initial part of the chapter will focus on those selected strategies used in center-based programs or classrooms. Teaching strategies from the field of early childhood and early childhood special education will be discussed. Many of the strategies are appropriate for use with younger children who receive early intervention services in centers or at home. Additionally, the second part of this chapter provides suggestions for adapting, and modifying the environment, materials, and instructional delivery to young children with special needs. For ease of communication, young children are discussed using noncategorical descriptors. Where appropriate, children will be discussed using more traditional categorical terminology as some young children already meet guidelines for specific disabilities (visual impairment or hearing impairment). Table 9–1 identifies early indicators or signs of possible problems in specific areas of development. It is important to realize that these are possible characteristics or early indicators of delay or disability. A disability may not manifest itself in the same way or at the same age for every child with that same disability. The presence of one (or some) of these early indicators does not always indicate a delay.

Table 9–1 Early Indicators of Potential Problems in Development in Young Children

Vision
- Pupil of the eye does not react to light source
- Seems inattentive to visual stimuli, unless in close proximity or only when a sound (noise) accompanies visual stimuli
- Does not gaze (or visually explore) surroundings
- Does not attend or track (visually follow) a moving object
- Eyelids are red, encrusted, watery, or swollen
- Eye has a visible abnormality (i.e., drooping eyelid)
- Appears to be excessively sensitive to light

Hearing
- Failure to exhibit a startle response (eyes blinking, rapid increase in sucking, whole body movement)
- Failure to localize (turn head or rotate eyes in the direction of a sound source)
- Failure to discriminate voices (startles/cries at the sound of a familiar adult, doesn't show preferences for familiar adult)
- Presence of ear discharge or persistent ear infections
- Pulling of ear(s)
- Delay in language development (failure to reproduce language, does not imitate sounds, words)

Motor Delays
- Structural abnormalities (presence of a physical abnormality that impacts motor development or movement)
- Motor dysfunction (abnormal reflex patterns, lack of coordination of movements for age, occurrence of repetitious motor patterns or unexplained pauses in motor movement, poor balance, poor muscle tone)
- Delays in motor development (fails to meet developmental milestones at appropriate age, such as head control, rolling over, trunk control, sitting, pull to stand, creeping, etc.)
- Motor regression (motor or muscle tone appears to be deteriorating instead of becoming more mature and sophisticated)
- Neurological dysfunction (abnormalities in sucking behavior, grasping, posture reflexes, muscle tone, delays in locomotion)

Health Issues
- Changes in behavior indicating illness (energy level, loss of appetite, excessive crankiness, presence of body rash, fever, headaches, dull eyes)
- Changes in bodily functions (diarrhea, color/odor of urine or bowel movements, unusual or excessive bleeding or poor clotting of blood with minor scratches)
- Irregularities in appearance (discoloration of skin, size is notably smaller than age mates, excessively bloated or thin, muscle weakness or poor coordination)
- Worrisome patterns of illness (constant colds, repeated bouts of diarrhea, headaches, constipation, longer recovery time when ill, extended loss of energy, labored breathing)

Cognitive Delays
- Exhibits a slow rate of learning
- Exhibits difficulty with memory (remembering)
- Is not an incidental learner (does not learn by observing others)
- Exhibits delays in expressive and receptive language development (diminished vocabulary, late in language production)
- Exhibits overly aggressive behavior
- Self-stimulatory and/or self-injurious behavior

Delays in Social or Emotional Development
- Experience sleep disturbances
- May be described as an irritable/fussy infant/toddler
- Withdrawn, noncompliant, or aggressive
- Limited attention span
- Easily distracted
- Exhibits impulsive behavior
- Does not use cries to express needs (of hunger, for comfort, attention, protest)
- Does not attend to sound source

Language Delays
- Exhibits limited nonverbal communication efforts (raise arms to be picked up, social smile to familiar people, reach, point)
- Vocalizes infrequently
- Does not coo, babble, or play with sounds
- Does not imitate sound
- Does not look at or give familiar objects when named
- Acquires language at a slow rate

Strategies for Including Young Children with Special Needs

Recently, educators have questioned the idea that students requiring intensive specialized services should receive them outside a general education setting such as a resource center or self-contained classroom (McLeskey & Waldron, 1996). Relatively few attempts have been made to provide the needed assistance within the general education classroom so that students could be educated with their nondisabled peers. A significant influence in the field of early childhood special education has been a movement toward the inclusion of students with their typically developing peers. The placement of young children with disabilities in inclusive settings is one of the most complex and controversial practices in early childhood today. Inclusion is more than the physical placement of children with disabilities in educational settings alongside typically developing children. It requires teachers to examine the child in each setting to determine if he/she is actively engaged in all aspects of their environment. (See Chapter 6 for a complete discussion of this issue.) For the purpose of this discussion, **engagement** will be defined as consistent, active involvement with the people (teachers, parents, classmates), activities (snack time, play time, group-time participation, center selection/participation), and materials (use of toys, art supplies, water-play materials) throughout the child's day. The initial part of this chapter will focus on selected strategies that will be organized into the following categories: (a) teacher-mediated strategies, (b) peer-mediated strategies, (c) routine-based strategies, and (d) naturalistic (milieu) strategies. While the discussion focuses on strategies used in center-based programs or classrooms, many of the strategies are appropriate for use with younger children who receive early intervention services in centers or at home.

Teacher-Mediated Strategies

The term **teacher-mediated** has typically been used to describe teacher-directed interventions designed to promote social interaction (McEvoy, Odom, & McConnell, 1992). We will broaden the term teacher-mediated to include many techniques that an adult (teacher or parent) can implement before or during activities that promote child engagement with people, materials, or activities. Teacher-mediated strategies include arranging the environment, promoting acceptance, providing of prompts and praise, accepting differential levels/types of participation, and monitoring communicative input.

Environmental Arrangements **Environmental arrangements** are one of the least intrusive steps that a teacher can take to promote engagement of children within their educational setting. Current guidelines are available with suggestions for the organization, structure, and operation of optimal learning environments for children with diverse abilities (Bredekamp & Copple, 1997; Bredekamp & Rosegrant, 1992; McLean & Odom, 1993). Three strategies will be discussed that fit within these guidelines: the arragement of physical space, the selection and use of materials, and the provision of structure to activities.

The typical guidelines used when arranging any learning environment need attention. These include the following: quiet areas are located away from noisy areas; the high-interest materials are accessible to children; materials are safe and stimulating; adequate space is provided for easy movement throughout the classroom; and the environment can be easily monitored by adults (McEvoy, 1990). However, research has shown that some additional environmental strategies are warranted when children with disabilities are included within the educational setting. For example, a relationship exists between the amount of space available and children's behavior. As noted earlier, too little space may result in increases in negative behavior and too much space may result in reduced interactions among children (Sainato & Carta, 1992). Even within the space, other aspects of the environment warrant attention including: limiting the amount of materials available to children, monitoring the number of adults and their behavior, and the specific considerations related to the individual child with the disability (such as use of walker or adaptive seating to maintain trunk control) (Bailey & Wolery, 1992).

Attention should be given to the selection and use of materials. Materials should be safe, multidimensional and developmentally appropriate for the children within the classroom. In addition, teachers can select toys known to promote high levels of engagement, select toys based on the child's preference, monitor the child's access to materials (Kaiser, Yoder, & Keetz, 1992), and adapt the use of toys or materials (Davis, Kilgo & Gamel-McCormick, 1998).

Some toys or materials result in more isolated play, while others appear to result in more interactive play (Odom & Strain, 1984). Toys that are more likely to result in higher social interactions are blocks, dolls, trucks and cars, social dramatic play (dress-up, cooking), and games that have multiple parts (such as Mr. Potato Head, farm or zoo animals). Materials that are more likely to result in solitary play include books, puzzles, and art activities (paints, paper and pencil drawing). Obviously, how a teacher structures the use of these more isolating materials will impact the level of interaction. For example, preschoolers can share a book, each taking turns reading, holding, and turning the pages. The selection of the materials should be driven by the goals of the teacher in the structured play setting. At times the goal may be to promote interactive play, which involves more social and communicative exchanges, while at other times it may be to promote the use of appropriate toy play behavior.

Material selection should also be determined by the level of interest and preferences of the child. Children with disabilities are more likely to engage with high-interest toys and materials. Preschoolers with disabilities are more likely to show high levels of engagement (Kaiser et al., 1992) and are less likely to engage in inappropriate behavior (Dyer, Dunlap, & Winterling, 1990) when participating in high-interest activities. Asking parents, family members, or the child is an excellent way to ensure that the activities, materials, and toys are preferred by the child.

While child choice and preference are important, a teacher or parent may want to provide some guidance to youngsters who consistently select the same activities, materials, or toys. The adult could observe the child as he makes choices of toys, materials, and activities across a specific period of time. Then, the adult could provide suggestions for play or introduce new materials with a high-preference toy as a way of expanding a child's choice to new, and per-

haps more challenging activities. This could be done by coupling the child's choice with that of the adult's. For example, every day Analise, age three, selects blocks during play. One day the teacher adds farm animals, suggesting that together they build barns, corrals, and beds for the animals. On another day, the teacher adds zoo animals to the block activity and asks Analise, "What could we do with these animals and blocks?" Peter, age two, chooses to bang toy objects (blocks, pretend food, etc.) on a daily basis and appears to be reinforced by the noise he makes while playing. The teacher could add containers (with big spoons for stirring) to the activity and suggest that they cook. Later, dolls and bears could be added to the activity for a pretend snack time. In this way, the teacher has extended his play with the materials and still provided an auditory reinforcer as the blocks (or food) are stirred. In both of these examples, the teacher has still provided the child with a choice (using the preferred materials), while expanding the activity or the way the child uses the materials.

Another environmental strategy that could enhance engagement is the provision of structure within the activity. DeKlyen and Odom (1989) found that structured activities resulted in increased social interactions between children with and without disabilities. Examples of structure include setting rules for a specific activity, identifying child roles within the activity, asking children to generate ways that they could play within an activity, identifying the theme for the play ("Let's make pizza with the playdough. What kind of pizza will you make today?"). Another way of structuring the activity is to analyze and monitor the accessibility of the materials. An infant or toddler who has easy access to every toy may have a decreased need for communicating or socializing within their environment. McGee, Daly, Izeman, Mann, and Risley (1991) found that altering the availability of some materials and toys across the day or week to be an effective strategy for promoting engagement. In essence the novelty or a toy is maintained through the periodic rotation of materials. Kaiser et al. (1992) found that restricting access to high-interest toys may result in higher levels of communicative attempts. By placing preferred materials within the child's field of vision, but out of reach, resulted in child requests for preferred toys and snacks.

Peer-mediated strategies are often effective in promoting social and communication skills in young children with disabilities.

Promoting Acceptance   Promoting acceptance is a strategy that can be viewed as creating and preparing the social environment to be more accepting of a child with a disability. It is a strategy that supports engagement with peers and one that is easily overlooked when preparing a class for young children with disabilities.

While positive attitudes toward children with disabilities (and subsequent social relationships among children with and without disabilities) is an anticipated benefit of inclusion (Guralnick, 1990), empirical evidence is inconsistent. Research shows that children form perceptions and attitudes about persons with disabilities as early as four and five years of age (Diamond, 1993; Favazza & Odom, 1996, 1997). Across studies, it is apparent that the placement of children with disabilities alongside nondisabled peers does not ensure acceptance without adult mediation (that is, actively promoting understanding and acceptance of children with disabilities). Acceptance of children with disabilities may be one of the essential elements for achieving authentic inclusion (Haring, 1991).

Guidelines are available that provide suggestions for creating accepting environments for young children (Favazza, 1998; McCracken, 1993). In addition, teachers can use specific strategies within the early childhood setting to actively promote acceptance of children with disabilities. Prior to the transition of a child with a disability into a general early childhood

classroom, teachers can prepare nondisabled children by providing information about the child with the disability (Chandler, 1992). Effective strategies for increasing understanding and promoting acceptance of children with diverse abilities include the use of cooperative activities, stories, and guided discussions that highlight similarities as opposed to differences (McPhee, Favazza, & Lewis, 1998), and structured social opportunities, or a combination of these activities (Favazza & Odom, 1997; Favazza, LaRoe, & Odom, 1999). Favazza and Odom (1997) found that kindergartners who had contact with children with disabilities expressed low levels of acceptance of children with disabilities. After a nine-week intervention, the same kindergartners who were provided with (a) stories and guided discussions about children with disabilities, and (b) opportunities for social interaction with children with disabilities, had more accepting attitudes than children who did not have these types of experiences. The authors speculate that what contributed to acceptance was the children's exposure to these components as well as the fact that the stories and guided discussions (about children with disabilities) were also provided for the parents of the nondisabled children. In this way, teachers and parents alike were involved in promoting acceptance of children with diverse abilities.

In addition to actively promoting acceptance through interventions within a center-based program, teachers (and parents) can examine the environment to determine if nondisabled children are exposed to individuals with disabilities. Using an environmental rating scale such as the Inventory of Disability Representation (IDR), Favazza and Odom (1997) found that typical kindergarten classes did not have materials (books, toys, or displays) depicting children with diverse abilities (see Table 9–2). Similar results were found when the IDR was readministered to a larger number of early childhood teachers (Favazza, Kumar, & Phillipsen, 1996).

Using inventories such as the IDR, teachers and parents can examine their environments to determine if children with disabilities are represented in toys, displays, materials, and media, and *how* they are depicted (in ways that highlight similarities? as contributing members of society? in a variety of roles?). In addition, teachers need to be discriminating when selecting materials like books about children with

Table 9–2   Inventory of Disability Representation (IDR)

Visual/Aesthetic Environment

1. Are there images of children with disabilities in your room? (Photos, pictures reflecting persons with differing abilities?) (If you answer "NO," please skip down to number 5 and continue. If you answer "YES," please continue with 2.)	YES	NO
2. Do these images reflect current daily lives in the U.S.? (Photos and pictures are up-to-date)	YES	NO
3. Do these images have an adequate balance? (Is there more than just one "token" image of a disabled person?)	YES	NO
4. Do these images show differently abled people		
a) of various ethnic backgrounds	YES	NO
b) of various ages (adults and children)	YES	NO
c) doing work	YES	NO
d) doing recreational activities	YES	NO
e) with families	YES	NO
f) in a positive way (active, independent)	YES	NO
5. When images of important individuals (past and present) are presented in your class curriculum, are differently abled people represented?	YES	NO
6. When images of persons in different occupations are presented, are differently abled people represented?	YES	NO

Books

7. Do children have access to books in your room that reflect children/adults with special needs and abilities?	YES	NO
8. Do children have access to books in your room that reflect different languages, such as the sign language alphabet, examples of Braille?	YES	NO

Dramatic Play

9. Do children have accessibility and exploration of tools used by persons with various special needs? (Such as crutches, braces, wheelchair, walker, cane, heavy glasses)	YES	NO
10. Are there any dolls (bought or homemade) with different kinds of abilities? (If you answer "NO," skip down to number 13. If you answer "YES," continue with 11.)	YES	NO
11. If yes, do they reflect both genders?	YES	NO
12. If yes, do they reflect different racial/ethnic backgrounds?	YES	NO

Language

13. Do children in your class have opportunities in current curriculum to see and hear various languages including sign language and Braille? (Opportunities might include labeling materials, alphabet and number posters, songs, finger games)	YES	NO

School Programs

14. Is there a school-wide program for your students that promotes and encourages interactions between children with and without disabilities?	YES	NO
15. Is there a component of the counseling program that provides information about children with disabilities?	YES	NO

SOURCE: P. Favazza, J. LaRoe, & S. Odom, *Special Friends.* (Boulder, CO: Roots & Wings) 1.800.833.787.

disabilities. It is important for books to be selected that promote acceptance and emphasize similarities as opposed to differences and abilities as opposed to disabilities. Research clearly indicates that placement alone will not guarantee acceptance. However, teachers and parents can actively promote acceptance and create more accepting environments utilizing some of the previously mentioned strategies.

The Provision of Prompts and Praise   Teacher-mediated or direct instruction involves the choosing of the behavior to be taught. The teacher selects a specific time to teach the behavior directly to the child. Through discussion, instructions, demonstration, modeling, and use of concrete examples the teacher provides direct instruction and practice opportunities. The teacher then follows the instruction with prompts and praise. The provision of prompts and praise is a strategy that teachers can employ to promote engagement within the inclusive preschool setting. Praise can be defined as the provision of a verbal reinforcement ("I like the way you are sharing those blocks") or a tangible reinforcer (stickers, access to desired activities, or "happy faces"). The provision of praise is an effective technique for promoting child engagement among children who have special needs. **Prompts** are defined as anything given to assist or help a young child to make a desired response (Wolery, Bailey, & Sugai, 1988). There are a variety of types of prompts that can be identified by the type of assistance they provide. Common prompts include direct and indirect verbal prompts, model prompts, partial or full physical prompts, spatial prompts, pictorial prompts, and cued prompts (Noonan & McCormick, 1993; Wolery, 1994b).

- *Direct verbal prompts* are simple statements that provide support for a child in his or her current task. For example, when a child is trying unsuccessfully to turn on the faucet, a teacher (parent or peer) could say, "Try turning it the other way." This simple statement may be enough for the child to be successful as he/she attempts to turn on the faucet.
- *Model prompts* actually supply the child with the desired behavior. The model prompt can be verbal or gestural or a combination of the two. For example, a teacher may velcro the child's shoe

while saying, "I'll do this one, and you do the next one." In this way, the child is supported in the dressing activity by a modeled verbal and gestural prompt.

- *Physical prompts* can provide partial or physical support. Guiding a child's elbow as they lift their spoon, cup, or lunch tray is an example of a partial physical prompt. A full physical prompt for the same behavior might involve hand-over-hand assistance with the teacher holding the child's hands as he/she is grasping the object (spoon, cup, or tray).
- *Spatial prompts* involve placing an object in a location that will more than likely increase a desired response. For example, placing paper towels (for wiping paint off of hands) near the sink or clips on the clothesline where children will go to hang their completed art work are examples of spatial prompts.
- *Visual/Pictorial prompts* involve providing assistance through the use of pictures (drawings, photographs, Rebus cue cards), colors, or graphics. Using different colors for different children or placing a red mark or the letter "C" on Cathy's cup are examples of visual prompts. Placing photographs depicting the steps to handwashing above the sink is a pictorial prompt.
- *Cued prompts* can be verbal and/or gestural and involve drawing direct attention to a specific aspect or dimension of a stimulus or task. An example of a cue is "Pick up your paint brush (spoon)" or "It's time to paint (eat)" while pointing to the handle of the brush (spoon). Cued prompts are used to focus on the most relevant characteristic or dimension of the stimuli.

There are several important points to remember when using praise and/or prompts (Wolery, Ault, & Doyle, 1992). These include the following:

1. Teachers should carefully plan for the provision of praise/prompts. They should not be applied haphazardly or when they are not necessary to support the child's behavior. Providing unnecessary prompts could result in a child becoming overly dependent on the adult and decrease

his/her own level of independence (Odom & Strain, 1986). When possible, prompts and/or praise should be faded or removed to promote independence in the child's behavior and to lessen his/her dependence on the adult.

2. Teachers should be certain that they have the child's attention when presenting a prompt/praise. The impact or effectiveness of a prompt or praise may be lost unless the child is paying attention.

3. Prompts should be selected and praise should be provided that are the least intrusive while at the same time are the most effective with that individual child. For example, a cued prompt (touching the paintbrush) or physical assistance (moving their hand to the brush) with a young child with a visual impairment may be less effective and more intrusive than a verbal prompt of "We are going to paint. Everyone, find a paintbrush. Wow! Now we are ready to paint." Not only is the prompt (and subsequent praise) likely to be successful in assisting the child, it does not single him/her out from the rest of the group at the art table, and a spatial prompt (the paintbrush) has been provided for everyone.

4. The prompts/praise can be changed or faded as the situation warrants. Ideally, a child should perform a task with fewer and fewer prompts and less praise applied. This implies that the teacher should keep a careful watch as to the effectiveness and necessity of prompts and praise to sustain the child's behavior. If a particular strategy is not effective or is not producing the desired results, teachers should shift to another prompt/praise strategy.

5. Teachers should always consult with the related service personnel (speech-language pathologist occupational therapist, physical therapist) before applying prompts or changing prompts that they have recommended. Changes in child prompts could be harmful to a child or counterproductive to the objectives that the various therapists have recommended. In addition, it is important to have the same expectation for the use of prompts/praise across all caregivers (teacher, assistants, parents).

Accepting Different Levels and Types of Participation This teacher-mediated strategy allows a child with diverse abilities to become more engaged in a group activity (Noonan & McCormick, 1993; Wolery, 1994c). The approach requires the teacher to make adjustments in his expectations about levels or ways a child participates in group activities. When a child is unable to participate at the same level as his peers in a group activity, the expectations for participation can be adjusted. When a child uses only a portion of the response, it is referred to as **partial participation.** Examples of partial participation include the following: In a game of Simon Says, the leader says, "Touch your toes." The child extends his hands downward, but does not touch toes. In another situation, the teacher accepts a single word response as opposed to a whole or partial sentence response in a group discussion. For example, during sharing time a teacher may have two children come to the front of the group. The teacher prompts the first child to ask the other child questions about an object brought for sharing time. The prompted questions could be, "What do you have?" "What do you do with it?" and "Where did you get it?" The questions for the second child could be shortened to his/her accepted level of participation with verbalizations like, "What have?" or "Have?" "What do?" or "Do?" and "Where get?" or "Get." **Adapted participation** is when a child may also use an alternative means to participate. Examples would be a youngster who orients his head or eye gaze instead of pointing or verbalizing, a child with speech delays who uses a communication board, or a child with a visual impairment who uses a sensory ball (that emits an auditory signal) when at play. These are all examples of adapted participation that enable a child with a disability to fully participate in group activities.

Monitoring Communicative Input This is another strategy that enables children with diverse abilities to participate in group activities. The adjustment of the timing and complexity of a teacher's communication can impact a child's ability to interact within group activities. Examples include the use of simple vocabulary and shorter sentence length, a variation in intonation and rate of speech, contingent

3t   *Teacher Technology Tips*

Principles for Integrating Technology in the Classroom

1. Start with the curriculum, not the technology. Let the individual needs of the student and the curriculum designed drive the selection of the technologies and the ways that they are used.

2. Use the motivational value of technology, but don't limit its use to that of a reward or leisure time technology. Technology has much value as a teaching tool and its use should not be ignored in instruction.

3. Use technology to reinforce skills taught by the teacher. Technology can present guided practice activities, monitor student responses, and provide student with immediate feedback.

4. Select technology activities that match the goals of instruction and the level of the individual student. Teaching an irrelevant skill is a waste of time no matter how dazzling the technology or superb the instruction.

5. Customize the technology. Features such as the ability to control the content and instructional parameter make it easy to adapt activities to the students' needs.

6. Monitor student work at the computer or with other technologies as is used to monitor other types of classroom work. Use performance data collected by the technology in making instructional decisions

7. Use technology to present new information to students. While technology is not the only available instructional strategy, it does provide the teacher with an additional resource for introducing new material.

8. Enrich and extend the curriculum through technology. Technology opens doors to experiences that students can't access in other ways. These experiences expand the use of a standard curriculum.

9. Teach students to use technology as a tool. Provide opportunities and encouragement for practice. Technology can help students compensate for disabilities and allow for achievement of greater levels of independence.

10. Extend the benefits of technology to teachers. Technology is an important tool for teachers as well as students.

Source: Lewis, R. B. (1993) *Special education technology: Classroom applications* (Pacific Grove, CA: Brooks/Cole Publishing Company). pp. 102–103.

---

responses, and scaffolding. For example, while young children learn word meanings of objects, people, and actions that are in their immediate surrounding, they can typically understand and attend to input that is slightly above their level of comprehension. Videotaping a group activity is an excellent strategy for examining the level of communication used when speaking to children. Is it understandable by all children? Does the teacher need to alter his communicative input (simplify the vocabulary or shorten the length of sentences in directives)? In this way, the adult matches the receptive and cognitive levels of the child and thus enhances the possibility of every child's participation in group activities. Likewise,

videotaping a parent playing with his/her child is another way to use this strategy with younger children and provide consistency in communicative input across caregivers.

Exaggerated intonation is another strategy that increases attention to speech and to the speaker (Fernald, 1985). Similarly, providing verbal input to a child at a slower rate may allow for more processing time and provide more precise cues for relating language to actual events. For example, when giving directions to a child, a pause while the child is moving through steps enables the child to process each individual step along the way. In a handwashing activity, a teacher could say, "Go to the sink." (Pause as the child moves toward sink.) "Turn on the water." (Pause while the child reaches the sink and turns on the water.) "Wash your hands." (Pause while the child washes her hands.) This strategy could be coupled with task analysis when addressing self-care skill with younger children.

Peer-Mediated Strategies

Peer-mediated strategies enlist the use of classmates to promote (or mediate) learning and engagement of other children (McEvoy et al., 1992). Davis et al. (1998) define peer-mediated strategies or interventions as the teaching of a peer to interact with a particular child and to provide reinforcement to that child for targeted behaviors. Peer-mediated strategies have been effective in promoting social and communication skills in young children with disabilities (Goldstein & Gallagher, 1992). Peer-mediated strategies typically involve carefully selecting classmates (who are nondisabled), teaching selected classmates specific ways to engage their peers with disabilities, encouraging the classmates to persist in their attempts with children with disabilities, providing structured opportunities for the children to interact with one another (so as to use the skills taught), and providing support (reinforcement and prompts by teachers) during the structured opportunities (Wolery, 1994b). Two types of strategies that utilize peers to mediate learning will be discussed: (a) peer-initiation interventions, and (b) cooperative learning.

Peer-Initiation Interventions These interventions are among the most effective peer-mediated strategies used for increasing social behaviors such as initiating, responding, and sharing (Gillies & Ashman, 2000). A teacher selects typically developing classmates who are known to be highly social, attend school regularly, have little or no history of negative interactions, have adequate attention spans and the comprehension to participate in the training sessions, and have the willingness to participate in the special play groups. The teacher instructs the selected peers about ways to interact with children with disabilities, such as how to initiate an exchange

("Ask for a toy," or "Ask Sam to play with you.") or suggest a play theme ("Let's play grocery store. You be the clerk."). After practicing the strategies with the teacher and other typically developing peers, the children are then given brief structured play opportunities (10–15 minutes in length) for using the strategies with peers with disabilities. When creating structured play sessions, the teacher carefully arranges the environment to promote interactions (see section in this chapter on environmental arrangements). For example, during an art activity the teacher provides the supplies and suggests that the children make a picture to hang in the classroom. The teacher then prompts the peers to model cooperative behaviors such as sharing ("Please give T. J. a paint brush."); requesting materials ("Maria, say please give me the blue paint."); complimenting other children ("That's a colorful rainbow."); and making suggestions to the group ("You can add clouds to the sky, Sam"). During the structured play sessions, the teacher remains close by, providing prompts and reinforcement as needed. Instructional resources are available that provide guidelines for promoting social and communication skills such as sharing, initiating, responding, learning alternative ways to initiate, and utilizing persistence in social attempts (McConnell & Odom, 1993). Brown, McEvoy, and Bishop (1991) identify the following suggestions for teachers when planning naturalistic interventions with typically developing peers and children with disabilities. They suggest:

1. Pair a child with a disability with a more skilled partner.

2. Using small, well-defined play areas for activities like building, dramatic play, and computer use.

3. Introduce and facilitate play activity.

4. Model social skills, such as obtaining another's child's attention, responding to another child, requesting desired items, and negotiating during play.

5. Prompting and praising of social interactions. (pp. 37–38)

However, teachers are encouraged to adapt strategies according to the individual needs of the children in their particular class. For example, nondisabled children may need to be taught alternative means of communication (the use of a communication board), gestural methods of initiating (tapping a peer who has a hearing impairment, or waiting until the peer is looking before speaking).

Cooperative Learning   This is another strategy that can utilize peers to mediate learning and child engagement. Cooperative learning can be defined as an intervention strategy in which small groups of learners are actively involved in jointly accomplishing an activity (Gargiulo, 2003). The goals of cooperative learning are to foster cooperative interaction, to teach cooperative learning skills, and to promote positive self-esteem. Research has demonstrated the effectiveness of cooperative learning in promoting positive interactions and social interactions between children with and without disabilities (Jordan & Le Metais, 1997; Shachar & Sharan, 1994). For example, Gackowski, Kobe, and McCormick (1991) used cooperative learning as a strategy for promoting social and communication skills of preschoolers with disabilities in a typical preschool setting. Two preschool children with disabilities demonstrated gains in social and communication behaviors (taking turns, asking/offering assistance). In addition, increased rates of initiations were generalized to other activities during the school day.

According to Johnson and Johnson (1992) and Gackowski et al. (1991), cooperative learning uses the social dynamics of the group to support social interactions and friendships, teaches children to encourage one another, and celebrates the success of peers. The four essential elements of cooperative learning include: positive interdependence, communication (or face-to-face interactions), accountability of all members, and group process (with emphasis on interpersonal skills).

Positive interdependence is promoted. Because members of small groups work together to achieve a common goal, interdependence on one another is required.

Communication is required. To achieve the common goal as materials and resources are strategically distributed to encourage interactions, communication among the group members is necessary.

Accountability is expected. Every member of the group is held accountable (is responsible) for contributing to the final product. Within the activity, each child with a disability could have his/her individual objectives embedded into the activity. While students may be working on a common project, the objectives may vary according to the needs of the individual child.

Group process is expected. As two or three children work together, they are expected to follow basic formats such as taking turns, listening, initiating, and responding. Based on the work of Johnson and Johnson (1992) and Gackowski et al. (1991), specific strategies can be implemented with young children to address each of these elements (see Table 9–3).

In addition to these strategies, Noonan and McCormick (1993) provide several suggestions for adapting cooperative learning for use with young children.

- A unit with clear objectives should be selected, listing the cooperative skills to be taught.
- A series of lessons or activities can be planned in which the skills will be taught.
- Children can be assigned to dyads or three-member groups that remain intact for the duration of all lessons/activities within the unit. (One child with a disability should be within the dyad.)
- Cooperation should be encouraged by the way materials are distributed (see Table 9–3).

Young children with disabilities need learning environments that are accepting of all children.

Table 9–3 Cooperative Learning

Elements of Cooperative Learning	Specific Strategies
Positive Interdependence	• Divide the tasks, materials, roles to match abilities with tasks within activity • Carefully pair children so that one or two children can assist, model; guide • Create tasks whereby the child with the disability is "leader" among dyads or group • Create joint rewards (reinforcing to all)
Communication	• Intentionally distribute materials/resources so children must ask peers for items • Intentionally limit equipment (i.e., scissors) to promote sharing • Seat children far enough apart so that requests are necessary to reach items • Provide prompts if needed ("Ask Eva to help you." "Tell Ann what you need.")
Accountability	• Ask each child to name their contribution • Ask children to name what another child did well. (Serves to promote recall, acknowledges the contributions of all, promotes "team" mentality, self-esteem)
Group Process	• Using communication strategies listed above, this is an ideal format to promote sharing, turn-taking, listening, seeking assistance, and offering assistance.

• Activities should be with specific explanations and demonstrations of what it means to be cooperative ("Sit next to your partner." "Take turns with the glue.").

• Children should be assisted and monitored carefully, providing prompts and praise as warranted.

• Child should be evaluated and provided with feedback ("Did you like working together?" "What was the hardest or easiest part?" "How does it feel when you help a friend?" "Who helped you?").

Cooperative learning may be better suited for older preschoolers or primary age children and the teacher may need to be more involved the first few times that it is used to ensure that children understand the nature and process of the activity. Clearly, more research is needed in this area to determine how cooperative learning in early childhood settings could better utilize peers as models, guides, and partners in learning.

Routine-Based Strategies

Routine-based strategies take advantage of already occurring events such as play (Linder, 1993; Spodek & Saracho, 1994), predictable routine activities (such as snack time, diapering, circle time) (Bricker & Cripe, 1992), and transitions (Werts, Wolery, Holcombe, Vassilaros, & Billings, 1992). Many routine-based strategies are appropriate for use with infants as well as toddlers, preschoolers, and early primary students.

For routine-based strategies to be successful, teachers and parents need to understand that daily activities that have a specific purpose (snack time is for eating) can also serve as an instructional time. For example, snack time could also be a time for promoting fine motor skills such as reaching or using the neat pincer grasp to eat raisins, Cheerios, cheese cubes, as well as gross motor skills such as trunk control. The same activity could be used to promote communicative attempts such as requesting (verbally or gesturally) "more," making a choice when asked, "Do you want an apple or an orange," and responding by pointing, signing, or saying "Apple." Therefore, before starting routine-based instruction it would be important that all involved with the child (teachers, assistants, parents) are able to recognize the variety of skills that can be promoted within the same routine activity.

Play-Based Intervention (Strategies) Play is a logical and natural activity for incorporating skills of children with disabilities. Play provides an avenue for children to master their thoughts and actions, and contributes to the child's cognitive, physical, and social/emotional development (Fein & Schwartz, 1986). Through play children have opportunities for learning through exploration, self-expression, imitation and imagination, interpretation of situations, negotiation of relationships, and utilization of social and communicative behaviors such as turn-taking, sharing, initiating, and responding. (For an extensive discussion of the role of play see Spodek & Saracho 1988, 1994).

Linder (1993) has developed **play-based interventions (strategies)** for incorporating and promoting skill acquisition in the play arena. This approach utilizes a transdisciplinary model (see Chapter 6) whereby all service providers (teachers, assistant teachers, occupational therapist, speech-language pathologist, physical therapist) and parents observe and assess the child during play. Each service provider supplies information about the child related to his/her discipline area while watching the child at play with peers or an adult. The goals for the child are developed based on this transdisciplinary-based assessment and incorporated into the child's play times while at school. Using this approach, related service personnel provide support and consultation

to teachers for promoting and supporting child goals in regularly occurring play times. The transdisciplinary approach is characterized by sharing of expertise through frequent, ongoing communication with all caregivers and training these caregivers to implement interventions. For example, if a toddler exhibits delays in fine motor skills, the occupational therapist would provide information and training to the parents and teachers on how to address these skill deficits during play activities at home and at the center the child attends.

Dolinar, Boser, and Holm (1994) provide an excellent resource for teachers to integrate concepts and instructional goals of children with diverse abilities into play. For example, using wet and dry sand, fine motor skills (digging, shaking, grasping), as well as cognitive and communicative skills (vocabulary, concepts such as wet, dry, under, fast, slow, size, texture), are incorporated into sand play (see Figure 9–1). A teacher could examine typical play activities in the preschool setting (playdough, water play, dress-up, or transportation toys) and generate a variety of skills that can be addressed within the play setting (Bricker & Cripe, 1992). Likewise, the teacher can assist the parent in examining play materials at home and together they can generate ideas for promoting skill acquisition.

When setting up activities, it is important to provide a range of difficulty in order to support active engagement. This strategy enables everyone to be successful by participating at his/her own level with a variety of materials. For example, providing some puzzles with pegs for easy grasp, others without knobs, some with two to three pieces, and others with seven to eight pieces allows many options for children with varying levels of fine motor abilities. During art, a variety of drawing implements (brushes with adaptive grips or of different sizes) can be provided, or within the social-dramatic play area, clothing of different sizes with a variety of fastening devices (snaps, buttons, zippers) and shoes that slip on, buckle, have velcro straps, and shoe strings can be provided. In this way, teachers can structure an activity so as to address the diverse abilities of children that will ultimately challenge and provide success for all.

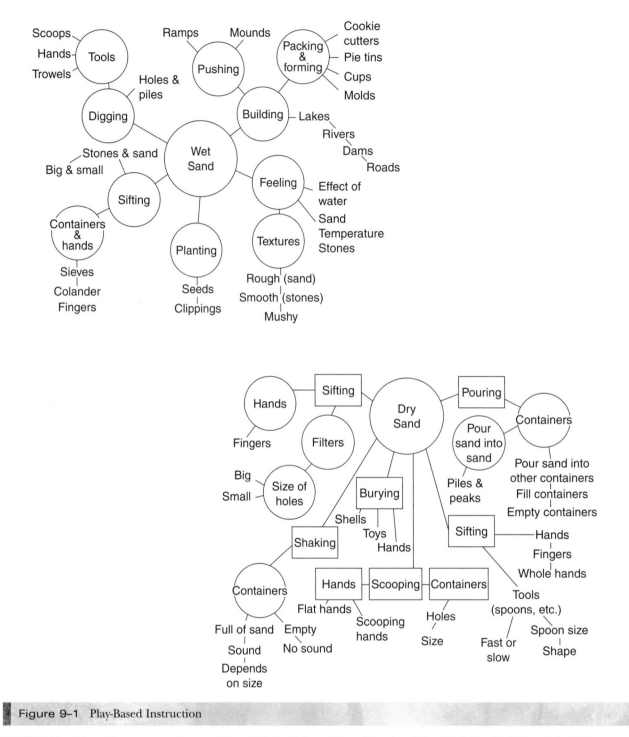

Figure 9–1   Play-Based Instruction

	Sabrina			Jana			
	Draws circles/lines	Uses 50 words	Two-step direction	Initiates interaction with peers	Gets into sitting position	Responds to communication from peers	Retrieves common objects
9:00 Arrival: Free play	X	X	X	X		X	
9:20 Opening circle		X	X	X	X	X	X
9:30 Planned activity	X	X	X	X	X	X	X
10:10 Outside play		X	X	X	X	X	X
10:30 Clean-up		X	X		X	X	X
10:45 Snack		X	X	X	X	X	X
11:00 Storytime— Book center		X	X	X	X	X	X
11:25 Centers	X	X	X	X	X	X	X
11:50 Closing circle		X	X	X	X	X	
12:00 Departure							X

Figure 9–2   Activity-Based Instruction

SOURCE: D. Bricker, K. Pretti-Frontczak, & N. McCornas, *An Activity-Based Approach to Early Intervention,* (2nd Edition) Baltimore: Paul H. Brookes, 1998. p. 112–113.

Activity-Based Instruction   Bricker and Cripe (1992) define **activity-based instruction** or intervention as "a child directed, transactional approach that embeds intervention of children's goals and objectives in routine, planned, or child initiated activities, and uses logical antecedents and consequences to develop functional and generative skills" (p. 40). While it was designed to be used with children with disabilities, it can easily be adapted for use with all students in an inclusive setting. Activity-based instruction utilizes the youngster's interest while addressing goals and objectives in routine, planned, or child-initiated activities. Activity-based instruction takes advantage of naturally occurring antecedents and consequences to develop skills that are functional and generalizable across people and settings. Two features of this approach are effective when working with young children. First, multiple goals from a variety of the developmental domains can be addressed in one activity. Additionally, the approach provides reinforcement for children for participating in planned activities that are motivating to them. It requires careful planning of the schedule

to ensure that activities will occur throughout the child's day in which the child's goals can be addressed. Bricker and Cripe (1992) demonstrate how the schedule from a typical preschool classroom can provide multiple opportunities to address a child's targeted goals (see Figure 9–2).

This is an excellent strategy for infants and toddlers whose objectives can be embedded into daily routine activities at home and at center-based programs. In this way, the likelihood of generalization of skills is increased as instruction occurs across settings within activities where the behavior naturally occurs. For example, a parent can address grasping and cross-midline reaching with an infant or toddler with cerebral palsy by careful placement of a cup of favorite juice during snack or a favorite tub toy during bath time. There are many aspects of activity-based instruction that make it appealing to programs that strive to be developmentally appropriate. It capitalizes on goals that are individually appropriate, it utilizes naturally occurring events and reinforcers (as opposed to applying artificial activities or reinforcement), it

3t Teacher Technology Tips

Technology Tips for Infants, Toddlers, and Preschoolers

Assistive technology devices can be used to increase, maintain or improve the abilities of all young children with disabilities. Using assistive technology to improve play abilities in young children is the goal of many early intervention and preschool programs. Some examples are listed below.

Adapted commercial toys	• Highlighters—outlines or emphasizers that help in focusing a child's attention • Attachers—links, shoelaces, elastic, ribbon that bring the toy to within the child's reach and allow retrieval • Extenders—foam or molded plastic that may help children press small buttons or keys • Stabilizers—Velcro or non-slip materials that will hold a toy in place or connect a communication device to a crib • Confinement materials—planter bases, hula hoops, box tops that keep toys from getting out of the child's field of vision
Positioning items	• Sling Seats, Boppys®, E-Z Lyers, wedges, floor tables, corner seats, Sassy Seats and Exersaucers all support children so that their hands are free to interact with toys more readily
Mobility items	• Walkers such as toy shopping carts or activity centers with wheels that a child can stand and push to allow them to explore the environment • Low rocking and riding toys
Switches, adapted battery operated toys, and interfaces	• Switches that allow for on and off function, battery adapters, timers, latch devices, and series adapters
Computer hardware and software	• Single switch connection reduces control to a single key • Use of a touch window where the child presses any place on the screen to operate the computer
Communication items	• Devices that use recorded messages to incorporate language into play or provide a way to use a voice to communicate, such as One-Step, Say It/Play It or Cheaptalk

Source: Lane, S. & Mistrett, S. (2002). Let's play! Assistive technology interventions for play. *Young Exceptional Children, 5,* 24–27.

capitalizes on child-initiated transactions, and can be used by teachers and parents alike in addressing child goals.

Changing the Content of an Existing Activity
Changing the content of an existing activity is another strategy for embedding child goals into routine activities. For example, appropriate expression of, and response to, affectionate behavior may be a goal for a young child with autism who has difficulty demonstrating and receiving affection (hugs, pats on back, or handshakes). Research suggests that the modification of well-known games/songs is effective in promoting affection activities because children are paired with peers in pleasurable, non-threatening activities, and there appears to be a desensitization to peer interaction during the activity (Danko & Buyesse, 2002). Brown et al. (1988) used typical group games

and songs such as "The Farmer in the Dell" and "Simon Says" to incorporate affection activities (pat on the back, hug, handshake, high fives), and songs such as "When You're Happy and You Know It" that incorporated such phrases as "shake a friend's hand, give a friend a hug, pat your friend on the back." As a result of this change in the routine song, children interacted more with one another within the group activity and during the play time the following day. At bath time, one dad chose to sing to his toddler, "This is the way we wash our tummy, wash our tummy, wash our tummy (foot, hand, etc.) . . . early in the morning." The child's goal was to increase language. The dad was providing names of body parts and naming the behavior (washing) within an enjoyable routine activity.

Transition-Based Instruction Transition-based instruction is another example of using daily routine as an opportunity for learning. In using this strategy, the adult presents an opportunity for participating within the group while children are transitioning to other activities (Werts et al., 1992). Examples of regularly occurring transitions might include going from free play to the snack table, lining up for outdoor play, or arrival and departure times. During this transition time, the teacher obtains the attention of the children and asks them to respond to questions ("What is this?" or "I spy something yellow, what could it be?") that match their level of functioning. It is an activity that is effective in teaching preacademic skills such as letter names, shapes, and colors, while utilizing the frequently occurring transitions in the child's daily routine. Some children may respond by saying the word, others may respond with a word approximation, and others may use an initial letter sound. Likewise, singing songs during transition times is a strategy that allows for group responding at a variety of levels. In addition, transitions provide an excellent vehicle for using fine motor skills (such as clean-up activities) or gross motor skills (mobility or ambulation).

There are several advantages to using routine activities/games/songs to incorporate skills. It does not require using new materials or a change in the existing structure or routine of the day (at school or home). It does not require changes in personnel,

except informing all personnel of how multiple skills can be incorporated in already occurring routines. The child with a disability can receive the attention needed without singling him or her out from the rest of the group. In addition, it may increase the likelihood of the generalization of skills when the instruction occurs in the place and time when the desired behavior typically occurs. However, to be effective, routine-based instruction does require preplanning, ongoing monitoring for changes that are needed, and coordination with all personnel involved with the child. It is an ideal way to incorporate skills that related service personnel (occupational therapist, physical therapist, speech/language pathologist, etc.) typically address when they take children out of the classroom for therapy. Through the use of routine-based instruction, related service personnel can consult with the teacher and parents, identifying times when child goals can logically be supported and promoted in daily routine activities.

Specific Naturalistic (Milieu) Strategies

Milieu strategies are ideal in early childhood settings in that they reflect developmentally appropriate practice (Bredekamp & Copple, 1997) by using procedures that are child-directed and teacher-guided. Milieu strategies are used to facilitate language skills (especially social interaction context) that take advantage of the natural environment (people, materials, activities) to support learning. Variations of these naturalistic strategies include the use of incidental teaching, models and expansions, the mand-model procedure, time delay, and interrupted routines.

Incidental Teaching Incidental teaching is a naturalistic strategy that has been effective in promoting communication skills in young children with diverse abilities (Kaiser et al., 1992). Incidental teaching is the use of naturally arising situations to teach skills. It is *always* child-initiated. The adult takes advantage of child initiations to promote communicative attempts and model more sophisticated language. In addition to providing models, the teacher can incorporate expansions, mands, and time delays within incidental teaching. The steps for using incidental teaching include:

1. Identifying the communication goals of the child and activities or opportune times for addressing these goals.

2. Arranging the environment to increase the likelihood of initiations from the child. This could involve placing high-interest materials/toys within view, but out of reach, intentionally selecting materials in which the child will need assistance (such as opening the playdough can), selecting materials that are new or novel to the child, or intentionally providing materials that have some pieces/parts missing.

3. Being within close proximity of child, watching and waiting for their initiation.

4. When the child initiates, following the steps below:
   a. Focusing on precisely what it is the child is requesting.
   b. Asking for more elaborate language by saying, "Use your words," "What about the ball (swing, playdough, cup, etc.)," "What do you need?"
   c. Waiting expectantly for a more sophisticated response from the child. ("Want ball," "Yellow ball," "Push swing," "Top off")
   d. If the child provides more language; praising her, expanding her statement, and providing the desired object or action. ("You want the yellow ball." "Push swing please." "You want the top off.")
   e. If the child does not respond adequately, providing a model coupled with an expectant look and waiting again for her to respond. Once the child imitates the model, providing what is needed (that is, assistance or the desired object).

The Model and Expansion The model and expansion technique involves (a) providing a verbal or gestural model for the child, and (b) providing an expansion (new information). For example, after showing the child the desired object (ball, cup of juice), the adult would say, "Ball" or "Say ball." The adult would then pause expectantly looking at the child. Once the child gives the desired response, the adult (a) provides the desired object or action, and (b) provides an expansion of what the child said ("O.K., you want the *blue* ball.").

The Mand-Model The mand-model technique involves presenting the child or children with a direction, command, or question that requires a verbal or gestural response from the child. The mand model is a directive and therefore more intrusive technique that can successfully be used in conjunction with and to augment child-initiated activities. For example, when the child finishes the juice and obviously wants more (begins looking around for juice or looks inside cup), the adult would say "Tell (or show) me what you want." The directive is always related to *exactly* what/where the child's attention is focused at the time. If the child responds, the child is given what he or she wants and is provided with a verbal confirmation and expansion. For example, using the previous example, if the child responds by saying "Juice," the adult could say "Oh, you want the *orange* juice," "Oh, you want *more* juice," or "You want the *delicious* juice." In this way, the adult has confirmed his/her response, provided the desired object, and provided an expansion of their response with an additional word or descriptor. If the child does not respond (or does not respond correctly), a model should be provided for the child followed by the desired object or action. The adult would say, "Say swing," then push her in the swing.

Time Delay The time-delay procedure systematically employs a brief waiting period to teach the child to initiate an interaction. Time delay is particularly effective in teaching language and response behavior to preschool children and older children with moderate and severe disabilities (Sandell, McLean & Smith, 2000). For example, a child may be presented with high-preference objects, within view, but out of reach at the snack table. Once the child shows an interest in an object (juice, food, spoon), the adult waits briefly for the child to emit a desired behavior (look expectantly at the adult, say "more," say "juice," orient eye gaze, reach, etc.). The desired behavior or range of desired behaviors is predetermined based on the child's individual goals. According to Schwartz, Anderson, and Halle (1989) some steps in a time delay approach include the following:

1. The adult should face the child with an expectant look while having desired object within his or her field of vision (favorite toy, snack items, paints or water play pieces).

2. The adult should wait a brief period of time (5 seconds, 10 seconds) for the child to initiate a request. The adult should remain silent while maintaining eye contact.

3. If the child responds, the adult provides the desired object.

4. If the child does not respond, the adult provides a verbal prompt ("Show me what you want."), or a physical prompt (hand-over-hand assistance in reaching toward the desired object), and reinforces the response by providing the desired object.

For an example of the use of time-delay approach that is embedded within daily instruction, see Feature 9–1.

Interrupted Routine   Interrupting a routine activity is another strategy that can be used to promote child engagement and for teaching communication, social, cognitive, motor, and self-care skills (Bricker & Cripe, 1993). Daily routines include caregiving routines (diaper changing, snack time, dressing and undressing), social routines (greeting and departure times, waking up from naptime), and activity routines (specific steps or actions that typically occur with a song or game).

There are three ways of applying interrupted routines: the provision of incomplete set of materials, withholding or delaying the provision of expected or high-interest items or events, and making "silly" mistakes. Many routines or activities require a set of materials such as clothing when dressing; food, drink, plates and cups when at snack; paints, brushes, and paper during art. The adult simply sets up the materials for the activity or routine, but does not provide all the needed materials in order to prompt an initiation by the child. The adult waits until the child says something about the missing item(s). For this procedure to be effective, the routine should be reinforcing and it must require a known set of materials.

Withholding or delaying an expected action, event, or object is another way of applying interrupted routines. For example, during the finger play "Eensy weensy Spider," the adult "forgets" to do the next action in the sequence of hand motions. Or during snack time, the adult passes out the napkins and juice cups (but withholds the crackers) and tells them "Eat your crackers." The omitted action or object will likely result in a protest response from the child or children. Purposefully withholding the object from one student could also prompt other children to tell the child, "Tell Miss Micki that you did not get crackers."

Making "silly mistakes" involves violating the function of an object or what children know to be the correct action or word. Examples of "silly mistakes" while dressing include putting shoes on hands or hats on feet. Or, the dad who routinely sang as he bathed his toddler, changed some of the words once the routine and words were familiar to the child. He would sing, "This is the way we wash our hands," while he was washing the tummy. As he made the silly mistake, he looked at the toddler with an expectant gaze (raised eyebrows, mouth and eyes wide open) waiting for the toddler's protest, "Tummy, Daddy! Tummy!" Another example with older children would be to give the wrong response in a counting or color identification activity. These types of exchanges can increase child engagement and communication, but require that the children know the correct or expected behavior. When considering routines in which to use the interrupted routine strategy, the following characteristics need attention: (a) the routine should be established whereby the child can anticipate the steps in the routine, (b) the routine should involve a variety of high-interest objects, (c) the whole routine should be completed quickly to increase the potential for multiple interactions, and (d) the routine should be functional to increase the probability of generalization. See Figure 9–3 for application of these naturalistic and routine strategies.

Feature 9-1   Plan to Embed and Distribute Time Delay for Maria's Goals

Steps for Using Time Delay	Using Words to Request	Using Words for Actions	Increase Muscle Strength and Fine Motor Skills
Step 1: Identify the skills to be taught.	Naming food and drink items. Using "Want ____" or "____, please" forms. Naming toys when given the choice between two.	Naming actions she is performing (e.g., stacking, pushing, drinking, building cooking, sliding, and eating).	Using utensils, (e.g., spoon, fork, toothbrush) and writing tools (e.g. crayons, markers).
Step 2: Identify the activities and routines for teaching.	Snack, lunch, and when given a choice of toys during free play.	Free play and during play on the playground.	Breakfast, lunch or snack time and during art or writing activities.
Step 3: Decide how many and how often trials will be used.	Every time she makes a nonverbal request.	10 times per day. At least 2 minutes between trials and no more than 10 minutes.	About 4 times per day; every time she engages in art or writing activities at centers or free choice centers.
Step 4: Select an intervals time-delay procedure.	Constant time delay-response intervals are all the same.	Progressive time delay-response time gradually increases over trials or days.	Constant time delay-response are all the same.
Step 5: Identify a task table; cue and controlling prompt.	Her nonverbal request (sign or gesture) and any choice she is given; the prompt is the verbal model.	Prompt is the verbal model, "Maria, what are you doing?"	Hand-over-hand at the center or prompt is physical guide.
Step 6: Select a reinforcer.	Receives the item she requested.	Continuing to play; praise for approximation or word Maria used.	Item and activity she enjoys and adult praise.
Step 7: Determine the number of 0-second trials to use.	4 days of 0-second trials.	4 days of 0-second trials.	4 days of 0-second trials.
Step 8: Determine the length of the response interval.	10 seconds.	Increase by 1 second increments every 2 days; stop at 10 seconds.	10 seconds.
Step 9: Select and use a monitoring system.	Count the number of requests, number of verbal requests using a prompt, number of nonverbal requests.	Count the number of questions, number of action words using a prompt, and number of no responses.	Count the number of steps before the prompt and number of steps wrong before the prompt.
Step 10: Implement the plan and monitor use and effects.	Record how many requests occur and if the steps of time delay were completed correctly.	Record how many questions were asked and if the steps of time delay were completed correctly.	Keep track of the number of opportunities of using utensils and art/writing tools in which she was taught and if the steps of time delay were completed correctly.

Source: Adapted from Wolery, M. (2001). Embedding time delay procedures in classroom activities. In M. Ostrosky & S. Sandall (Eds.), *Teaching strategies: What to do to support young children's development* (Longmont, CO: Sopris West). pp. 81–90.

Based on the information presented in the vignette on Maria (see page 54) and the information on young children with cognitive delays, there are a variety of strategies that could be used to address the unique needs of Maria in the *home setting*.

For example, Maria has the following goals: (a) to verbally request items that she wants, (b) using words for actions she is doing (pushing, running, cooking, drawing), (c) to increase muscle strength and fine motor skills, especially her ability to use utensils (e.g., spoon, toothbrush) and writing tools (e.g., crayons). Based on these goals, Maria's daily schedule could be examined to determine opportunities for addressing these skills in her routine activities. Specifically, during breakfast, lunch, or dinner, Maria could use eating utensils and during an art activity she could use a paintbrush, markers, and crayons. (In a discussion with the family, they noted that one of her favorite activities is art.) Both of these activities could serve to strengthen her fine motor skills. Also, during each of these activities, materials could be withheld to encourage Maria to request the items she wants and needs. For example, she could be given the art paper without the paint or paintbrushes. The teacher could request Maria to name the action she is doing during the art activity. If Maria needs a model, the teacher could say, "You are drawing, Maria." or "You are painting with the paintbrush." During mealtime, she could be given her cup without the juice. In this way, she would be provided with multiple opportunities to use the skills she is developing in a naturalistic setting (e.g., home) within routine activities.

Figure 9–3 Strategies for Using Classroom Goals in Naturalistic Settings

Adapting the Home and School Setting, Materials, and Instruction

Young Children with Sensory Impairments: Vision

Children with visual impairments are generally identified as partially sighted or blind. (For the federal definition of visual impairment see Appendix A.) The impact of a visual impairment depends on the age of onset, the amount of functional vision, etiology (is it progressive or nonprogressive?), mobility, and the presence of other disabling conditions. The presence of a visual impairment has the potential of having adverse effects on social, language, cognitive, and perceptual motor development if needs are not met at an early age (Barraga & Erin, 1991). Cox and Dykes, (2001) identify several areas that may require additional attention when working with young children with visual impairments. These include attention to locomotion (crawling, walking), fine motor skills, classification, social interaction, communication, and sensory coordination.

Considerations Related to Adapting the Home and Classroom Setting The home and class setting should have good lighting and the child should be seated away from glares, shadows, or flickering lights (Jacobson, 1993). Poor lighting or changing lighting may interfere with the limited vision that the child does have. Even the centers (block area, reading corner, etc.) should have high-quality lighting. The noise level should be monitored to ensure that it does not interfere with the child's ability to use auditory cues. For example, Tameka, a 5-year-old child with a visual impairment, relies heavily on auditory cues to know where to go, what is happening next, and what she is supposed to be doing. Each morning, Lisa, a 2-year-old with limited vision, relies on the auditory cues from the kitchen (mommy removing the dishes from the cabinet, refrigerator humming, dad listening to the radio) to navigate her way to the kitchen. Refer to Feature 9–2 for a list of common environmental adaptations for students with visual impairments.

Attention must be given to the layout and arrangement of the environment. The child needs to orient herself to the home as she is learning to crawl/walk and to the class setting prior to placement. In both settings, she needs to demonstrate that she has access to all aspects of the class. A teacher should enlist the assistance of an Orientation and Mobility specialist who can work with the child to enhance her mobility and level of independent movement about the home or classroom. **Mobility** refers to

Feature 9–2   Environmental Adaptations for Students with Visual Impairments

Lighting

What to observe:

- Variety of lighting situations
- Lighting at different times of day
- Low vision devices used

What to do:

- Light sensitivity—shades, visors, tinted spectacles
- Low light—lamp or illuminated low vision device
- Room obstructions—preferential seating, furniture placement
- Glare—non-glare surface on areas such as blackboards, computer screens, desktop, paper, maps, globes

Desired results:

- Better posture
- Greater concentration
- Less fatigue

Color and Contrast

What to observe:

- Contrast between object and background
- Color contrast
- Tactile tasks such as locker for books

What to use:

- Bold line paper
- Black print on white background
- Dark markers
- One sided writing on paper
- Dark placemat for contrast during eating
- Floor contrast for mobility ease
- Tactile markings for outline discrimination
- Contrast to define borders on walls
- Lock-and-key is preferred over combination locker

Desired results:

- Better visual efficiency
- Less fatigue
- Safe travel

Size and Distance

Observe placement and size of:

- Objects at near
- Objects at far

What to do:

- Enlarge materials
- Preferred seating
- Electronic devices
- Magnification
- Optical character recognition
- Adjustment of desks, tables, and chairs
- Additional storage space for Braille, large-print books, low vision devices near each work station

Desired results:

- Ease of viewing
- Appropriate adaptations for specific vision loss

Time

Observe time for completion of:

- Visual discrimination during tasks

What to do:

- Verbal cues for actions in classroom
- Increase time for task completion
- Call student by name
- Announce when entering or leaving room
- Encourage participation in demonstrations
- Provide opportunity to observe materials prior to lesson
- Use authentic manipulative objects
- Schedule instructional time in early part of day
- Convenient use and storage of materials

Desired results:

- Less fatigue
- Inclusion in class activities
- Time efficiency

Source: Gargiulo, R. (2003). *Special education in contemporary society: An Introduction to exceptionality* (Belmont, CA: Wadsworth) p. 474.

the ability to move about in one's environment and **orientation** refers to the process of using one's senses to determine one's position in relation to other objects in the environment (Anthony, 1994). The use of orientation and mobility skills will facilitate movement within the current environments, and support total independence in future settings.

Adapting Materials and Equipment Adaptations for children with visual impairments fall into one of three categories: visual, tactile, or auditory aids (Todd, 1986). Examples of visual aids include book stands, bold line paper, closed circuit television, high-intensity lamps, large-print materials, and acetate and felt tip pens. When using visual aids, the main focus is to create a contrast. For example, when offering the child a choice (of toys, clothing, etc.) dark items should be against light backgrounds and vice versa. Or, if the toddler is eating in a high chair that is light, dark dishes should be used to assist her in finding the food. When working/playing with printed material, dark lines should be used around pictures or items in the books to guide the child using the material.

Tactile aids allow a child to obtain information through the sense of touch. Examples of tactile aids include Braille books, Braille writers (a machine used to type materials in Braille), raised line paper, abacus (for math calculations), and tactual maps. Toys with interesting tactile components include fabric balls with different textures or dominoes that require the child to match different textures. In addition, the use of Braille readiness materials is recommended. These would include materials that require the child to match raised line patterns, match textures, identify big/small shapes, etc. Tactual symbols could also be placed throughout the child's school and home environment to mark personal belongings or differentiate between similar items (such as different cans of food). Texture changes under a child's feet assist them in identifying different locations (for example, the carpeted area is the living room, the tile is in the kitchen). Teachers could also use carpet runners to assist the child in following specific paths across an open room (from doorway to play area, from doorway to bathroom, etc.).

Auditory aids allow children to obtain information through the sense of hearing. Examples of auditory aids include toys with auditory signals (for example, bells within a ball), talking books, clocks with auditory signals, tapes, or synthetic speech (computerized production of sound). It is important for a very young child with visual impairments to learn to reach, move toward, or follow a sound source. This skill will be critical as he learns to move independently about his environment. For example, as he learns to associate sounds in his surroundings (the kitchen has the refrigerator sound, the office has the hum of a computer, etc.), he will begin to understand the direction in which he must move in order to get where he wants to go. In addition to sounds that naturally occur in the environment, artificial sounds can be created to facilitate the location of specific objects. Placing a wind chime over the toy box and a music box at the dresser will enable the toddler to learn the location of objects in the room while he is in his crib. Creating a sound library can help the child to learn sounds associated with different places and activities. This involves tape recording sounds that might be heard in different environments such as sounds from school, sounds at the grocery store, sounds of a city bus, and so on. The use of auditory aids will support the child's understanding of the auditory signals in the environment and ultimately lead to greater engagement and independence.

When developing printed materials or visual media (such as posters, charts) attention should be given to the edging paperwork and the use of too much detail should be avoided. A child with partial vision may use tactile cues from the edging of the paper to determine where to begin writing (or even from the edging of furniture to determine where to place objects). For a child who is partially sighted, too much detail may clutter printed material, making it more difficult for the child to focus on the most critical aspects on the paper or poster (Amerson, 1999). The vision consultant within the local school district will be a valuable resource in determining the kind of adapted materials needed. The vision specialist will be able to advise families and other personnel on the many recent technological advances that have created

3t   *Teacher Technology Tips*

Technology Tips for Children with Sensory Impairments: Vision

Technology plays a vital role in the lives of children who are visually impaired. Examples of tools are listed below:

• Large-Print Materials	Books or materials printed at a larger than typical print.
• Low-Vision Devices	Optical devices that allow students to see or read print and to see objects at a distance such as magnifiers or telescopes.
• Braillewriter	A mechanical device developed for the writing of Braille.
• Closed Circuit Television	System used by students to enlarge print information. A television is mounted on a stand to input print and the student reads the enlarged print from a monitor.
• Specialized Computers	Computers equipped with screenreading software and a speech synthsizer enabling the student to listen to the information presented on the screen.
• Tape Recorded Materials	Tape recorded versions of books and other reading materials. Best known is *Talking Books,* a national program started in the 1950s and now called the Library of Congress National Library Service (NLS) for the Blind and Physically Handicapped. It provides free library services for persons with vision disabilities.

many products that are advantageous for young children with visual impairments. Equipment is available that helps children by "reading" printed material, providing Braille printout of what is displayed on a computer monitor, and converting Braille to print. Scanners with optical character recognition (machines that "read") or speech synthesis is a technology that "talks" or speaks aloud anything on a computer disk. Television and video programming is made accessible to viewers with blindness or low vision by video description. Brief, spoken descriptions of on-screen action are inserted into the video when no dialog is occurring allowing the viewer to follow the story (Cullotta, Tompkins, & Werts, 2003). Adaptations and changes in instructional materials should occur only when necessary and should be based on the individual needs of the child. It would be a mistake to think that every child with a visual impairment requires the same adaptations.

Adapting Instruction Ferrell (1986) offers some guidelines for working with young children with visual impairments. Some of these include the following:

- *Teachers and caregivers should be consistent when providing directives about a particular skill the child is addressing.* Using different words for the same object ("jacket," "overcoat," "parka," etc.) may be confusing for the child who cannot see.

- *Teachers and caregivers should work from behind the child, putting him through the movements of what is expected of him while providing feedback.* A child with vision can observe the movements of others, monitor and change his actions, and understand what is expected of him. Because a young child with a visual impairment does not have this input, it is necessary to demonstrate what is expected using a hand-over-hand approach and provide feedback about what he is doing right and what he needs to do differently. When demonstrating, the teacher should work from behind the child. In this way the teacher provides a sense of security and allows the child to feel the natural fluidity of movement. Furthermore, it enables the teacher to be more responsive to the child. However, as with any assistance, it is important that the level of assistance be gradually decreased in order to increase independence in the child.

- *Teachers and caregivers should listen and explain every day environmental sounds and visual information.* Individuals with sight take in so much with their vision. Sight enables individuals to connect a sound with a sound source by seeing something happen, understand what sound belongs to what source, and locate the direction from which the sound came. By identifying sounds (for example, the cabinet doors opening and closing, or the humming of air conditioner unit), teachers can provide the child with an understanding of the sounds in his environment and enable him to use the auditory cues as landmarks for organizing his environment. In addition, whenever visual information is presented, auditory input should also be provided. For example, the parent may say out loud *what* he is doing while he is doing it, ("I am tying your shoe." "I am stirring the cereal."). The teacher should tell a child what is being written on the chalkboard or describe materials or pictures (Spenciner, 1992). In this way, *all* children within the class have access to visual information.

- *Skills should be taught, especially self-care skills, in the places and at the times where they naturally occur.* Ferrell offers the example of a child who is toilet trained on a potty chair in the kitchen and then must transition to toileting in the bathroom. The two environments have very different smells and sounds, and may be confusing for a child who cannot see. This approach is consistent with activity-based instruction (Bricker & Cripe, 1992), which stresses embedding skills within the natural environment or daily routines to promote skill acquisition and generalization.

- *Students should be encouraged to become familiar with objects before the instruction.* Teachers using models,

manipulatives, or other equipment should introduce students with visual impairments to the materials before teaching the lesson. If children have the opportunity to explore the materials before the activity begins, they will be more able to concentrate on the concept being taught rather than on the equipment (Cox & Dykes, 2001).

According to Noonan and McCormick (1993), there are some considerations when teaching a young child with a corrected visual impairment. Before, during, and after instruction, teachers must be attentive to whether the prescription for new optical aides or glasses is correct for the child. An incorrect prescription could cause eye damage, result in headaches, or cause eye fatigue. If changes in child behavior occur (such as complaints of headaches or rubbing of eyes after use of new optical aides), the parent should be notified to determine if a follow-up examination is needed.

Teachers should be attentive to the length of time the pupil wears glasses. When glasses are first worn by a child or there is a change in the prescription, the child may be required to wear the glasses for a specified length of time. In addition, the child may have an adjustment period associated with the way the glasses feel or look and may be reluctant to wear the glasses. It may be necessary to provide incentives for wearing glasses or optical aides and to create a

Children with visual impairments can experience success within their learning environment with appropriate adaptations.

need to see. High-preference activities should be provided that require him or her to wear the new glasses in order to participate. This would be one way of creating a need to see that might be highly reinforcing to a young child. For preschoolers or early primary children it may also be necessary to provide a unit on feelings, providing children with an outlet for talking about self-awareness and feelings related to the way they look in their new glasses.

Another instructional consideration is the modality of input. A young child with a visual impairment may need the parent, teacher, and peers to provide information that utilizes other senses. For example, Mary Kate, a four-year-old who is blind, relies on her sense of hearing and smell to navigate her way around the classroom. By providing an olfactory cue (an apple, bowl of potpourri, or flowers) on the teacher's desk, she is readily able to locate the teacher's desk using her sense of smell. Placing the cage for the pet gerbil by the door to the playground provides an olfactory cue (and sometimes audible cue) as to where the door is located for Joyce, who is enrolled in a half-day early intervention program. Coupling a verbal directive, such as "Put your cups here" with auditory cues such as tapping on the table top, enables the child to place the cups in the designated location. The unobtrusive nature of these adaptations make them particularly appealing since it does not single out the child with a disability.

Teachers must recognize that for a child with a visual impairment, learning may require more time, more practice, more verbal mediation, and more encouragement (Spenciner, 1992). This is, of course, highly dependent on the individual. But it may require a teacher to find creative ways to reteach skills that were not achieved the first time around, to examine lessons presented to determine if a visual element to the lesson interfered with learning, and to allow sufficient time for the child to complete a task successfully.

Young Children with Sensory Impairments: Hearing

Children with hearing impairments can be classified as having a mild, moderate, severe, or profound hearing loss (Bowe, 2000; Cullotta, Thompkins & Werts, 2002).

Getting Connected

Websites Related to Visual Impairments

American Foundation for the Blind
http://www.afb.org

American Printing House for the Blind
http://www.aph.org

Division on Visual Impairments, Council for Exceptional Children
http://www.cec.sped.org

Blindness Resource Center
http://www.nyise.org/blind

American Council for the Blind
http://www.acb.org

National Library Service for the Blind and Physically Handicapped
http://lcweb.loc.gov/nls

International Braille Research Center
http://www.braille.org

(See Appendix A for federal definitions associated with hearing impairments.) Typically, a young child with a mild to moderate hearing loss is considered hard of hearing, while a child with a severe or profound hearing loss is considered deaf (Cullotta et al., 2002). A child who is deaf has a hearing loss that is so significant that he or she is unable to process the spoken language without the use of amplified hearing devices (such as hearing aids, FM auditory training devices, and cochlear implants). A child who is hard of hearing has a less significant hearing loss and may be able to process spoken language (hear and speak) with or without the support of amplified hearing devices. Some children have a pre-lingual hearing loss (developed the hearing loss prior to language acquisition), while others have a post-lingual hearing loss (developed a hearing impairment after they had acquired language). While children with hearing impairments represent a diverse group, there are some common issues and considerations related to adapting the environment, materials, and instruction.

Adapting the Home and Classroom Setting
Attention should be given to the light source in the home and classroom setting, making sure that there

is adequate lighting and that the speaker is not standing in a shadow or location where a glare is present. The child may be using the visual cues of speech reading (or lipreading), body language, facial expressions, sign language, or natural gestures to supplement hearing.

Attention should be given to seating and positioning. It may be necessary to seat a child with a hearing impairment directly in front of the teacher or to the left or right of the teacher if he is dependent on one ear for auditory input. It might be necessary to allow the child to move about the room in order to see the the speaker (Compton, 1991). All caregivers (parents, teachers, assistants) should be encouraged to position themselves at the child's level to allow easy access to visual cues given when speaking. Teachers should not talk with their backs to the child (for instance, while searching for items inside the closet) or obscure their lips with anything (for example, their hands, a book, the newspaper). The child with a hearing impairment may be heavily dependent on the movement of lips as the teacher is speaking. Teachers should remember to monitor classroom noise and background noise. When a student wears a hearing aid, all sounds in the environment are amplified (Compton, 1991; Cullotta et al., 2002).

Adapting Materials and Equipment   There are several considerations related to hearing aids that are worn by young children with hearing impairments (Noonan & McCormick, 1993). It is important to know how to manipulate the controls and what to do if and when the hearing aid "whistles." Parents are excellent resources and can familiarize a teacher with their child's hearing device (such as knowing how to determine if the hearing aid is on or off). Even a young child may learn quickly how to turn the hearing aid off (and go about doing their own thing!). In addition, it is important to have a spare set of batteries on hand at home and at school and to frequently check them to ensure that they are still working. Teachers should make note if the hearing aid appears to fit improperly or has a damaged ear mold and notify the parent accordingly. A periodic visual examination of the ear (for redness or soreness), the cords

Getting Connected

Websites Related to Hearing Impairments

American Speech-Language-Hearing Association
http://www.asha.org

Alexander Graham Bell Association for the Deaf and Hard of Hearing
http://www.agbell.org

National Association for the Deaf
http://www.nad.org

DeafWorld
http://www.icdri.org/dhhi/dww

Laurent Clere National Deaf Education Center
http://clerccenter.gallaudet.edu/InfoToGo/

Gallaudet University
http://www.gallaudet.edu

Self-Help for Hard of Hearing People
http://www.hearingloss.org

of the hearing aid (to determine if they are worn and need replacing), and the mold (for split or broken pieces) takes very little time and can ensure that the child is properly fitted.

Adapting Instruction   A young child with a hearing impairment may lag behind in development as language becomes more intertwined with other areas such as social or cognitive development, and because they have been denied auditory input necessary for development. For example, a two-year-old with a hearing impairment may not be producing sounds, word approximations, or words. A four-year-old child with a hearing impairment may experience a high level of social isolation and solitary play or may fail to initiate or respond (Antia & Kreimeyer, 1992). Young children who are deaf typically have less language interaction during play and appear to prefer groups of two rather than a large group size. These patterns may be attributed to the difficulty of dividing their attention, which is visual in nature, and their poorer knowledge of language appropriate for play situations. They also engage in less pretend play, possibly because language deficits impede their

3t *Teacher Technology Tips*

Technology Tips for Children with Sensory Impairments: Hearing

Technology is an important component in the lives of individuals with disabilities. Nowhere are the effects of technological advances more evident than in those for students with hearing impairments. Examples of technology for students with hearing impairments are listed below.

Amplification of Auditory Information

- Personal hearing aids
- Assistive listening devices
- Auditory training devices or FM systems
- Sound field systems
- Cochlear implants

Computers

- Specialized software for speech drill, auditory training, speechreading, and sign language instruction
- Synthesized speech from keyboards to input and transcribe speech onto a printed display screen

Alerting Devices

- Wristwatches with vibratory alarm devices
- Doorbells, fire alarms, and alarm clocks with vibratory mechanisms or flashing lights

Captioning Devices

- Provides captioning for many current television programs, movies, and videos

Telecommunication Devices

- A Telecommunication Device for the Deaf (TDD) is a small keyboard with an electronic display screen and a modem. Messages are typed onto the keyboard and carried as different sets of tones over the telephone to the other party's telephone, which must be linked to another TDD.
- Amplified telephones

ability to script elaborate imaginary situations. Children who are deaf spend less time in cooperative peer play (Gargiulo, 2003). The implication for the teacher is to utilize other modalities (tactile or visual methods or materials such as using photos, pictures, charts, or gestures) and to provide multiple opportunities for social interaction. (See teacher-mediated and peer-mediated strategies earlier in this chapter).

One of the largest concerns for parents and teachers of young children with hearing impairment is the decision of the communication mode for the child. Also of great concern is the method or educational approach that is chosen to use when teaching the child who is hard of hearing or deaf. Three possible educational approaches are oralism, bilingual-bicultural, and total communication. *Auditory-oral* is an educational approach that emphasizes the development of speech, speechreading, and listening with appropriate amplification. Neither sign language nor gesture is used with this approach. *Bilingual-bicultural* is an approach that emphasizes the early use of American Sign Language (ASL) because it is thought to be the natural language that permits children who are deaf to advance through the normal stages of language acquisition. American Sign Language is used as the language of instruction, and English is taught by reading and writing. Both English and American

Table 9-4   Educational Approaches Used When Working with Students with Hearing Impairments

Bilingual-Bicultural

Basic Position:	Considers American Sign Language (ASL) to be the natural language of the deaf culture and urges recognition of ASL as the primary language choice with English considered a second language
Objective:	Provide a foundation in the use of ASL with its unique vocabulary and syntax rules; ESL instruction provided for English vocabulary and syntax rules
Method of Communication:	ASL (American Sign Language)

Total Communication

Basic Position:	Supports the belief that simultaneous use of multiple communication techniques enhances an individual's ability to communicate, comprehend, and learn
Objective:	Provide a multifaceted approach to communication to facilitate whichever method(s) works best for each individual
Method of Communication:	Simultaneous combination of sign language (accepts the use of any of the sign language systems), fingerspelling, and speechreading

Auditory-Oral

Basic Position:	Supports the belief that children with hearing impairments can develop listening/receptive language and oral language expression (English) skills with the emphasis placed on using residual hearing (the level of hearing an individual possesses), amplification (hearing aids, auditory training, etc.), and speech/language training
Objective:	Facilitate the development of spoken (oral) English
Method of Communication:	Spoken (oral) English

SOURCE: Gargiulo, R. (2003). *Special education in contemporary society: An introduction to exceptionality* (Belmont, CA: Wadsworth), p. 430.

Sign Language are valued as educational tools in this method. *Total communication* focuses on using the individual child's preferred modes of communication. It includes oral, auditory, speechreading, sign language, writing, and gestures as methods for teaching. For a detailed view of the educational approaches used when working with students with hearing impairments see Table 9–4.

Consulting with the speech/language pathologist enables the teacher to learn first-hand about the mode of communication that is supported by the family and therapists. Likewise, the peers and all adults that interact with the child (especially the parents) should know how to communicate with the child. For everyone to learn the same mode of communication the child uses (sign language or total communication) is one strat-egy, as well as peers using the same communication techniques as the teacher (face the child when speaking or using touch) is another strategy.

A normal voice, gestures, and touch (when appropriate) should be used in communicating with a child with a hearing impairment (Heyward, 2003). For example, a light touch on the shoulder (to gain the child's attention) or gestural motion (pointing to the door) are subtle visual cues that allow the child to understand what is happening or where to go. Noonan and McCormick (1993) caution teachers, however, not to "over gesture" as it could clutter the visual cues of a child who is dependent upon speech reading. For a list of classroom adaptations and accommodations for children with hearing impairments, refer to Feature 9–3.

Feature 9-3   Suggestions for Teaching Students with Hearing Impairments

What to Do

Promote acceptance of your students. Your student will benefit from a classroom where he/she feels accepted and where modifications are made without undue attention.

How to Do It

- Welcome the student to your class. Your positive attitude will help other students accept him/her.
- Discuss your student's hearing loss with him/her; let him/her know you are willing to help.
- As appropriate, have your student, the audiologist, or another person explain the student's hearing loss to your entire class.
- Make modifications seem as natural as possible so the student is not singled out.
- Accept your student as an individual; be aware of his/her assets as well as his/her limitations.
- Encourage your student's special abilities or interests.

Be sure hearing aids and other amplification devices are used when recommended. This will enable your student to use his/her hearing maximally.

- Realize that hearing aids make sounds louder, but not necessarily clearer. Hearing aids don't make hearing normal.
- Be sure your student's hearing aids or other devices are checked daily to see that they are working properly.
- Encourage the student to care for his/her hearing aid(s) by putting it on, telling you when it is not functioning properly, etc.
- Be sure your student always has a spare battery at school.
- Know who to contact if your student's device is not working properly.

Provide preferential seating. Appropriate seating will enhance your student's ability to hear and understand what is said in the classroom.

- Seat near where you typically teach. It will be helpful if your student is at one side of the classroom so he/she can easily turn and follow classroom dialogue.
- Seat where your student can easily watch your face without straining to look straight up. Typically the second or third row is best.
- Seat away from noise sources, including hallways, radiators, pencil sharpeners, etc.
- Seat where light is on your face and not in your student's eyes.
- If there is a better ear, place it toward the classroom.
- Allow your student to move to other seats when necessary for demonstrations, classroom discussions, or other activities.

Feature 9–3 *(continued)*

What to Do	How to Do It

Increase visual information. Your student will use lipreading and other visual information to supplement what he/she hears.	• Remember your student needs to see your face in order to lipread!
	  – Try to stay in one place while talking to the class so your student does not have to lipread a "moving target."
	  – Avoid talking while writing on the chalkboard.
	  – Avoid putting your hands, papers, or books in front of your face when talking.
	  – Avoid talking with your face turned downward while reading.
	  – Keep the light on your face, not at your back. Avoid standing in front of windows where the glare will make it difficult for your student to see your face.
	• Use visual aids, such as pictures and diagrams, when possible.
	• Demonstrate what you want the student to understand when possible. Use natural gestures, such as pointing to objects being discussed, to help clarify what you say.
	• Use the chalkboard—write assignments, new vocabulary words, key words, etc. on it.

Minimize classroom noise. Even a small amount of noise will make it very difficult for your student to hear and understand what is said.	• Seat your student away from noisy parts of your classroom. • Want until your class is quiet before talking to them.
Modify teaching procedures. Modifications will allow your student to benefit from your instruction and will decrease the need for repetition.	• Be sure your student is watching and listening when you are talking to him/her. • Be sure your student understands what is said by having him/her repeat information or answer questions. • Rephrase, rather than repeat, questions and instructions if your student has not understood them. • Write key words, new words, new topics, etc., on the chalkboard. • Repeat or phrase things said by other students during classroom discussions. • Introduce new vocabulary to the student in advance. The speech-language pathologist or parents may be able to help with this. • Use a "buddy" to alert your student to listen and to be sure your student has understood all information correctly.

Feature 9–3 *(continued)*

What to Do	How to Do It
Have realistic expectations. This will help your student succeed in your classroom.	• Remember that your student cannot understand everything all of the time, no matter how hard he/she tries. Encourage him/her to ask for repetition. • Be patient when student asks for repetition. • Give breaks from listening when necessary. Your student may fatigue easily because he/she is straining to listen and understand. • Expect student to follow classroom routine. Do not spoil or pamper your student. • Expect your student to accept the same responsibilities for considerate behavior, homework, and dependability, as you require of other students in your classroom. • Ask the student to repeat if you can't understand him/her. Your student's speech may be distorted because he/she does not hear sounds clearly. Work with the speech-language pathologist to help your student improve his/her speech as much as possible. • Be alert for fluctuations of hearing due to middle ear problems. • Request support from the audiologist, the speech-language pathologist, or others when you feel uncertain about your student and what is best for him/her.

Source: Johnson, C., Benson, P., and Seaton, J. *Educational audiology handbook* (San Diego: Singular, 1997). pp. 370–371.

Young Children with Delays in Motor Development and Health Impairments

Youngsters with physical and/or health impairments represent a very diverse group with children having health impairments such as asthma, cystic fibrosis, leukemia, diabetes or physical impairments such as spina bifida, cerebral palsy, muscular dystrophy, and spinal cord injury (Hallahan & Kauffman, 2003). (See Appendix A for federal definitions associated with physical and health impairments.) Because

young children with physical and health impairments reflect a wide range of etiologies and disabilities, early signs or indicators vary, as does the age of onset. However, children with physical or health impairments may share some common issues and considerations related to adapting the environment, instruction, and materials.

Adapting the Home and School Setting Because the child may be using adaptive equipment (wheelchair, walker, adaptive seating, etc.), ample space is needed for the child to move independently about the classroom. Prior to the child coming to the class, it must be determined how accessible the travel paths are within the classroom and doorways. Are there any changes in the layout of the home or class setting that are necessary to facilitate mobility? All areas (toy shelf, bookcases, coat racks, sensory tables, activity centers and so forth) should be accessible to all children. Are railings needed? The match between the height of the work surface and the child's seating should be examined to ensure that the child has access to all of the tabletop activities. Material should be presented at the child's eye level and should be stored at child height to promote independence in retrieving and replacing items. Depending on the child's abilities and his/her goals, location of objects and materials needs careful attention. For example, Mike is a right-handed toddler with cerebral palsy who has a limited range of motion in his right hand and arm, but has excellent grasping ability. If his goal is to promote independent play or eating, it would be important to place objects such as toys, food, drink in a position within his reach. Or, if his goal is to increase cross-midline reaching, objects should be placed on the left side of his lapboard to encourage cross-midline reaching. The accessibility and architectural specifications of the home or school should be examined to determine if the child will need adaptations (for example, the use of ramps or railings) to gain access to restrooms, water fountains, and doorways as well as passageways within the class.

Proper seating and positioning can combat poor circulation, muscle tightness, pressure sores, and contribute to digestion, respiration, and physical development. In addition, proper seating can promote feelings of physical security and safety, positively affect the use of the upper body, and reduce the possibility of developing additional deformities (McEwen, 1995). Because of the importance of seating and positioning, there are several aspects of the environment that need attention. There should be many seating options within the home and school such as adaptive chairs, corner chairs, or prop sitting with pillows or wedges. See Figure 9–4.

If necessary, an abduction block (a pummel, block, wedge, or cushion that the child's legs can straddle) can be used to prevent the child from sliding out of the chair. A seat belt and/or shoulder and chest strap may be necessary to maintain an appropriate upright position. In addition, to ensure maximum trunk control, adding a footstool may be warranted to ensure that the child's feet rest firmly on a flat surface. Prior to any changes in seating or prompting a young child to walk or move with or without adaptive equipment, an accredited specialist (physical or occupational therapist) should be consulted (Chiarello & Effgen, 1992).

A child may require medication or have specific nutritional needs. Therefore, when creating an environment that supports this child, attention is warranted regarding safety precautions and side effects associated with medication or nutrition. Written authorizations from the parents and physician are required related to the administration of medication or alternative nutritional needs of the child (such as a child with diabetes). At the school level, a determination must be made regarding who will administer medication, record medication administration, store medication in a secure, locked location, and monitor any changes in child behavior associated with nutritional or medication needs. In addition, teachers need to be aware of medication or special diets that the child is on while at home. For example, medication administered at home could result in side effects (such as altered behavior) during school hours. Therefore, teachers and parents need to have regular communication about the nutritional and medication needs of the child.

Adapting Materials and Equipment   The physical and occupational therapists should work closely with the teacher and parents to provide the information and consultation that is necessary for each individual child. Specialized equipment for standing, sitting, and ambulation may be necessary because of abnormal muscle tone. **Hypotonic muscle tone** (floppy muscles) or **hypertonic muscle tone** (tight muscles) may thwart movement patterns and physical growth. Adaptive equipment and **orthotic devices** offer a variety of options to optimize learning potential of a young child with a physical or health impairment. **Prosthetic devices** support the child in the learning environment, but without careful attention, can restrict range of motion, cause discomfort and

Alternative seating: (a) chair without legs and with added post in front of chair to promote abduction of hips; (b) chair with arms and footrests—runners or skis can be added to keep chair from tipping; (c) sandbags as supports; (d) and (e) corner seats (with lap straps, leg positioners, and perhaps a tray)

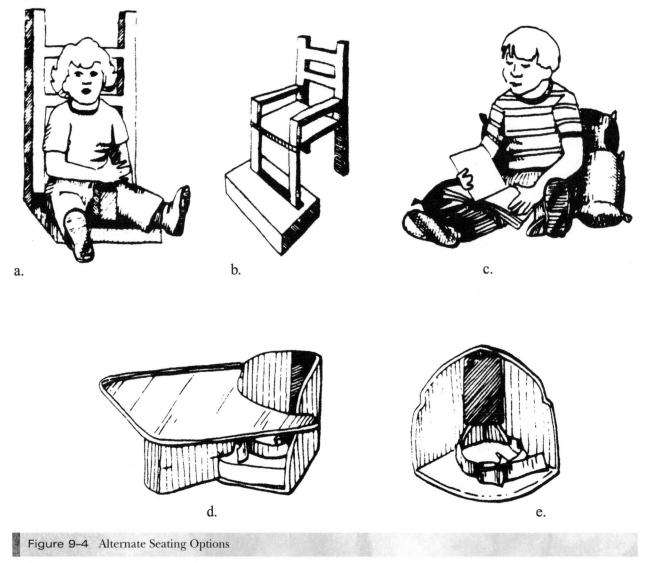

a.   b.   c.

d.   e.

Figure 9–4   Alternate Seating Options

SOURCE: Bigge, J. L., Best, S. J., & Heller, K. W. (2001). Facilitating participation across environments in *Teaching individuals with physical, health, or multiple disabilities,* 4th ed. (Upper Saddle River, NJ: Merrill/Prentice Hall). p. 204.

abrasions, or interfere with circulation if not properly fitted. If special equipment such as a wheelchair is used, periodic inspections are necessary to ensure proper fit, comfort, and that the equipment is in good working order. In addition, because of limited physical strength, it may be necessary to examine the weight of materials that the child will be expected to manipulate to determine if adaptations are warranted.

Teachers should always enlist the help of therapists (and parents) to adjust and adapt equipment

3t *Teacher Technology Tips*

Technology Tips for Children with Delays in Motor Development and Health Impairments

Children with physical or health disabilities use technology for academic tasks, leisure, and socialization. Computers are widely used. Depending on the severity of the disability, many modifications can be made to individualize its use to the specific needs of the user. Examples of high and low technology solutions are listed below.

Activity	Low Technology	High Technology
Reading	Book-stand Turn page with mouth stick Ruler to keep place on page	Electric page-turner Software to scan book into computer or read text aloud
Writing	Pencil with built-up grip Wider-spaced paper Mouth stick with attached pencil	Computer with alternative input (switch or voice recognition)
Math	Counter Abacus Money cards	Graphing calculator Software that positions the cursor for regrouping
Eating	Spoon with built-up handle Hand splint to hold spoon Adaptive cup Scoop dish	Electric feeder Robotic arm
Leisure	Card holder Larger baseball	Sport wheelchair Adapted bicycle Computer games

Source: Gargiulo, R. (2003). *Special education in contemporary society: An introduction to exceptionality* (Belmont, CA: Wadsworth). p. 585.

or materials. It is important to remember that simple modifications of everyday materials may be preferred as it might be less stigmatizing. For example, if a child cannot use the same materials (for example, scissors or drinking cup) as classmates, adapted scissors or adapted cups can be provided or made from standard materials and equipment. Clothing with velcro fasteners may increase independent dressing. Velcro straps added to a musical instrument may allow a child who has an unsteady grasp to hold the tambourine while playing it. A spoon handle built up with layers of tape may be enough of an adaptation for a student to grasp the handle and feed himself. (For an extensive discussion on adaptations for home, school, and leisure activities see York and Rainforth [1987]). **Physical therapists** and **occupa-**

tional therapists can also support the teacher by demonstrating effective techniques for using adaptive equipment or positioning, lifting, carrying, and transfer strategies that can be utilized with confidence and without harm to the caregiver.

Adapting Instruction   Children with physical and/or health impairment may exhibit fatigue, limited stamina and vitality, or require limited physical activity. This may require the teacher and parent to examine the schedule (at home and at school), the length of activities, and the pace of the curriculum. The teacher may need to determine the optimal time to schedule certain activities, adjust the length of activities, or create alternative ways for the child who is less active to participate.

For children who experience problems with fatigue and endurance, it is important that teachers plan for ambulation when setting up activities for the classroom. Teachers must think through the movements that will be needed, as well as equipment and materials necessary to maximize learning. Some questions that can be asked include:

- Does the class really need to transition after this activity?

- How long will the transition take?

- Can the student make this transition within the time allotted, with enough time to move independently, or is the teacher (or assistant) always carrying him (and fostering dependence)?

- Is it better to do two activities at the same table or do you want to utilize the transition to another area to allow an opportunity for the child to use his/her new walker?

- Is time a factor? To mobilize several children who are nonambulatory takes time. Therefore, before everyone is moved to new space, it is important that teachers be thoughtful about the transition.

- Is the wait time or transition movement utilized (to address fine motor and gross motor skills, language and listening skills)?

- Is the child supported in his own planning related to movement? The child may need assistance with the thinking and reasoning skills related to his own independent mobility. For example, when it's time to go outside, Sam, age two and one-half, may need a verbal prompt from the caregiver, "Sam, what do you need to get to the door?" He replies, "My walker." She responds, "That's right, go get your walker."

Restrictions in movement, including locomotion and voluntary gross and fine motor actions can occur and interfere with the mastery of other developmental skills. For example, a young child who has motor delays and is not able to freely explore his surroundings could exhibit delays in other areas such as speech, language, and social development due to limited exploration of new objects, limited vocabulary, or limited social experiences. The implication is for

For a young child with physical limitations, adaptations and accommodations are often needed for maximum participation in all aspects of the learning environment.

teachers and parents to provide a language-rich environment, integrating language into all areas of learning and ensuring that the child has as much mobility and accessibility as possible within a stimulating home and school setting.

Within the class and home setting, there are many opportunities for children to take on responsibilities (assist in daily events and activities) or leadership roles. Allowing children to participate in this capacity promotes leadership, independence, and positive self-esteem. It would be important that the child with a physical or health impairment, who is typically on the receiving end of assistance, be included in the leadership roles available in the home and school. For example, Annette, a five-year-old with spina bifida, was selected to carry books to and from the library using the tray that fit onto her wheelchair. In this way, she was provided with leadership opportunities like her classmates and the use of the wheelchair tray has become an asset for her as opposed to something that separates her from her classmates. Even when she was three years old, she assisted at home by clearing the table and taking folded clothes to the hall closet using her lapboard (attached to her wheelchair). At a very early age, she was participating in family activities that supported her sense of belonging, positive self-esteem, and leadership abilities.

Frequent and/or prolonged absences are not uncommon among this population and warrant attention. For a young child, this may have a negative impact on various areas of development, such as the development of friendships, security in the school setting, as well as the parent-child relationship. In addition, the child may qualify for homebound or hospitalized educational services, depending on the guidelines within the local school district.

Adjustments and accommodations for a student with a physical and/or health impairment may present a unique set of issues for teachers, parents, and other family members. For example, one child may have a physical impairment that does not progress (such as spina bifida), while another may have a physical or health impairment that is progressive in nature (such as muscular dystrophy) or has episodic (re-occurring) events (seizures or asthmatic attacks). Still another youngster may be sensitive to his own body related to the use of a prosthesis. Other issues relate to stress from repeated hospitalizations, daily or crisis care events, or the anxiety related to life-threatening illness or accident (like muscular dystrophy, leukemia, or spinal cord injury). Parents and teachers alike may be overprotective or have difficulty balancing the amount of attention given to the child with the health problem versus siblings or other children in the class. Likewise, it may be difficult to promote independence in a student who has been sick and become dependent on adults and others for sup-port and assistance. Because of these unique stressors, different types of support, such as counseling, may be required for a young child related to his health or physical impairment.

In addition, peers may have a need for counseling related to their friend with a disability. For example, Joe, a three-year-old youngster with muscular dystrophy, was progressively losing control of his gross and fine motor abilities, which negatively impacted his ability to walk, play ball, color or paint, carry his belongings, or feed himself. Several peers (ages three–five) expressed concern and anxiety about themselves ("Will I catch what he has"? "My leg hurts today. Does that mean I will be sick like Joe?"). Others expressed concerns about Joe as his illness progressed and resulted in frequent hospitalizations ("I feel sad about Joe. Is he going to ever walk again? Is he going to die?").

Teachers need to recognize signs of anxiety or stress that may warrant consultation with the school counselor (Goldman, 1994). Likewise, parents and teachers may have counseling and support needs related to the death of a child with a disability (Smith, Alberto, Briggs, & Heller, 1991). Therefore, it is critical that professionals understand the nature of the grief process and find healthy ways of addressing it if the situation occurs (Chomicki, Sobsey, Sauvageot, & Wilgosh, 1995).

Getting Connected

Websites Related to Physical or Health Disabilities

Division for Physical and Health Disabilities, Council for Exceptional Children http://www.cec.sped.org

Centers for Disease Control and Prevention http://www.cdc.gov

United Cerebral Palsy Association http://www.ucpa.org

Epilepsy Foundation http://epilepsyfoundation.org

Muscular Dystrophy Association http://mdausa.org

The Spina Bifida Association of America http://www.sbaa.org

Feature 9–4   Classroom Modifications Checklist for Students with Physical and Health Impairments

Area   **Comments**

I. Type of Condition and Effects

II. Physical/Health Monitoring
____ Pain/discomfort
____ Fatigue/endurance
____ Functional physical limitations
____ Medication or treatment effects
____ Health care procedures
____ Seizure monitoring
____ Absenteeism
____ Activity restrictions
____ Diet restrictions
____ Allergy
____ Other (Specify)

III. Environmental Arrangement
____ Modified day
____ Scheduled rest breaks
____ Proximity of classrooms
____ Need for homeroom to be near an exit
____ Special bathroom accommodations
____ Need to leave early to get to next class
____ Preferential seating
____ Widened aisles
____ Student requires special chair, desk, other
____ Work surface modifications
____ Materials need to be specially positioned. Location:
____ Materials need to be stabilized. How:
____ Assistance needed in manipulating materials
____ Specialized emergency evacuation plan (Specify)
____ Other (Specify)

IV. Communication
____ No adaptations in this area
____ Needs a longer time to respond
____ Uses an alternate form of response (Specify)
____ Uses AAC system (Specify)
____ Communicates correct answer with multiple choice
        format (with __ number of choices) by:
        ____ pointing to answer
        ____ eye gazing
        ____ marking with pencil
        ____ signaling when oral choices given
        ____ using switch to scanning device
        ____ other
____ Other means of communication

Feature 9–4 *(continued)*

Area	Comments

V. Instructional and Curricular Modifications
____ Provide study outline
____ Provide extra repetition
____ More frequent feedback from teacher
____ Directions should be:
____ written down, ____ read orally, ____ demonstrated
____ Provide material in lower grade reading level
____ Requires individualized instruction
____ Alter material
____ Alter curriculum
____ Organizational modifications
____ Requires extra set of books
____ Other (Specify)

VI. Modifications and Assistive Technology
for Specific Content Areas
____ Computer modifications (Specify)
____ Keyboard modifications
____ Alternative keyboard
____ On-screen keyboard
____ Alternative Input Device (e.g., switch)
____ Voice recognition
____ Output modifications
____ Writing
Modifications/assistive technology needs:
____ Spelling
Modifications/assistive technology needs:
____ Reading
Modifications/assistive technology needs:
____ Math
Modifications/assistive technology needs:
____ Specific content areas_____ (Specify)
Modifications/assistive technology needs:
____ Life management/daily living
Modifications/assistive technology needs:
____ Recreation/leisure
Modifications/assistive technology needs:
____ Prevocational areas
Modifications/assistive technology needs:
____ Other areas
Modifications/assistive technology needs:

VII. Class Participation
____ Requires extended time to respond
____ Give student question(s) to answer in advance
____ Uses modified response/ communication system

Area   **Comments**

VII. Class Participation (Continued)
    ____ Gains teacher attention by:
        ____ raising hand, ____ signaling device,
        ____ AAC system.
    ____ Works best:
        ____ individually, ____ teams of two,
        ____ small group, ____ large group
    ____ Needs encouragement to participate
    in class discussions
    ____ Other (Specify)

VIII. Assignments/Classroom Tests
    ____ Abbreviate assignments/tests
    ____ Break up into shorter segments
    ____ Provide extended time
    ____ Modify reading level
    ____ Reduce paper/pencil tasks
    ____ Allow computer use for assignments
    ____ Allow alternate responding (see communication)
    ____ Alternate test/assignment format
    ____ Peer helper for assignments
    ____ Alternate grading
    ____ Other (Specify)

IX. Other Modifications
    ____ Assistance needed in transferring
    ____ Assistance needed in moving chair up to desk
    ____ Assistance needed in mobility
    ____ Assistance needed in bathrooming
    ____ Assistance needed in eating
    ____ Other (Specify)

X. Sensory & Perceptual Modifications
    ____ Need to decrease visual clutter
    ____ Needs extra lighting or low lighting (Specify)
    ____ Needs material to be high contrast
    ____ Materials need to be modified visually or tactually
    (Specify)
    ____ Student uses a LVD (low vision device), CCTV,
    or other adaptations (Specify)
    ____ Student needs everything described orally
    ____ Student uses hearing aides or other adaptations.
    (Specify)
    ____ Student requires visual presentation
    ____ Student requires set of notes in appropriate format
    ____ Other:

XI. Other

Source: Gargiulo, R. (2003) *Special education in contemporary society: An introduction in exceptionality* (Belmont, CA: Wadsworth). pp. 571–573.

Young Children with Delays in Cognitive Development

Children with cognitive delays represent a diverse population. Children with cognitive delays may learn at a slower rate, experience a high rate of forgetting, and have difficulty regulating their own behavior and transferring (generalizing) learning to new events, situations, or people (Hallahan & Kauffman, 1997). They may require more adult guidance and direct instruction, may require activities that are concrete versus abstract, and may not readily understand lengthy verbal instructions. Because these characteristics are variable from one child to the next, it would be a mistake to assume that all children with cognitive delays exhibit the same characteristics or learning difficulties.

Adapting the Home and Classroom Setting
Creating a rich and stimulating environment for children with cognitive delays is critical to their development. As with all children, the teacher and parent should capitalize on the interests of children. Children should be observed or parents should be asked about what toys, foods, or activities they like. Using the child's interest will ensure that some aspect of the tasks and activities is reinforcing to the child. For example, Matt, a five-year-old with Down syndrome, enjoyed playing with race cars. The teacher incorporated the race cars into the center for color, number, and letter identification. Each car was a different color and had a letter or number attached to it. While at the car center, children raced the cars, then identified the winning cars by color and letter/number. The use of a child's interest offers multiple learning opportunities across the child's day in the early childhood environment. Many professionals recommend embedding instruction into typical classroom activities and routines (e.g., Bricker & Cripe, 1992; Davis et al., 1998; Noonan & McCormick, 1995; Wolery & Wilburs, 1994). **Embedding** is defined as ". . . a procedure in which children are given opportunities to practice individual goals and objectives that are included in an activity or task that expands, modifies, adapts the task/activity while remaining meaningful and interesting to children" (Bricker, Pretti-Frontczak, & McComas, 1998, p. 13). By embedding effective instruction into activities that are fun

and motivating for children, learning occurs more quickly. The children learn the skills in a natural setting. With embedded objectives, the classroom activities and routines become the structure for supporting the child's learning in the early childhood classroom.

As with all young children, consistency in the routine provides the child with security and promotes self-assuredness ("I know what I am supposed to be doing here."). This is especially important for the young learner with cognitive delays. A consistent routine facilitates memory for a child who may have difficulty remembering items or activities that occur out of sequence. Establishing a routine, remaining faithful to the routine when possible, and preparing the child for changes in the routine when necessary are possible strategies. In addition, teachers should ensure that there is adequate time to finish tasks within the established routine for the child who may take a little longer to complete activities.

Unlike typically developing children, a child with cognitive delays does not necessarily acquire cognitive, language, or social skills during social interactions and play with others without support to promote these skills (Odom, McConnell, & McEvoy, 1992). Therefore, it is important for teachers to examine the schedule to determine if there are multiple opportunities in the day for socialization and speech/language production at home and at school. This is consistent with activity-based intervention discussed later in this chapter. Structured play with typically developing peers is an excellent strategy for providing models for language development and socialization.

Adapting Materials and Equipment As much as possible, hands-on, concrete materials need to be available for a young child with cognitive delays. Especially when teaching abstract concepts (up, down, in, out) or common preacademic skills (letter recognition, number, color, shapes), it is critical for teachers to have multiple ways of presenting these abstract concepts in concrete ways. Using predictable games with an infant or toddler is an ideal way to address this issue. During play, a parent lifts the toddler up saying, "Up, up, up!", followed by "Down, down, down!" as the child is lowered. In this way the abstract concepts (up, down) are embedded within an enjoyable, predictable game sequence.

Substituting favorite toys within the same routine extends the play routine with the same concepts, encourages generalization, and sustains interest. With a preschooler or early primary age child, the use of real pennies (instead of toy money) when counting, real food when measuring, or talking about colors of clothing when matching socks are all examples of concrete learning materials/activities. Not only are these more hands-on ways to promote skills acquisition, they are also activities that relate learning to the child's real world (Bredekamp & Copple, 1997) and increase the likelihood of generalization of skills.

A variety of materials may be needed to accommodate for young children with diverse cognitive abilities. Blocks of different sizes or busy boxes with a variety of switches (representing different levels of difficulty) might enable a toddler to have some successes and some challenges. Puzzles with varying degrees of difficulty could be available in the free play corner or books with different levels of difficulty in the reading corner. Likewise, it is important that materials or toys are selected that are more likely to increase social interactions (McLean, Bailey, & Wolery, 1996). Children with cognitive delays may exhibit memory deficits requiring visual cues to prompt behavior. For example, when photographs are placed above each cubby, children can find their photograph when trying to locate their cubby. Pictures of the steps to washing hands can be placed by the sink at the children's eye level to support independence in handwashing.

Adapting Instruction   Every child has strengths—even children with cognitive delays have some areas in which they excel. It is critical to capitalize on the child's strengths when planning activities so as to increase the likelihood of success, promote positive self-esteem, maintain interest, and diminish frustration. For example, Maria, a child with Down syndrome, exhibited cognitive and language delays but excelled in gross motor activities. As a toddler, her mother reported that she sat independently, crawled, and walked early but she did not use words until she was three years old. As a preschooler, she enjoys outdoor play equipment (slide, swings) and the obstacle

course. Her parents and teachers often incorporated language skills within a gross motor activity where Maria finds success and enjoyment. When she is on the swing, waiting for someone to push her, the teacher waits for Maria to indicate or communicate what she wants. Initially even an approximation of "pu" for "push" is accepted, and later, the desired vocalizations is modeled, "Say *push*" and expanded "Say *push swing*." (These models are consistent with activity-based intervention and incidental teaching presented earlier in this chapter.)

Children with cognitive delays may have a smaller vocabulary, use less complex sentence structures, use language less frequently, and have difficulty making friends (Gargiulo, 2003). As mentioned previously, play with typically developing classmates is an excellent context for promoting these skills. However, even within these structured play opportunities, children need to be frequently monitored and supported in their interactions (using prompts, praise, or milieu strategies [discussed earlier in this chapter]) to maximize socialization and communication. Without such supports, children may engage in fewer social interactions and less mature social behavior, may be rejected by peers (Asher, 1990; Favazza & Odom, 1996, 1997), and ultimately have difficulty developing social relationships (Haring, 1991). In addition, to

Selecting materials and making adaptations according to each child's abilities and interests will maximize learning opportunities.

expand the child's communicative and social attempts, language should be integrated into all aspects of the curriculum including transition activities ("Where are we going next?"), self-help activities ("Tell me what you are doing."), and play activities ("James, ask Francie to help you."). The assistance of speech-language therapists can be sought to offer suggestions to teachers about how to insert language goals into daily activities.

Because children with cognitive delays often have memory problems it is not unusual for children to have difficulty transferring or generalizing knowledge or skills acquired in one context to a new or different setting (Gargiulo, 2003). **Generalization** refers to the ability to take what is learned in one setting and apply it within a different context. Wolery, Bailey, and Sugai (1988) suggest several strategies for promoting generalization.

- A *variety of adults can be involved when teaching skills.* For example, periodically a classroom assistant or volunteer can teach a particular skill so that a child becomes accustomed to different people. It is important that the directives and expectations for the child are consistent across people. This implies that communication needs to occur among teachers, parents, and other caregivers to ensure consistency across settings.

- *Skills can be embedded into naturally occurring activities.* For example, if putting socks on and off is a skill area that the child needs to focus on, instruction should occur during the dressing and undressing routines during the day (such as before/after nap). The use of the neat pincer grasp can be promoted during snack time (eating crackers or cheese cubes), during art (picking up tissue squares or pebbles to glue on art project), and during dressing routines (button, unbutton, or zip).

- *Activities can be created in the instructional setting that are as similar as possible to the generalization setting.* Warren and Kaiser (1986) found that the greater the differences between the educational setting and other settings, the less likely generalization will occur. For example, if the child is learning to drink from a two-handled cup at home, the same type of cup should be used at school.

- *The instructional setting should be varied.* By expanding the settings and activities in which the child utilizes targeted skills and the people they utilize them with, the probability of the generalization of skills can be increased.

A strategy often used with children with delays in the cognitive and adaptive domains is **task analysis.** Task analysis involves breaking down a skill or activity into smaller, more manageable steps (see Table 9–5 for a sample task analysis). McLean et al. (1996), offer working guidelines that define the basic steps for conducting a task analysis:

1. Identify the long-term objective.
2. Break the behavior into smaller steps.
3. Eliminate unnecessary and redundant behaviors.
4. Sequence the steps for teaching.
5. Specify the prerequisite behaviors that must be acquired before teaching the behavior.

Table 9–5   Task Analysis for Washing Hands (Sequenced by order in which to be performed)

1. Step up on stepstool to sink.
2. Pull up on sink stopper.
3. Place hands on faucet handles.
4. Turn water on (faucets automatically turn off).
5. Place hands in water.
6. Find the soap.
7. Rub hands together with soap.
8. Put soap back on soapdish.
9. Rub hands together and over back and front.
10. Rinse hands in sink.
11. Push down stopper.
12. Ask for towel.
13. Dry hands on towel.
14. Give towel to trainer.
15. Step down off stepstool.

SOURCE: N. Peterson, *Early Intervention for Handicapped and At-Risk Children.* (Denver: Love, 1987), p. 461.

Feature 9-5   Implementation of an Embedded Learning Opportunity

The implementation of an embedded learning opportunity is one of the strategies that Maria's teachers use to practice individual goals and objectives that are meaningful and interesting to her. The teachers embed the learning activities using the natural routine across the activities, people, and materials in the inclusive classroom. Using the daily routine at snack time, when Maria's glass is empty, she signs "more." The teacher asks Maria, "More what?" Maria signs "more" again. The teacher uses the opportunity to model for Maria. She signs, "more drink" and gives Maria a questioning look. Maria imitates and signs, "more drink" and receives more juice. At block center Maria needs more blocks for the tower she is building. She asks the teacher for "more blocks" and receives them. This is an example of an embedded objective that crosses activities throughout Maria's day. Later at free play, Maria asks the teacher for "more toys" and receives them. In this example the embedded learning objective has crossed to other adults in the classroom environment. Maria's objective was practiced within the natural routine, with different activities, with different adults, and with different materials within her classroom setting.

This strategy involves breaking down a skill or activity into smaller, more manageable steps. With younger children, pictures of each step can be provided to support the child in independent completion of a particular task. For example, pictures of each step used in washing hands could be placed near the sink area at the child's eye level. In this way, an unobtrusive prompt serves as a reminder for all children. Teaching young children phrases or songs that accompany daily activities is another strategy for providing the steps to a task. It is not only enjoyable and fun, but it is also functional because the child can use the phrase or song wherever he/she goes. For example, creating a phrase or song to accompany the motions or steps for tying shoes can be used over and over by a young child at school or at home.

Task analysis can also be individualized with younger toddlers using backward chaining. For example, for a toddler who offers no assistance in dressing or undressing, the parent or teacher could complete all of the steps of a task analysis (for pulling up pants) and leave the last step for him to complete, such as pulling pants from mid-thigh to hips. In this way, the child begins to assist in dressing, successfully completes the new skill, and is off to an enjoyable (and reinforcing) activity (for example, play or snack). Once this step is achieved with consistency, the parent or teacher can raise the expectation that he should pull his pants from the knees, from the

Getting Connected

Websites Related to Cognitive Impairments

The Arc (formerly the Association for Retarded Citizens of the United States)
http://www.thearc.org

American Association on Mental Retardation (AAMR)
http://www.aamr.org

National Down Syndrome Society
http://www.ndss.org

Down Syndrome WWW Page
http://www.nas.com/downsyn

President's Committee on Mental Retardation–The Administration for Children and Families
http://www.acf.dhhs.gov

National Center on Birth Defects and Developmental Disabilities
http://www.cdc.gov/ncbddd/

ankles, and so on. This example of backward chaining starts with the last step of a task analysis. It is typically used with younger children or children who are lower functioning because they can successfully complete the last steps(s) and are immediately reinforced by moving on to the next enjoyable activity.

One final strategy for children with delays in cognitive and adaptive skills is called scaffolding. This technique helps children become independent, proficient problem solvers. In this teacher directed strategy, various forms of support are provided as the child initially engages in learning a new task or skill. As the student becomes competent, the supports or "scaffolds" are gradually removed. This instructional strategy begins with what the child knows and attempts to connect new information with previously learned material. New information is presented in a logical sequence building on the child's knowledge base. Pupils are given the opportunity to apply and practice the new skill.

Young Children with Delays in Social and Emotional Development

The term *behavior disorder* is used to describe a wide variety of social and emotional challenges that include, but are not limited to, attention deficient and/or hyperactivity, conduct disorder (aggressiveness, disruptive or destructive behaviors), anxiety disorders (separation anxiety, overanxiousness, avoidance, or withdrawal) (Coleman, 1992). Typically very young children are not given these labels, but might exhibit some early signs that may later develop into behavioral problems. Because of the diversity of children who have delays in this area of development, it is critical to individualize strategies used with each child. However, there are some issues and considerations that may be applicable across children who exhibit problems in social and emotional development when adapting the environment, materials, and instruction.

Considerations When Adapting the Home and Classroom Setting   Teachers should make note of when and where behavior challenges occur. Some questions that might be asked include: Are there aspects of the home or school environment that trigger inappropriate behavior? For example, is the schedule realistic or is there too little time to complete activities? Are activities too long, and if so, are there planned activities for the child to move on to when his attention is waning? Is there too little or too much space for each child? Sainato and Carta (1992) found that providing too little space can con-

tribute to disruptive behavior, and that placing small numbers of children in very large, open spaces can lead to increased aggression. It is important to compare the number of children and amount of space to determine if space is contributing to unwanted behaviors. Are there enough materials or has the lack of materials lead to problems? Are the expectations realistic? (Remember, young children often have not learned to share yet. Therefore, it is not uncommon to have some problems when materials are limited.) Does the inappropriate behavior always involve the same children or the same activity? Do problems occur at the same time of the day (when the child is overtired, seated next to a specific peer, or after snack)? Is there something happening in the home setting that is contributing to problems at school (birth of a sibling, move to a new house, or other transition events)?

For a child with behavior problems, it is critical that he or she has a predictable, consistent environment. Ground rules should be established and maintained for the class *with* the children and the rules should be consistently applied. A routine should be established and

Families and service providers should work together to ensure that young children feel secure in their daily routines within their environment.

children should be prepared for changes in the routine. Warning signals (bell, music, or singing a "clean-up" song) can be provided to give notice that a transition is about to happen. These are simple environmental strategies that allow all young children to feel secure, knowing what is happening throughout their day.

Adapting Materials and Equipment   There are some adaptations related to materials that warrant attention. For example, does the child have special medication or nutritional needs? If so, these require careful administration, communication with parents, and monitoring for changes in behavior related to side effects from nutritional intake or medication.

Are there materials that encourage self-expression (modeling clay, paints, playdough, writing supplies, tape recorders)? One teacher provided a tape recorder and drawing materials to children who acted out. While they were pulled aside to "sit and watch" others engaging in appropriate play, the child would tell what happened using either the art supplies or the tape recorder before talking with the teacher about the incident. The tape or picture was then passed on to the parents to keep them informed of behaviors at school. Another teacher had the child dictate what happened, which was then sent home to the parents.

Are materials safe and do they promote the kind of interactions that should be encouraged? Some materials and activities suggest aggressive themes and will likely result in aggressive behavior (Slaby, Roedell, Arezzo, & Hendrix, 1995). Even with toddlers, it may become apparent that a particular toy or activity (such as toy guns, books or cartoons with aggressive themes) is involved when disruptive behavior occurs. It is important for teachers to observe children at play, removing the objects that are associated with problems, or discontinuing exposure to books or programming that lead to imitations of aggressive play behavior.

Are there enough materials? Teachers need to judge the amount of materials needed in the classroom. On the one hand, teachers need to promote sharing among preschool age children; on the other, they want to avoid conflicts over limited resources. Is recreational equipment available that naturally promotes cooperative play? Seesaws, rocking boats, and wagon rides are all examples of equipment that rewards cooperative play as they require children to play together.

Are the materials (and activities) reinforcing (high-interest, motivating) to children? It is critical that children have choices of materials that are of interest, especially if access to preferred materials or activities is contingent on behavior.

Adapting Instruction   One of the first steps for instruction is to determine, with the parent's help, the cause of a behavior problem, noting when, where, and with whom a particular inappropriate behavior occurs. This process of gathering information and data about the particular behavior is called a *functional behavior analysis.* Is the behavior something that can be ignored? Or is it a behavior that warrants attention (it is interfering with performance or it is not safe for the child or others). Are there environmental elements that are contributing to problem behaviors? For example, almost daily, Amy exhibits disruptive behavior when it is time to transition to another activity such as nap or snack. When she was given a little more time to complete activities, the disruptive behavior subsided.

If it is determined that the behavior warrants attention, an individualized behavior plan with positive behavioral supports plan can be created to address the behavioral problems. Specific strategies can be discussed with the family and other caregivers (teaching assistants, volunteers) to ensure consistency across people in the home and school setting. Strategies can be selected for reinforcing desired behaviors that include activities, materials, and people that are reinforcing to the child. For example, if adult attention is sought by Micki, a child who exhibits frequent tantrums, the teachers should make sure she receives adequate adult attention for desired behaviors ("That's a great picture; tell me about it." "I like the way you and Roy are playing together.") while withholding adult attention for undesired behavior.

When possible provide choices for children instead of placing demands on them. For example if T. J. refuses to leave the block area to come to small group circle, the teacher may give him choices by saying, "T. J., we need to sit for circle time. You may bring a red or blue block to the circle area with you." Or, "You can hop like a bunny or jump like a frog to the circle." In this way the teacher has given T. J. a choice. T. J. has the choice of the way he comes to the circle and the teacher has accomplished the desired behavior.

Multiple opportunities should be provided for "choice making" throughout the day (centers, art supplies, snack, or toys) so that children have a sense of control over some aspects of the environment. Opportunities should be provided for self-expression (art, music, or social dramatic play), which serve as channels for appropriate self-expression for a child who might have difficulty expressing himself in acceptable ways. When creating small group activities, peers should be carefully selected who can serve as good models for behavior, socialization, and communication.

Providing a child with a time-out when aggressive behavior occurs has been shown to be effective when dealing with aggression (Hobbs & Forehand, 1977). Time out is a strategy that involves removing

a child to a location a way from reinforcing conditions (Davis et. al., 1998) The child is briefly removed (1 minute for each year of chronological age) from rewarding activities (including attention from people). There is some discussion as to the appropriateness of time-out with young children (Slaby et al., 1995) as it can be overused and misused. Examples of misuse include:

- being placed in time-out too frequently and without the child understanding the reasons,
- being placed out of view of teachers,
- use without other strategies that promote desired behavior (that is, without talking about the behavior with the child),
- use as the first and only option when dealing with behavior problems,
- use without the knowledge or consent of parents, and
- placement in time-out for long periods of time.

Feature 9–6   Guidelines for Using Time-Out Successfully

1. Immediately go to the child and say calmly, "You were _____ " (Tell the child what he/she did that was a misbehavior, for example, hitting.) "That is not allowed. You must go to time-out."
2. Don't say more. Don't get into the conversation trap! Take the child to time-out. Use a timer! Set the timer for no longer than two minutes. Do not talk or make eye contact with the child during the time-out. In some cases it may be necessary the first few times to use a gentle arm across the child's lap to keep him/her in time-out. Providing a location near to the continuing class activities can sometimes be effective in allowing the child to observe the other children engaging in appropriate behavior.
3. When the timer goes off, immediately say to the child, "Time-out is over. You can go _____ " (Direct the child to the appropriate activity.) "Remember that _____ [the misbehavior] is not allowed."

4. Quickly help the child engage in positive behavior that you can praise and reinforce!

Points to Remember

1. Time-out should not be the major behavior management strategy you use. It is only a supplement to a plan that provides positive behavioral supports.
2. Remeber time-out only teaches the child what not to do. It is essential to to teach and reinforce positive behaviors.
3. Always have a plan.
4. Always keep records. Something is wrong if time-outs are not becoming less frequent.

Source: Davis, M., Kilgo, J., & Gamel-McCormick, M. (1998). *Young children with special needs: A developmentally appropriate approach* (Allyn and Bacon: Boston). p. 222.

Based on the information presented in the vignette on T. J. (see page 54) and the information on characteristics of young children with behavioral problems, there are several strategies that could be utilized to address the unique needs of T. J. For example, because of his aggressive behavior, it would be important to create an individualized plan to address behavioral issues. The parent is very concerned about her son and can provide useful information about her son. She can be asked what kinds of strategies she has used at home to mediate behavior including the ones that are successful as well as those that have been unsuccessful. It is important to pay attention to *when* the aggression typically occurs, if it is directed at *specific individuals* or preceded by *predictable events.* A plan of action can be created with the mother and T. J. so that he understands what is expected of him, understands the consequences of his actions, has opportunities for success and praise throughout his day, and sees that his mother is working closely with the teacher to help him.

T. J. should be provided with alternatives to aggressive behavior such as being encouraged to "Use his words;" provided with opportunities for choices and self expression through art, music, social dramatic play; or having peer-mediated social interventions used, whereby appropriate social skills are modeled and taught. In addition, it would be important for T. J. to hear praise for the things he is doing well, instead of receiving adult attention (in the form of reprimands) solely for inappropriate behavior.

It would be important for an examination of his social network to occur. Does he have friends and social relationships that are rewarding to him? It may be necessary for some of the strategies for promoting acceptance (found within this chapter) to be utilized if he does not have a social network within the class. Moreover, to address his problems with distractibility, it would be important for a determination to be made of his interest in materials and toys to ensure that high-interest items are available for instruction. Environment factors (too much noise, too much visual simulation, close proximity to others) that may be contributing to the distractibility should also be examined.

Figure 9–5   Strategies for Providing Positive Behavioral Supports for Young Children with Behavioral Problems

However, when thoughtfully used, time-out can be one of many valuable strategies for dealing with problem behavior. It provides children (and sometimes the adult) with a chance to control their own emotions. It separates the aggressor from the victim. It is best applied briefly, immediately, and in a matter-of-fact fashion without anger or reprimands. Explaining to children which behaviors will result in time-out, and why, will enable them to understand that it is one way to help them learn to change their behavior. Teachers and parents can demonstrate time-out procedures, showing children that they are provided a space and time to compose themselves before rejoining the group. One alternative to the traditional time-out is to have a child "sit and watch." In this way, the child can step aside briefly, watch other children at play or work, and learn from children who are demonstrating appropriate behaviors (Noonan & McCormick, 1993; Slaby et al., 1995).

A young child with behavior problems may lack communication skills and/or social competence needed to negotiate the interactions in their world (Coleman, 1992). For example, some children may not have the words to express their emotions of anger or anxiety, others may lack the appropriate social skills necessary for asking for a toy from a peer, or self control in a conflict situation. Some youngsters may require direct instruction (of words and/or social skills), while others may need prompts for appropriate self-expression ("Show me what you want." "Use your words." "Tell Jo Ann how you feel." "Tell him that it's your turn with the truck."). Likewise, a student may benefit from opportunities to interact with children who model appropriate communication and social skills. If the lack of communication skills is contributing to the problem, explore alternative ways of communicating (for example, use picture cards to express self). See Figure 9–5 for application of strategies in working with T. J., a child with behavioral problems.

Circle time is a favorite preschool activity for most children. This child, who was hitting other children during circle time, has "time out" from circle time.

Young Children with Delays in Communication and Language Development

Communication refers to the exchange of messages between a speaker and a listener. Language refers to the use of symbols (letter sounds that are used in various combinations to form words), syntax (rules that guide sentence structure), or grammar when communicating with one another. Speech is the oral-motor action used to communicate. (See Appendix A for the federal definition of language or communication delay.) In this area of development, a young child could have difficulty with one or all three of these aspects of development. Moreover, there are many potential causes of problems in language development. A language delay could be related to cognitive delays, sensory impairments (hearing loss or visual impairment), emotional problems, autism or pervasive developmental disorders, motor impairments (such as cerebral palsy), linguistic and cultural differences, and so on. Because the delay in communica-

tion and language development may be tied to a variety of etiologies, the early indicators could vary widely. For example, a young child with pervasive developmental delay may use *echolalic speech* patterns (repeats what is said, instead of generating an original sentence), a child with a cognitive delay may develop language at a slower pace and may not progress in his use of more complex language structures, or a child with a hearing loss may have difficulty following directions or exhibit poor articulation. Because of the interrelated nature of a communication or language delay with other disorders, the early indicators must be examined very carefully, keeping in mind that all children do not acquire language at the same pace and that many young children exhibit difficulty with articulation or fluency as they are developing language.

Adapting the Home and Classroom Setting
Adapting the home or school setting will depend, in part, on the cause of the language delay. However, some general guidelines would include the following.

Provide a language-rich home or classroom setting. Children should be exposed early on to music, conversation, and printed language (books). Children need immense amounts of stimulation to challenge their intellectual, social, and emotional development. A language-rich setting provides models for speech production, language structures, and social exchanges.

Children's nonverbal and verbal communications should be responded to by teachers and caregivers. Infants and toddlers communicate often through cries, gestures, eye gaze, and sound and word production. It is critical that infants and toddlers have a responsive caregiver (one who responds to early communicative efforts). Klein and Briggs (1987) provide an excellent communicative interaction checklist (see Figure 9–6) that enables caregivers to examine how responsive they are to a young child's communication attempts.

Turn-taking games should be used to have "conversations" with young children. Simple games such as "peek-a-boo" or "pat-a-cake" can be used to support turn-taking behavior that is a necessary component of communication.

Actions and objects in the child's surroundings should be labeled. For example, as mom is dressing her toddler, she could say, "Now, let's put on your socks and shoes. Socks go on. Shoes go on." In this way, the child is given labels for the actions and the objects in her surroundings. One mom commented that after doing this on a regular basis during dress-ing routines (with her son with Down syndrome), he began bringing the socks and shoes to her in anticipation of the dressing routine. Clearly, the labeling activity had an impact on her child's language development.

Adapting Equipment and Materials Materials should spark the child's interest and expand their development. Keep the following in mind when choosing materials.

Materials and activities that should be selected are appealing to his/her unique interests. For example, the parents of Andrea (who had a language delay) noted their child's keen interest in animals. They purchased many toys and books that depicted animals. Many of the toys had a feature that allowed the child to activate the animal sounds. Some of the first sounds the child made were imitations of these animals. She later went on to imitate other sounds and words in her environment. Likewise, activities that the child is interested in will be more enjoyable for him, maintain attention, and have greater potential for language production. Maggie was interested in dress-up activities. She demonstrated a great amount of self-talk during pretend play at home and school.

OBSERVATION OF COMMUNICATIVE INTERACTION (OCI)

Mother-Infant Communication Project

Infant' Name _____ Birthdate _____ Age _____

Setting _____ Date _____ Adjusted Age _____

Observer _____

	Rarely/Never	Sometimes	Often	Optimally	Not Applicable
1. Provides appropriate tactile and kinesthetic stimulation (e.g. gently strokes, pats, caresses, cuddles, rocks baby).	1	2	3	4	N/A
2. Displays pleasure while interacting with infant.	1	2	3	4	N/A

Figure 9–6 Observation of Communicative Interaction

SOURCE: M. Klien and M. Briggs, Facilitating mother-infant communicative interaction in mothers of high-risk infants. *Journal of Childhood Communication Disorders, 10*(2), 1987, p. 96.

	Rarely/Never	Sometimes	Often	Optimally	Not Applicable

3. Responds to child's distress.   1 2 3 4 N/A
    a. changes verbalization.
    b. changes infant's position, attempts to distract.
    c. provides positive physical stimuli (e.g. patting, rocking).
    d. avoids negative physical or verbal response.

4. Positions self and infant so eye-to-eye contant is possible (e.g., facing   1 2 3 4 N/A
    and 7 to 12 inches away).
    a. attempts to make eye contact.
    b. reciprocates eye gaze.

5. Smiles contingently at infant.   1 2 3 4 N/A
    a. consistently returns infant's smile.
    b. smiles in response to infant's vocalization.

6. Varies prosodic features.   1 2 3 4 N/A
    a. uses high pitch.
    b. talks more slowly.
    c. exaggerates "intonation."

7. Encourages "conversation."   1 2 3 4 N/A
    a. uses rising intonation questions.
    b. waits after saying something to infant, and looks expectantly, providing infant turn.
    c. imitates child's vocalization, or words.
    d. repeats own sounds, words, or phrases (e.g., "Here's the bottle. Bottle.").
    e. answers when infant vocalizes (e.g., "Oh, yeah?" "Okay." "Is that right?").

8. Responds contingently to infant's behavior.   1 2 3 4 N/A
    a. touches or responds with facial expression within 2 seconds after infant
    vocalization.
    b. vocalizes within 2 seconds after infant moves arms, head, etc.
    c. vocalizes within 2 seconds after infant vocalization.
    d. stops own activity or verbalization in response to interruption by infant's
    vocalization or movement.
    e. responds vocally to infant from a distance of more than 2 feet.

9. Modifies interaction in response to negative cues from infant.   1 2 3 4 N/A
    a. changes activity.
    b. reduces intensity of interaction.
    c. terminates attempts at interaction.

10. Uses communication to teach language and concepts.   1 2 3 4 N/A
    a. interprets infant's behavior appropriately (e.g., "Oh, you're hungry,
        aren't you?").
    b. comments on infant's attention to immediate environment and labels objects
        (e.g., "You see the doggie? That's the doggie.").
    c. matches child's vocalization, or word with slightly more elaborate language
        (e.g., baby says, "Ball" and adult says, "That's a ball." or "Big ball.").
    d. re-casts own sentences (e.g., adult says, "Shall we turn on the light?
        Turn on the light. There's the light.).

Figure 9–6 *(Continued)*

Materials should be placed in a location where the child can see them, but is unable to access them. This strategy provides a visual incentive for the child to request the materials he/she wants. While it may be easier to place all materials out for children, by following this strategy, a natural opportunity can be created for children with language delays to use language.

The materials or equipment should be limited. When preparing lunch, place the child's cup on the table without his favorite juice, while you pour your own cup with juice. In this way, the child will note something is missing and need to request the missing item. Again, this intentional limitation of materials creates a natural opportunity for the child to use language.

Materials should be used for "choice-making opportunities." By providing the child with multiple choices through her school and home routines, she gains more control and autonomy in her world and is supported in communication attempts. Many more strategies for adapting materials are provided in the milieu strategies found within this chapter.

Adapting Instruction *Every activity should be viewed as an opportunity for developing language.* Routine activities such as going to the grocery story, washing the dishes, playing after breakfast, daily walks in the neighborhood, or dressing routines are all opportunities to expose a young child to language. Times should be selected across the day at home and school where language skills can be addressed.

The child's actions and sounds should be imitated. Imitation of early actions and vocalizations is an ideal way to reinforce a toddler's motor and verbal movements. For example, Jonathan and his mother are playing with sand. His mother drops sand from her hand while saying, "ba, ba, ba." Pairing vocal models with physical imitation may encourage a child to use more complex and frequent vocalizations during play. When Jonathan pushes his fingers into the sand, his mother can imitate by pushing her fingers into the sand while adding the vocalization "da." Adults can model conventional gestures such as pointing to objects out of reach, shrugging one's shoulders, upturning the palms, nodding the head to indicate yes or no, waving, and making the "shhh" gesture. Imitation is a strategy that is effective for the teaching

of turn-taking behaviors and teaches the use of communication to regulate other's behaviors. Susan and her mother roll a ball back-and-forth. One day, instead of rolling the ball back, Susan's mother waits. After Susan looks at her mother and vocalizes "ba," her mother rolls the ball back to her.

The language that a child uses should be expanded. For example if Alina says "Down" when the ball falls down, the parent or caregiver could say, "Ball down" or "Ball fell down." In this way teachers and parents can capitalize on her initiation (and interest), imitate (reinforce) her vocalization and provide a model for expanding her vocalization. Elicitive modeling is an effective procedure used when a child has not yet acquired independent production of language. For example, Maria is playing with the teacher in the doll center. She says, "bottle" while reaching for the baby bottle. The teacher gives the model as she says, "Say, 'I want bottle.'" Maria responds with "Want bottle." The teacher then provides the corrective model by saying, "I want bottle." Maria then imitates, "I want bottle," and receives the bottle. The teacher follows with feedback and compliance with Maria's request by expanding the language by saying, "Yes, here is the bottle for your baby!"

Vocalizations can be coupled with gestures, if necessary. For example, a caregiver could say "No," while shaking her head, and "Yes," while nodding her head. This provides a visual cue as well as a vocal directive. Another example would be pointing to the door while saying, "Go to the door." Again, it provides the child with visual and auditory input while labeling the action as it occurs.

Pauses (verbally and physically) can be used to provide an opportunity to communicate. This seems like such an obvious strategy, but when trying to communicate with a child who has limited verbal skills, it is easy for caregivers to talk so much that the child does not have an opportunity to talk. Likewise, it is easy for caregivers to provide the child with all of the materials before they have indicated a need for them. This strategy requires the teacher or parent to make a conscious effort to slow down their own communication or sit back and wait to allow the child a chance to communicate what he/she wants.

Teachers should collaborate with the related service personnel (such as speech/language pathologist). It is critical that everyone working with the child use the same strategies and have the same expectations for addressing individualized language goals for each child. Collaboration will ensure consistency across settings and people and increase the likelihood of the generalization of skills. Moreover, the selection of effective strategies is highly dependent on the unique needs of each child. For example, if the child has a visual impairment, the strategies used to adapt instruction that will be used to facilitate language development may be different than those selected for a child with a hearing impairment. And, the related service personnel who are involved may vary. Therefore, it is important for teachers to look at each child individually and collaborate with the appropriate related service personnel. There are many more ways to adapt instruction that are discussed in detail earlier in this chapter. In particular, teachers should pay attention to monitoring communicative input, peer initiation intervention, cooperative learning strategies, routine-based strategies, and milieu strategies.

Summary

Teaching strategies from the field of early childhood and early childhood special education have been discussed. Both fields have provided general guidelines for creating appropriate educational experiences for young children with diverse abilities. Research has shaped these guidelines providing specific strategies that have proven to be effective when teaching children with diverse abilities. Current ideas about appropriate educational experiences for young children and strategies for creating less restrictive environments for children with disabilities should be continually examined to ensure that educational practice is informed by ongoing research and evaluation.

We have provided brief descriptors of young children with diverse abilities. It is important to realize that these are possible characteristics or early indicators of a delay or disability. However, a disability may not manifest itself in the same way or at the same age for every child with that same disability. And, the presence of one (or some) of these early indicators does not always indicate a delay.

Getting Connected

Websites Related to Communication and Language Impairments

Division for Children's Communication Development (DCCD), Council for Exceptional Children
http://www.ccc.sped.org

National Easter Seal Society
http://www.easter-seal.org

National Information Center for Children and Youth with Disabilities (NICIICY)
http://www.nichcy.org

American Speech and Hearing Association
http://www.asha.org

Stuttering Foundation of America
http://www.stuttersfa.org

The Center for Speech and Language Disorders
http://www.csld.com

Scottish Rite Centers for Childhood Language Disorders
http://www.srccld.org

While we have delineated several ways to adapt environments, materials, and instruction, one caution is needed. Above all else, children with disabilities are children first. They can and do learn. They may learn at a different rate, use different strategies, or learn through another modality, but they do learn. They may learn through exploration and child-initiated activities, but they may also need the additional support of, and direction from, a teacher. The key in creating appropriate educational experiences for any child is to *create a match* between the individual needs of the child and the environment, materials, and instruction. This may result in teachers and parents using a variety or combination of strategies to facilitate development.

Check Your Understanding

1. Each morning, a particular preschool classroom has circle time in class. Some children rarely or never participate in this activity. Describe two

teacher-mediated strategies that could be used to increase the level of child engagement during this group activity.

2. A child with delays in cognitive development is in your class. She uses sign language to communicate. One of her goals is to indicate when she wants items (to request) using the sign "more." Provide an example of how activity-based instruction could be used to address this goal.

3. What is the difference between a "time delay" and an "interrupted routine"?

4. Describe the kinds of strategies that can be used to prepare the physical environment and the social environment for children with delays.

5. Give an example of the model and expansion procedure.

6. How can the classroom setting and materials be adapted to accommodate for a child with a hearing impairment?

7. What are some of the issues that may need to be addressed if a child with muscular dystrophy is placed in a preschool classroom?

8. When teaching a young child with visual impairments, what are some considerations in adapting your instruction for this child?

9. Define the term *generalization* and provide examples of ways that can be used to ensure the generalization of skills.

References

Amerson, M., J. (1999). Helping children with visual and motor impairments make the most of their visual abilities. *Re: View, 31(1),* 17–21.

Anthony, T. (1994). Movement focus: Orientation and mobility for young blind and visually impaired children. In D. Fazzi & J. Lampert (Eds.), *Early focus: Working with young blind and visually impaired children and their families.* New York: American Foundation for the Blind.

Antia, S., & Kreimeyer, K. (1992). Social competence intervention for young children with hearing impairments. In S. Odom, S. McConnell, & M. McEvoy (Eds.), *Social competence of young children with disabilities* (pp. 113–134). Baltimore, MD: Paul H. Brookes.

Asher, S. (1990). Recent advances in the study of peer rejection. In S. Asher & J. Coie (Eds.), *Peer rejection in childhood* (pp. 3–14). New York: Cambridge University Press.

Bailey, D., & McWilliam, R. (1990). Normalizing early intervention. *Topics in Early Childhood Special Education, 10*(2), 33–47.

Bailey, D., & Wolery, M. (1992). *Teaching infants and preschoolers with disabilities* (2nd ed.). Columbus, OH: Merrill.

Barraga, N., & Erin, J. (1991). *Visual handicaps and learning: A developmental approach.* Austin, TX: PRO-ED.

Bigge, J., L., Best, S., J., & Heller, K., W. (2001). *Teaching individuals with physical, health, or multiple disabilities.* Upper Saddle River, NJ: Merrill Prentice Hall.

Billman, J. & Sherman, J. A. (1996). *Observation and participation in early childhood settings: A practicum guide.* Boston: Allyn & Bacon.

Blackman, J. A. (1995). *Technology in early intervention.* Gaithersburg, MD: Aspen Publications.

Bowe, F. (2000). *Physical, sensory, and health disabilities: An introduction* (2nd ed.). Upper Saddle River, NJ: Merrill/Prentice Hall.

Bredekamp, S., & Copple, C. (1997). *Developmentally appropriate practice in early childhood program.* (Revised Edition). Washington, DC: National Association for the Education of Young Children.

Bredekamp, S., & Rosegrant, T. (1992). *Reaching potentials: Appropriate curriculum and assessment for young children.* Washington, DC: National Association for the Education of Young Children.

Bricker, D., & Cripe, J. (1993). *An activity-based approach to early intervention.* Baltimore, MD: Paul H. Brookes.

Brown, W., McEvoy, M., & Bishop, N. (1991). Incidental teaching of social behavior: A naturalistic approach for promoting young children's peer interactions. *Teaching Exceptional Children, 24*(1), 35–38.

Brown, W., Ragland, E., & Fox, J. (1988). Effects of group socialization procedures on the social interactions of preschool children. *Research in Developmental Disabilities, 9,* 359–376.

Bunce, B. (1995). *Building a language-focused curriculum for the preschool classroom: Volume II, a planning guide.* Baltimore: Brookes.

Carbone, E. (2001). Arranging the classroom with and eye (and ear) to students with ADHD. *Teaching Exceptional Children, 34*(2), 72–81.

Chandler, L., (1992). Promoting children's social/survival skills as a strategy for transition to mainstreamed kindergarten programs. In S. Odom, S. McConnell, & M. McEvoy (Eds.), *Social competence of young children with disabilities* (pp. 245–276). Baltimore, MD: Paul H. Brookes.

Chiarello, L., Effgen, S., & Levinson, M. (1992). Parent-professional partnership in evaluation and development of individualized family service plans. *Pediatric Physical Therapy 4,*(2), 64–69.

Chomicki, S., Sobsey, D., Sauvageot, D., & Wilgosh, L. (1995). Surviving the loss of a child with a disability. *Physical Disabilities: Education and Related Services, 13* (2), 17–30.

Cohen, S., & deBettencourt, L. (1988). Teaching children to be independent learners: A step by step strategy. In E. Meyen, G. Vergason, & R. Whelan (Eds.), *Effective instructional strategies for exceptional children* (pp. 319–334). Denver: Love.

Coleman, M. (1992). *Behavior disorders.* Boston: Allyn & Bacon.

Compton, C. (1991). *Assistive devices: Doorways to independence.* Washington, DC: Gallaudet University.

Connor, C., M., Hieber, S., Arts, A., & Zwolan, T., A. (2000). Speech, vocabulary, and education of children using cochlear implants: Oral or total communication? *Journal of Speech, Language and Hearing Research, 43*(5), 1185–1205.

Cox, P., & Dykes, M. (2001). Effective classroom adaptations for students with visual impairments. *Teaching Exceptional Children, 33*(6), 68–74.

Crocker, A. D., & Orr, R. R. (1996). Social behaviors of children with visual impairments enrolled in preschool programs. *Exceptional Children, 62,* 451–461.

Cullotta, R.A., Tompkins, J. R., & Werts, M. G. (2003). *Fundamentals of special education: What every teacher needs to know.* Upper Saddle River, NJ: Merrill/Prentice Hall.

Danko, C., & Buysse, V. (2002). Thank you for being a friend: Fostering friendships for children with autism spectrum disorder in inclusive environments. *Young Exceptional Children, 6*(1), 2–9.

Davis, M., Kilgo, J., & Gamel-McCormick, M. (1998). *Young children with special needs: A developmentally appropriate approach.* Boston: Allyn & Bacon.

DeKlyen, M., & Odom, S. (1989). Activity structure and social interactions with peers in developmentally integrated playgroups. *Journal of Early Intervention, 13,* 342–352.

Derman-Sparks, J. (1989). *Anti-bias curriculum: Tools for empowering young children.* Washington, D.C. National Association for the Education of Young Children.

DeThorne, L., & Watkins, R. (2001). Five tools for teaching vocabulary in the preschool classroom. In M. Ostrosky & S. Sandall (Eds.), *Teaching strategies: What to do to support young children's development* (pp. 37–45). Longmont, CO: Sopris West.

Diamond, K. (1993). Preschool children's concepts of disability in their peers. *Early Education and Development, 4,* 123–129.

Dolinar, K., Boser, C., & Holm, E. (1994). *Learning through play: Curriculum and activities for the inclusive classroom.* Albany, NY: Delmar.

Drew, C., Logan, D., & Hardman, M. (1992). *Mental retardation* (5th ed.). New York: Merrill/Macmillan.

Dyer, K., Dunlap, G., & Winterling, V. (1990). Effects of choice making on the serious problem behaviors of students with severe handicaps. *Journal of Applied Behavior Analysis, 23,* 515–24.

Fallen, N., & Umansky, W. (1985). *Young children with special needs.* Columbus, OH: Merrill.

Favazza, P. (1998). Preparing for children with disabilities in early childhood classrooms. *Early Childhood Education Journal, 25*(4), 255–258.

Favazza, P., Kumar, P., & Phillipsen, L. (December, 1996). *Strategies for promoting social relationships between young children with and without disabilities: Implications for research.* Paper presented at International Division for Early Childhood, CEC Annual Conference. Phoenix, AZ.

Favazza, P., LaRoe, J., & Odom, S. (1999). *Special friends.* Boulder, CO: Roots and Wings.

Favazza, P., & Odom, S. (1996). Use of the Acceptance Scale with kindergarten-age children. *Journal of Early Intervention, 20*(3), 232–248.

Favazza, P., & Odom, S. (1997). Promoting positive attitudes of kindergarten-age children toward children with disabilities. *Exceptional Children, 63*(3), 405–418.

Fein, G. G., & Schwartz, S. S. (1986). The social coordination of pretense in preschool children. In G. Fein & M. Rivkin (Eds.), *The young child at play: Reviews of research,* vol. 4, Washington, D.C.: National Association for the Education of Young Children.

Fernald, A. (1985). Four-month-old infants prefer to listen to mothers. *Infant Behavior and Development, 10,* 181–195.

Ferrell, K. (1986). Infancy and early childhood. In G. Scholl (Ed.), *Foundations of education for blind and visually handicapped children and youth* (pp.119–136). New York: American Foundation for the Blind.

Fielder, B. (2001). Considering placements and educational approaches for students who are deaf and hard of hearing. *Teaching Exceptional Children, 34*(6), 68–74.

Forness, S., & Kavale, K. (1993). Strategies to improve basic learning and memory deficits in mental retardation: A meta-analysis of experimental studies. *Education and Training in Mental Retardation, 28,* 99–110.

Friend, M. & Bursuck, W. D. (1999). *Including students with special needs: A practical guide for classroom teachers* (2nd ed.). Boston: Allyn and Bacon.

Gackowski, C., Kobe, K., & McCormick, L. (1991). *Cooperative learning: A means to enhance the social interactions of preschoolers with special needs and typically developing peers.* Unpublished manuscript, University of Hawaii, Department of Special Education, Honolulu.

Gargiulo, R. (2003). *Special education in contemporary society: An introduction to exceptionality.* Belmont, CA: Wadsworth.

Gestwicki, C. (1999). *Developmentally appropriate practice: Curriculum and development in early education.* Albany, NY: Delmar.

Gillies, R., & Ashman, A. (1996) Teaching collaborative skills to primary age school children in classroom based workgroups. *Learning and Instruction, 6,* 187–200.

Gillies, R. M., & Ashman, A. F. (2000). The effects of cooperative learning on students with learning difficulties in the lower elementary school. *Journal of Special Education 34*(1), 19–27.

Goldman, L. (1994). *Life and loss.* Muncie, IN: Accelerate Development, Inc.

Goldstein, H., & Gallagher, T. (1992). Strategies for promoting the social-communicative competence of young children with specific language impairment. In S. Odom, S. McConnell, & M. McEvoy (Eds.), *Social competence of young children with disabilities* (pp.189–213). Baltimore, MD: Paul H. Brookes.

Guralnick, M. (1990). Major accomplishments and future directions in early childhood mainstreaming. *Topics in Early Childhood Special Education, 10*(2), 1–17.

Guralnick, M. (Ed.). (2001). *Early childhood inclusion: Focus on change.* Baltimore: Brookes.

Hallahan, D., & Kauffman, J. (1997). *Exceptional learners* (9th ed.). Boston: Allyn & Bacon.

Halle, J., Alpert, C., & Anderson, S. (1984). Natural environment language assessment and intervention with severely impaired preschoolers. *Topics in Early Childhood Special Education, 4,* 29–37.

Halle, J., Baer, D., & Spradlin, J. (1981). Teachers' generalized use of delay as a stimulus control procedure to increase language use in handicapped children. *Journal of Applied Behavior Analysis, 14,* 389–411.

Haring, T. (1991). Social relationships. In L. Meyer, C. Peck, & L. Brown (Eds.), *Critical issues in the lives of people with severe disabilities* (pp.195–217). Baltimore, MD: Paul H. Brookes.

Heward, W. L. (2003). *Exceptional children* (7th ed.). Upper Saddle River, NJ: Merrill/Prentice Hall.

Hobbs, S., & Forehand, R. (1977). Effects of differential release from timeout on children's deviant behavior. *Journal of Behavior Therapy and Experimental Psychiatry, 6,* 256–57.

Horn, E., Lieber, J., Sandall, S., & Schwartz, I. (2001). Embedded learning opportunities as an instructional strategy for supporting children's learning in inclusive programs. In M. Ostrosky & S. Sandall (Eds.), *Teaching strategies: What to do to support young children's development* (pp. 59–70). Longmont, CO: Sopris West.

Huebner, K. (1986). Curricular adaptations. In G. Scholl (Ed.), *Foundations of education for blind and visually handicapped children and youth* (pp.363–403). New York: American Foundation for the Blind.

Jacobson, W.H. (1993). *The art and science of teaching orientation and mobility to persons with visual impairments.* New York: American Foundation for the Blind.

Johnson, D., & Johnson, R. (1986). Mainstreaming and cooperative learning strategies. *Exceptional Children, 52*(6), 553–561.

Johnson, D., & Johnson, R. (1992). *Learning together and alone: Cooperative, competitive, and individualistic learning* (3rd ed.). Englewood Cliffs, NJ: Prentice-Hall.

Jordan, D., & Le Metais, J. (1997). Social skilling through cooperative learning. *Educational Research, 39,* 3–21.

Kaiser, A., & Delany, E., (2001). Responsive conversations: Creating opportunities for naturalistic language teaching. In M. Ostrosky & S. Sandall (Eds.), *Teaching strategies: What to do to support young children's development* (pp. 13–23). Longmont, CO: Sopris West.

Kaiser, A., Yoder, P., & Keetz, A. (1992). Evaluating milieu teaching. In S. Warren & J. Reichle (Eds.), *Causes and effects in communication and language intervention* (pp.9–47). Baltimore, MD: Paul H. Brookes.

Kallioniatis, M., & Johnston, A. W. (1994). Visual environmental adaptations problems for partially sighted children. *Journal of Visual Impairment and Blindness, 88,* 234–243.

Klein, M., & Briggs, M. (1987). Facilitating mother-infant communicative interaction in mothers of high-risk infants. *Journal of Childhood Communication Disorders, 10*(2), 1–21.

Koenig, A. J. (1996). Growing into literacy. In M. C. Holbrook (Ed.), *Children with visual impairments: A parent's guide* (pp.227–257). Betheseda, MD: Woodbine House.

Kulick, B.J. (1999). Physical disabilities: Education and related services. *Physical Disabilities: Education and Related Services, 18*(1–2) 124–132.

Lane, S. J. & Mistrett, S. (2002). Let's play! Assistive technology interventions for play. *Young Exceptional Children, 5*(2), 19–27.

Lewis, R. B. (1993). *Special education technology: Classroom applications.* Pacific Grove, CA: Brooks/Cole.

Linder, T. (1993). *Transdisciplinary play-based intervention.* Baltimore, MD: Paul H. Brookes.

Luckner, J., Bowen, S., & Carter, K. (2001). Visual teaching strategies for students who are deaf or hard of hearing. *Teaching Exceptional Children, 33*(3), 38–43.

McCathren, R., & Watson, A. (2001). Facilitating the development of intentional communication. In M. Ostrosky & S. Sandall (Eds.), *Teaching strategies: What to do to support young children's development* (pp. 25–35). Longmont, CO: Sopris West.

McConnell, S., & Odom, S. (1993). *Play time, social time.* Tucson, AZ: Communication Skill Builders.

McCracken, J. (1993). *Valuing diversity: The primary years.* Washington, DC: National Association for the Education of Young Children.

McEvoy, M. (1990). The organization of caregiving environments: Critical issues and suggestions for future research. *Education and Treatment of Children, 13*, 26–73.

McEvoy, M., Odom, S., & McConnell, S. (1992). Peer social competence interventions for young children with disabilities. In S. Odom, S. McConnell, & M. McEvoy (Eds.), *Social competence of young children with disabilities: Issues and strategies for intervention* (pp. 113–133). Baltimore, MD: Paul H. Brookes.

McEwen, E. (1995). *Occupational and physical therapy in educational environments.* Binghamton, NY: Haworth Press.

McGee, G., Daly, T., Izeman, S., Mann, L., & Risley, T. (1991). Use of classroom materials to promote preschool engagement. *Teaching Exceptional Children, 23*, 44–47.

McLean, M., Bailey, D., & Wolery, M. (1996). *Assessing infants and preschoolers with special needs* (2nd ed.). Upper Saddle River, NJ: Prentice-Hall, Inc.

McLean, M., & Odom, S. (1993). Practices for young children with and without disabilities: A comparison of DEC and NAEYC identified practices. *Topics in Early Childhood Special Education, 13*, 274–292.

McLesky, J., & Waldron, N. L. (1996). Responses to questions teachers and administrators frequently ask about inclusive school programs. *Phi Delta Kappan, 78*, 150–156.

McPhee, N., Favazza, P., & Lewis, E. (1998). *Sensitivity and awareness: A guide for developing understanding among children* (3rd ed.). Hollidaysburg: PA: Jason & Nordic.

Noonan, M., & McCormick, L. (1993). *Early intervention in natural environments: Methods and procedures.* Pacific Grove, CA: Brooks/Cole.

Odom, S., McConnell, S., & McEvoy, M. (1992). Peer-related social competence and its significance for young children with disabilities. In S. Odom, S. McConnell, & M. McEvoy (Eds.), *Social competence of young children with disabilities* (pp. 3–35). Baltimore, MD: Paul H. Brookes.

Odom, S., & McLean, M. (Eds.). (1996). *Early intervention/Early childhood special education: Recommended practices.* Austin: PRO-ED.

Odom, S., McLean, M., Johnson, L., & LaMontagne, M. (1995). Recommended practices in early childhood special education: Validation of current use. *Journal of Early Intervention, 19*, 1–17.

Odom, S., & Strain, P. (1984). Classroom-based social skills instruction for severely handicapped preschool children. *Topics in Early Childhood Special Education, 4*, 97–116.

Odom, S., & Strain, P. (1986). A comparison of peer initiation and teacher-antecedent interventions for promoting reciprocal social interaction of autistic preschoolers. *Journal of Applied Behavioral Analysis, 19*, 59–72.

Odom, S. (2000). Preschool inclusion: What we know and where we go from here. *Topics in Early Childhood Special Education, 20*(1), 20–27.

Putnam, J., Rynders, J., Johnson, R., & Johnson, D. (1989). Collaborative skill instruction for promoting positive interactions between mentally handicapped and non-handicapped children. *Exceptional Children, 55*, 550–557.

Rainforth, B., & York, J. (1987). Handling and positioning. In F. Orelove & D. Sobsey (Eds.), *Educating children with multiple disabilities* (pp. 67–104). Baltimore, MD: Paul H. Brookes.

Ramsey, P. (1980). Solving the dilemma of sharing. *Day Care and Early Education, 8*, 6–10.

Recchia, S. L. (1997). Play and concept development in infants and young children with severe visual impairments: A constructivist view. *Journal of Visual Impairment and Blindness, 97*(4), 401–407.

Rettig, M. (1994). The play of young children with visual impairments: Characteristics and interventions. *Journal of Visual Impairment and Blindness, 88*, 410–420.

Rosenberg, M. (1983). *My friend Leslie.* New York: Lothrop, Lee & Sheppard.

Sadler, P. (2001). The itinerant teacher hits the road: A map for instruction in young children's social skills. *Teaching Exceptional Children, 34*(1), 60–65.

Sainato, D., & Carta, J. (1992). Classroom influences on the development of social competence in young children with disabilities. In S. Odom, S. McConnell, & M. McEvoy (Eds.), *Social competence of young children with disabilities: Issues and strategies for intervention* (pp. 93–109). Baltimore, MD: Paul H. Brookes.

Sandall, S., McLean, M. E, & Smith, B. J. (2000). *DEC recommended practices in early intervention/early childhood special education.* Longmont, CO: Sopris West.

Saracho, O. (1985). Young children's play behaviors and cognitive styles. *Early Child Development and Care, 21,* 1–18.

Schwartz, I. S., Anderson, S. R., & Halle, J. W. (1989). Training teachers to use naturalistic time delay: Effects on teacher behavior and on the language use of students. *Journal of the Association for Persons with Severe Handicaps, 14,* 48–57.

Shachar, H., & Sharan, S., (1994). Talking, relating, and achieving: Effects of cooperative learning and whole class instruction. *Cognition and Instruction, 12,* 313–353.

Sigafoos, J., & Littlewood, R. (1999). Communication intervention on the playground: A case study on teaching requesting to a young child with autism. *International Journal of Disability, Development and Education, 46*(3), 427–429.

Slaby, R., Roedell, W., Arezzo, D., & Hendrix, K. (1995). *Early violence prevention: Tools for teachers of young children.* Washington, DC: National Association for the Education of Young Children.

Smith, M., Alberto, P., Briggs, A., & Heller, K. (1991). Special educators' need for assistance in dealing with death and dying. *Division of Physically Handicapped Journal, 12,* 28–34.

Snell, M., & Gast, D. (1981). Applying time delay procedure to the instruction of the severely handicapped. *Journal of the Association for Persons with Severe Handicaps, 6*(3), 3–14.

Spenciner, L. (1992). Mainstreaming the child with a visual impairment. In L. Cohen (Ed.), *Children with exceptional needs in regular classrooms* (pp. 82–97). Washington, DC: National Education Association.

Spodek, B., & Saracho, O. (1994). Using educational play. In B. Spodek & O. Saracho (Eds.), *Dealing with individual differences in early childhood classrooms* (pp. 199–232). New York: Longman.

Spodek, B., & Saracho, O. (1988). The challenge of educational play. In Bergen (Ed.), *Play as a medium for learning and development: A handbook of theory and practice* (pp. 9–22). Portsmouth, NH: Heinemann.

Strain, P., & Fox, J. (1981). Peer social initiations and the modifications of social withdrawal: A review for future perspective. *Journal of Pediatric Psychology, 6,* 413–433.

Tremblay, A., Strain, P., Hendrickson, J., & Shores, R. (1981). Social interactions of normal preschool children. *Behavior Modification, 5,* 237–253.

Visoky, A., & Poe, B. (2000). Can preschoolers be effective peer models? An action research project. *Teaching Exceptional Children, 33*(2), 68–73.

Warren S., & Kaiser, A. (1986). Generalization of treatment effects by young language-delayed children: A longitudinal analysis. *Journal of Speech and Hearing Disorders, 51,* 239–251.

Werts, M., Wolery, M., Holcombe, M., Vassilaros, R., & Billings, S. (1992). Efficacy of transition-based teaching with instructive feedback. *Education and Treatment of Children, 15,* 320–34.

Winterman, K., G., & Sapona, R. H. (2002). Supporting young children with autism spectrum disorders in a responsive classroom learning environment. *Teaching Exceptional Children, 35*(1), 30–35.

Wolery, M. (1994a). Designing inclusive environments for young children with special needs. In M. Wolery and J. Wilbers (Eds.), *Including children with special needs in early childhood programs* (pp. 97–118). Washington, DC: National Association for the Education of Young Children.

Wolery, M. (1994b). Instructional strategies for teaching young children with special needs. In M. Wolery and J. Wilbers (Eds.), *Including children with special needs in early childhood programs* (pp. 119–140). Washington, DC: National Association for the Education of Young Children.

Wolery, M. (1994c). Implementing instruction for young children with special needs in early childhood classrooms. In M. Wolery and J. Wilbers (Eds.), *Including children with special needs in early childhood programs* (pp. 151–166). Washington, DC: National Association for the Education of Young Children.

Wolery, M. (2000). Recommended practices in child-focused interventions. In S. Sandall, M. E. McLean, & B. J. Smith (Eds.), *DEC recommended practices in early intervention/early childhood special education* (pp. 29–37). Longmont, CO: Sopris West.

Wolery, M. (2001). Embedding time delay procedures in classroom activities. In M. Ostrosky & S. Sandall (Eds.), *Teaching strategies: What to do to support young children's development* (pp. 81–90). Longmont, CO: Sopris West.

Wolery, M., Ault, M., & Doyle, P. (1992). *Teaching students with moderate and severe disabilities: Use of response prompting strategies.* White Plains, NY: Longman.

Wolery, M., Bailey, D., & Sugai, G. (1988). *Effective teaching: Principles and procedures of applied behavior analysis with exceptional students.* Boston: Allyn & Bacon.

Wolfe, V., Boyd, L., & Wolfe, D. (1983). Teaching cooperative play to behavior problem preschool children. *Education and Treatment of Children, 6,* 1–9.

York, J., & Rainforth, B. (1987). Developing instructional adaptations. In F. Orelove & D. Sobsey (Eds.), *Educating children with multiple disabilities* (pp. 183–217). Baltimore, MD: Paul H. Brookes.

A Look to the Future

Contemporary Issues and Challenges
in Early Childhood Special Education

Chapter 10

CHAPTER

10

Contemporary Issues and Challenges in Early Childhood Special Education

Celebrating Cultural Diversity

Culture

Early Childhood Special Education
and Cultural Diversity

Emerging Populations of Young Children with Special Needs

Homelessness

Child Abuse and Neglect

Young Children with Special Health
Needs

Preparation of Early Childhood Special Educators

Summary

Check Your Understanding

References

Key Terminology

Culture

Ethnocentric behavior

Physical abuse

Neglect

Emotional abuse

Sexual abuse

Acquired Immune Deficiency Syndrome
(AIDS)

Human immunodeficiency virus (HIV)

Children with special health needs

Few would argue that the field of early childhood special education has dramatically changed in the past twenty-five years. We can only speculate what the next decade will hold for young children with special needs and their families. The only safe assumption is that change will continue to occur affecting service providers, caregivers, and the youngsters themselves. We foresee change occurring in several different arenas. Issues such as the full inclusion movement (which we fully discussed in Chapter 6), our response to an increasingly diverse student population, in addition to questions about the professional preparation of early childhood special educators, are only a few of the topics that will present a myriad of challenges to the field. Early childhood professionals must be prepared to respond to these issues and the impact they will have on the children and families we serve. The purpose of this chapter is to consider three topics which we believe are individually important to the professional development of teachers and have meaning for the field as well.

Celebrating Cultural Diversity

The United States is an immensely diverse society. We live in a nation of many different people and cultures. We are rich in our diversity of national origins, languages, foods, music, folk ways, values, religious practices, and traditions. As a nation we greatly bene-fit from this mix—it is a strength of our country rather than a flaw (Graves, Gargiulo, & Sluder, 1996).

While we celebrate and value this richness of diversity, all too often cultural differences generate stereotypes, misunderstandings, and in some instances, outright prejudice and discrimination. Our educational system is not immune to this faulty pattern of thinking. In fact, in the opinion of some educators, business leaders, and policymakers, the educational system encountered by youngsters from minority populations can be characterized as inadequate, damaging, and openly hostile (Quality Education for Minorities Project, 1990). It is indeed unfortunate that in many of our public schools cultural differences are still considered deviant and the pupils often identified as disadvantaged (Poplin & Wright, 1983). Professionally, as well as personally, this is unacceptable. As early childhood special educators working in an increasingly culturally diverse society we need to model respect for, and sensitivity to, the cultural characteristics of our students and their families.

The makeup of America's population is rapidly changing. The number of children from culturally and linguistically diverse backgrounds is increasing at an extraordinary rate. Our classrooms in the coming years will become especially heterogeneous and evidence greater diversity than we find today. Changing demographics will present a multitude of new challenges to early intervention and early childhood special education programs and the professionals who work therein. By the year 2020, children of color are projected to make up almost half of all school-age youth (Pallas, Natriello, & McDill, 1989). In fact, at the present time, "minority" children are actually the majority of students in many of our urban areas and in several states as well (Hodgkinson, 1993; Lustig & Koestner, 1996). By the middle of this century, it is projected that white Americans will barely comprise half of the country's population (Martin & Midgley, 1994). Thus, the concept of a minority population has become an increasingly meaningless term in many communities across the U.S. (McLean, Bailey, & Wolery, 1996). The effectiveness of our schools in meeting the needs of an expanding culturally diverse population will largely depend upon teachers' ability to be responsive to cultural differences.

While it is axiomatic that early childhood special educators are sensitive to the individual differences of their pupils, increasing emphasis is being placed on cultural and linguistic differences. The current DEC guidelines on recommended practices for young children with special needs and their families reflect the importance of cultural awareness and sensitivity as a crucial component in the delivery of services. The guidelines call for professionals to "acknowledge not only the individual needs of children or families, but also the individual value system of the cultural group with whom they identify" (DEC Task Force on Recommended Practices, 1993, p. 4).

Recognition of cultural diversity is also an important element of developmentally appropriate practice. One aspect of individual appropriateness is the various cultures that the youngsters bring to the classroom (Davis, Kilgo, & Gamel-McCormick, 1998). The key is to include this diversity in all aspects of the curriculum, or what Derman-Sparks (1993) calls "authentic multiculturalism."

Culture

Perhaps we should offer our interpretation of the word **culture** before continuing this discussion. Simply defined, culture can be viewed as the attitudes, values, belief systems, norms, and traditions shared by a particular group of people, which collectively form their heritage. A culture is transmitted from one generation to another. It is typically reflected in language, religion, dress, diet, social customs, and other aspects of a particular lifestyle.

Tiedt and Tiedt (2002) echo this thought. They write that culture "denotes a complex integrated system of values, beliefs, and behaviors common to a large group of people. A culture may include shared history and folklore, ideas about right and wrong, and specific communication styles—the 'truths' accepted by members of the group" (p. 23). These authors further state that every student grows up belonging to a particular culture. The cultural background of the student frequently influences their response to the educational process and must be considered when planning instruction.

Zirpoli (1995) adds an appropriate cautionary note. He reminds professionals to guard against generalizing and stereotyping when working with young children from various cultural groups. Even within specific groups, each youngster is unique and special despite the fact that they share similar group characteristics. Stated another way, teachers need to be cognizant of youngsters' intra-individual differences regardless of shared cultural heritage. Two preschoolers from the same racial group will most likely perform quite differently in the classroom irrespective of their common background.

Early Childhood Special Education and Cultural Diversity

For some youngsters with special needs, entrance into an early intervention or early childhood special education program may be their first exposure to a culture and a language that is different from that of their home. The values of the youngster's home and the values of society typically confront each other for the first time in school (Kirk, Gallagher, & Anastasiow, 2000). Thus, there is the potential for cultural conflict as roles, relationships, and expectations may clash. Hanson and Zercher (2001) write, if "preschool goals, and values for children's learning, social and behavioral expectations, and demands for interactional and communication abilities differ from those that the children and their families possess, then potential differences [conflict] may arise" (p. 418). Language, race, and ethnicity also often influence access to early intervention and special education services and supports (Sandall, McLean, & Smith, 2000). Early childhood special educators must be alert to these possibilities. They must also communicate to the child and his or her family that they value and respect the child's cultural heritage. Effectiveness in working with culturally diverse students further requires that teachers understand and are comfortable with their own cultural background (Gollnick & Chinn, 1998).

One particular challenge confronting early childhood special educators is distinguishing between ethnicity and exceptionality. Professionals who work with young children and their families need to ensure that ethnicity is not mistaken for educational exceptionality (Hallahan & Kauffman, 2003). This can easily occur when teachers view their own cultural group as setting the standard against which other groups are to be measured. When this happens teachers are guilty of exhibiting **ethnocentric behavior,** whereby they view their own cultural group characteristics as correct or superior and the ways of other groups are thought of as odd or inferior. Consequently, actions which are considered atypical or deviant by the early childhood special educator may, in fact, be fairly typical and adaptive within the youngster's culture (Hallahan & Kauffman). It is important to recognize that we all view other people and the world around us through "culturally-tinted lenses" (Barrera, 2000); different cultural groups interpret behavior differently—it all depends on one's perspective. Table 10–1 illustrates examples of these various perspectives. Morrow (1987) believes that these divergent viewpoints often result in differences in behaviors and achievement levels among pupils from these groups.

We offer the following note of caution: do not generalize or stereotype on the basis of the information contained in Table 10–1. Also, do not assume that all individuals within a particular cultural group will perform or react in a predetermined fashion (Raver, 1999). Always view the child and his or her family as individuals. Remember, differences do *not* equate to dysfunction or deficits.

Cultural differences should not routinely translate into disabilities. Far too often, however, belonging to a particular ethnic group results in an automatic assumption that the child will behave in certain ways. Possible reasons for this situation are that differences are sometimes not valued or are easily misunderstood, while in some cases it is the direct result of prejudice and stereotyping (Hallahan & Kauffman, 2003). This frequently leads to the overrepresentation of minority populations in some special education programs (such as those for youngsters with mental retardation) and an underrepresentation in others (such as programs for the gifted). Bowe (2000) reports data that suggests that between 25–33% of the enrollment in early childhood special education programs are youngsters from minority populations; even in regions of our country which are not that ethnically diverse. The percentage is dramatically higher in our urban areas. While there are a myriad of possible reasons for this relationship, we agree with Bowe's analysis that it is best understood as a relationship between family socioeconomic status and disability rather than being an issue of disability and minority group status per se. Report after report and survey after survey routinely indicate an overrepresentation of minority groups living in poverty (Children's Defense Fund, 2000; 2001). Poverty contributes to limited access to health care, poor nutrition, and inadequate living conditions among other adverse circumstances. All of these variables increase the probability of the young child being at-risk for future learning and development difficulties. Cultural and language differences only exacerbate the youngster's problems and heighten the likelihood of their needing special education services.

As the numbers of infants, toddlers, and preschoolers with special needs continues to grow at a rapid pace (U.S. Department of Education, 2002), one can reasonably anticipate a corresponding increase in the numbers of young children with special needs from culturally diverse groups; unfortunately, the numbers of teachers who share a similar cultural heritage with these youngsters is failing to expand. Almost 90 percent of teachers in this country are white, 7 to 9 percent are African American, and a mere 3 percent are Hispanic or of other racial groups (Cook & Boe, 1995). This means that teachers working in early intervention and early childhood special education programs, the majority of whom are white, will have to exhibit heightened cultural sensitivity as

Table 10–1 Familial and School Related Values: Perspectives of Anglo- and Non-Anglo-Americans

Group	Family Orientation	Relationship with Family	Socialization	Relationship with Group	Recognition
Anglo-American	Nuclear family-oriented	Individualistic, independent behavior	Children socialized to be independent, competitive, and self-reliant	Competition is valued	Status based on achievement
Hispanic-American	Extended family-oriented	Family unit is important, comes before the individual	Children taught to be obedient, cooperative, and dependent	Cooperation is valued; emphasis on sharing, group work	Humility is valued
Asian-American	Extended family-oriented	Family central focus; basis of society	Children taught to be obedient, cooperative, and dependent	Cooperation is valued; welfare of group	Humility is valued
African-American	Nuclear and extended family-oriented; strong sense of kinship	Expressive individuality tied to family and community	Children taught dependence on family and community	Loyalty to family and network	Individual accomplishment valued and encouraged
Native American	Extended family and large network units; clan, tribe	Belief in rights of individual as well as others; family important	Children are encouraged to be independent, to make own decisions	Cooperation is valued; stress working as a group; competition de-emphasized	Excellence is related to the contribution to group, not personal glory or individual recognition

Group	Time	Respect	Eye Contact	Personal Interactions	Planning
Anglo-American	Time is valuable; events are tightly scheduled; punctuality is important	Teachers and adults are not automatically respected	Direct eye contact	People express themselves and attempt to impress others through speech	Plan for future
Hispanic-American	Time is relaxed, flexible; events are not tightly scheduled	Parents and elders are highly respected	Children lower their eyes when reprimanded	Interact assertively; stand up for self	Live in the present
Asian-American	Time is "elastic," can be stretched or contracted	Teachers and parents are highly respected; reverence for elders	Lack of eye contact in deference to authority; indication of respect	Quiet/nonverbal, silence is valued; confrontation with issues and problems are avoided—saving "face"	Live on day-to-day basis

Table 10–1 (Continued)

Group	Time	Respect	Eye Contact	Personal Interactions	Planning
African-American	Most have mainstream time concept; some have flexible time concept	Parents, elders, and community leaders are highly respected	Eye contact is variable	Highly verbal and expressive; assertive	Live in the present
Native-American	Time is flexible; not critical	Wisdom of age and experience is respected	Limited eye contact	Quiet/nonverbal; express self and ideas through actions	Live in the present

Group	Education	Support System
Anglo-American	Parents likely to value education; education for grades	Seek support; trust outside agencies
Hispanic-American	For low-income families, daily survival is important—more than education	Use of family, neighbors, and religious leaders rather than outside agencies
Asian-American	Parents highly value education; academic achievement encouraged	Dissociate from others outside of culture; agencies are last resort—usually when problem is extremely serious
African-American	Parents respond well if school demonstrates interest; education seen as a means to better life	Extended family and church provide primary support; need to develop trust in professionals
Native-American	Parents are influenced by staff sensitive to their values and needs; education for knowledge sake	Extended family and others within culture first; then outside agencies as last resort

SOURCE: Adapted from S. Salend. *Effective Mainstreaming* (New York: Macmillan, 1990), p. 68. Adapted from E. Nuttall, B. DeLeon, and M. Valle, Best Practices in Considering Cultural Factors in *Best Practices in School Psychology II*. Edited by A. Thomas and J. Grimes (Washington, DC: National Association of School Psychologists, 1990), p. 230. Copyright 1990 by the National Association of School Psychologists. Reprinted by permission of the publisher.

they work with an increasingly culturally diverse student population. This will present many unique challenges to early childhood special educators. Cultural differences may present themselves in several ways. Examples of some of the issues that may confront teachers include: cultural interpretations of the etiology of disability; the family's perception of the disabled child; the perceived value of early childhood special education services; child-rearing practices; family coping strategies; medical practices and traditions; the role of family members; and the acceptance of "outsiders" who offer assistance with the youngster's care and education (Lynch & Hanson, 1998; Hanson, Lynch, & Wayman, 1990). It would not be uncommon for the best intentions of professionals to be misinterpreted due to their failure to consider the family's value system and cultural traditions.

Hanson et al. (1990) recognize the difficulty of the task confronting early childhood special educators as they work with families of culturally and linguistically diverse children. These experts believe that teachers of young children with special needs must not only acknowledge different cultural perspectives, but they must also learn "how to work effectively within the boundaries that are comfortable for the family" (p. 117). This will require that service providers become ethnically competent. It is not necessary, however, for the professional to know everything about a particular culture to provide sensitive and appropriate services (Lynch & Hanson, 1998). What is required, according to Hanson and Zercher (2001), is an attitude of openness and respect for the many beliefs, values, practices, and behaviors presented by the children and their families. Service providers who are open and eager to learn, respectful of differences, willing to conduct honest and reflective self-examinations and make changes when necessary are capable of developing cultural competence.

We cannot emphasize enough the importance of early childhood special educators demonstrating cultural awareness and sensitivity. In future years, the success of our early intervention and early education efforts may well depend upon the ability of teachers to exhibit culturally sensitive behavior while providing culturally competent services as mandated by PL 102-119. McLean et al. (1996) agree with this think-

America's classrooms are becoming increasingly culturally and linguistically diverse.

ing. They also believe that "services for young children and their families must be delivered in a culturally competent way by individuals sensitive to, respectful of, and knowledgeable about the families' cultural practices, values, and folkways" (p. 71).

We conclude this section by offering the following suggestions (Graves et al., 1996) as examples of some of the types of activities that can help early childhood special educators incorporate cultural diversity into their programs while working effectively with culturally diverse families. We realize, of course, that no list of ideas can guarantee that services to young children with special needs and their families will be provided in a culturally sensitive fashion.

- Instructional materials and assessment activities should be appropriate to the cultural background of the children
- Books, visual displays, learning activities, and computer software should be free of bias and stereotype
- Incorporate fully the holidays and festivals of different ethnic groups into classroom celebrations
- Communications with non-English speaking parents/caregivers should be in their native language; interpreters may be necessary for home visits, IFSP and IEP meetings, as well as in-school contacts

- Routinely invite professionals, parents, grandparents, community leaders, and other role models who represent the diversity of the community to visit the classroom where they can talk about their profession, demonstrate unique skills, and share the customs, traditions, heritage, and folklore of their native lands

- Community volunteers can help teachers develop survival vocabulary—greetings and common words or phrases appropriate to the background of the youngsters enrolled in the program

Emerging Populations of Young Children with Special Needs

The professional issues confronting early childhood special educators are many. We have identified only a select few of these challenges. Other issues, which seem to be a product of our times, are also affecting the lives of our youngest citizens and the professionals who serve them. It is indeed unfortunate that our children are not immune to the myriad of ills that are rampant in our society. Homelessness, child abuse, and children suffering the effects of parental/caregiver substance abuse are only some of the problems facing teachers. Consider the following portrait of contemporary life in the United States:

- Over 216,000 preschool age children are homeless; almost 40% of the homeless population are families with children.

- Fetal alcohol syndrome (FAS) is recognized as one of the leading causes of mental retardation in the United States.

- A child is reported abused or neglected every 11 minutes; almost 2.67 million cases of abuse and neglect were reported in 2001.

- Eighteen percent of children younger than age six or over 4.1 million youngsters were living in poverty in 1999.

- One in seven children are without health insurance.

- Human immunodeficiency virus (HIV) is the leading infectious cause of pediatric mental retardation in America.

- Every 2 minutes a baby is born at low birthweight (less than 5.8 pounds).

- In 1999 only 78% of two-year-olds were immunized against preventable childhood illnesses.

- Between 3.3 and 10 million youngsters are exposed to domestic violence each year (Children's Defense Fund, 1998, 2000, 2001; Gargiulo, 2003).

The preceding data are truly frightening, especially when one considers the implications for our educational system. Historically, schools have responded to the needs of society. The challenges that are now upon us dictate, therefore, that teachers have greater awareness of the magnitude of the crisis and are positioned to deal effectively with changing societal conditions and the resulting changing clientele.

Our goal in this section of the chapter is to highlight a few of the areas of concern. Selected for brief review are the issues of homelessness, child abuse, and young children with special health needs (such as children with AIDS, youngsters prenatally exposed to cocaine, and medically fragile youngsters). Research (May, Kundert, & Akpan, 1994) suggests that special education teachers are lacking in knowledge about many contemporary societal issues and are inadequately prepared to deal with the problems they will encounter in their classrooms.

Homelessness

The problem of homelessness in America is growing. The homeless population is also changing. Two decades ago adult males were the primary group of citizens without permanent shelter. Today, however, families with children are the fastest growing segment of homeless Americans (Children's Defense Fund, 1995; Williams & DeSander, 1999), accounting for almost 40% of the homeless population (Children's Defense Fund, 2001). It is believed that more than 1 million children are homeless every night including 250,000 preschoolers (Nunez & Collignon, 1997). Other reports suggest that there are about 850,000 homeless children in the United States of which approximately 216,000 preschoolers are without permanent shelter (Children's Defense Fund, 2000). Eight out of ten homeless families with children are female-headed households; a disproportionate percentage of these families are members of racial or ethnic minority groups (Interagency Council on the Homeless, 1999; Williams & DeSander, 1999). Of course, the transient status of these families leads to a significant problem of underreporting the actual incidence of homelessness.

The educational needs of homeless children are often neglected. Homeless youngsters are frequently at risk for missing school. It is estimated that approximately 10% of homeless children do not attend school (Interagency Council on the Homeless, 1999). Those students who are able to attend often experience both academic and behavioral difficulties (Eddowes & Hranitz, 1989; Stronge & Tenhouse, 1990). Although many of these children are eligible for special education services, the transient nature of their family's lifestyle prohibits the effective delivery of needed services.

Homelessness takes a toll on the very young child. In a national survey (Interagency Council on the Homeless, 1999) the U.S. government found that over 40% of children who are homeless are age five or younger. Homelessness, according to Russell and Williams (1988), is a breeding ground for disabling conditions. Research supports this assertion. In one investigation (Bassuk & Rosenberg, 1990), 50% of a sample of homeless preschoolers evidenced significant delays on the Denver Developmental Screening Test as compared to 16% of housed peers. The Children's Defense Fund (1988) reports that almost half of the homeless children who are younger than age five display significant developmental delays. Serious behavioral and emotional disorders are also quite typical in preschoolers who are homeless (Rescoria, Parker, & Stolley, 1991). Spodek and Saracho (1994) observe that homeless youngsters who attend child care centers frequently exhibit a number of problem behaviors. Common difficulties include short attention span, delayed speech, withdrawal, poor impulse control, and aggressive behavior, among other problems. Obviously, homelessness affects children not only educationally but emotionally and physically as well. Severe health problems, child abuse, psychosocial disorders, and clinical depression are but a few of the common consequences of homelessness (Heflin & Rudy, 1991). The repercussions of homelessness significantly increase the chances of developmental delays and the possibility of future learning and developmental difficulties.

The educational plight of homeless children has not gone unrecognized. Thanks to PL 101-382, the Improving America's Schools Act (Education for Homeless Children and Youth Program), local school districts are mandated to allow homeless children to attend, to the greatest extent possible, the school requested by their parents. The 1994 amendments to PL 100–77, the Stewart B. McKinney Homeless Assistance Act of 1987, requires that the state educational agency assure a free and appropriate education to preschool children who are homeless. In 1994 a Washington, D.C. federal appeals court ruled in *Lampkin v. District of Columbia* (27 F.3d 605) that homeless youngsters have an enforceable right to a public education under federal law. The Children's Defense Fund (1995) notes that individual states are enacting legislation providing for the education of homeless children. Illinois law, for example, requires local public schools to arrange for school transportation, in addition to mandating the enrollment of homeless children even if needed documentation like proof of residency and medical records are unavailable.

Early childhood special educators need to be especially sensitive to the plight of children who are homeless. Eddowes (1994) believes that schools can serve as safe harbor for these youngsters. Besides offering appropriate educational experiences schools can also provide special services like bathing facilities, clean clothes, and nutritious meals. The value of an education for homeless children cannot be underestimated. "One of the most efficient methods," Heflin and Rudy (1991) believe, "of enabling a student to overcome the detrimental effects of homelessness is to provide an appropriate education" (p. 20). Young students without a permanent address need more than just access to an education; they require an individually tailored instructional program designed to compensate for negative life stressors (Kayne, 1989).

Eddowes and Hranitz (1989) recommend that teachers plan for, and incorporate, pupils who are homeless into their programs regardless of the length of the child's attendance. At this point in time, an appropriate education is the most promising intervention tactic available. It has the potential of assisting youngsters in overcoming the harmful effects of homelessness (Heflin & Rudy, 1989). Early childhood special educators can thus play a vital role in securing a brighter future for these children.

Child Abuse and Neglect

Child abuse and neglect has reached epidemic proportions in the United States. On an almost daily basis the media exposes us to accounts of various acts of cruelty inflicted on children by adult perpetrators. Tragic illustrations secured from the files of the Ohio Department of Public Welfare (Gargiulo, 1990, p. 1) include:

- A father [who] poured lighter fluid on his child's arm and lit it
- A 42-month-old child [who] had been beaten and sexually abused by a babysitter
- A small child [who] was kicked in the face for simply making a noise
- A child [who] was left alone in a locked car on a 90° summer day
- A parent [who] failed to regularly send her child to school
- A mother [who] refused to seek medical care for her children

As teachers we have a legal, and perhaps more importantly, a moral obligation to see that such actions do not continue. Abuse flourishes due to secrecy, privacy, and a lack of attention. Greater awareness and active involvement on the part of teachers can help break the cycle of child abuse and may even save the life of a youngster.

Definitions   How does one define the terms *abuse* and *neglect*? What might seem to be a simple task is actually quite difficult due to varying accepted practices of child rearing. Societal and community standards generally dictate what is considered abuse.

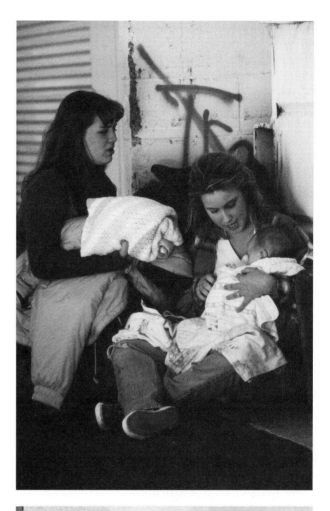

The educational needs of homeless children are frequently neglected.

SOURCE: GettyImages.

Most people, for example, oppose the beating of children; yet, some parents use physical punishment as a typical means of disciplining their children and corporal punishment is very common in a large number of schools.

One simple way of distinguishing between physical abuse and neglect is to view the former as an act of commission, while the latter implies an act of omission. The four major types of child maltreatment include physical abuse, neglect, emotional abuse, and sexual abuse. Although the definition of these terms varies according to individual state law, many definitions reflect the following thinking. **Physical abuse** is an act of commission. It refers to an assault on a child designed to cause physical injury or harm. Examples include hitting, kicking, shaking, stabbing, and other nonaccidental inflictions. Spanking is usually considered a disciplinary action; however, if the child is injured or bruised it can be classified as abusive.

Neglect is an act of omission and involves a variety of caregiver behaviors that include such things as abandonment, inadequate physical supervision, failure to provide basic necessities (shelter, adequate nourishment, attention and affection, clothing) as well as the failure to provide necessary medical treatment. Chronic school truancy also constitutes neglect (English, 1998).

Emotional abuse, is a difficult term to define, and can be an act of commission or omission. It is generally distinguished by a constellation of interactions instigated by the caregiver and designed to be psychologically destructive for the child. Verbal attacks on the youngster's self-esteem and self-image by constant screaming, criticizing, and humiliation illustrate one form of emotional maltreatment. Rejection and inadequate nurturance also defines emotional abuse whose effect is cumulative. In many instances, psychological injury is a byproduct of physical abuse, neglect, and sexual abuse (Gargiulo, 1990).

A description of **sexual abuse,** which is an act of commission, contains two parts: sexual abuse and sexual exploitation. Kempe (1978) defines sexual abuse as "the involvement of dependent, developmentally immature children and adolescents in sexual relations that they do not fully comprehend, to which they are unable to give informed consent or that violate the social taboos of families" (p. 382). The sexual exploitation of children occurs when they serve as prostitutes, engage in pornographic activities, or provide for the sexual gratification of adults (Brenner, 1984). According to Gargiulo (1990) sexual abuse is hidden by a conspiracy of silence and represents the most underreported form of child abuse.

Federal statutes also define child abuse and neglect. Unfortunately, like state law, much of the legislation is ambiguous and lacks precision when describing types of child maltreatment.

Prevalence   The number of cases of child abuse and neglect is increasing at an alarming rate. It is difficult, however, to obtain accurate and reliable data because definitions vary from state to state and the fact that there is a significant problem of underreporting. Not all cases of abuse and neglect are reported. Goldman (1995) notes that underreporting is especially severe in the case of preschoolers who have limited access to adults outside of their immediate family. These problems notwithstanding, national surveys reveal that every 11 minutes a child is abused or neglected (Children's Defense Fund, 2001). According to the U.S. Department of Health and Human Services (2003), approximately 2.67 million children were reported for suspected abuse or neglect in 2001. Over 1.02 million youngsters were confirmed victims of maltreatment. In comparison, only 1.9 million cases were filed in 1985 and less than 700,000 were recorded in 1976 (National Center on Child Abuse and Neglect, 1986).

An analysis of child abuse and neglect statistics by the Children's Defense Fund (2001) indicates that more than half of the confirmed cases of child maltreatment involve neglect, while just over one-third of the victims suffered physical or sexual abuse. One-quarter of the children were victims of more than one type of maltreatment. As noted in previous years, infants and toddlers had the highest abuse and neglect rates.

What the preceding data fail to reveal are the number of children who die each year at the hands of their parents or caregivers. An average of five children each day die as a result of abuse or neglect. Almost 80% of the victims are younger than age five (Children's Defense Fund, 2001). Estimates suggest that between 2,000 and 5,000 youngsters die each year as a result of child abuse and neglect (Gargiulo, 1990), while approximately 140,000 children are seriously injured—many of whom are disabled for life (Children's Defense Fund, 1996).

Child Characteristics   Child abuse requires three elements—the perpetrator, the victim, and a precipitating crisis, like the loss of employment or severe health problems. *All* parents have the potential to be abusive and some youngsters are more vulnerable to abuse and neglect than others. Our focus here is on the role that the child plays in the abuse triangle.

Research (Ammerman, Hersen, Van Hasselt, Lubetsky & Sieck 1994; Cosmos, 2001; Goldman, 1993; Zirpoli, 1990) suggests that children with special needs are particularly vulnerable to abuse. Youngsters with disabilities are overrepresented in samples of abused children (Zirpoli, 1986). Children who are perceived as different or difficult to raise are often at risk for abuse. Children with mild or moderate disabilities (versus those with severe impairments) seem to especially be in peril (Embry, 1980). Age also plays a role. Preschool children have the greatest risk for physical abuse as well as neglect (Goldman, 1995). According to both Gargiulo (1990) and Goldman (1990), some of the specific variables that heighten a youngster's vulnerability include:

- low birthweight
- mental retardation
- prematurity
- orthopedic impairments (cerebral palsy, spina bifida)
- emotional/behavioral disorders
- developmental delays
- provocative or unmanageable behavior (colic, hyperactivity)
- impairment in mother-infant bonding
- language and speech delays
- impaired social skills

An intriguing question that frequently arises is whether a particular characteristic, such as mental retardation or hyperactivity, is the cause or consequence of abuse. A conclusive answer is presently not available. Contemporary best thinking suggests that some youngsters are part of a reciprocal process whereby specific behaviors provoke abuse, which in turn exacerbates the situation and thus gives rise to additional maltreatment (Gargiulo, 1990). One must remember, however, that a youngster's characteristics or actions, in and of themselves, do not cause abuse. Specific individual traits are only one factor in the formula for abuse. Child abuse is the outcome of the interplay of parental/caregiver characteristics, cultural factors, environmental considerations, and a precipitating event. It is rare that the etiology of abuse can be linked to a sole condition (Gargiulo,

1990). The interrelationship among the aforementioned variables is illustrated in Figure 10–1.

A Role for Schools and the Early Childhood Special Educator   The toll of abuse and neglect on the young child is almost unimaginable. It affects them emotionally, socially, physically, and intellectually (Cosmos, 2001). Teachers, however, can play a vital role in the identification and prevention of child

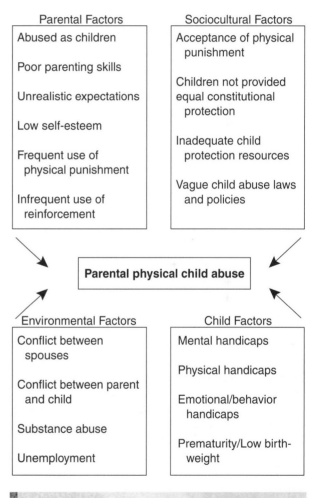

Figure 10–1   A Model of the Interaction of Primary Factors Contributing to Parental Physical Child Abuse

Note: The conditions provided under each primary factor represent only a limited number of examples.

SOURCE: T. Zirpoli, Child Abuse and Children with Handicaps, *Remedial and Special Education, 7,* 1986. p. 42.

abuse and neglect. They may well be the only professional who has daily and continuous contact with the youngster. Early childhood special educators are in a unique position, therefore, to intervene and assist in breaking the intergenerational cycle of child abuse and neglect.

Recognizing the signs of abuse and neglect can sometimes be difficult. Table 10–2 provides a list of some of the possible indicators of child abuse and neglect. If a number of these signs are evident or there are repeated occurrences, then you should be alert to the possibility of maltreatment.

Every state has child abuse reporting laws. Teachers, in fact, are mandated reporters. They are legally required to report their suspicion of instances of abuse and neglect to the appropriate law enforcement agency or child protective service. The purpose of this legislation is to protect abused and neglected children, not to punish perpetrators. To make a report proof is not necessary. Reasonable cause to suspect maltreatment is all that is required. Educators who act in good faith, and without malice, are protected from civil or criminal liability. Yet, failure to report can lead to legal problems for the teacher. The greatest tragedy, however, is the continued harm to the child and possibly their death (Gargiulo, 1990; Goldman, 1993).

Teachers are frequently unwilling to report abuse and neglect (Goldman, 1990). A variety of reasons exist for this reluctance. Excuses range from ignorance of their mandated status to the absence of school board policy to the fear of termination (if untenured) due to their reporting. We recommend that all schools have a written policy outlining the steps to be taken in recording suspected episodes of abuse and neglect. Schools are also a logical place for prevention programs to begin. Examples of such activities include inservice workshops on abuse and neglect for staff and administrators as well as parent education programs possibly sponsored by the parent-teacher organization offering hints and suggestions on child care, behavior management techniques, and parenting skills. Schools can also spearhead community awareness programs on abuse and neglect. Schools are in a unique position, as Goldman and Gargiulo (1987) observe, to bring about change in the community and subsequently improve the lives of countless children.

The eradication of child abuse and neglect is not possible. Informed and concerned special educators, however, are vital in attempts to bring this crisis under control. By being informed and vigilant, the quality of life for many young children with special needs will be improved and maybe the veil of secrecy surrounding child abuse and neglect will be lifted.

Getting Connected

For additional information about child abuse and neglect visit the following Websites:

Child Help USA
http://www.childhelpusa.org/

National Clearinghouse on Child Abuse and Neglect
http://www.calib.com/nccanch/

Prevent Child Abuse America
http://www.preventchildabuse.org/

Child Abuse Prevent Network
http://www.child-abuse.com/

Young Children with Special Health Needs

There are a large number of health issues that affect the quality of life of preschoolers. Increasingly, teachers are encountering youngsters with infectious and chronic conditions. Schools, therefore, are playing a larger role in the health care arena. One result of this expanded role are new professional and personal challenges, which now confront the early childhood special educator. Chosen for brief discussion are three contemporary health issues: children with AIDS, youngsters prenatally exposed to cocaine, and children identified as medically fragile.

Pediatric AIDS Since the early days of the **Acquired Immune Deficiency Syndrome (AIDS)** epidemic in 1981 there has been a significant amount of fear and misunderstanding about this disease. Part of the fear about AIDS resides in the fact that, at the present time, it is incurable.

Table 10–2   Examples of Possible Indicators of Abuse and Neglect

Physical Indicators of Abuse

- Bruises on face, lips, or mouth
- "Stocking burns" or doughnut shaped burns on buttocks
- Subdural hematomas caused by hitting or shaking
- Lacerations and abrasions on back of arms, legs, torso
- Cigarette or cigar burns on the palms of hands, soles of feet, or genitals

Behavioral Indicators of Abuse

- Overly compliant, passive
- Fearful of physical contact
- Arrives early for school, stays late
- Is often sleepy in class
- Inappropriate neatness while playing or eating
- Excessive school absence and/or tardiness

Physical Indicators of Neglect

- Abandonment
- Poor personal hygiene
- Absence of needed medical or dental care
- Inappropriate or inadequate clothing
- Complaints of being constantly hungry

Behavioral Indicators of Neglect

- Falls asleep in school, lethargic
- Dull, apathetic appearance
- Failure to thrive among infants
- Begs or steals food, eats classmate's leftovers
- Irregular school attendance

Physical Indicators of Emotional Abuse

- Absence of positive self-image
- Impulsive, defiant, antisocial behavior
- Overly fearful, vigilant
- Behavior inappropriate for chronological age: too adult-like or too infantile
- Difficulty in establishing and maintaining peer relationships

Physical Indicators of Sexual Abuse

- Torn, stained, or bloody undergarments
- Bruises of or bleeding from external genitalia, vagina, or anal region
- Presence of sexually transmitted diseases
- Hymen stretched at a very young age
- Complaints of difficulty with urination

Behavioral Indicators of Sexual Abuse

- Sexually precocious, sexual promiscuity
- Withdrawal from social relationships
- Acts in a seductive fashion in the presence of peers and/or adults
- School work (stories, poems, artwork) that manifest sexual themes
- Reluctance to participate in physical activities

SOURCE: Adapted from R. Gargiulo, Child Abuse and Neglect: An Overview, In R. Goldman & R. Gargiulo (Eds.), *Children at Risk* (Austin, TX: Pro-Ed, 1990). pp. 19–23.

Feature 10–1

**I Am Your Child
and I Need you Badly.**

Please look at me carefully the next time you see me.
Please notice that I am small and weak.
Please listen to me carefully the next time you see me.
Please notice that I don't know much.
Like you, I was born helpless. And growing up so I can take care of myself will take me a long time, too.
I need food.
I need rest.
I need to be kept clean.
I need to be kept warm in winter and cool in summer.
I need to be taken in your arms or sat on your lap.
I need to feel your skin against my skin.
I need you to help heal my hurts.
I need you to play with just so you and I can have some good times together.
I need you to teach me everything you can so I'll have a chance in this world when I grow up.
I need your patience. I know I'm not very orderly. I cry out for things like food and attention the second I need them. I can't help it, and I know that bothers you sometimes. All I can hope is that you will be patient with me until I can learn to be patient, too.
Above all, I need to know you love me. Even if your parents gave you no love, try to give a little to me so I can give a little to my children and they can give a little to their children. I need so much from you, yet I have only one thing I can give you in return.
That is my love.
Today and tomorrow and as long as I live.

Source: Pilkington Libbey-Owens-Ford, Toledo, Ohio. Published by the kind permission of Pilkington Libbey-Owens-Ford, Toledo, Ohio.

AIDS is caused by the **human immunodeficiency virus (HIV).** HIV contributes to the breakdown of the child's natural immunity system, leaving the youngster very susceptible to certain infectious and opportunistic illnesses (illnesses that can be serious due to a weakened immune system like chicken pox or influenza). The HIV virus may be spread through sexual intercourse, blood contact, or sharing contaminated hypodermic needles. Pediatric AIDS is usually the result of the youngster's mother being infected and transmitting the virus to her baby. About 90% of the youngsters diagnosed with HIV acquire the infection from their mothers (Spiegel & Bonwit, 2002). Transmission can occur during pregnancy, at birth, and via breast-feeding. Most instances of pediatric AIDS occur in utero (Armstrong, Seidel, & Swales, 1993). Approximately 30–50% of infants born to HIV mothers are infected (Caldwell, Sirvis, Todaro, & Accouloumire, 1991; Johnson, 1993). The Centers for Disease Control (CDC) identified almost 9,100 cases of pediatric AIDS as of December 2001 (Centers for Disease Control and Prevention, 2002). Yet, this data is somewhat suspect; more youngsters are likely to have AIDS than the CDC figures suggest due to their rigid standards for classifying pediatric AIDS cases. For every child reported with AIDS, another two to three are HIV-infected (Rathlev, 1994). Rosen and Granger (1992) predict that HIV infection will become the single most prevalent cause of developmental disability. It is already one of the most common infectious causes of mental retardation (Armstrong et al., 1993).

HIV infection is a source of significant stress for families. In fact, Lesar and her colleagues (Lesar, Gerber, & Semmel, 1996) view it as a family disease because it threatens the youngster's entire caregiving system. The impact of infection has devastating consequences on young children. Although the course of the disease is different for each child, and difficult to predict, pediatric AIDS contributes to significant developmental delays and debilitating motor, cognitive, language, and social development. Developmental regression and deterioration is also not uncommon (Johnson, 1993; Lesar & Maldonado, 1994). Some of the other possible adverse outcomes of pediatric AIDS include:

- impaired fine and gross motor skills
- chronic bacterial and viral infections

- failure to thrive
- acute diarrhea
- enlarged spleen and liver
- weight loss
- attention deficits
- frequent respiratory problems
- central nervous system damage
- sensory impairments

Early intervention and special education services are almost always necessary for children with AIDS. Some states serve very young children under the category of being at-risk for developmental delay while older youngsters with HIV receive services via the "Other Health Impaired" label found in IDEA.

Special educators need not worry about contracting AIDS as a result of teaching these children. Researchers note (Centers for Disease Control, 1998; Rutstein, Conlon, & Batshaw, 1997) that, to date, there has *not* been one reported instance of AIDS transmission from child to classmate or child to teacher in any early childhood program. It is safe, therefore, for children to play with a peer who has AIDS and for teachers to serve them. "HIV is not transmitted through vomit, sweat, stool, or nasal secretions" (Byrom & Katz, 1991, p. 10). Casual contact such as hugging, touching, coughing or the sharing of clothing items has not been shown to spread the infection (Le Roy, Powell, & Kelker, 1994). Of course, appropriate hygiene practices and universal infection control procedures are required, such as wearing disposable gloves when treating a bloody nose, vigorous handwashing (soap and water destroy the HIV virus), and cleaning soiled surfaces like toys, countertops, and bathrooms with a disinfectant like common household bleach.

Young children who are HIV positive or have AIDS are able, in most cases, to participate in early childhood programs; in fact, the Americans with Disabilities Act (PL 101–336) guarantees this right. All children with HIV infection should, according to the American Academy of Pediatrics, receive an appropriate education designed to meet their evolving needs (American Academy of Pediatrics, 1991). (See Table 10–3 for a checklist of strategies designed to accommodate children with AIDS in the classroom.) There is no logical reason for excluding a student with HIV infection if the youngster's health permits attendance at school (Rutstein et al., 1997). Some pupils, however, may require alternative instructional programs such as homebound instruction. This

Table 10–3   Teacher Checklist for Accommodating Students with AIDS

- Observe guidelines for confidentiality of information.
- Assess the student for eligibility under IDEA or Section 504.
- Obtain copies of state and local policies for inclusion of students with AIDS.
- Get the facts about AIDS and how it affects learning.
- Assemble a team to develop an individualized education program (IEP) that addresses educational needs and health-related supports.
- Plan modifications of instructional methods and curriculum to meet the student's individual needs.
- Design ways to include the student who has AIDS in typical classroom activities.
- Build flexibility into the student's IEP to allow for hospitalizations and frequent absences.
- Arrange for training in infection control procedures (e.g., universal precautions).
- Educate parents about communicable disease policies and the use of universal precautions.
- Answer students' questions about terminal illness.

SOURCE: K. Kelker, A. Hecimovic, and C. LeRoy, Designing a Classroom and School Environment for Students with AIDS. *Teaching Exceptional Children, 26* (4), 1994. p. 52.

strategy should only be used in response to the student's illness and not to the fears of the community (Byrom & Katz, 1991; Caldwell et al., 1991).

Schools and teachers have a unique role and responsibility in our nation's response to the AIDS crisis. (See Table 10–4 for a list of responsibilities of special educators.) Educating our students (and their parents), fellow professionals, and community members about AIDS and HIV infection prevention is an important first step. Accurate information is a powerful tool for combating unwarranted fears. We fully endorse preservice and inservice training experi-

---

Getting Connected

For additional information about HIV and AIDS visit the following Websites:

HIV/AIDS Fact Sheets
http://www.cdc.gov/hiv/pubs/facts.htm

National Pediatric and Family Resource Center
http://www.pedhivaids.org

Table 10–4   Responsibilities of Special Educators for Serving Children with AIDS

1. *Inclusion in schools.* There is no justification for excluding a child with AIDS from school, assuming that the child's health permits inclusion.

2. *Interdisciplinary team management.* The design of proper education programs is an important secondary consideration for improving the child's quality of life. The special educator's role is . . . [to ensure that] services are provided in the most inclusive and normal settings possible.

3. *Early and frequent assessment.* . . . [A]ssessments should be tied directly to the delivery of instruction and needed services.

4. *Provide a family focus.* Family support services must be provided within natural settings are they must build on family strengths and resources in a manner that encourages independence and decision making.

5. *Sensitive and nonjudgmental services.* Providing a nonjudgmental environment will enhance the effectiveness of special education services . . . [and] build trust between the family and special educators. . . .

6. *Confidentiality.* Decisions as to who should receive information on a child's condition should be made by the parents, the child's physician, and a school administrator. . . . [P]rograms that treat individuals with AIDS should develop a specific AIDS confidentiality policy.

7. *Providing safety.* Teachers should employ universal precautions . . . when dealing with body fluids.

8. *Keeping current.* The facts surrounding AIDS are changing rapidly. Keeping current with the latest information is the least we can do for our students and ourselves.

9. *Providing education programs that focus on prevention.* It is essential for special educators to help prevent the spread of AIDS. This can best be accomplished through prevention education. . . . [Help parents to] become involved in their children's AIDS education.

10. *Preparing the educational team.* All members of the educational team, including teachers, related education professionals, paraprofessionals, support staff, and administrators must be properly prepared to provide supportive learning environments for these children.

11. *Attention to quality of life.* A guiding consideration for all aspects of the child's education is how the child's quality of life can be enhanced.

12. *Advocacy.* The special education teacher is in one of the best positions to champion the rights of these children. . . .

SOURCE: Adapted from C. LeRoy, T. Powell, and P. Keller, Meeting Our Responsibilities in Special Education, *Teaching Exceptional Children, 26* (4), 1994. pp. 40–44.

ences for teachers. We also believe that preschoolers should be taught health concepts and good health behaviors; for example, avoiding contact with blood and handwashing before eating and after toileting. Health care professionals believe that the early years are an appropriate time to begin developing health and safety habits.

Prenatal Cocaine Exposure Professionals who work with young children are presently being challenged by a new community of youngsters considered to be one of the fastest growing at-risk populations in America: children prenatally exposed to cocaine (Kinnison, Sluder, & Cates, 1995). Much of the attention focused on this group is the result of an epidemic of cocaine and crack use, especially by pregnant women, in the mid- to late 1980s. Conservative estimates suggest that between 375,000 and 500,000 children are prenatally exposed to illicit drugs on an annual basis. Of these youngsters, approximately 30,000 to 50,000, or about 8–10%, are exposed to crack cocaine (Chapman & Eliott, 1995; Kinnison et al., 1995).

In the early 1990s the print and electronic media vividly portrayed the appearance of so-called "crack babies" in early childhood programs. Many of these early news reports were overly sensational, unduly pessimistic, and somewhat hysterical. They did, however, capture the attention of professionals and the public alike.

Prenatal cocaine exposure results in a constellation of medical, neurological, and behavioral difficulties for the developing fetus, and later, the child. Examples of adverse risks and consequences include heightened probability of prematurity, low birthweight, smaller head circumference, physical deformities, sleep irregularities, and the physiological effects of drug withdrawal. We emphasize, however, that the effects of prenatal cocaine exposure vary greatly, with problems ranging from mild to severe (Mayes & Bornstein, 1995; Vincent, Poulsen, Cole, Woodruff, & Griffith, 1991). Furthermore, we know very little about the long-term influences of maternal cocaine use on children (Thomas, 2000). What we do know is that these children usually present a complex array of learning and behavioral problems. Many of these youngsters can be considered at-risk for school

failure and developmental difficulties. Early childhood special educators will likely encounter children who have motor, cognitive, language, and affective-social disorders. Poor impulse control, attentional deficits, decreased task persistence, perceptual disorders, lower tolerance for frustration, and withdrawal are additional factors that will likely hinder their future success in school (Kinnison et al., 1995; Mayfield & Chapman, 1998); however, there is no typical profile which defines this population (Carta, 2003). Whether these difficulties are transient or result in permanent disabilities awaits the outcome of carefully conducted research. We should also point out that not all youngsters that are prenatally exposed exhibit problems in learning, development, and behavior. Some researchers believe that many of these children will fail to exhibit developmental or behavioral deficits (Frank, Augustyn, Knight, Pell & Zuckerman, 2001). As Vincent et al. (1991) note, "Children who were prenatally exposed to substances are unique, but as a whole they are more like than different from other children" (p. 24).

Services for children suffering from maternal cocaine abuse must focus on both biological and environmental factors (Carta, Atwater, Greenwood, McConnell, McEvoy, & Williams, 2001; Shonkoff & Marshall, 2000). Many of the problems displayed by these children may be the result of the interaction of these variables (Carta et al., 2001). In fact, confounding conditions like poverty, homelessness, family instability, and child abuse may be as harmful as the exposure itself. Yet, one must be cautious realizing that illicit drug use cuts across all socioeconomic classes, racial/ethnic backgrounds, and lifestyles, thereby contributing to the absence of a typical family profile. The environments in which children prenatally exposed to cocaine live are as varied as the youngsters themselves (Vincent et al., 1991).

While the complex needs of these children and their families are beyond the scope of any one social service agency, schools can play a very important role in the lives of children who were prenatally exposed to cocaine. Kinnison et al. (1995) believe that the early learning environment and the professionals who work therein may well be one of the most stable elements in the child's world. Successful intervention

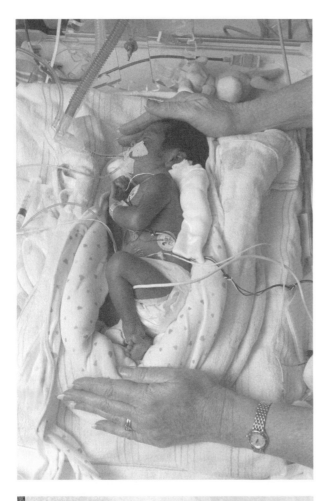

Children with special health needs present many challenges to our schools.

efforts with drug-exposed children necessitates a secure and predictable environment. Unfortunately, the cognitive and behavioral extremes associated with these students prohibits an explicit list of "best practices" or pedagogical approaches. Carta (2003) is of the opinion that prenatally exposed pupils do not require a special curriculum or instructional strategies; what they do require is the systematic application of effective early intervention tactics focusing on specific skill deficiencies. Furthermore, the majority of these students are able to receive services in settings designed for typical youngsters. (See Table 10–5 for a list of classroom guidelines.) We encourage the early childhood special educator to recognize the children's strengths and to see the ways in which they are more like their typical peers than different.

Medically Fragile Children   Our final example of young children with special health needs are preschoolers typically identified as "medically fragile" (we will soon point out, however, that this is *not* the term of choice). This population is growing due to rapid medical and technological advances that are saving lives and improving the quality of life for many of these children. As this population continues to grow, schools will encounter new challenges in service delivery as increasingly these children seek school services. The Council for Exceptional Children (CEC) predicts that most classroom teachers, at least once in their career, will encounter a pupil who requires some type of medical assistance (CEC Today, 1998). The right of children with complex health care needs to receive an appropriate education in the least restrictive environment is guaranteed by statute (PL 105-17) and reinforced by substantial legal precedents (e.g., *Irving Independent School District v. Tatro; Timothy W. v. Rochester New Hampshire School District; Cedar Rapids School District v. Garett F.*).

Who are these children who will present early childhood special educators with personal and professional challenges? This question defies a simple answer. We believe that there are two reasons for this difficulty. The first reason is due to differences in terminology and the second one is due to the complexity of health issues usually found in this population. Teachers will frequently encounter descriptive labels such as chronically ill, technologically dependent, medically fragile, or the IDEA term of other health impaired. Contemporary thinking suggests, however, that these labels are inappropriate as they perpetuate stereotypes and imply inaccurate information about the actual health status of these individuals. "Medically fragile is a status," Smith (2001) writes, "it is not assigned to any specific condition but rather reflects the individual's health situation. Students can move in and out of fragile status" (p. 376). The preferred term, therefore, is **children with special health needs** (Rueve, Robinson, Worthington, & Gargiulo, 2000). This label keeps the primary focus on the

Table 10–5   General Intervention Guidelines for Early Childhood Settings That Include Children with Prenatal Drug Exposure

Structure the learning environment

- Establish supportive home-school relationships and encourage family participation whenever possible
- Set up small designated learning areas rather than a large open area
- Organize the environment and define boundaries
- Use area signs or drawings to help children associate specific behaviors, activities, and materials with a particular space
- Rotate materials; do not put everything out at once
- Limit the number of classroom rules, and keep them positive
- Make daily routine as predictable as possible; limit interruptions
- Keep adult-child ratios low

Encourage teacher-child interactions

- Address children by name and make eye contact or touch children before making a verbal request if these are appropriate in their cultures
- Focus children's attention by limiting distractions and providing engaging activities
- Praise verbally and specifically rather than with just hugs or smiles
- Encourage decisions making by providing daily opportunities for choices; talk about consequences of choices
- Structure and limit the number and length of transitions; prepare children for transitions with verbal cues and role playing
- Encourage attachments and respect
- Provide role models and direct instruction if needed for appropriate classroom behaviors such as sharing, greeting, and thanking
- Encourage communication; respond to all attempts to verbalize
- Urge children to verbally express their wants and needs

Plan engaging activities

- Structure, model, and guide appropriate play activities; provide individual instruction to support play behaviors, such as how to join a group or welcome another child
- Initiate opportunities for children to engage in parallel and small-group play
- Implement a developmentally appropriate, integrated curriculum
- Promote active participation in group activities

SOURCE: P. Mayfield and K. Chapman. Children's Prenatal Exposure to Drugs: Implications for Early Childhood Educators, *Dimensions of Early Childhood,* 26 (3–4), 1998. p. 40.

child while his or her unique health needs are secondary. We will adopt this term.

As we just observed, part of the problem in defining this population is the diversity of medical conditions embraced by the concept of young children with special health needs. These youngsters do not present a single set of characteristics. Included in this group are students with chronic problems like asthma, those with physical deformities, congenital defects, infectious conditions, heredity difficulties, and life-threatening illnesses (Giardino, Kohrt, Arye, & Wells, 2002). Due to the great variety of conditions represented, generalizations are difficult to make. Yet, we feel safe in stating that one of the keys to working with this group of students is for educators to appreciate the highly individualized nature of each child's condition. While pupils might share a similar medical condition, muscular dystrophy, for example, the course and severity of the disease or illness and its impact on the child and his or her family is uniquely personal.

Medical and educational services for young children with special health needs reflect the contemporary belief that early childhood experiences should be as normalized as possible. This philosophy has contributed to the growth of community-based care and the opportunity for these youngsters to attend a variety of early childhood programs in their local communities (Crocker & Porter, 2001). Although young children with special health needs have traditionally not been served by early childhood educators, legal opinions and legislation, coupled with demands from families, have resulted in an increasing number of student's seeking services alongside their healthy classmates.

We fully agree with Crocker and Porter (2001) who argue that the inclusion of youngsters with special health care needs in early childhood settings should be seen as the norm, not an exception. Yet, such a decision requires that parents, teachers, and other professionals carefully weigh medical judgment about potential harm to the child with the desire to have the youngster participate in normalized school activities (Hallahan & Kauffman, 2003).

An integral aspect of providing for these children, regardless of the educational setting, is the development of a detailed health care plan (see Figure 10–2). This document, which is a critical element of the student's IEP, "should contain all of the information necessary in order to provide complete medical and educational services to the child with special health needs" (Rueve et al., 2000, p. 16). School personnel must also be prepared for unforeseen circumstances, the "What do I do if" incidents, which hopefully will never materialize. A written plan for potential emergency situations should be created based on the student's particular health needs. (See Figure 10–3 for an example of an emergency medical plan.) We recommend that copies of this plan be located in the classroom and other sites frequented by the child (lunch room, school bus, gymnasium).

Providing an appropriate education to youngsters with unique health care needs is a relatively new role for the early special childhood educator and will require increasing collaboration and cooperation with families and the agencies that provide the necessary services. It also requires open lines of communication with professionals from a variety of disciplines. Services for the youngster with special health needs, regardless of where they are delivered, is a shared responsibility. Successful preschool experiences demand, according to Peterson and her colleagues (Peterson, Barber, & Ault 1994), teamwork, flexibility, and the familiar themes of individualized, normalized, and family-focused services. A successful preschool experience also necessitates indepth staff training as early childhood educators are often ill-prepared to effectively meet the needs of these youngsters (Rueve et al., 2000). The Council for Exceptional Children recommends that preservice, inservice, and continuing education programs contain the following eight components:

- Awareness and understanding of student's health care, emotional, and educational needs.
- Knowledge of common medical and health terms.
- Knowledge of medical characteristics including etiology and implications.
- Knowledge of physical, developmental, and emotional characteristics.
- Knowledge of appropriate curricular and environmental modifications.
- Knowledge of the roles and responsibilities of the health care professional in the classroom.
- Knowledge of the importance and necessity for establishing support systems for personnel, students, and families.
- Knowledge of resources for the family. (Council for Exceptional Children, 1988, p. 5–6)

Student: _____ DOB: _____ Age: _____ Grade/Class: _____
Primary Caregivers: _____ Daytime Phone: _____
_____ Daytime Phone: _____
Primary Health Care Provider: _____ Phone: _____
Date Plan Approved: _____ Frequency of Plan Review: _____ Date Plan Last Updated: _____

Team Members

Team Member Signature	Title	Role/Responsibility	Phone	Alt. Phone (P) or Beeper (B)

Alternate Team Members

AlternateTeam Member Name	Title	Role/Responsibility	Phone	Alt. Phone (P) or Beeper (B)

Training Requirements

Team Member	Health Care Procedure, Assistive Technology, or Medical Equipment Training Required	Frequency of Initial and Ongoing Training	Date of Last Training

Brief Medical History

Current Medical Condition

Positioning or handling requirements:

Precautions/possible adverse reactions to health care procedures:

Restricted activities:

Behavior considerations:

Medical Management

Description of Health Care Procedure	Frequency and Number of Repetitions	Location

Figure 10–2 Sample Individual Health Care Plan

SOURCE: B. Rueve, M. Robinson, L. Worthington, and R. Gargiulo. Children with Special Health Needs in Inclusive Settings: Writing Health Care Plans, *Physical Disabilities Education and Related Services 19* (1), 2000. pp. 17–18.

Medical Management Log

Description of Health Care Procedure	Frequency and Number of Repetitions	Location	Date/Time	Authorized Care Giver	Signature of Caregiver

Feeding and Nutritional Needs

Special Feeding Instructions: Amount of Food; Temperature of Food; Number of Feedings, etc.	Nutrition Offered	Frequency and Time	Notable Concerns

Feeding and Nutritional Needs Log

Nutrition Offered	Date	Time	Notable Concerns	Caregiver Signature

Special Equipment and Devices

Assistive Technology Device or Medical Equipment Required	Details on the Use and Maintenance of Apparatus

Transportation Needs

Transportation Needs	Destination	Provider of Transportation	Provider Phone
Transportation to School			
Transportation from School			
Transportation Around School			
Field Trips			
Emergency Transportation			
Other			

Adaptations/Accommodations Req'd: ☐ None ☐ Bus Lift ☐ Seat Belt ☐ Wheel Chair Lockdown ☐ Chest Harness ☐ Booster Seat
☐ Other: _____ Method of Mobility: _____

Family/Caregiver Requests

Health Status Profile Leading to Emergency Interventions

Description of Change/Symptoms of Distress	Interventions

Figure 10–2 *(Continued)*

Student: _____ DOB: _____ Age: _____ Grade/Class: _____

Date Plan Approved: _____ Frequency of Plan Review: _____ Date Plan Last Updated: _____

Emergency Contact Information

Emergency Contact	Relation to Student	Contact for What Type of Emergency?	Daytime Phone	Alt. Phone (P) or Beeper (B)
	Primary Physician			
	Dentist			
	Ambulance			
	EMT			
	Hospital			
	Fire Department			
	Medical Supplier			

Emergency Procedures

Description of Medical Emergency	What To Do	Location of Medication/ Equipment	Transportation Requirement

Figure 10–3 Sample Medical Emergency Plan

SOURCE: B. Rueve, M. Robinson, L. Worthington, and R. Gargiulo (2000). Children with Special Health Needs in Inclusive Settings: Writing Health Care Plans, *Physical Disabilities Education and Related Services, 19* (1), 2000. p. 22.

Staff development activities should also allow for student-specific training wherein particular management techniques and health issues can be identified and planned for.

Regardless of the medical condition presented by the student—be it pediatric AIDS, cancer, or some form of neurological disorder—these children, like all infants, toddlers, and preschoolers, have a right to expect high-quality care and beneficial early education experiences from their teachers.

Preparation of Early Childhood Special Educators

It is our opinion that high-quality early intervention and childhood special education programs are the result of many factors, one of which is the quality of the personnel. Good programs for young children with special needs rely on competent teachers. Educators are the key to providing effective services to infants, toddlers, and preschoolers with disabilities and their families. Regrettably, there is a nationwide shortage of qualified teachers. This problem is long standing. Shortages were noted even prior to the enactment of PL 99-457; but, with the passage of IDEA and the resulting growth in the number of infants, toddlers, and preschoolers being served, this situation only grew worse. Recently, the U.S. Department of Education (2002) reported approximately 600 vacancies for preschool special educators with an additional 3,200 positions filled by teachers not fully certified in early childhood special education. A notable lack of trained professionals to work with infants and toddlers with delays and disabilities is also an area of growing concern (Klein & Gilkerson, 2000). We envision these critical shortages to continue into the foreseeable future despite attempts by colleges and universities to dramatically increase the number of qualified personnel.

Producing a sufficient cadre of well-trained and effective professionals is only one of the problems the field is encountering. Another matter confronting early childhood special education is the issue of inclusion of young children with special needs. Research over the past two decades strongly supports the conclusion that integrated early childhood programs are of significant benefit to both typical and atypical youngsters (Guralnick, 2001). As a result, a growing number of young children with delays and disabilities are receiving services in normalized or natural early childhood settings. Qualified staff, however, are not always available to deliver the needed instruction. An alarming example of this is the investigation by Wolery, Martin, Schroeder, Huffman, Venn, Holcombe, Brookfield, and Fleming (1994), who surveyed almost 500 preschool programs across the United States. They found that only about 25% of the programs serving children with and without disabilities employed an early childhood special educator. In fact, nearly three-fourths of the programs engaged in providing integrated services did not have *any* professionals on staff with preparation in special education. Likewise, a more recent study by McDonnell, Brownell, and Wolery (1997) found that less than half of the teachers in inclusive, community-based early childhood programs had the benefit of the expertise of an early childhood special educator.

We believe that this sort of data has implications for teacher preparation programs. As a profession, we not only need to produce more early childhood special educators, we also need to train professionals who can effectively serve young children in inclusive settings. The lack of appropriately prepared personnel is a huge barrier to the implementation of interventions in natural learning environments (Bruder, 2001). An innovative teacher training program might be one strategy to help alleviate the situation. We issue a call, therefore, for a collaborative or integrative personnel preparation program. We are not the originators of this idea. Support for this model of teacher preparation is growing in both early childhood circles and the field of early childhood special education (Blanton, Griffin, Winn, & Pugach, 1997; Miller & Stayton, 1998, 2000; Stayton & McCollum, 2002). The time is right to question whether or not we can continue to legitimately train early childhood professionals in distinct preparation programs. Miller (1992) is of the opinion that

> the practice of educating teachers to work with either "regular" or "nonregular" preschoolers can no longer be supported. Fractionation in teacher education programs is contradictory to all legal, philosophical, empirical, economic, and moral reasoning for early childhood education. Such segregation practices in teacher training perpetuate the myth that particular types of children need teachers who have trained in discrete bodies of knowledge and pedagogy accessible only to members of specialized fields of expertise. (p. 39)

Kemple and her colleagues (Kemple, Hartle, Correa, & Fox, 1994) believe that the educational segregation of children with disabilities is due, in large part, to the segregated manner in which teachers are prepared. The question that then confronts us, according to Lowenthal (1992), is "how to best train early childhood personnel, both regular and special, to meet the challenges of teaching in integrated settings" (p. 121). As we think about reformulating our teacher training programs there is a particular need to develop models that support inclusionary practices.

A unified teacher training program that prepares professionals to serve *all* young children holds strong promise for improving the delivery of services. Teachers can draw upon effective practices from each field and thus provide early education services that are both developmentally and age-appropriate, in addition to being responsive to the specific teaching and learning requirements of each youngster (Burton, Hains, Hanline, McLean, & McCormick, 1992). Rather than having two distinct preparation tracks we envision a seamless system for preparing teachers of young children. The merging of professional standards across the two fields would ensure that early childhood educators have the ability to meet the needs of typical as well as atypical youngsters regardless of the type of program in which they are enrolled.

Quality programs for young children with special needs demand well-trained service providers.

Integrative teacher training experiences dictate that personnel preparation standards be built around mutually agreed upon critical competencies, common philosophical assumptions, as well as a common core of knowledge and skills appropriate to all young children. An example of this type of consensus can be found in the NAEYC document on preparing early childhood professionals (National Association for the Education of Young Children, 1996). Its recommendations for personnel preparation, which meets the needs of both typical children and youngsters with special needs and their families, includes a conceptual foundation that articulates the six following components:

- the uniqueness of early childhood as a developmental phase;
- the significant role of families in early child hood development and early education and intervention;
- the role of developmentally and individually appropriate practices;
- the preference for service delivery in inclusive settings;
- the importance of culturally competent professional actions and
- the importance of collaborative interpersonal and interprofessional actions.

The competencies of a well-trained early childhood special educator should also reflect the theoretical as well as the research knowledge bases of both early childhood and special education (Klein & Campbell, 1990). Teachers must be prepared to fulfill their role as a pedagogical expert (Wolery, 1991); one who has the primary responsibility of facilitating the child's development in areas of social, motor, communication, cognitive, self-help, and behavioral domains (Klein & Gilkerson, 2000). Teacher education curricula will need to integrate special education content as well as content from the fields of early childhood education and child development. Proposals by Blanton, et al. (1997), Kemple et al. (1994), and Miller and Stayton (1998) for training early childhood special educators illustrate the type of merging of philosophical and conceptual foundations that will have to take place. A unified model of preparation at the early education level makes good sense because the knowledge base and practices are very similar (Kemple et al., 1994). Lowenthal (1992) believes that there is a great deal of similarity in the competencies required of regular and early childhood special educators. She writes that

> what is good early childhood practice for typical children in most cases appears to be good for those who have special needs. The presence of children with disabilities does

not require a different style of teaching from that which is appropriate for most other youngsters. (p. 123)

Critical to the success of our call is the required collaboration of professional organizations such as the Association of Teacher Educators (ATE), the National Association for the Education of Young Children (NAEYC), and the Division for Early Childhood (DEC) of the Council for Exceptional Children. Fortunately, a shared vision and mutual concern about segregated personnel preparation models has resulted in a joint position statement on personnel standards (see Appendix D). Collectively these three associations are in a strong position to influence state departments of education who are responsible for the credentialling and licensing of early childhood special educators. Many teacher education programs are exclusively formulated around specific state certification requirements. Thus, state departments of education will have a large voice in whether or not colleges and universities can develop integrative teacher training programs.

At the present time, the professional qualifications of those who work with young children with special needs greatly vary. Common standards of personnel preparation do not exist; in fact, not all states have a specific certification for early childhood special education. States typically use a wide variety of models or configurations to certify their teachers. In several instances multiple certification options are available. In a recent national survey Danaher and Kraus (2002) found that 17 states require a preschool special education certificate or license for teachers working with young children with special needs, while an equal number allow for a single certificate for both early childhood and early childhood special education. On the other hand, 21 states will certify teachers to work with preschoolers with special needs on the basis of a special education certificate without a preschool specialization or endorsement. Certificates in these states typically allow teachers to serve students from birth to age twenty-one, three to age twenty-one, or some similar configuration. Because of the lack of concordance regarding state certification standards, ATE, NAEYC, and DEC seek to develop some type of uniform state certification guidelines as well as a free-standing certificate with a specialization focusing on children birth through age eight (National Association for the Education of Young Children, 1996).

We fully agree with the DEC Task Force on Recommended Practices (1993) that the time has arrived to put an end to segregated, categorical teacher preparation programs. A unified early childhood/early childhood special education teacher training model has the potential to meet the growing need for well-trained professionals who have multiple competencies and can deliver high quality services in a variety of settings. Teachers trained in such a fashion will be well-suited to meet the challenges in the workplace of the twenty-first century.

Summary

We have attempted to identify several challenges that will confront early childhood special educators in the coming years. A growing list of social issues and professional concerns suggest that significant change in early childhood special education programs is on the horizon.

We live in a nation that is rich in its cultural diversity. Our schools are serving growing numbers of young children with culturally and linguistically diverse backgrounds. For some youngsters, entrance into school may represent their first exposure to a culture and a language that is different from that of their home. Because of this, teachers must guard against stereotyping and be certain that ethnicity is not misinterpreted as exceptionality. It is not uncommon for cultural differences to routinely translate into disabilities. Early childhood special educators, therefore, must model respect for, and sensitivity to, the cultural heritage of their students. For early childhood special education programs to be successful, services must be offered by professionals who are ethnically competent and demonstrate cultural awareness and sensitivity.

A variety of contemporary social ills will result in early childhood special education teachers serving a growing population of students who evidence the deleterious consequences of homelessness, child abuse, pediatric AIDS, prenatal cocaine exposure, and numerous other special health conditions. The cause of many of these problems is beyond the control of the early childhood special educator. Teachers can, however, provide a safe, stable, and nurturing learning environment where children can develop to their maximum potential. As teachers of infants, toddlers, and preschoolers it is our duty to fulfill our role as purveyors of care and education to all youngsters, but especially to those most in need.

Finally, competent teachers are the key to providing effective services to young children with special needs and their families. Unfortunately, there is a shortage of trained personnel. Coupled with this shortfall are the increasing numbers of young children with special needs who are receiving services in inclusive early childhood settings. In many instances, qualified staff are not available to provide the needed instruction. We believe that this scenario has implications for how we prepare early childhood special educators. We support the concept of a collaborative personnel preparation program wherein competencies, knowledge, and skills appropriate to the fields of early childhood education and early childhood special education are merged into a single model for preparing teachers of young children. An integrative teacher training model has the potential to meet the growing need for well-trained teachers who have multiple competencies and can provide high quality services in a variety of instructional settings.

Check Your Understanding

1. Explain the difference between ethnicity and exceptionality.

2. Why is it important for early childhood special educators to understand and respect the cultural heritage of their students?

3. Provide examples of the four major types of child maltreatment.

4. What role do schools play in providing services to young children with special health needs?

5. Should teachers of young children with special needs have professional preparation in both early childhood and special education? Support your viewpoint.

References

American Academy of Pediatrics. (1991). Education of children with human immunodeficiency virus infection. *Pediatrics, 88*(3), 640–641.

Ammerman, R., Hersen, M., Van Hasselt, V., Lubetsky, M., & Sieck, W. (1994). Maltreatment in psychiatrically hospitalized children and adolescents with developmental disabilities: Prevalence and correlates. *Journal of the American Academy of Child and Adolescent Psychiatry, 33,* 567–576.

Armstrong, F., Seidel, J., & Swales, T. (1993). Pediatric HIV infection: A neuropsychological and educational challenge. *Journal of Learning Disabilities, 26,* 92–101.

Barrera, I. (2000). Honoring differences: Essential features of appropriate ECSE services for young children from diverse sociocultural environments. *Young Exceptional Children, 3*(4), 17–24.

Bassuk, F., & Rosenberg, L. (1990). Psychosocial characteristics of homeless children and children with homes. *Pediatrics, 85,* 257–261.

Blanton, L., Griffin, C., Winn, J., & Pugach, M. (1997). *Teacher education in transition: Collaborative programs to prepare general and special educators.* Denver, CO: Love.

Bowe, F. (2000). *Birth to five: Early childhood special education.* (2nd ed.) Albany, NY: Delmar.

Brenner, A. (1984). *Helping children cope with stress.* Lexington, MA: Lexington Books.

Bruder, M. (2001). Inclusion of infants and toddlers: Outcomes and ecology. In M. Guralnick (Ed.), *Early childhood inclusion: Focus on change* (pp. 203–228). Baltimore: Paul H. Brookes.

Burton, C., Hains, A., Hanline, M., McLean, M., & McCormick, K. (1992). Early childhood intervention and education: The urgency of professional unification. *Topics in Early Childhood Special Education, 11*(4), 53–69.

Byrom, E., & Katz, G. (1991). *HIV prevention and AIDS education: Resources for special educators.* Reston, VA: Council for Exceptional Children.

Caldwell, T., Sirvis, B., Todaro, A., & Accouloumre, D. (1991). *Special health care in the school.* Reston, VA: Council for Exceptional Children.

Carta, J. (2003). Educating young children prenatally exposed to illegal drugs. Feature presentation in W. Heward, *Exceptional children* (7th ed., pp. 168–169). Upper Saddle River, NJ: Pearson Education.

Carta, J., Atwater, J., Greenwood, C., McConnell, S., McEvoy, M., & Williams, R. (2001). Effects of cumulative prenatal substance exposure and environmental risks on children's developmental trajectories. *Journal of Clinical Child Psychology, 30*(3), 327–337.

CEC Today. (1998). Growing challenges for teachers—providing medical procedures for students. *5*(3), 1, 5, 15.

Centers for Disease Control and Prevention. (1998). *AIDS surveillance by race/ethnicity.* Atlanta, GA: Author.

Centers for Disease Control and Prevention. (2002, September). *HIV/AIDS surveillance report.* Washington, DC: U.S. Department of Health and Human Services.

Chapman, J., & Elliott, R. (1995). Preschoolers exposed to cocaine: Early childhood special education and Head Start preparation. *Journal of Early Intervention, 19*(2), 118–129.

Children's Defense Fund. (1988). *What every American should be asking political leaders in 1988.* Washington, DC: Author.

Children's Defense Fund. (1995). *The state of America's children yearbook.* Washington, DC: Author.

Children's Defense Fund. (1996). *The state of America's children yearbook.* Washington, DC: Author.

Children's Defense Fund. (1998). *The state of America's children yearbook.* Washington, DC: Author.

Children's Defense Fund. (2000). *The state of America's children yearbook.* Washington, DC: Author.

Children's Defense Fund. (2001). *The state of America's children yearbook.* Washington, DC: Author.

Cook, L., & Boe, E. (1995). Who is teaching students with disabilities? *Teaching Exceptional Children, 28*(1), 70–72.

Cosmos, C. (2001). Abuse of children with disabilities. *CEC Today, 8*(2), 1, 2, 5, 8, 12, 14, 15.

Council for Exceptional Children. (1988). *Report to the Council for Exceptional Children ad hoc committee on medically fragile students.* Reston, VA: Author.

Crocker, A., & Porter, S. (2001). Inclusion of young children with complex health care needs. In M. Guralnick (Ed.), *Early childhood inclusion: Focus on change* (pp. 399–412). Baltimore: Paul H. Brookes.

Danaher, J., & Kraus, R. (Eds.). (2002). *Section 619 profile* (11th ed.). Chapel Hill, NC: National Early Childhood Technical Assistance Center.

Davis, M., Kilgo, J., & Gamel-McCormick, M. (1998). *Young children with special needs: A developmentally appropriate approach.* Needham Heights, MA: Allyn & Bacon.

DEC Task Force on Recommended Practices. (1993). *DEC recommended practices: Indicators of quality in programs for infants and young children with special needs and their families.* Reston, VA: Council for Exceptional Children.

Derman-Sparks, L. (1993). Revisiting multicultural education: What children need to live in a diverse society. *Dimensions, 14*(3), 4–7.

Eddowes, E. (1994). Schools providing safer environments for homeless children. *Childhood Education, 70,* 271–273.

Eddowes, A., & Hrantitz, J. (1989). Educating children of the homeless. *Childhood Education, 65*(4), 197–200.

Embry, L. (1980). Family support for handicapped preschool children at risk for abuse. In J. Gallagher (Ed.), *New directions for exceptional children* (pp. 29–57). San Francisco: Jossey-Bass.

English, D. (1998). The extent and consequences of child maltreatment. *The Future of Children: Protecting Children from Abuse and Neglect, 8*(1), 39–53.

Frank, D., Augustyn, M., Knight, W., Pell, T., & Zuckerman, B. (2001). Growth, development, and behavior in early childhood following prenatal cocaine exposure: A systematic review. *Journal of the American Medical Association, 285*(12), 1613–1625.

Gargiulo, R. (2003). *Special education in contemporary society: An introduction to exceptionality.* Belmont, CA: Wadsworth.

Gargiulo, R. (1990). Child abuse and neglect: An overview. In R. Goldman & R. Gargiulo (Eds.), *Children at risk* (pp. 1–36). Austin, TX: PRO-ED.

Giardino, A., Kohrt, A., Arye, L., & Wells, N. (2002). Health care delivery systems and financing issues. In M. Batshaw (Ed.), *Children with disabilities* (5th ed., pp. 123–139). Baltimore: Paul H. Brookes.

Goldman, R. (1990). An educational perspective on abuse. In R. Goldman & R. Gargiulo (Eds.), *Children at risk* (pp. 37–72). Austin, TX: PRO-ED.

Goldman, R. (1993). Sexual abuse of young children with special needs: Are they safe in day care? *Day Care and Early Education, 20*(4), 37–38.

Goldman, R. (1995). Recognizing child abuse and neglect in child care settings. *Day Care and Early Education, 22*(3), 12–15.

Goldman, R., & Gargiulo, R. (1987). Special needs children: A population at risk for sexual abuse. *Reading Improvement, 24*(2), 84–88.

Gollnick, D., & Chinn, P. (1998). *Multicultural education in a pluralistic society* (5th ed.). Upper Saddle River, NJ: Prentice Hall.

Guralnick, M. (Ed.). (2001). *Early childhood inclusion: Focus on change.* Baltimore: Paul H. Brookes.

Hallahan, D., & Kauffman, J. (2003). *Exceptional learners* (9th ed.). Needham Heights, MA: Allyn & Bacon.

Hanson, M., & Lynch, E., & Wayman, K. (1990). Honoring the cultural diversity of families when gathering data. *Topics in Early Childhood Special Education, 10*(1), 112–131.

Hanson, M., & Zercher, C. (2001). The impact of cultural and linguistic diversity in inclusive preschool environments. In M. Guralnick (Ed.), *Early childhood inclusion: Focus on change* (pp. 413–431). Baltimore: Paul H. Brookes.

Heflin, L., & Rudy, K. (1991). *Homeless and in need of special education.* Reston, VA: Council for Exceptional Children.

Hodgkinson, H. (1993). American education: The good, the bad, and the task. *Phi Delta Kappan, 74*(8), 619–625.

Interagency Council on the Homeless. (1999). *Homelessness: Programs and the people they serve.* Washington, DC: U.S. Department of Housing and Urban Development.

Johnson, C. (1993). Developmental issues: Children infected with the human immunodeficiency virus. *Infants and Young Children, 6*(1), 1–10.

Kayne, A. (1989). *Annotated bibliography of social science literature concerning the education of homeless children.* Cambridge, MA: Center for Law and Education.

Kempe, C. (1978). Sexual abuse, another hidden pediatric problem: The 1977 C. Anderson Aldrich Lecture. *Pediatrics, 62,* 382–389.

Kemple, K., Hartle, L., Correa, V., & Fox, L. (1994). Preparing teachers for inclusive education: The development of a unified teacher education program in early childhood and early childhood special education. *Teacher Education and Special Education, 17*(1), 38–51.

Kinnison, L., Sluder, L., & Cates, D. (1995). Prenatal drug exposure: Implications for teachers of young children. *Day Care and Early Education, 22*(3), 35–37.

Kirk, S., Gallagher, J., & Anastasiow, N. (2000). *Educating exceptional children* (9th ed.). Boston: Houghton Mifflin.

Klein, N., & Campbell, P. (1990). Preparing personnel to serve at-risk and disabled infants, toddlers, and preschoolers. In S. Meisels & J. Shonkoff (Eds.), *Handbook of early childhood intervention* (pp. 679–699). New York: Cambridge University Press.

Klein, N., & Gilkerson, L. (2000). Personnel preparation for early childhood intervention programs. In J. Shonkoff & S. Meisels (Eds.), *Handbook of early childhood intervention* (2nd ed., pp. 454–483). Cambridge, England: Cambridge University Press.

Le Roy, C., Powell, T., & Kelker, P. (1994). Meeting our responsibilities in special education. *Teaching Exceptional Children, 26*(4), 37–44.

Lesar, S., Gerber, M., & Semmel, M. (1996). HIV infection in children: Family stress, social support, and adaptation. *Exceptional Children, 62*(3), 224–236.

Lesar, S., & Maldonado, Y. (1994). Infants and young children with HIV infection: Service delivery considerations for family support. *Infants and Young Children, 6*(4), 70–81.

Lowenthal, B. (1992). Collaborative training in the education of early childhood educators. *Teaching Exceptional Children, 24*(4), 25–29.

Lustig, M., & Koestner, J. (1996). *Intercultural competence: Interpersonal communication across cultures* (2nd ed.). New York: HarperCollins.

Lynch, E., & Hanson, M. (Eds.). (1998). *Developing cross-cultural competence* (2nd ed.). Baltimore: Paul H. Brookes.

Martin, P., & Midgley, E. (1994). Immigration to the United States: Journey to an uncertain destination. *Population Bulletin, 49*(2), 2–47.

May, D., Kundert, D., & Akpan, C. (1994). Are we preparing special educators for the issues facing schools in the 1990s? *Teacher Education and Special Education, 17*(3), 192–199.

Mayes, L., & Bornstein, M. (1995). Developmental dilemmas for cocaine-abusing parents and their children. In M. Lewis & M. Bendersky (Eds.), *Mothers, babies, and cocaine: The role of toxins in development* (pp. 251–272). Hillsdale, NJ: Erlbaum.

Mayfield, P., & Chapman, J. (1998). Children's prenatal exposure to drugs: Implications for early childhood educators. *Dimensions of Early Childhood, 26*(3–4), 38–42.

McDonnell, A., Brownell, K., & Wolery, M. (1997). Teaching experience and specialist support: A survey of preschool teachers employed in programs accredited by NAEYC. *Topics in Early Childhood Special Education, 17*(3), 263–285.

McLean, M., Bailey, D., & Wolery, M. (1996). *Assessing infants and preschoolers with special needs* (2nd ed.). Englewood Cliffs, NJ: Prentice Hall.

Meier, J., & Sloan, M. (1984). The severely handicapped and child abuse. In J. Blacker (Ed.), *Severely handicapped young children and their families* (pp. 247–272). New York: Academic Press.

Miller, P. (1992). Segregated programs of teacher education in early childhood: Immoral and inefficient practice. *Topics in Early Childhood Special Education, 11*(4), 39–52.

Miller, P., & Stayton, V. (1998). Blended interdisciplinary teacher preparation in early education and intervention: A national study. *Topics in Early Childhood Special Education, 18*(1), 49–58.

Miller, P., & Stayton, V. (2000). Recommended practices in personnel preparation. In S. Sandall, M. McLean, & B. Smith (Eds.), *DEC recommended practices in early intervention/early childhood special education* (pp. 77–88). Longmont, CO: Sopris West.

Morrow, R. (1987). Cultural differences—be aware. *Academic Therapy, 23,* 143–149.

National Association for the Education of Young Children. (1996). *Guidelines for preparation of early childhood professionals.* Washington, DC: Author.

National Center on Child Abuse and Neglect. (1986). *Child abuse and neglect: An informed approach to a shared concern.* (No. 20-01016). Washington, DC: Author.

Nunez, R., & Collignon, K. (1997). Creating a community of learning for homeless children. *Educational Leadership, 55*(2), 56–60.

Pallas, A., Natriello, G., & McDill, E. (1989). The changing nature of the disadvantaged population: Current dimensions and future trends. *Educational Researcher, 18*(5), 16–22.

Peterson, N., Barber, P., & Ault, M. (1994). Young children with special health care needs. In P. Safford (Ed.), *Early childhood special education.* (Yearbook in early childhood special education, Vol. 5) (pp. 165–191). New York: Teachers College Press.

Poplin, M., & Wright, P. (1983). The concept of cultural pluralism: Issues in special education. *Learning Disabilities Quarterly, 6,* 367–371.

Quality Education for Minorities Project. (1990). *Education that works: An action plan for the education of minorities.* Cambridge, MA: Massachusetts Institute of Technology.

Rathlev, M. (1994). Universal precautions in early intervention and child care. *Infants and Young Children, 6*(3), 54–64.

Raver, S. (1999). *Intervention strategies for infants and toddlers with special needs* (2nd ed.). Upper Saddle River, NJ: Prentice Hall.

Rescoria, L., Parker, R., & Stolley, P. (1991). Ability, achievement, and adjustment in homeless children. *American Journal of Orthopsychiatry, 61*(2), 210–220.

Rosen, S., & Granger, M. (1992). Early interventions and school programs. In A. Crocker, H. Cohen, & T. Kastner (Eds.), *HIV infection and developmental disabilities* (pp. 75–84). Baltimore: Paul H. Brookes.

Rueve, B., Robinson, M., Worthington, L., & Gargiulo, R. (2000). Children with special health needs in inclusive settings: Writing health care plans. *Physical Disabilities Education and Related Services, 19*(1), 11–24.

Russell, S., & Williams, E. (1988). Homeless handicapped children: A special education perspective. *Children's Environments Quarterly, 5*(1), 3–7.

Rutstein, M., Conlon, C., & Batshaw, M. (1997). HIV and AIDS. In M. Batshaw (Ed.), *Children with disabilities* (4th ed., pp. 162–182). Baltimore: Brookes.

Sandall, S., McLean, M., & Smith, B. (Eds.). (2000). *DEC recommended practices in early intervention/early childhood special education.* Longmont, CO: Sopris West.

Shonkoff, J., & Marshall, P. (2000). The biology of developmental vulnerability. In J. Shonkoff & S. Meisels (Eds.), *Handbook of early childhood intervention* (2nd ed., pp. 35–53). Cambridge, England: Cambridge University Press.

Smith, D. (2001). *Introduction to special education* (4th ed.). Needham Heights, MA: Allyn & Bacon.

Spiegel, H., & Bonwit, A. (2002). HIV in children. In M. Batshaw (Ed.), *Children with disabilities* (5th ed., pp. 123–139). Baltimore: Paul H. Brookes.

Spodek, B., & Saracho, O. (1994). *Right from the start.* Needham Heights, MA: Allyn & Bacon.

Stayton, V., & McCollum, J. (2002). Unifying general and special education: What does the research tell us? *Teacher Education and Special Education, 25*(3), 211–218.

Stronge, J., & Tenhouse, C. (1990). *Educating homeless children: Issues and answers.* Bloomington, IN: Phi Delta Kappa Educational Foundation.

Thomas, J. (2000). Falling through the cracks. Crack-exposed children in the U.S. public schools: An educational policy issue. *Journal of Educational Policy, 15*(5), 575–583.

Tiedt, P., & Tiedt, I. (2002). *Multicultural teaching: A handbook of activities, information, and resources* (6th ed.). Needham Heights, MA: Allyn & Bacon.

U.S. Department of Education. (2001). *Twenty-third annual report to Congress on the implementation of the Individuals with Disabilities Education Act.* Washington, DC: U.S. Government Printing Office.

U.S. Department of Education. (2002). *Twenty-fourth annual report to Congress on the implementation of the Individuals with Disabilities Education Act.* Washington, DC: U.S. Government Printing Office.

U.S. Department of Health and Human Services. (2003). *Child maltreatment 2001: Reports from the states to the National Child Abuse and Neglect Data System.* Washington, DC: U.S. Government Printing Office.

Vincent, L., Poulsen, M., Cole, C., Woodruff, G., & Griffith, D. (1991). *Born substance exposed, educationally vulnerable.* Reston, VA: Council for Exceptional Children.

Williams, B., & DeSander, M. (1999). Dueling legislation: The impact of incongruent federal statutes on homeless and other special-needs students. *Journal for Just and Caring Education, 5*(1), 34–50.

Wolery, M. (1991). Instruction in early childhood special education: "Seeing through a glass darkly . . . knowing in part." *Exceptional Children, 58*(2), 127–135.

Wolery, M., Martin, C., Schroeder, C., Huffman, K., Venn, M., Holcombe, A., Brookfield, J., & Fleming, L. (1994). Employment of educators in preschool mainstreaming: A survey of general educators. *Journal of Early Intervention, 18*(1), 64–77.

Zirpoli, T. (1986). Child abuse and children with handicaps. *Remedial and Special Education, 7*(2), 39–48.

Zirpoli, T. (1990). Physical abuse: Are children with disabilities at greater risk? *Intervention in School and Clinic, 26*(1), 6–11.

Zirpoli, T. (1995). *Understanding and affecting the behavior of young children.* Englewood Cliffs, NJ: Prentice-Hall.

Appendixes

Federal Definitions of Disabilities

Autism means a developmental disability significantly affecting verbal and nonverbal communication and social interaction, generally evident before age three, that adversely affects educational performance. Other characteristics often associated with autism are engagement in repetitive activities and stereotyped movements, resistance to environmental change or change in daily routines, and unusual responses to sensory experiences. The term does not apply if a child's educational performance is adversely affected primarily because the child has an emotional disturbance as defined below.

A child who manifests the characteristics of "autism" after age three could be diagnosed as having "autism" if the criteria in this paragraph are satisfied.

Deaf-blindness means concomitant hearing and visual impairments, the combination of which causes such severe communication and other developmental and educational problems that they cannot be accommodated in special education programs solely for children with deafness or children with blindness.

Deafness means a hearing impairment that is so severe that the child is impaired in processing linguistic information through hearing, with or without amplification, adversely affecting educational performance.

Emotional disturbance is defined as follows:

(i) The term means a condition exhibiting one or more of the following characteristics over a long period of time and to a marked degree that adversely affects a child's educational performance:
   (A) an inability to learn that cannot be explained by intellectual, sensory, or health factors,
   (B) an inability to build or maintain satisfactory interpersonal relationships with peers and teachers,
   (C) inappropriate types of behavior or feelings under normal circumstances,
   (D) a general pervasive mood of unhappiness or depression, or
   (E) a tendency to develop physical symptoms or fears associated with personal or school problems.

(ii) The term includes schizophrenia. The term does not apply to children who are socially maladjusted, unless it is determined that they have an emotional disturbance.

Hearing impairment means an impairment in hearing, whether permanent or fluctuating, which adversely affects a child's educational performance but that is not included under the definition of "deafness" in this section.

Mental retardation means significantly subaverage general intellectual functioning existing concurrently with deficits in adaptive behavior and manifested during the developmental period that adversely affects a child's educational performance.

Multiple disabilities means concomitant impairments (such as mental retardation-blindness, mental retardation-orthopedic impairment, etc.), the combination of which causes such severe educational needs that they cannot be accommodated in special education programs solely for one of the impairments. The term does not include deaf-blindness.

Orthopedic impairment means a severe orthopedic impairment that adversely affects a child's educational performance. The term includes impairments caused by congenital anomaly (e.g., clubfoot, absence of some member, etc.), impairments caused by disease (e.g., poliomyelitis, bone tuberculosis, etc.), and impairments from other causes (e.g., cerebral palsy, amputations, and fractures or burns that cause contractures).

Other health impairments means having limited strength, vitality, or alertness, including a heightened alertness to environmental stimuli that results in limited alertness with respect to the educational environment that

(i) is due to chronic or acute health problems such as asthma, attention deficit disorder or attention deficit hyperactivity disorder, diabetes, epilepsy, a heart condition, hemophilia, lead poisoning, leukemia, nephritis, rheumatic fever, and sickle cell anemia; and

(ii) adversely affects a child's educational performance.

Specific learning disability is defined as follows:

(i) **General.** The term means a disorder in one or more of the basic psychological processes involved in understanding or in using language, spoken or written, that may manifest itself in an imperfect ability to listen, think, speak, read, write, spell, or to do mathematical calculations, including conditions such as perceptual disabilities, brain injury, minimal brain dysfunction, dyslexia, and developmental aphasia.

(ii) **Disorders not included.** The term does not include learning problems that are primarily the result of visual, hearing, or motor disabilities, of mental retardation, of emotional disturbance, or of environmental, cultural, or economic disadvantage.

Speech or language impairment means a communication disorder such as stuttering, impaired articulation, a language impairment, or a voice impairment that adversely affects a child's educational performance.

Traumatic brain injury means an acquired injury to the brain caused by an external physical force, resulting in total or partial functional disability or psychosocial impairment, or both, that adversely affects a child's educational performance. The term applies to open or closed head injuries resulting in impairments in one or more areas, such as cognition; language; memory; attention; reasoning; abstract thinking; judgment; problem-solving; sensory, perceptual, and motor abilities; psychosocial behavior; physical function; information processing; and speech. The term does not apply to brain injuries that are congenital or degenerative or brain injuries induced by birth trauma.

Visual impairment, including blindness, means an impairment in vision that, even with correction, adversely affects a child's educational performance. The term includes both partial sight and blindness.

SOURCE: Individuals with Disabilities Education Act 34 CFR 300.7.

B

Preschool Environmental Rating Scale

Barbara Fromm—Michelle Rourke—Tom Buggey

Table of Contents

Introduction

The Preschool Environmental Rating Scale (PERS) is a judgment-based measure of the adequacy of providing a positive preschool learning environment for children. The Subsections of Physical Layout, Materials, Basic Care Needs, Curriculum, Adult/Interpersonal, and Activities are assessed. To avoid rater bias, it is suggested that at least two independent raters use the scale and then compare results to obtain a composite score. Scores obtained by raters should be averaged. The PERS is also meant to be a formative measure. Results are best used in team discussions of how to improve service delivery.

Physical Layout

Safety
Furnishings
Personal Space
Attractiveness
Accessibility
Cleanliness
Allow for Exploration

Curriculum

Fine Motor
Gross Motor
Language
Self-Care
Social Skills
Cognitive
Adaptable

Materials

Gross Motor
Art Equipment
Books & Tapes
Play Equipment
Nap Provision
Adaptable for Disabled
Age/Ability Appropriate

Adult/Interpersonal

Parent Relations
Child Interaction
Staff Coordination
Adult Areas
Supervision
Preparation
Professional Development

Basic Care Needs

Toileting
Nutrition
Clothing
First Aid
Medical Access
Nurturance

Activities

Variety
Structured Play
Transitions
Free Play
Scheduling
Dramatic Play

Directions

Each subsection is scored on a scale from 1 to 5. Subsection totals are tallied to give a raw score for each section and then recorded on the scoresheet and graph. The Total column on the far right of the graph can be used to indicate a mean score of the subsections. Subsections falling below a horizontal line drawn across the chart from the total may indicate areas in need of improvement.

1 = Totally inadequate—Criteria are not or cannot be obtained.

2 = Poor—Criteria for meeting objectives present, but are not being utilized.

3 = Average—Criteria present. Some movement to utilize for attainment.

4 = Good—Positive environmental contingencies utilized effectively for goal attainment.

5 = Superior—Maximum use of environment for goal attainment.

▌Physical Layout

Safety
1   2   3   4   5
Notes:

Furnishings
1   2   3   4   5
Notes:

Personal Space
1   2   3   4   5
Notes:

Attractiveness
1   2   3   4   5
Notes:

Accessibility
1   2   3   4   5
Notes:

Cleanliness
1   2   3   4   5
Notes:

Exploration
1   2   3   4   5
Notes:

Section Total =   /35

Materials

Art Equipment

1   2   3   4   5

Notes:

Play Equipment

1   2   3   4   5

Notes:

Books & Tapes

1   2   3   4   5

Notes:

Nap Provisions

1   2   3   4   5

Notes:

Gross Motor

1   2   3   4   5

Notes:

Adaptability

1   2   3   4   5

Notes:

Age/Ability Appropriate

1   2   3   4   5

Notes:

Section Total =   /35

Basic Care Needs

Toileting

1   2   3   4   5

Notes:

Nutrition

1   2   3   4   5

Notes:

Clothing

1   2   3   4   5

Notes:

First Aid

1   2   3   4   5

Notes:

Access to Medical Needs

1   2   3   4   5

Notes:

Nurturance

1   2   3   4   5

Notes:

Section Total =   /30

▌Curriculum

Fine Motor

1   2   3   4   5

Notes:

Gross Motor

1   2   3   4   5

Notes:

Language

1   2   3   4   5

Notes:

Self-Care

1   2   3   4   5

Notes:

Social Skills

1   2   3   4   5

Notes:

Cognitive

1   2   3   4   5

Notes:

Adaptability

1   2   3   4   5

Notes:

Section Total =   /35

Adult/Interpersonal

Parent
Relations

1   2   3   4   5

Notes:

Child
Interaction

1   2   3   4   5

Notes:

Staff
Coordination

1   2   3   4   5

Notes:

Adult Areas

1   2   3   4   5

Notes:

Supervision

1   2   3   4   5

Notes:

Preparation

1   2   3   4   5

Notes:

Professional
Development

1   2   3   4   5

Notes:

Section Total =   /35

Activities

Variety

1   2   3   4   5

Notes:

Structured
Play

1   2   3   4   5

Notes:

Transitions

1   2   3   4   5

Notes:

Free Play

1   2   3   4   5

Notes:

Scheduling

1   2   3   4   5

Notes:

Dramatic Play

1   2   3   4   5

Notes:

Section Total =   /30

▮ Scoring Chart

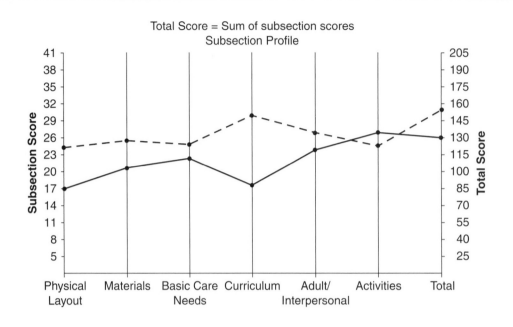

Total Score = Sum of subsection scores
Subsection Profile

Subsection

Note: The Scoring Chart should only be used to gain a rough visual profile of performance on subsections and to track improvements over time in reevaluations. When identifying weaknessess in program, take into account that subsections have different total scores possible because of unequal items. Using mean (average) subsection scores would provide more accurate across-subsection comparisons. Item analysis is the preferred method for analyzing results on the PERS.

Key: August 2004   Ms. Jefferson _____   December 2004   Ms. Novack ——
                      Mr. Simpson   Ms. Noll

Physical Layout

	Poor 1	2	Average 3	4	Excellent 5
Safety	Little consideration for safety built into room; little supervision during playtime; danger areas not highlighted; equipment and furniture not designed for safety.		Some consideration for safety built into class design; children are supervised during play; improvements could be made in environment to ensure safety; safety rules covered in curriculum.		Excellent use of safety features in the design of room and equipment; safety is stressed in the curriculum. Children are well supervised during playtime; structure of room allows for good field of view.
Furnishings	Furnishings are not age appropriate; they do not offer a variety of comfort and/or utility; they are in poor physical condition and in need of repair; drab unappealing appearance; little use of adaptive furnishings.		Furnishings seem appropriate for age; fairly good physical condition; offers some appeal and comfort. Some furnishings adapted for children with disabilities.		Furnishings are appealing and comfortable; appropriate for all ages attending; excellent adaptations to accommodate children with sensory and motor disabilities. Furnishings lend themselves well to overall educational program.
Personal Space	No space provided for personal privacy; room is cramped and allows little room for movement.		Space available for personal privacy; adequate space but it is not used to its full potential in class activities.		Personal space is available and is used to potential in classroom activities.
Attractiveness	Classroom is unappealing; makes little use of attention-catching stimuli; drab and unmotivating environment.		Room is fairly attractive in appearance; makes some use of attractiveness to stimulate child interest; some opportunities to use attractiveness within educational program.		Very attractive environment; attractiveness is manipulated to direct attention to program-relevant features. Room invites exploration but is not cluttered.
Accessible	Very little consideration for accessibility of children with disabilities in the design of class.		Some modification of environment to accommodate child with special needs; barriers still exist, restricting use of all areas by children with disabilities		Classroom is barrier free.
Cleanliness	Environment is cluttered and dirty.		Fairly clean environment.		Environment is very clean and uncluttered.
Exploration	Classroom gives little or no motivation for exploration.		Rooms present opportunities for exploration, but lack of structure evident.		Very motivating, exploratory environment; space and planning designed with exploration in mind.

375

Materials

	Poor		Average		Excellent
	1	**2**	**3**	**4**	**5**
Art Equipment	Little or no supplies; supplies present are dangerous; materials are not easily accessed by children.		Limited variety of equipment; supplies are generally safe; access to supplies is limited.		Safe supplies with much variety; materials neatly displayed and stored; accessible to children.
Play Equipment	No toys available or those present are not safe.		Toys present, but inadequate variety; toys not displayed or used in most efficient manner.		Many toys; variety across age ranges; displayed to encourage play and ease in clean-up.
Books & Tapes	No or few books/tapes; those present inaccessible to children; age inappropriate.		Few books/tapes; those present are accessible to children but are not displayed to best advantage; limited variety.		Many books with a variety of age appropriateness and subjects; very accessible and displayed in eye-catching manner.
Nap Provisions	No nap provisions; children lie on carpet, etc.; no blankets supplied; no privacy.		Mats or other similar provisions; little opportunity for comfort or privacy; blankets offered.		Cots or other comfortable provisions made; each child has own blanket; privacy is maximized.
Gross Motor Equipment	Little or no equipment available; what is available is considered unsafe.		Safe, but limited equipment available.		Equipment is safe; wide variety is available.
Adaptability	Equipment not adaptable for children with disabilities; inadequate sensory stimuli to all senses; inaccessible for children with motoric disability.		Materials accessible to all children; may be somewhat limited in all sensory stimuli areas.		Material accessible to all children; good opportunities for sensory stimuli across modalities;
Age/Ability Appropriate	A majority or all materials at inappropriate age and ability levels.		Equipment and materials at roughly appropriate levels (may be slightly immature or too sophisticated).		Equipment at appropriate levels that allow for safe and enjoyable play while giving the opportunity to develop.

Basic Care Needs

	Poor 1	2	Average 3	4	Excellent 5
Toileting	No area for changing; inadequate supply of diapers; bathrooms far from room; not child sized; no toilet-training facilities; no adaptations for persons with disabilities.		Diapering tables but no separate diapering area; bathrooms located conveniently and child-sized; training potties; some adaptation for youngsters with disabilities.		Separate diapering area; diapering tables and adequate supplies of diapers (cloth and disposable); bathrooms close by and child-sized; training potties; well-adapted facilities for children with disabilities.
Nutrition	Snacks erratically served; lack of nutrition; small portions.		Nutritious snacks; portions adequate and served on regular schedule.		Nutritious snacks; adequate portions; regular schedule; special dietary needs taken into consideration; meals used as teaching time (life skills).
Clothing	No extra clothing/underwear on hand; children allowed outside without sufficient clothing.		Extra clothing/underwear accessible; children dressed properly for outside activity.		Extra clothing/underwear; changes used as teachable moments; dress is proper for outside play.
First-Aid	No first-aid kit available; staff not trained in first-aid;		Medical kit with basic supplies; staff has some first-aid training.		Well-supplied medical kit; staff well trained in first-aid procedures; needs of children with disabilities taken into consideration.
Access to Medical Needs	Little or no access to medical support services.		School nurse on call; staff aware of medical needs.		Full-time school nurse available; staff in communication with doctors and very aware of medical needs.
Nurturance	Little or no consideration for emotional needs.		Private areas, respect for individual space; decorations/posters that emphasize positive emotions evident.		Total environment and staff exude sense of warmth and respect. Emotional needs and expression built into curriculum.

Curriculum*

	Poor 1	2	Average 3	4	Excellent 5
Fine-Motor **Gross-Motor** **Language** **Self-Care** **Social Skills**	Little or no evidence of curriculum area being applied in classroom; little evidence of planning and coordination of lessons. Materials inappropriate for ability levels; limited curriculum scope. Lessons appear directed to whole class rather than individual pupil. Lessons are isolated to one curriculum area (no carry-over to other curriculum areas).		Curriculum area is addressed beyond acquisition level (some indication of maintenance and generalization instruction). Curriculum gains are documented; planning is well coordinated among staff; instruction is individualized. Curriculum area is broader in scope; lessons are reinforced in other curriculum areas; individual goals are listed.		Curriculum area has well-defined individual goals; materials are completely adequate to support goal attainment. Planning is excellent among staff and objectives are reinforced across curriculum. Planning takes into account the maintenance, fluency, and generalization of skills; proper reinforcement schedules are used; all gains are systematically documented. Curriculum is very broad in scope.
Cognitive **Adaptability**	Little or no use of adaptations for students with special needs.		Lessons and materials are adapted so that the majority of students can actively participate in most activities.		All lessons are adapted so that all students can actively participate.

*Note: Make note of any other curriculum areas present in the program. All curriculum areas can be rated using same scale.

Adult /Interpersonal

	Poor 1	2	Average 3	4	Excellent 5
Parent Relations	Little or no communication with parents; no method or physical area for meetings. Little opportunity for parents to observe or participate in class activities.		Communication with parents not actively pursued but procedure and place for meetings is communicated. Opportunity to observe present but restricted.		Good communications with parents/caregivers; frequent conferences encouraged (place and procedure readily available). Parents are welcome to observe.
Child Interactions	Staff seems unresponsive to children's needs or ignores them.		Staff attends to children's needs and maintains order; but exhibit limited consistency and ability to positively reinforce behaviors.		Staff anticipates children's needs and effectively interacts with children at all times.
Staff Coordination	Staff does not communicate or coordinate planning among themselves. No formal meetings planned.		Staff communicates and coordinates but not in systematic manner; improvement needed in efficiency of teamwork.		Staff communication is organized and effectively transferred to instructional activities. Staff works as a coordinated team at maximum efficiency.
Adult Areas	Little or no opportunity or space for staff breaks; little or no considerations for adult/staff comfort.		Space and time limited for adult/staff breaks; considerations for adult comfort present but of limited adequacy.		Adult space available and comfortable. Time for staff breaks built into schedule to maximize morale and staff efficiency.
Supervision	Too few staff present to adequately supervise or those present are inattentive. Children left unsupervised during crucial times and/or long periods.		Adequate number of staff but lapses in adequate supervision apparent.		Good supervision at all times; staff members aware of child's location and needs.
Preparation	Teachers show little or no lesson preparation.		Teachers exhibit adequate preparation and organization.		Lessons are very well organized. Excellent preparation and follow-through are obvious.
Professional Development	No opportunity present for staff development.		Reading material available but few professional meetings and no time off for conferences or seminars.		Opportunities such as reading materials, professional consultants and in-service available on-site. Time allocated for attending seminars

Activities

	Poor 1	2	Average 3	4	Excellent 5
Variety	Very little change in day-to-day activities. Little or no diversity in daily activities.		Good balance of active and passive activities; frequent changes of types of activities available.		Same as 3 but with needs of children with disabilities taken into consideration. Activities very child-centered; allows for exploration and experimentation.
Structured Play	Not provided for.		Structured play built into curriculum; areas set up for play.		Same as 3 with clearly stated developmental goals. Structured play planned daily; reinforces other curricular goals.
Transition Time	Teacher declares abruptly time to change activities; children allowed to mill around; much "dead time" between activities.		Transition planned and orderly; students who finish early still have "dead time."		Transitions well planned and orderly. Children know expectations; extra activities planned for those who finish early.
Free Play	Very little for children to play with; toys in poor condition and/or not age-appropriate. Time for free play extremely limited.		Fair variety of toys; set time for free play. Children allowed to choose.		Same as 3 but with staff joining in when invited. More than one of most popular toys available to prevent disputes. Staff alert to possible problems.
Scheduling	Staff seems confused as to when activities are to occur; poor planning and communication among staff.		Staff aware of time-order of activities; activities planned well ahead of time. Parents informed of special events.		Same as 3 but children are also aware of schedule of activities; parents informed of special events.
Dramatic Play	Not provided for.		Dramatic play built into curriculum; planned to occur several times per week.		Same as 3 but with great deal of variety of dramatic activities. Integrated with other areas of curriculum.

380

Personnel Standards for Early Education and Early Intervention

A Position of The Association of Teacher Educators (ATE)
The Division for Early Childhood (DEC)
The National Association for the Education of Young Children (NAEYC)

It is the position of ATE, DEC, and NAEYC that individuals who work with children in early childhood settings must possess, to a degree congruent with their roles, the knowledge and skills for working with young children with special learning and developmental needs and their families. The increasing capacity internationally to provide comprehensive, coordinated services for young children with special learning and developmental needs and their families has significant implications for personnel preparation and credentialling. There is a need to ensure that personnel are both available and adequately prepared to meet the challenges identified by the field. There is a particular need to develop personnel standards that support the practice of inclusion, providing services for young children with disabilities in general early childhood programs and other community-based settings in which typically developing young children are also served. There is also a need to develop personnel standards that support the emerging trend for the development of unified early childhood/early childhood special education teacher training programs and unified state certification. These personnel standards are necessary for individuals functioning in a variety of roles, including but not limited to, the following: a) early childhood educators who work directly with young children in a variety of early childhood settings, who must accommodate children with a range of abilities and special needs and who must work collaboratively with families and other professionals; b) early childhood special educators who possess specialized knowledge and skills about young children with disabilities and their families and who may work directly with young children with disabilities or work in a collaborative relationship with early childhood educators, family members, and other professionals serving young children with special learning and developmental needs and their families; and c) related services professionals who provide consultation and support to families and other professionals, as well as direct treatment.

In recommending the development of personnel standards that apply to all of these roles, ATE, DEC and NAEYC recognize that the collaboration of professional organizations is critical to this process. The articulation of shared standards will provide a base from which states can develop certification, licensure, and credentialling guidelines. The desirable outcomes will be coherence of state standards and certification guidelines, congruence between personnel standards and standards of recommended practice in early childhood service delivery, an increased probability that services to young children with disabilities are delivered in the context of services to all young children, and that those services are provided by appropriately prepared personnel.

Philosophy and Assumptions Guiding Personnel Recommendations

ATE, DEC and NAEYC recommend that personnel standards be derived from empirically defensible knowledge and clearly articulated philosophical assumptions about what constitutes effective early education and early intervention for young children with special learning and developmental needs and their families. These include:

- The uniqueness of early childhood as a developmental phase,
- The significant role of families in early childhood development and early education and intervention,
- The role of developmentally and individually appropriate practices,
- The preference for service delivery in inclusive settings,
- The importance of culturally competent professional actions, and
- The importance of collaborative interpersonal and interprofessional actions.

The Structure of Certification

It is the intention of ATE, DEC, and NAEYC to provide a framework for personnel standards that is sufficiently flexible to allow states to plan within the context of local limitations, while also maintaining "content-congruence" (ATE/NAEYC, 1991) with the philosophy and assumptions. In developing a structure for certification standards, it is recommended that:

1. State agencies responsible for credentialling, certification, and/or licensure develop standards for all individuals who may be working with young children with disabilities, to include at least early childhood educators, early childhood special educators, and related services professionals.

2. As a first step in influencing the credentialling of all individuals working with young children, states develop free-standing certification or licensure guidelines for educational professionals working with young children and that these be separate from either existing general education or special education certifications. Certification/ licensure standards should be clearly delineated for: a) an early childhood professional who will possess knowledge and skills related to general early childhood education as well as a common core of knowledge and skills related to young children with disabilities and their families; and, b) an early childhood special education professional who will possess specialized knowledge and skills related to young children with disabilities and their families, including those related to consultation with team members, as well as common core knowledge and skills related to general early childhood education. Such separate certifications should be linked clearly to enable professional mobility between roles and should be constructed so as to support the possibility of unified early childhood/early childhood special education teacher training programs.

3. State certification standards apply to the birth-to-eight age range. Further, recognizing that it is difficult to prepare individuals to be skillful across this broad age range, it is recommended that certification standards incorporate options for subspecializations of birth-to-age three, age three-to-five, or age five-to-eight, with the opportunity to specialize in no more than two of these in a pre-service program.

Content of Certification Standards

Personnel standards must articulate common core knowledge and skills necessary for all individuals who work with young children with special learning and developmental needs and their families, as well as the specialization knowledge and skills required for each of these roles. The identification of the content of credentialling standards should follow directly from the articulated philosophy and assumptions and reflect the spirit and letter of appropriate federal regulations related to serving young children with disabilities and their families. Credentialling standards should recognized such that graduate level training is seen as a desirable part of a career ladder for all professionals working with young children and that, as such, it has the potential for improving the quality of services to all young children. Finally, credentialling standards should be outcome-based, not course-based, and ensure that personnel possess the knowledge and skills to work collaboratively as members of family-professional teams in planning and implementing appropriate services for young children with disabilities in a variety of community settings.

Representative Organizations Concerned with Young Children with Special Needs and Their Families

American Foundation for the Blind (AFB)
11 Penn Plaza, Suite 300
New York, NY 10011
(800) 232-5463
http://www.afb.org

American Speech-Language-Hearing Association (ASHA)
10801 Rockville Pike
Rockville, MD 20852
(301) 897-5700; (800) 638-8255
http://www.asha.org

The ARC of the United States
1010 Wayne Ave., Suite 650
Silver Spring, MD 20910
(301) 565-3842
http:www.thearc.org

The Association for Persons with Severe Handicaps (TASH)
29 W. Susquehanna Ave., Suite 210
Baltimore, MD 21204
(410) 828-8274
http://www.tash.org

Autism Society of America
7910 Woodmont Avenue, Suite 300
Bethesda, MD 20814
(301) 657-0881; (800) 328-8476
http://www.autism-society.org

Beach Center on Families & Disability
University of Kansas
3136 Haworth Hall
Lawrence, KS 66045
(785) 864-7600
http://www.beachcenter.org

Division for Early Childhood (DEC), Council for Exceptional Children (CEC)
634 Eddy Avenue
Missoula, MT 59812
(406) 243-5898
http://www.dec-sped.org

ERIC Clearinghouse on Disabilities and Gifted Education
1110 North Glebe Road
Arlington, VA 22201
(800) 328-0272
http://www.ericec.ed.gov

Federation for Children with Special Needs
1135 Tremont Street Suite 420
Boston, MA 02120
(617) 236-7210
http://www.fcsn.org

National Association of the Deaf
814 Thayer Avenue
Silver Spring, MD 20910-4500
(301) 587-1788
http:ww.nad.org/

National Association for the Education of Young Children (NAEYC)
1509 16th Street, NW
Washington, DC 20036-1426
(800) 424-2460; (202) 232-8777
http://www.naeyc.org

National Coalition for Parent Involvement in Education (NCPIE)
3929 Old Lee Highway
Suite 91-A
Fairfax, VA 22030
(703) 359-8973
http:www.ncpie.org

National Deaf Education Center
Gallaudet University
800 Florida Avenue, NE
Washington, DC 20002
(202) 651-5031
http://clercenter.gallaudet.edu/

National Down Syndrome Congress
1370 Center Drive Suite 102
Atlanta, GA 30338
(800) 232-6372
http://www.ndsccenter.org/

National Down Syndrome Society
666 Broadway, Suite 810
New York, NY 10012-2317
(212) 460-9330; (800) 221-4602
http://ndss.org

National Early Childhood Technical Assistance Center (NECTAC)
137 East Franklin Street, Suite 500
Chapel Hill, NC 27514
(919) 962-2001
http://www.nectac.org/

National Dissemination Center for Children with Disabilities (NICHCY)
P. O. Box 1492
Washington, DC 20013-1492
(800) 695-0285
http://www.nichcy.org

Parents Helping Parents: The Parent-Directed Family Resource Center for Children with Special Needs
535 Race Street, Suite 140
San Jose, CA 95126
(408) 288-5010
http://www.php.com

United Cerebral Palsy Association
1660 L St. NW, Suite 700
Washington, DC 20036
(800) 872-5827
http://www.ucpa.org

Glossary

Academic (preacademic) skills curriculum model. A model that focuses on reading, writing, arithmetic, and other skills needed in a school setting.

Accessibility. Adaptations of the environment aimed at equalizing participation opportunities for persons with disabilities.

Accommodation. According to Piaget, an alteration of existing cognitive structures to allow for new information; involves a change in understanding.

Acquired Immune Deficiency Syndrome (AIDS). Caused by the human immunodeficiency virus (HIV), which destroys the body's natural immune system; almost always fatal.

Activity area. Organized space within a classroom dedicated to activities based on a theme or developmental domain. Typically designed to accommodate small groups of children and a teacher.

Activity-based instruction. Systematic distribution of teaching and learning across routine activities, planned activities, or child-initiated activities at school and at home.

Activity-based intervention. A curriculum approach that embeds training on a child's individual IFSP or IEP goals and objectives into routine or planned activities.

Adaptability. In family systems theory, this is a concept used to describe a family's ability to change in response to a crisis or stressful situation.

Adapted participation. Use of an alternative means of participation (i.e., orient head or eye gaze instead of pointing; use of communication board instead of speaking).

Adaptive skills. Those skills that promote independence and facilitate a child's ability to fit into his or her environment.

Age appropriateness. A component of the developmentally appropriate practice (DAP) guidelines, which refers to the need for the learning environment and curriculum to be based on the typical development of children.

Apgar Scale. A screening procedure for newborns given at one-minute and again at five-minutes following their birth to measure heart rate, respiration, reflex response, muscle tone, and color.

Arena assessment. A team process in which one team member conducts the assessment while the other team members observe and contribute.

Assessment. The process of gathering information for the purpose of making a decision about children with known or suspected disabilities in the areas of screening, diagnosis, eligibility, program planning, and/or progress monitoring and evaluation.

Assimilation. In Piaget's terms, the inclusion of new information and experiences into already present cognitive schemes or structures.

At-risk. Describing a child with exposure to certain adverse conditions and circumstances known to have a high probability of resulting in learning and development difficulties.

Authentic assessment. The process of observing, recording, collecting, and otherwise documenting what children do and how they do it for the purpose of making educational decisions.

Auto-education. In Montessori terms, the self-learning that occurs as a result of a child independently interacting with a carefully planned environment.

Behavior disorder. A term used to describe a wide variety of social and emotional problems that include, but are not limited to, attention and/or hyperactivity, conduct, and anxiety disorders.

Behavior trapping. A method of instruction in which the environment is arranged to provide for the positive reinforcement of behaviors. Typically used to promote social behaviors.

Behavioral curriculum model. A model, based on learning principles of behavioral psychology, which emphasizes direct instruction through a prescribed sequence of instructional activities.

Biological risk. Young children with a history of pre-, peri-, and postnatal conditions and developmental events that heighten the potential for later atypical development.

Center-based programs. Group-oriented service delivery model for young children with special needs. Intervention and educational services provided in settings other than the child's home.

Child Find. The process of finding and identifying children who have a delay or disability.

Children with special health needs. A general term referring to youngsters with a wide variety of serious, and oftentimes unique, health care concerns.

Cognitive skills. A child's evolving mental and intellectual ability.

Cohesion. According to family systems theory, this is a concept used to describe the degree of freedom and independence experienced by each family member within a family unit.

Combination programs. A service delivery model for young children with special needs that combines elements of home-based and center-based program models.

Compensatory education. Early experiences and intervention efforts aimed at ameliorating the consequences of living in poverty; goal is to better prepare young children for school.

Communication. The exchange of messages between a speaker and a listener.

Concurrent validity. A type of validity that refers to how well a test correlates with other accepted measures of performance administered close in time to the first.

Construct validity. A type of validity that refers to the degree to which a test addresses the constructs on which it is based.

Content validity. A specific type of validity that refers to how well a test represents the content it purports to measure.

Criterion-referenced instruments. A type of measure used to determine whether a child's performance meets an established criteria or a certain level of mastery within various developmental domains or set of objectives.

Culturally biased assessment. A measure that focuses on skills and abilities of the dominant Western culture and places children from non-Western, non-dominant cultures at a disadvantage.

Culture. The attitudes, values, belief system, norms, and traditions shared by a particular group of people, which collectively form their heritage.

Curriculum. What is to be learned in an early childhood program; it flows from the theoretical or philosophical perspectives on which the program is based.

Curriculum-referenced instruments. A type of measure that is used to interpret a child's performance or abilities in relation to specific curricular objectives.

Development curriculum model. A model based on the theories of typical child development, which suggests that skills are acquired in a predictable sequence.

Developmental-cognitive curriculum model. A theory-driven model, based on the work of Piaget, which emphasizes the domain of cognitive skill development.

Developmental delay. A concept defined by individual states when referring to young children with special needs. A delay is usually determined on the basis of various developmental assessments and/or informed clinical opinion.

Developmental domains. The key skill areas that are typically addressed in a comprehensive assessment, including cognitive, motor, self-care, communication, play, social, and emotional skills.

Developmentally appropriate practices. A set of guidelines established by the National Association for the Education of Young Children (NAEYC) to articulate appropriate practices for the early education of young children.

Diagnosis. The process of confirming the presence or absence of a delay or disability.

Diagnostic assessment. A type of assessment procedure that is designed to determine the existence of a disability.

Didactic materials. Instructional items used in Montessori programs.

Disability. An inability to do something; a reduced capacity to perform in a specific way.

Early childhood special education. The provision of customized services uniquely crafted to meet the individual needs of youngsters with disabilities between three and five years of age.

Early Head Start. A federal program providing a variety of services to low-income families with infants and toddlers as well as women who are pregnant.

Early intervention. The delivery of a coordinated and comprehensive set of specialized services of infants and toddlers (birth through age two) with developmental delays or at-risk conditions and their families.

Echolalic speech. A condition in which someone repeats what is said rather than generating an original sentence.

Ecological assessment. An assessment that considers all dimensions and requirements of the child's natural environment in determining goals and objectives.

Ecological perspective. The basic tenets of this perspective are that individuals or family units are influenced by the events and experiences that occur in their lives (their ecology), and that these events and experiences can be understood and influenced to promote healthy modes of development and learning in families.

Ecology. The interrelationships and interactions of the various environments or contexts that affect the child and are affected by the youngster.

Eligibility. A comprehensive diagnostic process to determine if a child meets the criteria to be eligible for special services.

Emotional abuse. A type of child maltreatment distinguished by caregiver actions that are designed to be psychologically harmful to the youngster.

Empathy. The action of understanding, being aware of, being sensitive to, and vicariously experiencing the feelings, thoughts, and experiences of another.

Empowerment. The process of applying strategies whereby individuals gain a sense of control over their future as a result of their own efforts and activities.

Engagement. Consistent, active involvement with the people (i.e., teachers, parents, classmates), activities (i.e., snack time, play time, group time participation, center selection/participation), and materials (i.e., use of toys, art supplies, water play materials) throughout the child's day.

Environmental arrangements. Any changes in the environment that are used to facilitate child engagement such as altering the physical space, selection and use of materials, and altering the structure of an activity.

Environmental risk. Biologically typical children who encounter life experiences or environmental conditions that are so limiting that the possibility of future delayed development exists.

Equilibration. According to Piaget's theorizing, the cognitive process by which a person attempts to balance new information with already existing data.

Established risk. Youngsters with a diagnosed medical disorder of known etiology and predictable prognosis or outcome.

Ethnocentric behavior. The viewpoint that the practices and behavior of one particular cultural group are natural and correct, while considering the actions of other groups as inferior or odd.

Exceptional children. Children who differ from society's view of normalcy.

Exosystems. According to Bronfenbrenner, the social systems that exert an influence on the development of the individual.

Expressive language. The ability to communicate one's ideas or feelings through vocalizations, words, and other behaviors used to relay information.

False negative. Designation of a child who needs special services but was not referred by a screening.

False positive. Designation of a child who has been referred by a screening but does not need special services.

Family. A group of people, related by blood or circumstances, who rely upon one another for security, sustenance, support, socialization, and stimulation.

Family-based practices. Those practices used in early-intervention/education designed to have child, parent, and family strengthening and competency enhancing consequences.

Family-centered practices. A philosophy of working with families, whereby specific techniques and methods are used that stress family strengths, the enhancement of family skills, and the development of mutual partnerships between families and professionals.

Family characteristics. According to family systems theory, this is the component that refers to the dimensions that make each family unique such as its socioeconomic status, cultural heritage, number of family members, as well as other distinguishing characteristics.

Family functions. One of the components of family systems theory that refers to a variety of interrelated activities considered necessary to fulfill the collective needs of a family (e.g., affection, economics, recreation, and education).

Family interactions. According to family systems theory, these are the relationships and interactions that occur among and between various family subsystems like the marital subsystem.

Family life cycle. According to family systems theory, the changes that occur in families that influence their resources, interactions, and functions.

Family systems theory. A model that suggests that the family is an interdependent unit; whatever affects one family member has repercussions for the other members of the unit. Adoption of a family systems approach means that professionals focus their attention on the entire family constellation instead of only the child with a disability.

Fine motor skills. The ability to use small muscle groups such as those in the hands, face, and feet.

Formal testing. A type of assessment in which standardized measures are used with a specific purpose in mind, such as screening or eligibility determination.

Formative evaluation. Evaluation that takes place while a program is in progress.

Full inclusion. The belief that all children with disabilities should be educated in regular education classrooms in their neighborhood schools. Placements should be age- and grade-appropriate.

Functional curriculum model. A model in which the skills or behaviors are emphasized that have immediate relevance to a child.

Functional skills. Those skills that will be useful to a child and will be used often by the child in his or her natural environment.

Generalization. The ability to apply what is learned in one context to different settings, different materials, or different people.

Gifts. A Froebelian term referring to manipulative objects, such as balls and wooden blocks, used as tools for learning in Froebel's curriculum.

Gross motor skills. The type of skills that involve the movement and control of large muscle groups used to function in the environment.

Handicap. The consequences or impact encountered by or imposed on a child with a disability as he or she attempts to function and interact in the environment.

Home-based programs. A type of service delivery model for young children with special needs. Intervention provided in the youngster's home by the primary caregiver. Professionals make regular visits to work directly with the child and to provide instruction to the caregiver.

Home Start. A derivation of the Head Start program; designed to provide comprehensive services to young children and their parents in the home through the utilization of home visitors.

Human immunodeficiency virus (HIV). The specific virus that causes acquired immune deficiency syndrome (AIDS).

Hypertonic muscle tone. Tight muscles.

Hypotonic muscle tone. Floppy muscles that exhibit resistance to being stretched.

Individual appropriateness. A component of the developmentally appropriate practice (DAP) guidelines, which calls for the learning environment and curriculum to be responsive to the individual differences and needs of each child.

Individual transition plan (ITP). Document required by federal law whose purpose is to assist adolescents with disabilities in moving from school to postschool functions.

Individualized education program (IEP). Required by federal legislation. A customized educational plan, constructed by a team, for each child with special needs.

Individualized family service plan (IFSP). A written document mandated by federal law. Designed as a guide for services for infants, toddlers, and their families. Developed by a team of professionals and the parent(s).

Instructional validity. A type of validity that refers to the extent to which the information gained from an assessment instrument would be useful in planning intervention programs.

Intelligence tests. Standardized measures of intellectual functioning that are often referred to as I.Q. tests.

Interdisciplinary. A type of teaming model utilized in delivering services to young children with special needs. Team members typically perform their evaluations independently; however, program development and recommendations for services are the results of sharing information and joint planning.

Interviews. A form of assessment used to gather information from families or other caregivers about a child's abilities; the families concerns, priorities, and resources; or other relevant information.

Labeling. The assignment of a disability label such as deaf or mentally retarded.

Language. The use of symbols, syntax, or grammar when communicating with one another.

Learned helplessness. A condition of hopelessness resulting from inconsistent or negative feedback. Persons with learned helplessness feel they have little control over elements of their environment.

Least restrictive environment (LRE). A concept requiring that children with special needs be educated, to the maximum extent appropriate, with their typical classmates. Settings are individually determined for each pupil.

Macrosystems. The ideological, cultural, and institutional contexts that encompass the micro-, meso-, and exosystems.

Mainstreaming. The process of integrating children with special needs into educational settings primarily designed to serve youngsters without disabilities.

Mesosystems. The relationships between the various environments of the microsystems.

Meta-analysis. A comprehensive statistical procedure, whereby research studies are evaluated in an effort to ascertain global statistical patterns, which yield "effect size," reported as standard deviations.

Microsystems. As proposed by Bronfenbrenner, the immediate environments in which a person develops such as a youngster's home and neighborhood.

Milieu strategies. Strategies to facilitate language skills (especially social interaction context) that take advantage of the natural environment (people, materials, activities) to support learning. Milieu strategies include a variety of specific procedures (i.e., time delay, mand-model, incidental teaching).

Milieu teaching. A teaching method based on arranging the environment to facilitate instruction through use of functional and relevant contexts.

Mobility. The process of using one's senses to determine their position in relation to other objects in the environment.

Multidisciplinary team. A type of teaming model utilized in delivering services to young children with special needs. This approach utilizes the expertise of professionals from several disciplines, each of whom usually perform their activities independent of each other.

Natural environments. A philosophy that emphasizes providing early intervention in settings viewed as typical for youngster without disabilities.

Naturalistic observation. A systematic process of gathering information by looking at individuals and their behavior in their environments.

Neglect. A form of child maltreatment; characterized by a variety of caregiver actions, which may include failure to provide basic necessities, inadequate physical supervision or render needed medical treatment.

Normalization. A principle advocating that individuals with disabilities should be integrated, to the maximum extent possible, into all aspects of every day living.

Norm-referenced tests. A type of measure that provides a score that compares a child's performance to other children from a particular group.

Occupational therapist. A professional who deals with the improvement of a person's strength and movement in the lower and upper limbs.

Occupations. A Froebelian concept describing arts and crafts type activities used to develop eye-hand coordination and fine motor skills.

Orientation. The ability to move around in one's environment.

Orthotic devices. A device used to promote body alignment, stabilize joints, or increase motor functioning.

Parent. Any adult who fulfills the essential caregiving duties and responsibilities for a particular child.

Partial participation. Use of only a portion of the response instead of full response (i.e., when told to touch the picture of the tree, a child moves his/her hand in direction of the correct picture, but does not actually touch the picture).

Peer-mediated strategies. Strategies or approaches that utilize peers (or classmates) to promote learning.

Physical abuse. A type of child maltreatment. An assault on a youngster designed to cause physical injury or harm to the child.

Physical therapist. A professional who deals with the improvement of a person's mobility skills, strength, endurance, and movement.

PKU screening. A procedure used to detect the metabolic disorder phenylketonuria (PKU) in infants.

Play-based assessment. A systematic procedure for observing children during play to determine their level of development.

Play-based strategy (intervention). The intentional use of play as the context for implementing interventions.

Portfolio. The format followed during the assessment process which includes the specific skill areas, skills, and/or behaviors to be observed or measured.

Portfolio assessment. A systematic and organized collection of children's work and records of their behaviors, which can serve as evidence to be used to monitor their progress.

Predictive validity. A type of validity that refers to the extent to which a test relates to some future measure of performance.

Premacking. Arranging sequences of activities so that low-probability (desirable) behaviors are followed by high-probability (motivating) behaviors.

Prepared environment. An important component in a Montessori classroom; a planned and orderly setting containing specially developed tasks and materials designed to promote children's learning.

Program evaluation. A process that addresses a program's progress in achieving overall outcomes and effectiveness.

Program planning. A procedure used to identify desired goals/outcomes for the IFSP/IEP and intervention.

Program planning assessment. Assessment that focuses on a child's skill level, needs, background, experiences, environmental demands, and interests as the basis for constructing and maintaining individualized programs.

Progress monitoring. The process of collecting information about how children are progressing towards meeting their individual goals and objectives.

Progress monitoring and evaluation. A process of collecting information about a child's progress, the family's satisfaction with services, and overall program effectiveness.

Progressivism. A school of thought founded by John Dewey. Emphasis placed on interest of children rather than activities chosen by the teacher.

Project Follow-Through. A federal program that attempts to continue the gains developed through Head Start. Funding is available for children in kindergarten through the third grade. Children receive educational, health, and social service benefits.

Project Head Start. A federally funded program aimed at young children in poverty; designed to increase the chances of success in school and opportunity for achievement.

Prompts. Any systematic assistance provided to an individual to enable them to respond, including verbal prompts, physical prompts (assistance), pictorial prompts.

Prosthetic device. An artificial device used to replace a missing body part.

Protocol. A format to be followed during an assessment which can include the skill areas on which to focus and/or the specific skills to be observed.

Receptive language. The ability to understand and comprehend both verbal and nonverbal information.

Referral. When a professional comes in contact with a child whom they suspect of having a disability and recommends further assessment.

Regular education initiative (REI). An approach for educating children with special needs; special and regular educators work cooperatively in providing services to pupils with exceptionalities in the regular classroom.

Reliability. The consistency of a test in measuring what it is supposed to assess in a dependable or consistent manner.

Responsivity. The quality of the environment that provides immediate and consistent feedback for child interaction.

Routine-based strategies. The intentional use of predictable routine activities (i.e., snack time, dressing, etc.), transitions (i.e., departure and arrival time, daily transition to the cafeteria, etc.) and routine group activities (i.e., circle time) to implement interventions.

Scaffolding. A Vygotskian concept referring to the assistance rendered to the learner by adults or peers, which allows the person to function independently.

Schema. According to Piaget, a cognitive organizational pattern or framework that provides a foundation for the development of cognitive structures used in thinking.

Screening. A procedure designed to identify the children who need to be referred for more in-depth assessment.

Self-care skills. Those skills that allow a child to independently care for him or herself, are basic for maintaining life, and deal with bodily functions.

Self-fulfilling prophecy. An expectation that individuals who are labeled will achieve at a predetermined level.

Sensitive periods. Stages of development early in life during which, according to Montessori, a child is especially capable of learning practicular skills or behaviors.

Sensitivity. A screening instrument's ability to identify children who need additional assessment.

Sexual abuse. A form of child maltreatment in which developmentally immature individuals engage in sexual activities, which they do not fully comprehend or are unable to give informed consent. Sexual abuse may also include issues of sexual exploitation.

Social and cultural appropriateness. A component of the developmentally appropriate practice (DAP) guidelines, which calls for curriculum and learning experience to be based on each child's unique social and cultural experiences.

Social and emotional skills. A broad range of behaviors that describe how children interact with others and react in social situations.

Specificity. The capacity of a screening instrument to accurately select out children who should not be identified.

Speech. The oral motor action used to communicate.

Stimulus-control. A behavioral science concept that states that future behaviors are more likely to occur in the presence of specific stimuli while the behavior is initially being reinforced.

Summative evaluation. Evaluation that takes place at the completion of services.

Tabula rasa. Concept attributed to John Locke. Young children seen very much like a blank slate. Learning is not innate but rather the result of experiences and activities.

Task analysis. The process of breaking down a task or skill (i.e., brushing teeth, getting a drink of water, putting on a shirt, turning on a computer, etc.) into sequential steps.

Teacher-mediated. Intervention directed by teachers to promote social interactions.

Tests. Predetermined collections of questions or tasks to which predetermined types of responses are sought.

Transdisciplinary. A type of teaming model utilized in delivering services to young children with special needs. Building on an interdisciplinary model, this approach also includes sharing of roles and interventions delivered by a primary service provider. Support and consultation from other team members is important.

Transition. The process of moving from one type of educational program or setting to another.

Validity. The extent to which a test measures what it was intended to measure.

Zone of proximal development (ZPD). According to Vygotsky, this term refers to the distance between the child's actual development level as determined by independent problem solving and the level of potential development as determined through problem solving under adult guidance or in collaboration with more capable peers.

Index